The Aviation Book

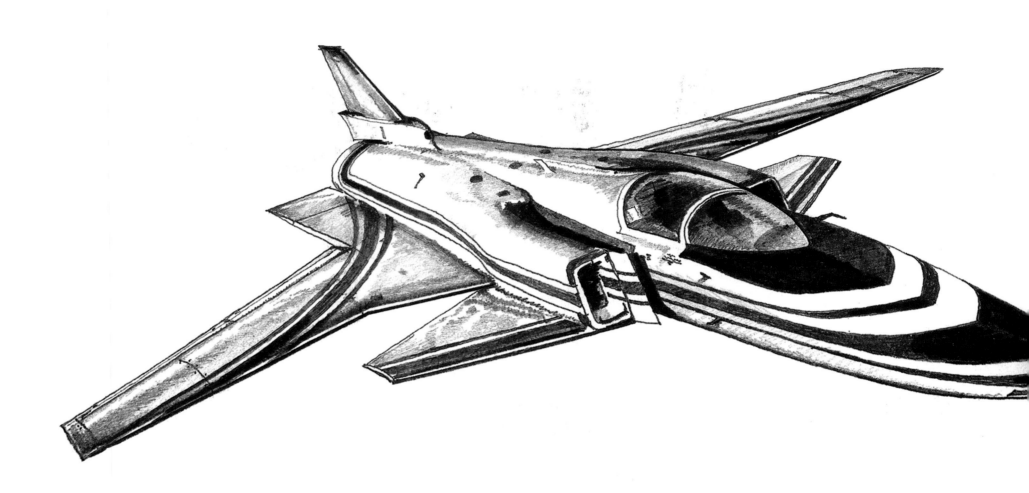

Fia O Caoimh

The Aviation Book

The World's Aircraft A-Z

Thames & Hudson

In memory of Tom McNamara who never failed
to empathize and enthuse at each of his many
grandchildren's interests and undertakings.

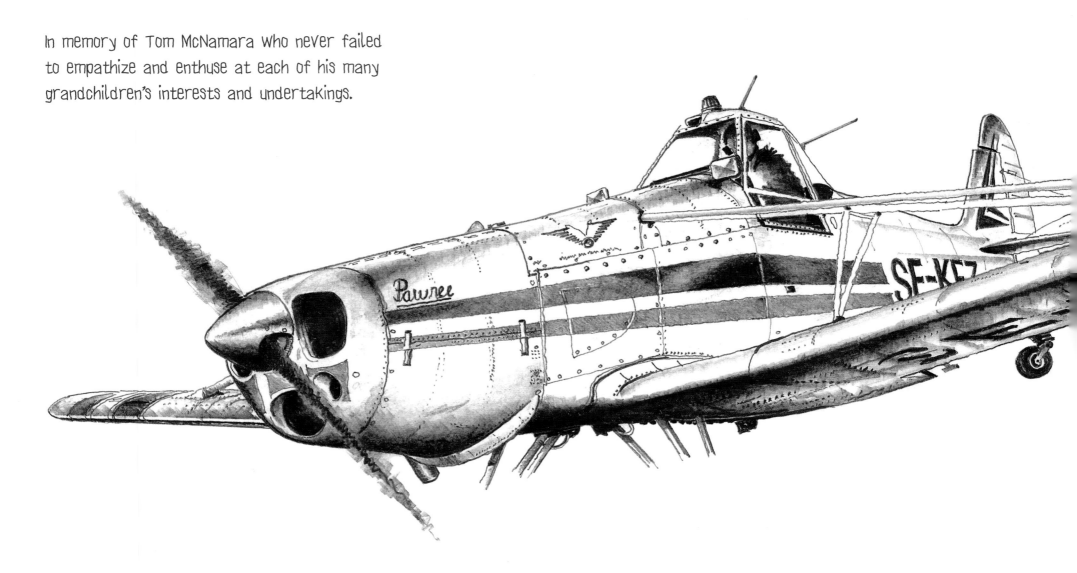

First published in the United Kingdom in 2006 by Thames & Hudson Ltd,
181A High Holborn, London WC1V 7QX

www.thamesandhudson.com

Text, design and drawings © 2006 Fia O Caoimh

British Library Cataloguing-in-Publication Data
A catalogue record for this book is available from the British Library

ISBN-13:   978-0-500-51303-3
ISBN-10:   0-500-51303-1

Printed and bound in China by SNP Leefung Printers Limited

All the illustrations for this book have been produced from the author's original drawings,
made in pencil on white cartridge paper over a ten-year period (1996-2006).
The backgrounds that appear in a number of the illustrations are from his own
photographs (often taken while flying with the other hand).

Every effort has been made to ensure that terminology and technical specifications used
in describing the aircraft are as accurate as possible. It is to be noted that standard
works and expert accounts often differ in matters of detail. Any comments received will
be carefully considered, and amendments will be made, if necessary, in future editions.
Thanks are due to François Besse, the translator of the French edition, for his many
helpful comments and suggestions during the preparation of this book.

To find out more about the author's work go to www.theaviationbook.com

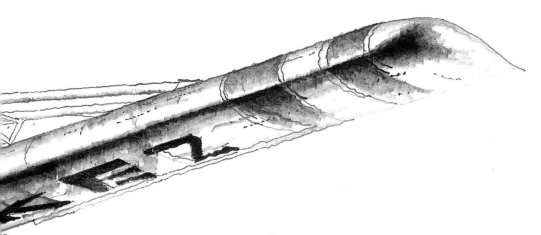

Contents

Preface

'The Aviation Book' is a compilation of extracts from my sketchbooks of 1996 to 2006, featuring a collection of diverse aircraft types from classic and antique to the latest commercial and military jets. Special emphasis, however, is placed on unusual or forgotten types and, indeed, the book contains some very rare and eccentric gems of aviation.

For many years I have been fascinated with the varied shapes and forms of aircraft types and the multitude of new configurations that aircraft designers have used to achieve flight. The rapid pace of innovation and development within the world of aviation, fuelled by competition and war, provides an engrossing field of study. In its early years aviation was governed by a crude and unforgiving form of natural selection. Unsuccessful aircraft types and their designer-pilots often met their ends very quickly. Other aircraft were simply outdated even before they reached production. Many of these obscure and unfortunate pioneering aircraft have been lost to history for ever but, working from old drawings and photographic plates, I have attempted to bring a few of them back to life.

Great care has been taken to ensure that the spread of aircraft types represented is such that the story of aviation is well told. The merit of a particular aircraft in the overall development of flight has a bearing on its inclusion, as may its longevity or its place in popular culture. Some have been selected on account of the aesthetic appeal of the airframes, where markings and colour schemes provide particular interest. In all of these cases these markings and colour schemes are genuine and accurate. Throughout the book, care has been taken to ensure that the materials from which individual aircraft have been built are accurately represented, or represented as faithfully and clearly as is possible within the context of a sketch drawing. Rivet lines, stitching lines and fabric stretch lines have been drawn with a small degree of artistic selectivity. In all cases, however, these vital construction details are genuine and accurate. Indeed, my involvement over the years in airframe construction has helped immeasurably in allowing me to represent these complex and minute details in drawn format. Perhaps the most difficult sketch subjects were the new generation of commercial passenger jet transports which, by virtue of their seamless bonded-skin technologies, left me almost nothing to draw. In these cases I have introduced the minimum possible number of seam lines required to express their essential character and to suggest their three-dimensional form.

This collection is presented broadly alphabetically by manufacturer with the intention of providing order and structure to this large body of work while accommodating sketches of various sizes on page layouts that are pleasing to the eye. The text accompanying each of the drawings is presented following the format of my sketchbooks and in a font developed from my own handwriting that complements the sketch drawings and gives the book an individual flavour. The commentary is intentionally more anecdotal in character than most other aviation books, placing emphasis on the stories and the folklore behind each of the aircraft types.

A small number of sketches have been presented on photographic backgrounds. Each of these photographs has been taken by myself while in the skies of Ireland, the US and Canada, usually while flying the aircraft with one hand and holding my camera in the other.

The Technical Data provides, where it was available, the technical information and performance figures for each aircraft type. Airframe specifications, and in particular performance figures, have not been adjusted to take into account standard atmospheric conditions or flight levels. Dimensions and figures will vary between different models within given aircraft types. The main headings refer to aircraft types, while the subheading 'Subject' refers to the particular aircraft I have drawn. A second subheading, 'Statistics', gives the related model to which the schedule of technical information applies; where possible, figures are given for the model indicated on the heading panel. Taken together, this information should provide the reader with a broad sense of an aircraft type.

In addition to the technical data I have included details of museums where you can see preserved examples of particular aircraft or airframes. I hope you are as inspired by them as I was.

Fia O Caoimh

Introduction

From the beginning of time man has had a fascination with flight, yet throughout its short and dramatic history, the story of aviation has been closely linked to the evolution of modern warfare. That one of mankind's most wondrous inventions should be linked so closely with the arms industry is a source of great sadness, but the need of that industry to continually reinvent itself has driven it to the limits of technical possibility and has, in turn, driven the progress of aviation at a pace that would otherwise have been unsustainable. Aircraft design progressed rapidly from the time of Wilbur and Orville Wright's first tentative flight in 1903, but it was only with the advent of the First World War that organized governmental resources were pumped into aircraft design and, in particular, the design of aircraft with military applications. Across Europe and America substantial contracts were awarded for the development of fighting aircraft and light bombers and the powerful piston engines needed to carry them into battle. The fledgling aviation industry responded admirably, and within a few years the evolution of both airframe and powerplant design had surged forward. For the remainder of the first century of flight the needs of various military and governmental bodies would continue to provide the dominant driving forces within the aviation industry. Throughout these years the majority of research into the development of reciprocating engines, turboprop powerplants, pulse jets, turbojets and rocket engines was directed into military applications. Aerodynamic design, too, advanced at a remarkable pace but again the majority of governmental resources were directed into military projects or into research projects with specific military aspirations. Commercial aviation therefore, and in particular general aviation, was carried along with the tide of progress, which was a by-product of the prolific and thriving military aviation industry.

In the space of just 100 years the aircraft has changed the course of human progress for ever. At the start of the 20th century, only small numbers of people travelled more than 50 or 100 miles from their place of birth. Today, however, we travel vast distances across oceans and continents on holidays and business trips; journeys that would have taken the early crusaders and explorers large portions of their lives to complete. The advent of flight has also brought about huge political and economic change. Countries formerly isolated and peripheral to the great empires and centres of population of earlier times can now be reached within hours. Other countries, such as France, Britain and the USA, have used aviation to great effect to expand their influence on the world. The USA, in particular, embraced aviation from its earliest days, viewing it as a means of traversing its vast lands and overcoming the geographical problems posed by its isolated location between the vast Atlantic and Pacific oceans. Indeed, the USA's singular dedication to the development of aviation and new systems of telephony and electronic communications was so successful and all-encompassing that it resulted in massive benefits to the US economy and, ultimately, caused most of us to view our positions in the world relative to the USA rather than to any of the traditional European centres of population.

Stories of god-like flying heroes have adorned the traditions and the cultures of almost all recorded civilizations. It was not until the identification of hydrogen gas by Henry Cavendish in 1766, however, that the possibility of lighter-than-air flight was identified as a possibility. Cavendish was able to demonstrate that his 'inflammable air' could not only be made to explode violently but that it was substantially lighter than air. It took 17 years, however, before J.A.C. Charles demonstrated the world's first hydrogen balloon, a rudimentary affair but a promise of greater things to come. Within months, brothers Joseph and Etienne Montgolfier were astounding King Louis XVI and Marie-Antoinette of France with their extraordinary hot-air balloon and its pioneering cargo of farm animals. The cream of Parisian society was even more enthralled when Jean-François Pilatre de Rozier became the first man to ascend in a hot-air balloon, achieving an altitude of 85 feet. Thereafter, ballooning demonstrations became one of the great social pastimes of the upper classes of Paris and the other principal European cities. The Montgolfier brothers went on to great things, while aviation's earliest royal enthusiasts, Louis XVI and Marie-Antoinette, lost their heads in the French Revolution.

The staunch religious work ethic of the Wright brothers would simply not let them rely on the findings and the formulae of the aeronautical pioneers who had gone before them. Through the services of that agony uncle of early aviation, Octave Chanute, the 2 bicycle-makers from Dayton, Ohio had access to the drawings and writings of many of aviation's greatest fathers. From the writings of Otto Lilienthal, who had made thousands of successful gliding descents in Germany, to the proclamations of Hiram Maxim, who was a strong advocate of steam-powered aircraft, Chanute generously and enthusiastically circulated all the material that he felt would advance the path to aviation. Wilbur Wright, in particular, was not keen to assume that this information was correct and he set about the tiresome task of building hundreds of aerofoil models to prove Lilienthal's figures and to find the ideal aerofoil profile. So it was, then, that some of aviation's most colourful and charismatic characters paraded their unsuccessful flying machines before a sceptical public while the Wrights worked away patiently at the back of their workshop building their aerofoil sections and testing them in the world's first wind tunnel. By now the 2 principal components necessary for flight, the glider and the compact petrol engine, were reaching an advanced stage of development and the race to become the first into the air became a matter of great public speculation and some derision, particularly after such large-scale public exhibitions as Samuel Pierpont Langley's unsuccessful Great Aerodrome fiasco of 1903. The Wright brothers, however, were not distracted from their task and continued to work methodically. Overcoming each of their design goals and progressing from wind-tunnel models to flying prototypes, they tested their first man-carrying gliders in privacy on the remote sand flats and dunes of Kitty Hawk, North Carolina. It was here on Tuesday 17 December 1903, in their third year of flight testing, that the Wright Flyer finally took to the air and the world was changed for ever. Hard work, lateral thinking and a scientific approach had allowed the Wrights to make one of the greatest steps in the history of human endeavour.

In December 1903, therefore, heavier-than-air flight had become a reality but, apart from a handful of curious onlookers and the helpful lifeguards from the Kill Devil Hills lifeguard station, few other people knew of the remarkable event. Rumours of the flight were mentioned in some of the smaller provincial newspapers but the press release was ignored by all of the major newspapers and, in particular, by Frank Tunison, editor of the 'Dayton Journal', whose scepticism caused him to turn down one of the greatest exclusives of all time, a decision which haunted his career forever afterwards. Wilbur and Orville Wright, meanwhile, began to be struck by the enormity of what they had achieved and they became obsessed with secrecy and the battle to keep other would-be aviators from copying their ideas. The brothers returned from Kitty Hawk and locked their flying machine away while they began the slow process of filing patents and perfecting their flight control system. By 1905 their improved Flyer was capable of staying aloft for 30 minutes and yet they continued to keep out of the limelight. Their confidence was shaken, however, when the intrepid Brazilian Alberto Santos Dumont achieved a flight of 200 metres in 1906. Suddenly, the newspapers were filled with stories of rapid and simultaneous developments in flying machines. It was Henri Farman's record-breaking 1-kilometre flight of 1908, however, which finally stirred the brothers into action. They had waited too long and they would have to act rapidly and decisively if their great achievement was not to be lost to the pioneering aviators of Europe. The latest Wright Flyer with its improved flight control system and its 2-seat payload was

carefully crated and Wilbur set off for France while Orville stayed in the USA and continued his protracted attempts to generate interest within the US War Department in the new flying machine.

France had become the unofficial capital of the world of aviation by 1908, with unprecedented levels of patronage and public following. By the beginning of August Wilbur was established in his simple shed by the Hunaudieres Race Track at Le Mans and he carefully uncrated his flying machine. As he painstakingly assembled his aircraft the newspapers laid siege to his quarters, and spectators thronged to the racecourse in the hope of seeing the curious American. By 8 August, Wilbur was ready. In front of a substantial crowd of stunned onlookers and newspapermen Wilbur sped down his launch rail and lifted into the air. Wilbur cruised above the racetrack at a height of 30 feet and displayed graceful and controlled banking turns as he followed the circuit below. Although his flight lasted only 1 minute 45 seconds the crowd was ecstatic and it was clear that the Wright brothers' mastery of the air far surpassed anything that had gone before. Wilbur became the shy and reluctant toast of Europe and was visited and congratulated at Le Mans by many of the great political and royal heads of Europe and many of the other great aviation pioneers.

The evolution of flight progressed more rapidly after 1908. In Europe and the Americas a host of aircraft projects began to take shape. Fed by relentless newspaper coverage, public interest in aviation was remarkable. The 1909 crossing of the English Channel by Frenchman Louis Blériot marked a huge milestone in aviation. In just 36 minutes Blériot's dramatic crossing secured his place in history and changed the relationship between Britain and Europe for ever. In 1909 the first International air rally, held just outside the French city of Reims, was attended by more than 250,000 spectators, who witnessed 23 aviators flying 9 types of aircraft. The Grande Semaine d'Aviation de la Champagne was a superbly organized and well-financed affair with substantial prizes for those aircraft that could fly the fastest, the highest and the furthest. From across Europe the rich and famous came to view history in the making, including presidents, royalty, politicians and some of the world's highest-ranking military figures. Most of the great aviation pioneers, too, were there, including Henri Farman, Glenn Curtiss and George Cockburn. Notable for their absence were the Wright brothers, although 2 of their latest Wright Flyers did perform daily routines in the hands of Eugene Lefebvre and Paul Tissandier. During the week more than 120 flights were made, a remarkable tally given that it was just 6 years since the first flight at Kitty Hawk. Among the records set at Reims was Glenn Curtiss's 47mph (75km/h) closed-course speed record, Hubert Latham's brave 508ft (155m) altitude record, and Henri Farman's 3-hour-long 112-mile (180km) distance record. It was just 1 year since Wilbur and Orville Wright had unveiled their flying machine, and already the shared momentum of development within aviation was passing them by.

Lighter-than-air aircraft, meanwhile, had begun to flourish with the application of new lightweight petrol engines to provide thrust and direction. No longer were these vast balloon-shaped flying machines carried along at the whim of the prevailing winds. The bulbous balloon shapes soon gave way to elongated forms, which could better cut through the air, and then to the pointed internally framed forms which we now associate with the great airships. Britain and Germany, in particular, embraced the airship race but Germany, under the direction of Count Ferdinand Von Zeppelin, was always ahead of the field with its sophisticated series of zeppelin airships. By 1906, his prototype LZ-3 airship was demonstrating flights of 8 hours endurance. Zeppelin fever gripped Germany, and when financial ruin followed the loss of LZ-4 in a storm, the German public spontaneously donated more than 6 million marks to ensure that the work of the great airship designer could continue. By 1910, Zeppelin was ready to carry fare-paying passengers, and the world's first scheduled flights began. Between 1910 and the outbreak of the First World War more than 37,000 passengers were carried by Germany's great airships, a total that far exceeded the numbers carried by heavier-than-air aircraft. By 1912, Hamburg and Berlin had scheduled airship links to many of the other European cities, and the Zeppelin became one of the world's dominant symbols of national prestige. With the advent of hostilities in 1914, however, the role of the Zeppelin changed radically. The use of newly developed lightweight aluminium-copper alloy in place of steelwork for Zeppelin's airship structures had brought huge reductions in airframe weight and allowed large amounts of munitions to be carried. The first aerial bombing of London on 31 May 1915 was a stunningly daring raid which brought the war right to Britain's doorstep. From a clear night sky the LV-38 dumped tons of bombs and incendiaries over the city and, although only 8 of its citizens were killed, the raid clearly illustrated that metropolitan populations would forever afterwards be vulnerable to attack from the air. The great airships would have their own terrible tragedies, however, and Henry Cavendish's 'inflammable air', which carried them into the air would also be their downfall. Ludwig Durr, chief engineer of the Zeppelin works, replaced the rubber-coated cotton material used to form the airships' hydrogen airbags with 'goldbeaters' skin', a lightweight membrane derived from cattle intestines. Its primary advantage, apart from its reduced weight, was its softness and the reduced likelihood that it would collect static electricity and generate sparks. The great airships were a precarious mix of explosive gas and static-collecting materials, a veritable accident waiting to happen. The loss of the Hindenburg in May 1937, although not the first airship disaster, was a tragedy of unprecedented proportions. The images caught live on camera and radio were so horrific that the days of the great rigid airships were immediately over.

After the events at Reims, aviation took hold of Europe and the Americas, and aviators and adventurers continued to push back the boundaries of aviation. By 1910 the first air freight was carried by a Wright biplane when a consignment of silk was ferried by Philip Parmalee from Dayton to Columbus, Ohio. In the same year the world's first seaplane lifted off the water at Martigues in France with Henri Fabre at the controls. Georges Chavez of Peru demonstrated to a fascinated public that even mountains could not defeat this new science of aeronautics. His 1910 crossing of the Alps in a Blériot monoplane was successful although he died in a simple flying accident as he landed in Italy. American Cal Rogers, meanwhile, fascinated the general public with his epic flight across the

American continent. It was his stubborn determination to keep going despite crashing 19 times, rather than his flying abilities, however, that intrigued the public. More practically, airmail was carried for the first time in February of 1911 when Frenchman Henri Pequet airlifted 6,500 letters across India's Jumna River. Aviation was becoming a worldwide phenomenon.

The military world had been greatly divided on the subject of aviation but, after its exposure to the highest levels of political and military leadership at Reims, aircraft began to find their way into the inventories of many of the world's armies. The Italians were the first to use an aircraft in action when on 22 October 1911, the Blériot of flying officer Capitano Piazza undertook a reconnaissance mission against Turkish forces in North Africa. Just 1 week later, his fellow officer, 2nd Lieutenant Giulio Gavotti, dropped explosive devices over the Turkish forces at Taguira Oasis, the first offensive action by any aircraft.

Britain's Royal Flying Corps, the forerunner of today's Royal Air Force, was formed in 1912 and many of the other European countries formed similarly dedicated air forces and flying wings. In the years leading up to the First World War, the rising tension within European politics was reflected by large-scale procurement of aircraft by European military and governmental establishments. By 1914, Henri Farman's aircraft works was employing more than 1,000 workers while the manufacturers of the successful Gnome aero-engine employed even more. Other early mass producers of military aircraft included Short Brothers of the UK, Junkers of Germany, and the Curtiss Aeroplane and Motor Company Inc. of the USA. Military aircraft were still a novelty and military leaders were unsure how they would be employed in a battlefield situation. Clearly flying machines promised great advantages in the areas of reconnaissance and artillery direction but, apart from these roles, there was much division on the usefulness of the new apparatus. Within the aviation community, however, there was little doubt that aircraft would play a major part in all future conflicts. As far back as June 1910 Glenn Curtiss had dropped dummy bombs from 1 of his biplanes onto a simulated battleship target over Lake Keuka, New York. Just 2 months later, Curtiss was again involved when Lieutenant Jacob Fickel of the US Army fired at ground-based targets from the passenger seat of a stock Curtiss biplane. By 1912, flying machines were a little more robust and engines more powerful, and in June of that year the first machine gun was fired from a Wright Model B Flyer. The age of military aviation was fast approaching.

On 28 June 1914, when the assassination of Archduke Franz Ferdinand in Sarajevo threw Europe into turmoil, the number of aircraft in the inventories of European armies was still very low. Germany held just over 230 aircraft and a number of giant Zeppelin airships. France held 156 aircraft while the combined Royal Flying Corps and Royal Naval Air Forces of Britain had a total force of 154 landplanes and seaplanes, and 7 giant airships. These numbers would increase massively over the war years as the aviation industry struggled to meet the increasing demands of the protagonist armies. By 1918, when the Armistice was signed, the aviation industry within Britain alone had grown to employ more than 350,000 workers and had demonstrated its ability to produce more than 30,000 aircraft a year. The combined stocks of surviving French, German, British and US aircraft at the end of the war are estimated to have been more than 75,000, an extraordinary total given that aviation was only in its 15th year.

The First World War, however, was unlike any past wars. The combatant forces entered it with grand 19th-century notions of horseback cavalry charges, buglers and standard-bearers. Instead they found themselves locked for years in a deadly quagmire of trenches that stretched hundreds of miles across the Eastern and Western Fronts. The introduction of the machine gun, and the mass production of artillery pieces and explosive shells, had changed the nature of warfare for ever and produced a tragic stalemate of unprecedented proportions where bewildered officers sent hundreds of thousands of hapless soldiers to a certain death for little or no military advantage. It was an appalling situation, in both military and human terms, and it was the introduction of the armoured tank and the development of more effective fighting aircraft which, as much as sheer numbers, eventually managed to break the stalemate. Military aviation, which had begun the war in the docile role of aerial observation only, developed at a remarkable pace during the war years. In 1914 flying machines had practically no margin for payload other than the pilot and his observer, and only very limited endurance. Observation flights were flown from behind the front lines with the intention of providing accurate information for the operators of the giant field guns and artillery pieces on the battlefield below. From this height the observer could monitor the entire frontline resources of the enemy, including his supply lines and his areas of concentration. With the introduction of better engines and more robust airframes, however, it became the norm to install a machine gun in the observer's station and, where payload margins allowed, a second machine gun in the pilot's station. Even with these weapons, however, it was immensely difficult to score a hit on an enemy aircraft. It was only with the invention of the interrupter mechanism by Anthony Fokker's engineering staff that the true military fighter was born. This mechanism 'timed' the bullets from one or more forward-firing machine guns so that they would pass through the arc of a spinning propeller. Fokker's innovation paid dividends in the skies above the trenches of France and for a period of months the combined Allied air forces were pounded by the German fighters. By early 1916 the Allies had begun to introduce the synchronous forward-firing gun to their own fighting fleet and so, for the first time, the tide of military warfare was decided, not on the battlefield, but in the design shops and research facilities of Germany, Britain and the US. From now on wars would be won by the application of technology and mass production.

On all sides the flying classes were also the officer classes. Many career cavalry officers found their way into the observer corps and several of those who survived long enough became aces with numerous enemy 'kills'. France's Captain Rene Fonck scored 75 kills, 6 of them in one day, and still went on to survive the war. Germany's Baron Manfred Von Richthofen, the infamous Red Baron, downed a record 80 enemy aircraft before himself being shot down in April 1918.

Lieutenant Albert Ball and Major James McCudden, for Great Britain, downed 101 aircraft between them before they too were lost in action. Dogfighting was a perilous occupation and the careers of most fighter pilots were tragically short. Even if they survived the fierce aerial combat there was the possibility that their engines would fail, their airframe fold up, or that they would fall victim to small-arms fire from below. Many of the less experienced pilots lasted only hours in frontline combat.

It was Hauptmann Oswalde Boelcke who introduced the feared German 'hunting packs', tight formations of fighters trained to attack from above and behind, flying out of the sun to maximize the element of surprise. His simple tactics brought great success in battle and went on to become the basic premise of aerial combat. The Allied forces, for their part, were the first to undertake a complex strategic bombing mission when in November of 1914, 3 Avro 505s of the Royal Navy took off from Belfort in France and flew 125 miles up the Rhine Valley to attack the giant Zeppelin sheds at Friedrichshafen. Even more ambitious was the June 1918 raid on the Zeppelin sheds at Tondern, where the improvised aircraft carrier HMS Furious approached the German coast and launched 7 bomb-laden Sopwith Camel biplanes. The raiders destroyed 2 Zeppelin airships in their sheds and one large captive balloon. It was an important victory for the Allied forces and a testament to the great strides made in naval aviation since the beginning of the war. Airframes and aircraft engines had improved dramatically, range and payload margins had increased substantially and the frail pre-war flying machines had been replaced by a tough breed of new fighting aircraft.

Suddenly the world was at peace and the surplus military aircraft were scrapped or sold into private ownership. The aviation industry, too, which had grown substantially during the war, was faced with adapting to meet the needs of the new peace-based economies. The difficulty was that there was little money about and many of the aircraft which survived the war were unsuitable for conversion to freight or passenger usage. By 1919 aviators were again stretching the boundaries of aviation, but now with the advantage of greatly improved technologies. The direct crossing of the Atlantic Ocean was perhaps the most ambitious challenge of the day and publishing giant Lord Northcliffe's 1913 offer of 50,000 dollars for the first direct Atlantic crossing was still unclaimed. In May 1919 the US Navy paved the way by flying 3 Curtiss NC-4 flying boats in stages from Newfoundland, via the Azores, to Lisbon. In the same month 12 aircraft, all modified military airframes, were at an advanced stage of preparation in the race to be the first to make it directly across the Atlantic. Lieutenant-Commander Kenneth Mckenzie-Grieve and Harry Hawker (later of Hawker Aircraft fame) were first to set out from Newfoundland but their modified Sopwith biplane was lost at sea. For a week they were mourned across the world before being miraculously picked up by the crew of a Danish merchant ship. By 14 June, the weather had again settled and Captain John Alcock and Lieutenant Arthur Whitten Brown flew their modified Vickers Vimy from Newfoundland east towards Ireland. During a gruelling 16-hour battle with hail, snow, lightning and low-level cloud, Brown at one point had to climb out onto the wings to de-ice the engine intakes. Eventually the Vimy crossed the coast of Ireland and the 2 jaded airmen ditched it unceremoniously into a bog outside Clifden, County Galway. The spell of the Atlantic had at last been broken.

A spate of pioneering adventures and record-breaking flights followed. In July 1919, the Atlantic was crossed for the first time by an airship when Britain's R-34 made a 2-way crossing from London to New York and back with its complement of 31 crew and 1 stowaway. During November and December 1919 Keith and Ross Smith of Australia flew their modified Vickers Vimy more than 11,000 miles for 28 days from Darwin to London. Frenchman Lucien Bossoutrot blazed a trail into Africa in his Farman Goliath, only to spend 6 terrifying days wrecked off the coast of Mauritania. Arctic explorer Roald Amundsen of Norway had reached the South Pole by foot in 1911 and now turned to aviation to bring him to the North Pole. In 1925, his Dornier-Wal seaplane had carried him within 150 miles of the Pole before it failed and the expedition had to be abandoned. The following year he returned with the airship Norge piloted by Italian Umberto Nobile, but as the Norge was readied to depart Spitzbergen, Commander Richard E. Byrd of the US Navy arrived to mount a US expedition. A dismayed Amundsen was left watching as Byrd's Fokker Trimotor set out before him to reach the Pole. Although Byrd did fly over the top of the world from Spitzbergen to Alaska there has always been controversy surrounding his claim to be the first to fly over the North Pole.

One of the most practical and obvious uses for aircraft was the transport of mail, and many ex-military pilots found themselves back in the air carrying mailbags for the US mail service. It was a tough business and accidents and fatalities were common. To provide a truly efficient airmail service would entail night flights, and in 1921 the mail service undertook the first night-flying experiments. By the mid-1920s a system of lighted airways was being built right across the USA with powerful rotating beacons located on hilltops and towers at 10-mile (16km) intervals. By 1933 the USA had more than 18,000 miles (28,800km) of lighted airways, and night flights were being undertaken with more success. One airmail pilot who aptly demonstrated the perilous nature of working for the mail service was Charles Lindbergh, who had to parachute from his aircraft on 2 mail flights: once when his aircraft ran out of fuel above dense ground fog, and once when he got caught in extreme weather conditions at low level. Lindbergh, the son of a Minnesota congressman, was fascinated by the challenges presented by aviation and, responding to the 25,000-dollar prize fund offered by hotelier Raymond Orteig, he decided to enter the New York-Paris race. Already the challenge had cost the lives of several aircrews, some of them on preparatory flights, others on take-off with maximum fuel and, perhaps worst of all, in the case of former war aces Charles Nungesser and Francois Coli, somewhere over the Atlantic Ocean between Le Bourget and New York. On 20 May 1927, Lindbergh's 'Spirit of St Louis' lifted off the wet grass at New York's Roosevelt Field and headed east over the Atlantic. With no radio, no sextant, and just 5 sandwiches and 2 flasks of water, Lindbergh struggled to stay awake hour after hour through appalling weather conditions. When at last he sighted fishing-boats off

the coast of Ireland he was fatigued to the point of hallucination. Remarkably, however, he was on course and he headed south-east for France. As he crossed the French coast news of his arrival had already reached Paris and hundreds of thousands of Parisians raced out to Le Bourget to greet him. Lindbergh had flown 3,600 miles over 33 hours 30 minutes to become an aviation icon.

By the early 1920s it was realized that until aviation could provide a reliable means of transporting passengers it would never fully thrive. The military surplus aircraft left over after the war were unsuitable even for conversion to such transports. Therefore an entirely new fleet of passenger carriers would have to be developed and many of the larger wartime manufacturers began to divert resources to this task. Among the earlier of these transports was the Handley Page Pullman of 1919, which served in-flight meals, and the de Havilland DH-34 of 1922, which had a toilet and baggage compartment but left the unfortunate pilot exposed to the elements in an open cockpit. Gradually the early airliners began to take shape and a small number of aircraft designers began to lead the industry. Professor Hugo Junkers of Germany developed a succession of excellent all-metal passenger transports which led the field throughout the 1920s and culminated in the superb Ju-52 of 1932, one of the great aircraft designs of the era. Handley Page, meanwhile, perfected its passenger transports in a series of improving models which led to the mammoth Handley Page HP-42 biplane of 1930. The advent of passenger transports soon led to the formation of the first airlines and these early operators quickly began to identify what they required of an aircraft if it was to make money. Despite the state of the German economy and the scale of war reparations to be paid to its neighbours, Lufthansa thrived and established routes across Europe and beyond. Britain's Imperial Airways, too, pioneered new scheduled flights to Europe and to Britain's many far-flung Commonwealth interests. But it was on the far side of the Atlantic that the real battle of the airlines was to take place as giant rivals Pan American Airways, Trans World Airlines and American Airlines pushed for bigger, faster, more comfortable airliners with which to win customers and expand their networks. Henry Ford, keen to expand into aircraft production, had William Stout design the 12-seat Ford Trimotor of 1926 which borrowed heavily from the earlier offerings of Hugo Junkers and Anthony Fokker. In response to a detailed brief from United Air Lines, Bill Boeing developed the 11-seat Boeing 247 of 1930 which, with a low monoplane wing, integrated flight deck and retractable undercarriage, was a major breakthrough. Boeing, however, had promised all of his production to United Air Lines, so rival Trans World Airlines turned to Donald Douglas of The Douglas Aircraft Company for help. For TWA it was a lucky move: the prototype DC-1 of 1933 was a stunning improvement on all that had gone before. Manufactured as the 14-seat DC-2, it was so highly prized by airline operators that the Douglas assembly line scaled up to produce 1 aircraft every 3 days. By 17 December 1935, 32 years to the day after the first flight by the Wright brothers, the remarkable DC-3 flew for the first time. Airline transport had at last come of age. By the end of the 1930s US operators were carrying more than 3 million passengers per year, 90 per cent of them on DC-3s and Boeing 247s.

The slow demise of the great airships from 1930 left airline transport over the world's oceans exclusively to flying boats and there followed a brief golden age when the lumbering hulled aircraft of Boeing, Sikorsky, Dornier, Latecoere and Short plied their way across the waters of the Atlantic and the Pacific. Associated always with glamour and intrigue, it was thought that they provided better safety when flying over water although, in truth, they were capable of alighting only onto medium-to-light levels of swell. Having conquered much of the USA with his land-based fleet, Pan American Airways' charismatic Juan Trippe himself accompanied Charles Lindbergh and wife Anne Morrow on a clever publicity tour across the Caribbean Islands and into Central America. The American public watched their Sikorsky S-38 flying boat on the newsreels and decided that flying boats did represent style and glamour. Across the world a network of carefully positioned flying-boat bases was developed, many of them, including Gander in Newfoundland and Foynes in Ireland, selected by Lindbergh himself. The golden age of the great flying boats was short, however. Although they did provide an invaluable link between Britain and the US throughout the War, the advances in airframe and powerplant technology which resulted from the war were to render them instantly obsolete in a post-war society.

By the late 1930s the politics of Europe were in a state of disarray. Spain was engaged in a vicious civil war, Italy in the grip of a Fascist dictatorship, and the shadow of communism loomed threateningly in the East. Worst of all, Germany was clearly building up its army, navy, and air strength at an alarming rate despite the strict limitations of the Treaty of Versailles. From absolute ruin after the First World War it had rebuilt its economy at a remarkable rate and had developed an industrial, military and technological might that far surpassed those of its neighbours. By 1936 Germany's Messerschmitt Bf-109 fighters and Heinkel He-111 bombers were openly supporting the Nationalist cause in Spain with unprecedented effectiveness. Its apocalyptic bombing of Guernica, in particular, caused great shock and anxiety right across Europe, particularly in France, which rushed to expand and update its air force. New fighting aircraft were developed and rushed into service and military officers scoured the USA for suitable frontline fighters and bombers.

When the forces of Nazi Germany poured into Poland in September 1939 their near-perfect synchronization of fast-moving Panzer columns and overwhelming air power were unprecedented. Germany's devastating Blitzkrieg tactics relied on waves of close-support Stuka dive bombers and high-level He-111s to pave the way for its highly mobile ground forces. The Polish air force, for its part, put up fierce resistance but its PZL P-11C fighters were no match for the swarms of modern Bf-109 fighters pouring into its airspace. Already, in the opening hours of the Second World War, it was technology and sheer numbers which were deciding the fate of armies and nations. For the remainder of the war the outcome of its many battles and campaigns would be decided, not by the combatant forces, but by the vast armies of scientists, mathematicians, engineers, aerodynamicists, radar specialists and code breakers who forged deep paths into previously unknown technologies in the battle to maximize military advantage.

In 1939 Germany's Luftwaffe summarily dealt with each of Europe's air forces. Britain's island status, however, afforded it a level of protection and it was not until June 1940 that the resources of the Reich became focused on it, in the form of Operation Sea Lion. To successfully cross the Channel, however, overwhelming air superiority would be required and so the RAF would have to be engaged and obliterated. The Luftwaffe's offensive, when it came, was on a scale hitherto unknown over the skies of southern England. The Battle of Britain had begun. For the first time, the fate of a nation lay entirely in the hands of its air force. Every day for 5 months large formations of He-111 bombers and Bf-109 escort fighters flew over Britain to be met by fierce opposition from the Hurricanes and Spitfires of the RAF. Piloted by crews from Britain, France, Poland, Czechoslovakia, Australia, New Zealand, Canada and the USA, the RAF held its ground at great cost to both sides. Even the Luftwaffe could not sustain such losses, sometimes up to 72 aircraft per day, and so in the last days of November the offensive was ended. Britain had been spared by the great bravery, tenacity and sacrifice of an extraordinary band of aviators. The fight to repulse night raiders and Blitz bombers would, however, still continue for several years. Both sides were now relying heavily on new wartime technologies, the German bombers navigating accurately to their targets using directional radio beacons, and the British using the rudimentary but highly effective Chain Home radar system to gain advance warning of the intruders. It was the discovery of the magnetron and the development of new lightweight airborne radar detection systems, however, which gave the Allies their biggest break of the war, allowing them to home in accurately on enemy aircraft by day or night and, in so doing, to greatly increase the attrition rate of the enemy fleet. This same technology, successfully concealed from the Axis powers for most of the war, could also be used to locate U-boats with precision. The ageing Fairey Swordfish biplane anti-submarine torpedo bomber was now joined by a new breed of sophisticated radar-equipped submarine-hunters which had the range and endurance to search the oceans for the elusive U-boat packs.

Japan's airborne attack on Pearl Harbor on 7 December 1941 marks one of the great turning points in history and one of the most dramatic and tragic milestones in naval aviation. It was not the first successful carrier-based assault: the Royal Navy had successfully launched an attack on Taranto in November 1940 which had famously crippled much of the Italian fleet. It was the sheer enormity, precision and audacity of the Pearl Harbor attack, however, which most shocked America and the world. In a moment the USA went from peace to war and national mourning. The lives of thousands of servicemen had been lost and the Pacific fleet was all but decimated. It was a demoralizing opening salvo in a war that would be fought over vast expanses of ocean. It would require new technologies and new aircraft with the range and the capacity to carry troops, weapons and even vehicles across the Pacific Ocean. Japan hoped the United States would have little stomach for fighting such a war but it had badly underestimated the USA's resolve, ingenuity and astonishing industrial capacity.

With the addition of the US to the Allied war effort, vast quantities of armaments and military aircraft began to arrive in Britain. Germany's encounter with the Soviet Union too, although not actually a defeat as such, had absorbed considerable weaponry and manpower for little or no return. Gradually the tide of war turned and the Allies began to gain the upper hand. The industrial might of the USA was applied to the mass production of new heavy bombers and escort fighters. Its B-17 Flying Fortresses and B-24 Liberators were among the most effective bombers of the war and its P-51 Mustang escort fighters were more than a match for the Luftwaffe's Bf-109s. Allied bombing raids on the cities and industrial centres of Germany grew in size and frequency until, late in the war, massive raids comprising many hundreds of bombers and escort fighters, were, daily and nightly, striking deep into Germany's industrial heart.

On all sides of the conflict, aircraft became central to some of the most daring operations and, in so doing, entered common folklore and the history books. The airborne rescue of Mussolini from captivity was one of aviation's earliest and most sophisticated special-operations coups and it remained a source of German national pride for the rest of the war. In a remarkable demonstration of efficiency and daring, Otto Skorzeny and his raiding party used silent assault gliders to storm the Gran Sasso mountain lodge, where Mussolini was being held, and then spirited the deposed Fascist leader away in a 3-seat Fieseler Storch light plane. Britain, too, has always held the exploits of its wartime airmen dear to its heart but none more so than the raid on the dams of the Ruhr Valley by the specially designed bouncing bombs of the aeronautical designer, Barnes Wallis.

The jet engine was first discovered in 1930 by Frank Whittle, a 23-year-old officer of the Royal Air Force. The British Air Ministry, however, was not impressed with his radical new powerplant and refused to support his work. So the design of the world's first jet engine was filed away for almost 10 years and its inventor relegated to more mundane research duties. In Germany, however, new sciences and technologies were embraced and supported, and although it stumbled on jet power many years after Whittle it quickly recognized its immense potential and set about making it its own. By 1939 Germany's rudimentary turbojet-powered Heinkel He-178 had flown. By April 1941 it had advanced turbojet technology to the point of launching its prototype Heinkel He-280, the world's first workable and fully armed jet fighter. Although workable it was not put into production, and it was the Me-262 jet fighter which finally made it into operational service in the last months of the war. With a maximum level speed of 539mph (867km/h), it was substantially faster than its adversaries and it could have had a significant bearing on the outcome of the war had it become operational just 1 year earlier. Britain, the USA and the Soviet Union, meanwhile, were all developing their own jet-fighter prototypes, with Britain and the USA achieving their first jet-powered flights in 1941 and the Soviet Union flying its first jet fighter in 1945.

By the beginning of 1945 it was clear to all but the most fanatical that Germany was about to collapse under pressure from the Allied armies. From January 1945, increasing numbers of German scientists, mathematicians and aerodynamicists began to surrender to the advancing Allied forces in anticipation of the coming defeat. Among these defectors were teams of aerodynamicists and project engineers from some of the leading aircraft design shops, and many of them went on to work in the research facilities of the USA, the Soviet Union and Britain. Germany's V2 missile design team, headed by Werner Von Braun, became one of the most invaluable spoils of war of all time when they surrendered to the American forces. Von Braun and his team and the V2 ballistic missile became the basis on which the American space programme would be built.

After the end of the war in Europe and the devastating airborne release of atomic weapons over Hiroshima and Nagasaki, the world should have returned to peace, but new perceived threats instead brought tension and the start of what would become the Cold War. Its first great test, the Berlin Airlift, was accomplished by a remarkable army of aircraft armed, not with weapons of war, but with the foodstuffs and vital supplies for the people of that city. Throughout the Cold War, the development of new military aircraft would become one of the principal areas in which East and West would compete. It was confrontation with minimal bloodshed. From the first generation of post-war operational jet fighters such as the North American Sabre, the Gloster Meteor and the Mig-15, to the sophisticated supersonic aircraft of the 1980s, the Cold War brought development in military aviation such as one might expect of a wartime economy.

Aviation has come of age. From those tentative first flights by the 2 Dayton bicycle-makers to today's sophisticated fly-by-wire military jets, aviation has travelled an extraordinary route and has developed more quickly than the other sciences. Where it will develop in the next 100 years is difficult to say, but if it continues to progress as it has done in the past, it promises an exciting and intriguing spectacle for all of us who hold it dear.

The Timeline of Aviation

Some of the most important or influential events in the development of flight, and some of the more interesting stories of perseverance, innovation and eccentricity.

Pre-1200 — Legends, myths and crazy tower-jumpers

From the very earliest of times man has had a fascination with flight, and all civilizations have incorporated legends and tales of great flying heroes into their traditions and folklore. From the ancient and unfortunate Icarus right up to the contemporary Superman, story tellers have embraced the wonder and the mystery of flight in the fabric of their creations. History records many eccentric individuals, too, who have tried to unravel the mysteries of flight with the aid of cloaks, feathers and church towers. For the most part these brave innovators have had very short careers.

1200s — Giant man-lifting kites in 13th-century China

The Chinese mastered the art of building and flying kites at least 3,000 years ago and the flying of huge colourful kites was absorbed into the country's wonderfully rich culture. During the 13th century, adventurer Marco Polo witnessed huge kites that could lift humans into the air. Man-lifting kites would become fashionable again in 19th-century Europe.

1500s — Leonardo da Vinci studied the anatomy of flight

The extraordinary Leonardo da Vinci applied science and logic to his examination of flight. He studied the anatomy and muscle groups of birds and developed his own theoretical flying machine, essentially an early ornithopter. He invented the airscrew, essentially a propeller, and he devised the first ever parachute device.

1766 — Henry Cavendish isolated 'inflammable air'

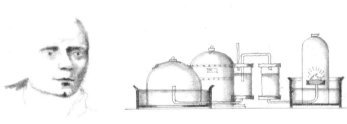

Henry Cavendish was an oddball and an eccentric but he was one of the great scientists of his day. In 1766 his experiments into the specific gravities of gases led him to isolate and identify 'inflammable air' or hydrogen gas. Cavendish soon realized that the gas was lighter than air, a discovery that would change the face of both science and aviation for ever.

1783 — J.A.C. Charles built the first hydrogen balloon

From the discovery of hydrogen gas to the flight of the first hydrogen-filled balloon took a matter of only 17 years. The J.A.C. Charles balloon was basic and simple but, with the aid of Cavendish's 'inflammable air', it did achieve flight. The Charles balloon did not carry a basket or a passenger but it was a clear promise of things to come.

1783 — Montgolfier bros demonstrated the hot-air balloon

Brothers Joseph and Etienne Montgolfier demonstrated their hot-air balloon to the stunned King Louis XVI of France, his Queen Marie-Antoinette and the cream of Parisian society. The first aviators were not humans but a sheep, a cock and a duck. The Montgolfier brothers would go on to great things but Louis and Marie-Antoinette would lose their heads in the French Revolution.

1783 — Man's first flight in a hot-air balloon

Jean-François Pilatre de Rozier became the very first true aviator when he ascended to a height of 85 feet, nothing by today's standards but a massive advance for 1783. At that time science and the pursuit of flight were the playthings of a few wealthy eccentrics, and production of large volumes of hydrogen gas was a major hurdle for de Rozier and his fellow aviators. Within months, however, word of the first aviator or 'Pilatre' had raced across Europe, and society notables and gentlemen in all of its capitals began to emulate the great events in Paris. Balloon experts and balloon workshops began to appear in the most unlikely locations, and fortunes and reputations were made by those who were successful in the new art of aerial construction and navigation.

1785
First balloon to cross the English Channel

Frenchman Jean-Pierre Blanchard and American Dr John Jeffries were the first aviators to cross the English Channel by balloon, an extraordinary achievement given that the first manned balloon had flown only 2 years earlier. The flight was made in a 'Charles' hydrogen balloon, the type having advanced rapidly in size and performance in the intervening 2 years.

1797
World's first parachute jump by André J. Garnerin

France was very much the centre of the ballooning revolution in its early years and the intrepid aviators fascinated Parisian society and became great public figures. In 1797, Frenchman André Jacques Garnerin made the very first parachute jump, a feat of the most extraordinary valour and blind faith in the most basic and rudimentary of parachute devices.

1871
Otto Lilienthal, the real father of flight

Otto Lilienthal commenced his research into aviation in 1871. For 25 years he crunched numbers and built and flew his many many gliders. He used his data to design and incorporate a system of horizontal stabilizers and rudders. He flew reliably and frequently and corresponded in his later years with the Wright brothers. Lilienthal was killed when his glider stalled in 1896.

1896
Langley flew giant steam-powered model aircraft

Professor Samuel Langley built a large tandem-wing steam-powered aircraft that was to be launched from the top of a houseboat moored in the middle of the Potomac River at Quantico, Virginia. The aircraft, although not piloted, did lift off and flew briefly before landing into the river. Langley's later efforts at flight proved to be very contentious and much less successful.

1899
Percy Pilcher killed in powered hill launch

The aviation bug was spreading across the world and all manner of local flying attempts were being made. Scotsman Percy Pilcher built and flew his own gliders and by 1899, had added an engine to give powered flight. On 30 September 1899, Pilcher was killed while demonstrating his glider at Market Harborough, England. His powered version was never flown.

1899
The Wright brothers began the study of flight

The Wright brothers of Dayton, Ohio used logic, hard work and the writings of Lilienthal to build up an understanding of the mechanics of flight. They developed the world's first wind tunnel and with it they determined the most successful aerofoil shapes. They used their bicycle-making skills to construct a series of gliders which they flew at a remote beach at Kitty Hawk, North Carolina.

1900
First flight of the Zeppelin LZ-1 dirigible

The LZ-1 dirigible of 1900 was the prototype for the great Zeppelin series that was, without doubt, the most successful of all the airship lines. The enormous size and the directional steering abilities of the LZ-1 made a huge press impact. For a few short years aviation was divided between the ardently followed 'lighter-than-air' and 'heavier-than-air' camps.

1903
First powered flight by the Wright brothers

The Wright brothers worked quietly without attracting the attention that other aviators seemed to court. By 1903 they had mastered the art of gliding and could exercise reasonable directional control. On 17 December 1903 their newly engined 'Flyer' made history with the first flight of just 12 seconds. The aircraft flew a total of 4 times that day.

1905 — Wright Flyer No 3 could fly non-stop for 30 minutes

In both Europe and the Americas the press was fascinated by the accelerating race to be first into the air. Newspapers kept the waiting public informed of all developments and, indeed, many rumours also. The Wrights, meanwhile, worked away in relative privacy perfecting their machine and writing patents. By 1905 they could fly for a full 30 minutes with complete directional control.

1906 — Brazilian Alberto Dumont flew nearly 200 feet

The diminutive Brazilian Alberto Santos Dumont was one of the great characters of aviation: rich, magnanimous and greatly loved by the press. In 1906 his '14 Bis' Flyer took off and flew all of 200 feet. The people of France were jubilant and heralded Dumont as the first to fly. The Wright brothers' pursuit of privacy and patent rights could cost them their place in history.

1908 — Henry Farman's Voisin Biplane flew 1km

Flying a Voisin Biplane, Henry Farman flew a closed circular route of 1km to win a prize of 50,000 francs, a huge windfall in its day. The Wright brothers, on hearing of the many great advances in European aviation, became alarmed and decided that they must bring their latest Flyer to the attention of Europe and the world.

1908 — Glenn Curtiss broke the 1km barrier in his June Bug

Glenn Curtiss became an instant celebrity when his 'June Bug' biplane successfully flew a 1-kilometre course making Curtiss the first American to achieve that milestone. The Wright flights were still not public knowledge. Curtiss went on to become one of the world's greatest and most prolific aircraft designers and founder of the Curtiss Wright Corporation.

1908 — Wilbur Wright revealed the Wright Flyer at Le Mans

Wilbur Wright set up shop in a shed adjacent to the Le Mans race course and then began a series of flight demonstrations which amazed the crowds and brought worldwide acclaim. The Wright Flyer was clearly far superior to all of the European machines, flying under complete control and even, on one occasion, circling the race course 77 times in a 2.5-hour flight.

1908 — Lt Thomas Selfridge: the first aircraft fatality

While Wilbur Wright headed to France, Orville stayed in the USA to demonstrate the new Flyer to the US Army and to other interested business parties. On 17 September 1908 Orville, with Lt Thomas E. Selfridge on board, stalled the aircraft and crashed violently to the ground. Lt Selfridge's injuries were severe and he became the first-ever aviation fatality.

1909 — Louis Blériot crossed the English Channel

On 25 July 1909 Frenchman Louis Blériot crossed the 23-mile-wide English Channel in a time of 37 minutes and won himself a place in aviation history. Blériot was an instant celebrity and was cheered by thousands in London. On his return to Paris more than 100,000 people lined the streets to welcome their new hero.

1910 — Zeppelin LZ-7 carried the first paying passengers

By 1910 the Zeppelin LZ-7 was ready to commence the carriage of passengers. Despite the huge envelope of dangerous hydrogen overhead, the airship proved to be a most popular way for the rich and famous to travel, with no less than 35,000 passengers being carried before the outbreak of the First World War. The fare between Dusseldorf and Frankfurt was not cheap at 200 marks.

1910
Cal Rogers crashed 19 times while crossing the USA

Cal Rogers was a colourful character who was greatly loved by the press and public alike. When publisher William Randolph Hearst offered a prize of $50,000 to the first aviator to cross the USA in less than 30 days, Rogers took the challenge. Unfortunately, however, his aircraft was a disaster from the start and he crash landed 19 times before completion.

1911
Lilian Bland, first woman to design and build an aircraft

Having read about the Channel crossing by Blériot, Irishwoman Lilian Bland attended an English aviation meeting and carefully studied the aircraft. On returning to Ireland she then set about designing, building and flying her own machine. The completed aircraft flew successfully giving Ms Bland a place in history.

1911
Meli Besse experienced male chauvinist pilots

German student pilot Meli Besse was shocked to be harassed by her fellow male pilots in the hours before her final flight test. It seems that, while they were prepared to tolerate her taking pilot lessons, they were not happy to have her gain a full pilot's licence. The intolerant males drained her fuel tanks and even tampered with her aircraft's steering mechanism. Throughout the early years of aviation the flying movement was closely shadowed by the suffragette movement and, indeed, a large number of the great aviation pioneers were women. Here was a brand new area of endeavour where women could compete with men. Gravity and the emerging laws of aerodynamics applied to men and women in equal proportion with sometimes tragic results.

1912
Harriet Quimby, first woman to cross the Channel

Harriet Quimby, the first American woman to hold a pilot's licence, successfully crossed the English Channel on 16 April 1912. Unlike Blériot's reception, however, Ms Quimby's achievement was overshadowed by the coinciding tragic sinking of the Titanic, and the newspapers, giving blanket coverage to the demise of the great White Star liner, scarcely reported her exploit.

1912
Britain's Royal Flying Corps was formed

Britain's Royal Flying Corps was founded and similar army and naval forces were established in many countries across the world. From now on military forces would be the main purchasers of aircraft and, indeed, would shortly be specifying the nature, size and performance details of most new aircraft types.

1914
First World War changed aviation for ever

The coming of the First World War changed aviation for ever. The great adventurous heroes of the fledgling days of aviation were replaced by new military heroes: the short-lived 'aces', who killed their enemies in the air and were, themselves, usually killed in turn. A more mundane usage of aircraft, however, was the gunning of troops as they hid in their trenches.

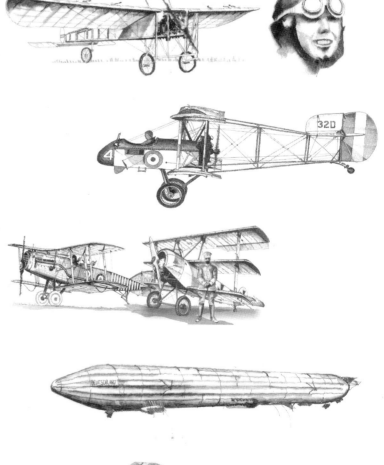

1915
Aerial bombardment of London by Zeppelin LZ-38

On a clear moonlit night on 31 May 1915 the Zeppelin LZ-38, commanded by one Captain Linnartz, flew over the London Docks and dropped bombs and incendiaries over Stoke Newington, Hoxton and Stepney. Londoners were shocked that the war had come to their doorstep and, although only 7 people were killed, the raid illustrated the vulnerability of civilian populations.

1915
First flight of Junkers all-metal aircraft

In Germany, Junkers Aircraft rolled out the first all-metal aircraft, the 'J-1 Tin Donkey'. Compared to other aircraft the type was tough and robust and, unlike the fabric-covered aircraft of the day, it provided great protection against enemy bullets. The Tin Donkey would go on to inspire a broad range of aircraft for many many years to come.

1916 Very first members of the 'Mile-High Club'

The distinction of being the very first members of the 'Mile-High Club' belongs to a Mr Laurence Sperry and a Mrs Polk. Mr Sperry, a wealthy socialite and man-about-town, was the inventor of the Sperry autopilot. Mrs Polk, whose husband was driving an ambulance on the European battlefront, was his student. It seems, however, that she was getting much more than flying lessons. In 1916, while flying with Mrs Polk in a Curtiss Flying Boat, Sperry engaged his newly invented autopilot. After some time, however, the device failed and the intrepid pair ended up crash-landing into the river. When rescued, both pilots were found to be completely naked. The next day's newspapers carried the headline 'aerial petting leads to wetting'.

1916 A new culture of war heroes and aces

Over the course of the war a new breed of flying aces and war heroes emerged within each of the warring nations. Many of these aces had brilliantly distinguished but very short flying careers. Other poor unfortunates lasted only hours in the battlefields of the skies. To the troops in the trenches below their twisting dogfights must have been an awesome sight.

1917 First ever landing on a ship under way

On 2 August 1917 Flight Commander E.H. Dunning landed his Sopwith Pup onto the deck of the HMS Furious while she was under steam. His attempt to repeat the feat only 2 days later ended in tragedy when 1 of his tyres burst and he cartwheeled into the sea. By the time a rescue party had managed to reach the stricken aircraft and release him, Dunning had met his death.

1919 Alcock & Brown first to cross the Atlantic Ocean

On 14 June 1919 the Vickers Vimy of Charles Alcock and Arthur Brown departed Newfoundland, Canada, on its brave transatlantic flight to Ireland. Conditions over the huge ocean were terrible with rain and fog, but the pair fought hour after hour until they at last sighted dry land. Photographs taken the day after the flight clearly show the stress and strain on the faces of the pilots.

1919 Vickers Vimy flew from England to Australia

On 12 November 1919 Vickers Vimy G-EAOU carried Captain Ross Smith and his crew of 3 all the way from London to Port Darwin, Australia. The flying time was 136 hours and the distance flown was 11,080 miles. The aircraft had stopped liberally on the journey and the overall trip duration was almost 28 days. Given that flight was only 16 years old this is a remarkable achievement.

1920 The era of barnstorming and wingwalking

With the release of large numbers of army-surplus aircraft after the war the barnstorming era really took off. Stunt pilots, wingwalkers and a multitude of other crazies vied with each other for the attentions of the paying public. It was a hard way to make a living and pilots had to resort to ever more dangerous tasks to satisfy the appetites of spectators. There were many accidents.

1921 First sinking of a battleship by an aircraft

On 21 July 1921 in a joint service exercise the captured German battleship 'Ostfriesland' was sunk by 11 1,000lb and 2,000lb bombs dropped from above by Brigadier General Billy Mitchell's bombers. US and British forces disposed of large quantities of captured materials and munitions and many ships were simply used for target practice and despatched to the bottom of the sea.

1921 The world's first crop-dusting aircraft

The ever-inventive Glenn Curtiss developed an agricultural crop-dusting version of his robust and successful Curtiss JN-4D aircraft. On 4 August 1912, the first crop-dusting exercise took place with stunning results. In a 15-minute fly-past pilot Lt John McCready managed to apply insecticide to 5,000 young Catalpa trees. The era of crop-dusting had arrived.

1922
The world's first aircraft carrier USS 'Langley'

The first aircraft carrier was the USS 'Langley', a conversion of the collier 'Jupiter'. To provide a working flight deck the superstructure was substantially removed and a new, level flight deck was constructed overhead. The ship's funnels were diverted to the port side of the 'runway' in order that the approach path of the landing aircraft would be clear.

1923
Juan de la Cierva crossed the Channel by autogyro

Spanish designer Don Juan de la Cierva began working on the theory of autogyros in 1920. Over the following 2 years he built a series of prototype autogyros which could not sustain balanced flight. Finally his C-4 autogyro of 1923 was successful and the designer of the world's first rotary wing aircraft went on to demonstrate his aircraft in a series of dazzling flights.

1924
2 Douglas DWC Cruisers circumnavigated the globe

In 1908 aviators were struggling to break the 1 kilometre distance barrier. Now only 16 years later the first round-the-world flight set off into the unknown. 4 Douglas World Cruisers of the US Army Air Service set out and, while 2 of the aircraft were lost en route, the crews were saved and the remaining 2 aircraft completed the 27,533-mile journey in 175 days.

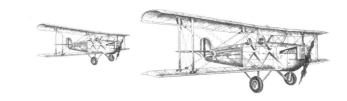

1927
Charles Lindbergh flew New York to Paris solo

In May of 1927 Charles Lindbergh astounded the world by flying solo and non-stop from New York directly to Paris. The 33.5 hour journey was a miracle of navigation and Lindbergh went on to fame and fortune. His arrival in Paris and later in New York was greeted by vast crowds, all anxious to have sight of the great new aviation pioneer.

1928
'Bremen' made first East to West Atlantic flight

Crossing the Atlantic from East to West would entail battling headwinds all the way. The 'Bremen', a modified German Junkers 33, set out from Ireland's Baldonel Aerodrome on 12 April 1928 and, after battling drizzle and fog for much of the journey, landed roughly on Greenly Island, Canada. Again huge media interest and notoriety greeted the brave aircrew.

1929
First stowaway to make it across the Atlantic

Journalist Arthur Schreiber, anxious to get a scoop, concealed himself in the rear of the French 'l'oiseau Canari' immediately before take-off from Maine on its South Atlantic crossing. The aircraft was sluggish in the climb, which led to the discovery of the stowaway. The crew continued the 28-hour journey to Spain even though Schreiber's weight greatly reduced their safety margins.

1929
First in-flight motion picture entertainment

The very first in-flight motion picture was screened during the summer of 1929 on board a Transcontinental Air transport over Columbus, Ohio. The motion picture was, of course, black and white and there was no sound save for the droning of the aircraft's engines. Two short programmes were shown, a comedy reel and a news reel.

1930
Amy Johnson flew England to Australia in 19 days

Amy Johnson became the first woman to fly solo from England to Australia. In an extraordinary adventure she covered the difficult route in a mere 19 days. Her open-cockpit de Havilland Gipsy Moth biplane was one of de Havilland's greatest designs and, after several successful record-breaking flights, it went on to be manufactured in very great numbers.

1930
23-year-old Frank Whittle patented his jet engine

At 23 years of age Royal Air Force officer Frank Whittle began his studies of propulsion systems and patented the world's first jet engine. The British Air Ministry, however, was unimpressed with Whittle's ideas and they refused to support his work. Whittle continued his experiments at a low level and established many of the ground rules which govern propulsion systems.

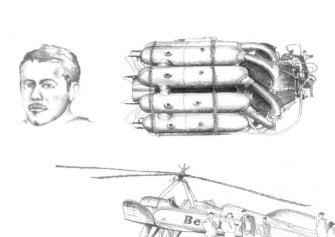

1931
Amelia Earhart set a new autogyro altitude record

On 22 April 1931 Amelia Earhart established a new altitude record for autogyros. Reaching 18,400 feet she came to the point where the machine would simply not climb anymore. The flight entailed battling extreme cold, and oxygen deprivation. For auto gyro designers, new engines offered new opportunities and new limitations.

1931
Lindberghs surveyed routes to Orient & Americas

Charles Lindbergh and his wife, Anne Morrow, carried out a series of extraordinarily long and adventurous pioneering flights to establish commercial air routes from the USA to the Orient (1931) and later from the USA across the North and South Atlantic (1933). The Lindberghs remained in the eye of the public for much of their natural lives.

1932
Amelia Earhart's Atlantic solo flight

Amelia Earheart's Lockheed Vega 5B departed Newfoundland on 20 May 1932, arriving in Northern Ireland 14 hours and 56 minutes later. Aircraft were becoming faster and the Vega had virtually halved the time required to complete the 2,026-mile journey. This was one of the great aerial achievements of the day and it was greeted with great enthusiasm by press and public alike.

1933
Fairey Monoplane flew England to South Africa

The flight of the Fairey long-range Monoplane from RAF Cranwell non-stop to Walvis Bay, South Africa, set a new distance record and was, in its time, an extraordinary aviation achievement. Covering a distance of 5,410 miles without stopping or refuelling, the flight took a total of 57 hours and 25 minutes.

1933
Wiley Post solo-circumnavigated the world

The Lockheed Vega was the plane selected by Wiley Post to attempt the very first solo circumnavigation of the globe. The 'Winnie Mae' was perhaps the world's most advanced aircraft in 1933 and it already had a string of difficult endurance and record flights to its credit. The flight covered a distance of 15,600 miles and took a total of 7 days, 18 hours and 49 minutes.

1933
First flight over the summit of Mount Everest

The first flight over the summit of Mount Everest was on 3 April 1933 by a Westland PV3 aircraft which was specially modified to support the Houston Everest expedition of 1933. Later, during the Second World War, buzzing the summit of Everest would become a favourite pastime of US fighter pilots who would divert hundreds of miles off-route to buzz the snowcapped peak.

1935
Fred and Algene Key flew 27 days without landing

Fred and Algene Key took off from Meridian Mississippi in their tiny Curtiss Robin J-1. Once in the air they received food and fuel through a sliding door in the roof of the aircraft. The engine was serviced by way of a frighteningly flimsy external catwalk. Their record-breaking flight lasted an amazing 27 days, by which time they must have been much relieved to return to earth.

1935 Douglas Aircraft introduced the DC-3 airliner

1935 saw the first flight of the prototype Douglas DC-3, a truly outstanding 28-seat airliner which set new standards of reliability, performance and longevity. Indeed, there are places in the world where DC-3 aircraft are still in service today. The military version of the type was the C-47 transport which, after the war, became available to hundreds of tiny new airlines.

1937 Guernica, Spain, suffered massive aerial bombing

The Spanish town of Guernica was devastated by massive aerial bombardment by German aircraft operating in support of Spain's right-wing nationalist rebels. The bombing was unprecedented in its ferocity and high explosives rained down on the town's unfortunate inhabitants for 4 hours killing most of its people and inspiring Picasso's harrowing artwork, 'Guernica'.

1937 The Hindenburg tragedy ended the days of airships

In one moment in New Jersey the fortunes of the great airships came to a sudden and tragic end. As the magnificent and luxurious Zeppelin LZ-129 'Hindenburg' moored after a transatlantic passage the entire airship was engulfed in an enormous fireball. All on board were instantly killed and a series of frightening images were published right around the world.

1937 Amelia Earhart lost over the Pacific Ocean

1937 was also the year that Amelia Earhart was lost. Adored by the press and never far out of the limelight, Earhart attracted huge interest when she set out to circumnavigate the globe. Her luck ran out, however, and she and Fred Noonan, her mechanic, disappeared over the Pacific. Over the years there have been many rumours of intrigue but it is likely that she simply became lost at sea.

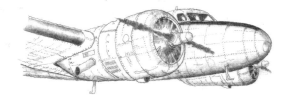

1938 Howard Hughes circled the globe in 3 days 19 hours

On 10 July 1938 Howard Hughes, entrepreneur, womanizer, and eccentric, set out in Lockheed's latest and greatest, the L-14 Super Electra, to establish a new speed record for circumnavigation of the globe. Hughes and his crew of 4 completed the pioneering 14,791-mile flight in a mere 3 days, 19 hours and 8 minutes. The world was, indeed, becoming a smaller place.

1938 'Wrongway' Corrigan misread his compass

On 18 December 1938 one Douglas Corrigan came to the attention of the world's media for all the wrong reasons. Setting out westwards from New York to Los Angeles, Corrigan 'accidentally' went the wrong way and flew right across the Atlantic Ocean landing instead at Baldonel Aerodrome in Ireland. In a world that was building up to war he was a welcome diversion and became a great hero.

1938 First flight of the world's first pressurized airliner

The world's first pressurized airliner was built by Boeing. The Model 307 Stratoliner was a capable and innovative 4-engined transport which, with the benefit of pressurization, could ensure a smooth ride at altitudes far above normal atmospheric turbulence. It was overtaken by the war, however, when the emphasis was very much on fighters and bombers, and only 10 of the type were produced.

1939 The Second World War brought death from the air

The tragic scale of the killing and the suffering which came with the Second World War changed the world for ever. Aviation, too, would never be the same. New specially designed aircraft had facilitated the industrial-scale bombing of civilian populations by all sides. Where in the past wars had been fought on the battlefields, the aeroplane had brought the killing to the people.

1939

Heinkel He-178, the world's first jet aircraft

At the outset of the war the German designers certainly seemed to have the advantage in terms of technology. On 27 August 1939 Flugkapitan Erich Warsitz lifted off in the He-178, the first-ever turbojet-powered aircraft. Britain, too, was working on a jet propulsion engine but it would be 1.5 years later before the Gloster E-28/39 would fly.

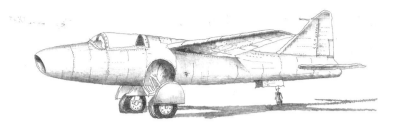

1940

12-year-old schoolboy was youngest to fly solo

Despite the constant deluge of mixed news from the war zones, life went on for those who remained at home. Aviation was still young and there were many records yet to be broken. In Canada one of the more trivial, or perhaps downright foolish, records to be broken was that of being the youngest-ever pilot to fly solo. In 1940 that honour went to 12-year-old Bob Martin of Toronto.

1940

Tom Dobney talked his way into the RAF, at 14

In 1940, young Tom Dobney ran away from home and, falsifying his age, enlisted in the RAF. Within weeks he was undergoing pilot training and within the year he had moved on to an operational training unit in preparation for transfer to a full operational fighter squadron. His tormented parents, however, located him at last and arrived to bring the young confidence trickster home.

1941

Germany's He-280 became first operational jet fighter

Clearly ahead of the posse in the area of jet propulsion, the Luftwaffe launched the He-280, the first workable turbojet fighter in April of 1941. Although this aircraft did not proceed past flying prototype stage the type was a major influence on the Luftwaffe's later twin turbojet fighter, the Me-262, which did itself see operational service in the later years of the war.

1941

Massive carrier-launched attack on Pearl Harbor

Japan's massive surprise attack on the US naval fleet at Pearl Harbor was like a bolt out of the blue for the US. The sheer distance across the Pacific Ocean caused the Japanese threat to be treated with great complacency by politicians and armed forces alike. The Japanese task force, however, sailed within 260 miles of Honolulu before releasing its 360 deadly fighter bombers.

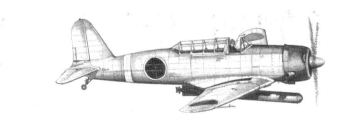

1942

Messerschmitt's Me-262 jet exceeded 539 mph

The Messerschmitt Me-262 is the aircraft that might have changed the outcome of the war! With a max level speed of 539mph and a range of 700 miles, the Me-262 was more than a measure for any of the Allied piston-powered aircraft. Hitler, however, was insistent that maximum effort should be put into the development of bombers and not fighters and so the project was stalled.

1943

The Lockheed Constellation airliner flew

1943 saw the first flight of the Lockheed Constellation, the aircraft which more than any other brought air travel to the masses. Designed to meet exacting specifications set down by Trans World Airlines (TWA), the Constellation could fly more than 3,500 miles non-stop, giving it a routine transatlantic range. During the war years, production of the type was primarily military.

1943

The extraordinary airborne rescue of Mussolini

The rescue of Mussolini from the Gran Sasso was one of aviation's earliest and most successful special-operations coups. Hitler selected the highly capable Otto Skorzeny as the leader of the raiding party, and Skorzeny used silent assault gliders to sneak up on his prey, followed by the extraordinary Fieseler Storch STOL light plane to spirit away the deposed Fascist leader.

1944

First V2 ballistic missiles fired at London

Londoners were already aware of the V1 'Doodlebugs' but when the first V2s came crashing down from a height of 50 miles the poor citizens were absolutely terrified. These devastating weapons, the first ballistic missiles, could fall on any part of the city without warning and without mercy. By 1945 everybody knew somebody whose life had been cut short by a V1 or a V2.

1944

First Japanese 'kamikaze' missions

By late 1944 the Japanese were being hard pressed by American forces right across the Pacific. The sheer number of fighters and the amount of flak that was being thrown up by the US carrier fleet was so great that it was extremely difficult for the Japanese pilots to score a hit. The extraordinary Japanese 'kamikaze' pilots, however, inflicted mortal blows on many US warships.

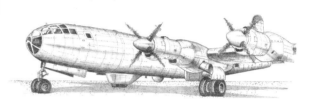

1945

B-29 'Enola Gay' dropped an atom bomb on Hiroshima

On 6 August 1945, Boeing B-29 Superfortress 'Enola Gay' released the terrible atom bomb over Hiroshima. The Manhattan Project team had designed the bomb to detonate some 2,000 feet above the city to ensure maximum destruction of the city and its unfortunate population. The bomb's descent was slowed to allow the crew of 'Enola Gay' to make a clean getaway.

1947

Chuck Yeager broke the sound barrier in the Bell X-1

Aerodynamicists were not sure what would happen when an aircraft broke the sound barrier, so they sent Chuck Yeager up to find out. On 14 October 1947 Yeager strapped himself into the Bell X-1 rocket-powered research aircraft and, at an altitude of 42,000ft (12,600m) accelerated to Mach 1.015 or 700mph. The sound barrier had at last been broken.

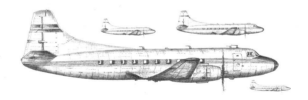

1948

The Berlin Airlift began

Following the Russian blockade of the road and rail links to Berlin, Operation Vittles or the great Berlin Airlift began. Everything had to be carried into the city by air while the population, already deprived for the war years, had to live as frugally as possible. Every type of western heavy-lift transport was pressed into service before the blockade ended in May of 1949.

1949

de Havilland's Comet became the first jet airliner

The 1949 flight of the de Havilland DH-106 Comet heralded a new era of jet airline travel. In May of 1952 the world's first pressurized jet airliner went into operation with BOAC on the 6,724-mile London-to-Johannesburg route. Despite several disastrous in-flight structural failures in its first years, the Comet went on to service the world's longest and busiest air routes for many years.

1950

The world's first all-jet combat

The very first all-jet combat encounter took place between a US Air Force Lockheed F-80 Shooting Star and a Soviet-designed MiG-15 of North Korea. Despite the superb manoeuvrability and performance of the MiG-15, the F-80 was successful in winning the joust, most probably because the pilot training procedures adopted by the US Air Force were very elaborate and sophisticated.

1952

First helicopters to cross the Atlantic Ocean

On 1 August 1952, 2 stripped-down Sikorsky S-55 helicopters set out from Westover in the USA to fly a direct transatlantic route to Prestwick in Scotland. The 3,400-mile adventure kept US Air Force pilots McGovern and Moore in the air for more than 42 hours. The Sikorsky S-55 was later manufactured under licence in Britain as the Westland Whirlwind.

1953 Scott Crossfield exceeded Mach 2

Just 50 years after the Wright brothers made those first tentative hops into the air, Scott Crossfield's Douglas D-558-2 'Skyrocket' dropped from the underbelly of its B-29 mothership and, entering a shallow dive, gathered speed to exceed the speed of sound, not once, but twice. Crossfield was the first person to fly an aircraft at speeds in excess of Mach 2.

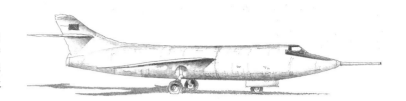

1954 Prototype Boeing 707 flew for the first time

While the de Havilland Comet had introduced the new era of jet airliners, it was the Boeing 707 which brought mass airline travel within reach of the ordinary man. Here at last was an aircraft which combined large seating capacities with speed, range and reliability. Indeed, the 707 presented such a leap in mission reliability that Pan Am introduced a round-the-world service.

1955 1st aircraft to carry an operational nuclear reactor

Scientists were interested in developing an aircraft which would, in theory, be capable of sustained and infinite flight. In an era where nuclear fission was being liberally and casually thrown about, some bright spark installed a working nuclear reactor in a ConVair B-36. The intention was to monitor the operation of the reactor and the crew working immediately adjacent.

1956 Bell X-2 set new 126,000-foot altitude record

The Bell X-2 earned its place in history when on 2 September 1956, in the hands of Captain Ivan Kincheloe, it reached an altitude of 126,000 feet and set a new world altitude record for rocket-powered aircraft. 2 X-2 prototypes were built to progress the research into supersonic and transonic flight earlier begun by the X-1. The X-2 was lost in a fatal Mach 3.2 breakup.

1956 First landing by an aircraft at the South Pole

A specially prepared ski-equipped US Navy R-4D transport, the military equivalent of the DC-3, was the first aircraft to touch down on the South Pole. Philosophically named 'Que Sera Sera' the R-4D landed at the Pole on 31 October 1956. Many surplus R-4Ds became available to operators after the War and, indeed, some continue to work to this day.

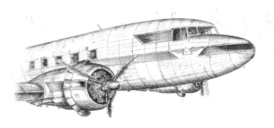

1958 Cessna 172 flew non-stop for 64 days

Pilots John Cook and Robert Timm chose the cooler winter months to set a new world record for endurance in their Cessna 172. Using in-flight transfer of fuel and foods the Nevada-based pair stayed aloft for an extraordinary 64 days, 22 hours and 19 minutes, which is more than 2 full months in the air. Exactly how they went to the toilet was a matter of much media speculation.

1959 Gary Powers' U-2 was shot down over USSR

The Russians were well aware that the American U-2 Spyplanes were making regular overflights. The U-2 pilots, for their part, would see the Russian missiles coming up to meet them but they would simply fall away before reaching the U-2's 80,000-foot cruising altitude. Eventually, however, USSR missile technology improved and Gary Powers was shot down leading to a huge international incident.

1960 16-mile freefall parachute jump from 102,800 feet

On 16 August 1960, US Air Force pilot Joe Kittinger jumped out of a balloon gondola from a height of 102,800 feet above sea level. Kittinger wore a high-altitude pressure suit on the 16-mile downward freefall. The journey upwards took 1 hour and 43 minutes while the world record-breaking descent took only 13 minutes and 45 seconds. For much of the duration of the fall Kittinger was travelling at well in excess of the speed of sound, although, in the later stages of the fall, the gradually increasing atmospheric pressure helped to slow his descent rate to just that of a standard freefall jumper. The other great danger faced by Kittinger was the effect of pressure altitude on his bloodstream, effectively the opposite of the 'bends'.

1961 Yuri Gagarin became the first man in space

When the tiny Vostok spacecraft completed its 90-minute orbit of the earth and Yuri Gagarin was returned alive and well, Khruschev and the Soviet people were jubilant. Red Square filled with ecstatic crowds to cheer the return of the first man in space. The prize of being first into space had been whisked from the Americans and NASA now began to focus on a moon-landing.

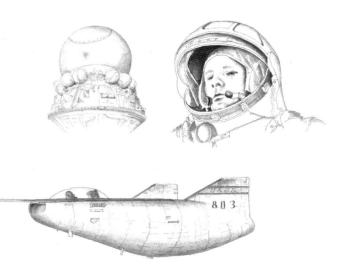

1963 First flight of a lifting-body prototype

The Northrop/NASA M2-F series of lifting-body prototypes were designed to explore the flight characteristics of lifting-body aircraft, that is aircraft where the fuselage itself generates the lift and there are no wings as such. Milton Thompson handled the craft on 3 September 1963 becoming the first man to pilot a lifting-body aircraft.

1964 Mrs Mock circumnavigated the globe in a Cessna 180

The first solo circumnavigation of the globe by a woman was the wonderful 1964 adventure by Mrs Mock in her tiny Cessna 180 'Spirit of Columbus'. The epic journey began on 19 March at Columbus, Ohio and, after 29 days, 11 hours and 59 minutes, Mrs Mock completed the 23,100-mile journey. Arrival back in Columbus on 17 April 1964 won her a place in aviation history.

1965 Lockheed's SR-71 Blackbird exceeded Mach 3

It was at Lockheed's top-secret prototype workshop, The Skunk Works, that the truly stunning SR-71 Blackbird high-altitude strategic reconnaissance aircraft was developed. Under the leadership of designer Kelly Johnson the SR-71 project broke new ground on all fronts including metallurgy and aerodynamics. In May of 1965 the SR-71 exceeded Mach 3, another great first.

1967 Boeing's 737 took to the skies

The prototype Boeing 737 flew for the first time on 9 April 1967. Initial orders for the type were slow and Boeing even considered halting production. With the placement of large orders by some of the bigger carriers, however, the fortunes of the type picked up. Now, 39 years after its first flight, the 737 is still in production and the type is the world's best-selling airliner.

1968 Soviet Tu-144 became the world's first supersonic airliner

The Soviet Union's Tu-144 airliner, the equivalent of Concorde, flew for the first time on 31 December 1968. Although a superb performer the type had no clear place in a non-market-led economy. When a Tu-144 crashed tragically and publicly at the 1973 Paris Air Show the type's international flights were scaled back. After a second crash in 1978 it was taken out of service.

1969 Boeing's 747 'Jumbo Jet' prototype flew

Boeing's prototype B-747 'Jumbo' fascinated the world when it took to the air for the first time on 9 February 1969. With seating for 450 passengers and a generous lounge for the first-class passengers on the upper deck, the Jumbo was simply out of scale with what we were used to. In flight it proved to be an excellent performer and a docile and intuitive aircraft to fly.

1969 First flight of Concorde

Populations on both sides of the English Channel were filled with national pride on 2 March 1969 when the Concorde prototype flew for the first time. Unlike the Soviet Tu-144, the free-market-led economies of the West suited the commercial ideology of Concorde, where the rich and famous were whisked around the world at more than 2.2 times the speed of sound.

1969 Apollo 11 carried Neil Armstrong to the moon

'That's One small step for man, one giant leap for mankind.' The words spoken by Neil Armstrong as he stepped down onto the surface of the moon will be remembered forever. Throughout the world we gathered in hushed silence around monochrome television sets and marvelled that we were witnessing such a defining moment in the history of mankind.

1971 Senate rejected US Supersonic Transport Program

March of 1971 saw the US Government withdraw financial support from the United States Supersonic Transport Program. There was much public debate and much public name-calling over this near-split decision but public monies were in short supply and, in this economic climate, the US Senate could not justify the transfer of such massive funds to a non-essential project. It was a decision which would shape the future of US commercial aviation development for years to come with the US taking, for the first time, a back seat to the European and Soviet supersonic development programmes. Despite great public disquiet in the US, however, the superb subsonic offerings from the major US manufacturers continued to win market share.

1973 Soviet Union's Tu-144 crashed at the Paris Air Show

The tragic loss of the Soviet Union's flagship Tupolev Tu-144 supersonic airliner at the Paris Air Show caused worldwide headlines. Suffering a disastrous structural failure the aircraft crashed to the ground killing all 6 crew members and 8 people on the ground. It would be within miles of this location that the rival Concorde would be lost in a great air tragedy in 2000.

1974 The Airbus A-330 prototype flew

It was the US Airline industry, and particularly Boeing, who dominated the world wide civil airline market for many years. It was only with the formation of the giant Airbus consortium that European manufacturers could challenge the market incumbents. The A-330 presented airlines with greater levels of efficiency and economy and the type quickly won a large market share.

1977 2 Jumbos collided on the ground at Tenerife

With the size of passenger aircraft increasing all the time it followed that aviation disasters too, when they occurred, would bring tragedy and grief of greatly increased magnitude. On 27 March 1977 at Tenerife's Los Rodeos airport a packed KLM Boeing 747 collided on the ground with a similar Boeing 747 of Pan Am. The death toll was a frightening and unprecedented 583 souls.

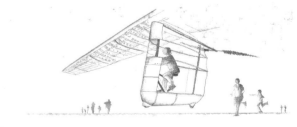

1979 Man-powered Gossamer Albatross crossed Channel

Following the stunning success of the Gossamer Condor, came the first man-powered aircraft capable of sustained and controlled flight. The Gossamer team set their sights on being first to 'cycle' across the Channel. On 23 August 1979 the Gossamer Albatross, with professional cyclist Bryan Allen at the pedals, lifted off from the English coast and took 2 hours 49 minutes to reach France.

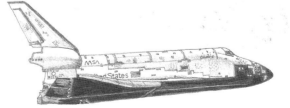

1981 The Space Shuttle heralded a new era of space travel

The world watched nervously and excitedly in April of 1981 when the Space Shuttle 'Columbia' glided back to earth for its first dead-stick landing. The era of efficient and re-usable space craft was at hand. From now on travel into space would be relatively routine, even if still unbelievably expensive.

1982 'Lawnchair Larry' flew his deckchair to 16,000 feet

Larry Walters of Los Angeles attached 45 helium-filled army-surplus balloons to his tethered garden chair. Then, taking with him some sandwiches, a 6-pack of Miller, and a pellet gun, he cut himself free hoping to float up to a height of about 30 feet. Unfortunately, however, Walters shot up to 16,000 ft and drifted dangerously across the approach path of LAX International airport.

1986 Rutan's non-stop non-refuelled global flight

Burt Rutan's amazing non-stop non-refuelled Voyager global flight is as much a testament to the power of collective volunteer dynamics as it is to the immense ingenuity of the man himself. Designed initially on a paper napkin over a cup of coffee, the extraordinary Voyager circled the earth in 216 hours, or 9 days, covering a distance of 24,987 miles.

1986 Space Shuttle 'Challenger' exploded on take-off

On 28 January 1986 we watched in horror as the Space Shuttle 'Challenger' exploded just 1 minute after lift-off. The graphic live TV coverage of the tragedy was made even more harrowing by the repeated commentaries on the exceptional lives of the 7 crew members, both male and female. It was a tragedy which became personal to ordinary people all over the world.

1991 Pan Am, Juan Trippe's airline, ceased operations

On 4 December 1991 Pan Am, the airline formed by Juan Trippe in 1928, ceased operations. Times were tough in the airline industry and the beleaguered Pan Am had been through several radical restructurings before it was forced to close. Now the Pan Am name and trademark, which had set the standard in the aviation industry, were auctioned off for a mere 1 million dollars.

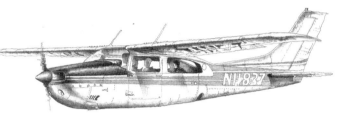

1994 Vicki Van Meter, age 12, flew across the Atlantic

Following her record-breaking 1993 flight across the continental USA, 12-year-old Vicki Van Meter set out across the Atlantic Ocean in a Cessna 210. With her on this epic flight were her father, James, and her flight instructor, Bob Baumgartner. On completion of this extremely dangerous journey Vicki Van Meter became the youngest pilot to fly across the Atlantic.

2000 Air France Concorde crashed on take-off

On 25 July 2000 an Air France Concorde exploded only moments after take-off from Paris Charles de Gaulle Airport. The airliner fell in a giant fireball onto a small hotel killing all 109 on board as well as one unfortunate hotel employee. This was the first fatality in the Concorde fleet in its 31 years of service. From that day forward the future of the Concorde was in great jeopardy.

2001 Russia's 15-year-old Mir station fell to earth

The return of Mir to earth was witnessed in countries across the globe but it was the Pacific Rim countries which had ringside seats. The giant Mir space station had been circling the earth at a height of 212 miles for a full 15 years. Now it was due to crash back to earth and concerns were raised all along its projected flight path as to where the 20-ton molten ball would land.

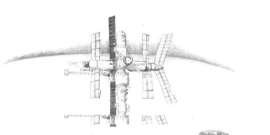

2001 Millionaire Dennis Tito became the first space tourist

With massive changes in Soviet political and economic life, money was in extremely short supply and millionaire Dennis Tito's offer of 20 million dollars for a trip to the International Space Station was taken up. Public comment on the deal was mixed, with some people deeply unhappy that money should open such doors. Tito had few duties on the voyage, being, essentially, a paying passenger.

2001 NASA's 'Helios' solar aircraft reached 85,100 feet

On 13 August 2001, the NASA designed 'Helios' solar-powered aircraft reached an altitude of 85,000 feet, a stunning achievement for a solar-powered vehicle and a new altitude record for a non-rocket-powered aircraft. Flown from the ground by remote control, the Helios was powered by 14 electric motors all supplied with power by the aircraft's 62,000 wing-mounted solar cells.

2001 4 hijacked airliners wreaked havoc on the USA

At 8.55 am on 11 September 2001 hijackers crashed a packed airliner into the North Tower of the World Trade Center, New York. 10 minutes later a second aircraft smashed into the South Tower. A third targeted the Pentagon while a fourth was heroically brought down by its passengers. The world watched in absolute horror as the most tragic and terrible events unfolded. The twin towers of the World Trade Center managed to withstand the initial impact of the packed jet airliners but the massive fires caused by burning jet fuel raged so hot that the steel framing of the 2 great towers buckled, and they suffered catastrophic collapse, one after the other, with terrible loss of life.

2001 All aircraft within US grounded for 2 days

The magnitude of the events of 11 September and the stark horror of the images which were replayed over and over again on TV sets traumatized the USA and, indeed, the whole world. The multiple nature of the attacks and the uncertainty of what was still to come caused the US authorities, for the first time ever, to ground all aircraft within and en route to the USA.

2001 Sabena was the first of many airline casualties

Following the events of 11 September the aviation business was hit by a sharp and sudden downturn. Nobody wanted to fly. Trading figures for all of the big airlines declined dramatically. Those airlines which were already struggling were first to go. Sabena, in operation since 1923, ceased operations on 7 November 2001 followed, within months, by many others.

2002 Acts of Congress on air marshalls & armed pilots

Aviation had changed for ever. In the hands of radicals armed with cardboard cutters any jet airliner could become a lethal missile. Airport security was dramatically tightened. A programme of strengthening pilot-cabin doors and bulkheads was introduced and completed well ahead of schedule. In the US Congress introduced legislation to facilitate air marshalls and arming of pilots. Right across the world airliners were regarded with a new sense of concern and trepidation. Wherever possible flight paths were routed away from areas of population but the proximity of many airports to city locations required that overflights could not be avoided. Standing patrols of armed fighters were provided over certain city locations.

2003 Concorde flew for the last time

Concorde had been given a reprieve in November of 2001 when, following local strengthening of the skin beneath the wing fuel tanks, the type was allowed back into the air. Passenger numbers were low, however, and the Concorde fleet insurances had dramatically increased in cost. On 10 April 2003, in a nostalgic and moving finale, the Concorde fleet flew for the last time.

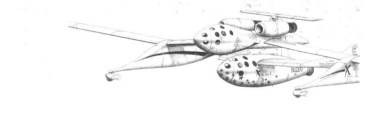

2004 First non-governmental venture into space

Burt Rutan's Scaled Composites developed the extraordinary combination of the White Knight and Space Ship One. On 21 June 2004, the White Knight mothership released Space Ship One at 50,000 feet, at which point the tiny spaceship's ground-breaking rocket propulsion system was fired. Burning a mix of nitrous oxide and rubber pellets, the craft reached an altitude of 328,491 feet.

2005 Airbus rolled out the double deck A380

The roll-out of the Airbus A380 revealed a truly massive aircraft, the first to provide 2 decks over the entire length of the airframe. The A-380 will carry up to 555 passengers on some of the world's longest and busiest air routes. Its unveiling marks a most important milestone for the giant European Airbus consortium, whose products closely rival those of market leader, Boeing.

2005 Global Flyer flew unrefuelled around the globe

Again Burt Rutan and again Scaled Composites, this time designing and constructing the Virgin Global Flyer to facilitate Steve Fossett's record-breaking non-stop non-refuelled circumnavigation of the globe. Burt Rutan excels in the design of aircraft where unusual and novel configurations are mixed with the requirement for great ingenuity, performance and efficiency.

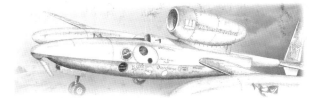

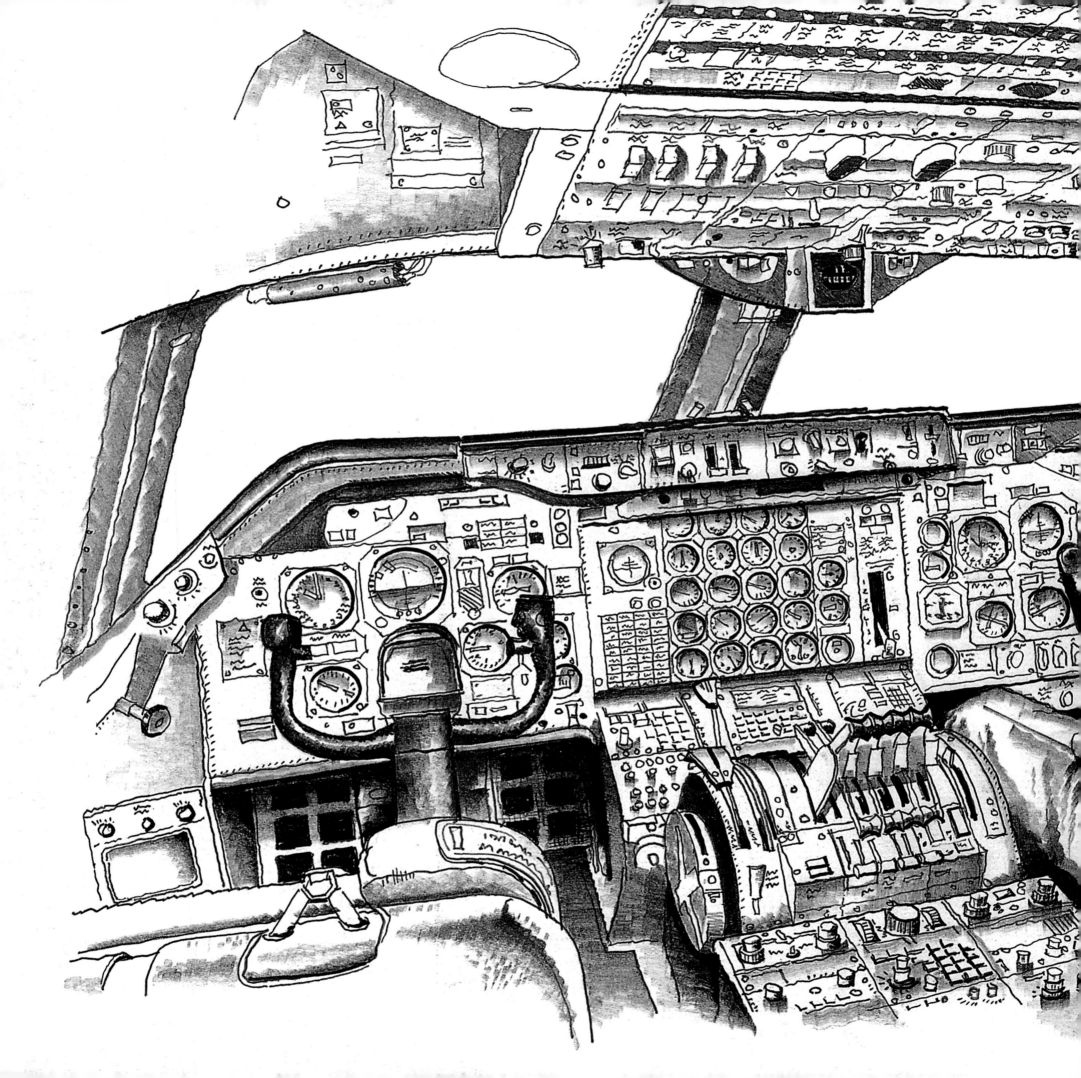

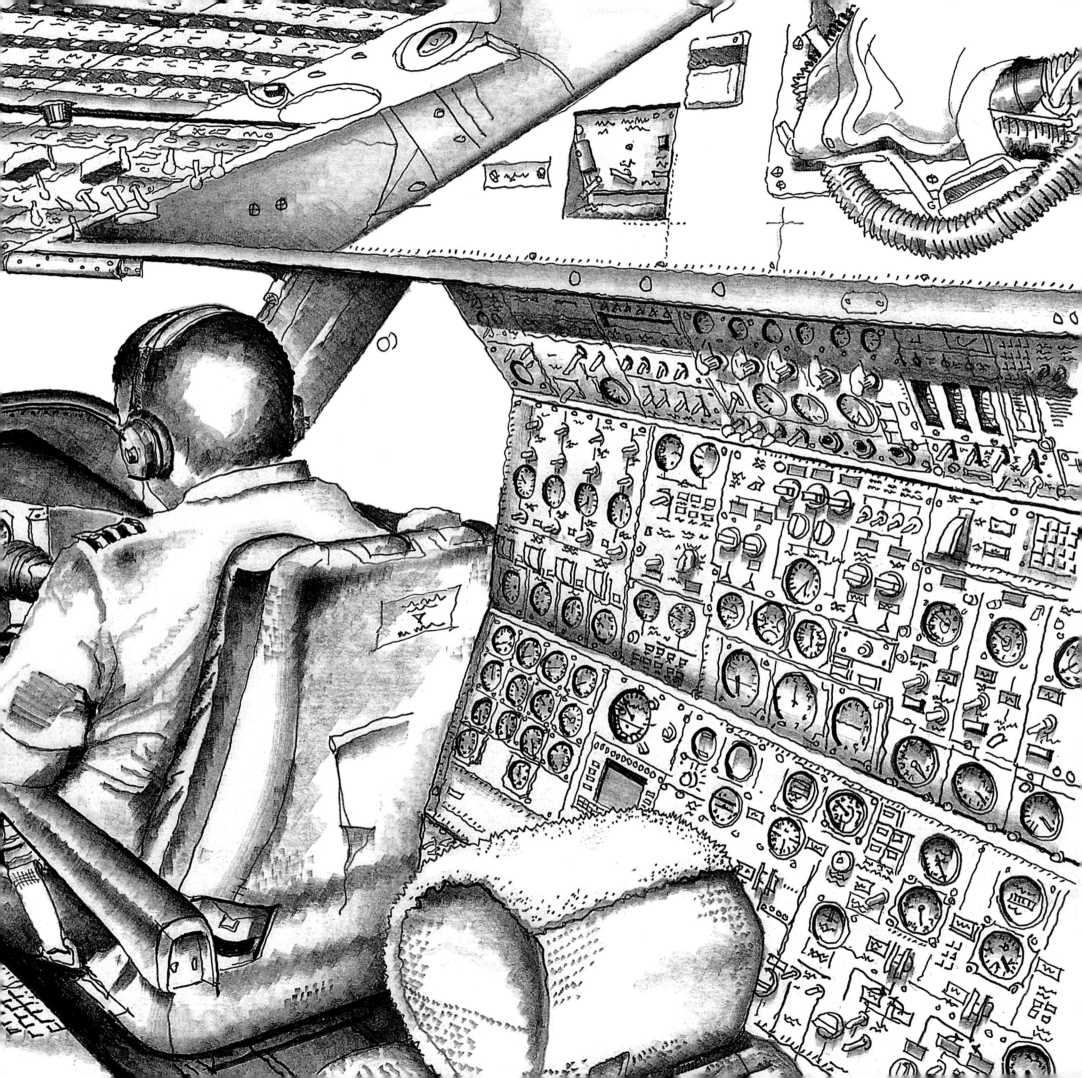

Aviation A-Z

Adam Aircraft Industries A-500

FF 2002 USA

Colorado-based Adam Aircraft employed highly advanced composite structures and shaping techniques to produce its extremely efficient A-500 airframe. With its centreline push/pull engine configuration, the type has all of the valuable flight advantages of the earlier Cessna 337 Super Skymaster, which could operate after the loss of an engine without the problems of asymmetrical

flight that are inherent in most twins. The A-500 has been granted certification.

Adam Aircraft Industries A-700

FF 2003 USA

Following a very strong market reception by the A-500, Adam immediately commenced the development of the A-700, a jet-powered upgrade based on the A-500 fuselage and wing. Certification is under way and due to be completed in 2006.

Aeronca 7AC Champ

FF 1944 USA

Flying a Champ is flying at its very best. Its simplicity and its ability to get you into any tiny airstrip make every flight an adventure to be savoured. Designed to compete directly with the ubiquitous Piper Cub, the Champ first flew in May 1944. Faced with diminishing order books most of the aircraft manufacturers began to develop light civilian models and the Champ was perhaps the most successful of these. In 1945 it could be bought for $2,095 and, at this price, they sold like hot-cakes. More than 10,000 were built between 1945 and 1951 alone. The Champ was progressively improved over the years and is much treasured to this day.

Aeronca 7AC Floatplane

FF 1946 USA

With the coming of peace to Europe and the USA in 1945, civil aircraft manufacturing was resumed. Manufacturers, expanded by wartime demand, now fought to produce sport aircraft for a new, confident generation of flyers and ex-military pilots. Aeronca's wonderful floatplane was aimed at this new and emerging market and, indeed, was conspicuous in being deliberately and consciously targeted at women as well as men.

Aeronca C-3

FF 1931 USA

The Aeronautical Corporation of America changed its name to Aeronca Aircraft Corporation in 1941. Aeronca's simple C-3 2-seat parasol-wing monoplane was among its most lasting achievements. Powered by a 36hp (26.8kW) Aeronca E-113C 2-cylinder engine, the C-3 had a maximum speed of 93mph (149km/h). Still to be found at airfields and fly-ins today, these airworthy Aeroncas are always a source of great attention and wonder. With its fabric-covered structure and its odd, snub-nosed engine fairing, the presence of airworthy C-3s is a tribute to the ruggedness and the longevity of the type. This small craft must surely be one of the most endearing flying machines of all time.

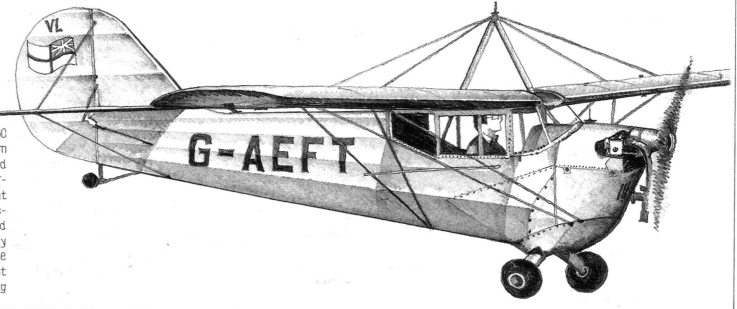

Aeronca L-16 FF-1946 USA

Aeronca's popular and prolific Model 7AC Champ drew the attentions of the US Air Force and US Army. With the installation of an uprated engine and larger plexiglass windows, the L-16 military observation and reconaissance utility was born. This was a simple aircraft which could be flown off short, unpaved airstrips in support of ground troops and heavy artillery units. Indeed the diminutive L-16 served in large numbers in Korea and in many other troubled parts of the world. In recent years L-16s have become much-treasured and sought-after aviation collectables.

Aero Spacelines Super Guppy FF 1962 USA

Aero Spacelines Inc. was formed in 1961 to carry out the conversion of a Boeing B-377 Stratocruiser for specialist airlifting duties. They stretched the airframe by 16 foot and constructed a circular-section bubble atop the fuselage. The first

of the series was the Pregnant Guppy (B-377PG), to lift Saturn rocket sections for the Apollo space program. The later Super Guppy could take loads of up to 25ft (7.62m) in diameter. 2 of the series were used in Europe to ferry components for the giant Airbus programme.

Aérospatiale SA-321 Super Frelon FF 1959 France

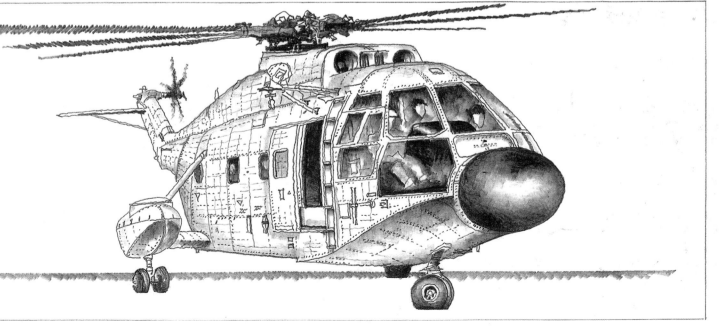

Developed originally by Sud-Aviation, the Super Frelon went on to be built by Aérospatiale and the type was manufactured for France's Armée de l'Air and Aeronavale, as well as for export to the armed services of Iraq, Israel, South Africa and Libya. Of the 120 airframes delivered, many are still in service today. The Super Frelon differs from the basic Frelon by virtue of its integral boat hull, which offers increased levels of safety for protracted flights over water. It can be configured for medium-lift general transport duties or for a range of specialist covert mission, mine laying, and Search-and-Rescue duties. Aérospatiale developed a commercial variant of the type but it attracted little market interest.

Aérospatiale TB-30 Epsilon

FF 1979 France

Aérospatiale SOCATA developed the TB-30 Epsilon in response to a specification from the Armée de l'Air. The airframe was the TB-20 structure with a much slimmed-down fuselage and a fully retractable undercarriage. With its narrow frontal area and its 300hp (224kW) Lycoming piston powerplant the Epsilon is a real performer, with a 236mph (380km/h) maximum speed and a climb rate of 1,850fpm (564m/min). Total production of the type was in excess of 172 with the Armée de l'Air receiving 150, the Portugese Air Force 18, and the military forces of Togo receiving 4 airframes complete with weapons hardpoints. The Omega was a later turboprop development.

Aérospatiale SE-3 Alouette II

FF 1955 France

Helicopter design was at a very early stage in 1955 when the Alouette II first took to the skies. The simple, open-trussed structure, so reminiscent of the early Bell designs, may have been rudimentary in appearance but it produced a helicopter which was faultless in terms of flying manners. The Alouette II's open-trussed framework, combined with its beautifully formed plexiglass bubble canopy, became a familiar sight across Europe and indeed the world. The type served with the air forces of France, UK, Austria, Germany, Switzerland, Belgian Congo, Cambodia, Indonesia, Israel, and many other countries. Designed as a military utility transport, the Alouette served its many governmental operators in a wide variety of roles from observation and liaison, to Search-and-Rescue, primary trainer, and ground-attack platform. A specialist medevac variant was capable of airlifting injured personnel off the battlefield in 2 external stretcher panniers strapped to the outside of the helicopter, a daunting prospect, especially when under enemy fire. Over the years, army surplus Alouettes IIs have been released to the private market in several countries and many of these airframes are still actively flying. It is a tribute to the engineering and the longevity of the Alouette programme to see these veteran airframes in airworthy condition after 50 years of military service.

Aérospatiale SA-365 Dauphin 2

FF 1975 France

The latest derivative of the basic Dauphin design employs lightweight carbon-fibre composite components as well as a new, retractable undercarriage to produce a more efficient aerodynamic envelope. The type has been well received in both its military and commercial configurations and a wide variety of variants have been developed over the years. The SA-365N is a 10- to 14-seat military utility transport, while the SA-365F is a modified variant with folding rotors for carrier-based operations. A specialized Search-and-Rescue variant, the SA-366, provides medium-range Search-and-Rescue services.

Aérospatiale Fouga Magister

FF 1952 France

Dubbed 'The Whistling Turtle' by the Belgian air force, the Fouga Magister was better known for many years as the mount of the world-famous Patrouille de France aerobatic team. The squat, low trainer was designed by engineers Castello & Mauboussin of the Air Fouga Company, now long absorbed into the giant Aérospatiale consortium. Air Fouga had previously specialized in the design of sailplanes and this early influence can clearly be seen in the sleek, clean lines of the jet trainer. The design was an immediate success and was ordered in large numbers by the French Armée de l'Air. In subsequent years it was exported to many other air forces across the world and, in all, a total of 916 were built. In recent years the Fouga has been substantially relieved in its role as primary trainer but several privately owned air-force surplus Fougas provide delight and thrills to their owners to this day.

Aérospatiale SA-342L Gazelle
FF 1967 France

The Gazelle was the first helicopter to introduce the trademark Aérospatiale shrouded-fenestron tail-rotor system. The new arrangement greatly reduced the levels of turbulent wash which developed at the point where the downward main rotor flow met the horizontal tail-rotor flow. The distinctive sound of the shrouded tail-rotor helicopter was born and the Gazelle went on to be produced in large numbers by Aérospatiale. The type was also produced under licence by Westland in the UK, by Soko in former Yugoslavia, and by ABHCo in Egypt. A total of 1,250 of all types were built.

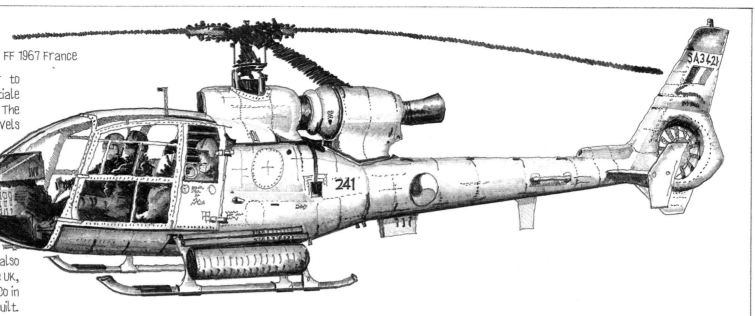

Aérospatiale Puma HC
FF 1965 France

Designed to carry troops and medium slung loads, the Puma has been built by both Aérospatiale in France and under licence by Westland in the UK.

Aérospatiale SE-210 Caravelle
FF 1955 France

The Caravelle SE-210 originated from a specification set down by the French government for a large jet-powered transport which was required principally to link France to its many far-flung interests. A total of 280 of the type were produced by SNCASE, by Sud Aviation, and later again by Aérospatiale. The Caravelle served on some of the great airline routes of the 1950s and 1960s linking Paris to Rome, North Africa and Istanbul.

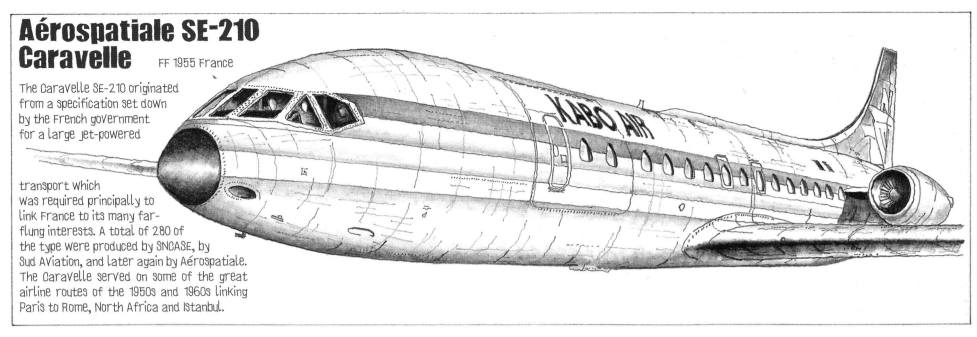

Aérospatiale TB-31 Omega
FF 1985 France

The TB-31 Omega resulted from Aérospatiale's 1985 attempt to secure a very large training airframe contract with the French air force. The TB-31 comprised an uprated and enhanced TB-30 Epsilon airframe with a powerful new Turbomeca Arrius 1-D turboprop powerplant. The result was a sophisticated advanced training platform complete with ejection seats, weapons hardpoints, and all of the military accoutrements that would be expected in an advanced trainer. Despite Aérospatiale's valiant efforts, however, the French government selected the Embraer Tucano and the TB-31 Omega was never put into series production.

Aérospatiale SOCATA TB-9 Tampico
FF 1977 France

The Tampico is the Renault 30 of the skies, decidedly French in styling with lots of dials, lights, and buttons. An excellent touring aircraft with lots of space for friends and their baggage. The Tampico has a most reassuring and effective set of ground brakes.

Aérospatiale SOCATA Trinidad TB-20
FF 1980 France

If the Tampico is the Renault 30 of the skies, the Trinidad is the top of the range Citroen XM. A wonderfully powerful personal transport with retractable undercarriage and the very highest levels of avionics and interior fittings.

Aérospatiale Super Puma

FF 1970 France

When Sud Aviation was absorbed into Aérospatiale in 1970 the giant conglomerate inherited the Puma series of medium-lift troop-assault helicopters. Numerous variants have evolved from the type over the years, the most notable being the stretched and upgraded Super Puma. Designed originally to meet a French army specification, the project was given a major boost when it was adapted in the tactical transport role by Britain's Royal Air Force. In subsequent years it has been adopted by many other countries. Designed to fly in all weather conditions, the Super Puma is a tough, versatile performer which has been built in very large numbers.

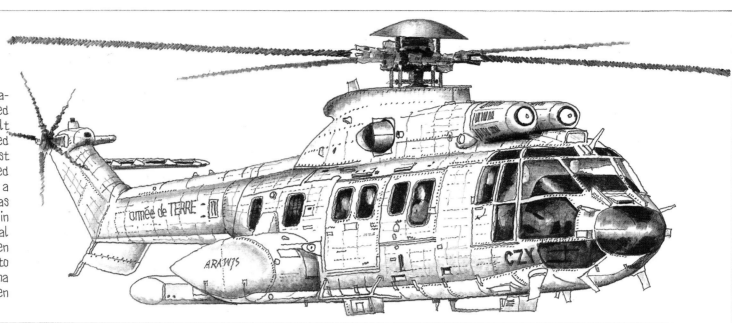

Aérospatiale/ SOCATA TBM-700

FF 1988 France

Every operator dreams of an aircraft which will deliver jet-like performance for the cost of a piston twin and it was this goal that was set at the outset of the TBM-700 development programme. Indeed, it must be accepted that the TBM comes very close to fully achieving this aim. This sleek, pressurized turboprop single burns only 50 gallons of Jet A1 per hour to cruise at 280mph (450km/h), with a ceiling of 30,000ft (9,144m) and a range of 1,784 miles (2,870km).

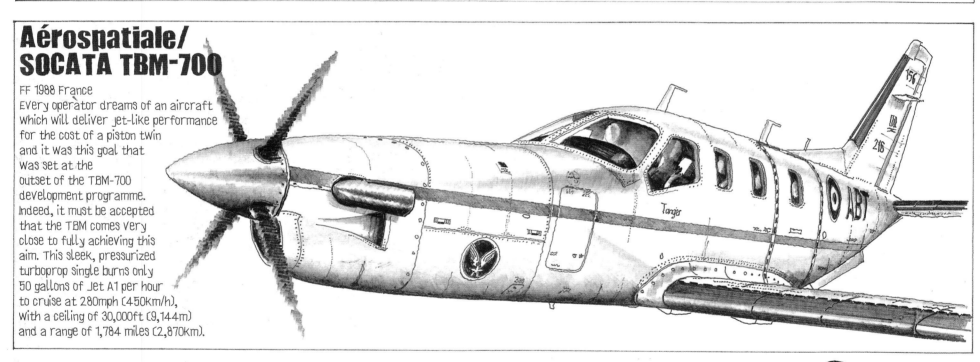

Aero Vodochody L-39 Albatross

FF 1968 Czechoslovakia

Surely this is the ultimate toy for the man who has everything. The Eastern Bloc's superbly capable L-39 advanced jet trainer can now be bought for the same price as a top-level sports car. Training and servicing are generally provided by specialist companies operating out of former Eastern Bloc countries. Fuel, on the other hand, must still be sourced locally and, with an enormous burn rate, very deep pockets are mandatory.

Aero Vodochody L-29 Delfin

FF 1959
Czechoslovakia

In 1961 competitive trials were held to select an all-new advanced jet trainer to serve the Warsaw Pact countries and it was former Czechoslovakia's all-new L-29 Delfin which scooped the prestigious prize. The win was an important boost to the Eastern European state, not just for status reasons, but because the

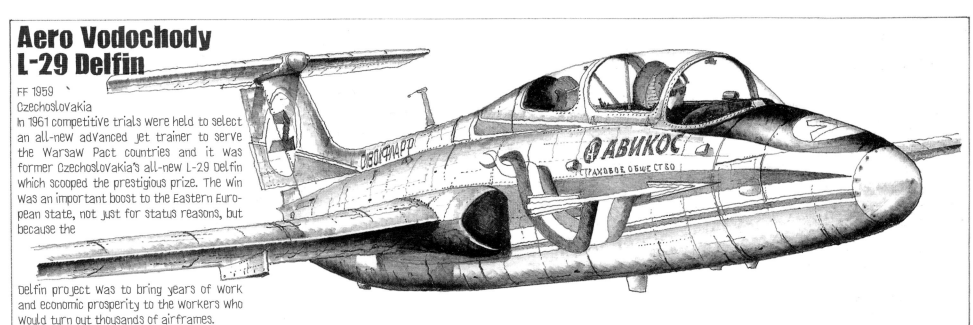

Delfin project was to bring years of work and economic prosperity to the workers who would turn out thousands of airframes.

Airbus A330

FF 1992 EU

The 1986 announcement by Airbus of its new A330 aircraft development project saw the escalation of the great rivalry between the fledgling European consortium and the giant market leader, Boeing. Could the diverse European teams stay clear of the obvious political influences and would the all-new aircraft, designed by committee, be a fitting match for the great Boeing market leader. It was! The aircraft's first flight in October 1992 revealed an aircraft that far exceeded design expectations. Low drag combined with winglets and efficient engines resulted in huge operator savings and a full order book.

Airbus A319

FF 1995 EU

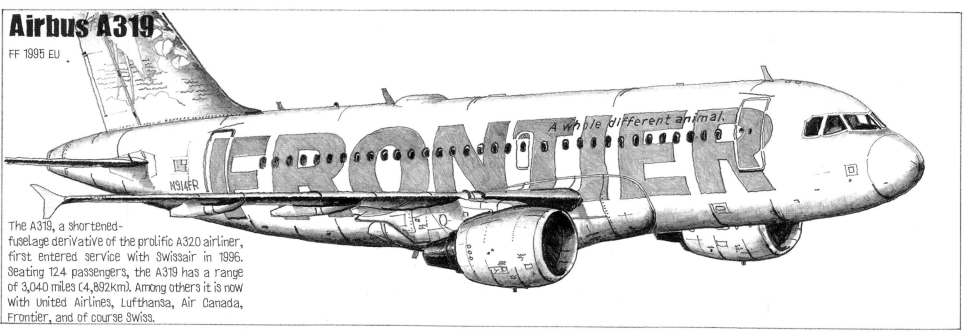

The A319, a shortened-
fuselage derivative of the prolific A320 airliner,
first entered service with Swissair in 1996.
Seating 124 passengers, the A319 has a range
of 3,040 miles (4,892km). Among others it is now
with United Airlines, Lufthansa, Air Canada,
Frontier, and of course Swiss.

Airbus A340

FF 1991 EU

The A340 range was designed to specialize
in the high-volume, long-range sector
of the commercial aviation market,
its main attraction to operators
being its lower fuel burn and its
very fast turn-around time. As
with all of the Airbus fleet, the
work of the flight engineer is
managed by the flight-management
system with some minor intervention by
the 2-man flight crew where necessary.
Airbus has maintained a very high level of
commonality between its airliners, both to
reduce costs and to provide an incentive
to its client operators to gradually move over
to Airbus-only fleets.

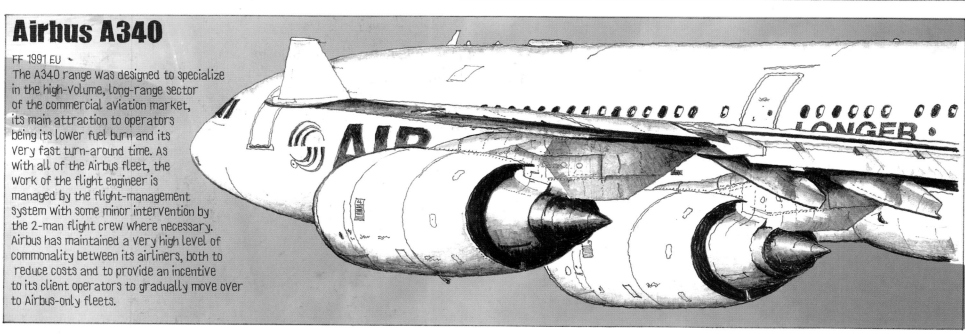

Airbus A380

FF 2005 EU

With seating for
555 passengers over 2
decks, the extraordinary new A380
has 49% more floor area, but only 35% more
seating, than the 747 Jumbo. This extra floor
space opens up, for the first time, new possibilities
in passenger amenities such as in-flight gymnasi-
ums, bars, and shopping outlets.

Airbus A300-600ST Beluga

FF 1994 EU

Designed to haul the very largest of components between Airbus manufacturing plants.

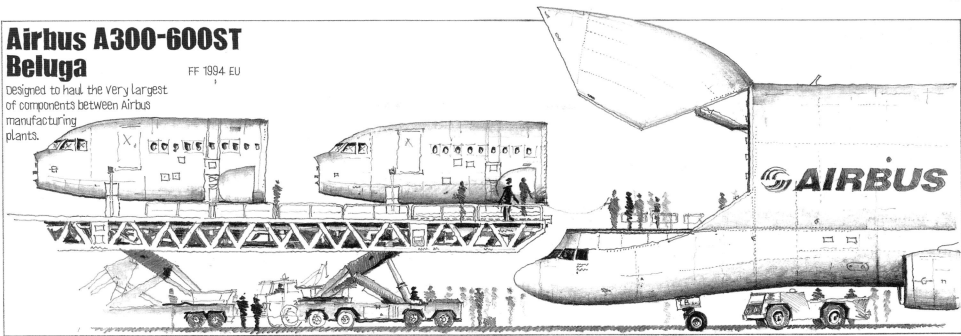

Airco/de Havilland DH-2

FF 1915 UK

By 1915 the First World War was raging and Geoffrey de Havilland was set the task of producing an aircraft to outfly and outmanoeuvre the Fokker scourge. The synchronous machine gun had not yet been perfected and de Havilland positioned a rear-facing engine behind the pilot in order to facilitate the mounting of a fixed forward-facing gun. For some months the DH-2 led the way until the rapid pace of aircraft development rendered it dangerously obsolete. Approximately 400 were built and the type served with the Royal Flying Corps on the Western Front and later in Palestine.

Airco/de Havilland DH-4

FF 1917 UK & USA

The DH-4 was designed by Geoffrey de Havilland in England but it was greatly modified by the Dayton-Wright Airplane Co. when they paired it with the great American Liberty powerplant. Over 4,846 of the type were made for the US Army, many of which were shipped to Europe to serve as observation platforms and artillery spotters in the last years of the First World War. The DH-4 served well in its few short months in Europe and it remained in active army service until 1932. Others of the type were adapted for use by the US Mail Service.

Air Tractor AT-802 Fireboss

FF 1973 USA

The AT series of crop-sprayers and water-bombers was designed by Air Tractor founder and chief designer, Leland Snow. He had been involved in the design of many agricultural crop-dusting aircraft including the Snow S-2, which was built by Rockwell and later by Ayers. The Fireboss is one of a long succession of upgrades of the type, its 1,424hp (1,062kW) turboprop powerplant making it the largest and most powerful single-engined agricultural/water bombing aircraft in current production. Over 1,500 of the series have been built.

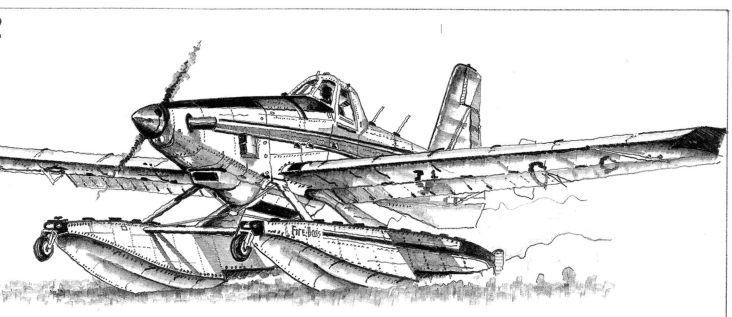

Antonov An-2 Colt

FF 1947 USSR/Poland

More than 5,000 of Antonov's wonderful An-2 workhorses were built in the Ukraine before production was relocated to Poland, where a further 12,000 were built by PZL. The Chinese, too, found that the versatility and ruggedness of the type was ideally suited to its needs and its economy, and it built a further 1,000 examples of the type. The An-2 is ponderous and slow but it is tough and durable and it can land and take off from any small patch of ground.

Antonov An-12 Cub

FF 1958 USSR

For many years all Soviet airliners were derived from military transports and carried the trademark military glazed nose and rear gun emplacements. The logic was that these civil transports would be pressed into service by the military authorities if ever required. To see one of these airliners on a western ramp was always a chilling reminder of the great tension and mistrust which existed for many years between East and West.

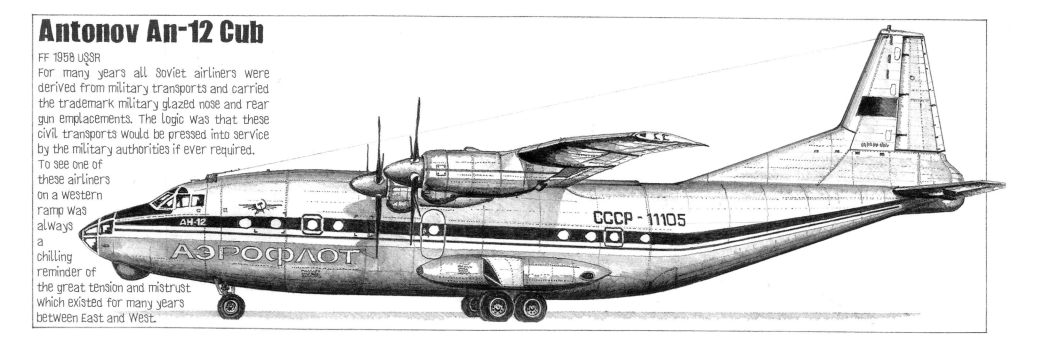

Antonov An-14 Clod

FF 1958 USSR

Antonov's An-14 or 'Little Bee' was given the rather derogatory title 'Clod' by NATO. This was a STOL feederliner and freighter designed to be able to access even the smallest and most remote of rough airfields so that they could be linked back into Aeroflot's giant route network. The type was no beauty but it was reliable and simple and it could be operated by pilots with relatively little experience, a staffing policy which would cause enormous public outcry if it was to be adapted today.

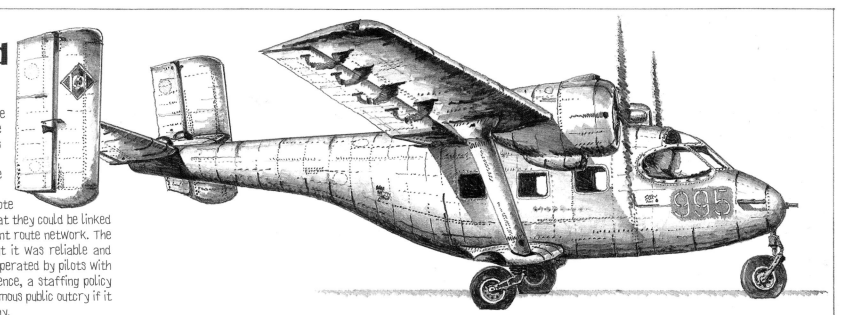

Antonov An-28 Cash

FF 1969 USSR/Poland

The Antonov Bureau's An-28 short-range twin-turboprop light transport was developed from the earlier An-14 airframe. Carrying 17 to 19 passengers, the NATO-codenamed Cash can fly sectors of up to 800 miles (1,300km). In some of its other roles as freighter, ambulance, and crop-sprayer, this range is significantly reduced. While the prototype airframes were equipped with a completely retractable undercarriage, all production models sport a simple fixed tricycle-gear arrangement.

Antonov An-72 Coaler FF 1977 USSR

The twin-turbofan-powered An-72 Coaler STOL freighter has the same general configuration as the unfortunate Boeing YC-14. The coanda effect created by positioning the turbofan engines tight onto the high-set wings gives greatly improved lift and take-off performance. The Coaler can operate from short, unpaved runways providing the ideal freighter airframe for military operations and civil work.

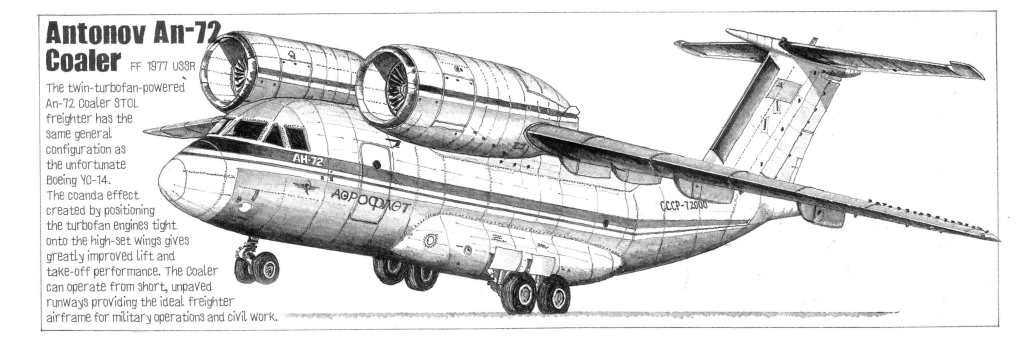

Armstrong Whitworth Apollo
FF 1949 UK

A large civilian turboprop airliner from this long-established UK manufacturer. Despite the great successes of earlier AW types the Apollo met with little commercial success.

Armstrong Whitworth 101 Argosy
FF 1959 UK

The Argosy heralded a new era in the early 1960s when the rich and famous could ferry their favourite custom-built Bentleys and Jaguars to Europe for their touring holidays. The type was adopted by outsize-load specialists on both sides of the Atlantic.

Arrow Aircraft Active II
FF 1932 UK

Arrow Aircraft Ltd of Leeds produced only 2 Arrow Active biplanes before a total lack of customer orders forced them to withdraw from the aircraft-manufacturing business. Indeed, Arthur Thornton's wonderful biplane design might have been forgotten forever had 1 of the 2 airframes not fallen into the hands of enthusiast Desmond Penrose, who spent many years bringing the aircraft back to its original flying condition. G-ABVE is now based with the Shuttleworth Trust and it is 1 of a number of superb vintage aircraft which the Trust maintains in full flying condition, and which fly at regular Shuttleworth open days and flying events.

Arrow Sport
FF 1926 USA

The Arrow Aircraft & Motor Corporation of Havelock, Nebraska, cleverly marketed its new biplane as a side-by-side sport-plane and pilot trainer. With a 1929 price tag of just $3,000 to $3,500, the Arrow Sport's novel configuration appealed to pilots and flying schools alike and the type quickly became a big commercial success. The Arrow Sport was a superbly designed aircraft with excellent flying manners.
In its original configuration it required no interplane struts or wire bracing whatsoever, although simple struts were later added to allay the concerns of its customer base.

Auster AOP-9

FF 1955 USA/UK

The Auster AOP (Air Observation Post) series was developed from the earlier Taylorcraft 3-seat Mk 5 artillery guidance and observation platform. Almost 1,600 of these spotters were delivered to the RAF and other Allied air forces over the course of the war. Now in 1946 Auster released an improved and heavily modified version, the AOP-6, followed by the AOP-9 of 1955. These tough military aircraft were made with longevity in mind and many ex-army Austers and Taylorcraft are now in private ownership and are still flying today. The type has excellent short field performance, wonderful visibility in flight, and the best of flying manners. This is flying with a touch of class and nostalgia thrown in.

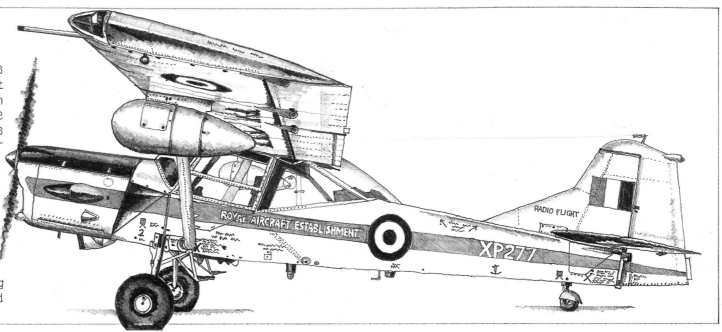

Auster B-4 Ambulance/Freighter

FF 1955 UK

Auster's B-4 was a most unusual affair with a high-boom tail configuration and twin rear tail-dragging wheels. Bearing all of the signature Auster cowlings and forward fuselage details, the type had a large rear-facing loading door through which light freight or stretchers could be loaded. The B-4 project was a private venture, the Auster Company hoping to market it to its military customer base as an air-ambulance platform and light freighter which would have high levels of commonality with the AOP series, which they were already operating. The B-4 was truly a case of form following function and the result, while not being pretty, does possess a certain rugged simplicity which is most appealing.

AVE Mizar Flying Car

FF 1973 USA

Man's fascination with the concept of winged horses dates back to the days of the Ancient Greeks but it took 20th-century technology, a Ford Pinto, and engineer Henry Smolinski to finally make it happen. AVE, owned by the former Northrop engineer, mated the rear portion of a Cessna Skymaster with a stock Ford Pinto and created a massive US-wide distribution network to market the resulting flying Pinto (horse). The distribution rights alone reputedly netted millions for Smolinski and he duly proceeded with flight testing. Unfortunately, however, the Mizar folded up in mid-flight and Smolinski and his dream died in a tragic fireball.

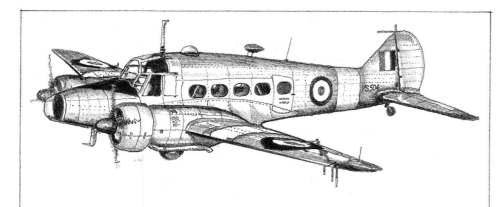

Avro 652-A Anson (T-1 to T-22) FF 1935 UK

The Anson was one of the first European aircraft to adopt the new low cantilever wing layout which was beginning to appear on American aircraft. With reduced drag and more efficient aerofoil profiling the Anson was a capable performer which was built in very large numbers and exported to many countries across the world.

Avro 701 Athena FF 1948 UK

Designed as a 2-seat advanced trainer, the Athena had very clean lines and a powerful 12-cylinder Rolls-Royce Merlin powerplant under the hood. With 1,280 horses at hand the 701 had a maximum cruise speed of 297mph and a service ceiling of 29,500ft. 1 rapid-firing Browning .303 machine gun was inset into the port wing.

Avro Lancastrian

FF 1949 UK

A high-speed long-range conversion of the trusted wartime Lancaster. At the end of the Second World War, Victory Aircraft Ltd of Canada converted the first Lancasters to produce the civilian Lancastrian. Glass turrets were removed, civilian interiors fitted, and new Packard-built Merlin engines installed. This sketch depicts a test-bed airframe used to test new turbo jet engines.

49

Avro Shackleton MR-3-3

FF 1949 UK

If longevity is a measure of an aircraft's success then the Shackleton must surely be among the most successful of all time. First entering service with the RAF in 1951, the type was continually upgraded and remained in service right up into the mid-1990s. In a time of great political uncertainty the Shackleton airborne early warning (AEW) platform was a vital part of Britain's defence system and its electronics suite was continuously enhanced.

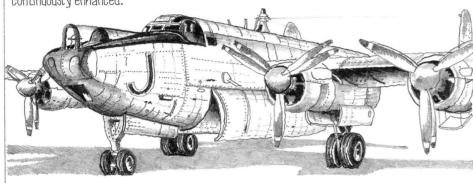

Ayers Thrush Turbo

FF 1956 USA

Ag-pilot and engineer Leland Snow designed the original Snow 2 which evolved and changed hands many times over the last 50 years to become the Ag Commander, the Thrush Commander, and eventually after 1977, the Ayers Thrush Commander 600 and Thrush Turbo. With every change and every upgrade the sturdy agricultural crop-duster's engine got bigger, culminating in Ayers' massively powerful and capable turboprop versions.

Avro Tudor

FF 1945 UK

Roy Chadwick, Avro's leading designer, was keen to ensure that Avro lined up a new and capable civil airliner for the years immediately following the war. Because of wartime materials restrictions, however, he found that he could not start from scratch but had to source the components for his design from earlier Avro stocks and tooling. It was from these humble mongrel beginnings that Britain's first pressurized airliner emerged. The service life of the Tudor began well with good market orders and a wide spread of airline customers. In January of 1948 and 1949, however, 2 Tudors disappeared in mysterious circumstances and the type never recovered.

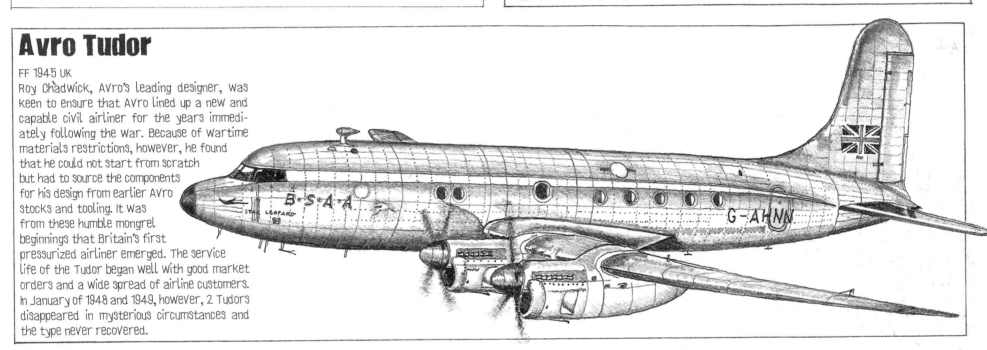

Avro 685 York

FF 1942
UK

Winston Churchill, a great aircraft enthusiast, expressed delight when the all-new Avro York replaced his personal transport. Throughout the Second World War he spent long periods of time travelling to far-flung theatres of war and attending vital battle summits. With Europe essentially occupied, his pilot had to route down the centre of the Atlantic to reach North Africa, and a dependable 4-engined transport was required.

FF 1981 UK

BAe 146 Whisper Jet

The BAe 146 series brought new levels of refinement and polish to the feederliner market when it was first introduced in May of 1983. Here at last was a miniature and cost effective 70-seat airliner with 4 engines and the highest levels of airliner detailing and interior finishes. Its ability to access smaller airports in noise-sensitive city centre locations will ensure its position in the commuter market for some time to come.

BAC/Hunting Jet Provost

FF 1954 UK

When Hunting Aircraft was absorbed into the British Aircraft Corporation in 1964, production of the P-84 was continued under the new title of BAC Jet Provost. This 2-seat turbojet became the standard basic jet trainer of the RAF. It was only the coming of the BAe Hawk advanced trainer that led to the replacement of the Jet Provost. The UK, Singapore, Sudan, Sri Lanka, Iraq and Venezuela all operated the type, and a range of variants evolved during its long years of production. The Jet Provost T3 was an unpressurized trainer with a Rolls-Royce Viper Mk 102 turbojet engine. The Jet Provost T5 was an uprated pressurized variant with improved instrumentation, an elongated nose, and a revised wing. With its Rolls-Royce Viper Mk 202 turbojet, the T5 variant has a max level speed of 404mph (650km/h) and a range of 900 miles (1,450km).

Beagle A-61 Terrier 2

FF 1962 UK

When Auster Aircraft was purchased by The Pressed Steel Company in 1960 the Beagle marque was founded and the newly formed manufacturer immediately set about re-badging and revitalizing its inventory. Auster's well-established AOP-9 series now became the new Beagle Terrier, with a greatly improved level of specification.

BAC Jet Provost

FF 1954 UK

Imagine if your first flying lesson was given in a fast jet instead of a clapped-out Cessna 152. The Jet Provost was designed in response to an RAF specification for an all-new ab initio jet trainer. After trials alongside the old piston-powered Provost trainer the RAF confirmed that student pilots experienced no great difficulty in receiving their initial training on the jet and, indeed, those students flying the jet achieved solo flight status earlier than those on the traditional piston-engined Provost. It's just not fair.

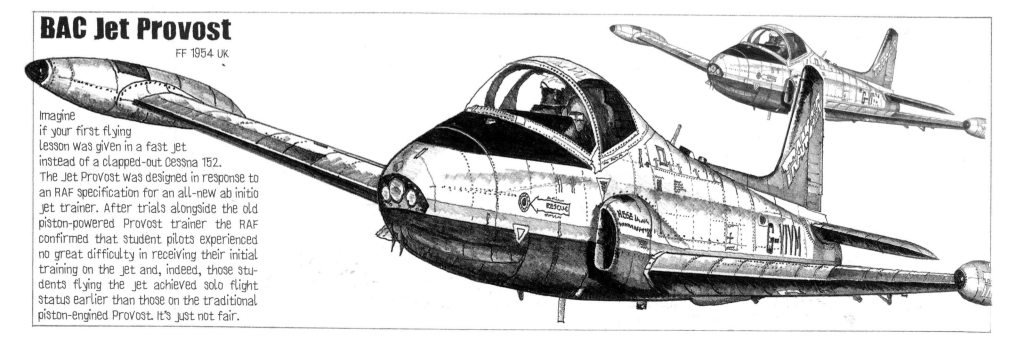

BAe Harrier T-10

FF 1966 UK

The ability of the Harrier Jump Jet to lift vertically into the air is surely one of the most extraordinary and impressive feats of aerodynamic engineering of our day. Indeed, this is old technology really, the first tentative hovers and lifts having been completed almost 40 years ago now. Entering service with the RAF in April of 1969, the Harrier was the first and only operational VTOL military fighter in the world. Designed to be dispersed to unprepared sites in close proximity to a forward battle area, the Harrier is capable of lifting off vertically without runway or other prepared groundworks. While lift-off could be entirely vertical the type can carry an additional weapons load if space for a very short take-off run is available.

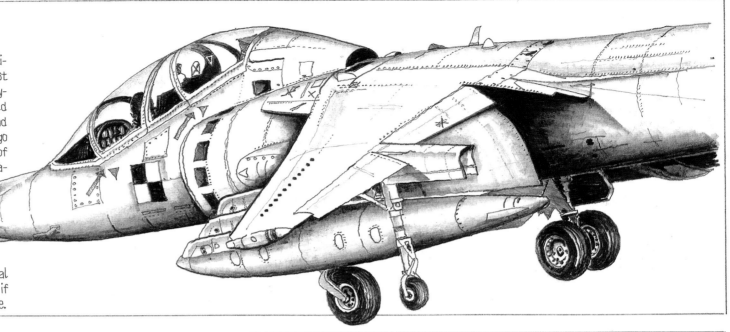

BAe/Aérospatiale Concorde

FF 1969 UK/France

Graceful on the ground and truly stunning in the air. Crossing the Atlantic at twice the speed of sound became a favourite pastime of the rich and famous. Concorde's last flight in 2003 marked the end of an era.

BAe (de Havilland) HS-125

FF 1962 UK

De Havilland were already producing the DH-125 executive transport when they were absorbed into the huge Hawker Siddeley Group. Development progressed and the HS-125 went through a succession of powerplant and avionics upgrades to keep it at the very forefront of the executive-jet market. With the absorption of the Hawker Siddeley Group into the giant British Aerospace consortium the newly titled BAe-125 continued to flourish. This mid-sized business jet continues to be used today and, while being slightly more dated and thirsty than some, is a capable performer.

Beagle 206 Basset

FF 1961 UK

Designed in the late 1950s to meet an RAF need for a dedicated transport to facilitate the positioning of V-bomber support crews, the 206 entered service late in 1965. A total of 20 Bassets were produced for the Royal Air Force with further derivatives for the commercial market and for the Royal Flying Doctor Service of New South Wales. Of the 79 airframes produced, many are still in service today.

Beagle B-121 Pup

FF 1967 UK

Beagle Aircraft Ltd was formed in 1960 following the merger of those 2 stalwarts of British aviation, Auster and Miles. In one fell swoop, 2 of the most beautiful marques in aviation disappeared for ever, to be replaced by the practical but decidedly lacklustre Pup. Modernity had triumphed over beauty and nostalgia but at a great cost to Britain's rich aviation heritage. Within 10 years Beagle was experiencing severe financial difficulty and it finally closed its doors in January of 1970. The Beagle B-125 Bulldog was a basic military training development of the type and was adopted by the RAF as a primary basic trainer.

Bede BD-5 Micro

FF 1971 USA

Jim Bede's ambitious marketing of his tiny BD-5 kitplane fired the public imagination and within months more than 4,000 kits had been sold. The Micro was all that it promised to be: extremely fast, efficient, responsive, and best of all, it looked like a tiny jet. Filled with enthusiasm, Jim Bede's army of home-builders set to work. As they toiled away on fuselages and wings Jim Bede himself was perfecting the powerplant. The problem was, however, that a suitable engine could not be found and the project floundered amid great controversy in 1979.

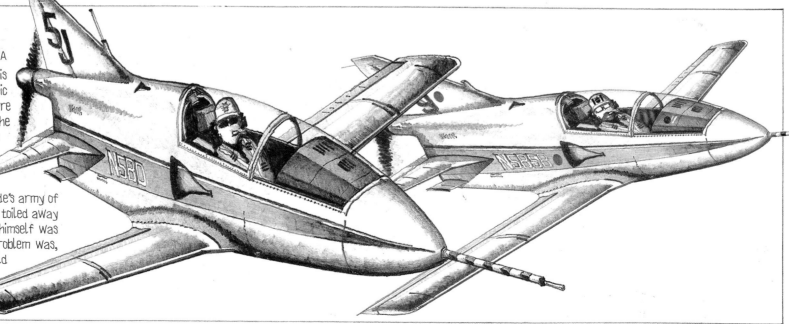

Beechcraft Model 35 Bonanza

FF 1945 USA

The best designs last the longest and on this basis the Bonanza must surely rate among the very best aircraft designs of its day. Flying first in 1945 the model 35 remained in production right up to 1982, a production period of 35 years, during which more than 10,400 variants were built. The type is still widely flown to this day.

With its retractable undercarriage and its efficient aerodynamic profile the Bonanza is a capable and versatile performer.

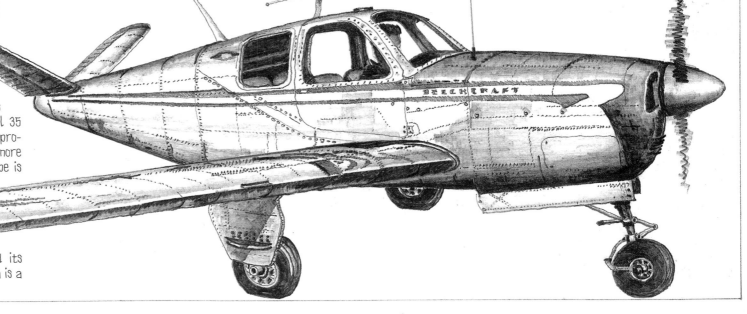

Beechcraft Model 55 Baron

FF 1960 USA

Competition between aircraft manufacturers has meant that designers are forever trying to identify new niche markets for their aircraft products, and Beechcraft carried out exhaustive surveys before commencing the development of its new Model 55. Having established the market's appetite for size, weight, horsepower and cost, Beechcraft set to work with the aim of producing the perfect aircraft and has not been far off the mark as the type remained in production for 44 years.

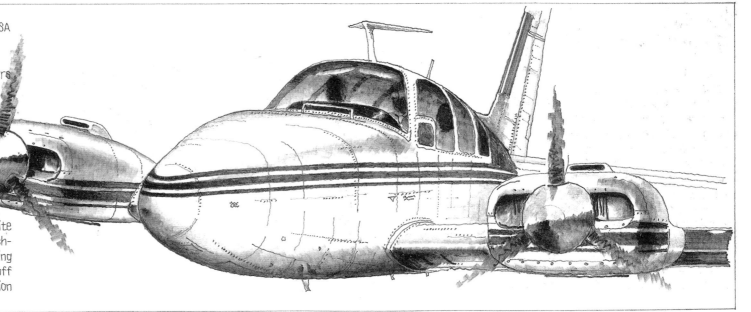

Beechcraft 99 Airliner

FF 1966 USA

By the early 1960s, the airline industry had begun to identify the need for small efficient commuter aircraft to feed into the larger hub networks. To meet this demand Beech developed the Beech 99 Airliner which was based closely on its earlier Beech Queen Air. With substantial stretch of the fuselage and a pair of Pratt & Whitney's prolific and reliable PT6A-20 turboprops, the Beech 99 Airliner was well-received by feederliner and commuter operators alike and almost 240 of the type were built. Indeed, many of these airframes are still in service today.

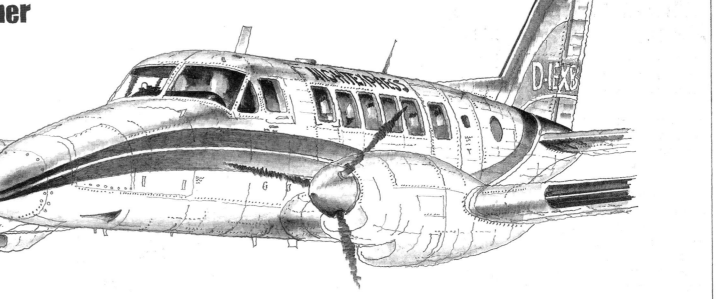

Beechcraft 390 Premier 1

FF 1998 USA
Beechcraft's latest corporate runabout with seating for just 6 passengers in a single cabin configuration. The ultimate toy for the executive who has everything.

Beechcraft Starship

FF 1983 USA

Designed for Beechcraft by aviation guru Burt Rutan, the Starship was developed to flying prototype stage by Rutan's own Skunk Works, Scaled Composites Inc. The Starship is unique among executive transports, its configuration being essentially identical to Rutan's hugely successful Long Ez, with canard foreplane, John Roncz aerofoils, and winglet technology. The aircraft exceeded all of the targets set out at design stage but later ran into difficulties with weight when Beechcraft's avionics suite grew in size.

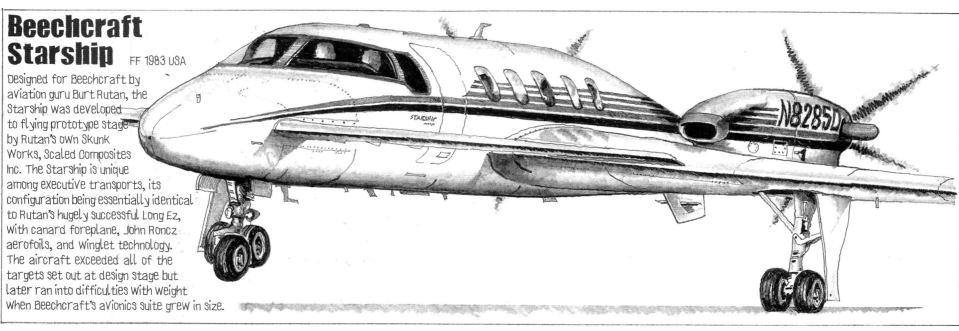

Beechcraft T-34 Mentor

FF 1948 USA
The owner of this stunning T-34 Mentor attended one of Florida's Sun 'n Fun air extravaganzas, where I was bowled over by its wonderful presentation. Maintaining an original warbird in this peak condition is a major labour of love entailing long working hours and meticulous standards of craftsmanship. If pleasure is to be found in seeing a job well done, however, this owner must be very happy in the knowledge that his project is maintaining this piece of history in peak condition. Added to this is the sheer joy of flying, the adventure of flying to an airshow, and the camaraderie and friendship which develop between enthusiasts of any specialist persuasion.

Bell Model 30 Genevieve

FF 1942 USA

The Genevieve was Bell's first helicopter and it represented the beginning of a huge change in direction for that firm, from airframes manufacturer to rotorcraft specialist.

Bensen B-8M Autogyro

FF 1957 USA

Dr Igor B. Bensen, formerly chief engineer of Kaman Helicopter Corporation, developed a series of lightweight autogyros, initially for research purposes but later for home-building. Bensen's creations used a range of modified engine types from McCulloch to Volkswagen.

FF 1932 USA

Beechcraft Model 17 Staggerwing

First flown in 1932, the Staggerwing quickly gained notoriety when it won the 1933 Miami Air Races' prestigious Texaco Trophy. Production began in 1934, and Model 17s of many evolving and improving designations variants were produced for sport air racing, for the US Army and Navy, for European diplomatic personnel transport, and for air-ambulance work. 781 of the type had been built by 1948 when production ceased.

Bell 47-3-B

FF 1945 USA

Many diverse variants of Bell's extraordinary Model 47 helicopter were developed over the years, from the standard military air ambulance variant which was used in large numbers in Korea to the float-equipped police and border-control platform with its outsized pneumatic floats. Production of the Model 47 continued in the USA right up until 1974 and in Italy until 1976. The longevity of the type established Bell as one of the world's leading helicopter producers and ensured financial security throughout many later years of helicopter development. The Bell 47-3-B illustrated right was an early production variant which was not provided with Bell's signature bubble canopy, surely a very cold and daunting prospect at any time of the year.

Bell Model 47-G-2A [on floats]

FF 1945 USA

When Larry Bell met the brilliant 23-year-old inventor and engineer Arthur Young, in 1941 he was immediately impressed by the obvious headway the young man had made into the aerodynamics of rotary flight. Other researchers into this area of aviation had built full-size helicopters and had proceeded dangerously and slowly with little collective success for all their effort. Young, on the other hand, built numerous simple remotely-controlled models to test the validity of his theories and so progressed rapidly from step to step. The value of these achievements was not lost on Larry Bell as he watched Young fly his latest model, and he quickly invited the young inventor to join him at Bell. Young's first full-scale prototype at Bell was the now-famous Model 30 Genevieve, which was remarkable for its ease of flight and its stability in the air. One of Young's simplest and most important contributions to flight was the incorporation of the stabilizer bar on the rotor mast, an invaluable device employed to dampen the oscillations inherent in rotary flight through any air mass. Bell's Model 47, built in vast numbers over many years, was in fact the production development of Arthur Young's Model 30. The combination of Arthur Young's inventive genius and Larry Bell's marketing skills produced the world's first fully certified helicopter.

Bell 206 LT Twin Ranger

FF 1991 USA

The Bell 206 derived originally from a detailed US Army brief. With its sights on both the military and the civilian markets, Bell flew 2 separate B-206 prototypes in late 1972. The 206 has progressed steadily on all fronts since those early days with greatly uprated avionics and engines, and with a new stretched Long Ranger airframe.

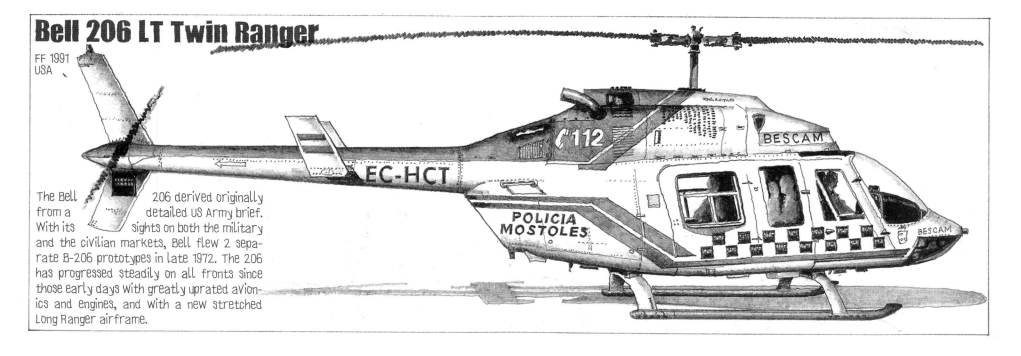

Bell Model 209 Huey Cobra

FF 1965 USA

The Huey Cobra is a high-performance close-support attack helicopter developed by Bell in response to a US Army specification. The type is based closely on the earlier Bell Iroquois helicopter, with similar structures and powerplant but a greatly thinned-down tandem-seat fuselage to reduce frontal profile and therefore the likelihood of an enemy hit. The type was configured specifically to carry a large array of weapons systems from rockets and laser-guided missiles to large-volume automatic machine guns. Great emphasis was placed on providing systems to allow these weapons to be delivered to target with deadly accuracy.

Bell 412

FF 1979 USA/Canada

The first 2 prototype 412s first flew in 1979 with certification being awarded in 1981 and first customer deliveries being made only 1 month later. The helicopter has evolved continually since those early days, with engine upgrades, enhanced avionics and modern EFIS systems. With a seating capacity of 15, the B-412 is employed in a wide variety of roles from executive to medevac to offshore utility.

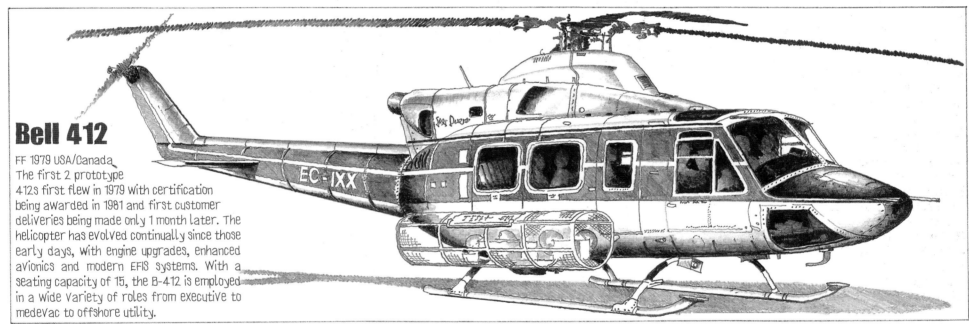

Bell P-63 Kingcobra

FF 1942 USA

The Bell P-39 Airacobra promised to provide a new level of firepower and performance with its sleek, tightly faired contours and its massive 37mm cannon, which fired through its hollow propeller shaft. In practice, however, the Airacobra had a disappointing mission debut with the RAF and the type was quickly relegated to training duties. The P-63 Kingcobra development of the type addressed many of the faults of the original Airacobra but, with an ever emerging crop of excellent fighter designs coming on stream, it failed to attract the attention it deserved.

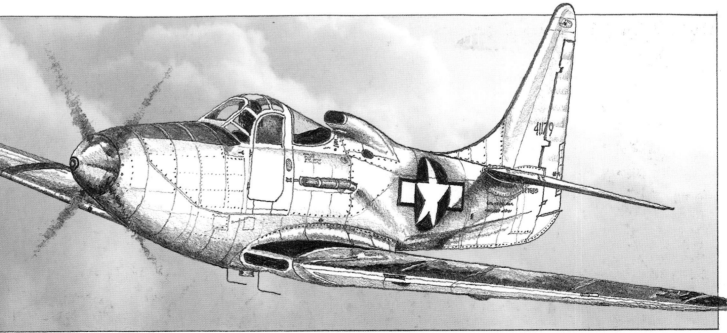

Bell X-14 Research Prototype

FF 1957 USA

Bell had long been one of the world's foremost designers of both aircraft and helicopters and so it was no surprise when it turned its attention to the production of a new hybrid convertiplane in 1956. The X-14 research test vehicle was something of a mongrel, being made up of a heavily modified T-34 Mentor fuselage mated with the wings of a Bonanza. It did, however, fly and it did greatly advance the available bank of knowledge into this elusive field of aeronautical dynamics. The Bell X-14's 2 Armstrong Siddeley Viper engines did lift the prototype into hover flight in 1957 and into full forward horizontal flight in 1958.

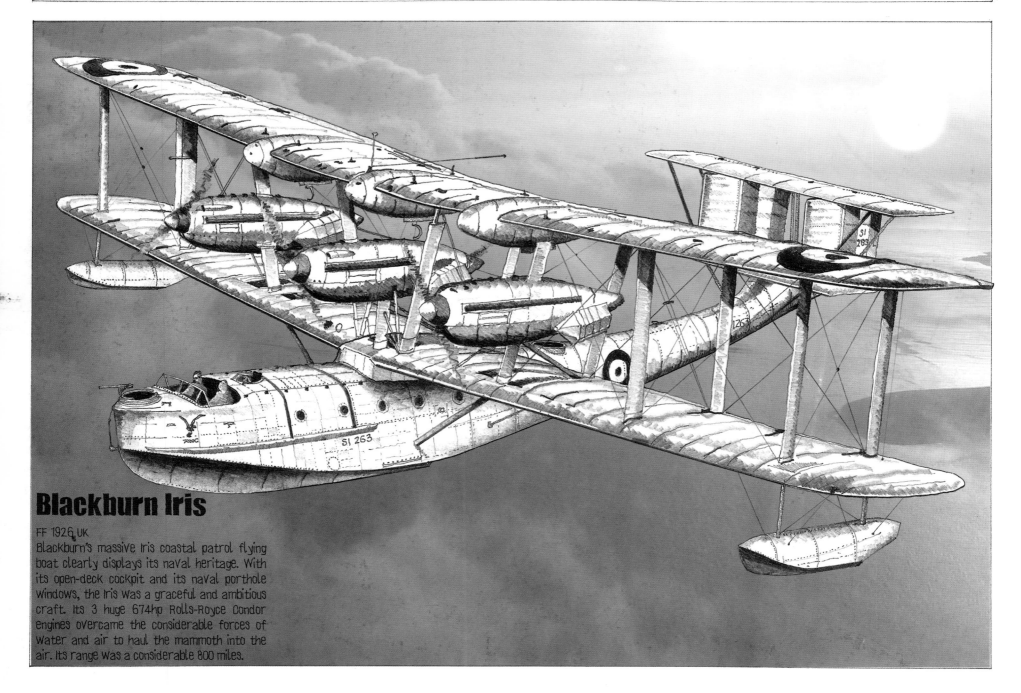

Blackburn Iris

FF 1926 UK

Blackburn's massive Iris coastal patrol flying boat clearly displays its naval heritage. With its open-deck cockpit and its naval porthole windows, the Iris was a graceful and ambitious craft. Its 3 huge 674hp Rolls-Royce Condor engines overcame the considerable forces of water and air to haul the mammoth into the air. Its range was a considerable 800 miles.

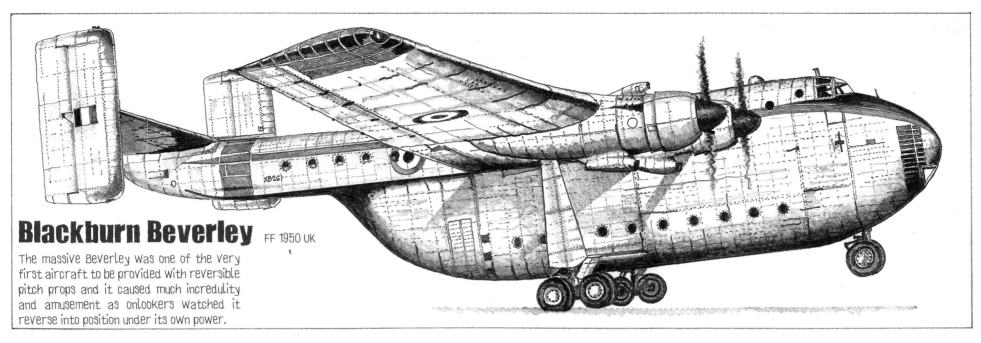

Blackburn Beverley

FF 1950 UK

The massive Beverley was one of the very first aircraft to be provided with reversible pitch props and it caused much incredulity and amusement as onlookers watched it reverse into position under its own power.

Blackburn B-24 Skua

FF 1937 UK

As the political clouds gathered in Europe in the years coming up to the Second World War the British Air Ministry placed large orders with many of the leading aircraft manufacturers. Germany had rearmed and the nature of its insatiable appetite to dominate Europe was becoming apparent. As Herr Hitler's rhetoric bamboozled the chanting throngs at his extraordinary Nazi Party rallies, Britain's Royal Navy and Royal Air Force were placing orders with anybody who could build aircraft. To meet the Royal Navy's urgent requirements a total of 190 Skuas were ordered from Blackburn in 1936, a full 6 months before the prototype even flew! Development and manufacture did, however, go to plan and the last of the 190 Skuas were delivered by March of 1940. Both HMS Ark Royal and HMS Furious were equipped with Skuas and the type saw much action during the early years of the war. Indeed, at the outset of the war the very first enemy aircraft to be shot down by a British aircraft was a Dornier Do-18 which was brought down by a Skua of No 803 Squadron. Perhaps the greatest moment ever for the type was the dramatic sinking of the German Königsberg battlecruiser which was caught sheltering in Bergen Harbour.

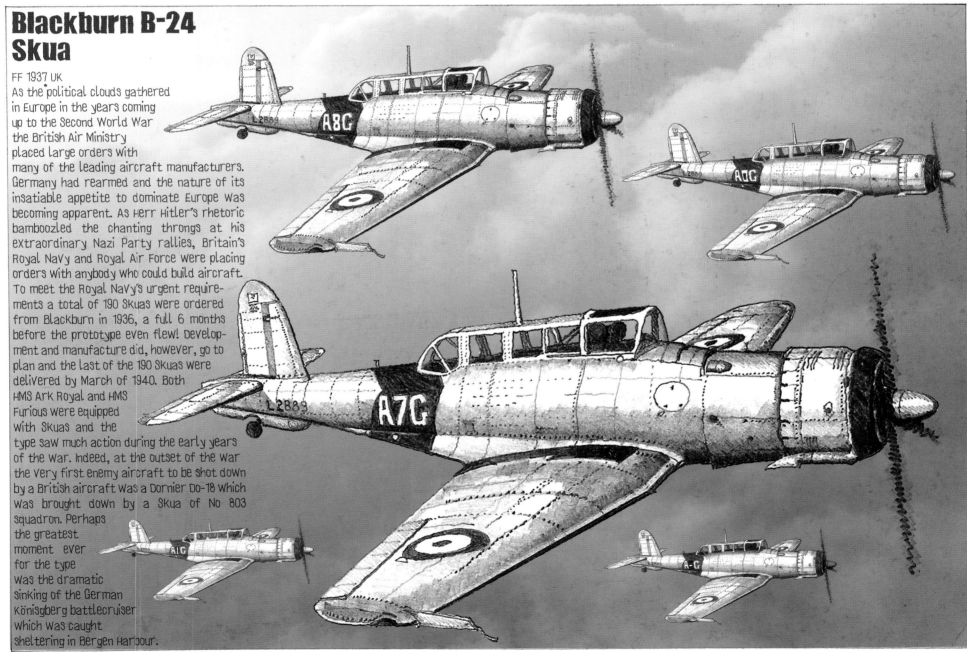

Boeing L-15 Scout

FF 1947 USA

The Scout was the last Boeing aircraft to be developed for the single-engine small-aircraft market. Like all of the other big aircraft manufacturers Boeing found that its order books were decimated by the end of the War and it raced to diversify into alternative markets. The Scout was designed as a ground-observation platform and was provided with high wings and large unobstructed 360-degree views. An innovative feature of the type was that it could be quickly dismantled and towed behind a jeep. With a massive surplus of aircraft available to it, the US Army was not in a buying mood and, in the end, only 12 of the type were manufactured.

Boeing Model 100

FF 1928 USA

Boeing's fabric-covered Model 100 was a most beautiful sight on the ground or in the air. Perfectly designed around the forces and functions of flight at its simplest and best, it was something of a hot-rod in its day.

Boeing F4B-3

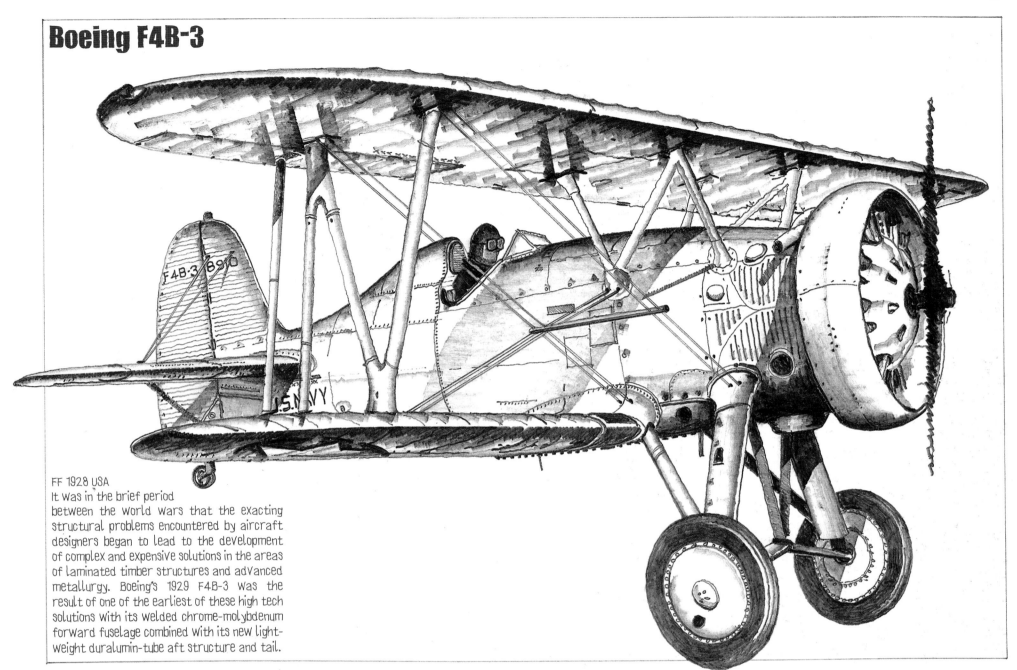

FF 1928 USA
It was in the brief period
between the world wars that the exacting
structural problems encountered by aircraft
designers began to lead to the development
of complex and expensive solutions in the areas
of laminated timber structures and advanced
metallurgy. Boeing's 1929 F4B-3 was the
result of one of the earliest of these high tech
solutions with its welded chrome-molybdenum
forward fuselage combined with its new lightweight duralumin-tube aft structure and tail.

Boeing KC-97F
Stratotanker

FF 1944 USA
The war in the Pacific brought massive
logistical problems with troop positions and
supply lines spread over vast, isolated
areas. To address these difficulties the US
Government invited the larger manufacturers
to make submissions for a long-range heavy-
lift, transport so the Stratocruiser and the
Stratotanker were born. Based on the airframe of the B-29 Superfortress and
retaining its lower fuselage, wings, powerplants, tail and landing gear, the mammoth
airframe could be configured to carry light
tanks, troops, stretchers, freight, or air-to-air
refuelling equipment. Many of the type were
converted for civilian use.

Boeing 737-500

FF 1967 USA

Surely the most prolific of all airliners in today's robust commercial market, Boeing's 737 has permeated every market and every country. The type presents operators with an ideal medium-range transport with high levels of efficiency both in terms of fuel burn and turn-about times. With its high level of market saturation, too, spare parts and trained service and flight personnel are readily available right across the world. Only in recent years has the 737's market share been slightly eroded by the the sophisticated new generation of offerings from Airbus. In this new competitive market

environment
Boeing continues to
re-invent its 737 with a constant
stream of upgrades from quiet,
efficient wide-fan engines to glass
cockpits and the very latest in
flight-management systems.

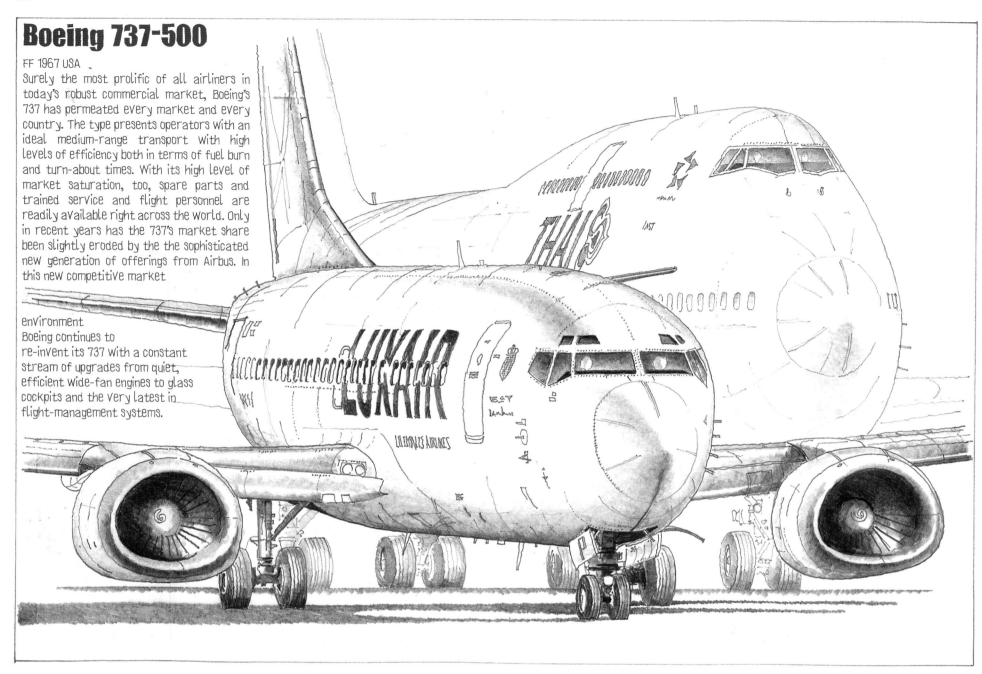

Boeing 747 NASA 905 Shuttle Carrier

FF 1977 USA

The NASA 905, a heavily
modified Boeing 747-123, was commissioned
by NASA to facilitate ferrying the Shuttle
between Edwards AFB, California, and Cape
Canaveral, Florida. The first combination flight
was made from the Dryden Flight Research
Centre, Edwards AFB, in February 1977.

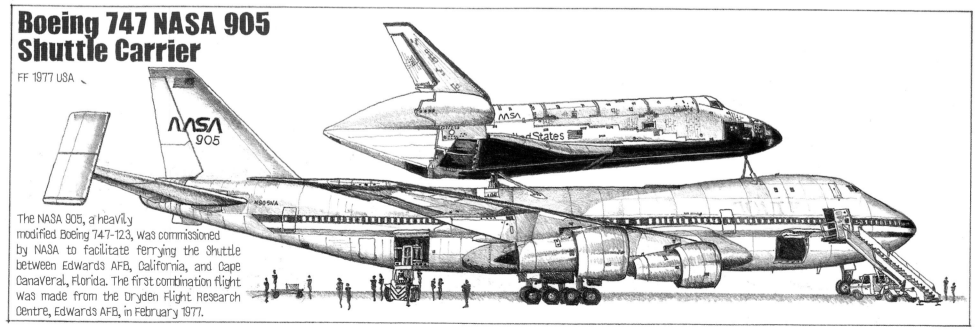

Boeing B-17 Flying Fortress
FF 1935 USA

Bristling with no less than 13 defensive guns, Boeing's B-17 Flying Fortress heavy bomber.

Boeing B-52 Stratofortress
FF 1952 USA

No other aircraft epitomizes the shadow of the Cold War like the massive B-52

strategic bomber. More than 740 of the type were produced, most of them nuclear-capable. Although the days of nuclear stand-off have now passed the US maintains a large B-52 fleet today.

Boeing KC-135 Tanker
FF 1954 USA

Boeing's 367-80 flight-refuelling airframe was a prototype for the KC-137 tanker. Taking to the air for the first time in July of 1954, it opened up for Boeing new challenges and new opportunities in the fledgling science of large-volume mid-air

refuelling.
Running in
parallel to the military
KC-137 project was the development of the first of a new generation of turbojet-powered widebody airliners, the Boeing 707.

Boeing C-17 Globemaster III
FF 1995 USA

The C-17 Globemaster was designed to provide US armed forces with an effective heavy-lift solution which would allow rapid deployment of combat equipment, troops and humanitarian aid. This is a mammoth aircraft with a cavernous interior, capable of lifting heavy tanks, battle helicopters, and an array of other outsized military loads. The

ability to rapidly position heavy forces in conflict areas provides the US with substantial political leverage.

Boeing 747-4J6
FF 1969 USA

For many years Boeing's 747 was the unrivalled queen of the skies. At its unveiling the world's press was staggered by the projected statistics of the new type. With a take-off weight of over 300 tons it would carry 530 passengers and fly some of the world's longest air routes non-stop. Public scepticism, however, was soon proved unfounded and the familiar 'Jumbo' title was born.

Boeing 757

FF 1982 USA

Based on new technologies and reflecting new levels of efficiency, the Boeing 757 carries up to 239 passengers on route sectors of up to 4,470 miles (7,195km).

Boeing 767

FF 1981 USA

Tailored to meet the needs of long-range high-density operators, the 767 brings new levels of fuel efficiency and new, improved flight management sytems.

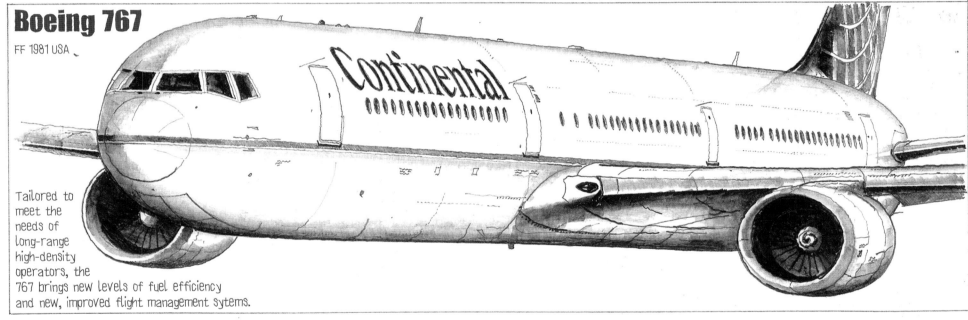

Boeing 777-300

FF 1994 USA

Boeing's new-generation widebody carrier marks significant improvements in both efficiency and range with the ability to fly some of the world's longest sectors non-stop.

Boeing Stearman PT-17 Kaydet

FF 1934 (PT series) USA

There is perhaps no other aircraft that is as beautiful on the ground or in the air as the Boeing Stearman PT-17. Its simplicity and its ruggedness are immediately apparent. The lines of the timber longeron formers, visible through its fabric covering, allow you to understand exactly how the structural loads are distributed across the airframe. The detailing, the stitching, and the timberwork tell of days gone past. The smells of leather and oil are rich and strong and, of course, that big noisy radial engine up front thunders out the power of 220 horses. The perfect aeroplane! It was Lloyd Stearman himself who designed the Model 70 series, which eventually evolved into the PT-17. The US Army had been discussing the requirement for a new pilot training aircraft for some considerable time but had, for financial reasons, not invited tenders. Stearman, nonetheless, decided to develop the Model 70 as a private venture. Unhampered by the usual military stipulations and red tape, he was able to produce the aircraft as he himself would have wished it to be. The Model 70/PT series was immediately successful and the rest is history! In 1939 the Stearman Aircraft Co., already a subsidiary of Boeing, became the new Wichita division of Boeing. Development of the PT series continued, eventually leading to the PT-17 Kaydet. It was known to many young pilots as the Yellow Peril, not because of its flying characteristics, but on account of the inherently dangerous nature of primary pilot training. More than 10,000 of the type were built and many are still flying to this day.

Boeing 307 Stratoliner

FF 1938 USA

Pan American and TWA were quick to recognize the merits of Boeing's new pressurized 307 airliner and they bought the first models straight off the plans. Howard Hughes, too, dug deep and purchased his own private Stratoliner, which was fitted out as a luxurious personal liner.

Boeing-Vertol CH-47 Chinook

FF 1961 USA
Twin-rotor heavy-lift military helicopter from Boeing-Vertol.

Boeing Stearman

FF 1934 USA

With the end of the Second World War many hundreds of Boeing Stearmans were released for sale to civilian pilots and air operators alike. With an abundance of aircraft and returning pilots many tiny training and carrier operations were established. Other Stearmans ended up being used as stunt planes, barnstorming their way across the US and Canada, making a meagre and uncertain living entertaining townsfolk and farming communities. The type was rugged and versatile with docile and reliable flying qualities which were loved and trusted by its display pilots. The build-quality of the type was such that many Stearmans remain in service to this day, providing a fascinating insight into those days when flying was at its best and when the training of military pilots in vast numbers was vital to the battle for freedom from tyranny and oppression.

Boulton Paul Defiant FF 1937 UK

The logic behind the RAF's specification for the Defiant was that any enemy aircraft undertaking a pursuing attack would be quickly overwhelmed by the new fighter's power-operated gun turret with its 4 rapid-firing 0.303 Browning machine guns.

In the early days of the Battle of Britain the Defiant shot down a record number of enemy fighters. Within weeks, however, the German pilots realized that the type was entirely defenceless in a frontal attack or when approached from below.

Bristol Beaufighter

FF 1939 UK

At the outset of the war the RAF found that its fighters did not have the range required to reach deep into Continental Europe. To reach deep into Germany a twin-engined fighter would be required. To answer this need The Bristol Aeroplane Company developed the Beaufighter. It took 8 months and it entered service with the RAF 15 months later. The Beau' was a capable night fighter with an abundance of firepower.

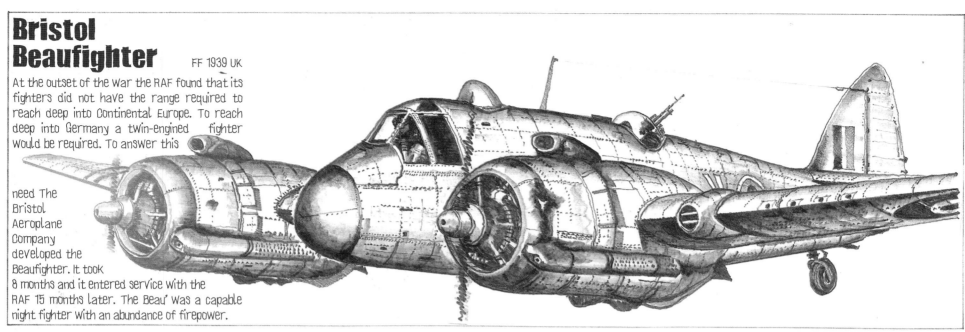

Bristol Beaufort Mk 1

FF 1938 UK

The 1938 Beaufort torpedo- and general-reconnaissance bomber served in all theatres of war and more than 2,100 were delivered to various Allied air forces right across Europe and Asia.

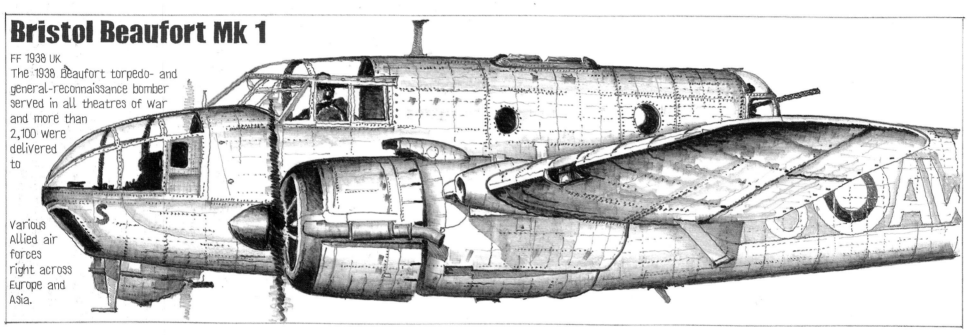

Bristol F-2B Brisfit

FF 1916 UK

The Bristol Brisfit's first venture into battle was a disaster for the new fighter. On 5 April 1917 6 brand-new RFC Brisfits engaged 5 of the older German Albatros D-III fighters over Douai, France. 4 of the Brisfits were lost, against no losses for the Germans. The RFC Brisfits took a pounding for the rest of April until they developed a series of diving-attack tactics with which they could beat the Germans. Suddenly they became a potent weapon which was greatly feared by the German aircrews. Designed by one Captain F. Barnwell of the British and Colonial Aeroplane Company, it had a maximum speed of 120mph (193km/h), and a range of 300 miles.

Bristol F-2B Fighter Brisfit

FF 1916 UK

Given that the first powered flight, by the Wright brothers, was only 13 years earlier, the speeds, manoeuvrability, and weaponry of many of the First World War fighters were extraordinary. In little more than a decade flight had advanced from its fledgling beginnings to the point where robust, capable aircraft would tangle in deadly mid-air combat. Aircraft like the Bristol F-2B were icons to the infantry troops in the muddy trenches below. They would watch in awe as the fortunes of their army pilots surged and fell in the fierce air battles raging overhead. To each side their pilots were like distant heroes or movie stars. They lived in different worlds. They met only when one of the tiny biplanes peeled off from the group and dived, trailing flames, into the ground below. Downed aircraft were always a source of great wonderment to the ground forces, and soldiers would travel long distances along the complex maze of trenches to view a crash scene.

On both sides the bodies of downed pilots were treated with far greater respect than those of the unfortunate ground troops and there were many instances where enemy pilots were buried with honours.

Bristol Britannia

FF 1952 UK

Designed to meet BOAC's 1947 specification, the Bristol Britannia's size grew from its intended 36-seat capacity to its eventual 139-seat capacity. This increase, influenced principally by the availability of new, powerful engines, meant that in its final configuration it was capable of flying some of the world's longest routes. Engine upgrades and stretches saw the capacity of the aircraft increase to 139 while its range was dramatically improved.

In 1957 Israeli carrier ElAl flew a partially stripped-down Britannia non-stop from New York to Tel Aviv, a distance of over 6,000 miles.

BAe Hawk 100

FF 1974 UK

An advanced military trainer and ground-attack aircraft from British Aerospace.

BAe Nimrod MR-2

FF 1967 UK

A production airframe based closely on the de Havilland Comet. The Nimrod's underbelly panniers, boom and steeply pointed nose profile are unmistakable on the ground or in the air.

British Aerospace
BAe 1000

FF 1990 UK

The BAe 1000 light corporate and executive transport is derived from the longstanding BAe-125 series. Developed in the 1960s by de Havilland, the type has had a long and colourful series of designations over the years. At various stages in its lifetime it has been called the de Havilland 125, Hawker Siddeley 125, Beech 125 and British Aerospace 125, but in the end it is the simple nickname Hawker which has endured. Each consecutive variant of the series from 400 to 800 was a thorough refinement of the type involving uprated engines, aerodynamic improvements, and radical equipment fit-outs. Now the BAe 1000 variant is the ultimate culmination of this development process, and it again places the veteran airframe at the forefront of the range of executive aircraft available today. Each of its quiet Pratt & Whitney PW-305 engines produces 5,225lb of thrust to speedily carry the aircraft to a new ceiling of 43,000ft (13,107m). Fuel consumption, and therefore range, is greatly enhanced with the BAe 1000's new FADEC digital engine direct authority control system. When fully laden with fuel the new 1000 series carries only 1,400lb of fuel more than the 800 series and yet the 1000 has a range which is all of 700 miles (1,126km) greater than its predecessor. Its range is 3,525 miles (5,672km) and seating is provided for 8 to 12 passengers in an executive configuration.

Bücker Bü-133 Jungmeister

FF 1935 Germany
The wonderful Bücker Bü-133 Jungmeister aerobatic biplane was born in the years leading up to the Second World War when the German government was engaged in playing ducks and drakes with the onerous armament-limiting conditions of the Treaty of Versailles. The Jungmeister was designed to dominate the world of aerobatics and to allow Germany to develop large numbers of trained pilots without seemingly expanding its air force. The Bü-133 was a dream to fly, responsive and extremely controllable during aerobatic manoeuvres. Its many competition wins created an early propaganda victory for the Third Reich.

CAP 231-EX   FF 1981 France

A capable and highly strung aerobatic monoplane designed to compete at the highest levels in contemporary aerobatic championships. The CAP 231 is a phenomenal performer with remarkably precise control and handling characteristics. 12 times winner of the world aerobatic championships, it is rigged to perform rapid and repeated rotations on every axis and to recover quickly from even the most extreme

of manoeuvres. Of course, for $250,000 you would expect no less of any small aeroplane.

Caproni Stipa

FF 1932 Italy
Count Gianni Caproni di Taliedo built many wonderful aircraft and, indeed, owned or sat on the boards of management of up to 20 of Italy's best-known aircraft-manufacturing companies. In 1932 Caproni financed and built the amazing ducted-fan Caproni Stipa, designed by controversial Italian designer Luigi Stipa.
The 'Flying Barrel',
as it became known, was used to investigate the flight characteristics of ducted-fan propulsion units and hollow-chord fuselage designs. In recent years a team of Falco builders from Richmond, Virginia, have built and flown a 65%-scale copy of the original Stipa. The new Flying Barrel collects a crowd whenever its hangar doors are opened.

Capella XS

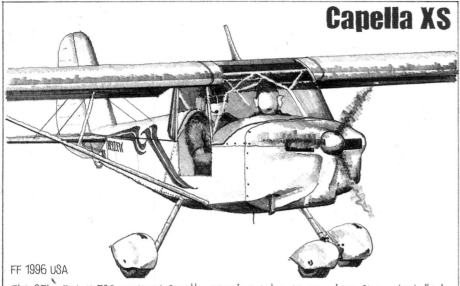

FF 1996 USA

The 65hp Rotax-582-powered Capella experimental category aircraft can be built in tricycle or taildragger configuration. An attractive and highly efficient home-build.

Catalina II Home-build

FF 1996 USA

Borrowing its title from the great Catalina of the 1940s, the tiny Catalina II amateur-build flying-boat may not be as impressive but is float flying at its simplest and best.

CASA/IPTN CN-235

FF 1983 Spain & Indonesia

A regional airliner, feederliner and tactical military transport, the CN-235 was developed jointly by CASA of Spain and IPTN of Indonesia. CASA of Spain build the inboard portions of the wings as well as the centre and forward fuselage assemblies, while the outer wings rear fuselage and tail sections are built by IPTN of Indonesia. The 235 is configured to carry a total of 45 passengers in its airline configuration, or a combination troops and specialist freight containers in its dedicated military configuration.

Caudron G-4

FF 1915 France

René and Gaston Caudron were 2 of the great characters and innovators of the early days of aviation. The brothers, from the French town of Romiotte were farmers when they developed their first interest in flying. By the start of the First World War the 2 brothers had built an ever improving succession of aircraft and were now supplying the Caudron G-3 artillery spotter to the French army. By the second half of 1914 the brothers were working on the G-4, a twin-engined biplane fighter-bomber with greatly increased range and firepower. For months the type was among the most successful weapons of the air until the rapid wartime development of fighting machines rendered it suddenly obsolete.

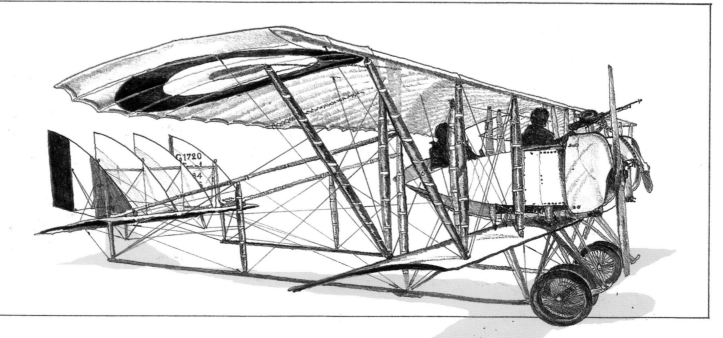

Cessna Model 140

FF 1945 USA

Clyde Cessna led a remarkable life even before he founded the Cessna Aeroplane Company. Born in Iowa, Cessna built his first aeroplane in 1911 and, teaching himself to fly, he became the first American to achieve flight west of the Mississippi. Moving to Kansas, Cessna risked his life as an exhibition pilot. It was during this period that his ability to innovate with mechanical devices started to appear and he began to develop and build his first aircraft designs. In 1924 he was approached by Lloyd Stearman and Walter Beech, and the rest is history. Cessna's wonderful Model 140 had excellent flying characteristics and was built in very large numbers over a long period.

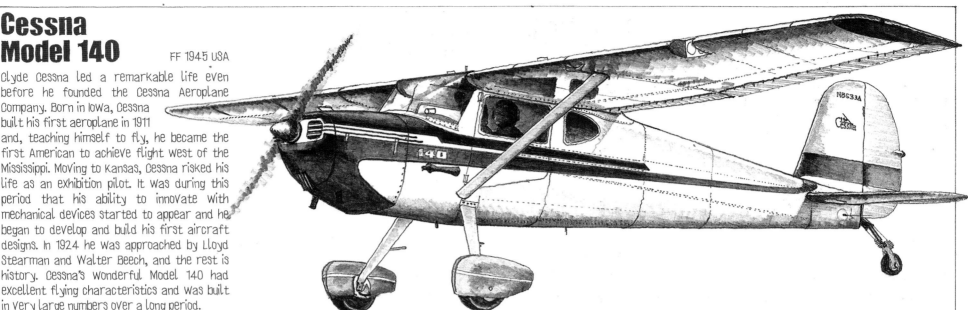

Cessna O-1

FF 1949 USA

The US armed forces employed the O-1 as an artillery-spotting platform in many areas of conflict across the world including Vietnam and Korea. With clear 360-degree visibility its observer could view the entire area of battle and provide radio instructions to the artillery batteries below. While the type was only employed in areas where the US forces had overwhelming air supremacy its relatively slow airspeed left it completely open to small-arms fire from below. Flying the Bird Dog in a hostile environment could be a particularly dangerous occupation and pilots developed new random weaving patterns to remove all pre-dictability from their flight paths.

Cessna Super Stol 150

FF 1957 USA

Pilots have always been intrigued by the prospect of reducing their aircraft's stall speed. A low stall speed allows for a reduced approach speed and a shorter landing run. Inversely a wing that picks up quickly will allow a shorter take-off run and greater margins of safety in flight. The trick is to ensure that the 10 to 15 knot reduction in stall speed does not adversely affect the performance of the aircraft at the upper end, that is at maximum cruise speed. A variety of STOL devices and upgrade kits are available for certain aircraft models, each aiming to reduce stall speed by way of causing the boundary layer to adhere more tightly to the wing surface.

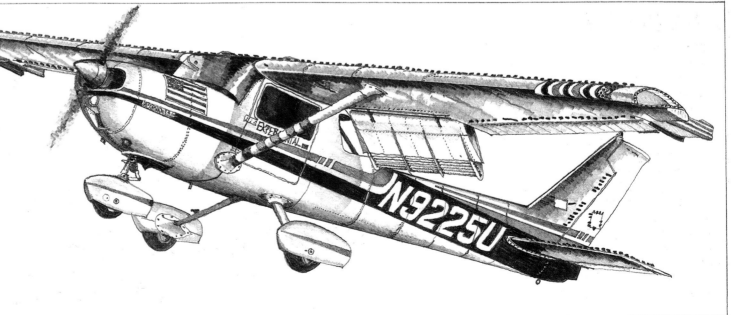

Cessna 172 Skyhawk

FF 1955 USA

With a total production run of over 42,500 of all types, the Cessna 172 is undoubtedly one of the most prolific aircraft types of all time. Back in production again as the 172 R/S Skyhawk, the type looks set to dominate the training and touring market for some considerable time to come. Developed originally as a tricycle-undercarriage variant of the Cessna 170 taildragger, the 172 was warmly received by the GA market of the 1950s as a rugged, docile and forgiving flyer with an affordable price tag. The rest is history! The aircraft permeated aviation across the world and multiple Cessna 172s are to be found at practically every aerodrome, owned by aeroclubs or small syndicates of pilots who share the burden of paperwork and costs.

Cessna 404 Titan FF 1976 USA

Cessna developed a stretched variant of the earlier Model 402 airliner to plug a gap in the lucrative commuter/cargo market. In its commuter configuration the Model 404 Titan could seat 13 passengers as well as the pilot while, with seating removed, it could efficiently haul large volumes of cargo over distances of over 2,000 miles (3,200km). United Kingdom-registered Titan G-TASK is fitted-out for specialist survey work and continues to operate to this day.

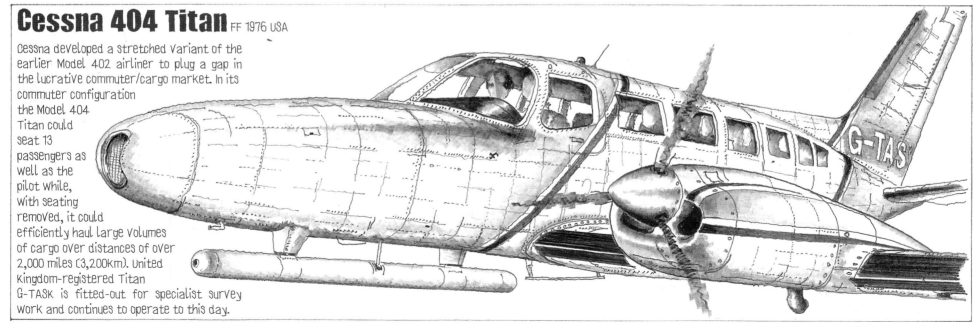

Cessna 190/195 Businessliner

FF 1947 USA

When Clyde Cessna introduced the Cessna 195 in 1947 the type was as near to a cabin-class single as one could get and Cessna pitched his new model as a 4- to 5-seat airliner, not a light plane. While Cessna might have believed his own sales talk, the market did not and they chose, instead, the rival Bonanza with its ultra-modern retractable tricycle gear. The Businessliner, nonetheless, went on to sell 1,183 units, a respectable tally by any standard. The interior of the big radial taildragger was clearly influenced by elements of 1920s Art Deco industrial design, a nostalgic and unusual inclusion in any aircraft presentation.

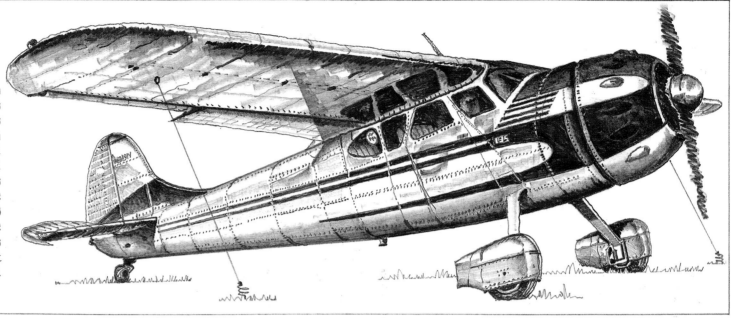

Cessna 208 Caravan

FF 1982 USA

Cessna's 208 Caravan is a tough and capable workhorse which was designed as a freight carrier and regional feederliner. The Caravan marque has become much associated with carrier Federal Express over the years and, indeed, Cessna developed a stretched 208 Super Cargomaster variant to meet FedEx-specific requirements. On floats, skis, or with a standard fixed undercarriage, the 208 Caravan is a superb working aircraft.

Cessna Model 318/T-37 Tweet

FF 1954 USA

A total of 1,272 T-37s had been delivered by the time production ceased in 1977. While most of these jet trainers went to the US Air Force a substantial number were controversially supplied to foreign governments under the US Military Assistance Program. Many of these 1970s armament-supply arrangements turned out to have been ill-advised and poorly judged, in some cases allowing semi-dictators to inflict years of oppression and neglect on their unfortunate populations.

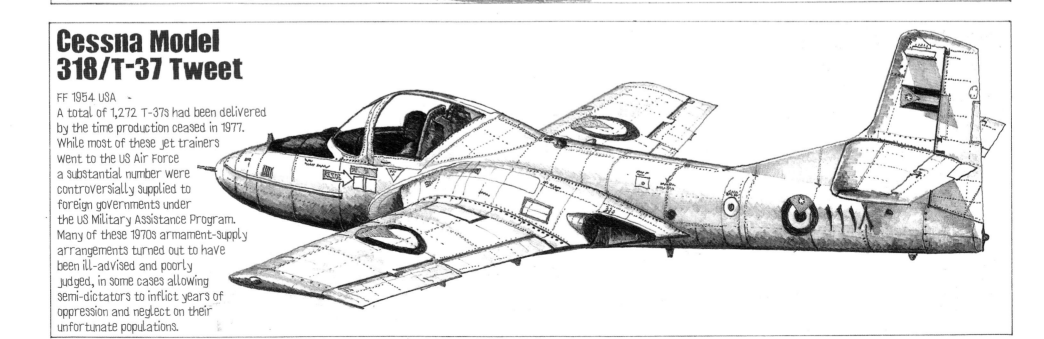

Cessna
L-19A-O-1 Bird Dog

FF 1949 USA

When the US Army advertised a design competition for a new 2-seat liaison and observation aircraft Cessna responded by remodelling their longstanding Cessna 170 design and entering it against such notable competition as Stinson and Piper. The little Cessna won, however, and so the L-19 Bird Dog was born. With seating for pilot and observer only, and with accommodation for one stretcher, the L-19 had greatly enhanced visibility with a reduced turtle deck and clear perspex panels above. As an observation platform it was second to none and, in the end, a total of 3,400 of all variants were built.

Cessna 210
Centurion

FF 1957 USA

The Cessna 210's strongest attribute is its very high cruise speed. This is the next step up from the prolific Cessna 172 for the pilot who needs to travel further or faster or, indeed, the salesperson who is using the aircraft to cover vast areas of territory. Clyde Cessna had it all worked out: an aircraft for every purpose and for every pilot. His range of aircraft varied in size and mission capability from the very smallest VFR singles to the most capable and sophisticated of all-weather twins. Of course, the Cessna 210 is no shrinking violet and it can eat up money like the best of them. Contrary to Clyde Cessna's master plan, most 210 Centurions are owned by flying groups or syndicates with pilots sharing the considerable costs and burdens of ownership and paperwork.

Cessna CJ3 Citation Jet

FF 1969 USA

Over the last 35 years Cessna's superb Citation series has been continually upgraded and enhanced to ensure that it is always at the leading edge of the executive jet market. The CJ3 series continues this trend with a 20-inch cabin stretch, more powerful engines and a 480 mph/(768km/h) maximum cruise speed. The aircraft's interior finishes and build quality make it more akin to the high-end corporate jets than the earlier Cessna models. The CJ3 will carry its lucky corporate client to 45,000 feet in just 27 minutes and can make it possible to effortlessly attend meetings over a

range of 2,160 miles (3,475km).

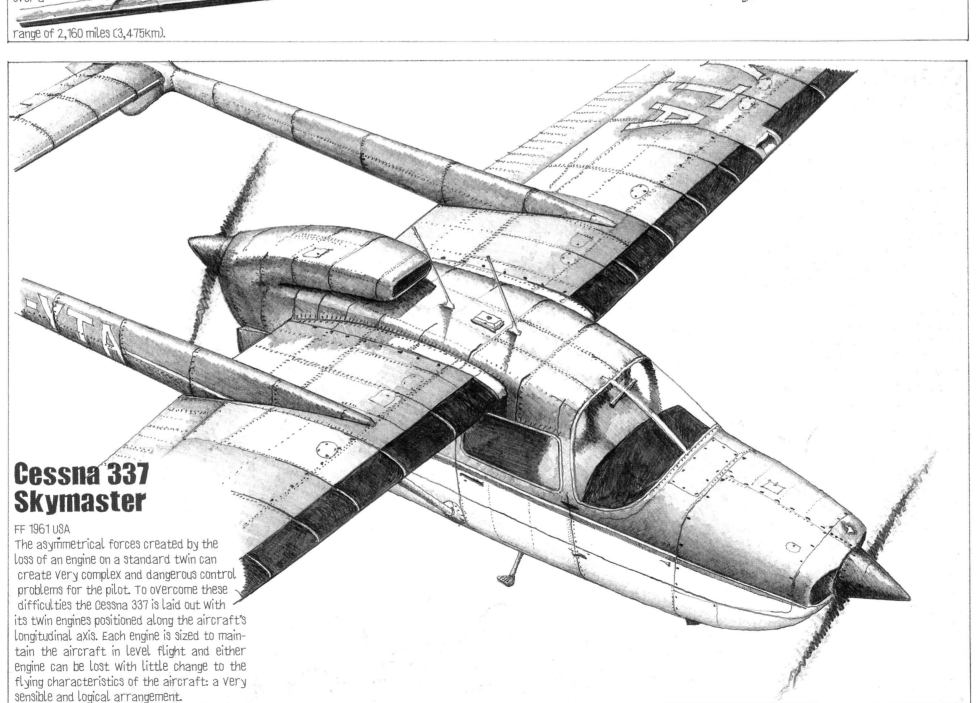

Cessna 337 Skymaster

FF 1961 USA

The asymmetrical forces created by the loss of an engine on a standard twin can create very complex and dangerous control problems for the pilot. To overcome these difficulties the Cessna 337 is laid out with its twin engines positioned along the aircraft's longitudinal axis. Each engine is sized to maintain the aircraft in level flight and either engine can be lost with little change to the flying characteristics of the aircraft: a very sensible and logical arrangement.

Champion Lancer 402

FF 1960 USA

The Lancer was a high-wing, fixed-gear twin, designed to provide twin-engine pilot training at an affordable price. Essentially it was the ultimate simple and rudimentary twin with no frills and no aspirations of distant travel or high speeds. The Lancer was cheap to operate and so provided the most inexpensive twin training around. The problem was that it was a dog to fly, ponderous and underpowered and very slow in the climb. The type provided students with some mind-bending moments during engine failure procedures as the propeller of the failed engine could not be feathered and so the asymmetrical yaw could be extreme. The Lancer held little appeal outside training circles and only 26 were built.

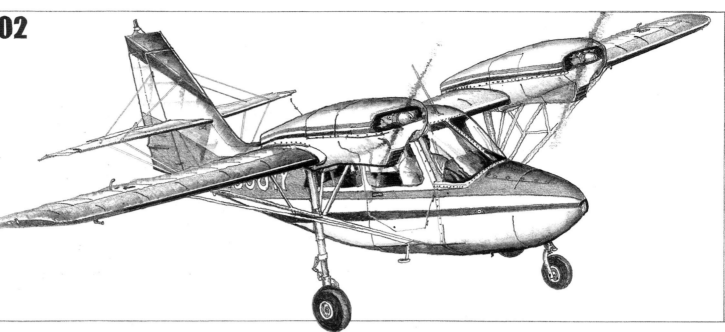

Chrislea CH-3 Super Ace

FF 1946 UK

The Chrislea Aircraft works produced a series of 4-seat light aircraft powered by Lycoming's 125hp (93kW) and 145hp (108kW) engines. Despite good flying qualities, sales of the type were, at best, lacklustre, principally because Chrislea installed the pilot's flight controls in a non-standard format. The CH-3 Super Ace, intended as an airborne observation platform, was the culmination of the type, with a higher level of specification.

Comper CLA-7 Swift

FF 1929 UK

Of the 41 Comper Swifts built in the 1930s only 2 airframes survive today. G-ACTF, now preserved in flying condition by the Shuttleworth Trust, has had a colourful history, seeing service in India in the 1930s and eventually flying all the way back to the UK.

Christen Eagle

FF 1977 USA

Frank Christensen's superb Christen Eagle aerobatic biplane is surely among the most beautiful and complex aircraft projects ever to be made available to amateur builders. That's right! You can do it at home! You buy a painstakingly detailed set of plans from the designer and set to work constructing each of the aircraft components to the very high standards and tolerances set down by the designer. This is a hobby that consumes all in its path, both time and money. It does, however, provide some of the most satisfying of moments just like a good game of golf or a successful afternoon's fishing. Prospective home-builders should be sure, too, that they enjoy the building process and not just the completed result, as most will never finish.

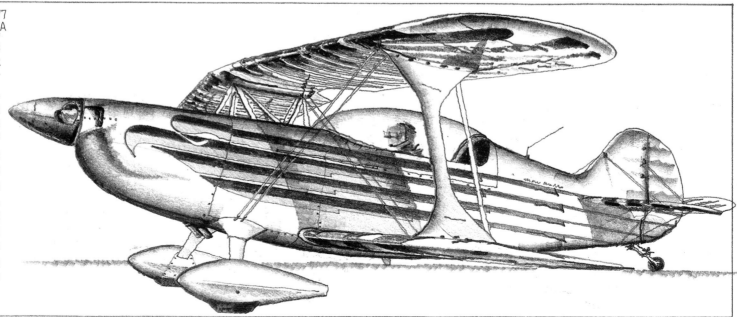

Civilian Aircraft Co. Coupé

FF 1929
UK

Harold D. Boultbee of Burton-on-Trent formed the Civilian Aircraft Co. in 1929. Boultbee was formerly assistant chief designer at the Handley Page aircraft works and he now turned his talents to producing his own range of aircraft. All did not go to plan, however, because the company produced only 1 design and the production line closed after only 6 examples. Civilian Coupé EI-AAV was based in Ireland for many years before being reintroduced to the British register.

Commonwealth Wirraway

FF 1939 Australia

The Commonwealth Aircraft Corporation of Australia purchased the production rights for the North American NA-33 and transported an example back to Australia for study. Similar in configuration to the original but fabricated largely of timber, the Wirraway prototype first flew in 1939. 3 months later the first production units were rushed into service with the RAAF. Over 755 of the type were built between 1939 and the end of 1946.

Consolidated-Vultee Convaircar

FF 1947 USA

Theodore P. Hall was the Consolidate-Vultee project leader who was responsible for the development of the extraordinary Convaircar flying car. He brought the great industrial designer Henry Dreyfuss, designer of the Bell telephone and the Polaroid camera, in to apply his talents and flair to the project. The Convaircar was to revolutionize personal transport, simplifying flight and bringing personal air travel to the ordinary man. Hall's vision never came to pass, however. Despite great media hype the project was not without its problems. In November 1947 the first prototype Convaircar crashed in the desert and, with public confidence shattered, the project quickly floundered.

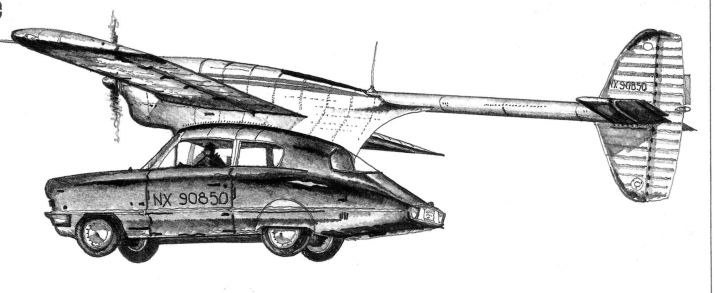

Consolidated PB4Y-2 Privateer
FF 1943 USA

Initiated in 1943 as a long-range maritime patrol/bomber, the Privateer was one of many aircraft developed during the Second World War.

After the war many Privateers were converted to civilian use.

Consolidated B-24 Liberator
FF 1939 USA

The Consolidated Aircraft Corporation developed the B-24 Liberator series, one of the most poignant symbols

of the Second World War, and one of the best-known warbirds of all time. Capable of long-range bombing, extended anti-submarine duties, and transatlantic ferry operations, the B-24 was first flown in 1939 at the very outset of the war. The series designations A to M describe the USAF's evolving variants of the type, while the designations B-24 i to ix describe those of the RAF. Over the course of the war years more than 18,000 B-24s (mostly bombers) were built. Various configurations of the type were flown in each theatre of war by the USA, Britain, Canada and France. Novel and functional innovations incorporated into the B-24 included the catwalk linking the rear fuselage to the flight deck, and the unusually large retractable landing gear. Other innovations included the extensive use of de-icing boots and the compact vertical stowage of bombs within the bomb bay. With a maximum speed of 300mph (483km/h) the B-24 required all of its 10 1/2-inch machine guns to keep fast-moving enemy predators at bay.

Consolidated PBY-5A Catalina
FF 1935 USA

The Catalina will forever be remembered as the US Navy aircraft that located the Japanese fleet at the outset of the Battle of Midway. Indeed, the Catalina played a central role in many of the great naval engagements of the Second World War. In particular, its vital role in the fight against marauding U-boats played a significant part in the Battle of the Atlantic and the breaking of the German sub-marine stranglehold on vital Allied shipping supplies from the USA. With the introduction of new lightweight radar sets the Catalina became a potent and much-feared anti-submarine weapons platform.

Cozy Mk IV
FF 1982 USA

For $500 you can buy the full set of Cozy plans from Aircraft Spruce & Speciality Inc. Building the aircraft itself, however, will make this first outlay seem very insignificant indeed. The Cozy was developed by veteran home-builder Nat Puffer, who was convinced that a new 3-seat side-by-side variant of the Long Ez could combine the very best characteristics of Rutan's canard design with the practical and social advantages of a side-by-side seating arrangement. The Cozy was well received by the home-building community and, as the first examples rolled out of garages and hobby-shops, Puffer put into place a comprehensive builder support network which won over many customers.

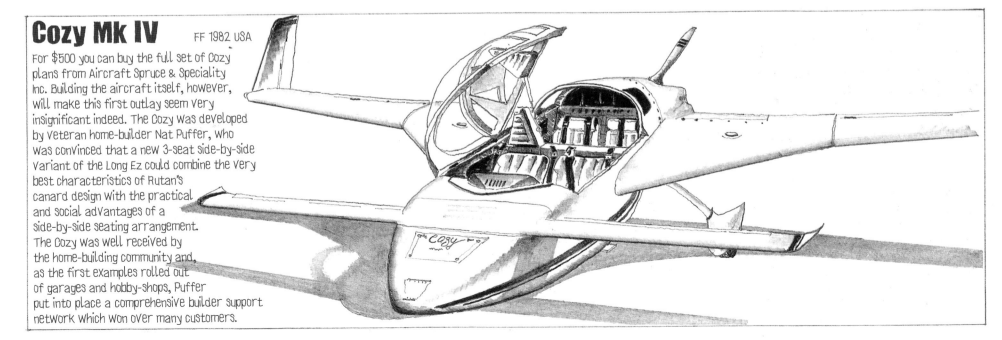

Convair XFY-1 Pogo

FF 1954 USA

Project Hummingbird of 1947
was a concerted effort by the
US Air Force and Navy to combine
what they already knew about VTOL
(vertical take-off and landing) with new
data retrieved from Germany's wartime
Focke Wulf Triebflugel (Trust Wing) programme. The intention was to develop an
interceptor fighter which could take off and
land vertically from destroyers, ships,
and even the smallest patches of level
ground. In 1951 the US Navy awarded
contracts to both Lockheed and Convair to
produce full-size prototypes of their VTOL
designs. Convair's XFY-1 Pogo was capable
of taking off and landing vertically using
its massive Allison YT-40 turboprop powerplants and its outsize tandem contra-
rotating propellers. Transition to horizontal flight was also achieved.

Curtiss P-40 Kittyhawk

FF 1938 USA

Throughout the Second World War the
Curtiss P-40 provided the Royal Air Force
with a reliable and potent aerial workhorse.
Known as the Warhawk by the US Air Force, and
the Kittyhawk or Tomahawk by the RAF, the
type was used in every theatre of war by
almost all of the Allied nations. While there
were faster and heavier fighting aircraft in the
Axis inventory, the P-40 was a lethal adver-
sary at altitudes of less than 15,000 feet and,
despite the arrival of sleek new fighters, the
type remained in service to the end of the war.
P-40s were produced in vast numbers throughout
the war, with Curtiss maintaining a
policy of ongoing progression
and upgrading.

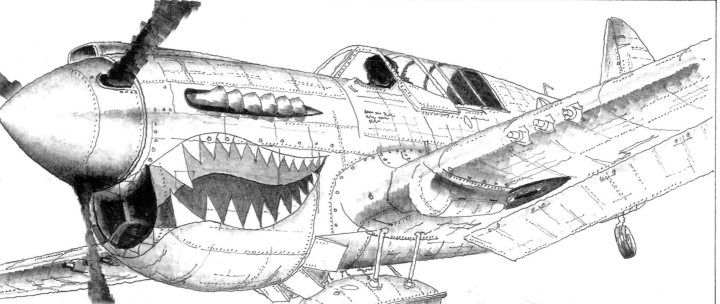

Curtiss BF2-C-1 Hawk

FF 1935 USA

The BF2-C-1 served aboard the USS Ranger and other fleet carriers from October 1936 to November 1937, surely one of the shortest operational lifespans of any military aircraft of the period. The Hawk's difficulty arose from the chance matching of the engine's cruise speed resonance with that of the all-metal wing structure. At design cruise speed the aircraft was simply shaking itself to pieces. Both Curtiss and the Navy used their wealth of experience to resolve the problem but, try what they might, the airframe continued to resonate dangerously

in sympathy with its powerful radial engine. With no apparent solution available to him, Curtiss bit the bullet and offered to replace all of the US Navy's BF2-C Hawk wings with a new all-wooden wing which could be guaranteed not to resonate. He must have been very relieved when the US Navy declined his offer on the basis that the design of carrier-borne aircraft was progressing so rapidly that the reconfigured Hawks would be obsolete before the corrective programme would be completed.

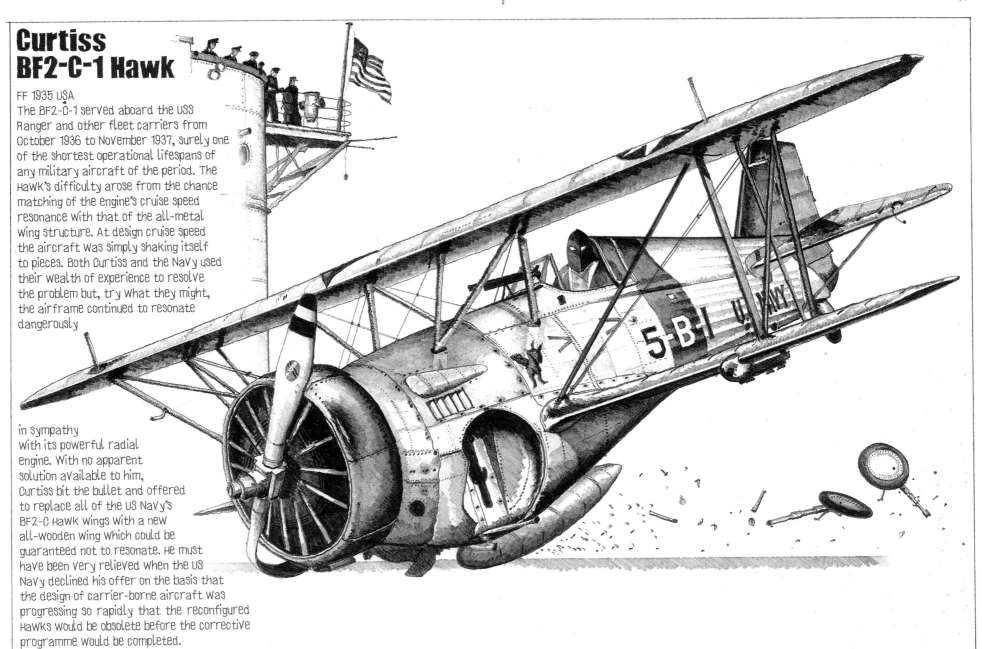

Curtiss P-40 Warhawk

FF 1938 USA

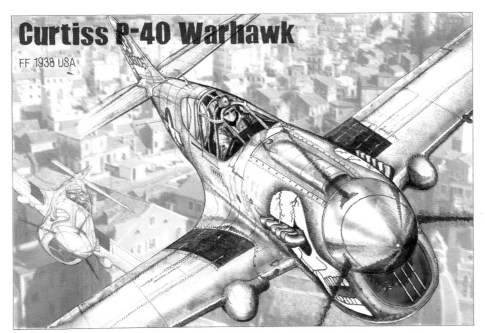

Curtiss H-75A-1 Hawk/Mohawk

FF 1935 USA

In the years leading up to the war the Curtiss Hawk was snapped up by France as it rushed to strengthen its air force in the face of overwhelming German rearmament. A hundred of the type were delivered to the beleaguered nation, the later portion of the order being shipped to Britain after the fall of France. The French Hawks fared well against Germany's prized Bf-109 fighters in the early days of the war, while the British Hawks (designated Mohawk IIIs) were used primarily to help defend Britain's Middle Eastern and Indian interests.

84

Curtiss C-46 Commando

FF 1940 USA

By the summer of 1940 Allied opposition to the relentless Nazi blitzkreig campaigns in Europe was going alarmingly badly and the US Air Force, anticipating being drawn into the conflict, placed massive orders for large troop transports with a number of suppliers including Curtiss. The initial order to Curtiss was for 200 of the C-46 but in the following year a

further 1,000 were ordered, and another 1,982 were ordered between 1943 and 1944. Over the course of the war the type served in all theatres of battle but it became especially well known for its crucial support of the India to China airlift, the opening of a massive military supply route across the Himalayas in support of General Chiang Kai-Shek of China, who was fighting a rearguard action against a ferocious Japanese war machine. With the coming of peace the same C-46s were pressed into civilian usage, becoming the basis of many of the hundreds of new airlines which sprang up right across the world.

Curtiss SBC-4 Helldiver

FF 1934 USA

The SBC-4 began life as a parasol-wing monoplane but, following a crash-landing in 1934, Curtiss designers rebuilt the single prototype in a biplane format. By 1939 the type was in service with the US Navy. France, meanwhile, was desperately trying to strengthen its air force and Franklin D. Roosevelt gathered 50 SBC-4s from active service and had them flown by civilian pilots to Nova Scotia, where the French aircraft-carrier Bearn awaited them. The aircraft never reached French soil, however, as news of the fall of France caused the Bearn to divert to Martinique. In 1942 the Martinique SBC-4s were set on fire to prevent them being used by Vichy forces.

Dassault-Breguet Atlantic 1150

FF 1961 France
Designed in association with
NATO's armaments committee,
the Atlantic is a multinational European
defence product. In service with France,
Germany, the Netherlands, Italy and Pakistan,
the type is configured for long-range maritime
patrol operations. With its complement of 12
crew it has a loiter speed of 195mph (320km/h)
and an endurance of 18 hours. Homing torpe-
does, depth charges, or anti-shipping mines can
be carried internally. Sensitive acoustic and
radar equipment is carried. In 1981 an
upgraded variant, the ATL-2, was given an
uprated airframe and more sensitive ELINT
gathering and computing systems.

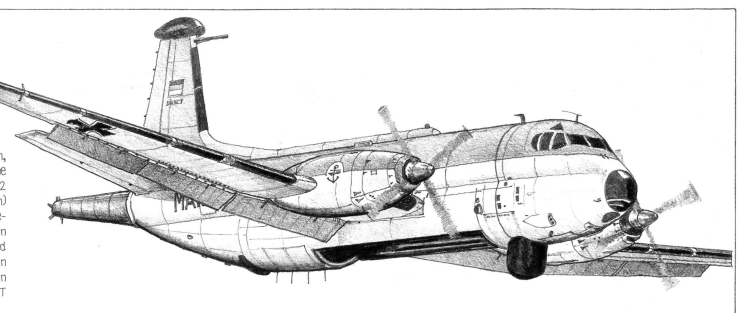

Dassault-Breguet Dornier-Alpha Jet

FF 1973 France
Following a 1969 agreement between the
French and German governments, Dassault-
Breguet of France and Dornier of
Germany were contracted
to develop

the Alpha Jet subsonic
tandem seat advanced jet trainer. The 2
countries each identified a need for 200 of the
type but the type went on to be exported to
many third nation clients also. The Alpha Jet
provides a compact and efficient advanced
training platform which is well capable of
being used in anger.

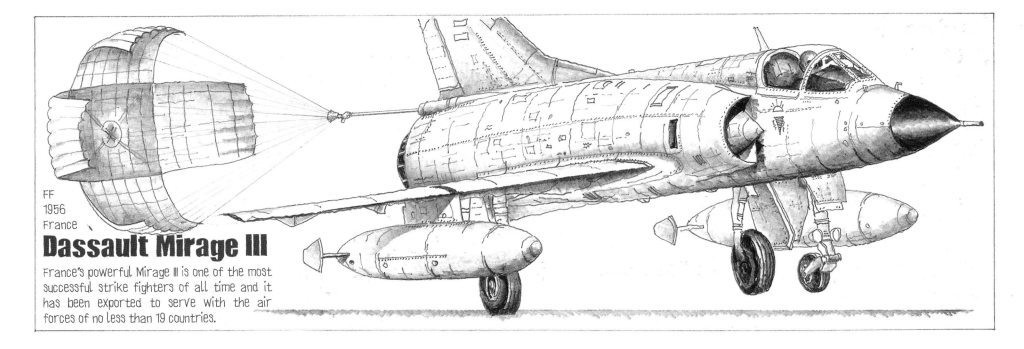

FF
1956
France

Dassault Mirage III

France's powerful Mirage III is one of the most
successful strike fighters of all time and it
has been exported to serve with the air
forces of no less than 19 countries.

de Havilland (Airco) DH-9A Ninak

FF 1917 UK

The DH-9A was one of the first truly rugged and reliable aircraft of all time. Flown for the first time only 14 years after the first flight at Kitty Hawk, the Ninak was tough, efficient, and extremely practical. Although some 800 DH-9As were built by the end of 1918 they saw very little use during the First World War. In the early 1920s, however, the DH-9A brought about massive changes to the policing policies throughout Britain's many colonies, allowing vast tracts of land to be policed by a tiny number of aircraft. The DH-9A served in India, Iran, Palestine and many other countries right up to the mid-1930s.

de Havilland DH-91 Albatross

FF 1937 UK

The fuselage of de Havilland's graceful Albatross was constructed of plywood outer and inner layers with balsa wood in between, certainly not a confidence-building detail for an aircraft designed to ply the lonely routes across the Atlantic. Only 7 of the type were produced, 2 for the British Air Ministry, and 5 for Imperial Airways. By 1939 all 5 were flying major air routes connecting Britain to Europe, Asia and India. With the outbreak of hostilities 2 Albatrosses were impressed into the Royal Air Force and operated on the London to Reykjavik route, now an important refuelling point on the long journey to the USA.

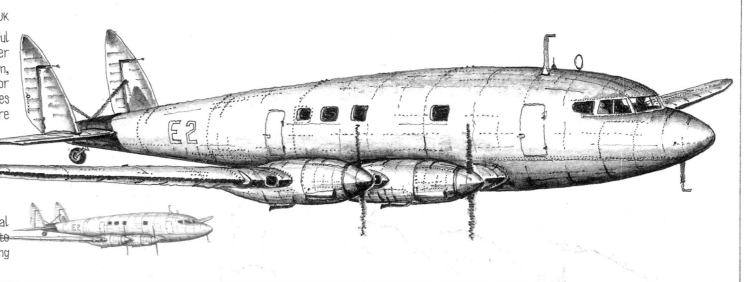

de Havilland DH-94 Moth Minor

FF 1937 UK

Just over 100 Moth Minors were completed before the rapid pace of 1930s aircraft development rendered the type dated and de Havilland moved on to its next model. The Moth Minor was a tandem 2-seat cantilever low-wing monoplane and production was undertaken in the UK and Australia. While many of the Australian examples were built in open-cockpit format, the UK variant tended to favour a hinged coupé arrangement.

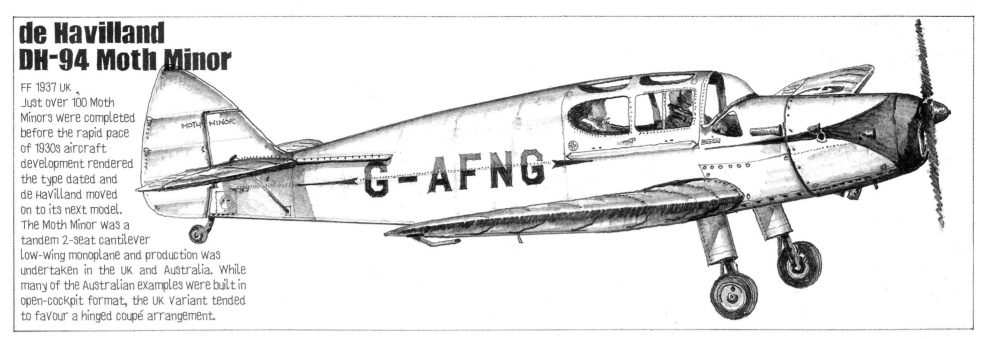

de Havilland DH-89 Dragon Rapide

FF 1934 UK

Over 700 wonderful Dragon Rapides were built over a period of 10 years and, indeed, several of the type are still flying today. With a cruise speed of 132mph (212km/h) and a range of 578 miles (925km) the Rapide was central to the development of civil airline routes throughout a wide range of Commonwealth and other countries.

de Havilland DH-100 Vampire

FF 1943 UK

A single-seat turbojet twin-boom fighter and interceptor from the de Havilland Aircraft Company. The type served with the RAF and many other air forces

across the world.
Its de Havilland Goblin 2 centrifugal-flow turbojet provided the power required to cruise at 480mph to a service ceiling of 40,000 feet. Originally the DH-100 was to be called the SpiderCrab but the Vampire name stuck.

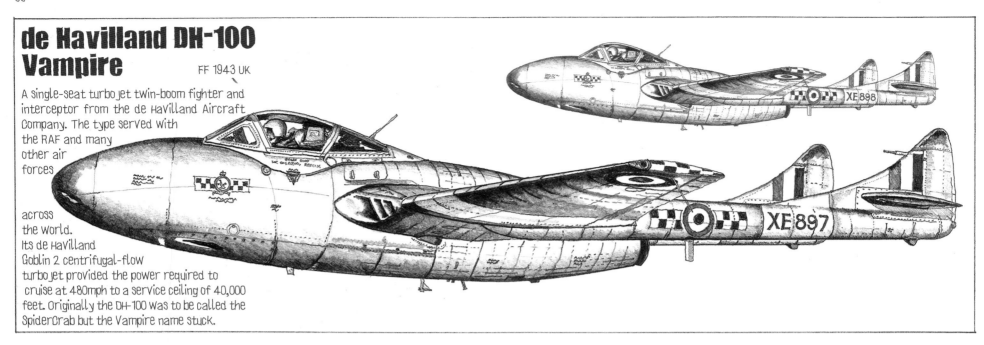

de Havilland DH-104 Devon

FF 1945 UK

As the Second World War finally came to a close it became apparent that the massive amounts of money expended on military R&D would now bring about a sea change in the area of commercial and military aviation. The new generation of aircraft now emerging from the design houses of Europe and the USA were vastly more sophisticated than those of the pre-war fleet. Among this new generation of aircraft was de Havilland's Dove and Devon series of light military transports. Advances in powerplant metallurgy, airframe structures, aerodynamics and fairing systems all combined to produce an aircraft which set new higher levels of performance, efficiency and mission safety.

de Havilland DH-106 Comet

FF 1949 UK

The new jet technology which appeared in the closing stages of the war was quickly adapted for civilian use by many of the main aircraft designers. De Havilland, too, was quick off the mark with its new DH-106 Comet and the type beat off stiff competition to become the world's first jet-powered airliner. BOAC Comets now linked London to Johannesburg and Tokyo with greatly reduced travel times and incomparable levels of in-flight comfort.

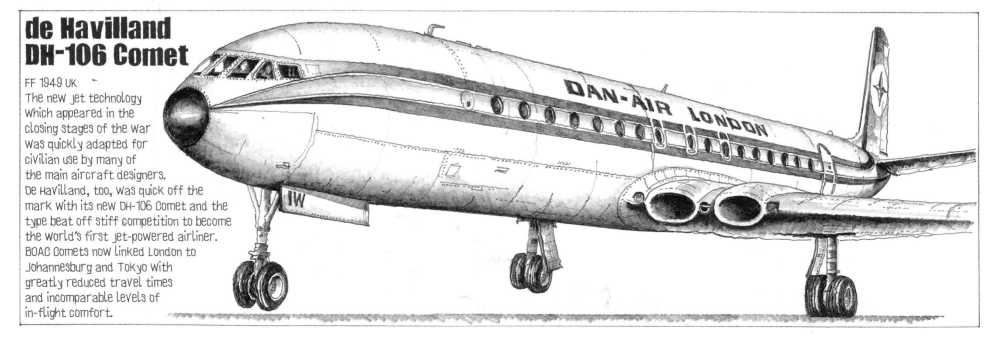

FF 1946 UK

de Havilland DH-108 Swallow

The DH-108, the first British aircraft to exceed the speed of sound, was a difficult and dangerous aircraft to control. All 3 prototypes crashed killing their unfortunate pilots.

Float-equipped variant of the ubiquitous Tiger Moth.

de Havilland Tiger Moth Sea Tiger

FF 1931 UK

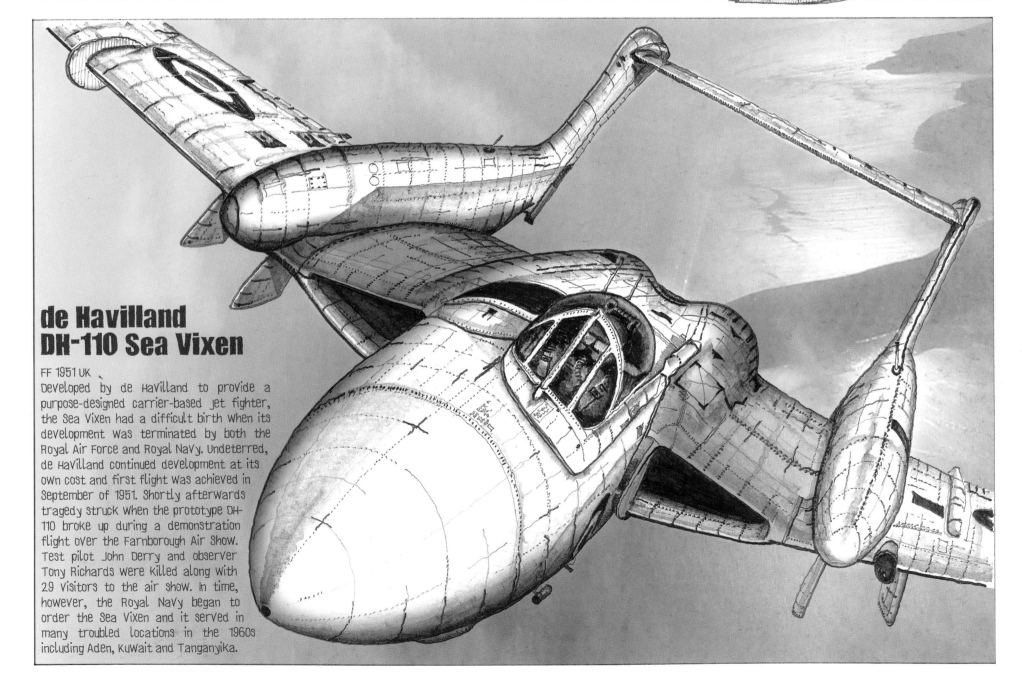

de Havilland DH-110 Sea Vixen

FF 1951 UK

Developed by de Havilland to provide a purpose-designed carrier-based jet fighter, the Sea Vixen had a difficult birth when its development was terminated by both the Royal Air Force and Royal Navy. Undeterred, de Havilland continued development at its own cost and first flight was achieved in September of 1951. Shortly afterwards tragedy struck when the prototype DH-110 broke up during a demonstration flight over the Farnborough Air Show. Test pilot John Derry and observer Tony Richards were killed along with 29 visitors to the air show. In time, however, the Royal Navy began to order the Sea Vixen and it served in many troubled locations in the 1960s including Aden, Kuwait and Tanganyika.

de Havilland CC3 DH-114 Heron

FF 1950 UK

The 4 de Havilland Herons of the Queen's Flight must have seen some fairly auspicious occasions in their day. Operated by the Royal Air Force, the aircraft were used to transport members of the Royal Family while attending official duties within the United Kingdom and nearer Europe. In the skies of Britain they were afforded purple airways status, that is, separate and preferential air traffic control treatment. The aircraft's interiors, always discreetly closed from view, were a matter of much interest and even more speculation. The Heron was later replaced in its privileged position by the larger Hawker Siddeley Andover.

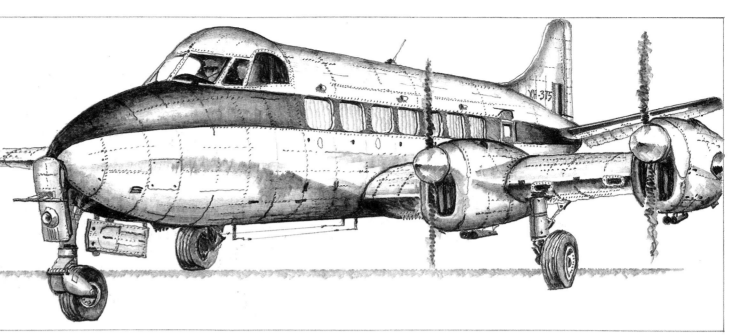

de Havilland Canada DHC-1 Chipmunk

FF 1946 Canada

The Chipmunk was designed by W. J. Jakimuil of de Havilland Canada and the type underwent its flight trials at Downsview, Toronto. Jakimuil, previously chief designer with PZL of Poland, was tasked with the job of designing a primary military trainer replacement for the venerable Tiger Moth. The Chipmunk, with its all-metal low-set wing and its tandem place configuration, was the perfect training aircraft and it went on to serve with many air forces across the world including Canada, Britain, Ireland, Malaysia and many others. de Havilland Canada built 158 Chipmunks while de Havilland UK produced 740 of the type.

de Havilland Canada DHC-2 Beaver
FF 1947 Canada

This single-engine STOL utility transport has seen civil and military service in over 65 countries. Provided in floatplane, wheeled format, or equipped with skis, the Mark 1 version is powered by a Pratt & Whitney R-985 Wasp Junior radial engine. 1,692 of this 8-seater were built. Requiring only a short landing run, it could be configured to land on rough grass strips, on water, or on snow skis. Its maximum speed is 134mph (217km/h) and range is in excess of 775 miles (1,252km). After a brief flirtation with a disappointing Mark 2 version, the Mark 3 Turbo-Beaver followed in 1963. Approximately 60 of this type were built, the broad radial being replaced by a long, thin turboprop.

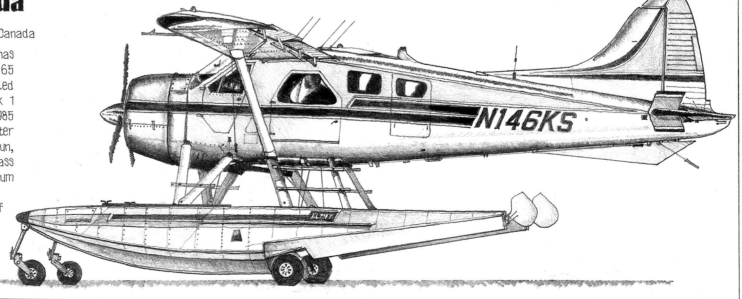

Delanne Duo-Mono
FF 1937 France

Maurice Henri Delanne was a most unusual man. Immediately before the Second World War his tiny aviation design shop was experimenting with tandem-wing aircraft such as the Delanne 10C-2. When France was overrun by the Germans in 1942 Delanne's designs and prototypes fell into the hands of the enemy. Delanne, caught up in the German advance, pretended to collaborate while striving to prevent the Reich making any headway with his designs. He altered his technical data, making it useless, and deliberately crashed his 10C-2 prototype into one of his fighter prototypes to ensure that his data was lost to the occupiers. Delanne's work for the Resistance eventually saw him imprisoned.

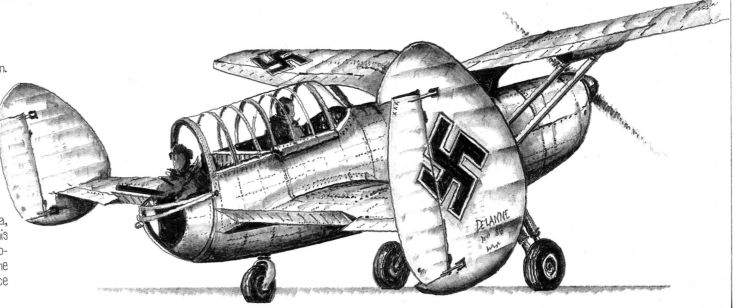

de Pischoff Flycycle
FF 1922 Austria/France

One of my favourite sketches and one of my favourite aircraft has to be de Pischoff's wonderfully simple Flycycle. Austrian aviator and inventor Alfred Ritter von Pischoff built a long string of biplanes dating back as far as 1911. His Flycycle was intended to allow the ordinary man to afford the joys of flight. Its clarity and simplicity are inspiring.

Diamond Aircraft DA20C-1 Katana

Diamond's Katana was selected by flying schools across Europe for its docile, forgiving flight characteristics and its meagre running costs. For most flying schools the margin between income and expenditure is extremely tight and the selection of a school aircraft type can be the difference between success and collapse.

FF 1992 Austria/Canada

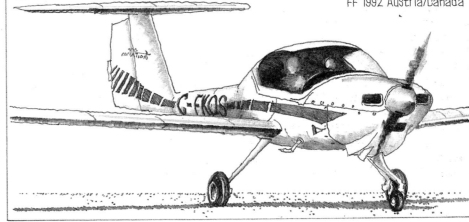

Diamond Aircraft DA-40 Diamond Star
FF 1997 Austria

Diamond's FAR/JAR Part 23 certificated DA-40 TDI Star burst onto the light plane market with its superb 135hp Thielert centurion turbo-diesel powerplant. This was a departure for a light plane manufacturer and it caught the attention of airmen right across the world. People had been talking about diesel aircraft engines for decades but, apart from a few lonely pioneers, nobody had followed through. Now Diamond were offering a highly refined and fully certified diesel aircraft. With its stunning finish and detailing the DA-40 is set for a promising future.

Diamond Aircraft DA-42 Twin Star

FF 2002 Austria

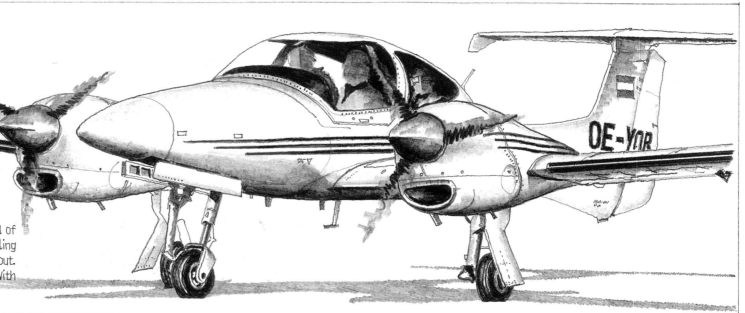

Like the DA-40, the DA-42's trump card is Diamond's ground-breaking certified diesel powerplant arrangement. Its 2 Thielert Centurion 1.7 4-cylinder turbodiesel engines burn just 45 litres per hour to give a very respectable cruise speed of 174mph (280km/h). Again, airframe detailing and interior finishes are stunning throughout. Inside the cockpit, too, the Diamond excels with its superb EFIS glass-cockpit avionics suite.

Dornier Do-228

FF 1981 Germany

With its high wing and its efficient Garrett turboprop engines the 228 is a popular and capable commuter transport. Designed to carry 19 passengers over short-haul routes of up to 750 miles, the type is in service with a wide range of commercial airlines and freight carriers right across the world.

Dornier 328

FF 1991 Germany

Following the success of the 228, Dornier developed the larger 328

turboprop regional airliner. With a full-height cabin interior, overhead bins, and lavatory, the 328 is a full airliner despite its very small size. The type has excellent hot-and-high performance and more than 100 examples have been delivered to operators and regional airlines across the world. In recent years a string of financial misfortunes have beset the project with both Fairchild Dornier and AVCraft Aviation declaring insolvency in 2002 and 2005 respectively. A superb aircraft and an ideal regional airliner.

Dornier Do-X

FF 1929 Germany/Switzerland

Claude Dornier's extraordinary Do-X flying boat created a new world record in 1929 when it lifted into the air with 169 persons on board, a truly stunning technical achievement for its day. Success for the Do-X would be elusive, however, as the introduction of the type clashed with the great and sudden Wall Street crash of 1929. Most of the world's economies fell into depression and both airlines and governments had no spare cash to spend on aircraft. The great Do-X airliner that should have been became a victim of the times and never made it into production.

Dornier Do-335A-6 Pfeil

FF 1943 Germany

In the years leading up to the Second World War, Germany's scientists and aerodynamicists probed the secrets of aerodynamics with an extraordinary level of efficiency. Dr Claude Dornier had patented the push/pull configuration used in the Pfeil as early as 1937 but it was not until 1942 that permission to develop the project was received. The Pfeil was an extremely powerful and capable night fighter with a 474mph (763km/h) maximum speed and powerful heavy cannon armaments. Although available in small numbers in the last months of the war the type saw little action against any of the Allied air forces.

Douglas C-124 Globemaster II

FF 1949 USA

56 years before the arrival of Airbus's much-heralded double-deck A380 the amazing C-124 of the US Air Force was in service carrying up to 200 fully laden troops or 127 stretchers on its 2 flight decks. The aircraft could accommodate tanks, field guns, trucks and helicopters through its massive undernose clamshell doors. 446 of the type were built before production ceased in 1955. 'Old Shakey', as she was called, saw service in many parts of the world supporting missions to Antarctica, lifting provisions into Berlin and evacuating refugees from the Congo.

Douglas SBD Dauntless

FF 1938 USA

Remembered forever as the dive-bomber that turned the tide of the naval war in the Pacific, the Dauntless was used in massive numbers during the critical battle of Midway. In that battle alone it sank 4 Japanese aircraft carriers and 1 heavy battlecruiser. In the following months it took part in almost all of the many fierce battles around the Pacific Rim. These were dangerous times when young, inexperienced pilots would fly extraordinary distances across wide oceans with minimal navigational aids.

More pilots were simply lost at sea or killed in flying accidents than were struck down in engagements with the enemy. On 24 June 1944, during the Battle of the Philippine Sea, a 200-strong fleet of aircraft returning for a night-time landing on the US aircraft carrier fleet was decimated as the aircraft crashed, one after an other, onto the heaving carrier decks. Others of the group ran out of fuel on the home run or were unable to locate the fleet at all. On that night, 80 aircraft, of the total force of 200, were lost, a terrible tragedy even in the context of the ferocious Pacific war battles. The Dauntless dive-bomber had a range of 1,115 miles and a maximum airspeed of 255mph.

Douglas R4-D

FF 1935 USA

In May of 1940 Franklin D. Roosevelt called for the production of 50,000 new aircraft annually by the American aviation industry. The R4-D, a military derivative of the DC-3, was an obvious choice and the US Army and Air Force immediately placed orders for 177 of the type. When production ceased in 1947 a total of 10,654 of all R4-D and DC-3 types had been completed. The type saw service throughout the world and many are flying to this day.

Douglas DC-4

FF 1939 USA

The market response to Douglas's groundbreaking DC-3 was so positive that Douglas immediately set about developing its successor, the DC-4. Each of the 5 biggest US airlines was consulted and Douglas developed the new airliner to meet their collective market forecasts. Compared with the DC-3, the new DC-4 had an increased passenger capacity, longer range, and a new, level non-taildragger fuselage configuration.

Douglas Dauntless

FF 1938 USA

Designed to provide the US Navy with a carrier-based dive-bomber and scout, the Dauntless was also used in the anti-submarine and reconnaissance roles. Serving throughout the war years in Europe and the Pacific, the Dauntless is linked forever to great aircraft carriers such as the Lexington and the Enterprise. The rapid technological advances which came with the war meant that the type was produced in an ever evolving series of designations from SBD 1 to 6. The A-24 variant, developed for the US Army, was identical to the SBD save for the omission of the carrier-deck landing hook.

Douglas DC-3 FF 1935 USA

To this day, more than 70 years after its first flight, there are up to 400 Douglas DC-3s still in commercial service, an extraordinary testament to this wonderful aircraft, to its longevity, and its ability to turn profits for its operators. There is perhaps no other aircraft which is as universally recognized and loved as the DC-3.

Edgley Aircraft EA-7 Optica

FF 1979 UK

The Optica story is a sad one. The aircraft itself was a novel and wonderful concept, superbly executed by John Edgley and his team. The Optica was designed for police work, border patrol and other aerial observation duties, providing maximum visibility and extended loiter endurance. Unique in configuration, the type comprised an all-glass bubble cockpit arrangement with a ducted fan behind. The project, however, was beset with troubles from the start. Its first day in police service was marred by a crash which shook investor confidence and was the prelude to a long series of financial difficulties. In 1987 an arson attack brought the venture to an end.

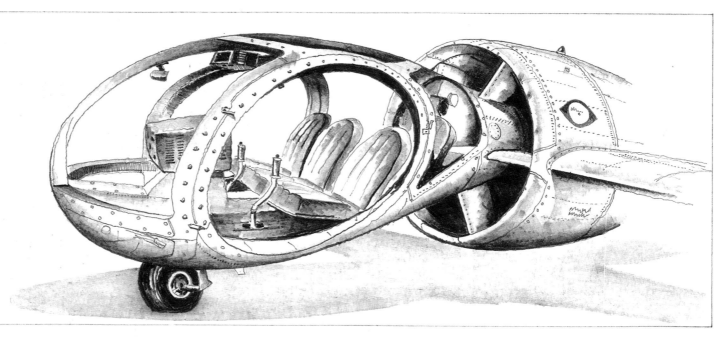

Embraer ERJ-135

FF 1998 Brazil

Following the success of Embraer's 50-seat ERJ-145, the company identified a need for a smaller regional airliner with reduced seating capacity. Given the ease with which the ERJ-145 had been accepted by operators it was decided that the new aircraft would be a cut-down derivative of the 145 rather than a stretch of one of Embraer's smaller airframes. Development of the project from inception to first flight took only 9 months, perhaps reflecting the type's similarity to the 145 as much as the efficiency and determination of the design team. The public launch of the type, too, was unusually successful, with substantial orders being placed by both American Eagle and Continental Express. Less than 1 year after roll-out the order book for the type stood at 145 with options on a further 75, an unusually healthy order book for any new design. The ERJ-135 is a capable and efficient carrier with good cruise speed, short turn-around times and excellent flying range. The type is in operation with some of the world's most competitive and canny operators as a feederliner and regional transport.

English Electric Wren

FF 1923 UK

Even the biggest oak trees start out as tiny acorns, and so it was with the English Electric Company of Coventry. Established in 1911 to manufacture fighters for the war effort, English Electric became involved in manufacturing flying boats immediately after the armistice. In much later years The English Electric Company's ambitious Canberra and Lightning projects would bring the company to the very forefront of world-class military aviation. In 1923, however, English Electric was still a small company and its management was quite open to the idea of building a motorized glider when suggested by one of their chief designers, Bill Manning. Manning was a Royal Aero Club observer in his spare time and he had been admiring some of the new low-drag gliders which had begun to appear at some of the club meetings. He wondered what would happen if he could combine these new low-drag measures with a powered aircraft. The tiny Wren did exactly that. For its time it was extremely clean and streamlined. All of its wire bracing was housed within its thick cantilever wing. In October of 1923 it entered the Daily Mail newspaper air trials at Lympne and it won an award and much publicity for flying 87.5 miles on a single gallon of fuel.

Erco Ercoupé 415C

FF 1937 USA

Throughout the 1930s, aviation had its fair share of characters and Fred Weick, designer and entrepreneur, was certainly one of them. Keen to bring aviation into the mainstream, Weick set about designing an aircraft for the common man: simple to pilot, safe in all stages of flight, and inexpensive to buy. Weick was not content to be confined to the airfield, and his superb Ercoupé tourer was even available for sale at Macy's. The Ercoupé was an excellent all-round performer and it remained in production right up to 1969.

Eurocopter EC-120B Colibri

FF 1995 France/Germany

The Colibri, or Hummingbird, is the result of a collaboration between a consortium of manufacturers from France, Germany, China and Singapore. With its Fenestron shrouded tail rotor and its superbly balanced Turbomeca TM-319Arrius turboshaft, the Humming-bird sounds wonderful in the air. Seating is provided for 4 passengers as well as the pilot. For certain missions this 5-person capacity is reduced. This is one of a new genera-tion of sophisticated light helicopters and it is enjoying a healthy and substantial order book ensuring continuity of production into the future.

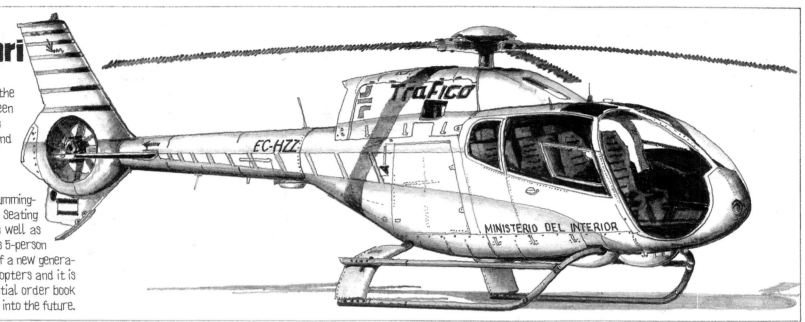

Eurocopter EC-145B

FF 1999 France/Germany/Japan

The EC-145 is the product of a joint venture between Eurocopter of France and Germany and Kawasaki Heavy Indus-tries of Japan. Derived principally from the venerable BK-117, the EC-145 was developed around the requirements of police work, border control duties, general utility and executive trans-port. A dedicated camera ship variant was offered for specialist aerial and filming work. Generous side openings and large rear doors provide unparalleled access facil-itating a multitude of mission roles.

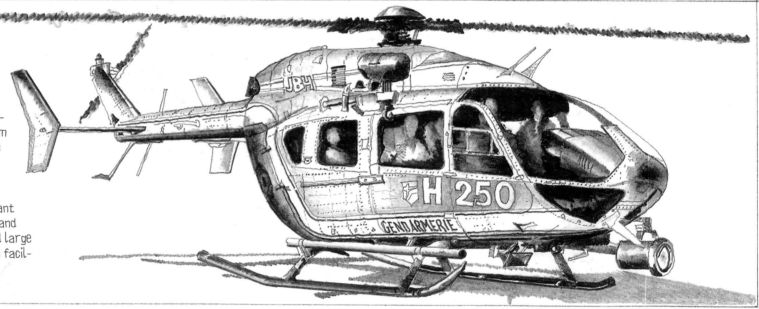

Eurocopter AS-350B Ecureuil

FF 1974 France/Germany

Eurocopter's 'Squirrel' 6-seat turbine-powered general utility helicopter has been a firm favourite with civilian operators and police forces right across the world since the days of its first customer deliveries in April 1978. The type has undergone an ongoing programme of refinements and improvements since those early days, with the introduction of more powerful engines, lighter composite body parts, and new and sophisticated avionics suites. Mission-specialized variants of the type have been produced for various defence force contracts and for dedi-cated police, TV and border patrol duties. The Esquilos is a licence-built Brazilian variant.

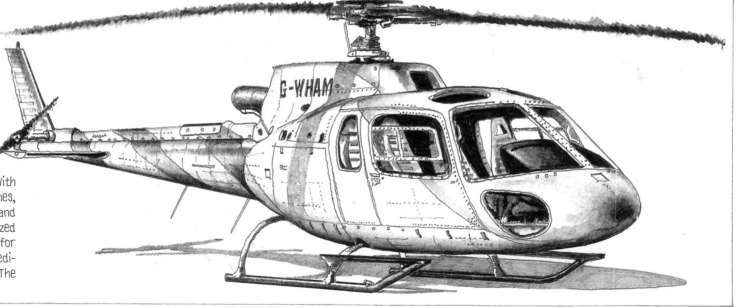

Eurofighter Typhoon
FF 1994 EU

The new multinational EF-2000 advanced-technology fighter is a product of all of the century's greatest lessons and advances in aeronautical engineering. Developed jointly by Britain, Germany, Spain and Italy, the Eurofighter will form the foundation stone of Europe's air defence for the next 25 years. With a top speed of 1,522mph (2,435km/h) and the ability to carry a diverse range of smart armaments and guided missiles, the Eurofighter is a world-class weapons platform equal to the very best of Russian and American jet technology.

Europa Aviation Europa XS
FF 1992 UK

Having completed the building of a Rutan Long-Ez, home-builder Ivan Shaw used his new-found skills with composite structures to develop his own design, the Europa. On completion the aircraft was an immediate hit with its very long range and its beautiful clean lines. Most unusual of all was its bulbous monowheel landing gear, which allowed it to land on some of the roughest and shortest of airfields. Ivan's design allowed pilots to tour ambitious distances while being based at smaller, cheaper airfields and the type became an immediate commercial success. Europa Aircraft has subsequently released a new tricycle-gear conversion for pilots who find the landing characteristics of the monowheel overly demanding.

Evans VP-1 Volksplane

FF 1969 UK

My first interest in aviation came about when I read a book about an English gentleman called Robert Lowe who built his own VP-1 aircraft. I was fascinated and immediately hooked. The VP-1 is the quintessential home-build project: cheap, simple to build, and great fun to fly. There is certainly no fear that the other pilots in the flying club will confuse the VP-1 with the run-of-the-mill factory production models. Every VP-1 is a one-off and a crowd-pleaser. Spectators are not in awe of the aircraft's speedy lines or throaty roar. They are simply astounded that it flies and that you are going to risk your life in it.

Extra 300L

FF 1988 Germany

An exceptional aerobatic performer from Extra GmbH of Germany.

Fairchild C-82 Packet

FF 1944 USA

The prototype Packet was first flown in 1944, when the full might of the USA's industrial muscle was churning out massive numbers of fighters and transports to support the war effort, which was, at last, turning the tide against the Axis powers. The C-82 was designed to carry heavy and outsized loads and, in particular, trucks, tanks, artillery and other bulky items. The Packet illustrated in this sketch is the modified jet version, a standard Packet with an additional jet engine mounted over the centre-section.

Fairchild Republic A-10 Thunderbolt

FF 1972 USA

I always liked this sketch. I caught this A-10 on the ground but felt that it would be more dramatic in flight.

Fairey Flycatcher

FF 1922 UK

Richard Fairey, later to be knighted Sir Richard Fairey, leased tiny premises at Hayes, Middlesex, to facilitate the building under licence of a series of 12 Short seaplanes. The fledgling workshop went from strength to strength, completing further manufacturing projects and opening an aerodrome at Harmondsworth, which later became part of Heathrow.

The Flycatcher was a single-seat naval fighter designed to operate off aircraft carriers or, with floats, to be launched off Navy ships. Its wooden biplane construction and fabric covering were light and strong allowing the Flycatcher to cruise at 130mph with a range of 310 miles. It could certainly not be said that the Flycatcher was a clean-cut design. Indeed, its many lines and its confusion of materials caused the type to look most eccentric. Airmen and naval flyers, nonetheless, loved the aircraft and it remained in service until 1935.

Fairey Fulmar Mk 1

FF 1940 UK

In Europe the demand for military aircraft increased dramatically with the deteriorating political climate in the 1930s. Fairey Aircraft Co. were developing new military prototype projects and courting favour with various governmental procurement agencies. Fairey's Fulmar carrier-borne fighter was ordered by the Royal Navy and it served for the first years of the war until replaced by Supermarine's more powerful and manoeuvrable Spitfire.

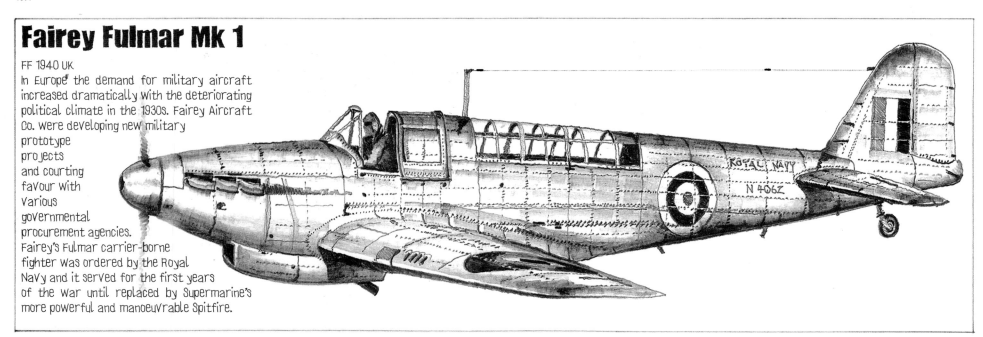

Fairey Gannet T-2

FF 1949 UK

Britain's near-calamitous struggle against Germany's remorseless U-boat packs caused the nation to view submarine warfare with trepidation. Design proposals for a new fleet of post-war aircraft carriers, too, indicated that the next generation of anti-submarine hunters would be more powerful and more compact than ever before.
The Gannet was designed to replace the ageing Avenger in the submarine-hunting role. In particular, its greatly increased range was designed to provide a much wider cloak of safety around the fleet in order to guard against the ever increasing speed and sophistication of modern strike aircraft. The Gannet was the first aircraft to combine the hunter and killer roles.

Fairey Primer

FF 1939 and 1948 Belgium

Fairey's Primer was intended to compete with the de Havilland Chipmunk for the lucrative Royal Air Force primary-training aircraft contract. Compared to de Havilland's wonderful, simple Chipmunk design, however, the Primer was simply no match and the contract was duly awarded to de Havilland. Small numbers of the Primer were sold to private owners.

Fairey Rotodyne Convertiplane

FF 1957 UK

Half helicopter and half aircraft, the Rotodyne combined a pair of Eland turboprop engines for forward thrust with pressure-jet-tipped rotor blades for vertical lift. This was an ambitious and brave effort for 1957. The project floundered, however, when it was found that the outrageously loud screaming noise produced by the rotor-tip jets could not be reduced or dissipated using existing technology.

Fairey Swordfish

FF 1934 UK

This 2-bay staggered biplane torpedo bomber was designed for carrier-borne operations and anti-submarine and convoy-protection duties. The Swordfish, soon to be called the Stringbag, served as a front-line naval attack bomber until the end of the Second World War. It served in many of the larger naval battles of the war and its superb handling qualities, even at low speeds and in atrocious weather conditions, earned it respect. 2,392 of all types of Swordfish were built. Carrying 1 large torpedo centrally below its fuselage, its big Pegasus radial engine provided a range of 1,028 miles and a maximum speed of 139mph. Its wings could be quickly folded for stowage on board cramped aircraft carriers.

Fiat G-59B

FF 1951 Italy

Fiat had used its German ally's DB-605 aircraft engine for its successful 1942 Model G-55 fighter. Now that the war was over, however, the German armaments industry was dismantled and the engine was no longer available. Fiat turned to Rolls-Royce for its legendary 1,130hp Merlin powerplant and developed the last upgrade of the G-55, the superb G-59. Over 100 of the type were manufactured, mostly for the Italian air force but also, in a heavily modified fighter/bomber format, for Syria. Armaments comprised of 4 12.7mm machine guns with hardpoints as required to carry up to 350lb (160kg) of rockets and gravity steel bombs. The 2-seat training variant was armed with 1 forward-firing 7.7mm machine gun.

Fieseler Fi-103 Piloted Flying Bomb

FF 1944 Germany

The Luftwaffe went to great lengths to point out the difference between their manned Fieseler Fi-103 and the Japanese version, the infamous Kugisho Kamikaze flying bomb. Essentially the Japanese pilot was sealed for ever into his cockpit, while the German pilot was intended to jump clear of his fiendish contraption just before impact. That the pilot would surely die in this split-second exit strategy, or else be sucked bodily into the jet engine, seemed to be overlooked by all. Fieseler built 175 of the type in the last desperate months of the Reich.

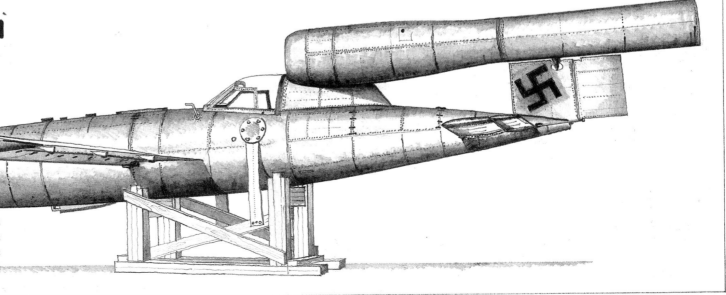

Fieseler Fi-156 Storch
FF 1936
Germany

The Storch will forever be remembered as the aircraft that spirited deposed dictator Benito Mussolini out of captivity and into German hands, a stunning propaganda coup in its day. SS officer Otto Skorzeny, leader of the 110-strong German paratroop task force, selected the Storch with its extraordinary 29mph stall speed to land between the scattered boulders on the 6,500 foot high mountain top. Officer Walter Gerlach, pilot of the Storch, was able to stop the aircraft in just 100ft and, after loading Skorzeny and a confused and dazed Mussolini, the aircraft took off and raced for the safety of the German lines. The fate of the others of the brave task force is less well known.

Flug & Fahrzeugwerke Ag C-3605
FF 1939/1968 Switzerland

Even as the Second World War raged savagely across Europe, Switzerland built its own independent fighter, the EKW C-3605. Over the course of the war years 158 of the type were built. It served until 1968 when F&W upgraded 24 airframes with a new 1,100hp Lycoming T53-L turboprop powerplant in a greatly extended and exaggerated nose stretch.

Flettner Fl-265

FF 1939 Germany

Anton Flettner had been tinkering with auto-gyros and helicopters since the early 1930s. In 1938 he received a small production contract from the German navy which led to the 1939 flight of his Fl-265 'synchropter'. This tiny prototype was a superb performer compared to the other helicopters of the day. All of the usual controllability problems appeared to have been solved and Flettner went on to develop the Fl-282 model, which actually saw service on many fronts in the later war years. Flettner Fl-282 Kolibris were evaluated at length by the German Kriegsmarine and several of the type were briefly operated off warship decks.

The enigmatic Fokker Triplane, mount of the legendary First World War ace, Baron Von Richthofen.

Fokker Dr1 Triplane

FF 1917 Germany

Fokker F-VII

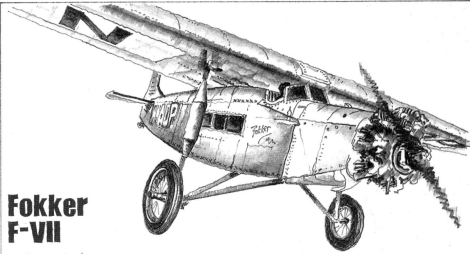

FF 1928 Netherlands

Anthony Fokker founded Fokker Aviatik GmbH as early as February of 1912. Over the following years he became one of Europe's leading aircraft manufacturers specializing first in biplane military fighters and, after the armistice, in large passenger-carrying liners.

Fokker F-70

FF 1993 Netherlands

Fokker removed 2 fuselage plugs from its F-100 airliner to produce the F-70 feederliner and regional jet. With a flight crew of 2 and accommodation for 79 passengers, it was hoped the F-70 would plug the gap left by the ageing Fokker F-28 fleet. An executive variant, the Executive Jet 70, was developed for corporate customers. With the 1996 collapse of Fokker new production of the F-70 was abandoned but operators continue to place great value on their airframes.

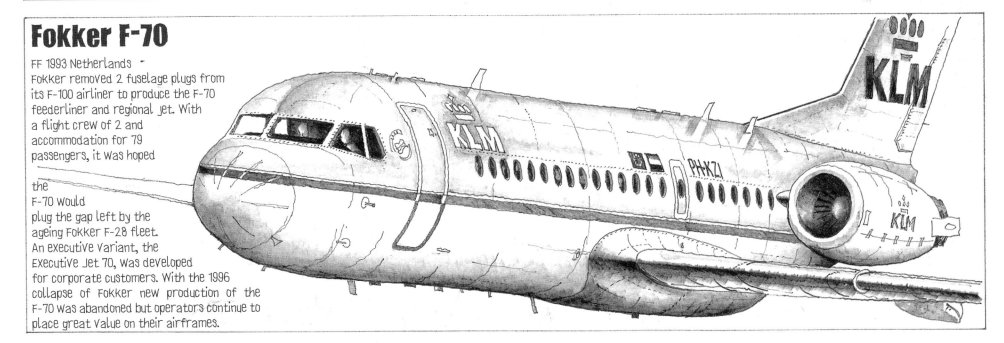

Gee Bee Model R-2 Racer

FF 1932 USA

The R-2 is not so much an aircraft as a massive engine with a tiny airframe and pilot attached. Jimmy Doolittle described flying the Granville brothers' extraordinary R-1 and R-2 racers as being akin to 'balancing a pencil on one's fingertips'. Always on the very limits of controllability, Doolittle found that the barrel-bellied wonder was likely to go into a crazy roll at any stage of flight and he abandoned the highly successful Granville team after just a few weeks. A series of terrible accidents then beset both the R-1 and R-2 marques and within weeks the Gee Bee's great success had turned to tragedy. When Zantford Granville himself was killed the story drew to a close.

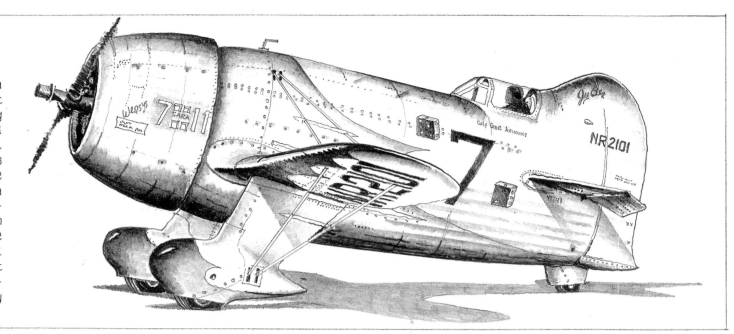

General Aircraft GAL-56

FF 1944 UK

The GAL-56 was one of a series of radical experimental prototype gliders developed by General Aircraft in the later years of the war. The project was designed to collect research data on airframe planforms and on a range of tailless swept-wing configurations. 4 GAL-56s were constructed, each with a different plan form and each formulated to illustrate the permissible boundaries of sweep and twist and the delicate balance which must be struck between these parameters if aircraft stability is to be maintained. 3 of the 4 prototypes undertook flight trials under tow from RAF Whitleys and Halifaxes and it was rumoured that all 3 were difficult to fly.

General Aircraft Hamilcar X

FF 1942 UK

The Allied forces knew that they would have to mount a massive invasion of France if the German military machine was to be stopped. The Hamilcar tank-carrying glider was designed to cheaply and quietly ferry light tanks and armoured vehicles to invasion zones. Capable of carrying Tetrarch and even Locust tanks, the Hamilcar would be towed to forward invasion zones where the tank crews could take up offensive positions near to or even behind enemy lines. When D-Day came almost 70 Hamilcars were towed by Stirlings and Halifaxes to Normandy, where a variety of landings and fates awaited their occupants. 2 Mercury 31 engines assisted take-off.

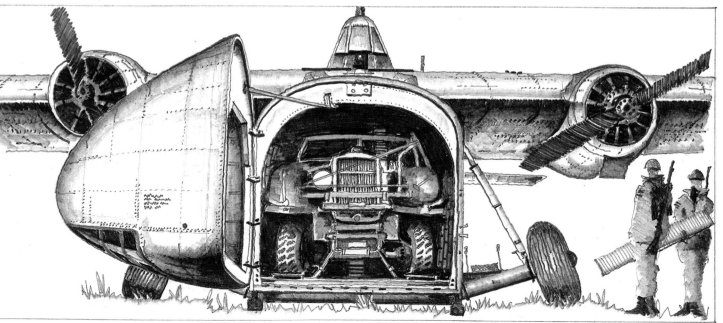

General Dynamics F-16 Fighting Falcon

FF 1974 USA
Few military aircraft combine grace and raw power as effortlessly as the General Dynamics F-16 Fighting Falcon. By any standards

this is a good-looking aircraft, sleek and wonderfully proportioned. Aviation's old adage 'If it looks good it will fly well' certainly applies in this case and the Falcon is a stunning performer. While its speed, range and awesome firepower are much discussed and recorded, there are few pleasures in aviation as satisfying as watching an F-16 performing aerobatics at an airshow.

GlasAir III

FF 1979 USA
The availability of new, lightweight composite aircraft materials brought a revolution in airframe structures. Strong, lightweight aircraft structures could now be formed with relative ease, and complex curved aerodynamically efficient shapes could be formed cheaply as never before. The GlasAir was among the first projects to take full advantage of the new structural opportunities afforded by these materials and, on first flight, its performance figures were found to be staggering. From the moment of its unveiling at the 1980 EAA Convention in Oshkosh the type was warmly received by pilots and kitbuilders alike. In that year alone GlasAir sold over 150 of its superbly complete pre-moulded kits.

GlasAir GlaStar

FF 1994 USA
Combining constant-chord aluminium wings and control surfaces with an all-new composite fuselage structure, the GlaStar sport-plane was designed to provide affordable flying to amateur kitbuilders. With a wealth of previous experience in the kitbuild market, GlaStar's kit was among the most complete and best presented available. A wide variety of build methods were available to builders from quick-build kits to do-it-all-yourself packages. For those who had more money than time, the jump-start GlaStar kit undertook to get you into the air quickly. There are many GlaStar projects under construction today, and builders of the type have developed a superb web-based support network.

Glass Goose Amphibian

USA

The perfect aircraft for fishing, hunting and camping, the Glass Goose's command of both land and water presents bold new options to flyers of the home-building and kitbuilding fraternities. $32,500 buys the basic parts kit short of engine, seating and avionics, and a well-motivated and dexterous builder might finish the project in about 2 years. Thereafter, weekends might be spent on remote mountain lakes in pursuit of fishing and outdoor adventure. Life is, however, not so simple and the rigours and financial pressures of daily life mean that most home-build projects take many years to complete and some projects never do reach completion.

Globe Aircraft Corp Swift

FF 1941 USA

The Swift was initially developed in 1941 but, with the outbreak of the Second World War, the Globe Aircraft Corporation found itself building Beech 18 transports for the US Government. By late 1944, however, the Allies were advancing steadily across Europe and Globe began to anticipate the hordes of returning pilots who would want to fly sport-planes after demobilization. However, on returning from war most pilots wanted to resume their own lives, or simply could not afford to fly. Almost 1,505 Swifts were built for the US civil market and for military customers including Belgium, Spain, and many others.

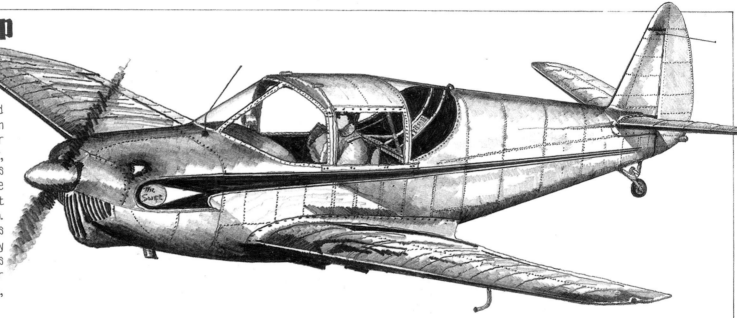

Gloster E-28/39

FF 1941 UK

Frank Whittle had written the first ever patent for a jet engine back in 1930, when he was just 23 years of age. In 1941 with Europe in turmoil, Whittle's top-secret turbojet power-plant was flown for the first time in a specially developed airframe, the Gloster Whittle E-28/39. This pioneering flight would change the face of British aviation for ever.

Grob G-115 Trainer

FF 1985 Germany

Grob GmbH had been specializing in lightweight composite aircraft structures and gliders for many years before the development of the G-115 series. Designed to serve as a primary-training platform and touring aircraft, the type offers fast cruising speeds and a clean, efficient airframe.

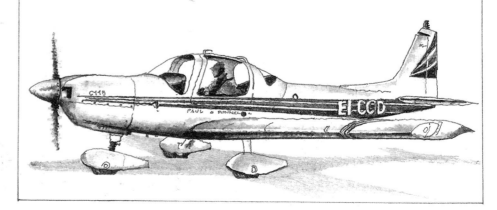

Gloster F-8 Meteor

FF 1943 UK

The first batch of 20 F-1 Meteors were rushed into service in early 1944 in an effort to stem the constant barrage of V1 flying bombs which were falling over London. By the last months of the war uprated Meteor F-4s were operational in the skies over Germany. The F-8 Meteor was of 1948 vintage.

Gloster Gamecock II

FF 1925 UK

When the first batch of 30 new Gloster Game-cocks was delivered to the RAF in 1928 it was found that the type was still suffering from tail flutter and spinning problems and, indeed, over the following 18 months there were 19 Gamecock accidents, 8 of which were fatal. Once these shortcomings had been addressed, however, the Gamecock became much loved by pilots and ground crew alike.

Gloster SS-37 Gladiator

FF 1934 UK

Between May and June of 1939 the Royal Air Force's No 263 Gloster Squadron, taking off from frozen lakes, carried out a series of stunningly daring attacks against the German forces who were occupying Norway. Over a period of 12 days the group flew a total of 389 sorties with 69 air combat engagements and at least 26 kills. After this intense period of combat those who had survived made a dash for HMS Glorious which was to ferry them home. On the journey Glorious was attacked by the heavy battleship Scharnhorst and sunk with the loss of 1,474 lives. Only 2 of the Gladiator pilots survived.

Grumman F9-F Cougar

FF 1951 USA

The Cougar was the US Navy's first operational carrier-based fighter to utilize swept-back wings. The Cougar development of the old Panther was rushed into operational service to provide an interceptor to rival the Soviet-designed swept-wing MiG-15 being encountered in dogfights over Korea. The Cougar performed well in its first operational sorties with a top speed of 705mph (1,135km/h).

Granger Brothers Archaeopteryx

FF 1930
UK

The 2 Granger brothers must have seemed eccentric to their neighbours in Nottingham, England, when they began to build their extraordinary Archaeopteryx. The brothers, who had no prior aeronautical experience, were fired with enthusiasm when they saw the remarkable swept-wing tailless Westland-Hill Pterodactyl. They began the design and construction of their own strange flying monster, finally achieving first flight in 1930. The aircraft flew frequently and successfully for some years in the Nottingham area and, indeed, it undertook some reasonably long journeys. By 1936 the airframe, with its 32hp Bristol Cherub flat-twin engine, was tiring and it was withdrawn to storage. The groundbreaking Archaeopteryx did continue, nonetheless, to create strong waves among aviation enthusiasts and designers, inspiring much interest in tailless aircraft and in swept-wing design. The airframe then floundered for many years until 1968, when it was handed into the safekeeping of the Shuttleworth Trust. Restoration was thorough and true and, after reintroduction to the civil aircraft register, G-ABXL flew again in 1971. It flew frequently for a short period of time and performed at several Shuttleworth airshows until it was decided that its unpredictable flying manners presented an unacceptable risk to modern display pilots. The amazing Archaeopteryx remains airworthy but grounded to this day.

Grumman U-16 Albatross

FF 1947 USA

Grumman produced 466 of its heavy Albatross military amphibians between 1947 and 1961 and the type served for many years with the US Navy, US Coast Guard and with many other armed forces across the world. In the mid-1980s, however, the type had the unique distinction of being bought back into stock by Grumman, who launched a programme of converting the airframes to G-111 civilian transports. Of the 57 airframes purchased back by Grumman just 12 were delivered to Resorts International Inc.

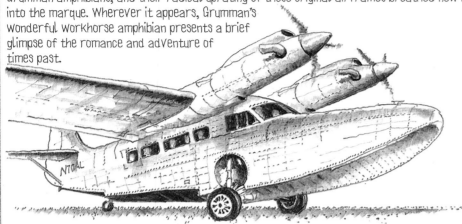

Grumman (McKinnon) TurboGoose
FF 1937 USA

McKinnon Enterprises Inc. of Oregon became specialists in the area of turboprop conversions of Grumman amphibians, and their radical uprating of these original airframes breathed new life into the marque. Wherever it appears, Grumman's wonderful workhorse amphibian presents a brief glimpse of the romance and adventure of times past.

Grumman Duck
FF 1933 USA

Grumman's superbly designed Duck plucked hundreds of water-treading sailors and pilots out of the sea.

Grumman F3F

FF 1935 USA

Landing the 'Flying Barrel' on the heaving deck of an aircraft carrier was looked on by many pilots with trepidation. The aircraft's speed had to be controlled very precisely in relation to that of the carrier. Extreme turbulence caused by disruption of wind across the carrier's superstructure, too, caused extreme buffeting in the moments immediately before landing. Lastly, the heaving action of the carrier's deck meant that the landing itself was, to a large extent, a matter of luck.

Handley Page Victor B-2 and K-2

FF 1952 UK

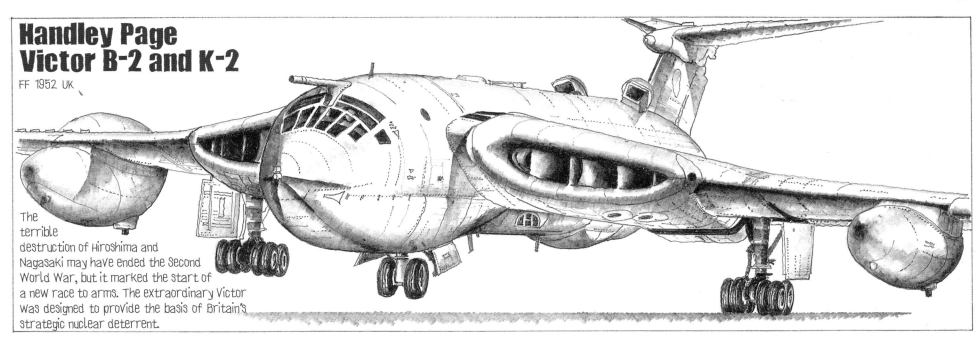

The terrible destruction of Hiroshima and Nagasaki may have ended the Second World War, but it marked the start of a new race to arms. The extraordinary Victor was designed to provide the basis of Britain's strategic nuclear deterrent.

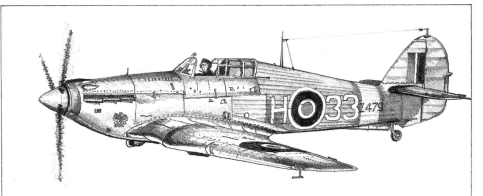

Hawker Hurricane

FF 1935 UK

Sydney Camm's wonderful Hurricane was Britain's main interceptor fighter over the months of the Battle of Britain when 620 Hurricanes and Spitfire fighters faced a massive 3,500 German Bf-109 and Bf-110 fighters and bombers. These were frightening times when Britain came within a hair's breadth of floundering under the overwhelming pressure of Germany's ruthlessly efficient Luftwaffe.

Hawker Siddeley C-1 Andover

FF 1965 UK

The Hawker Siddeley Andover was developed from the Avro 748 airliner to meet a Royal Air Force requirement for a STOL transport that could perform a variety of duties, from troop transport to paratroop carrier and freighter. Other uses included VIP transport and specialist calibration duties. 31 of the type were delivered to the RAF with further examples (including an HAL early-warning variant) being licence-built by HAL in India.

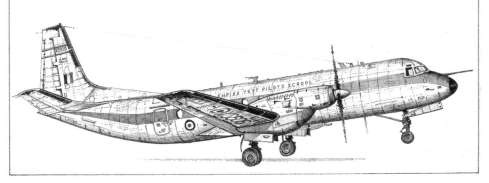

Hawker Siddeley HS-748 Srs 2-A

FF 1960 UK

1959 saw the merging of some of the great names of British aviation to form the Hawker Siddeley Group. The Avro, de Havilland, Armstrong Whitworth, Gloster Blackburn, Folland, and Hawker marques all disappeared for ever.

Hawker Siddeley Buccaneer

FF 1958 UK

During the early 1950s the Soviet navy was being expanded and transformed into a sophisticated and modern fighting force. To counter this threat, the Royal Air Force began the task of selecting a new

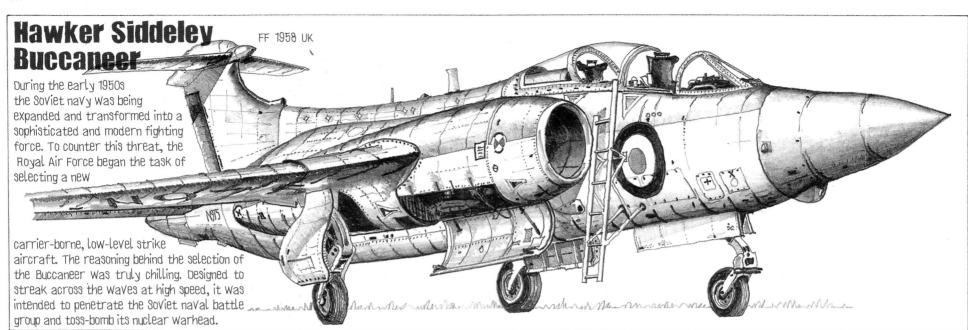

carrier-borne, low-level strike aircraft. The reasoning behind the selection of the Buccaneer was truly chilling. Designed to streak across the waves at high speed, it was intended to penetrate the Soviet naval battle group and toss-bomb its nuclear warhead.

Heinkel He-III

FF 1935 Germany

What were the young men in this He-III thinking as they made their way in over the south coast of England to drop their bombs over the houses and factories of London? Were they filled with fear for their own lives, with remorse for the civilian lives that would undoubtedly be lost, or were their minds filled with the aspirations and the rallying cries of the Fatherland? On all sides, but particularly on the Axis side, terrible tragedies were wrought on civilian populations by young, idealistic men who were answering the call of their leaders. That their idealism and their lives were being misused and callously traded by their political leaders was a great and terrible wrong to their generation.

Heinkel He-162A-2

FF 1944 Germany

When test pilot Gotthold Peter's Heinkel He-162 disintegrated at low level right in front of the collected Nazi Party officials, questions should have been raised about the new disposable jet fighter with its wood and glue construction. But there was little time to mourn the brave test pilot.

Germany was in deep trouble on all fronts and the new wonder weapon had to be rushed into service immediately. It was like rearranging the deck chairs on the Titanic. The Reich was now in its final months and few of the He-162s ever saw action.

Hughes Model 269-300

FF 1956 USA

The Hughes 269 light helicopter, although flown for the first time as far back as 1956, is still essentially in production to this day as the Schweizer 300C. Simple, rugged, efficient, and versatile in design, the type has been used for many years as an ab initio military trainer, a civilian primary trainer, and a police and border-patrol platform. Schweizer has continued to improve and upgrade the airframe over the years to ensure that the type continues to maintain its substantial niche in the light helicopter marketplace. Other Model 269 and 300 variants have included dedicated crop-sprayers and float-equipped helicopters.

Hughes Model 369E

FF 1963 USA

During the 2003 Cricket World Cup, South African authorities used one of their Hughes Model 369 police helicopters to dry out the rain-sodden cricket pitch, surely one of the most unusual and extravagant uses of a helicopter anywhere in the world. The Greenpeace Model 369E, too, must have seen some very unusual action, being used to support Greenpeace's missions in the southern seas and, in particular, its environmental programmes in Antarctica.

Hunting Pembroke

FF 1952 UK

The P-66 was developed from the earlier Percival Prince feederliner and executive transport. Flown by the Royal Air Force, the Royal Swedish Air Force, and military forces of many other European countries, the Pembroke has earned its name as a most reliable and versatile special-mission trans-port. Changing roles many times during the course of its long service life as other aircraft came and went, the Pembroke has been a freighter, air-ambulance, troop transport, and photographic reconaissance platform at various stages. Its 2 540hp (402.5kW) Alvis Leonides engines give it a max level speed of 224mph (360km/h) and a range of 1,150 miles (1,840km).

120

Hunting Percival Provost T-1

FF 1950 UK

Perhaps one of the greatest training aircraft of all time, the T-1 had already been brought to production by Percival Aircraft prior to its assimilation into the Hunting group in 1954. The Provost appealed immediately to various governments who wished to train military pilots, and it was soon serving in large numbers in Ireland, Rhodesia, Burma, Sudan, and Iraq. It carried a series of weapons hardpoints beneath its wings and was capable of light ground attack and primary weapons training. By the mid-1980s the last of the 461 Provosts were being retired in favour of newer and more efficient training aircraft. Derelict Provost airframes still occasionally turn up in Ireland, Britain, and the Middle East.

Ilyushin Il-12 Coach

FF 1946 USSR

Sergey Vladimirovich Ilyushin became a legend in the Soviet Union when 36,000 of his superb Il-2 Shturmovik armoured ground-attack fighters became a vital and integral part of the extraordinary push against Germany in 1944. It was about this time that Ilyushin began development of the Il-12, a twin-engine troop transport and freighter. The type entered service with the Soviet air force and later, in its civilian configuration, with Aeroflot. This capable and efficient aircraft would have been the equivalent of the West's Douglas DC-4.

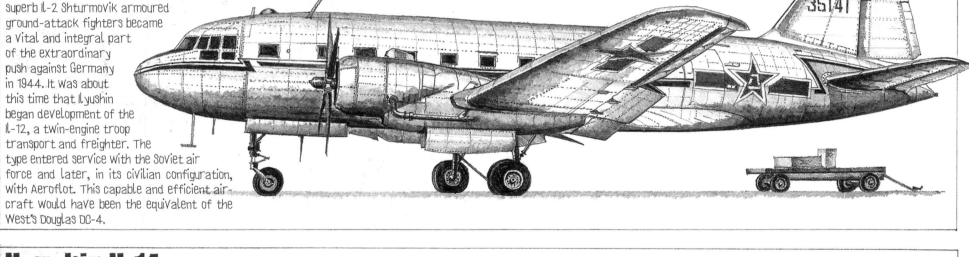

Ilyushin Il-14 Crate

FF 1953 USSR

Sergey Vladimirovich Ilyushin produced a constant stream of aircraft designs through his Ilyushin aircraft design bureau. The Il-14 must surely be among his greatest achievements. The simplicity, ruggedness, and sheer longevity of this aircraft were vital to Aeroflot in establishing its vast civil network right across the Eastern Bloc countries. Built first in the Soviet Union and later in both East Germany and Czechoslovakia, the Il-14 was deployed in many countries across the world. Its cruise speed was 198mph (320km/h) and its range 932 miles (1,500km).

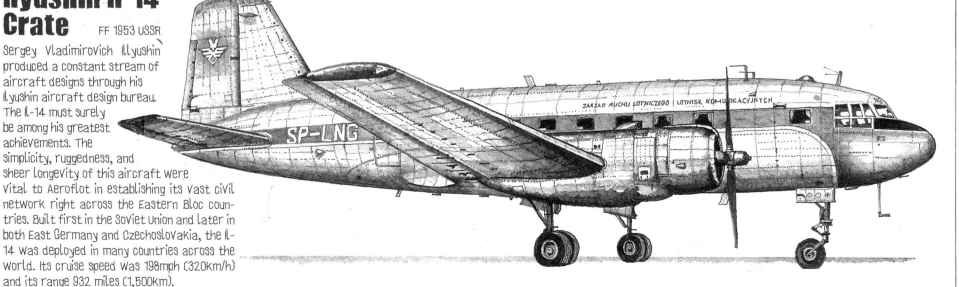

Ilyushin Il-18 Coot

FF 1957 USSR

Over 700 Ilyushin Il-18 Coot turboprop transports were built. The type served many countries across the globe including the former Czechoslovakia, Afghanistan, Algeria, Poland, Syria, Cuba, and, of course, the former Soviet Union. The Il-18D carried 122 passengers at cruise speeds of 388mph (625km/h) and had a range of 4,040 miles (6,500km). The Il-20 Coot-A electronic surveillance variant of the aircraft carried a large, under-fuselage pannier. Over 6,000 of all non-military variants were built and many Il-18s are still in service today.

Ilyushin Il-76 Candid

FF 1971 USSR

A heavy-lift medium/long-haul military strategic transport aircraft and commercial freighter, the Ilyushin Il-76 Candid provides the countries of the former Soviet Union with the equivalent of the Lockheed Starlifter. Its wide rear-loading ramp allows access to its cavernous interior for transport of large guns, tanks, and other heavy vehicles, while a system of modular cranes and a quick-fit seating system facilitates precise loading and rapid configuration. A specialist airborne early-warning and control variant is known as the Mainstay.

Ilyushin Il-76 Candid

FF 1971 USSR

Again the trademark Soviet glazed nose-and-tail turret positions are remnants of a tense and troubled past. All earlier Soviet aircraft were designed so that they could be recalled to military duty if required.

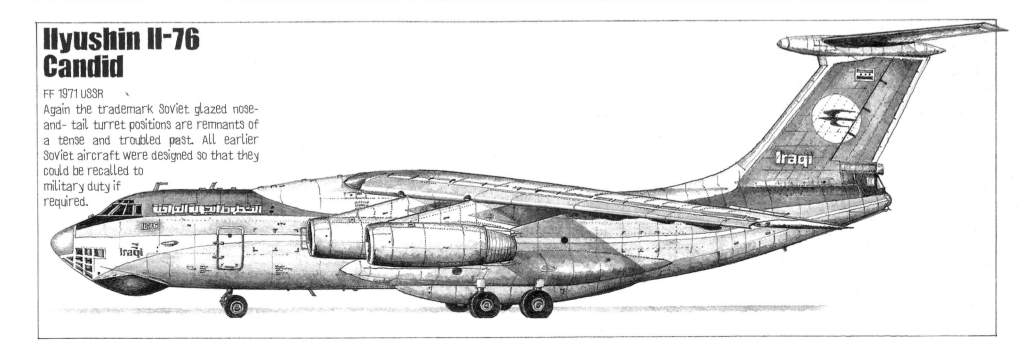

Ilyushin Il-86 Camber

FF 1976 USSR

The Soviet Union's first full wide-bodied transport, the Il-86, was powered by 4 Kuznetsov NK-86 turbofans. Capable of accommodating 350 passengers, it has a cruise speed of 560mph (900km/h) and a range of 2,875 miles (4,629km).

Ilyushin Il-96

FF 1988 USSR

The Ilyushin Il-96 incorporates all of the refinements of a modern and efficient transport. With drag-reducing winglets and a host of airframe improvements, this is the first of a new generation of Soviet aircraft.

Jungster 1

FF 1962 USA

The Jungster 1 Biplane was designed by Rim Kaminskas of Los Angeles, California, who was long fascinated by the great Bücker Jungmeister of the 1930s. A superb performer for homebuilding by amateur aircraft constructors.

An all-metal, low-wing monoplane. A groundbreaking achievement given its early vintage.

FF 1918 Germany
Junkers D1 (J9)

Junkers Ju-52
FF 1930 Germany

Throughout the 1930s, Junkers Ju-52s provided the airlines of Finland, Germany, Spain, and Sweden with a tough and reliable civilian transport. By the end of the war years more than 5,000 of the type had been built and the 'Auntie Ju' served in all roles and on all fronts.

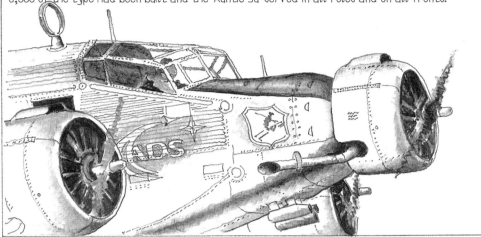

Junkers Ju-87 Stuka
FF 1935 Germany

The Junkers Ju-87 was a terrifying dive-bomber that was as legendary for its morale-breaking shrieking sirens as for its near-vertical diving ability and pinpoint accuracy. The Stuka was the equivalent of today's close-support A-10, a formidable and vicious weapon.

Kamov Ka-32S
FF 1980 USSR

Political and economic reforms in the former Soviet Union have led to huge changes in the worldwide aviation industry and, even more so, in the world of commercial helicopter operations. With very large numbers of available helicopters and a substantially lower cost base, newly commercialized operators from former Eastern Bloc countries are making heavy inroads into the helicopter operation industries of Europe and Asia. The Kamov Ka-32 Helix is widely used to carry heavy slung loads.

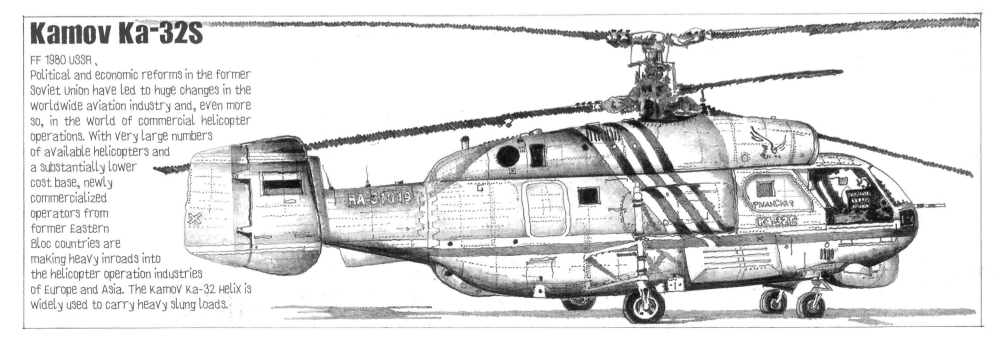

Karman-Petroczy Captive Helicopter

FF 1918 Austria

The PKZ-1 and PKZ-2 tethered helicopter projects were intended to provide the Austrian army with a captive observation post that could be quickly raised and lowered. Created by Stefan Petroczy, a lieutenant in the Austrian army, the PKZ-1 failed to lift off the ground. With the intervention of a young professor, Theodore Von Karman, however, the 2 huge contra-rotating wooden propellers did lift the device to a height of 165 feet. A second model, the PKZ-2, was developed. Complete with 3 120hp Le Rhône engines and topped by a very brave and foolhardy observer, it was flown many times until it crashed spectacularly, tragically ending the project.

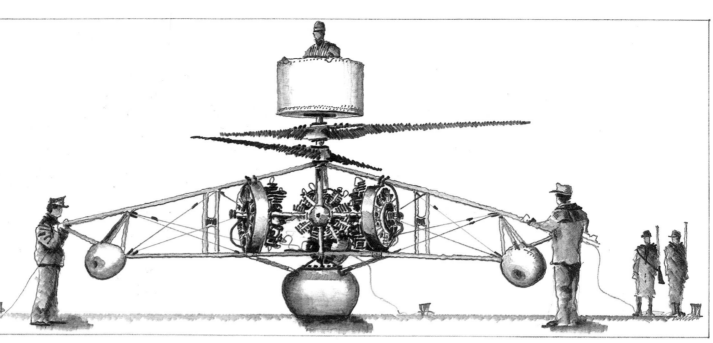

Keuthian Solaris Ultralight

USA

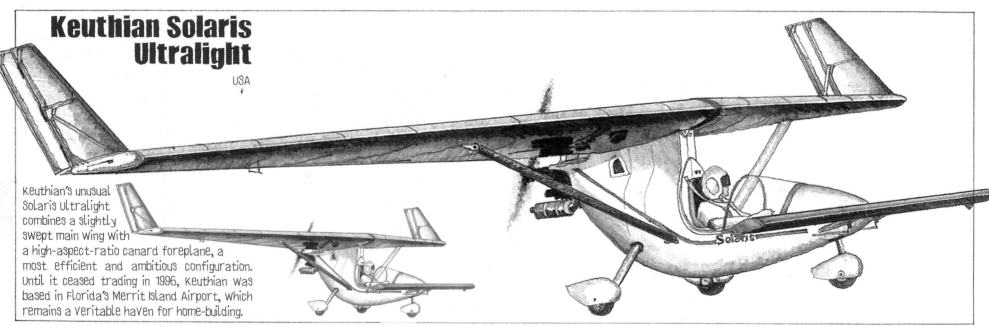

Keuthian's unusual Solaris ultralight combines a slightly swept main wing with a high-aspect-ratio canard foreplane, a most efficient and ambitious configuration. Until it ceased trading in 1996, Keuthian was based in Florida's Merrit Island Airport, which remains a veritable haven for home-building.

KIS Cruiser

FF 1996 USA

Rich Trickel's plastic-fantastic, the KIS Cruiser, is a comfortable, all-composite, 4-seat sport-and-touring aircraft. Its sleek aerodynamic lines allow it to cruise at 190mph at 10,000ft, a respectable touring speed for any light aircraft. Its range, at 950 miles, allows it to fly long distances without fuel stops. The aircraft's interior fit and avionics are generally designed by the individual owner/builder, and can vary from simple VFR arrangements to complex all-weather glass cockpit installations.

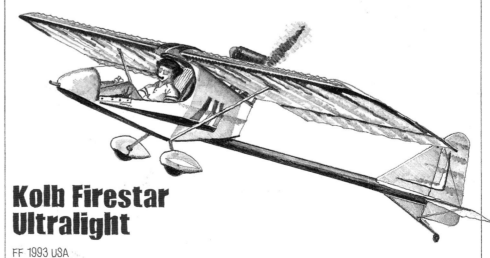

Kolb Firestar Ultralight

FF 1993 USA

This is flying at its very simplest and best with no canopy, no instrument array, and no huge costs. The Firestar brings the very best of flying manners along with the ultimate panoramic views of the world below. Just you and the sky and lots of fresh air.

KIS TR-1 Cruiser

FF 1991 USA

Rich Trickel's KIS Cruiser has now been absorbed into the well-known Pulsar marque, and all future airframes will come under the Pulsar 150 brand. California-based Pulsar Aircraft Corporation is a long-established and professional kitplane provider that has become synonymous with high-end sporting kitplanes. The project now comes in a series of elemental sub-kits, from fuselage shell to wings and undercarriage. This particular KIS Cruiser with its striking colour scheme attended Sun 'n Fun 2005.

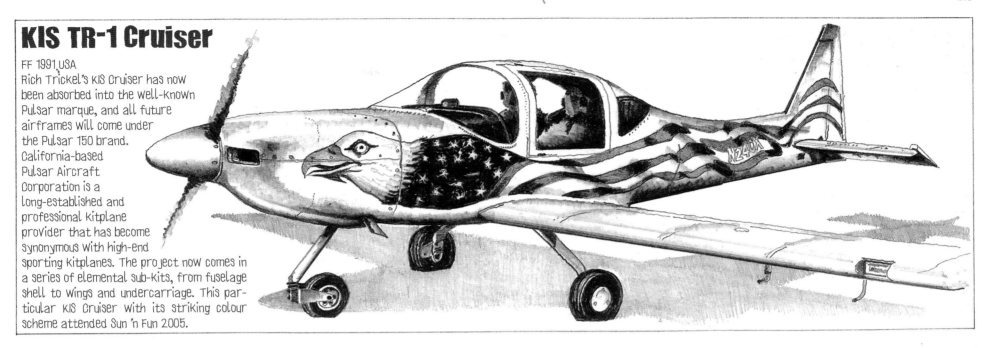

Kitfox Speedster

FF 1984 USA

Since 1984, over 4,000 Kitfox self-build kits have been delivered to home-builders right across the world. Indeed, additional Kitfox aircraft regularly appear on new registration listings to this day. Designed by Denny Aerocraft of Boise, Idaho, the 2-seat Kitfox sport-plane has excellent handling characteristics and superb STOL capabilities. Construction is of lightweight welded steel tubing with fabric covering. As with all kitplane manufacturers build-time guidelines are always grossly underestimated, but most home-builders revel in the opportunity to build and tinker, and, indeed, are often at a complete loss when their aircraft projects are finally completed.

Kugisho Ohka 22 Flying Bomb

FF 1945 Japan

In late 1944, as Allied air and sea forces continued to systematically crush the Japanese war machine, the extraordinary kamikaze squads began to wreak havoc on Allied shipping. By the time Japan finally surrendered, it is estimated that up to 5,000 kamikaze pilots had sacrificed all for their emperor. These attacks were flown in standard aircraft, however, and against carriers equipped with up to 75 flack guns, few actually reached their targets. The Ohka human-guided missile, with its rocket-powered engine, was designed to increase these odds. Its development, however, came too late in the war and only a small number were completed.

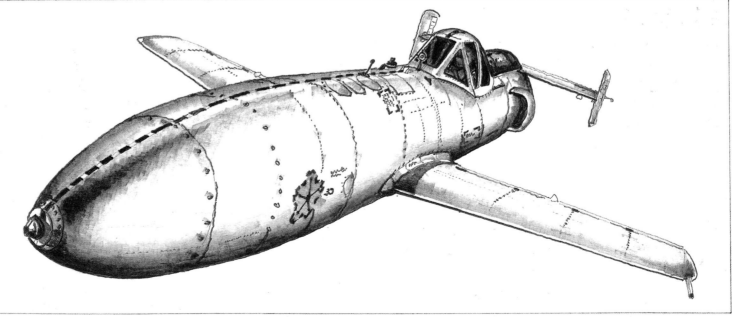

Lake Sport Mermaid

FF 2005 Czech Republic

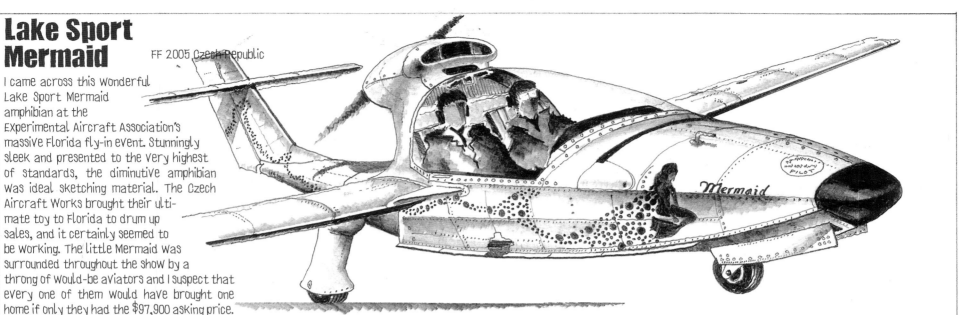

I came across this wonderful Lake Sport Mermaid amphibian at the Experimental Aircraft Association's massive Florida fly-in event. Stunningly sleek and presented to the very highest of standards, the diminutive amphibian was ideal sketching material. The Czech Aircraft Works brought their ultimate toy to Florida to drum up sales, and it certainly seemed to be working. The little Mermaid was surrounded throughout the show by a throng of would-be aviators and I suspect that every one of them would have brought one home if only they had the $97,900 asking price.

Lancair IV P

FF 1991 USA

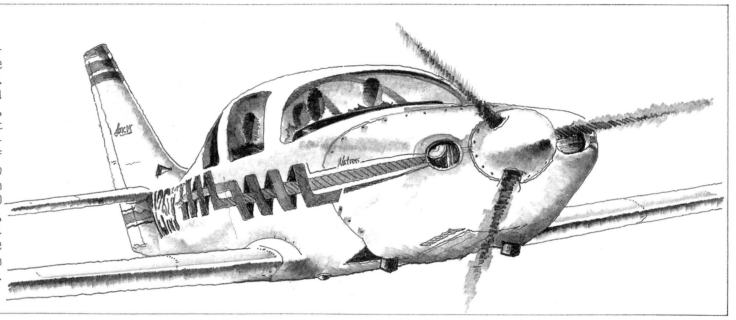

Lance Neibauer's superb Lancair series of high-performance sport-planes has always been the very top end of the kitbuild aircraft market. Now they can be bought fully certified and expertly built by Lancair. The Lancair is a sleek, aerodynamically efficient airframe that makes extensive use of new lightweight, super-strong composite materials. A variety of powerplants can be installed, from the 300hp (225kW) Continental flat-six piston to the twin turbocharged, twin intercooled 310hp (231kW) Continental TSIO-550-G. The avionics package, too, is designed to suit the pocket and skill levels of each of the owner-builders, with some examples being fitted out with the very latest in electronic wizardry and glass-cockpit technology.

Lavochkin LA-156

FF 1947 USSR

The end of the Second World War saw the seizure by the various Allied powers of the very best of Germany's aeronautical engineers, aerodynamicists, and engine designers. The war had shown, if nothing else, that technology would be the measure by which all future military and national might would be rated. Bolstered by the influx of specialist German jet-propulsion scientists, the Lavochkin design bureau, and indeed many of the other Soviet design shops, set about developing fledgling jet-powered fighter programmes. The LA-156 was one of the earliest of these and was powered by the RD-10F turbojet, essentially a rebadged Junkers Jumo 004B.

LET Aero 145 & Super Aero
FF 1947
Czechoslovakia

During the Second World War the Czech aircraft industry was forcibly pressed into service supplying the Nazis with German aircraft such as the Messerschmitt Bf-109 and other military fighters. Many of the aircraft built on these manufacturing lines incorporated the very latest technologies, and, as soon as the war was over, the Czechoslovakian aviation industry was quick to build on this knowledge and set about developing a range of technically advanced civil and military aircraft. The LET Aero 145 was one of these projects. Powered by 2 Czech-built Walter Minor engines, the type could accommodate 4 to 5 persons in an air-taxi configuration.

LET L-40 Meta-Sokol
FF 1956
Czechoslovakia

Although the former Czechoslovakia has always had a cutting-edge aviation industry the system made little allowance for general aviation, that is, recreational flying by private pilots. Where light aircraft were developed they were usually the result of demands from the state airlines for basic pilot-training airframes. The L-40 3-seat light plane, developed in the late 1940s, was an example of this. The Meta-Sokol's most unusual trait was its reverse tricycle undercarriage, which must have made landings very interesting indeed. This seems to have been carried over from the traditional taildragger configuration, prevalent in earlier aircraft types.

LET L-410 Turbolet

FF 1969 Czechoslovakia

The LET L-410 Turbolet light passenger/ freight transport has for many years provided Aeroflot and the airlines of other Eastern Bloc countries with a rugged and dedicated short-field carrier. Capable of carrying 17 to 19 passengers at 236mph (380km/h), the L-410 is configured for very short sectors. It is designed to operate in temperatures between +50 and -50 and, as such, is suited for use in some of the world's most inhospitable climates. Recent marketing drives have seen the LET L-410 competing for business with some of the West's short-haul STOL aircraft, in particular the DHC-6 Twin Otter. The latest LET L-410 is equipped with Walter 601E engines in lieu of the Pratt & Whitney Canada PT6A-27 engines used to date.

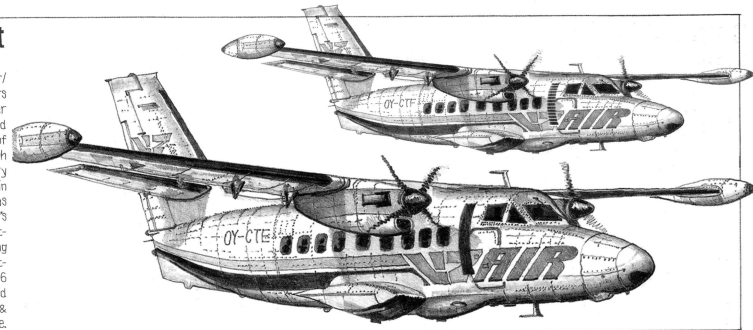

128

Lockheed SR-71 Blackbird

FF 1964 USA

Flying at over 80,000ft at speeds so fast that you are outpacing the setting sun must surely have been one of the great rushes of the 1970s. Developed by the now-infamous Kelly Johnson in Lockheed's top-secret Skunk Works, the Blackbird was perhaps the most remarkably innovative aircraft of all time. Over its short development period, Johnson stretched the boundaries of all disciplines of metallurgy and aerodynamics to build one of the greatest aircraft of all time.

Lockheed L-1049 Constellation

FF 1950 USA

The largest of the great piston-engined airliners, the Constellation evokes travel at its most colourful and daring. Its maiden flight was made in 1950 and the first 22 'Connies' were pressed into military service.

Lockheed HC-130J Hercules

FF 1954
USA

By the start of the 1950s, the huge stocks of aircraft leftover after the war were beginning to flounder and age. Turboprop technology, too, was now coming of age and the US Air Force issued a specification for a new turboprop transport that could lift an 18-ton outsize load from even the roughest of airstrips.

Lockheed P-38 Lightning

FF 1939 USA

Barely 2 minutes after the declaration of war with Germany a Lightning of the US Navy shot down a German reconnaissance aircraft over Iceland, the first US offensive action of the Second World War. The Lightning was a stunningly powerful aircraft, the first twin-engined fighter of the war. As the war progressed it was developed and upgraded continually with even bigger engines, better turbochargers, more weaponry, and new radar sets. Over 10,000 of the type were built and Lightnings served on all fronts. By late 1944 the Allies were making vast bombing raids over German cities, often despatching more than 1,000 bombers at a time. It was in this role as fighter escort that the P-38 was best known.

Lockheed F-104G Starfighter

FF 1954 USA

The awesome Starfighter was designed at Lockheed's top-secret Skunk Works facility under the direction

of Kelly Johnson, one of the greatest aircraft designers of all time. The heavily guarded Skunk Works was an extraordinary think-tank where the greatest scientists, aerodynamicists, metallurgists, and mathematicians of the day worked on some of the USA's most treasured and groundbreaking aviation projects. Other Skunk Works projects included the U-2 and the SR-71 Blackbird.

Lockheed U-2

FF 1955 USA

In July 1956 the highly classified U-2 spyplane made its first overflight of the Soviet Union. The Soviets were naturally incensed, but their existing missile stock simply could not reach the intruder at its 80,000ft cruising altitude. There followed a 3-year-long battle of cat and mouse in

which the American spyplane pilots could literally see the improving Russian missiles climbing higher and higher. Eventually, of course, pilot Gary Powers was shot down, an event which led to a famous and well-documented international incident.

Lockheed L-1011 TriStar

FF 1970 USA

The TriStar wide-body medium/long-range airliner was the first aircraft to incorporate the highly efficient Rolls-Royce RB211 big fan engine. Powerplants are mounted on pylons under each of the wings, with the third engine cradled at the base of the tail unit. Various configurations of the type were produced, including the long-range 1011-100, the shortened fuselage 1011-500, and the Advanced TriStar of 1979. The L1011-500 has a max cruise speed of 485mph (781km/h) and its max laden range is a massive 4,310 miles (6,896km). Accommodation is for 315 passengers. Lockheed ceased TriStar production in 1983 after 250 of the type were completed.

Lockheed Martin F-117 Nighthawk
FF 1981 USA

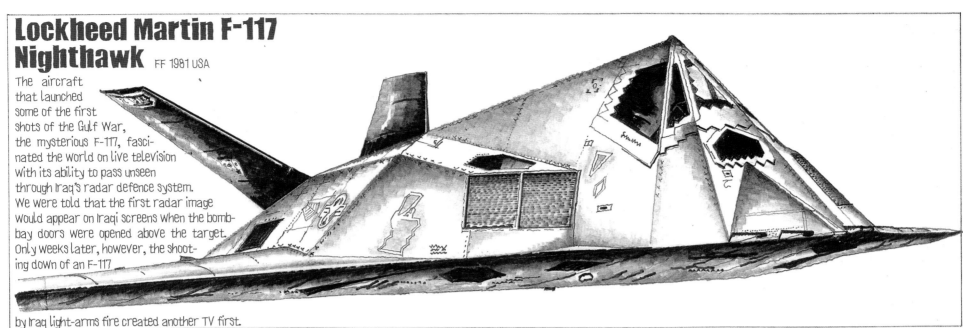

The aircraft that launched some of the first shots of the Gulf War, the mysterious F-117, fascinated the world on live television with its ability to pass unseen through Iraq's radar defence system. We were told that the first radar image would appear on Iraqi screens when the bomb-bay doors were opened above the target. Only weeks later, however, the shooting down of an F-117 by Iraq light-arms fire created another TV first.

Loening OA-1A Amphibian
FF 1923 USA

Aviation was still in its infancy when Grover Loening designed the wonderful Loening OA-1A amphibious observation aircraft for the US Navy. The type merged, for the first time, the features of a landplane and a seaplane with its huge hull-like centre structure and parallel undercarriage. This arrangement was immediately successful and the OA and OL series was pressed into service with the US Navy on a series of ambitious pioneering flights, from Commander Byrd's 6,000-mile Arctic exploration voyage of 1925, to the US Navy's 20,000-mile Pan-American flight that visited 26 South American countries in 1926.

LoPresti Piper Swift Fury
FF 1988 USA

Roy LoPresti was one of the great characters of aviation and, indeed, one of its greatest influences. Earning his pilot's licence while still a teenager, the young LoPresti went on to work over the course of his long career for Grumman, Mooney and Beech, where he designed a long succession of world-class aircraft. In 1991 he founded his own company, LoPresti Speed Merchants, which specialized in customizing existing factory-produced aircraft to increase performance by improving powerplant installations and reducing airframe drag. LoPresti's superb Swift Fury is a greatly improved, licence-built variant of the old Swift design, a truly stunning performer.

Luft-Verkehrs Gesellschaft CV-1

FF 1917 Germany

LVG CV-1 serial number 7198/18 was captured intact at the end of the First World War and shipped back to Britain, where it was test flown by the Royal Air Force who were keen to examine their opponent's aircraft in detail. After months of evaluation the aircraft was put into storage, where it remained for many years until it was acquired by the Shuttleworth Trust, who restored it to flying condition. The wonderful polished timberwork and fabric-covered wings of the CV-1 tell of an era when workmanship and tragedy were merged on a daily basis.

Luscombe Model 8 Silvaire

FF 1937 USA

Don Luscombe established the Luscombe Aircraft Engineering Company of Kansas City in 1934 and immediately set about producing a series of light aircraft of all-metal construction. In an era of timber struts and fabric coverings Luscombe's designs were unusually robust and durable, and the marque became greatly sought after. Luscombe's dependence on metal became a liability during the war years, however, when quality aluminium was unavailable and production had to be suspended until 1946. On resumption Luscombe concentrated on his Model 8 of 1937 and on an improved version, the Model 8 Silvaire.

Marchetti Avenger Gyrocopter

USA

A lightweight 2-seat gyrocopter aimed at the home-build market.

Martin SP-5B Marlin

FF 1948 USA

The Marlin was the US Navy's very last operational flying boat and its retirement in 1967 brought an end to a long-standing culture of deploying flying boats for maritime patrol and submarine detection duties. Land-based turboprop aircraft were now reaching very high standards of mission reliability and, with ever more fuel-efficient engines, could now loiter on station for very long periods of time.

Martin 4-0-4
FF 1950 USA

Glenn Martin's manufacturing plant took a financial battering at the end of the war years when military production was scaled back. In fact the world was awash with ex-military aircraft which were being adapted for civilian roles and so production of new aircraft was almost at a stop. The all-new 4-0-4 was Martin's hope for the future and he set about its design with great enthusiasm. Unfortunately, however, although Eastern Airlines and TWA ordered the 4-0-4 in quantity, only 103 airframes were actually purchased, and manufacturing soon came to a halt. In all its years of service only 2 4-0-4s were lost.

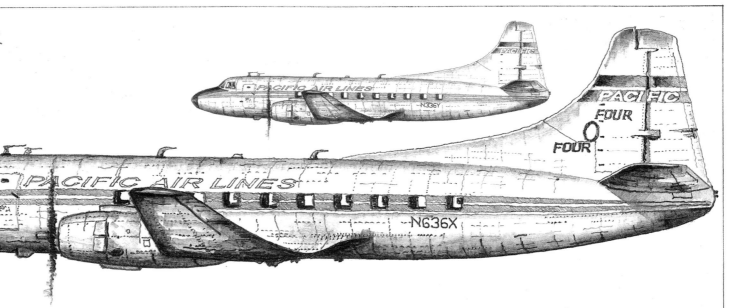

Martin B-26 Marauder
FF 1940 USA

With a landing speed of 152mph the B-26 was a handful on the approach. Indeed, many young pilots fell prey to its vicious stall in the landing configuration and, without adequate height to recover, spun into eternity. The resulting nickname 'The Widow Maker' was both unfortunate and inaccurate as the Marauder established a superb safety record as soon as aircrews were adequately rated and trained on the type. With a total of 12 machine guns in mechanized forward, dorsal and tail turrets, the B-26 was a formidable opponent. The aiming device for its 4,000lb bomb load was the very latest and best of its day, ensuring that every item of ordnance was deployed to maximum effect.

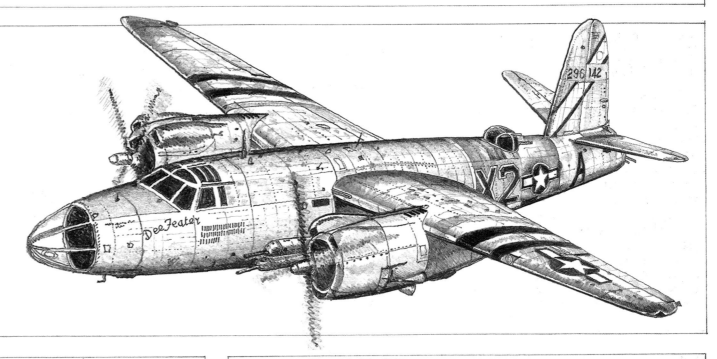

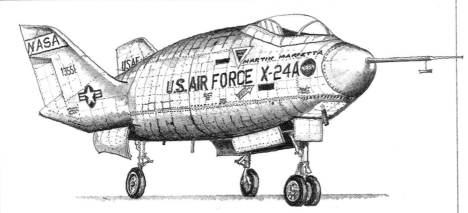

Martin Marietta X-24A
FF 1970 USA

Like many aircraft designers Martin Marietta was experimenting with new lifting-body technology in the 1970s. After a protracted development period the experimental X-24A lifting-body prototype made its first short, rocket-powered flight in March 1970.

MBB Bö-105 CBS-4
FF 1967 EU

Developed originally in the early 1970s by Messerschmitt-Bölkow-Blohm in Germany but now substantially improved and uprated, and listed by Eurocopter.

McDonnell Douglas MD-11

FF 1990 USA

The MD-11 was designed as a replacement and an upgrade of the long-serving MD-10. The design of the new airliner incorporated all of the latest innovations in the areas of aerodynamic efficiency, fuel economy and simplified maintenance schedules. New winglet technology and a sophisticated avionics suite added to the appeal of the widebody and set it apart as one of the new generation of modern cost-effective passenger transports. By 1998, however, the MD-11 order book was drying up and the production line began to wind down.

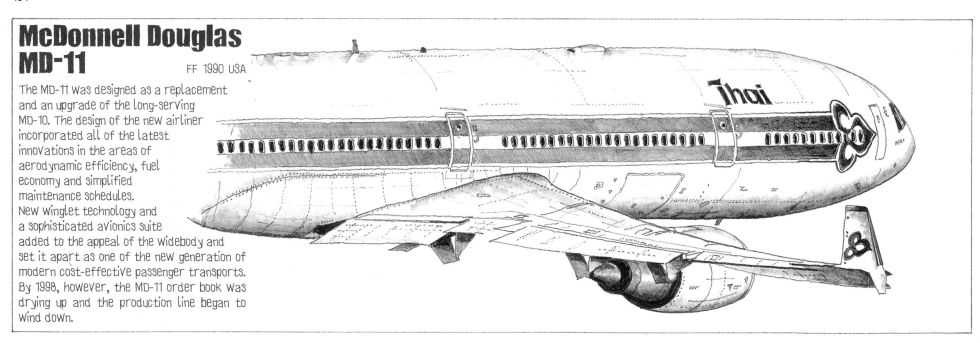

McDonnell Douglas F-4 Phantom

FF 1958 USA

The F-4 has served with the air forces of 11 nations as well as the US Air Force, US Marine Corps and US Navy. Large numbers of the type continue in operational service.

McDonnell Douglas F-15 Eagle

FF 1972 USA

The official Boeing website gives the F-15 Eagle's air combat score as 101 victories to zero defeats. It is no wonder, then, that air forces and governments across the world are queueing up to fork out $35,000,000 for the base model without sophisticated weaponry, electronic countermeasure systems, and all of the backup contracts necessary to maintain such a leading-edge fighter programme.

McDonnell Douglas F/A-18B Hornet

FF 1978 USA

The F/A-18 is the main fighter/attack aircraft of the US and other air forces including Canada, Australia, Finland and Spain. Specialized F/A-18 squadrons are operated from 10 of the US fleet aircraft carriers and, with a combat mission range of 2,070 miles (3,312km), there are few parts of the world which are beyond their reach. The Hornet is designed to provide traditional strike capacity or to act in a close-support role, both without compromising its own air combat fighting capabilities.

McDonnell Douglas Model 79

FF 1952 USA

The technicians working on the McDonnell Douglas Model 79 liked to call her 'Big Henry'. The tiny ram jet-powered helicopter prototype flew satisfactorily but made a ferocious noise. Its shrieking rotor-mounted ram jets were so loud that, even by 1950 standards, it was clear that operators and general public alike would not tolerate them. Fuel efficiency, too, was another insurmountable problem, as Big Henry was big on juice. The offending ram jets burned fuel at such a rate that the endurance of the type was far less than was commercially viable. Without prospects or customers the Model 79 was abandoned.

McDonnell Douglas XF-85 Goblin

FF 1948 USA

The tiny XF-85 Goblin fighter was designed to be carried by long-range conventional bombers to provide defensive cover where required. Both size and weight of the miniature parasite fighter were critical to the venture as the mother ship's bomb load would be reduced proportionally. The Goblin project was scaled down as the potential and the suitability of defensive missile technology became apparent. The amazing Goblin, however, is an icon of its time.

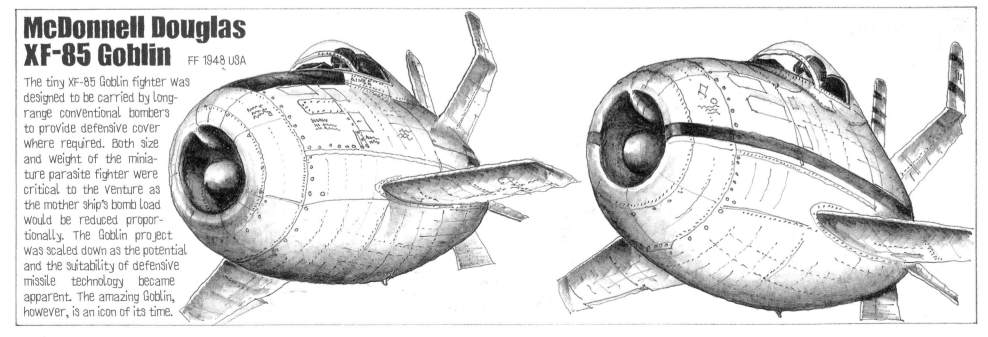

McDonnell Douglas (Hughes) 500-D

FF 1963 USA

The McDonnell Douglas 500-D, formerly the Hughes 500, is one of the world's most popular light turbine helicopters. Its single 420shp Allison C20B engine provides all the power required to ensure exceptional performance and the very highest levels of mission reliability. The MD-500 can be configured to take on a wide range of tasks from civil utility to military liaison, scout, anti-tank and ground attack. In its military role it comes equipped with an array of hardpoints to carry rockets, air-to-ground missiles, and a heavy-calibre machine gun. Maximum cruise speed is 160mph and range is 263 miles.

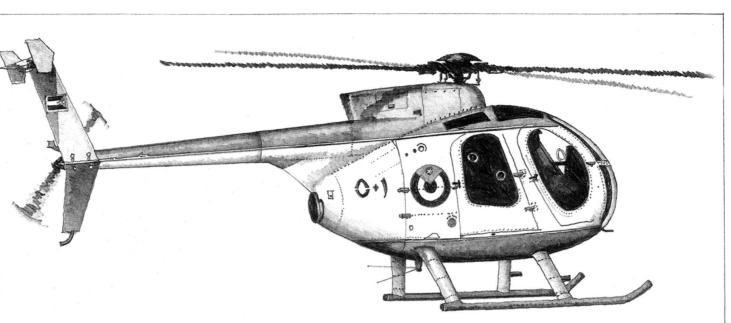

McDonnell Douglas MD-900

FF 1992 USA

When McDonnell Douglas set about designing the MD-900 they approached more than 170 operators to identify exactly what the market was looking for. The new helicopter was the first ever to be fully designed on a new generation of specialist aerodynamic computers. Using large numbers of composite parts as well as advanced flight- and engine-control systems, the type represents a substantial step in the evolution of light commercial helicopters. Its 14-foot-long internal floorplate is designed to facilitate many diverse mission configurations from executive transport to air-ambulance.

McDonnell Douglas XV-1 Convertiplane

FF 1955 USA

A sophisticated experimental convertiplane prototype test bed developed by McDonnell Douglas to investigate the feasibility of transitioning from vertical flight to horizontal, the XV-1 was half helicopter and half aeroplane, an experiment on a grand scale. Its pusher propeller was powered by a Continental R-975-19 piston powerplant while its rotors were driven by rotor-tip pressure jets, an ambitious and unusual arrangement. The XV-1 underwent a drawn-out programme of flight evaluation culminating in a transition from vertical to horizontal flight in April of 1955. Only in very recent years have convertiplanes become a technical reality.

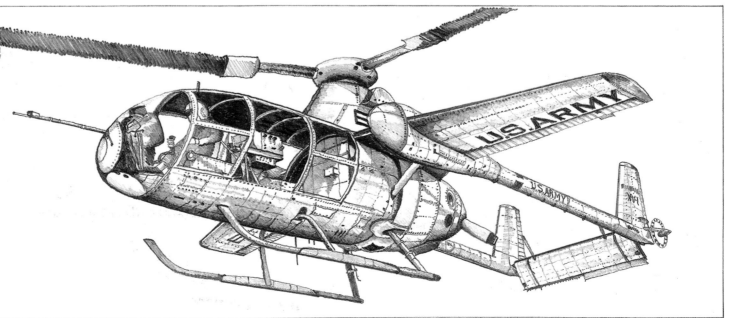

Messerschmitt Bf-109

FF 1935 Germany

The Bf-109 was the plane that terrorized Europe. Over 35,000 of the type were built to soften up enemy forces ahead of Hitler's rapidly mobile ground offensive. The Bf-109 and its pilots had already seen action during the Spanish Civil War and, by the time the Second World War started, both were fully battle-hardened and particularly effective. When used in large numbers in close combination with Hitler's elite panzer divisions the Bf-109 was a force that few armies could withstand and, indeed, in 1940 and 1941 the armies of Europe collapsed ahead of it.

Messerschmitt Me-262 FF 1942 Germany

The Schwalbe (Swallow) was the world's first operational turbojet fighter. Although Messerschmitt's revolutionary new airframe was ready by April of 1941 it took many months before BMW were ready to install its fledgling BMW-003 jet engines. The 262 flew for the first time in July of 1942 but its engines continued to prove unreliable, causing operational deployment to be delayed into late 1944. Although 1,430 of the type were built many were never fitted with engines and others were destroyed by large-scale Allied bombing. Only 300 of the type saw combat service.

Meyer P-51B Mustang Scaled replica

USA

The thriving home-build market offers a vast number of aircraft types to amateur home-builders for home construction. While some of these projects have great longevity and are built in large numbers, others are short-lived and are built in very small numbers only. Within this wondrous microcosm of aviation there exists another tiny sub-culture, the replica builders. Here enthusiasts lavish extraordinary amounts of skill and expertise on the construction of flying scaled replicas of some of the greatest aircraft of all time. The Meyer Mustang is stunning in both detail and performance.

Meyers M-200C

FF 1953 USA

Al Meyers' M-200C was one of the best-built private sport-planes of all time and to this day there has never been an AD (mandatory change) notification made against it. Each aircraft was hand-made by Meyer and his highly experienced team. When an order was received Meyer would lower the fabrication jigs from the rafters of his maintenance facility. When there were no live orders Meyer and his team would hoist the jigs up out of their way and set about repairing stock aircraft. I came across this pristine M-200C classic in April of 2005.

Henri Mignet's Mignet 'Pou-du-Ciel' Flying Flea

FF 1933 France

Frenchman Henri Mignet became quite famous in the early 1930s when Europe's newspapers carried stories of his new Pou-du-Ciel (Flying Louse) aeroplane. This tiny do-it-yourself aeroplane was simplicity itself and could be built by anybody, even those inexperienced with tools. Flea fever soon spread across Europe and within months thousands of plan sets had been sold. As the months passed and constructors completed and flew their Fleas, a pattern of air accidents began to emerge, 4 of which were fatal. By December of 1936 Britain had imposed a flying ban on the Flea. Unperturbed, Henri Mignet released plans for an improved version of the aircraft and, indeed, some of these Fleas were granted permits after 1936.

Mil Mi-2S Hoplite

FF 1961 USSR/Poland

The Mi-2 was designed by the Soviet Mikhail design bureau and later manufactured in very large numbers by PZL of Poland. The Mi-2 was one of the great flying workhorses of the Soviet Pact countries being used by many branches of the state services for military transport, air-ambulance, search and rescue, and simply for accessing remote and inhospitable locations. A specialized agricultural crop-spraying version with a 500-litre external chemical storage hopper was known as the Bazant (Pheasant). It served on the massive collective farms where vast tracts of intensely farmed land required to be treated with heavy doses of fertilizers. Many Mi-2 helicopters continue to earn their keep today.

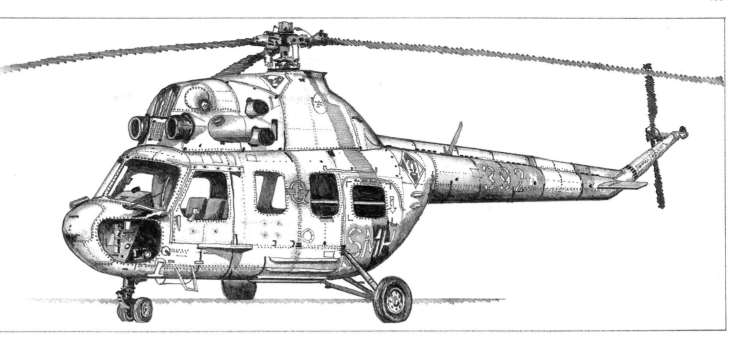

Mil Mi-4 Hound

FF 1952 USSR

Stalin is rumoured to have personally issued the directive that led to the development of the Mi-4 heavy transport helicopter. Soviet helicopter evolution had closely paralleled that of the West in the years immediately following the war but the West was now beginning to get ahead with the 1949 first flight of the Sikorsky S-55 and with the roll-out of several other truly practical machines. More than 3,500 of the piston-engined Mi-4 Hound were manufactured before production was suspended in 1969.

Mil Mi-8 Hip

FF 1961 USSR

With a production run of well over 10,000, the Soviet Mi-8 helicopter was one of the greatest and most prolific helicopter designs ever flown. Its twin turbines and its 5-blade main rotor powered a wide range of Mi-8 variants, each designed to perform a specific task for either the Soviet military or for giant state carrier, Aeroflot. The Hip was exported to many countries of Soviet influence and to many more who simply wanted to fly an efficient and sensibly priced helicopter. The type was a rough and robust workhorse, well-behaved in flight and easy to service. Indeed, very large numbers of Mi-8s, both military and civilian, are still in service today in countries right across the world.

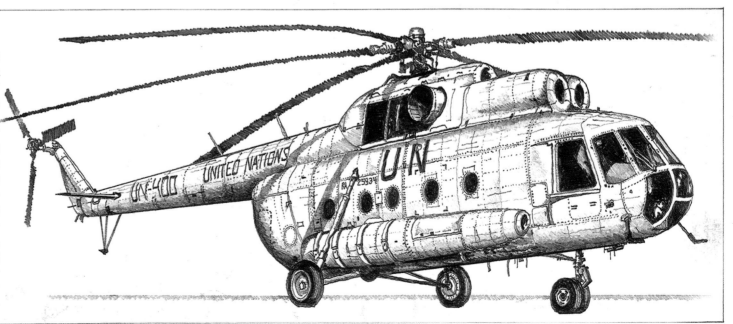

Mil Mi-9

FF 1961 USSR
Derived from the
Mi-8 heavy military
helicopter, the Soviet Union's Mi-9 was an
enhanced countermeasures variant with
additional electronics and antennas.

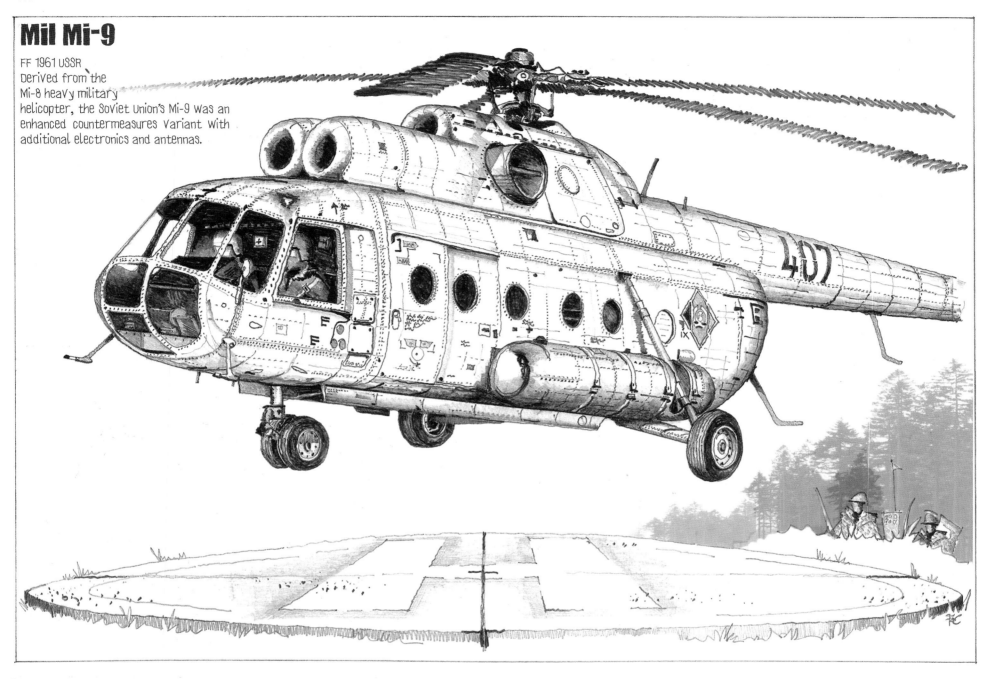

Mil Mi-14
Haze

FF 1974 USSR
From the time of its formation
in 1947 the Mil design bureau turned
out a succession of helicopter designs,
each tailored to advance the understanding of helicopter dynamics or to
meet the specific needs of the Soviet
Union's giant state bodies. Mil built specialist derivatives of its more common designs
where dedicated mission requirements dictated necessary airframe or performance
changes. The Mi-14, developed for the Soviet
navy, was derived from the earlier Mi-8 but
with the addition of a watertight hull and
sponsons for operations over water.

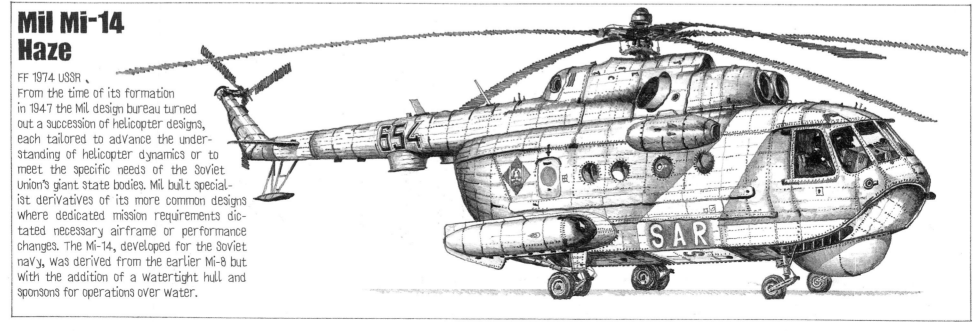

Mil Mi-24P

FF 1970 USSR

Built as a heavily armed attack transport and gunship, the Mi-24 Hind was derived from the engines and the technology of the earlier Mi-8 programme. Similar in configuration to the USA's AH-64 Apache attack helicopter, the Hind is designed to loiter low on the horizon, where it can acquire tanks, fortifications, and other military targets, and engage them with minimal risk. Unlike the Apache it can carry a complement of 8 fully laden troops in a compartment located immediately to the rear of the pilot and weapons-operator stations. Immense power is required to lift and propel this immensely heavy craft at speeds of up to 210mph (338km/h).

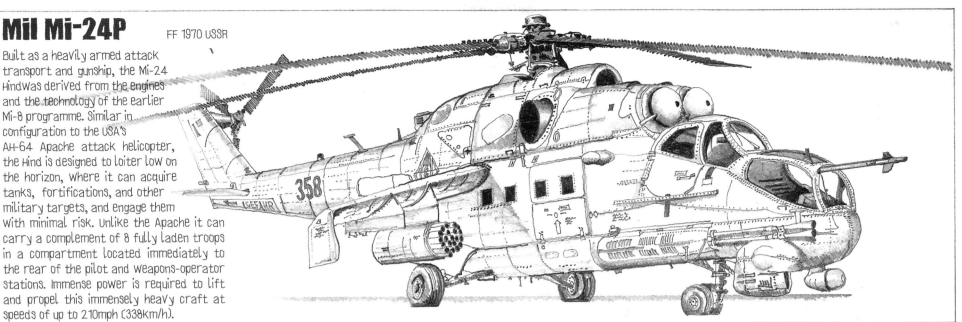

Mikoyan-Gurevich MiG-3

FF 1940 USSR

In August 1941 during the first air battles over Kiev the German pilots encountered the first MiG-3s. The new Russian fighters were clearly faster and more manoeuvrable than the feared German Bf-109s. The Luftwaffe's hierarchy were incensed that there had been no intelligence whatsoever of the new fighter, which clearly threatened German air superiority and therefore the whole basis of the German advance. In fact the MiG-3 did not fulfil its full potential as many of the Russian pilots were not as battle-hardened as the Germans, whose tactics were to draw the MiGs down to low level, where they had a reduced superiority.

Mikoyan-Gurevich MiG-15 Fagot

FF 1947 USSR

Developed in the years immediately after the Second World War, the MiG-15 was a superb performer given the very early stage of development of jet technology. Codenamed Fagot by NATO, it introduced many ingenious developments to produce a jet fighter which could reach speeds of 630mph while still maintaining extraordinary manoeuvrability and handling characteristics. Rugged and dependable, it was produced in great numbers and supplied to many of the Soviet satellite nations including North Korea, where it came face to face with its main western rival, the equally superb F-86 Sabre. The jet fighter was coming of age.

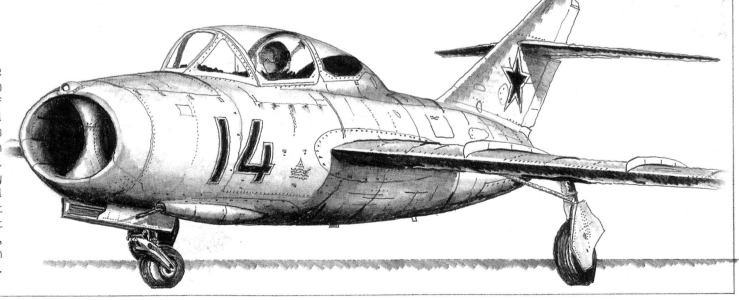

FF 1955 USSR

Mikoyan-Gurevich MiG-21 M Fishbed

Flown by all of the Soviet Pact air forces the Fishbed was, in its day, the most prolific of the Cold War jet fighters. Its ongoing development was watched intently by NATO and especially by the USA.

Mikoyan-Gurevich MiG-25 Foxbat   FF 1964 USSR

The MiG-25 was developed to counter the threat of the USA's Mach 3 XB-70 Valkyrie strategic bomber. When that project was terminated in 1961 work on the MiG-25 continued although the emphasis moved from strike interceptor to photographic and electronic reconaissance platform. The Foxbat was a stunningly good performer with maximum level speeds in the region of Mach 2.5 and a combat radius of 805 miles (1,300km). On 6 September 1976 a MiG-25 pilot defected from Sikharovka Air Base to Japan causing an international incident and affording western analysts a rare opportunity to examine the type.

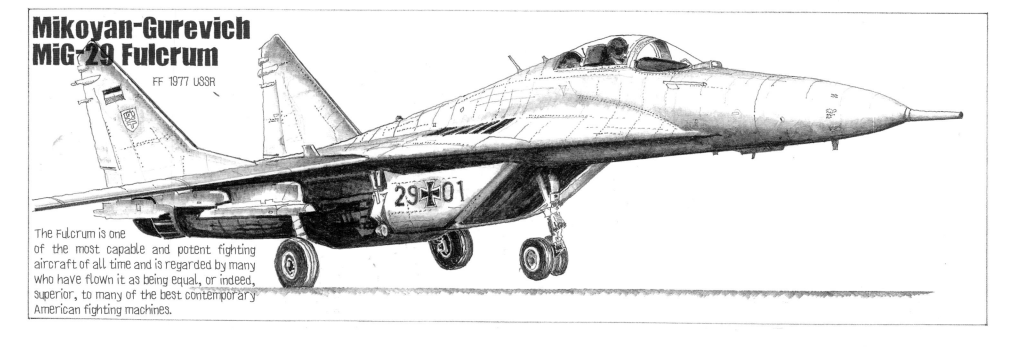

Mikoyan-Gurevich MiG-29 Fulcrum

FF 1977 USSR

The Fulcrum is one of the most capable and potent fighting aircraft of all time and is regarded by many who have flown it as being equal, or indeed, superior, to many of the best contemporary American fighting machines.

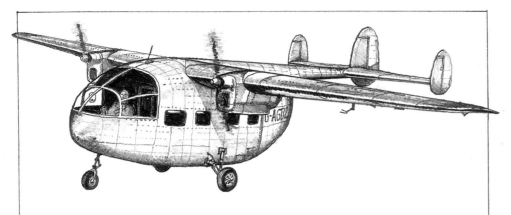

Miles M-57 Aerovan 1

FF 1945 UK

The Aerovan was a simple and efficient aircraft and the type remained in service for many years. The last record of an Aerovan in operational service was that of the prototype Mark VI Aerovan, which was certainly operating in Italy up until 1968. An Aerovan with an all-new prototype Hurel-Dubois high-aspect-ratio wing was flown in 1957.

Miles' twin-engined 4-seat cabin monoplane retained many of the individual components of its earlier M-38 Messenger single. While the design prototype was fitted with fixed landing gear the 149 production airframes had a retractable undercarriage arrangement.

Miles M-65 Gemini

FF 1945 UK

Miles M-57 Aerovan 1

FF 1945 UK

Miles was a most prolific and innovative aircraft designer and he regularly worked on a large number of aircraft projects at any one time. While many of his design drawings were destined to come to nothing, those that made it into production would be treasured for ever. His M-57 Aerovan, flown for the first time in January of 1945, was a low-cost twin-engine bulk-load carrier with a large rear hinged access door. The clever design with its high-boom tail allowed a single mid-sized car to be driven right up to and inside the aircraft. The arrangement was ideal for delivering outsized loads to islands and other remote locations. In total, 48 of the type were manufactured.

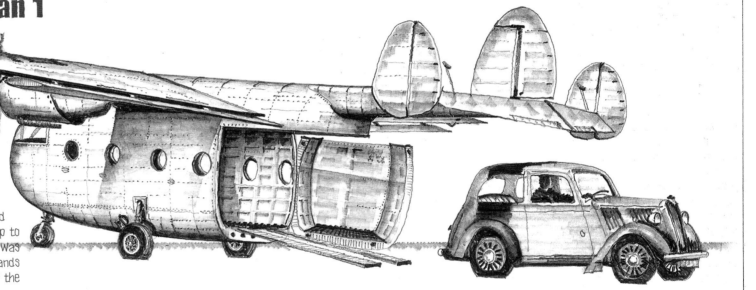

Miles M-25 Martinet

FF 1942 UK

That big Frankenstein bolt on the side of the Martinet is the winding drum for its target-towing cable. The type was developed by Miles in response to an RAF specification for a new target tug which would allow the ever increasing stream of trainee pilots to hone their interception skills on flying targets. Miles based the new tug on the original Miles Master airframe but still found it necessary to elongate the Master's nose to make up for the weight of the drum and drogue cabling. The Martinet continued in service throughout the War and earned a small but important role in modern history.

Miles M9-A Master

FF 1939 UK

At the start of the Second World War the RAF had just received its first 7 Miles Master advanced trainers. Before the end of the war over 3,250 of all variants of the type would be built to train the vast army of airmen who would be needed to sustain the beleaguered RAF in its desperate bid to stem the advancing threat from Germany. The Master was an ideal advanced trainer with its powerful 715hp Rolls-Royce Kestrel engine and its inbuilt wing-mounted Browning machine guns. Many of the type had their wings clipped in order to increase speed and improve agility in the air. The type remained in service until 1947 and, indeed, there are several Masters flying to this day.

Miles M-17 Monarch

FF 1938 UK.

A low-wing cantilever monoplane of spruce construction with laminated plywood covering, the Monarch was full of character and class. Built by Philips & Powis of Woodley, England, the type developed an excellent reputation and Monarchs served in many countries across the world including India, Australia, and the Middle East. Its de Havilland Gipsy Major engine developed 130hp to give a cruise speed of 125mph.

Miles M-2L Speed Hawk Six

FF 1934 UK.

The Hawk, the Hawk Major, the Hawk Trainer and the Speed Hawk Six were all derivatives of Miles's superb 1934 series, and all were imbued with the wonderful Miles character, nose fairings and faired undercarriage. These were the days when style was as important as performance, and wonderful timber detailing was presented alongside gracefully curved hand-beaten fairings to give a remarkably high standard of finish throughout. The Speed Hawk Six was a particularly well-rounded aircraft with a high level of specification, a comfortable touring interior and de Havilland's smooth 6-cylinder 200hp (149kW) Gipsy 6 under the bonnet.

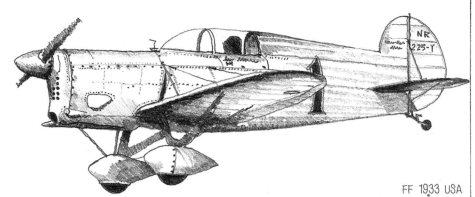

Miles & Atwood Special

FF 1933 USA

Leland Miles and Leon Atwood provided that perfect partnership of design ability and finance, which led to the wonderful 1933 Miles and Atwood Special. Miss Tulsa, as she became known, went on to win the 1934 Greve Trophy recording a track airspeed of 189.5mph, a very respectable tally for 1933. Leland Miles was tragically killed in Cleveland in 1937 when the wings of his Special folded after a bracing cable snapped in flight.

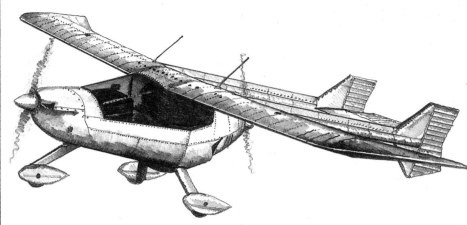

Minimaster

FF 1989 USA

An ultralight sport-plane designed to provide low-cost flying in an enclosed and comfortable environment. The Minimaster went on to inspire a generation of ultralight designs.

Mooney Ranger (M-20J) 201 Series

An unpressurised single-engine light plane, conspicuous for its distinctive unswept Mooney fin and rudder. The Mooney 201 first flew in 1953. For years its 191mph cruise speed gave it a 23 to 35 mph advantage over most aircraft of similar size and horsepower. Thereafter, years of constant refining and continued aerodynamic fine-tuning ensured that the Mooney was always a strong performer among piston singles. The Mooney MSE was a later development of the series, applying state-of-the-art stress-test analysis and aerodynamic programmes to produce a sleeker, lighter aircraft with a cruise speed of 191mph and an endurance of 5.9 hours.

FF 1953 USA

Morane-Saulnier MS-230

FF 1929 France

The MS-230 parasol single was intended to fulfil the duties of observation, gunnery, advanced pilot training and target towing. With its Salmson 230hp (171kW) radial engine it had a maximum level speed of 127mph (205km/h).

Morane-Saulnier D-3801 (MS-406)

FF 1935/1939 France

Morane-Saulnier had been supplying the French Armée de l'Air with its MS-406 single-seat piston fighter before the outbreak of war and more than 570 had been rushed into service by the time Germany turned its attentions to France. Unfortunately for the beleaguered Armée de l'Air, however, the pace of technological advancement within the Reich's aircraft design bureau was so rapid that the 406 was obsolete even before it entered service. 2 of the type were exported to Switzerland, where they were licensed for production as the D-3800 and 01.

Murphy Rebel

FF 1990 Canada
An all-aluminium, parasol-wing, side-by-side, touring aircraft which combines the best traditions of the classic taildragger with the very latest in contemporary technology and performance. Murphy Aircraft provide plan sets and kit parts to amateur builders throughout the USA and, indeed, the world. The Rebel is a rugged and versatile and, always a good measure of any type, there are many Rebels which have built up very large numbers of flying hours. After use, the Rebel's wings can be de-rigged for efficiency of storage removing the requirement for large expensive hangar spaces. Floats, skis and conventional landing gear can be installed.

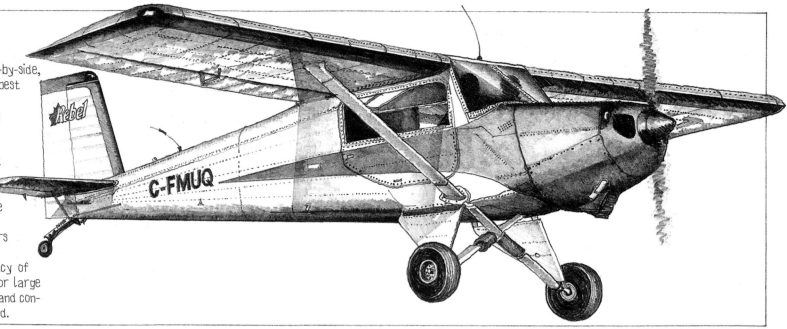

Murphy Renegade Spirit

FF 1985 Canada
The Renegade is a modern kitplane which is based on classic biplane lines and proven air handling qualities. With its open cockpit, strutted biplane configuration and its wonderful finish, the Renegade presents a brief glimpse of times past.

Myasishchev M-4 Bison

FF 1953 USSR

Vladimir Myasishchev's 4-engined strategic bomber was originally designed to deliver its nuclear warheads all the way to the cities of North America but difficulties with range caused many problems for the programme.

Nanchang CJ-6

FF 1958 People's Republic of China

More than 1,900 of Nanchang's CJ-6 primary military trainer were produced under licence from Yakovlev of the Soviet Union. The CJ-6 was a rugged and capable training airframe which was more than able to absorb all the punishment its student pilots could dish out. Today it continues in service with the air forces of Albania and North Korea. Others of the type have been released from military service in China and are beginning to appear in the West.

Nakajima B-5N Kate Torpedo bomber

FF 1937 Japan

When the Japanese task force sprung its devastating surprise attack on Pearl Harbor on 7 December 1941 the B-5N carrier-based dive-bomber was represented in large numbers. On that day more than 40 torpedo-equipped B-5Ns inflicted enormous damage on the anchored US Naval fleet while a further 105 B-5Ns dropped freefall bombs onto the hapless US battleships, corvettes and concentrations of Navy personnel. It was a disaster of massive proportions for the US Navy, brought about by a new and unprecedented scale of carrier-borne operations. The B-5N grew increasingly obsolescent as the war progressed.

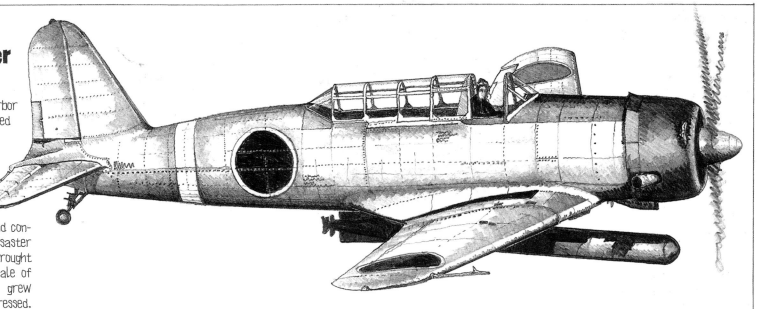

NAMC YS-11

FF 1962 Japan

Fuji, Kawasaki, Mitsubishi, Nippi, Shin Meiwa, and Showa all joined forces in June of 1959 to develop the NAMC YS-11 airliner. Each of the partners developed a series of large assemblies which were then mated to produce the completed airframe. The first flight took place in August of 1962 and the type first entered airline service in April of 1965. This was a most serviceable and efficient aircraft and a total of 159 were built for Japanese and US airline operators, with a further 23 going to various Japanese military forces. To this day many of the type are in daily operational use and the NAMC continues to present a relatively efficient operational prospect despite its age.

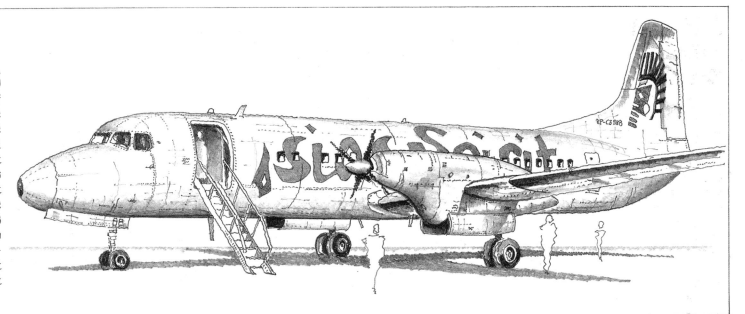

NASA Space Shuttle

FF 1981 USA

The shuttle's first nervous re-entry from space in April of 1981 and the tragic Challenger disaster of 1986 are 2 events that have become forever bound into modern memory and culture. The Space Shuttle was intended to open the doors to space and, although the programme was fraught with difficulties, it certainly did go some way to making space more accessible.

The recent ascents into space by Scaled Composites' lightweight Space Ship One, and imminent near-space flights by some of the other Ansari Competition contenders, are likely to set a new direction for future reusable space vehicles.

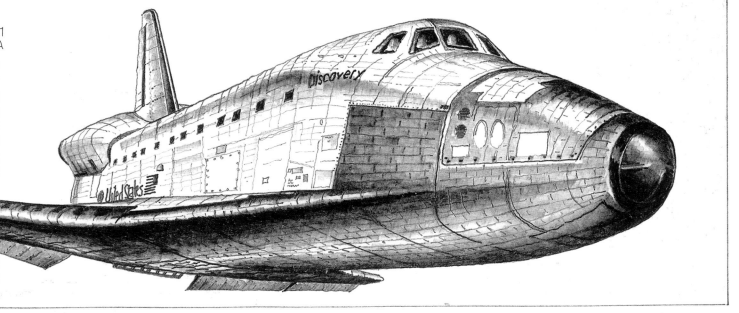

Nimrod AEW-3

FF 1967/1986 UK

Few development projects can have been as protracted and as politically live as the Nimrod AEW-3. Based on the de Havilland Comet airliner, the AEW-3's airframe was fitted with its distinctive bulbous GEC/Marconi radar antenna nose and tail units at the former Avro plant at Woodford, Manchester. Every step of the project, however, was beset by cost over-runs and difficulties with the electronic surveillance suite. In December 1986 the project was cancelled and Britain ordered a fleet of proprietary Boeing E3 Sentries (AWACS).

Nord N-1203 Norecrin II

FF 1946 France

Nord's N-1203 scooped up a host of prestigious awards before winning the 1948 Deauville speed race with a stunning performance of closed-circuit flying. The Norecrin II was a development of the Noralpha N-1101 with a new retractable undercarriage, more powerful engine, and improved

aerodynamic detailing. A total of 378 of the type were produced, many of them incorporating additional revisions and improvements.

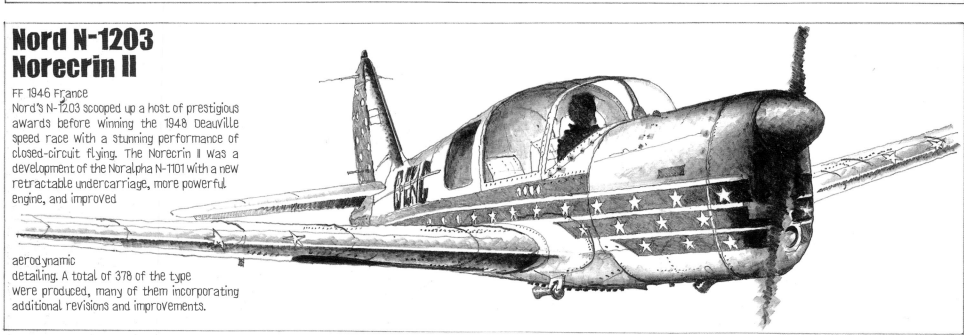

Nord N-2501 Noratlas

FF 1949 France

Developed by Nord to address the French air force's requirement for a heavy transport and paratroop-launch platform, the heavy, twin-boomed Noratlas provided a rugged and unique solution. A tough and versatile aircraft, the Noratlas has worked in some of the most inhospitable and undeveloped environments on Earth.

Nord N-1101 Noralpha

FF 1946 France

Known as the Noralpha in its civilian role and as the Ramier in its military role the Renault-powered 1101 strikes an unusual pose on the ground with its high nose and its exaggerated dihedral. A fast utility transport monoplane, the French-built Noralpha was heavily influenced by the Messerschmitt 108 and many of its parts have commonality with that infamous aircraft. In its military role it was employed as a reconaissance transport with its high cruising speed and, for the 1940s, its sleek, modern airframe. Noralphas can still be seen attending air shows today.

Noorduyn Aviation Norseman

FF 1935 Canada

Jazz band leader Glenn Miller was the unfortunate subject of one of the great mysteries of the Second World War. When the USA joined the war Miller was a hugely successful celebrity but, putting that life aside, he went to serve his country and after some time was stationed with the US Air Force in England. On 15 December 1944 Miller was being ferried across the English Channel to perform in Paris when the Noorduyn Norseman in which he was being carried disappeared never to be seen again. The tragedy was the source of huge speculation during the war years and ever since. So what did happen to the tiny Norseman on that fateful December night? There have been many rumours over the years. Witnesses stated that the night was damp and foggy suggesting that the unwitting pilot simply got into trouble over the Channel in dense clouds and fog. Another more colourful story told of Miller dying of heart failure in the arms of a prostitute in one of the seedier Parisian bordellos. Yet another story asserts that Miller was shot by a Parisian prisoner of war who found his way home only to find an American officer with his young wife. Incensed, the Frenchman is supposed to have shot both the American and his wife. The American, of course, turns out to be Miller. The last story, now thought to be the most likely, is that the Norseman crossed an area of water used by returning bombers to discard unused and volatile incendiary bombs and the unsuspecting Norseman simply wandered into the danger zone.

Nord N-1002 Pingouin II
FF 1945 France

The annual Private Flying Association 'fly-in' at Kemble always throws up some rare antique and classic aircraft types. This wonderfully refurbished Nord 1002 dropped in and became an immediate favourite. Presented in an unusual wartime desert camouflage scheme the 1002 would have been used during the war years for artillery spotting, transporting high-level personnel and for general communications duties.

North American P-51 Mustang
FF 1940 USA

It is a remarkable tribute to the P-51 Mustang to see it still providing one of the fastest and most agile unlimited aircraft racing platforms all these years after its inception. Unfortunately, however, it is these very qualities which are sadly bringing about its near-extinction, as airframe and engine stocks are becoming rapidly depleted by the pylon-racing circuit. The Mustang was designed over a period of 3 months in the summer of 1940 to meet a request from the British War Office and its first flight was recorded only 5 months after its inception. The new fighter incorporated the very latest advances in airframe and aerodynamic technologies including laminar-flow wings, wide-track landing gear, and greatly reduced airframe drag. The effect of all these innovative advances was to produce an airframe that was extraordinarily efficient resulting in an aircraft which could carry (internally) 4 times as much fuel as any of its contemporaries. It was this payload margin which gave the Mustang its great advantage. Very large quantities of either fuel or armaments could now be carried deep into enemy territory eventually affording fighter cover for bombers all the way to the target area. It was the 1942 match of the Mustang airframe with the new high-blown Merlin engine that finally released the Mustang's full might and magic. Suddenly the Mustang was the king of the skies over Europe and even over Germany. The type quickly became the main long-range escort fighter serving with all of the Allied forces on all fronts. 15,586 of all types of Mustang were delivered by 1945.

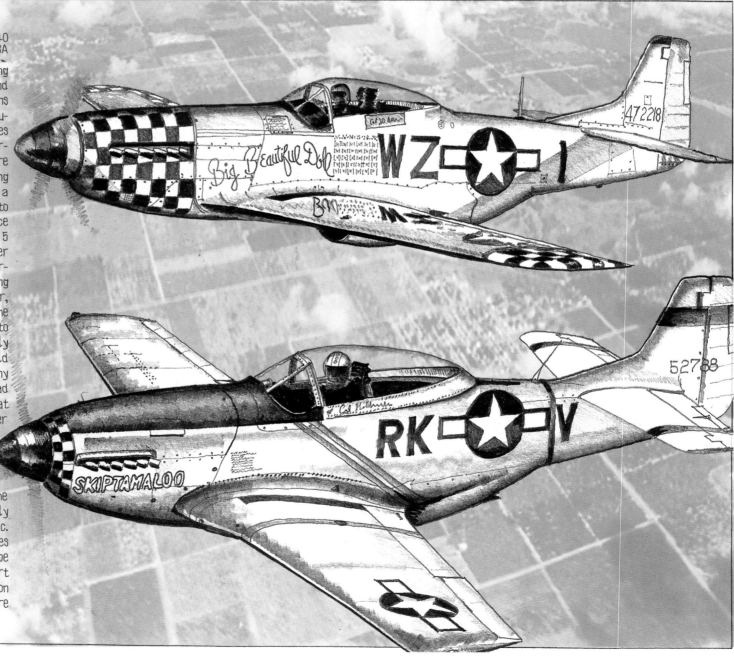

North American B-25 Mitchell

FF 1940 USA
On 18 April 1942 16 bomb-laden B-25 Mitchells lifted off the deck of the carrier USS Hornet. Their targets were Tokyo, Kobe, Yokohama and Nagoya on the Japanese Home Islands 700 miles away. That first raid on Japan secured the B-25's place in history.

North American Navion Rangemaster

FF 1946 and 1971 USA
Derived from the original North American-built military reconnaissance L-17 Navion of 1946, the Navion Rangemaster was re-engineered by Ryan as a high-performance civilian transport. The result was a powerful and capable personal transport with modern and well-appointed interior. Its first flight was in 1960 with series production starting in 1961. The Rangemaster cruises comfortably at 185mph with its 260hp Continental powerplant.

North American AT-6D Texan

FF 1937 USA
As the political clouds darkened over Europe the US Air Force began to churn out fighter pilots. By December 1941 when the USA entered the war the training period for combat pilots had been reduced to just 200 hours, an extraordinarily low threshold. By the end of the conflict more than 17,000 Texan trainers were in use by the US and other Allied nations.

Northrop XP-56 Black Bullet

FF 1943 USA

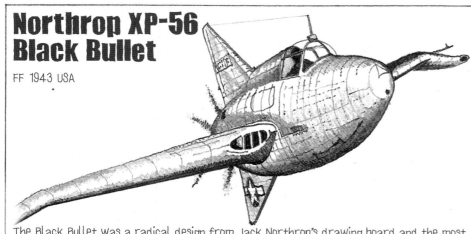

The Black Bullet was a radical design from Jack Northrop's drawing board and the most unusual submission made to the US Air Force in response to its Interceptor Competition R-40C. The tailless semi-flying-wing must have appealed to the Air Force chiefs, however, because an order for 1 flying prototype was placed in September 1940. Although the XP-56 project was finally abandoned in 1944, much invaluable data was collected by Northrop and it formed the basis of their later flying wing designs.

Northrop F-5E Tiger II

FF 1972 USA

In April of 1962 the US Department of Defense announced that the Northrop F-5 had been selected for its Military Assistance Program, essentially a mechanism for supplying world class lightweight affordable supersonic fighters to selected foreign governments. This was no army-surplus handout. The F-5 was designed from scratch for the task and was pitched at a level which provided third-party countries with a potent air superiority weapon without threatening existing US Air Force inventories.
The F-5E variant became well known as the standard 'aggressor' aircraft used at the US Air Force's Miramar Top Gun school.

North American F-86 Sabre

FF 1947 USA

Development of the Sabre began in 1944 but with the influx of German scientists and aerodynamicists immediately after the war, the project changed direction incorporating captured data derived from the Messerschmitt Me-262 and adapting a swept-wing configuration which would allow higher subsonic speeds.

PILOT
1ST LT HOOT GIBSON
CREW CHIEF
T/SGT. O SCRUGGS

North American
F-86 Sabre

FF 1947 USA

Sun 'n Fun 2005
brought out a rash of
wonderful classics, from vintage biplanes
to the latest fast jets. Perhaps the most
wonderful of all, however, was this gleaming
North American F-86 Sabre with its highly
burnished aluminium finish and its stunning
standard of workmanship.

Northrop XB-35
Flying Wing

FF 1946 USA

Jack Northrop's aircraft design studios have
always, it seems, been fascinated with the
concept of flying wings. The massive XB-35
heavy bomber was, however, the first such
project to reach the point of being ordered
for operational use by any air force. The
1946 order by the US Air Force for 14 of the
type was a first in aviation. Even as the airframes were being built Northrop were busy
working on replacing its 4 reciprocating
engines with a new jet-powered
arrangement.

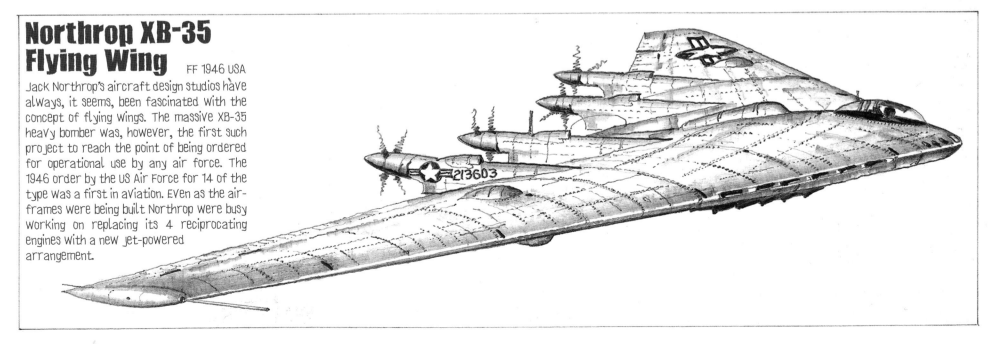

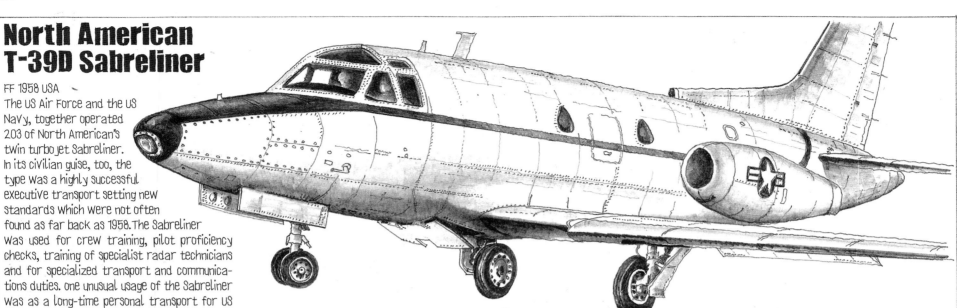

North American
T-39D Sabreliner

FF 1958 USA

The US Air Force and the US Navy, together operated 203 of North American's twin turbojet Sabreliner. In its civilian guise, too, the type was a highly successful executive transport setting new standards which were not often found as far back as 1958. The Sabreliner was used for crew training, pilot proficiency checks, training of specialist radar technicians and for specialized transport and communications duties. One unusual usage of the Sabreliner was as a long-time personal transport for US ex-president Lyndon B. Johnson.

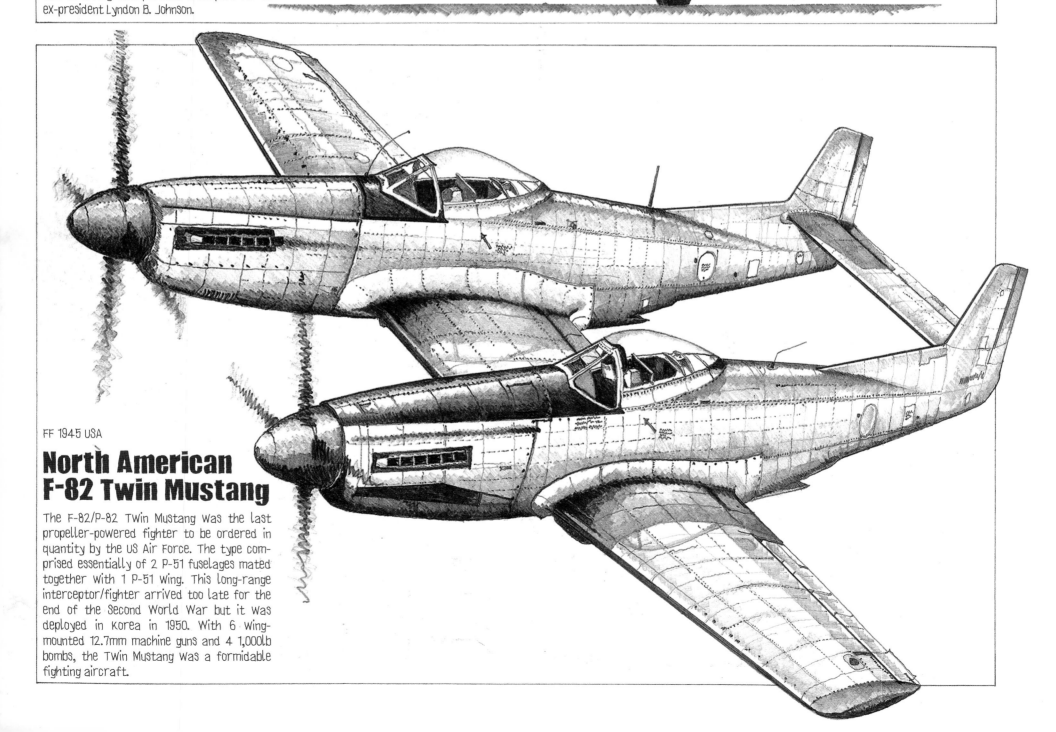

FF 1945 USA

North American
F-82 Twin Mustang

The F-82/P-82 Twin Mustang was the last propeller-powered fighter to be ordered in quantity by the US Air Force. The type comprised essentially of 2 P-51 fuselages mated together with 1 P-51 wing. This long-range interceptor/fighter arrived too late for the end of the Second World War but it was deployed in Korea in 1950. With 6 wing-mounted 12.7mm machine guns and 4 1,000lb bombs, the Twin Mustang was a formidable fighting aircraft.

Northrop/Grumman/ Boeing/GE B-2A Spirit

FF 1990 USA

The development and flight testing of the B-2 was among the world's best-guarded secrets, with rumours and counter-rumours of a strange flying-saucer-like aircraft flying about the desert skies in the dark of night. Behind the mystery and intrigue, however, was a dark motive which we seemed to accept without protest: the unde-tected delivery deep into enemy territory of gravity-released nuclear weapons. Indeed, the B-2 is ominously efficient in that role, being able to deliver a massive 8 gravity-fall nuclear weapons or a total of 16 stand off tactical nuclear warheads. The aircraft's 11,100-mile range, too, has completely rede-fined the rules of strike engagement, being able, with 1 in-flight refuelling stop, to target any location on earth from its own home base in the USA. The development of stealth technology brings with it entirely new concepts in terms of aeronautics and radar-dissipation techniques. The complexities of achieving a near-invisible radar signature greatly outweigh the normal challenges of overcoming gravity and friction to keep the aircraft in flight. Aerodynamic compromises are made where required and corrections are applied using sophisticated flight-control computers. The B-2 airframe is not massively different from the earlier flying wing prototypes produced by Northrop and other pioneering manufacturers in the 1950s.

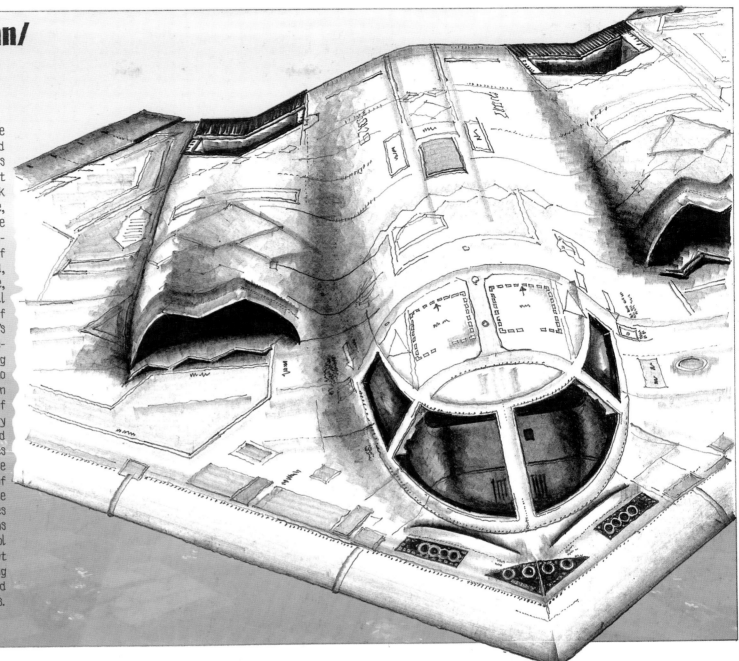

Panavia Tornado IDS

FF 1974 UK/Italy/Germany

The Panavia Tornado was developed jointly between by the UK, Italy and Germany, and work continued over a 12-year period to bring the all-weather supersonic tactical strike aircraft to completion.

The 3 partners divided the project into constituent parts, the UK building the nose and the rear fuse-lage, Italy building the wing assemblies, and Germany building the centre fuselage. The IDS Tornado variant was flown by both Germany and Italy and also by non-partner Saudi Arabia.

Panzl S-330
FF 2003 USA

This wonderfully chequered Panzl S-330 was sitting by the ramp at Florida's Kissimme airport as I waited my turn to fly aerobatics in the Warbird Adventures SNJ-6 Texan. The S-330's exciting lines and its extensive paint scheme promised a dramatic sketch, but I had to sever the under-carriage and take some liberties with perspective to fill the page.

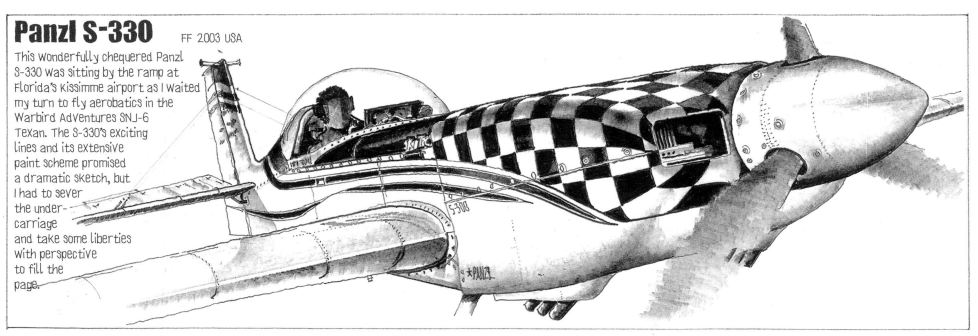

Payne Knight Twister

FF 1929 USA

Vernon Payne developed the original Payne Knight Twister in 1928 to liven up an aircraft design class he was teaching. Taking his outline sketch drawings home, Payne developed the design to produce the tiny Knight Twister biplane and ended up releasing the plans to amateur home-builders for individual licensed production. Payne continued to develop and support the design over the following 50 years and the later designs have been honed and shaped to produce very high standards of performance. No matter what the Vintage, every Knight Twister is a true thoroughbred.

FF 1986 Italy
Piaggio P-180 Avanti
Piaggio's stunningly sleek and efficient executive turboprop provides jet performance with lower costs.

Piaggio P-136L-1

FF 1948 Italy

Piaggio's 5-seat pusher amphibian used a gull-wing configuration to keep the propeller arcs well clear of the water. The type was adapted by Italy's military authorities as a Search-and-Rescue aircraft and 34 of them were deployed for many years along Italy's extensive and sunsoaked Adriatic and Mediterranean coastlines.

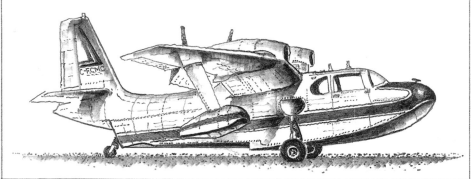

Pilatus Britten Norman Trislander
FF 1970 UK

When Britten Norman developed a stretched derivative of their popular Islander commuter transport they found that additional power was required to lift the newly enlarged aircraft with its increased payload. Rather than increasing the size of the 2 engines, however, Britten Norman opted to add a third engine, which they positioned on the new aircraft's tail. The result was the Trislander, a most unusual 16- to 18-seat commuter airliner. The type was manufactured between 1971 and 1982, by which time 73 had been completed and delivered to operators across the globe. Plans to build the Trislander in the US and Australia were abandoned.

Pilatus P-2

FF 1945 Switzerland

Swiss aircraft manufacturer Pilatus designed the P-2 advanced trainer to operate in Switzerland's rugged, mountainous environment. With its clean, low monoplane wing and its tightly cowled engine the P-2 was a capable performer and an efficient climber. It was powered by a Czech-built version of the 465hp (347kW) German Argus AS-410 engine. The P-2 was a docile and forgiving aircraft with excellent flying manners, perhaps the perfect trainer. It served Switzerland from 1946 right up to 1981, at which point the remaining airworthy airframes were sold into private ownership. Pilatus P-2 trainers, now classed as antique warbirds, can be found attending Swiss flying events today.

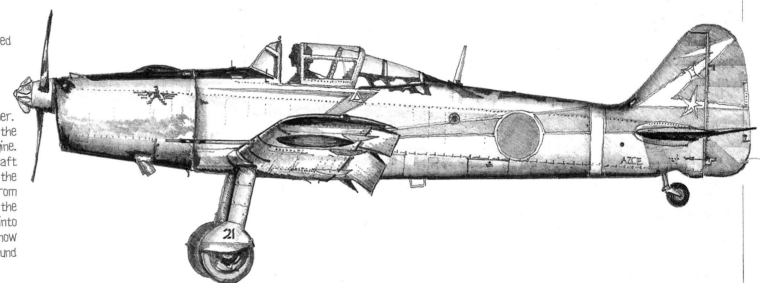

Pilatus PC-6 B2/H4 Turbo Porter

FF 1959 Switzerland

While the Porter flew for the first time in 1959 it was 2 years later that the type received its first turboprop engine and therefore its distinctive pointed nose profile. The PC-6 series quickly won a niche in the hot-and-high market, where short landings and take-offs and an ability to climb rapidly are the dominant performance requirements. Designed in Switzerland to cope with that country's acute mountainous terrain, the Porter is a tough and versatile workhorse which has been exported to many countries across the world.

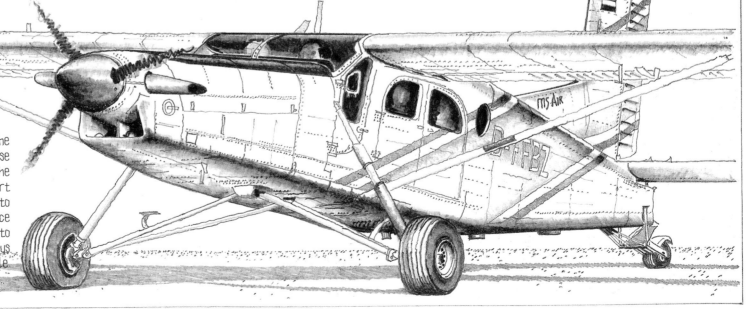

Piper PA-22 Tri Pacer

FF 1951 USA

7,629 Tri Pacers were built between 1951 and 1963 and, indeed, the type is still much treasured and flown to this day. In the 1930s the tricycle undercarriage became all the rage and punters began to favour those aircraft which had adopted the new tricycle format in lieu of the earlier taildragger layout. The PA-22 was essentially a robust tricycle upgrade of the earlier PA-20 Pacer and the type went on to win a most treasured and time-honoured place in the annals of aviation.

Piper PA-28 Cherokee Warrior

FF 1960 USA

This is Whiskey Romeo November, the PA-28 Cherokee Warrior on which I have done much of my flying in recent years. With a 1-wheel landing like this one, it can only be me at the controls.

Piper PA-31 Chieftain

FF 1973 USA

In 1972 Piper set about stretching its highly successful Navajo series to produce the PA-31 Chieftain range. The new 10-seater appealed to the smaller commuter- and cargo-carriers alike and the type was sold in large numbers right across the world. In its 6-seat executive format, too, it delivered on speed, range and comfort, and it quickly became a long-time market leader. Now, more than 30 years after its introduction, the type can still be found in service in many far-flung parts of the globe.

Piper PA-32 Saratoga II TC

FF 1980 USA

Piper's Saratoga II TC sales demonstrator was able to command a respectable turnover of admirers at 2005's EAA Show despite the fact that it has been around since 1979. Is it that people will throng around any display aeroplane, or is it that the type has been improved dramatically over the years? Perhaps it is a little of both. The Saratoga is by any measure a capable and well-appointed aircraft although it is certainly dated in comparison with the new composite offerings from the younger and more idealistic American and Eastern European manufacturers.

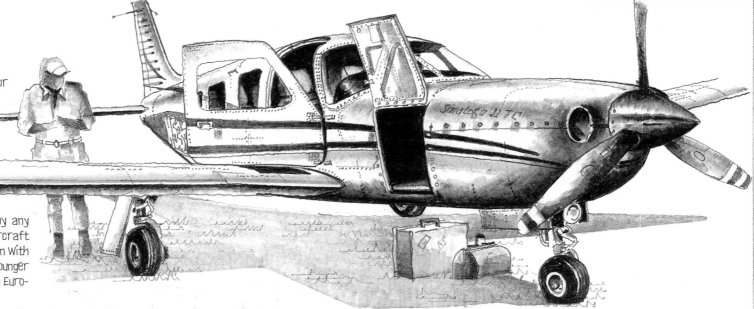

Piper PA-25 Pawnee

FF 1954 USA

I love this aeroplane. The Pawnee's whacky appearance gives every opportunity to produce an unusual and exciting sketch. Echo Zulu was parked and covered but I have taken some liberties showing it in flight and, indeed, lopping off any parts that upset the balance of the drawing. One of my favourite aircraft and one of my favourite sketches. To this day the 1962 PA-25 Pawnee is one of the greatest and most prolific workhorses of the agricultural crop-spraying world.

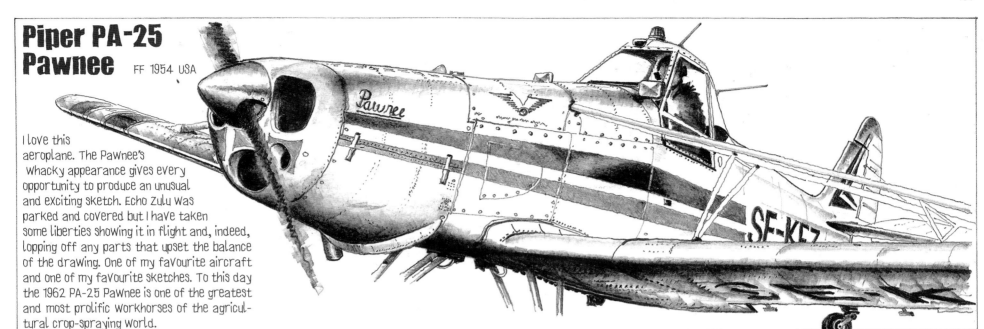

Piper PA-34 Seneca

FF 1969 USA

Piper created the PA-34 Seneca for those of us who hold our breath when flying over large expanses of water. Indeed, there is nothing as comforting as the sound of that second 220hp (164kW) Lycoming engine thundering away when you are still 90 minutes from landfall. Inside, the Seneca has all the trappings of home with deep leather seating and an executive fit-out for the pilot and his 5 passengers. Almost 4,790 Senecas have been built by Piper, with further examples being turned out by PZL of Poland and by Embraer of Brazil.

Pitts Special S-1 & S-2

FF 1944 USA

Curtis H. Pitts, with no formal training in engineering, designed the legendary Pitts Special aerobatic sport-plane. Perhaps the best-known of all competition aerobatic aircraft, it has collected a host of international aerobatic titles over the years. It began life as a single-seat S-1 in 1943/44 but an uprated 2-seat S-2 was developed and certified in 1971. The airframe has been beefed up many times over the years to accommodate bigger engines to compete in the ever more competitive world of aerobatics. After initially building samples of the type on a part-time basis, Pitts released plans of the aircraft for amateur home-building in 1962. These plans can still be obtained to this day from Christen Industries of Afton, Wyoming.

Portsmouth Aerocar
FF 1947
UK

The Portsmouth Aviation Co. was founded in 1932, initially formed to establish air transport routes to and from the Isle of Wight. The company found itself servicing aircraft of the RAF during the war years. With the coming of peace in 1945 many of the contractors who had manufactured and serviced aircraft during the war now developed their own aircraft programmes. The Aerocar was one of these projects. With its twin-boom high-wing configuration and its centre fuselage pod, the Aerocar 6-seater was an unusual sight in the air. Indeed, it soon became a rare sight, as only 1 prototype was built and the model was sadly never put into production.

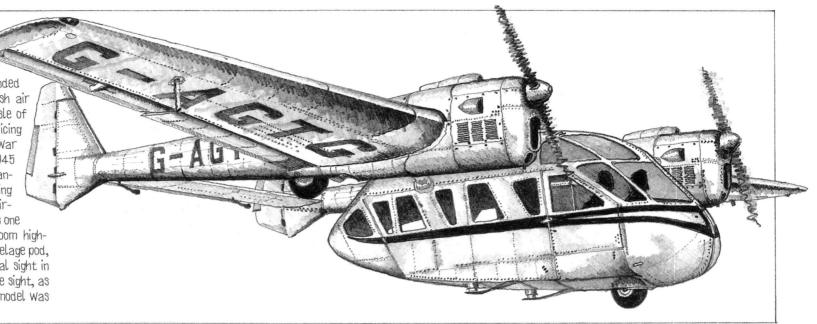

Pitcairn AC-35
FF 1936 USA

On 2 October 1936 James Ray, Vice-president of the Autogiro Company of America landed his roadable craft up to the doors of the US Department of Commerce. The AC-35 was 1 of 6 prototypes commissioned in an effort to foster private aircraft ownership.

Pitcairn AC-35 in a municipal park in the centre of Washington and, after folding up his rotorblades, drove

Pushy Galore
FF 1989 USA

The Pushy is a experimental-category high-performance aircraft designed specifically for competing in time-to-climb events. Designed and built by Texan Bruce Bohannon, the tiny racing airplane has collected a long series of trophies over the past 17 years.

PZL M-28B-1-TD Bryza
Poland

Given Poland's relatively short Baltic coastline PZL must have been hoping for large numbers of export orders for their sophisticated M-28B-1-TD Bryza maritime patrol platform. Even given the very high level of shipping and submarine traffic which passes through Poland's Baltic waters, the extraordinary levels of expenditure required to develop any state-of-the-art patrol and detection aircraft are such that they are unlikely to be sustained on the basis of 1 government order alone.

PZL 230F Skorpion
FF 1990 Poland

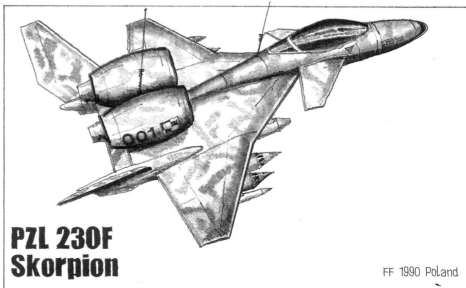

PZL of Poland developed the 230F Skorpion light battlefield attack platform. The type's compact lightweight airframe is not unlike the Aries fighter built by Burt Rutan.

PZL-Mielec M-26 Iskierka

FF 1986 Poland

Competition among manufacturers of military training aircraft has never been as intense, with designers worldwide coming under huge pressure to produce low-cost piston and turbine aircraft that closely approach the high-performance flying characteristics of advanced jet trainers. The M-26 is a Polish-built 2-seat military training aircraft. Student and tutor are seated in a tandem arrangement with the tutor in an elevated seat to enhance downward visibility in the landing phase. The M-26 is intended to provide an environment that will prepare ab initio students for advanced training in turbo-prop or jet-powered trainers.

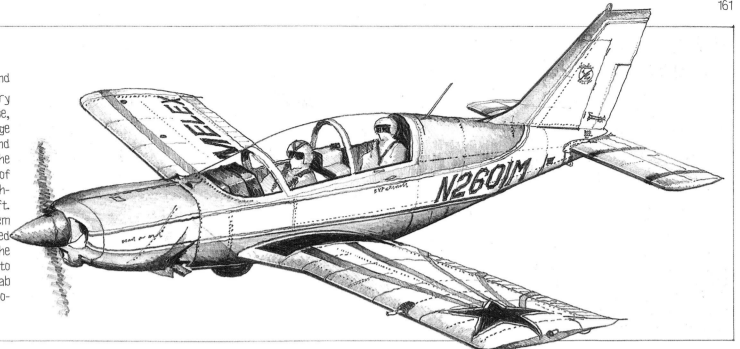

PZL-Mielec M-15-01 Belphegor

FF 1973 Poland

In the early 1970s the idea of a turbofan-powered agricultural crop-sprayer seemed plausible and PZL set about the design of its unique Belphegor biplane. The new jet wonder would replace the ponderous An-2 and would bring new-found levels of efficiency and speed to the collective farming system of the Eastern Bloc. But it was not to be. The type was quickly abandoned, whereas the trusted An-2 gives stalwart service to this day.

PZL 104 Wilga 35

FF 1962 Poland

Poland's unusual Wilga was designed to fulfil a wide variety of general aviation and flying club duties, flying first as the Wilga 1 in 1962. The upgraded Wilga 35 derivative followed in 1967. The Thrush can be found in several configurations, the most prolific being the W-35A (Aeroclub) flying club trainer and glider tug. Other variants include the W-35P 4-seat personnel transport, the W-35R agricultural crop duster, the W-35S air-ambulance and the float-equipped W-35H. With its Ivchenko AI-14RA supercharged radial engine, its maximum speed is 120mph (193km/h) and range is 350 miles (563km). Over 1,000 of the type have been produced.

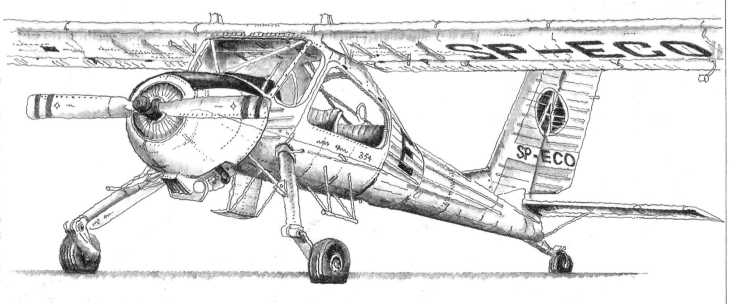

PZL-Swidnik (Mil) Mi-2 Hoplite

FF 1961 USSR/Poland

Codenamed Hoplite by NATO forces, the Mil Mi-2 was designed by the Soviet Mikhail design bureau. After its first flight in 1961 agreement was made that the new type would be manufactured, not in the Soviet Union, but in Poland, where PZL-Swidnik had the available resources and a large skilled workforce. Production commenced in 1965 and a programme of constant development and upgrading was pursued over the years resulting in a wide variety of variants. In all, more than 5,080 Mi-2s were produced, many of them specializing in areas of military transport but others being configured for police work, ambulance and medevac work, pipeline inspection, rescue and general utility.

The Mi-2 has been exported to many countries, earlier exports being predominantly to countries of Soviet influence, but later exports being to Western countries also.

The Mi-2 Kania, a heavily upgraded development of the type, received US certification in 1986 but was never put into large-scale production. The basic Hoplite, meanwhile, represents superb value to operators and it is a frequent sight in many of the Eastern European and African countries.

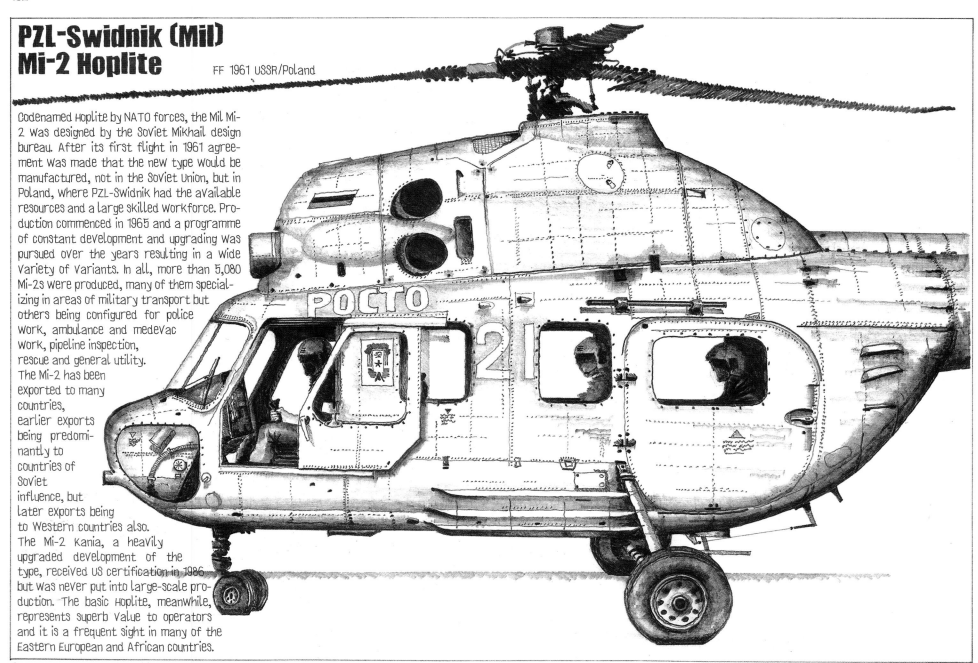

Potez 60

FF 1935 France

The Potez 60 2-seat parasol-wing monoplane was developed as a private touring aircraft and sport-plane. 155 of the type were manufactured complete with open cockpit, unusually long undercarriage legs, and a 60hp (44.7kW) Potez 3B reciprocating engine.

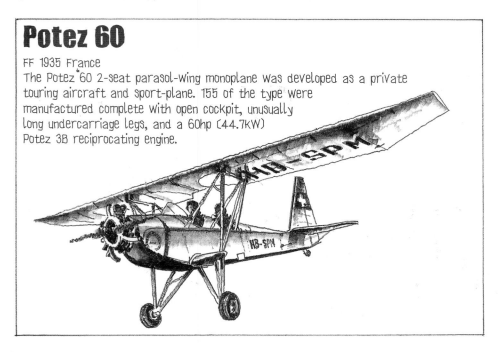

Questair Venture

FF 1987 USA

The unusually close-coupled Questair Venture was designed by Jim Griswold and Ed MacDonough, both former Piper engineers and both part of the Piper Malibu development team. Indeed, it is said that the Venture's match of Continental IO-550 powerplant and McCauley propeller was inspired by their work on the Malibu QEC. Installed on the compact Venture, however, the combination produced stunning results.

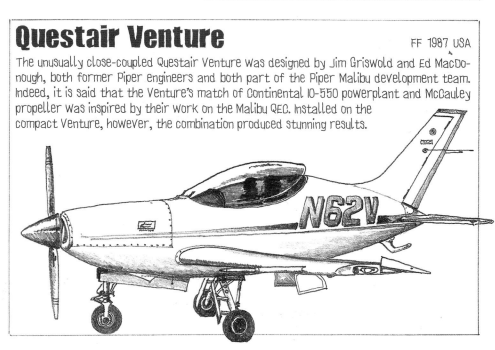

Quickie

FF 1977 USA

Roy Shannon began his Quickie project in 1997, a full 20 years after the revolutionary new Rutan-designed Quickie was awarded the 'Outstanding New Design' award by the Experimental Aircraft Association. On completion in 2003, Roy's first flight went superbly with only very minor changes required to the trim system. Powered by the tiny 22hp Onan (generator) engine the newborn aircraft cruises at 100mph while guzzling just 1.6 gallons of fuel per hour, an extraordinary achievement for any home-builder and a testament to the wonderful design skills of aviation legend Burt Rutan.

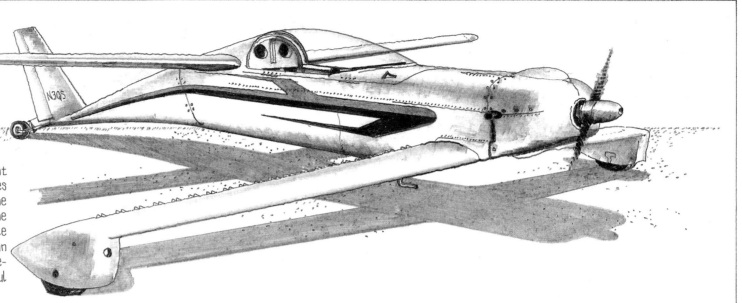

Republic Seabee

FF 1944 USA

The Seabee is one of the great icons of 1950s aviation but the story of Percival Hopkins Spencer, its intrepid designer, is even more fascinating. When still only 13 years of age, Spencer built his first hang-glider from plans published in an old copy of 'Popular Mechanics' magazine. At the age of 16 he re-built and re-engined a crashed Curtiss flying boat. In the course of its first taxi trials Spencer, who had no previous flying experience, accidently lifted the air-craft into the air and, somehow, managed to land again some 5 miles upriver. An extraordinary happening for a 16-year-old boy and all just 6 years after the first flight by the Wright brothers.

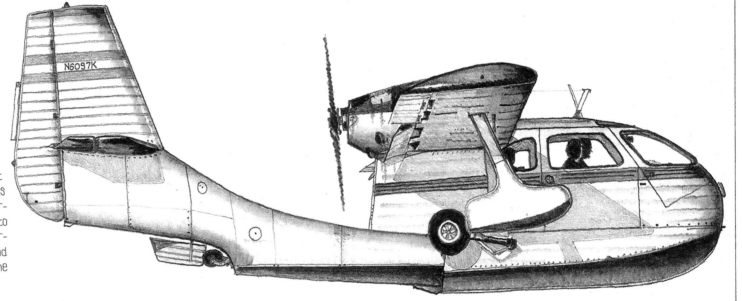

Republic RC-3 Seabee

FF 1944 USA

Some of the old classics are so good that you can not resist drawing them twice. I came across this Seabee at Sun 'n Fun 2005 and I knew immediately that it would make an ideal sketch. I have launched it into the air, retracted the landing gear, and conjured up a pair of suitably attired pilots. Magic!

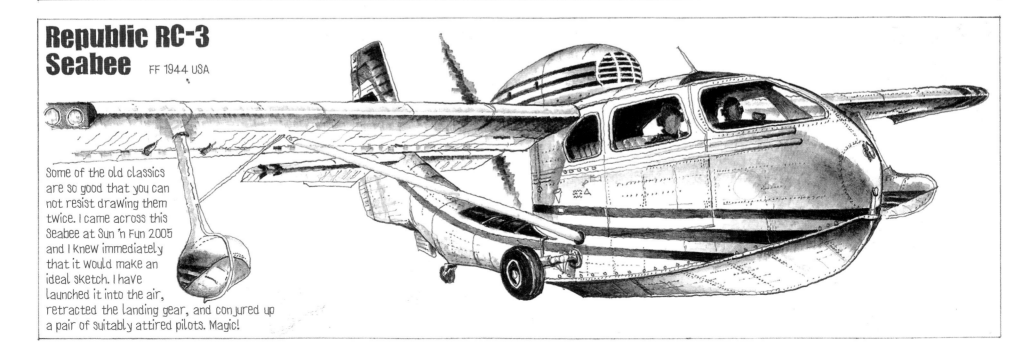

Republic P-47 Thunderbolt
FF 1941 USA

The Juggernaut, or 'Jug', was aptly named. As the largest and the heaviest of the Second World War fighters/escorts it could deliver huge firepower and survive punishing flak damage. Its turbocharged Pratt & Whitney R-2800 Double Wasp radial engine gave it a top speed of 428mph (690km/h) and a range of 590 miles (950km). The P-47 was built in a series of variants from long-range fighter escort (P-47, A, B and C), to ground-strafing fighter bombers (P-47 C, D and D-25). Some of the most interesting P-47 variants were the P-47N, an ultra-long-range variant used for Pacific escort duties, and the P-47M, a stripped-down version used across the South of England to chase flying bombs.

Republic P-47D
FF 1941 USA

The P-47D was a long-range fighter escort version of the powerful Thunderbolt. Designed to accompany bomber formations deep into enemy territory, the type could absorb astonishing levels of flak damage while still remaining operational. Right up to the end of the war, escort cover was an essential element of any long range operation as even a small number of enemy fighters could wreak havoc in the midst of formations of up to 1,000 bombers.

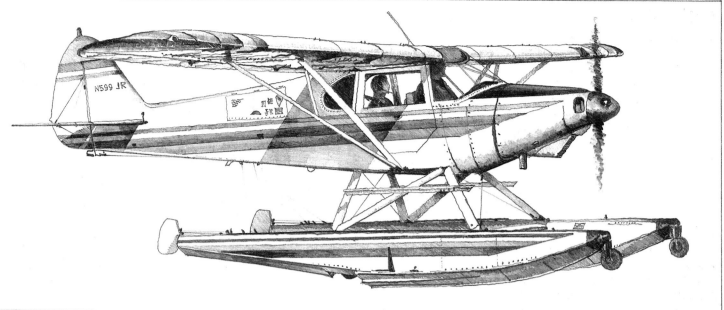

Ritter SDSC Floatplane

FF 1996 USA

At the time of completing this sketch John Ritter had clocked up 1,100 hours on his home-built Ritter Floatplane. It took some 4,000 working hours spread over a period of 4 years to bring the project to completion. When he was done John brought the aircraft to his local airstrip which, at 7,300ft was the highest public airstrip in Wyoming. With its high-aspect-ratio wings, its generous flaps, and its powerful 180hp Lycoming engine, N599JR performs admirably among the airfields and lakes which surround its mountainous home. John flies his EAA Grand Champion award-winning aircraft through all the seasons of the year, on floats, on bulbous tundra wheels, and even, during the winter months, on skis.

Robinson R-44 Astro

FF 1990 USA

Robinson's polished R-22 and R-44 helicopters have changed the face of light helicopter design for ever. In a short period of years the Robinson Helicopter Company has established a solid reputation for producing reliable and capable light helicopters at an affordable price. With the highest standards of specification and engineering Robinson have been able to simplify maintenance schedules to the point where no scheduled maintenance other than oil change is required between 100-hour inspections. Teflon-lined, elastomeric and sealed bearings further reduce wear and increase inspection intervals. To operators and owner/pilots alike, the simplicity and cost savings offered by this reduced maintenance regime make the Robinson a most attractive and cost-effective choice and the type's price tag, at a fraction of that of other similar light helicopters, seals the deal.

Robinson's R-44 range is dominated by the new R-44 Raven, which is configured for general utility, personal touring and flight training roles. With a cruise speed of 130mph and a fuel burn of just 15 gallons per hour the Raven can fly reasonably long sectors in comfort. Another dedicated R-44 variant is a specialized 'Newscopter' which is fitted out with a sophisticated news-reporting suite with digital motion-camera system and full audio and transmission installations.

For operations over water, Robinson's 'Clipper' range provides the assurance of large, rigid floats or, alternatively, compact pneumatic 'pop-out' floats. The Clipper is configured for operations over water and its lowered centre of gravity assures additional stability when flying on floats.

Rockwell 690 Turbo Commander

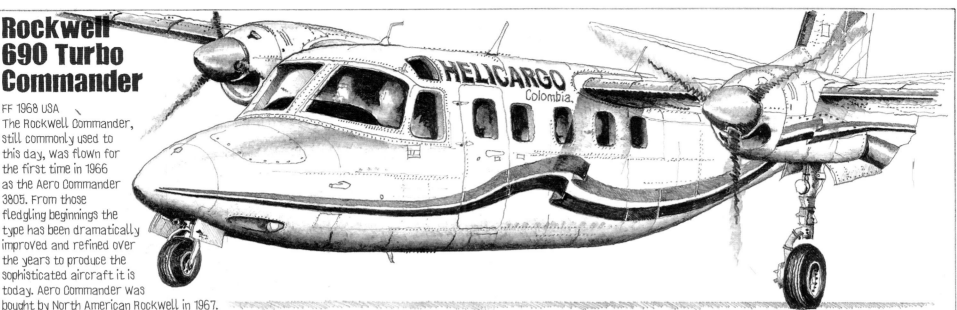

FF 1968 USA
The Rockwell Commander, still commonly used to this day, was flown for the first time in 1966 as the Aero Commander 3805. From those fledgling beginnings the type has been dramatically improved and refined over the years to produce the sophisticated aircraft it is today. Aero Commander was bought by North American Rockwell in 1967.

Rockwell International
B-1A and B-1B
B-1A 1974
B-1B 1984

The long-range B-1A supersonic strategic bomber was as much a casualty of politics as it was of technical difficulty, being first cancelled by the Carter administration only to be later resurrected in the B-1B format by that of Ronald Reagan. The B-1B was designed to penetrate deep into the Soviet Union while other Strategic Air Command aircraft were designed as stand-off weapons intended to deliver air-launched cruise missiles (ALCMs) to the boundaries of the Soviet Union. That the all-out trans-polar war so feared by both Americans and Soviets could in theory last only 1 day simply shows the madness on which this Cold War nuclear rivalry was built. SIOP, the American national plan for deployment of nuclear forces against the Soviet Union, was based on a computer-generated strategy which simulated a battle duration of only hours since a second day of such a war would be unlikely. It was in this environment of fear that the B1-B concept evolved. Although not possessing a stealth capability it carries, at low level, a radar signature of only one-hundredth of SAC's other workhorse, the B-52. With a crew of 4 the B1-B is intended to fly at speeds of up to Mach 1.25 where it is least likely to be detected by defensive radar systems. Its high-aspect variable-geometry wings allow it to cruise at supersonic speeds while still providing reasonable landing performance. Powered by 4 General Electric F101-GE-102 turbojets mounted in underwing boxed pairs, the aircraft can pull high levels of G-forces in manoeuvres.

Rotorway Exec
FF 1980 USA

Perhaps the best of the home-build helicopter kits, the Rotorway Exec is a polished and superbly presented performer. This is the very upper end of the kit market and Rotorway have honed their product to appeal to the builder/pilot whose finances will allow for fuel-injected engines, ACIS (Altitude Compensation Induction System) and FADEC (Fully Automatic Digital Control) systems, and a host of other sophisticated computing and control systems not normally found on Kitbuilt projects.

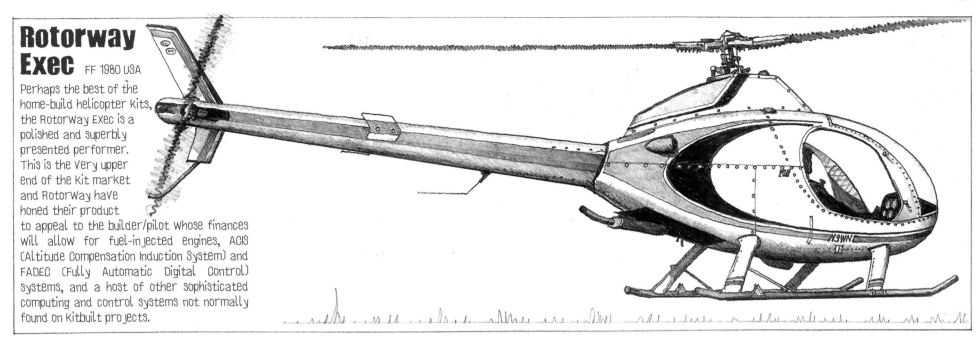

FF 1938
Hungary

Rubik
R-11B Cimbora

A superbly efficient glider designed by Erno Rubik, father of the famous academic and Rubik's cube inventor, Professor Ernő Rubik II.

Rutan Long Ez
FF 1979 USA

This excellent plan-built Rutan Long Ez is the pride and joy of Irish home-builder Dave Ryan. Dave has spent many years completing and perfecting his project and he has become, in the process, a leading authority on Rutan's extraordinary design. Many other home-builders benefit regularly from the self-taught and generously given skills of Dave and others like him. Indeed, I too, a long-time Long Ez builder, have enjoyed great kindness from other builders over the years. Long Ezes are relatively complex and sophisticated projects and build times are generally protracted. On completion, however, the rewards in flight are truly stunning. The freedom that comes with flying a plane that you have built with your own hands is truly exhilarating.

Rutan VariViggen

FF 1972 USA

When Burt Rutan revealed his swept-wing VariViggen at Oshkosh in 1973 the diminutive plan-build aircraft took the world of home-building by storm. Rutan had turned his back on all of the generally held perceptions of aerodynamics and produced an aircraft that seemed to have the engine at the wrong end, a sharply swept main wing set precariously far aft and, to top it all, a strange new canard fore-wing. But the VariViggen was a huge breakthrough for the home-building movement and for aviation in general and it became the inspiration for a multitude of new, radical airframe designs. Rutan now had almost all of the components that he would use to build a dazzling career in aerodynamics and aerospace design.

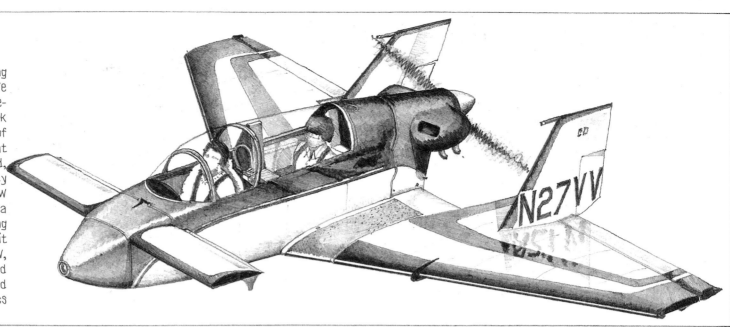

Royal Aircraft Factory SE-5A

FF 1916 UK

By the middle of 1917 the SE-5 and the more powerful SE-5A were in action high over the battlefields of the Western Front. At last the RFC had a potent and capable fighting machine. In the hands of a capable pilot the SE-5A was capable of coming off best in any aerial confrontation. Indeed, the celebrated ace pilot Edward Mannock chalked up a staggering 73 victories, most of them in his Royal Aircraft Factory-built SE-5A.

169

Ryan B-1 Brougham
FF 1927 USA

The Brougham was a commercial development of the pioneering 'Spirit of St Louis' that Lindbergh famously flew across the Atlantic. After Lindbergh's stunning triumph the fledgling Mahoney-Ryan Aircraft Corporation was flooded with requests for a production variant of the type. For almost a year the Brougham was the world's fastest-selling aeroplane. Turning out 20 a month, Ryan went on to build 150 before the rapid pace of aircraft development heralded the introduction of its next model. The B-1 Brougham had, however, won a place in history. It was identified with the 'Spirit of St Louis', and in 1928 it blazed a trail across China, piloted by 'China's Lindbergh', General Zhang Huichang.

Ryan L-17 Navion
FF 1946 USA

It was North American that first developed the L-17 Navion. The end of the Second World War brought massive cancellations of orders and staggering levels of redundancy in the aircraft manufacturing industry. North American hoped that the Navion and other, similar projects would allow them to hold onto a core group of experienced staff and so they accelerated the development programme. Manufacture of the type, in fact, changed hands many times over the years from North American to Ryan, and eventually to the Navion Rangemaster Corporation.

Ryan STM Trainer
FF 1934 USA

After severing his ties with the original Ryan Airline Company Claude Ryan re-entered the aircraft manufacturing business in 1933 with his ST tandem 2-seat open trainer and sport-plane. It was from this range that the Ryan STM was derived. The Menasco C-4S-powered STM was a lightweight fighter and advanced trainer which was bought in quantity by the US Air Force and by the Dutch armed services. The type served as a military training air-craft in the years leading up to the Second World War and, indeed, in some instances, is known to have been involved in skirmishes with enemy forces. A number of the Dutch colonial Ryan STMs are recorded to have been engaged and shot down by Japanese Zeros.

Saab J-29F

FF 1948 Sweden

As the Second World War raged on, the Swedish government raced to develop new jet aircraft which could compete with the powerful new weapons they knew were being developed by all of the combatants fighting above and around them. While they did manage to fly the rudimentary J-21R jet fighter in 1947, it was not until September of 1948 that the first world-class J-29 prototype fighter was flown. Developed by Saab, the performance figures for the early J-29 immediately exceeded all design expectations. Despite its chubby appearance it was superbly manoeuvrable and agile in the air. The much-loved 'Flying Barrel' was flown by Sweden and later by Austria and a total of 661 were manufactured.

Saab 35 Draken

FF 1955 Sweden

Sweden has learned from past conflicts that any large-scale incursion into Scandinavian territories would be made by overwhelming forces at lightning speed. In such a scenario it is likely that all of its air bases would be lost in the opening hours and so the Swedish Defence Forces have developed an aerial defence programme based on rapid dispersal of combat aircraft to forward roadside bases. Saab's fearsome Draken, or Dragon, is designed to take off from such impromptu forward dispersal bases and to intercept hostile targets at speeds in excess of Mach 2.

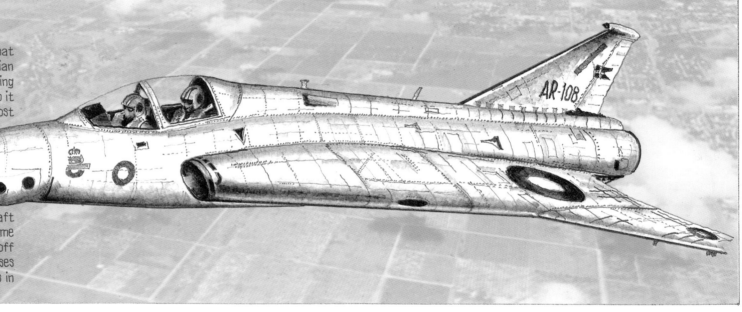

Saab Viggen

FF 1967 Sweden

Sweden's air forces have always pursued a novel and independent procurement policy fostering the development of their own national aircraft which are each designed to operate off tiny 500m airstrips and roadways. The Viggen was designed to meet these requirements and has fulfilled the role of tactical fighter from the time of its introduction in 1967 right up to the present day. The Viggen is a potent and sophisticated weapons platform.

Scaled Composites Pond Racer

FF 1990 USA

Bob Pond commissioned Burt Rutan to create a new unlimited-class racing aircraft for competition pylon racing. The development of such an aircraft would, in theory, demonstrate the advantages of new over old and, in so doing, would save countless Second World War warbirds from destruction at the hands of the racing fraternity. In 1991 Rutan's extraordinary Model 158 Pond Racer participated in the Reno air races for the first time. The following year it returned to Reno and came second in its class. In 1993, however, disaster struck when a fire in one of its 1,000hp Electromotive automobile engines led to the tragic loss of the prototype airframe and its experienced pilot, Rick Brickert, ending the Pond Racer project.

Saunders Roe SARO SR-A/1

FF 1947 UK

The war in the Pacific had illustrated, if anything, that a fast fighter which could operate off water would be an invaluable asset, particularly in the Pacific theatre where superiority in the air had to be won without the benefit of hard runways. Thus it was in 1944 that Britain issued a specification for a single-seat twin-engine jet fighter which could operate off water. Under the leadership of Henry Knowler the Saunders Roe SR-A/1 began to take shape, and its first flight was achieved in July 1947. Although the 3 prototypes performed well in trials the rapid development of land planes rendered them quickly obsolete.

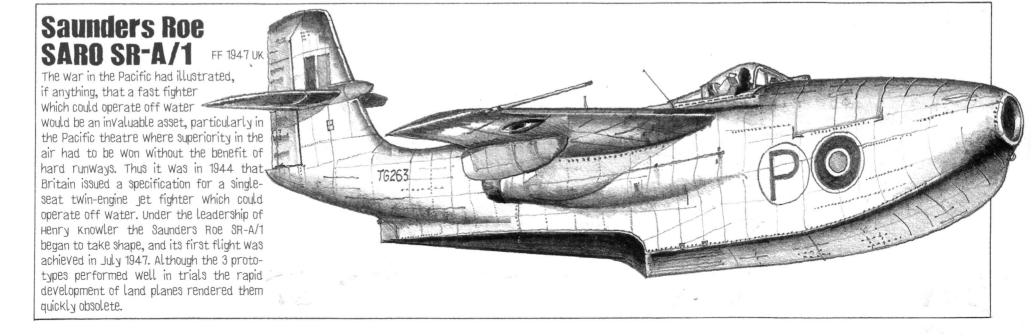

Saunders Roe AOP-12 Skeeter

FF 1948 UK

Tiny but full of character, this Saunders Roe product began its life with Cierva Autogyro Co.

Scottish Aviation Jetstream T2

FF 1967 UK

The Jetstream was developed initially by Handley Page as the HP-137, and a number of the type entered commercial operational service under that designation. Sales of the type were brisk and substantial numbers of Jetstreams continued to be built under the Scottish Aviation title. Eventually the Jetstream became a British Aerospace product and the type was much modified and improved to maintain its attractiveness within the marketplace. The Royal Navy T1 and T2 turboprop variants are still used to train specialized Navy radar technicians in the detection of maritime and sub-maritime threats.

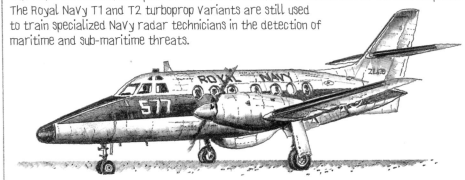

Scaled Composites Proteus

FF 1998 USA

Like Blohm & Voss's designs of the 1940s, Burt Rutan's are always eccentric, always ground-breaking, and usually weird and wonderful in configuration. Rutan, of course has the multiple advantages of modern lightweight composite materials, powerful jet engines, and new aerodynamic computing models with which to develop and refine his designs. All of these essential components, combined with Rutan's own brand of eccentric lateral thinking, have brought a wide array of superb aircraft which have redefined aeronautical thinking. His Halo-Proteus high-altitude communications platform has an interchangeable mid-section plug, designed to carry specialized communications and research equipment.

Scaled Composites Space Ship One

FF 2004 USA

Burt Rutan seems to have no boundaries when it comes to designing configurations for new prototype projects. Scaled Composites Inc., his very own private Skunk Works, has been established as an outlet for his unique brand of lateral aeronautical thinking and to develop and build his many flying prototypes. His latest ventures have been into space with the development of Space Ship One and its amazing mothership, The White Knight. With a budget of just over 10 million dollars, Rutan has opened the doors to private space travel and done what NASA spent billions doing.

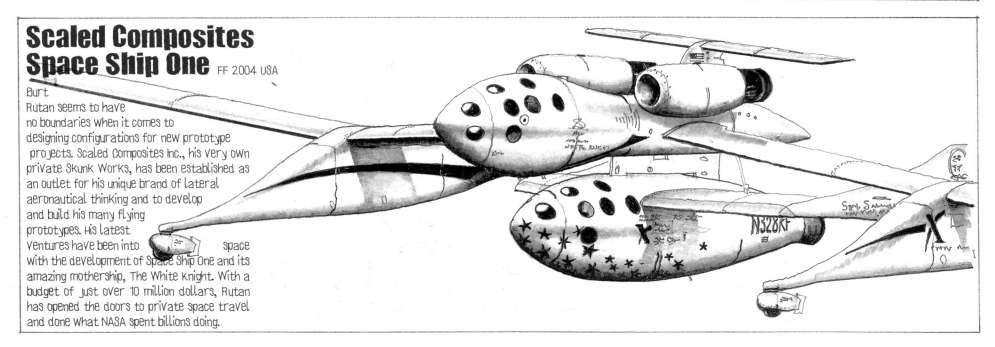

Schweizer BD-2 Phoenix
FF 1967 USA

For many years the infamous Jim Bede had been experimenting with the control and manipulation of wing boundary layers. In order to expand and verify his theories he built the high-altitude BD-2 research prototype, a heavily modified production Schweizer with removable undercarriage, revised wingtips, and a massive network of wing-mounted fuel cells which brought fuel capacity up to 575 gallons. Bede's creation behaved well at all altitudes and he went on to collect the required high altitude data. In 1969 he flew his BD-2 into the record books with a maximum endurance flight of 70.6 hours and a maximum distance record of 9,731 miles.

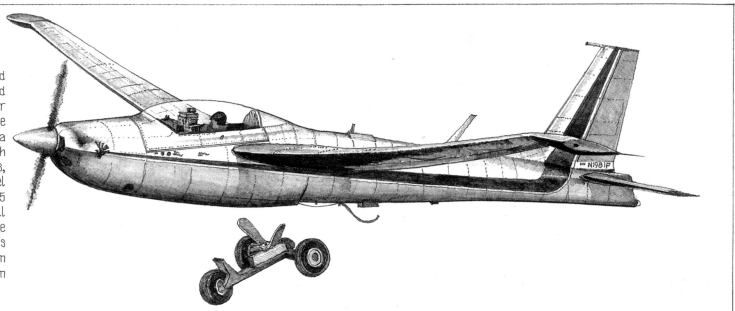

Schweizer 330 Sky Knight
FF 1988 USA

Schweizer, well known for its production of excellent gliders, closed a deal with McDonnell Douglas to allow it to manufacture the well-established Hughes 300 helicopter. After 4 years of producing the original 300 model, Schweizer announced a new turbine model with an improved airframe and avionics suite. The new 330 model would be aimed at entirely new and better-financed markets including law enforcement, border patrol and personal executive transport. Since certification in 1992 the 330 has performed well in the marketplace and a new-improved 330P model was announced in 1997. The SP will have an enlarged rotor hub and new composite parts.

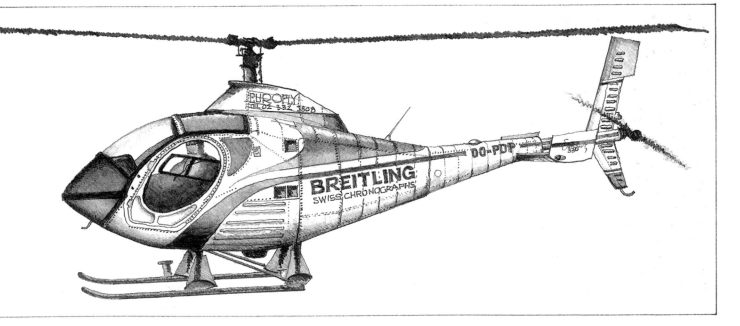

Shavrov Sh-2 Amphibian

FF 1930 USSR
Vadim Shavrov's Sh-2 amphibian remained in service for 34 years after its 1930 launch. Basic in form but robust and durable, the Sh-2 provided an ideal maritime patrol platform and utility transport for remote lakeside and coastal areas of the Soviet Union. With its exposed cockpit and its ponderous airspeed, flying the Sh-2 must have been a daunting experience in the freezing winter months.

Short Brothers S-10 Gurnard

FF 1929 UK

The Gurnard began life on the drawing boards of Short Brothers (Rochester and Bedford) Ltd, where the airframe was designed around the 525hp Rolls-Royce Kestrel 12-cylinder water-cooled engine. The S-10 was a capable and proficient performer, agile and forgiving, and fast by 1928 standards, with a max speed of 166mph. The type was well armed with one forward-facing Vickers machine gun firing through the arc of the propeller and a second observer-operated gimbal-mounted Lewis gun covering all other angles. The Gurnard served at home and abroad, usually in taildragger format but also at times in floatplane configuration.

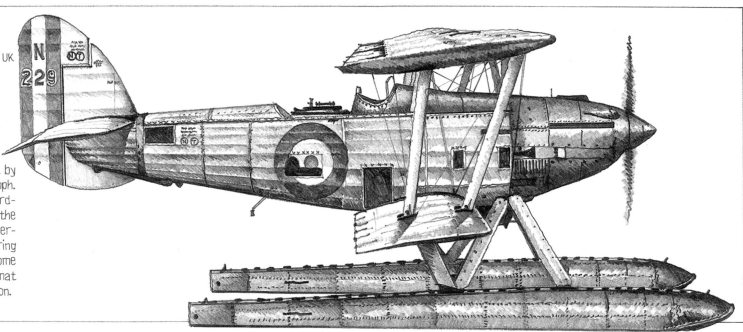

Shin Meiwa PS-1 & US-1

FF 1967 Japan

Developed for the Japanese Maritime Self-Defense Force (JMSDF) the PS-1 seaplane provides a valuable long-range anti-submarine patrol platform for this sea-bound nation. It first flew in 1967 and this was followed by a production run of 24 units. Production PS-1s carry sophisticated computing and radar-sensing equipment as well as a variety of internal and external armaments. The fully amphibious US-1 provided a very long-range Search-and-Rescue capability. This variant first flew in 1974 and approximately 10 units of the type were completed. The exceptionally low take-off and landing speeds of the US-1 provide it with a remarkable STOL capability. Careful control of the wing boundary layer, as well as outsize flaps, make these very low airspeeds possible. With its Ishikawajima-built General Electric T64-IHI-10 turboprops each producing a hefty 3,400hp, the PS-1's maximum speed is 318mph (511km/h) and its range is 2,370 miles (3,814km). The prototype PS-1 aircraft has since been converted to provide the Japanese National Fire Agency with a water-bomber test bed.

Short Solent III

FF 1946 UK

The Short Solent was developed from the Seaford which, in turn, was developed from the great Sunderland flying boat of 1937. BOAC ordered 12 Solents for its long-range overseas routes. Carrying 30 passengers and a crew of 7, the BOAC Solents reached out to the furthest corners of the world. In 1950, however, BOAC ended all of its flying-boat services and the Solents went into storage. The great flying-boat days were over for ever and the Solents went on to much more uncertain and rudimentary careers operating small charter and freight routes in some of of the more remote and underdeveloped parts of the world.

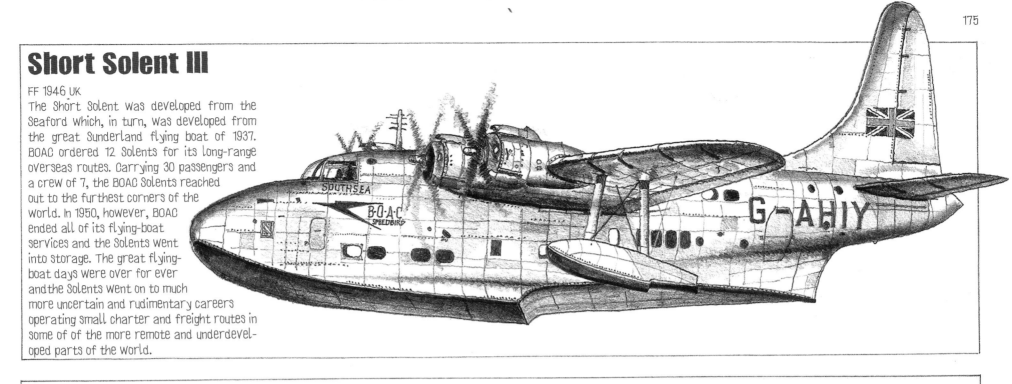

Short SC-1 VTOL

FF 1957/58 UK

By the mid-1950s the aerodynamic challenges of VTOL flight were being investigated in many countries and by many of the larger aircraft manufacturers. In Britain the government invited submissions for a VTOL test bed airframe and both Avro and Short tendered outline plans. After lengthy deliberation Short's SC-1 VTOL was selected and development of the design proceeded. The SC-1 was provided with 4 fuselage-mounted RB108 powerplants to provide the necessary lift while forward propulsion was provided by a fifth RB108. The type first flew in winged format in 1957 and graduated to hover and transitional flight the following year. The SC-1 became the inspiration for the Harrier jump jet series.

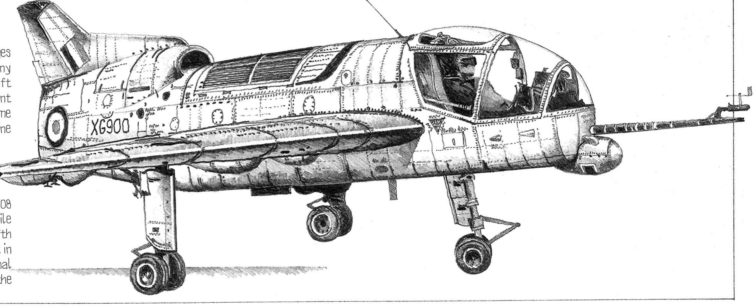

Short 360

FF 1981
UK/Northern Ireland

Northern Ireland-based Short Brothers Ltd developed the Short 360 from its earlier Short 330 utility transport. The stretched 36-seater was an immediate success with regional carriers and quickly carved a niche in the market that stretched all the way from the Americas to the Far East.

Unsympathetically dubbed the 'Vomit Comet' by some, the 360 was prone to turbulence with its large wing area and its slow cruise speed. Production continued up until 1991, by which time some 164 had been delivered. G-DAAS, the subject of this sketch, served with Channel Island-based Aurigny Airlines.

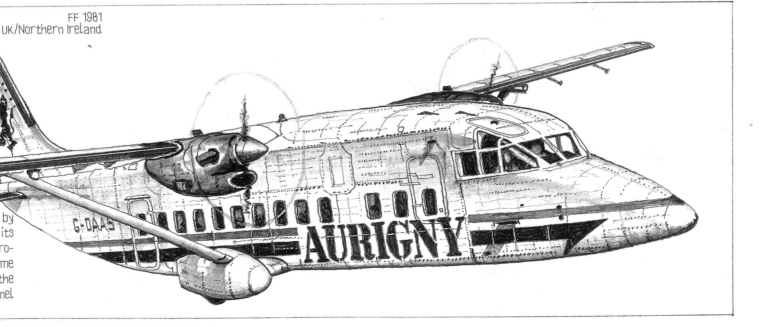

Short 360 Commuter

FF 1981 UK

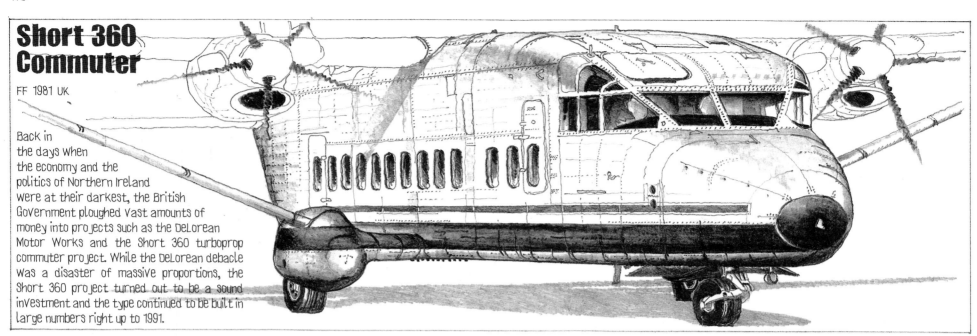

Back in the days when the economy and the politics of Northern Ireland were at their darkest, the British Government ploughed vast amounts of money into projects such as the DeLorean Motor Works and the Short 360 turboprop commuter project. While the DeLorean debacle was a disaster of massive proportions, the Short 360 project turned out to be a sound investment and the type continued to be built in large numbers right up to 1991.

FF 1946 UK

Short TT-2 Sturgeon

A carrier-based reconnaissance bomber and, in later years, a carrier-based tug.

Sikorsky R-4 Helicopter

FF 1942 USA

The first truly serviceable helicopter and the first to be put into full series production, the R-4 changed the course and the pace of helicopter development for ever. By 1943 the US War Shipping Administration was already carrying out ship-landing trials.

SIAI (Agusta) Marchetti SF-260

FF 1964 Italy

Designed in the early 1960s by Stelio Frati, the SF-260 began life as a civilian sport and touring aircraft. Known because of its performance and its perfect Italian detailing as 'The Ferrari of the Skies', the type was soon being ordered by air forces around the world as a training and ground-attack aircraft. Frati's design employed a 260hp (194kW) Lycoming O-540 engine with a constant-speed propeller to give a maximum level speed of 189mph (304km/h) and a range of 684 miles (1,100km). More than 1,000 of the type were completed and a turbocharged advanced-training version is now being manufactured.

Sikorsky S-38B

FF 1924 USA

Igor Sikorsky's S-38 of 1924 was an extraordinary affair, with struts, booms, braces, outrigger floats and heavy influences of naval architecture. It was a superb performer, however, and it attracted the interest of Juan Trippe and Pan Am. Trippe bought 38 of the type and so began some of the greatest adventures in the evolution of aviation with pioneering flights deep into South America and the formation of new mail and passenger services to Panama and Central America.

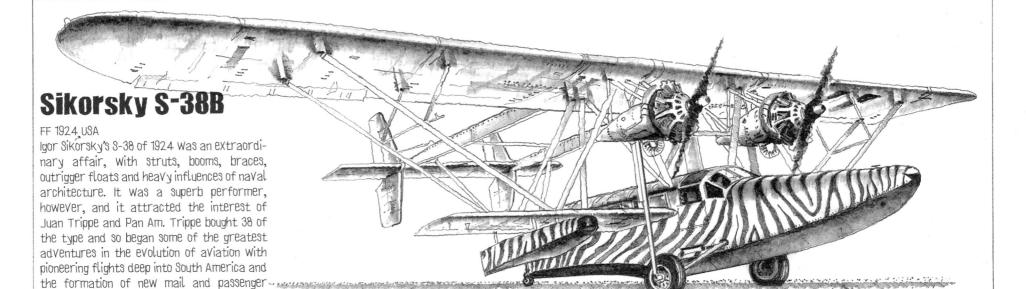

Sikorsky S-39

FF 1929 USA

Igor Sikorsky's wonderful S-39 amphibian could be bought for $20,000 in 1930, a vast sum of money at that time. But it was worth it. This was the plaything of the rich and famous, and the S-39 established many records, including being the first aircraft to be mounted on a private yacht. The S-39 was so stable in the air that test pilot Boris Sergievsky was happy to loop it on its first flight. The type soon became one of the icons of the 1930s.

Sikorsky S-51 FF 1946 USA
Westland Dragonfly

The first practical helicopters appeared at the very end of the Second World War. While both Britain and Germany did use small numbers of autogyros for gunnery observation duties, the helicopter was still at a tentative stage and its usage in active combat situations was very limited. Perhaps the nearest contenders were the technically advanced German Flettner Fl-282 Kolibri helicopter, which saw active service in the Mediterranean theatre, and the American Sikorsky YR-4 helicopter, which carried out the first successful medevac operation in the Burma theatre. It was from this fledgling background that the S-51 emerged in 1946 and it immediately presented an immensely serviceable and effective helicopter platform.

Sikorsky MH-60G Pave Hawk

FF 1974 USA

Operated by the USAF's Special Operations Command, the MH-60 Pave Hawk was designed for special infiltration missions and for the resupply of special-operations placements in all conditions and in all environments. The type was used extensively during Operation Desert Storm, where it provided combat recovery and Search-and-Rescue support to coalition air forces in Iraq, Kuwait and Saudi Arabia. The Pave Hawk crew comprises pilot, co-pilot, flight engineer and 2 paramedic winch operators. Drops and hoist extractions can be made from an altitude of 200ft above ground and up to 3 laden troops can be lifted at one time if required.

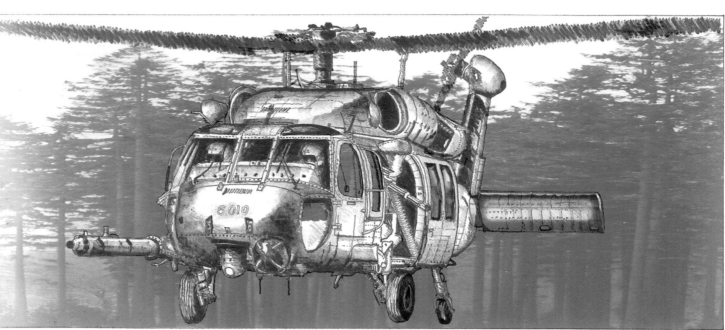

Sikorsky CH-54 Skycrane Tarhe

FF 1962 USA

Sikorsky's heavy-lift flying-crane was designed to provide the US with a specialized military lifting capability. Employing a cleverly designed system of standard interchangeable pods, the Tarhe is capable of carrying 45 fully equipped battle troops, or 24 stretchers or up to 20,000lb (9,070kg) of freight. Pods of standard dimension can be fitted out as communications or command posts or, indeed, as surgical units. Other pods are designed to accommodate minelaying and the bulk carriage of missiles. A platform pod unit can be attached to carry military vehicles and other pieces of tracked field equipment, and slung loads can be suspended where required. 6 of the CH-54B were ordered by the US Army in 1968, as well as 80 examples of the more powerful CH-54C. The S-64E and later S-64F provided a commercial equivalent for specialized civilian applications. With its 2 Pratt & Whitney JFTD-12-4A turboshaft engines the Skycrane has a maximum cruise speed of 126mph (203km/h) and a range of 230 miles (370km). In recent times several CH-64s have been fitted with a specialist firebombing pod which is capable of delivering very large volumes of water or dispersant as required.

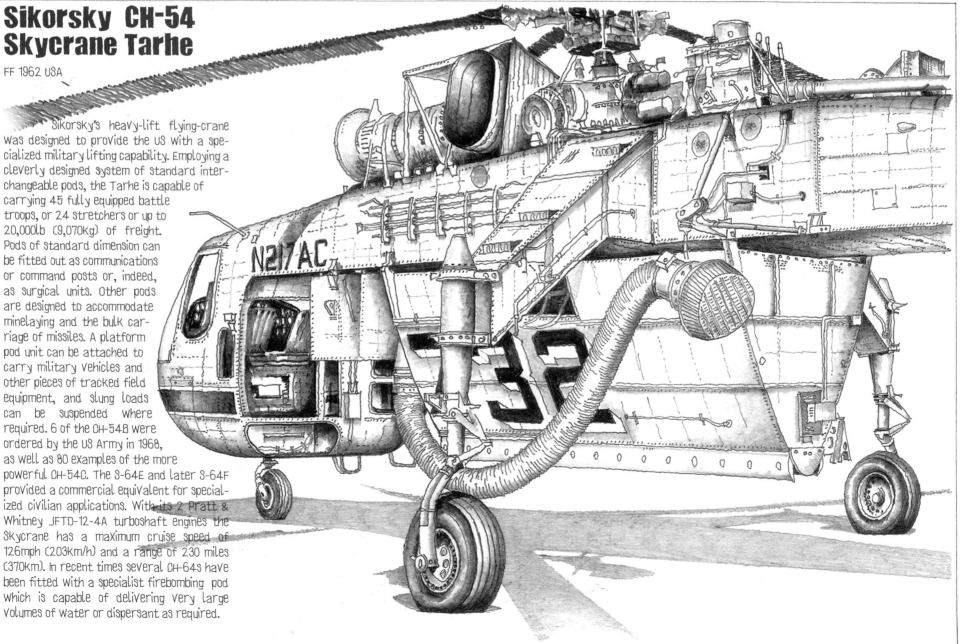

Sikorsky VH-60N White Hawk

FF 1974 USA

This Sikorsky VH-60N White Hawk helicopter is 1 of 10 airframes which are dedicated to facilitating the safe and timely transport of the US president. While the airframe is clearly based on the Sikorsky Hawk series, the exact specifications of the communications system and the defensive countermeasures systems are not clear. The VH-60N adopts the call sign 'Marine One' when the president is being carried aboard.

Sikorsky S-65

FF 1964 USA

The Sea Stallion heavy-lift assault helicopter first flew in 1964. Capable of carrying up to 44 fully equipped troops in a high-density arrangement, the type is provided with a rear loading ramp for rapid dissipation and for larger loads. Vehicles, field guns or freight can be carried. A load of up to 18 tons can be carried externally. Variants include the CH-53A heavy assault transport used by the USMC, the HH-53 used by the USAF, and the S-6 minesweeping patrol variant designated RH-530 by the US Navy. Its maximum speed is 196mph (315km/h) and range is 540 miles (864km).

Sikorsky S-70/UH-60A Black Hawk
FF 1974 USA

The S-70 Black Hawk, Winner of the US Army's utility tactical transport competition, has been delivered in very large numbers to the US Army, Navy, and Air Force as well as to the RAAF and to China. S-70 Variants include the S-70 Black Hawk assault transport designated UH-60A by the US Army, and the similar SH-60B Version of the US Navy. The HH-60A Night Hawk combat rescue Variant, meanwhile, was developed to meet the requirements of the US Air Force. A further specialist derivative of the type is the MH-60K which was designed for special mission operations and is complete with uprated powerplants, heavier armaments and a host of electronic countermeasures.

Sikorsky S-61N
FF 1959 USA

Well, I know the interior of the S-61 at first hand, as it once rescued me after the engine of the Piper PA-28 I was flying suddenly stopped in mid-flight. In truth, rescue is probably too dramatic a term for the event but the giant red-and-white helicopter was a most welcome sight as it hovered overhead and it certainly did save a long, long walk back to Waterford Airport. This minor mishap was, of course, a walk in the park for a helicopter designed to undertake Search-and-Rescue missions in the most unimaginable weather conditions at distances of up to 220 miles offshore. The S-61N was developed from the military Sea King of 1959 and in developing its civilian equivalents, the S-61L and S-61N, Sikorsky targeted oil rig resupply, airline logistical support and the delivery of humanitarian aid. The provision of long-range Search-and-Rescue coverage by specialist operators, too, became a major growth area with military SAR services being replaced in many places by more cost-effective civilian operations. For this growing market group Sikorsky's float-equipped S-61N has become the industry norm. Rugged, reliable, and with a superb service record, the S-61N is trusted by its crews and operators alike. On a typical mission the S-61N is operated by a flight crew of 2 as well as a Winchman and medevac specialists. Up to 30 passengers can be carried, although most of the type are provided with little in the way of fixed seating, while a large centre floor mattress allows for emergency medical care to be administered quickly to injured or hypothermic patients.

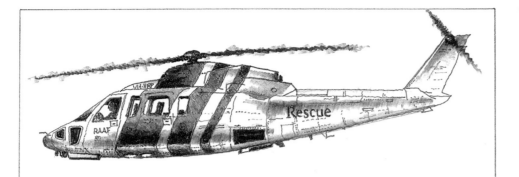

Sikorsky S-76

FF 1977 USA

Sikorsky's S-76 corporate and general utility helicopter has been tailored to meet a wide range of specialist mission duties from oil rig support to Search-and-Rescue platform. The S-76, with its clean lines and its fully retractable undercarriage, cruises at up to 167mph (268 km/h). Its range with 12 laden oil rig workers on board is 410 miles (656km).

SAI KZ VIII

FF 1949 Denmark

Danish showman Sylvest Jensen commissioned the KZ VIII aerobatic sport-plane for his Air Circus, which flew all over Denmark in the summer months of 1950, giving in all no less than 50 air shows. The aircraft was flown during many of these air shows by Peter Steen, who had flown fighters with the RAF during the war years.

SAI KZ II Trainer

FF 1937 Denmark

Danish engineers Viggo Kramme and Karl Zeuthen founded Skandinavisk Aero Industri (SAI) and went on to design the KZ series of aircraft. The 2 designers produced a broad range of single and twin designs specializing in military flight training, gliding training, air-ambulance work and artillery observation. These were simple, attractive, rugged designs and, indeed, several examples of their works are still flying to this day. The open-cockpit KZ II trainer was adapted as the standard primary trainer for the Danish air force and it remained in service in that role until 1955 when the 9 air-frames which were still airworthy were sold into private ownership.

Solar Challenger

FF 1980 USA

The name of Dr Paul McCready has become synonymous over the years with

advances in environmentally efficient systems for travel and high-altitude research. His extraordinary Solar Challenger of 1980 set an altitude record of 14,300ft, an amazing achievement for a solar-powered aircraft. The Solar Challenger later crossed the English Channel in a 163-mile flight that saw the aircraft fly non-stop for 5 hours and 23 minutes. McCready would later break his own record when his 1995 solar-powered 'Pathfinder' would reach an altitude of 50,500ft.

Spartan 7W Executive

FF 1936 USA

The Spartan's glistening polished aluminium contours and its orderly rows of rivets give a rare insight into the early days of executive flying, when vast amounts of labour, skill and care were lavished on these exotic aircraft for the few pilots and oil executives who were wealthy enough to fly them. The Executive was a 5-seat all-metal monoplane which, in 1937, could be yours for $23,500, a vast sum by any standards. The type heralded a new level of style and comfort for executive and personal transports with its lined interior and plush leather seating. Spartan's legendary 200mph Executive was as comfortable and opulent as any of the great limousines of its day.

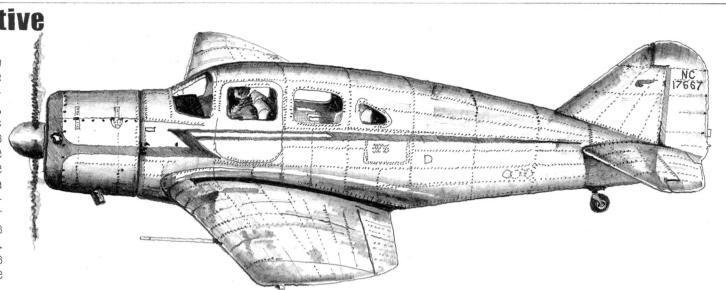

Stearman Hammond

FF 1936 USA

One of my favourite sketches and aeroplanes, Dean Hammond's wonderful Stearman Hammond was inspired by the 1934 'flivver' competition sponsored by the US Bureau of Air Commerce. Hammond's submission was selected as joint winner of this award and the Bureau ordered 15. This was to be the Volkswagen of the air, the plane that motorists could fly and every household could afford. Despite his best efforts and those of Lloyd Stearman, the aircraft's selling price could not be reduced below $3,000 and few orders were placed.

Stits Sky Baby

FF 1952 USA

The mantle of 'World's Smallest Aircraft' has changed hands many times over the years as designers and trivia fanatics competed to push the boundaries of miniature aircraft design ever further. The Wee Bee and the Stitts Junior were sub-miniature monoplanes which each held the title in their time. Designer Robert Starr, however, went one better. He designed the tiny Sky Baby which, because of its biplane configuration, was able to have its wingspan reduced to an incredible 7 foot (2.1m). From April to November of 1952 Starr flew his tiny wonder at air shows and public events before donating it to the National Air and Space Museum. Starr went on to build an even smaller aircraft, the 180mph Bumble Bee with its 5ft-5inch span.

Stout Amphibian

FF 1927 USA

William Stout was one of the fascinating characters of early aviation in the US. As a boy he
had followed the plans published in the popular
Youth's Companion and had been fascinated
when his model gliders actually flew. He was
hooked. Finishing his engineering studies he
became heavily involved
in the crackpot world of would-be
flyers. In 1907 Stout delivered a public
lecture on flight and displayed models
and lantern slides borrowed from that
great agony uncle of aviation, Octave Chanute.
Stout went on to start up his own aircraft
factory, where he built his own flying
machines. Although half blind he was a prolific
craftsman and, between projects, he crafted
all the furniture for his own house. He eventually sold out to Henry Ford.

Supermarine
Spitfire T-9

FF 1936 UK

The Spitfire is as much a part of the culture
and identity of the British Isles as the Houses
of Parliament or the London Bus. This is the
aircraft that saved the day back in summer
1940 when the Luftwaffe began the battle to
win aerial supremacy in preparation for Operation Sealion, the invasion of Britain. Hitler's
blitzkrieg tactics had overwhelmed Europe so
rapidly that few believed Britain would be
able to hold out for long. The Royal Air Force,
too, had lost substantial portions of its fighters in the many fierce battles over France
and the Low Countries. This was a time of

great national peril, Britain's
darkest hour. From June through to November
fierce air battles raged over the South of
England and heroes and victims alike fell to
chance and fate. It was in these days of great
danger that the inimitable spirit of the Spitfire became for ever bound into the history
and the psyche of the British people.

Supermarine 535 Swift
FF 1952 UK

The short flying career of Britain's first fully swept-wing fighter was tarnished by an ongoing series of handling difficulties and powerplant problems. The Swift was rushed into service, being presented for operational use while still under severe speed and service-ceiling restrictions. After a series of handling accidents the type was temporarily grounded on more than one occasion in late 1954.

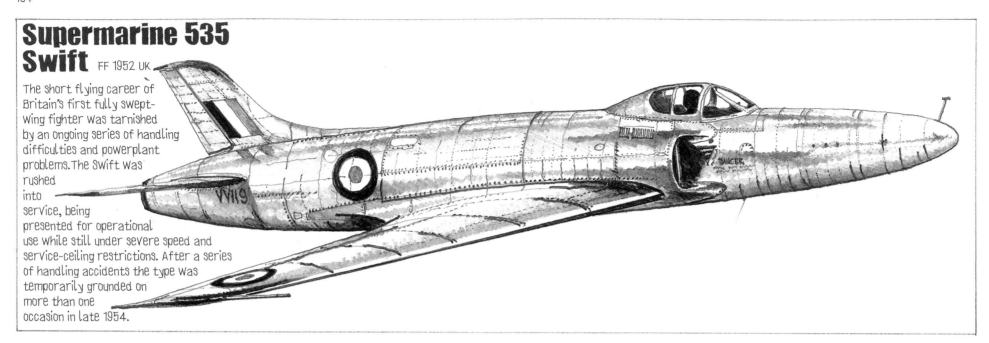

Supermarine Scimitar F-1

FF 1956 UK

From 1958 to 1966 the Supermarine Scimitar was the Fleet Air Arm's main heavy fighter bomber operating off the aircraft carriers HMS Ark Royal, Hermes, Eagle, Victorious and Centaur. Infamous for being difficult and unforgiving in the air and for weeping fuel across the carrier decks, the Scimitar was very much a stop-gap aircraft for the Royal Navy. Without radar and with poor flight endurance the type was retired from carrier-borne operations in 1966.

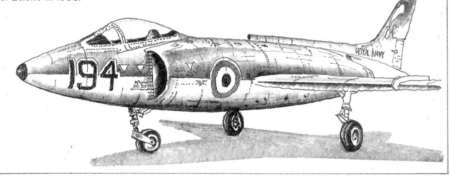

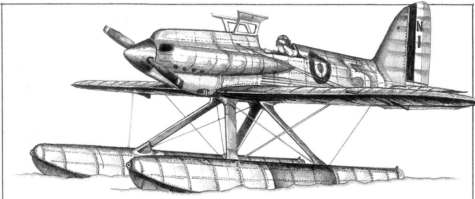

Supermarine S-5

FF 1926 UK

The international Schneider Trophy competition was one of the most important and most influential of all aviation events. Fostering the design of better aircraft, more compact engines and higher speeds, the Schneider Cup would help to shape aviation into the future. In 1927 Supermarine's S-5 swept the board with 1st- and 2nd-place wins.

Supermarine Stranraer
FF 1934 UK/Canada

A long-range reconnaissance and bomber, the Stranraer flying boat appeared in the twilight years of the great floatplane movement. With its 2 875hp (652kW) Bristol Pegasus X radial engines the Stranraer has a maximum level speed of 165mph (266km/h), a respectable pace for such a weighty and draggy flying machine. The type was designed to fly long endurance coastal patrol missions and the 28 Stranraers built in Britain and Canada served the Royal Air Force and the Royal Canadian Air Force in many parts of the world.

Swearingen SX-300 FF 1984 USA

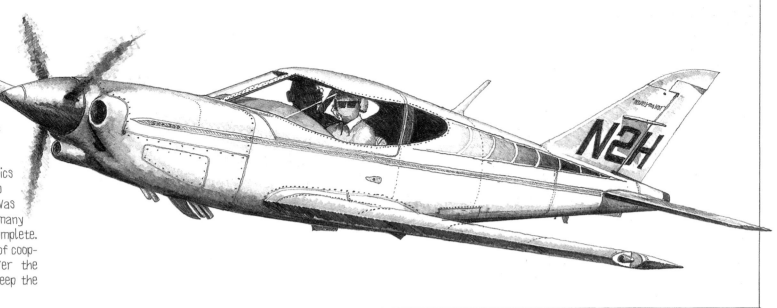

Ed Swearingen's superb SX-300 high-performance personal transport was marketed to amateur builders between 1984 and 1989. This was the very top end of the kitbuild market with the promise of cruising at 209mph with retractable undercarriage and sophisticated avionics suites. Indeed, the SX-300 was a superb performer although its manufacture was so complex and labour-intensive that many of the original kitbuilders failed to complete. SX-300 builders have set up a number of cooperative build-assist programmes over the years to share knowledge and to keep the fleet flying.

Supermarine Walrus FF 1933 UK

Over 700 of the Walrus, or 'Shagbat', were built by Supermarine as naval reconnaissance aircraft for coastal patrol work or for launch by catapult from battleships and cruisers. After 1942, small numbers of Walrus amphibians were fitted with ASV Mark 2 radar sets and used as catapult observation platforms for fleet protection and submarine spotting. It is in the Search-and-Rescue role, however, that the Walrus is best remembered by the numerous water-treading air crews who were plucked bodily from the sea.

Thomas Morse Scout

FF 1917 USA

William Thomas was a young Englishman who emigrated to the USA to work with the fledgling Glenn Curtiss Aircraft Company. By 1910, Morse's apprenticeship was complete and with his brother Oliver he founded Thomas Aircraft. By 1917 it had merged with the Morse Chain company and the legendary Thomas Morse Scout made its debut. The 'Tommie' trainer was greatly loved by tutors and students alike and, after the war, large numbers of the type were released for sale to flying schools, sports pilots, and ex-army pilots. There are several beautifully maintained Scouts flying to this day.

Molt Taylor's Taylor Aerocar

FF 1949 USA

Molt Taylor's wonderful 'Aerocar' is one of the great icons of 1950s America. These were the beginnings of days of plenty when households were being offered every manner of consumable from swimming pools to microwaves and over-the-top automobiles. It was in this environment that Molt Taylor introduced his Aerocar. At last the skies would be opened up to the ordinary American. The Taylor Aerocar did, indeed, resolve many of the problems which had beset flying automobiles in the past. It behaved superbly in the air and landed with ease. It could be turned from aircraft to car in 3 minutes and, although light compared with other American cars, it drove well on the road. After receiving CAA type approval Taylor became well

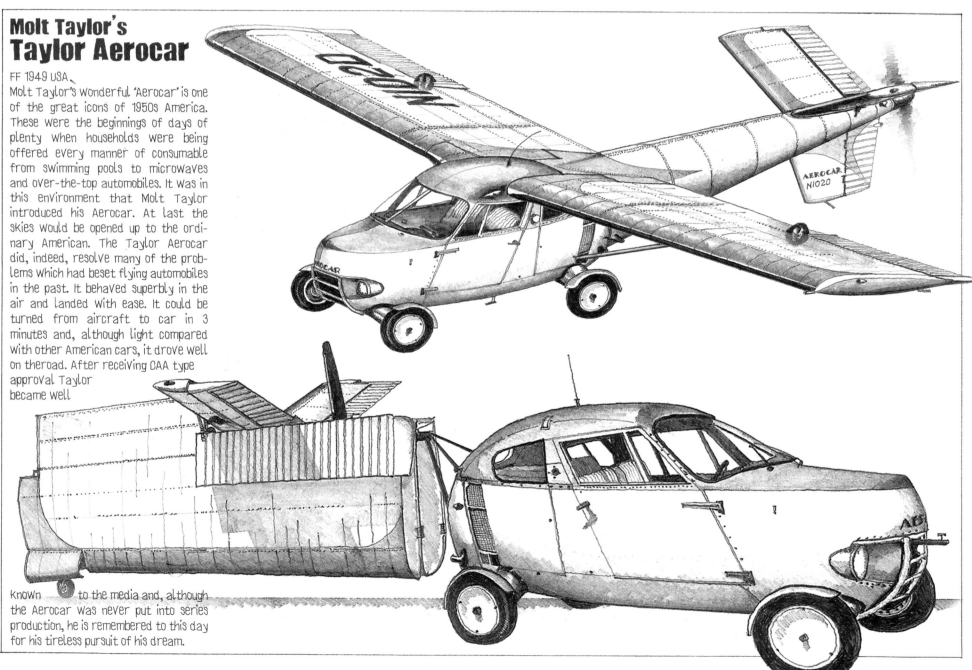

known to the media and, although the Aerocar was never put into series production, he is remembered to this day for his tireless pursuit of his dream.

Thorp T-18

FF 1964 USA

Don Taylor's 1976 circumnavigation of the globe in his tiny home-built Thorp T-18 caught the world's imagination. Retired Air Force pilot Taylor had constructed the aircraft from scratch in his garage before setting out on his 24,625-mile journey into the record books. On completion of his epic journey Taylor became the first pilot to fly a home-built aircraft around the globe. But he was only getting warmed up. In 1980 he flew his T-18 to Australia and New Zealand flying a record 19,000 miles over open Pacific waters. Later, in 1983 Taylor flew his long-suffering aircraft north into the Arctic wilderness to the very top of the world, the North Pole.

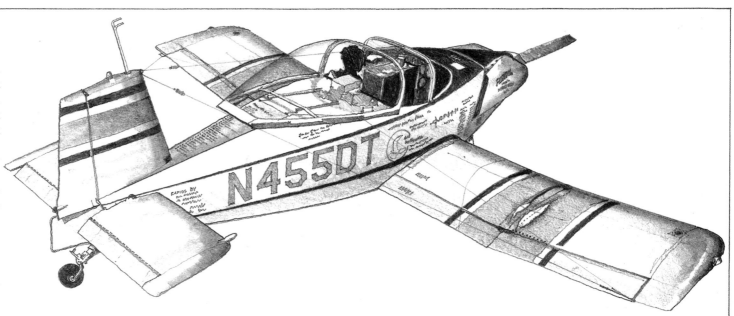

Tipsy Nipper T-66

FF 1957 Belgium

In 1952 Ernest Tips, citizen of Belgium and managing director of Avions Fairey SA, set about developing an aircraft which he hoped would set new levels of simplicity in terms of ease of construction and controllability in flight. Over the course of 1952 his tiny Tipsy Nipper took shape and quickly won a unique position in aviation as one of the most eccentric and capable aircraft of all time. Avions Fairey delivered 59 of the type before production was stopped to allow them assemble F-104 Starfighters for the Belgian air force. Graduating from Nippers to Starfighters must have been pretty interesting.

Turbine Legend

FF 1996 USA

For a paltry $120,000 Legend Aircraft Inc. will send you the materials package for its incredible Turbine Legend kitbuild airframe. To purchase the second half of the project, the turboprop powerplant and avionics, could easily set you back the same again. But an aircraft with a cruise speed of 300mph at 25,000ft is no ordinary kit plane. With prop-fighter performance and the very latest in airframe technology, the Turbine Legend breaks new ground for the home-build sector. New miniature jet engines, now appearing in the marketplace may bring further change.

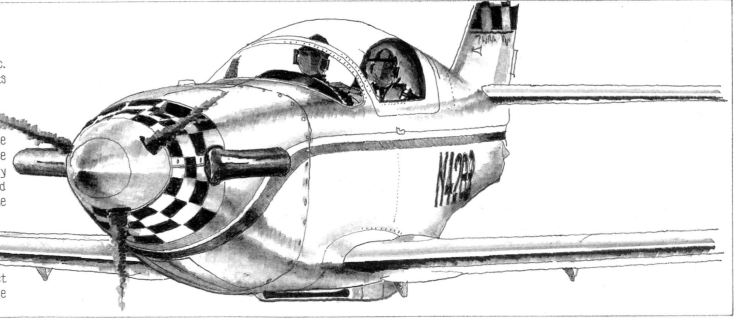

Tupolev Tu-154 Careless

FF 1968 USSR

A Soviet medium-haul T-tail tri-jet, similar in configuration to the West's Tristar, DC-9 or Boeing 727. Its landing gear is designed around a heavy-duty 6-wheel bogie main under-carriage, which makes it suitable for rough short-field operations. The type entered service with Aeroflot in 1972 and has since been widely exported to many countries. The Tu-154 seats 154 to 180 passengers and continues in service today.

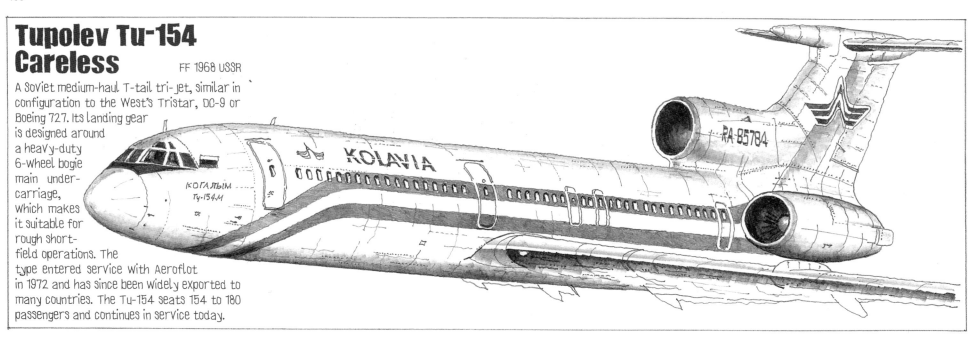

Tupolev Tu-4 FF 1947 USSR

In the last years of the Second World War the Soviets, who were not at war with Japan, became the lucky recipients of 3 of the USA's latest B-29 bombers, each of them after diverting inadvertently to escape Japanese territory. The 3 crews were allowed to 'escape' in a carefully staged operation but the B-29s stayed behind. The type was then copied bolt by bolt to become the Tu-4. This Chinese Tu-4 is an early AEW variant.

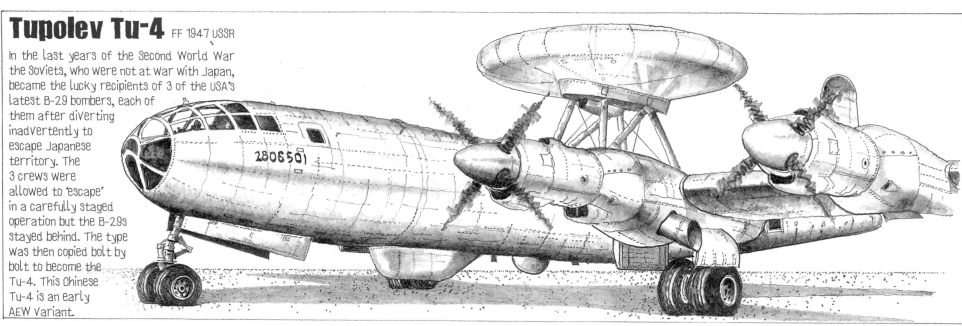

Ultravia Aero Pelican

FF 1982/1985 Canada

The Ultravia Aero Pelican uses a combination of composite fuselage and aluminium wings to produce an aircraft which is easy to build and cost effective to maintain. With the highly efficient Rotax 912S engine under the hood, the Pelican can cruise at 115mph, a respectable airspeed for any ultralight-category air-craft. The type is aimed firmly at the light plane sporting market, where prospective owner/builders can purchase kits which are up to 49% complete. In this way build time is min-imized while still allowing owners to operate their Pelicans under the EAA's more relaxed 'permit to fly' regulations. A robust, cost effective and rewarding project.

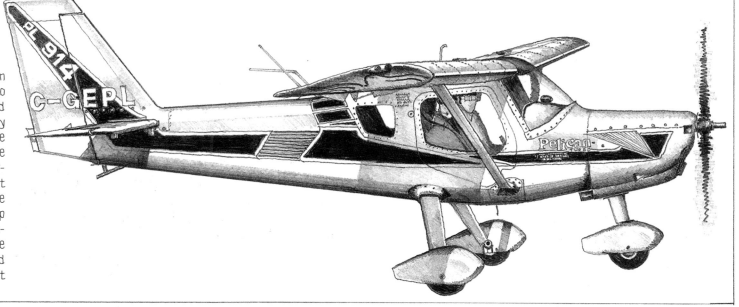

Vans RV-9A

FF 2002 USA

When you have built your own superb RV-9A from scratch you are allowed to paint on an 'over-the-top' and sentimental motif as this Florida-based owner has done. It looks great and it certainly made it interesting for me to draw. Vans Aircraft have applied computer modelling tools and sophisticated production techniques to ensure that their 'easy-build' kits can be assembled with a minimum of difficulty. All of the components are manufactured to previously unheard-of tolerances to ensure that all parts fit first time and that all jigging holes match perfectly.

Vickers Type 141 Scout

FF 1926 UK

Vickers developed the Type 141 Scout as a private speculative venture and registered it on the civilian register as G-EBNQ. The prototype was furnished with RAF roundels and Navy trial colours and submitted to the RAF and the Royal Navy for lengthy trials. Various modifications were made including the introduction of the Rolls-Royce F.X1 engine and the addition of a new carrier-landing arrester hook. In 1929 the Scout underwent protracted trials aboard HMS Furious, a light battlecruiser which had been fitted out with a hangar and a 'flying-off deck'. The trials were unsatisfactory and the Type 141 military trials were abandoned.

Vickers Varsity

FF 1949 UK

The Vickers Varsity was designed to replace the ageing fleet of Wellington T10s which were now visibly tiring after many years of intense service. Developed from the earlier Vickers Valetta, the Varsity adapted a new retractable tricycle undercarriage and an all-new under-fuselage pannier which could be used as a bomb-aimer's station. The service career of the Varsity was one of extraordinary versatility and longevity and the type remained in operational service from September 1953 to July 1992, a period of almost 39 years. It was tasked with a multitude of roles but configured firstly for the simultaneous training of pilots, flight engineers, radio navigators and bomb-aimers.

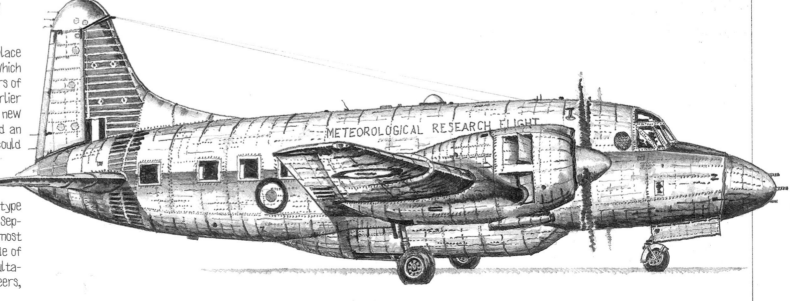

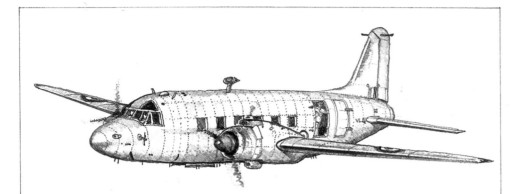

Vickers Valetta C-1

FF 1947 UK

Vickers-Armstrong Ltd built 263 of their Vickers Valetta military transport twin-engined taildraggers. With its 2 massive Bristol Hercules 230 9-cylinder radial engines each turning out 1,975hp the Valetta could cruise at 258mph over a range of 1,460 miles. The type was designed as a military transport and logistical support aircraft and was employed in many parts of the world in support of British military interests.

Vickers Viscount

FF 1948 UK

The post-war Vickers Viscount was the first turboprop airliner from any country to enter operational service. The smooth performance, seamless handling and superb reliability of the new turbine were clearly apparent to operators BEA, and the Viscount became an immediate success with airlines and passengers alike.

Vickers Vildebeest

FF 1928 UK

The Vickers Vildebeest had a service ceiling of 17,000ft, certainly an occasion for wearing extra scarves and socks. This extraordinary mammoth biplane was designed for coastal defence escort patrol, and torpedo-bombing duties. Designed to meet Royal Air Force Specification No 24/25, its range was 625 miles, giving it a very generous loiter patrol time. Successive improvements and upratings of the Bristol Pegasus radial engine led to a dramatic increase in load-bearing capacity, range and ceiling. The Vildebeest saw service as a coastal patrol platform with both the RAF and the RNZAF up to the early years of the Second World War.

Vultee Valiant
BT-13 & BT-15

FF 1939 USA

By 1939 a mounting array of international tensions led to a rapid expansion of the US Army and air forces. The pilot flight-training syllabus was standardized and the array of training aircraft was simplified and reduced to just a few selected types. Vultee's Valiant advanced trainer became the aircraft of choice for the later stages of flight training and 11,537 of the type were delivered to hastily established flight schools right across the states. Pilots honed their evasive flight manoeuvres first on the forgiving Valiant before moving on to the Texan Harvard for final training. The next stop would be a powerful frontline fighter and, indeed, war.

Vought V-173 Flying Pancake

FF 1942 USA

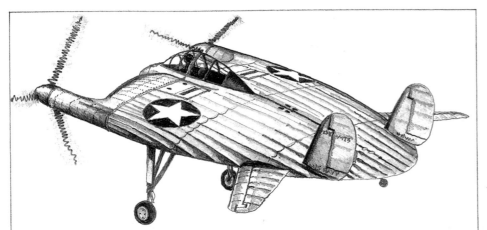

During the Second World War, new technologies and powerful engines opened up new and exciting avenues of exploration to aircraft designers. The V-173 Flying Pancake was Chance-Vought's groundbreaking exploration of the lifting body/flying wing concept.

Vought-Hiller-Ryan
XC-142A

FF 1964 USA

A VTOL convertiplane from Vought-Hiller-Ryan.

Vought A-7
Corsair II

FF 1965 USA

The A-7 Corsair was designed to provide close tactical support to ground forces and to facilitate rapid land-based advances by way of missile delivery to battle tanks and other hostile combat elements. From its first operational sorties in 1968 until its eventual retirement in 1992, the Corsair served with the US Air Force and US Navy and, indeed, with the air forces of many countries across the globe. In 1985 the Corsair was part of a joint strike operation which attacked targets in Libya in response to large-scale terrorist activity by Libyan Government-backed activists.

Vought F4U-4 Corsair

FF 1940 USA

When Chance Vought commenced design of the Corsair in 1938, Europe was in a state of upheaval, and war with the emerging Axis powers was looking ominously likely. In this environment, and with the growing threat posed by Japan in the East, the US Navy sought proposals for a new-generation carrier-borne fighter. Chance Vought's stunningly powerful Corsair was selected in this role and it went on to fight its way, island by island, across the Pacific Ocean.

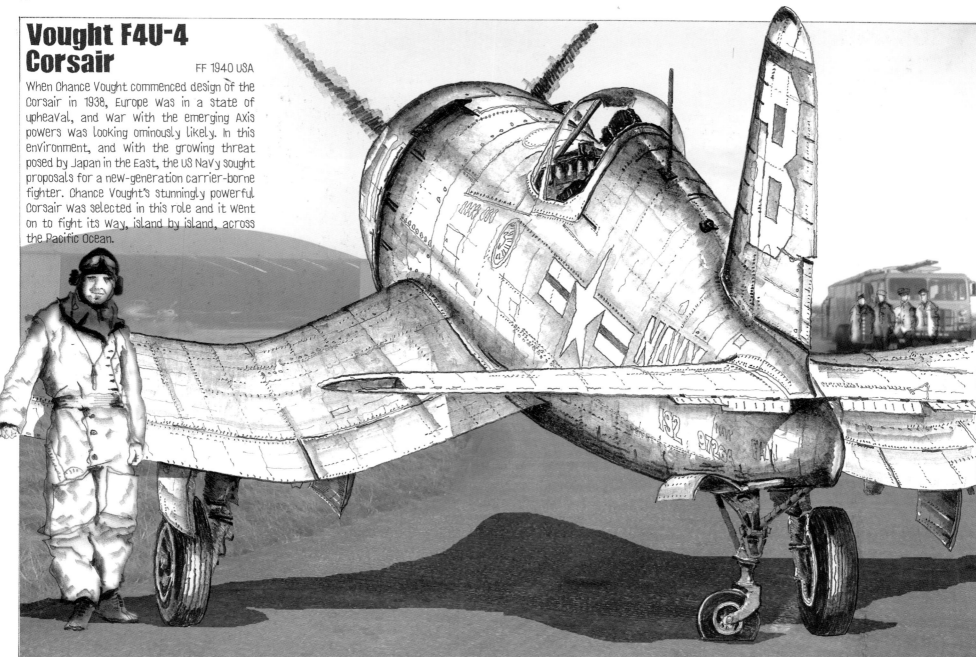

Waco CG-4A Hadrian

FF 1942 USA

Being the pilot of a Waco Hadrian during the war years was not an enviable job. If the slow-moving Hadrian was not picked off by enemy fire there was always the hazardous blind night landing to finish off the job. The 'legs up NOW' cry at the point of landing was a reference to the liklihood that the flimsy glider's bottom would collapse on landing and crush the legs of the 13 battle-ready troops behind. Other Hadrian pilots would be carrying jeeps and howitzers and their crews, and their worry was that if the glider stopped too suddenly on landing they would be run over by their own payload. The Allied forces were prepared, nonetheless, to accept such losses by its invasion forces and it ordered 13,900 of the type.

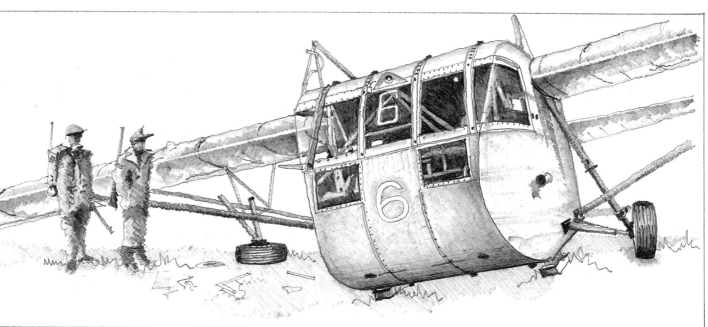

Waterman Arrowbile

FF 1937 USA

Waldo Waterman's fascination with flying cars began as far back as 1911 when he was still an associate of Glenn Curtiss. His 'Whatsit' of 1932 and his prototype Arrowplane each pointed the way to his crowning glory, the Arrowbile of 1937. This flying car came close to manufacture but the project ended when Waterman's financier died and engine supplier Studebaker got cold feet.

Watson GW-1 Windwagon

FF 1977 USA

When Gerry Watson of Newcastle, Texas flew his tiny home-designed Windwagon in 1977 he could not have anticipated the number of home-built projects it would inspire. One of the lowest-budget aircraft of all time, it was perhaps best known as the inspiration for Morry Hummel's miniature Volkswagen-powered single-seat Hummel Bird.

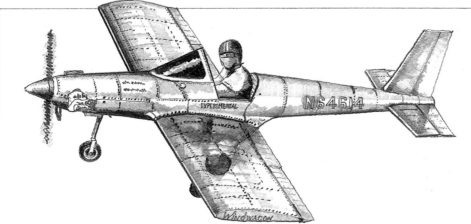

Westland Merlin EH-101

FF 1987 Italy and UK

The EH-101 Merlin is a collaborative development between Agusta SpA of Italy and GKN Westland Helicopters of Britain. The type is now manufactured in both Italy and Britain and is currently being marketed to third-party countries in both its military and civilian format.

Weick W-1

FF 1934 USA

Fred Weick was a prolific aircraft designer and self-promoter who designed many wonderful aircraft, including the 1937 Ercoupé which could be bought over the counter at Macy's department store. His 1934 Weick W-1, while not as well known as the Ercoupé, was another gem of aviation. Its system of slots and trailing-edge ailerons allowed it to take to the air in less than 120ft and to roll to a stop in less than 100ft. Weick entered his prototype design into the 1934 Bureau of Air Commerce design competition and his prototype was bought and given to Fairchild for evaluation and development. In 1938 it was scrapped after an accident.

Weir W-9 Helicopter

FF 1944 UK

Juan de la

Cierva had been associated with the Weir Company Ltd of Scotland since 1925 when they first sought his expertise. Now prompted by the successes of Sikorsky's R-4 and R-5 military helicopters, Cierva-Weir began development of the W-9, a large single-rotor helicopter. This project was most unusual by virtue of its usage of jet thrust to counteract rotor torque, a concept which has only recently been conquered in the form of the new McDonnell Douglas Notar helicopter. The W-9's jet thrust could be varied in strength to facilitate turning movements and this airflow down through the tubular fuselage boom provided much-needed cooling to the engine.

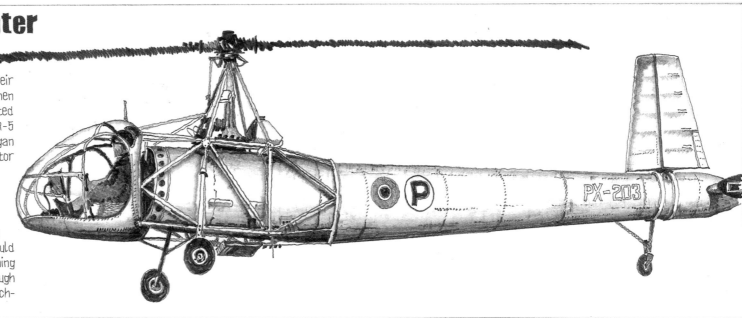

Westland Wessex HC-2

FF 1958 UK

The Wessex was a turbine-powered British development of the slightly earlier Sikorsky S-58, the Sikorsky flying for the first time in 1954 and the Wessex flying first in 1958. Developed initially as a troop carrier and ground-attack platform, the Wessex soon became the base model for a wide variety of mission specialist roles from anti-submarine duties to air-ambulance work, ship-borne troop shuttle, and even Queen's Flight. In its Search-and-Rescue role the Wessex brought salvation to many seafarers, its rounded shape and its bright yellow colouring becoming a symbol of hope to many who have been rescued at sea. The Wessex entered service in 1961 and served in all roles until its retirement in 2003.

Westland Lysander III

FF 1936 UK

The Lysander was designed by the Westland Aircraft Co., which took its name from the small Somerset Westland Farm where it began operations. The 'Lizzie' 2-seat army monoplane began service with the RAF in 1938 and, during the early years of the war, was widely used in France and North Africa. After its replacement as a frontline machine the Lysander's short take-off and landing performance caused it to be used on many occasions for inserting and extracting agents from occupied Europe. Powered by an 870hp Bristol Mercury 30 radial engine, the Lysander had a maximum speed of 229mph (369km/h) and a range of 600 miles (966km). Total production of the type, both in the UK and Canada, exceeded 1,600.

Westland AH-1 Scout

FF 1959 UK

Saunders Roe and Bristol Rotorcraft were incorporated into Westland in 1959 and so the Scout helicopter prototype, developed from the earlier SARO-P531, was designated Westland Scout AH-1. The type has served with the British Army in many parts of the world from Northern Ireland to the Falklands. A general utility and light attack helicopter, it could be quickly configured for medevac missions, anti-tank patrol, special counter-insurgency missions, and light troop deployment. The Westland Wasp was a naval variant which could be equipped with torpedos and specialized radar equipment. Its maximum speed was 131mph and range was 316 miles.

Westland Delanne Lysander

FF 1940 UK

During the Battle of France the ubiquitous 'Lizzie', or Lysander, was being shot down at an alarming rate. Of the 174 in the French theatre, more than 88 had been lost by April 1940. Something had to be done to protect it from the powerful Messerschmitts and it was decided that a heavy rear-facing gun was the answer. The proposal required substantial changes to the aircraft's centre of gravity and perhaps even an additional tandem wing. The expert was Frenchman Maurice Henri Delanne and so Westland sent their technical director and test pilot to Paris to collect vital information and to fly Delanne's own 20T prototype. In the end only one hybrid Delanne Lysander was built.

Westland-Hill Pterodactyl

FF 1925 UK

The Westland-Hill Pterodactyl V was one of a series of experimental fighter prototypes developed in Britain in the mid-1920s. Aviation, still in its infancy, was undergoing rapid advances with designers dabbling in unusual configurations. The extraordinary Pterodactyl was a radical departure from the conventional aeronautical thinking of its day. Its swept-wing, tailless design was years ahead of its time. Its wingtips pivoted to supply the forces normally provided by ailerons. Its perfectly balanced centre of gravity allowed the rear gunner's station to be positioned at the very rear of the fuselage, the optimum defensive arrangement. Although not put into production, the Pterodactyl became one of the great influences in aircraft design.

Westland Sea King

FF 1969 UK

By the late 1950s the Cold War was throwing a chill over the politics and economies of Europe and the Royal Navy began to intensify its watch over its territorial waters and those of the North Atlantic.
An all-new anti-submarine helicopter was to be developed with increased endurance, a vastly upgraded electronics suite, and a new advanced avionics package. Because the trusted Wessex was now getting older it was decided that the new platform should be based on a younger and more versatile helicopter. In 1959 Westland closed a deal with Sikorsky which allowed it to build its newly launched S-61B under licence. The new Royal Navy Sea King would combine the best of Sikorsky's design with a pair of Rolls-Royce Bristol Gnome turbine engines and the latest in radar and search technology from a range of specialist market leaders including Plessey, Marconi-Doppler and Sperry. The new Sea King flew for the first time in May 1969 and the first Royal Navy squadron was formed just 1 year later. In the interim the ageing Wessex helicopter was beginning to be retired and its role began to be filled by the Sea King. Mission-specialist airframes were developed for SAR (Search-and-Rescue), and a commando assault variant was developed for the RAF. Export derivatives were made for the navies of Pakistan, India, Australia, Norway, Belgium, Germany, and Egypt. Sea King Mark IV, the subject of this drawing, is an unusual development mock-up, being furnished with a prototype Blue Kestrel radome as part of trials for the Eurocopter EH-101 Merlin helicopter programme.

Wozniak Double Eagle

USA

In the early years of flight the majority of aircraft were custom-built or were one-offs. Not so today, when statutory certification and mass-production limitations mean that aircraft have to be made in very large numbers in order to justify mountains of paperwork and to offset production costs. Only within the home-built movement can builders express themselves in the construction of their aircraft. While most home-builders will adhere to plan sets produced by experienced designers, others will have the confidence and skills necessary to modify such plans or, indeed, to design their own aircraft from scratch.

Wright Flyer

FF 1903 USA

The Wright brothers' first tentative flight at Kitty Hawk was witnessed only by their new-found friends, the Kill Devil lifeguards, as well as by a shipwreck lumber trader and by 1 local youth. The men of the lifeguard station had been only too delighted to assist the eccentric brothers, who had become a source of great interest and intrigue in Kitty Hawk's remote and windswept environs. When news of the first flight reached Frank Tunison, editor of the Dayton Journal, however, he was sceptical and famously refused to run the story.

X-5 Seabird

USA

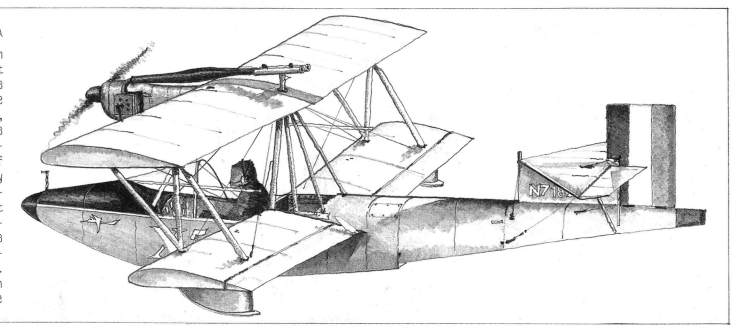

For 1 week every April the extraordinary Sun 'n Fun fly-in at Florida's Lakeland Linder Airport becomes home to one of the largest gatherings of aircraft in the world. During the event more than 15,000 aircraft will visit the airfield, many of them having travelled long distances across the US and Canada. This fly-in is the laid-back Woodstock of aviation and the centre of the world of aircraft home-building. For many home-builders this is a chance to source materials and to haggle with vendors over the most obscure of secondhand components. This is a no-frills event. Pilots can opt to sleep in tiny tents beneath the wings of their aircraft while visitors are accommodated in a tented village. Nearby the floatplane base is teeming with unusual and eccentric home-built projects like the X-5 Seabird.

Yakovlev Yak-7B

FF 1942 USSR
It's not every day that an original Yak-7B warbird will pull up beside you. An aircraft like this is history that can fly and if aeroplanes could talk then this one would surely have some stories to tell. The Yak-7 was a 2-seat training version of Alexander Yakovlev's earlier Yak-1 fighter. The Yak-1 of 1939 was a superb performer and, alongside the Spitfire and the P-51 Mustang, was surely one of the 3 best aircraft of the war.

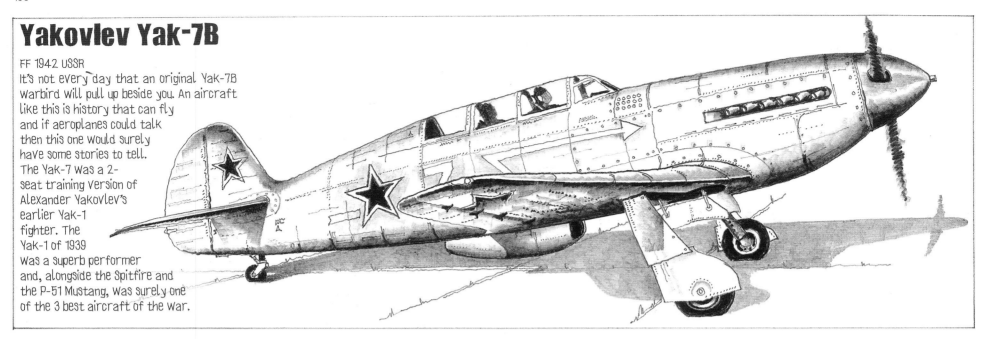

Yakovlev Yak-18T

FF 1967 USSR

A wonderful example of 1960s Soviet design which can be bought today for much the same price as an executive saloon car. The Yak-18T is a superb performer and perhaps the cheapest warbird available today.

Yakovlev Yak-42

FF 1975 USSR
Designed to meet Aeroflot's requirements for a short-range feederliner and regional airliner the Yak-42 was developed to serve, not only standard regional airports, but also isolated and unprepared landing strips. More than 200 of the type were built to serve the former Soviet Union's massive network of domestic routes.

Yakovlev Yak-52TW

FF 1979
USSR/Romania

The Yak-52, ab initio trainer of the Eastern Bloc countries, has been exported in large numbers into Western Europe and the USA. Despite its military lineage the type is

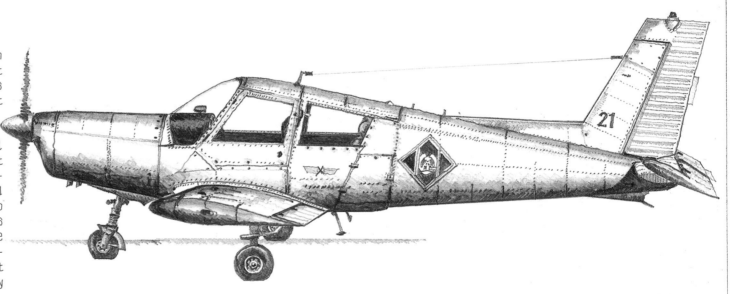

relatively affordable and it has displayed immense appeal to Western pilots, who see an opportunity to fly a potent Warbird at low cost. Fully aerobatic, and with perfect flying manners, the Yak-52 has all of the charisma and character that one would expect of an Iron Curtain contender.

Zlin Z-43

FF 1968 Czechoslovakia
One of a series of light training aircraft from Zlin of Czechoslovakia, the Z-43 was a 4-seat touring sport-plane and trainer. With its 210hp (157kW) Avia M337A piston powerplant the type had a maximum cruise speed of 146mph and was rated for light/medium aerobatics. Given the social and governmental structures in the Eastern Bloc countries at that time the end users of Zlin's completed Z-43s tended to be essentially institutional and cooperative, with most airframes going to training groups and agencies. Other airframes went to East Germany while more again were tailored for light military use in Czechoslovakia and Hungary. A sturdy touring aircraft which can be found in small numbers in many European countries today.

Zlin Z-526F

FF 1968 Czechoslovakia
Czechoslovakia has always had an extremely well-developed aircraft industry and to this day is clearly at the leading edge of light plane development in Eastern Europe. In 1947, when it became apparent that its fledgling aviation sector would require large numbers of basic trainers, the authorities turned to Zlin to fill the void. Zlin's more advanced Z-526F variant flew for the first time in 1968.

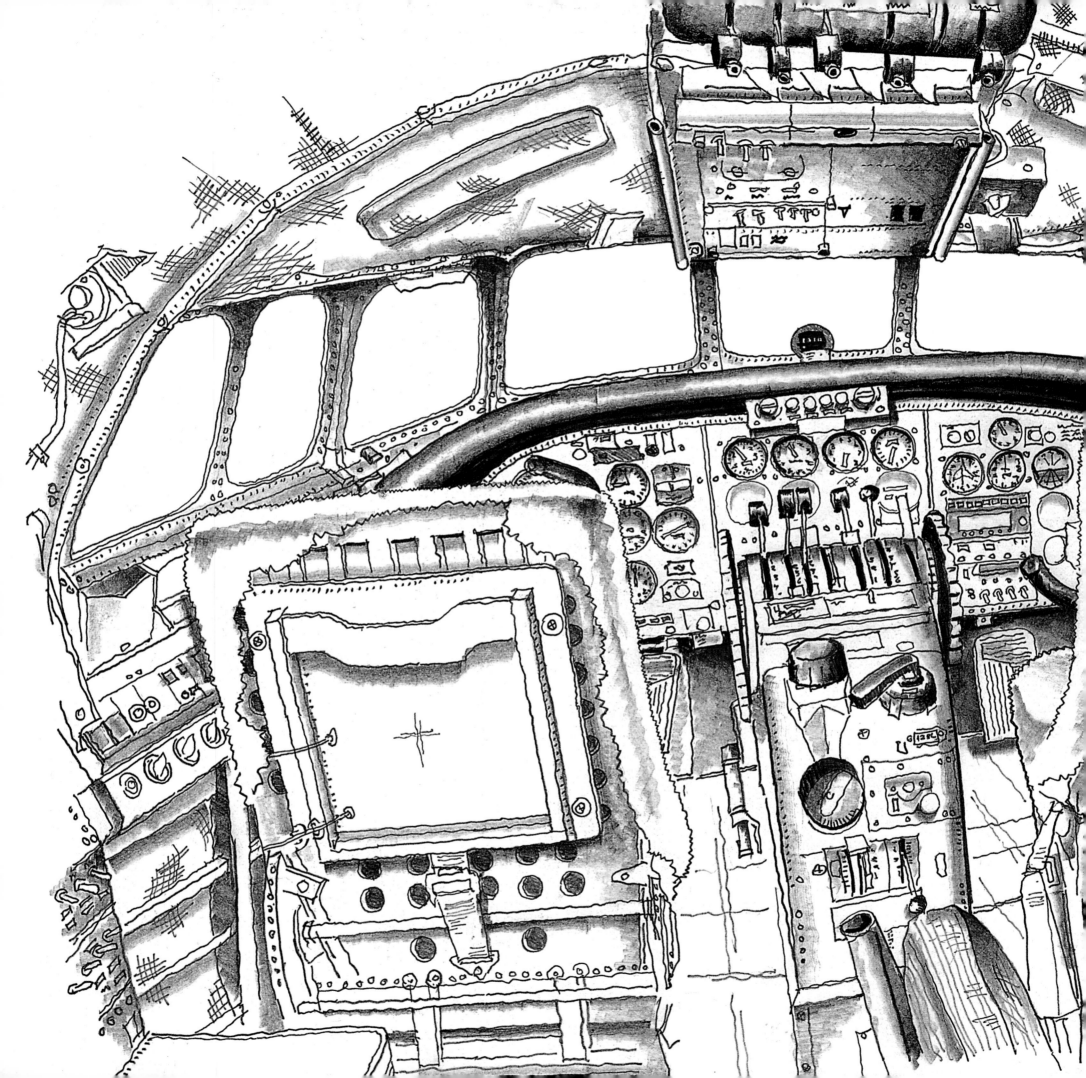

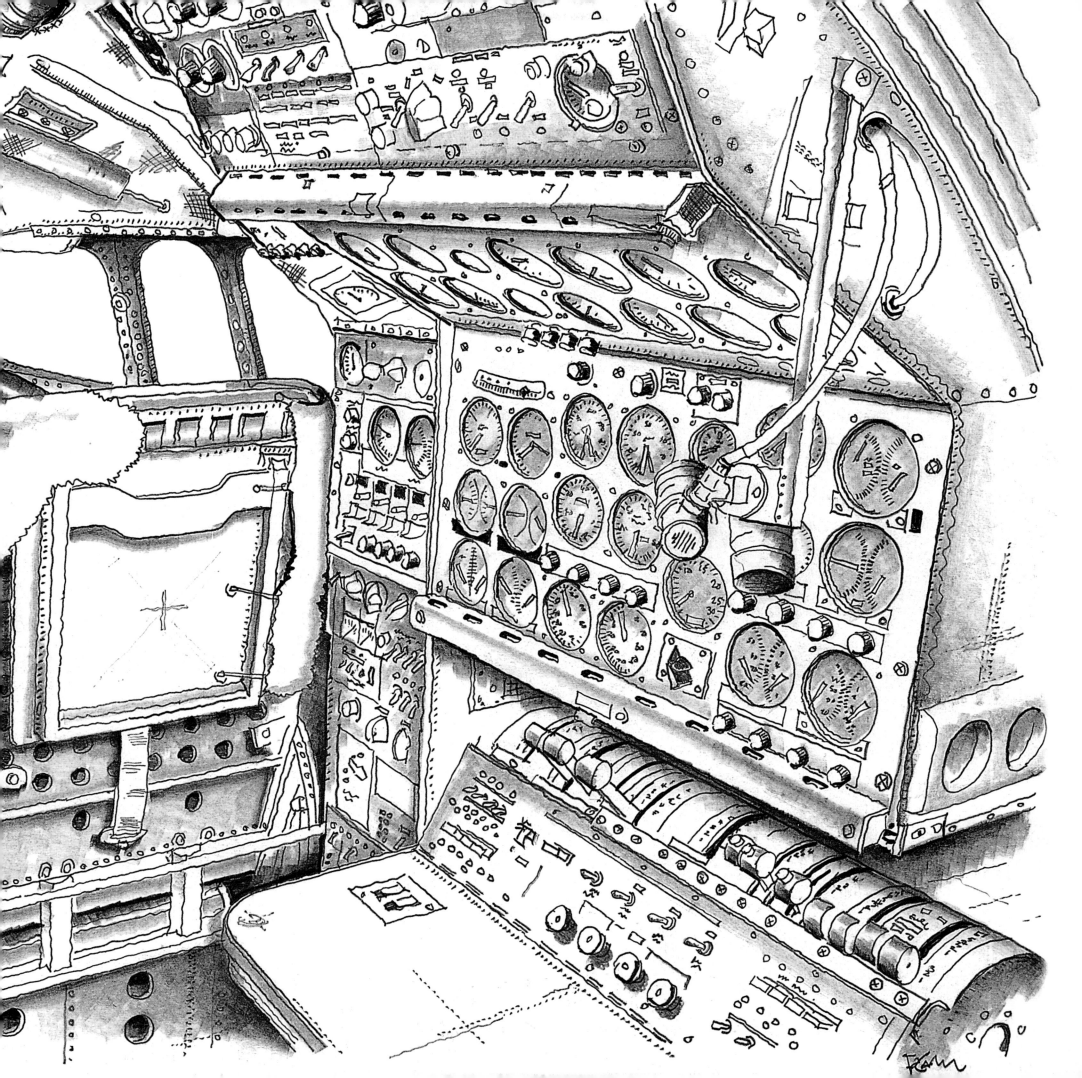

Technical Data

Adam Aircraft Industries Adam A-500

Subject: Adam A-500. Registration N501AX. Sun 'n Fun Fly-in 2005.
Statistics: Adam Aircraft Industries A-500.

The Adam A-500 transport is targeted firmly at the lower corporate transport market, aiming slightly below Citation Jet level but well above the level set by the standard twins. This is a big-feel cabin with all the trappings of a corporate jet but with greatly reduced fuel burn and maintenance costs. Indeed, too, it is hoped that the in-line positioning of the two Teledyne Continental engines will attract owner operators who might otherwise be put off by the complexities and the rigorous training procedures which are inherent in asymmetric flight. Adam has prepared better than most for its entry into this difficult market with as much emphasis on financial security and corporate investment as on the aircraft development itself. A measure of Adam's success in this regard is given by the close involvement of Goldman Sachs as the largest outside investor in the project.

Country of Origin:	USA
First Flight:	2002
Accommodation:	1 + 5
Wingspan:	44ft 0in (13.41m)
Length:	36ft 7in (10.27m)
Height:	9ft 6in (2.9m)
Empty Weight:	5,160lb (2,340kg)
Max Take Off Weight:	7,050lb (3,197kg)
Powerplant:	2 x Teledyne Continental
Cruise Speed:	200mph (322km/h)
Max Speed:	250mph (402km/h)
Service Ceiling:	25,000ft (7,620m)
Range:	1,150nm (2,130km)
Number Manufactured:	First airframes due for delivery end 2005.
Flying or in service:	1 development airframe.

Adam Aircraft Industries Adam A-700 Jet

Subject: Adam A-700. Registration N700AJ (previously N700JJ). Flying prototype as displayed at Sun 'n Fun Fly-in 2005.
Statistics: Adam Aircraft Industries A-700.

Even before deliveries of the piston-powered A-500 have commenced, Adam has set its sights on the lucrative corporate jet market. The A-700 defines a new executive 'micro-jet' market made possible by the development of smaller and less complex turbojet engines. Indeed, all of the main aircraft manufacturers expect this segment of the market to expand rapidly in the coming years as existing high-end piston and turboprop operators begin the transition to jet-powered aircraft. With the A-700 already beginning its certification trials, Adam hopes to be at the forefront of this new trend towards jet propulsion. To operators and clients alike the Adams A-700 executive jet will present an attractive and plausible airframe choice with its generous corporate-jet-sized cabin, its low running costs and its modest purchase price.

Country of Origin:	USA
First Flight:	2003
Accommodation:	1 + 5
Wingspan:	44ft 0in (13.41m)
Length:	40ft 9in (12.42m)
Height:	9ft 7in (2.93m)
Max Take Off:	10,000lb
Powerplant:	2 x Williams FJ-33 jet engines.
Cruise Speed:	340mph (547km/h)
Max Speed:	383mph (612km/h)
Service Ceiling:	41,000ft (12,500m)
Range:	1,611nm (2,985km)
Number Manufactured:	Production expected to commence 2006.
Flying or in service:	1

Aeronca 7AC Champ

Subject: Aeronca 7AC bearing the n-number N083102 is flown out of Costa Mesa, California. This pristine airframe first flew in 1946.
Statistics: Aeronca 7AC Champ.

The Champion 7 series comprised a wide range of civilian and military types which were custom-fitted to meet specific mission requirements from observation and artillery-spotting to club training and recreational floatplane fishing. The 7AC Champ was the primary civilian marque and it was built in very large numbers in response to an overwhelming market demand. The Champ was gifted with wonderful flying manners and its simplicity and forgiving nature made it a favourite with pilots of all proficiency levels. There are many Champs flying to this day and, indeed, the type can be found gracing flightlines all over the world.

Country of Origin:	USA
First Flight:	1944
Accommodation:	2
Wingspan:	35ft 0in (10.67m)
Length:	21ft 6in (6.55m)
Height:	7ft 0in (2.1m)
Empty Weight:	810lb (368kg)
Loaded:	1,320lb (600kg)
Powerplant:	1 x 65hp (48.4kW) Lycoming flat-four piston engine.
Cruise Speed:	85mph (136km/h)
Max Speed:	100mph (160km/h)
Service Ceiling:	12,400ft (3,780m) with 1 pilot. 8,900ft (2,712m) with 2 pilots
Range:	250 miles (399km)
Number Manufactured:	More than 10,200 of all 7 series types built between 1946 and 1971.
Flying or in service:	Several thousand Champs in active service to this day.
Airframes Preserved:	Museum of Aviation. Warner Robins AFB, Georgia, USA.
Preserved:	Ottumwa Airpower Museum, Iowa, USA. Mid-America Air Museum, Liberal, Kansas, USA.

Aeronca 7AC Floatplane

Subject: Aeronca 7AC floatplane. From a 1940s Aeronca proportional image by renowned aviation photographer Ben Ross.
Statistics: Aeronca 7AC (with floats).

Floatplane-equipped development of the original 7AC Champ. The type was also available with standard tricycle-wheeled undercarriage, with tundra tyres and with snow skis. Many Champs would be fitted with all 3 undercarriage types as the seasons progressed.

Country of Origin:	USA
First Flight:	1946
Accommodation:	2
Wingspan:	35ft 0in (10.67m)
Length:	21ft 6in (6.55m)
Height:	7ft 0in (2.13m)
Empty Weight:	740lb (336kg)
Max Take Off:	1,220lb (533kg)
Powerplant:	1 x 65hp (48.4kW) Lycoming flat-four piston engine.
Cruise Speed:	70mph (113km/h)
Max Speed:	87mph (140km/h)
Service Ceiling:	8,700ft (2,651.76m)
Range:	460 miles (740km)
Number Manufactured:	10,000 of all 7 series type built between 1946 and 1951.
Flying or in service:	Several in active flying service to this day.

Aeronca C-3

Subject: Aeronca C-3 registration G-AEFT based at Denham.
Statistics: Aeronca C-3.

Despite its small size the Aeronca C-3 was one of the great pioneers of general aviation, bringing cheap and affordable flight to many aviators right across the world. The 'flying bathtub' was produced from 1931 to 1937 and it was immensely popular with pilots and spectators alike. With just 36 horsepower available the C-3 was no stallion but it had the very best of manners in the air and, at a time when money was very scarce, it did over 20 miles per gallon. The C-3 was the first really successful light aircraft and it is often referred to as the true father of the private light-plane movement. In 1932 monies just $1,890 would buy an Aeronca C-3 that would open up the skies. By 1937, however, the US Government set down new minimum standards for aircraft construction and the rudimentary C-3 ceased production. Fortunately those C-3s which were already on the register were allowed to remain flying under a 'grandfather' clause.

Country of Origin:	USA
First Flight:	1931
Accommodation:	2
Wingspan:	36ft 0in (10.97m)
Length:	20ft 0in (6.09m)
Height:	7ft 6in (2.3m)
Empty Weight:	406lb (184kg)
Loaded:	875lb (397kg)
Powerplant:	1 x 36hp (26.85kW) Aeronca E-113 two-stroke powerplant.
Cruise Speed:	75mph (120.7km/h)
Max Speed:	80mph (128km/h)
Service Ceiling:	14,000ft (4,267m)
Range:	200 miles (322km)
Number Manufactured:	400 built between 1931 and 1937.
Flying or in service:	Many carefully cared-for examples still in airworthy condition.
Preserved:	Flying Tigers Air Museum, Kissimme, Florida, USA. Ottawa Aviation Museum, Ottawa, Canada. Ottumwa Airpower Museum, Iowa, USA. Seattle Museum of Flight, Washington, USA.

Aeronca L-16A

Subject: Aeronca L-16A registration 77124, formerly of the US Army, flew into Sun 'n Fun, Lakeland Linder Regional Airport, Florida.
Statistics: Aeronca L-16 Grasshopper.

Immediately after the Second World War when production of civil aircraft was resumed, Aeronca redesigned and repackaged its pre-war L-3 observation and instructional airframe. The resulting type became the Aeronca Model 7AC in its civilian role and the Aeronca L-16 in its military role. About 10,000 of the 7 series were produced in all variants, many of these for the US Army as trainers, observation platforms and, on occasions, as rescuecraft.

Country of Origin:	USA
First Flight:	1946
Accommodation:	Pilot & Observer
Wingspan:	35ft 2in (9.81m)
Length:	21ft 6in (6.58m)
Height:	7ft 0in (2.13m)
Empty Weight:	870lb (394kg)
Max Take Off:	1,300lb (590kg)
Powerplant:	1 x 90hp (67kW) Continental C-90-8F horizontally opposed piston.
Cruise Speed:	129mph (207km/h)
Max Speed:	135mph (217km/h)
Service Ceiling:	12,000ft (3,657m)
Range:	400 miles (643km)
Number Manufactured:	More than 10,000 of all variants.
Flying or in service:	Many of all types still actively flying.
Preserved:	US Army Aviation Museum, Fort Rucker, Ozark, Alabama, USA. Arkansas Air Museum, Fayetteville, Arkansas, USA.

Aero Spacelines Super Guppy

Subject: Super Guppy F-8TGV (cn 001) of Airbus Skylink.
Statistics: Aero Spacelines Super Guppy.

In 1961 Aero Spacelines began upgrading ex-military Boeing Stratocruisers to accommodate heavy and outsize loads such as rocket boosters, oil derricks and even locomotive rolling stock. With the coming of the Airbus project in Europe, Aero Spacelines found a new client with an ongoing need for airlifting of massive aircraft components, fuselages, and wing sections. In all, a total of 8 Guppys, Pregnant Guppys and Super Guppys were built, all of them slightly different in dimension and internal configuration. Loading of freight items into the airframe brought one of the most extraordinary sights in aviation as the entire nose section of the Guppy would swing open a full 110 degrees to allow unimpeded access to the aircraft's cavernous interior. The Airbus programme depended on the Guppy series for many years before Airbus began development of the massive Beluga, its own outsize load transporter, which was built around the airframe of the Airbus A300.

Country of Origin:	USA
First Flight:	1962 (Pregnant Guppy)
Accommodation:	3 + outsized loads of up to 112ft length X 25ft (34m X 7.7m) diameter
Wingspan:	156ft 0in (47.63m)
Length:	144ft 0in (43.84m)
Height:	48ft 0in (14.78m)
Empty Weight:	99,790lb (45,359kg)
Loaded:	169,644lb (77,111kg)
Powerplant:	4 X Allison 501 turboprops
Cruise Speed:	252mph (407km/h)
Max Speed:	287mph (463km/h)
Range:	504 miles (813km)
Number Manufactured:	8 Guppys of 6 different mission-specific configurations.
Flying or in service:	1 turboprop conversion flown by NASA.
Preserved:	4 mothballed, 1 of them at Prima AFB, Arizona and 1 each in UK, France, and Germany.

Aérospatiale SA-321 Super Frelon

Subject: Aérospatiale SA-321G Super Frelon of the French Navy.
Statistics: Aérospatiale SA-321G Super Frelon.

The Super Frelon was built as a military transport, assault helicopter and anti-submarine weapons platform. Developed originally by Sud Aviation, the Super Frelon was ordered by the French Armée de l'Air as well as by its Aéronavale and by the military forces of Israel, Iraq, South Africa and Libya. Further examples were sold into China and assembled there under licence as the Changhe Z-8. Many SA-321 Super Frelons continue in military service to this

day and the type has undergone a large number of avionics and weapons-systems upgrades over the years. A civilian variant of the type was developed but, despite protracted efforts to market it to civilian operators, interest was very low and only two of the type were built.

Country of Origin:	France
First Flight:	Frelon 1959 Super Frelon 1962
Accommodation:	Crew of up to 5 and capacity for 38 battle-equipped troops.
Rotor Diameter:	62ft 0in (18.9m)
Length:	75ft 6in (23.01m)
Height:	16ft 3in (4.95m)
Empty Weight:	14,576lbs (6,612kg)
Max Take Off:	28,660lbs (13,000kg)
Powerplant:	3 X 1570hp (1,171kW) Turbomeca 3C III Turbines.
Cruise Speed:	155mph (249km/h)
Max Speed:	171mph (275km/h)
Service Ceiling:	10,170ft (3,100m)
Range:	520 miles (837km)
Number Manufactured:	120 of all Super Frelon types including prototypes.
Flying or in service:	Still widely in operational service to this day.

Aérospatiale SOCATA TB-30 Epsilon

Subject: Aérospatiale TB-30B Epsilon in French military colours.
Statistics: Aérospatiale TB-30 Epsilon.

Aérospatiale developed the TB-30 Epsilon primary trainer to meet the exacting requirements of France's Armée de l'Air. Its development entailed substantial reconfiguration of the earlier TB-10 civilian runabout and included narrowing and stretching of the TB-10 fuselage to produce a tandem seat layout, and insertion of a new 300hp (224kW) powerplant in lieu of the TB-10's more mundane 180hp (134kW) piston engine. The resulting TB-30 Epsilon is a powerful and capable performer and an ideal airframe for pilot development work from ab initio training to advanced piston training and specialized navigational exercises.
Deliveries began in 1983 and continued through to 1989, by which time no less than 172 of all Epsilon variants were

completed. The type served with the military forces of both France and Togo and, indeed, Portugal operated a group of 18 Epsilon trainers which were assembled under licence in Portugal by OMGA.

Country of Origin:	France
First Flight:	1979
Accommodation:	2
Wingspan:	26ft 0in (7.92m)
Length:	24ft 11in (7.59m)
Height:	8ft 9in (2.66m)
Empty Weight:	2,055lb (932kg)
Max Take Off:	2,755lb (1,250kg)
Powerplant:	1 X 300hp (224kW) Lycoming AEIO-540 piston powerplant.
Cruise Speed:	222mph (358km/h)
Max Speed:	236mph (380km/h)
Service Ceiling:	24,000ft (7,315m)
Range:	830 miles (1,340km)
Number Manufactured:	In excess of 172 of all types delivered.
Flying or in service:	In service with, among others, the air forces of France, Portugal, and other nations.

Aérospatiale SE-3 Alouette II

Subject: Alouette II SE3-13B registered G-UGLY still flying after 40 years.
Statistics: Aérospatiale SE-3 Alouette II.

Aérospatiale's capable and efficient 5-seat general utility military and civil helicopter. Operated in large numbers by the French armed services and much favoured by civilian operators for light transport tasks, hoisting duties and power and pipeline surveys.

Country of Origin:	France
First Flight:	1955
Accommodation:	1 + 4
Rotor diameter:	33ft 6in (10.2m)
Length:	31ft 11in (9.48m)
Height:	9ft 0in (2.75)
Empty Weight:	1,973lb (895kg)
Max Take Off:	3,630lb (1,650kg)
Powerplant:	1 x 530shp (395kW) Turbomeca Astazou II turboshaft derated to 360shp (268kW).
Cruise Speed:	103mph (165km/h)
Max Speed:	112mph (180km/h)
Service Ceiling (Hover):	5,400ft
Range:	450 miles (724km)
Number Manufactured:	In excess of 1,679
Flying or in service:	Many ex military examples now in civilian ownership.
Preserved:	Israeli Air Force Museum, Hazerim, Beer Sheeva, Israel.

Aérospatiale Dauphin 1 & SA-365 Dauphin 2

Subject: Aérospatiale SA-365 Dauphin 2 of the US Coast Guard.
Statistics: Aérospatiale SA-365 Dauphin 2.

The prototype of Aérospatiale's sophisticated Dauphin 1 military and utility helicopter flew for the first time in 1972. In the months following its first flight Aérospatiale made numerous changes to the prototype airframe including the installation of a more powerful Astazou powerplant and the addition of damping weights to the rotor tips. Development of the more advanced twin-engine Dauphin 2 began just 1 year later with the first flight of this twin-engined helicopter being achieved in January of 1975.

Country of Origin:	France
First Flight:	1972
Accommodation:	1 + 9
Rotor Diameter:	37ft 9in (11.5m)
Length:	36ft 0in (10.98m)
Height:	11ft 6in (3.5m)
Empty Weight:	3,980lb (1,806kg)

Loaded:	7,495lb (3,400kg)
Powerplant:	1 x 1,050shp (785kW) Turbomeca Astazou XVIIIA turboshaft.
Cruise Speed:	152mph (245km/h)
Max Speed:	173mph (278km/h)
Service Ceiling:	8,040ft (2,450m)
Range:	295 miles (545km)
Flying or in service:	In service.
Preserved:	The Helicopter Museum, Weston-Super-Mare, Somerset, UK

Aérospatiale Fouga Magister

Subject: Aérospatiale Fouga Magister of the Irish Aer Corps Silver Swallow aerobatic team.
Statistics: Aérospatiale Fouga Magister.

Designers Castello and Mauboussin were well known for installing compact turbojet engines into smaller general aviation aircraft and gliders and, indeed, this early influence is clearly reflected in the 1951 design of the Fouga Magister primary jet trainer. Together they created one of the simplest and most efficient jet trainers of all time.

Country of Origin:	France
First Flight:	1952
Accommodation:	1 + 1
Wingspan:	36ft 9in (11.15m)
Length:	28ft 2in (8.59m)
Height:	9ft 5in (2.87m)
Empty Weight:	2,238lb (1,015kg)
Max Take Off:	3,800lb (1,725kg)
Powerplant:	2 x Turbomeca Marbore II or Marbore IV turbojets
Max Speed:	444mph (715km/h)
Service Ceiling:	36,000ft (10,973m)
Range:	575 miles (925km)
Number Manufactured:	576 built in France and 340 built between Germany, Finland and Israel.

Flying or in service:	Now beginning to reappear as private warbirds.
Preserved:	Ailes Anciennes Toulouse, France. Irish Aer Corps Collection, Baldonel, Dublin.

Aérospatiale SA-342L Gazelle

Subject: Aérospatiale SA-342L Gazelle of the Royal Air Force.
Statistics: Aérospatiale SA-342L Gazelle.

Under the Anglo-French helicopter co-operation programme Westland Helicopters Ltd was granted a licence to build large numbers of the Gazelle for the British Army and the Royal Air Force.

Country of Origin:	France
First Flight:	1967
Accommodation:	2
Rotor Diameter:	34ft 6in (10.5m)
Length:	31ft 3in (9.53m)
Height:	10ft 5in (3.18m)
Empty Weight:	2,149lb (975kg)
Max Take Off:	4,190lb (1,900kg)
Powerplant:	1 x 858shp (640kW) Turbomeca Astazou XIV turboshaft.
Cruise Speed:	148mph (238km/h)
Max Speed:	168mph (270km/h)
Service Ceiling:	16,400ft (5,000m)
Range:	424 miles (785km)
Number Manufactured:	1,250 built in France with further examples built in the UK and former Yugoslovakia.
Flying or in service:	Many ex-military Gazelles now appearing in civilian ownership.
Preserved:	Prototype Newark Air Museum, UK (SA 341). Israeli Air Force Museum, Hatzerim, Beer Sheeva, Israel.

Aérospatiale Puma HC

Subject: Aérospatiale Puma SA330B of the French Armée de Terre passes over the Customs House, Dublin, en route for home.
Statistics: Aérospatiale Puma HC.

Designed by Aérospatiale to meet the requirements of the French army, the Puma was an excellent all-weather medium lift helicopter. Many variants of the type were developed for specific missions, from military transport to gunship and electronic countermeasures platform. The Puma served with many countries across the world and it underwent a continuous and ongoing programme of improvements to ensure that it always retained its very strong market position.

Country of Origin:	France.
First Flight:	1965
Accommodation:	2 + 16 fully laden troops
Rotor Diameter:	49ft 2in (15.0m)
Length:	46ft 2in (14.08m)
Height:	16ft 11in (5.14m)
Empty Weight:	8,305lb (3,766kg)
Max Take Off:	16,535lb (7,500kg)
Powerplant:	2 x 1,575shp (1,175kW) Turbomeca Turmo IVC turboshafts.
Cruise Speed:	160mph (257km/h)
Max Speed:	162mph (262km/h)
Range:	297 miles (550km)
Number Manufactured:	696 Pumas of all variants were completed when production ceased in 1987.
Flying or in service:	Many still in military service.

Aérospatiale SE-210 Caravelle

Subject: Aérospatiale SE-210 Caravelle IIR registration HK-3325X in the colours of Kabo Air.
Statistics: Aérospatiale SE-210 Caravelle III.

The Caravelle was developed in response to a French government specification for a medium-range airliner which was intended to link France with its many interests abroad and particularly with its former territories in North Africa. 1955 saw the first flight of the prototype Caravelle and, after a certification process that lasted just 11 months, the first Caravelles began operational service with Air France in May of 1956. The SE-210 was to prove a most capable performer and a total of 280 airframes were produced in a series of ever improving variants. Seating capacity, engine size and avionics packages all improved and increased over the years and, indeed, many Caravelles continue to fly to this day.

Country of Origin:	France
First Flight:	1955
Accommodation:	86
Wingspan:	112ft 6in (34.3m)
Length:	105ft 1in (32.01m)
Height:	28ft 7in (8.72m)
Empty Weight:	53,319lb (24,185kg)
Max Take Off:	101,413lb (46,000kg)
Powerplant:	2 x 1,162lb (5.17 kN) Rolls-Royce Avon RA.29 Mk 527 rearmounted turbofans.
Cruise Speed:	497mph (800km/h) or Mach 0.67
Service Ceiling:	42,400ft (12,923m)
Range:	1,988 miles (3,200km)
Number Manufactured:	279 of all variants excluding prototypes.
Flying or in service:	Small numbers still in service.

Aérospatiale SOCATA TB-31 Omega

Subject: Aérospatiale prototype TB-31 Omega.
Statistics: Aérospatiale TB-31 Omega.

Aérospatiale was keen to secure the contract for the French air force's new advanced turboprop trainer and so they developed a turboprop variant of the trusted Epsilon airframe. This was a thorough and all-encompassing upgrade with new powerplant, avionics, weapons hardpoints and ejection seats. The prototype Omega flew for the first time in 1985 but, despite protracted trials, the project was overlooked in favour of the Tucano trainer, which had already proved itself with many other air forces around the world. It is unlikely now that the Omega will ever enter production, although the technology gained during the development stage will undoubtedly appear in some flying format in future years.

Country of Origin:	France
First Flight:	1985
Accommodation:	2
Wingspan:	25ft 11in (7.92m)
Length:	23ft 0in (7.0m)
Height:	12ft 0in (3.65m)
Empty Weight:	2,382lb (1,080kg)
Max Take Off:	3,307lb (1,500kg)
Powerplant:	1 x 359hp (268kW) Turbomeca Arrius 1-D.
Cruise Speed:	270mph (434km/h)
Max Speed:	323mph (519km/h)
Service Ceiling:	30,000ft (9,145 m)
Range:	808 miles (1,300km)
Number Manufactured:	1
Preserved:	1

Aérospatiale SOCATA TB-9 Tampico

Subject: TB-9 Tampico. Registration HB-KAU of
            Switzerland.
Statistics: Aérospatiale SOCATA TB-9 Tampico.

The little sister of the TB-20 Trinidad is the smaller
and somewhat less opulent TB-9 Tampico. SOCATA's
wonderfully named Caribbean series of Trinidad,
Tobago and TB-9 Tampico were each designed to capture
a specific portion of the general aviation market from
high-performance personal transport to basic club trainer.
The Tobago marks the centre of this range, providing 4
to 5 seats in a well-appointed and spacious touring cabin.
Power is provided by a 180hp Lycoming horizontally opposed
piston powerplant giving a cruise speed of 123mph, a
respectable tally for such a large airframe. As with all
of its offerings Aérospatiale SOCATA's Tampico is superbly
detailed both inside and out. Its sleek, smart profile and
its high, elongated cowlings are an impressive sight on the
ground and in the air. The TB-11 was a specialized aerobatic
variant which was produced in limited numbers only.

Country of Origin: France
First Flight: 1977
Accommodation: 1 + 3 to 4
Wingspan: 32ft 0in (9.76m)
Length: 25ft 0in (7.63m)
Height: 9ft 5in (2.9m)
Empty Weight: 1,477lb (670kg)
Max Take Off: 2,535lb (1,150kg)
Powerplant: 1 x 180hp (134.2kW) Lycoming
                        piston powerplant.
Cruise Speed: 123mph (198km/h)
Max Speed: 152mph (244.6km/h)
Service Ceiling: 13,000ft (3,962m)
Range: 863 miles (1,389km)
Number Manufactured: Over 725.
Flying or in service: In service.

Aérospatiale SOCATA TB-20 Trinidad

Subject: Aérospatiale SOCATA TB-20 Trinidad
            registration F-GEVU.
Statistics: Aérospatiale SOCATA Trinidad.

The French aviation industry has always had its own
unique and independent approach to aircraft design and
manufacture. Just when the US general aviation market
was in the doldrums with massive levels of litigation
and the closure of production lines, the Trinidad and
Tobago range of touring aircraft was launched. Complete
with gullwing doors and a most opulent automobile-type
instrument panel, the Trinidad's plush, spacious detailing
appealed to the American market as well as that of
Europe. This was a comfortable and well-appointed interior
all dressed up in a sleek and powerful airframe to give
fast cruising speeds and a 1,100nm touring range. A
sophisticated and capable top-end personal touring aircraft.

Country of Origin: France
First Flight: 1980
Accommodation: 1 + 3
Wingspan: 32ft 0in (9.76m)
Length: 25ft 0in (7.63m)
Height: 9ft 11in (3.03m)
Empty Weight: 1,744lb (791kg)
Max take off: 3,080lb (1,397kg)
Powerplant: 1 x 250hp (185kW) Textron
                        Lycoming IO-540 fuel-injected
                        flat-six piston engine.
Cruise Speed: 188mph (301km/h)
Max Speed: 195.6mph (314.8km/h)
Service Ceiling: 20,000ft (6,096m)
Range: 1,100nm (2,038km)
Number Manufactured: 680 Trinidad & Trinidad TC.
Flying or in service: Generally in service.

Aérospatiale Super Puma

Subject: Super Puma T-313 of the Swiss Air Force was
            based at Alpnach.
Statistics: Aérospatiale Super Puma.

The Super Puma is derived from the SA-330 Puma with
more powerful engines and an enhanced rotor system. It is
used in a wide variety of military and civilian roles such
as offshore oil-rig support and marine rescue.

Country of Origin: France
First Flight: 1970
Accommodation: 2 + 19 fully laden troops.
Rotor Diameter: 50ft 7in (15.6m)
Height: 16ft 4in (4.92m)
Empty Weight: 6,613lb (3,000kg)
Max Take Off: 9,260lb (4,200kg)
Powerplant: 2 x 1,840hp (1,372kW)
                        Turbomeca Makila 1A
                        turboshafts.
Cruise Speed: 173mph (278km/h)
Service Ceiling: 15,091ft (4,600m)
Range: 385 miles (620km)
Number Manufactured: 696 Pumas of all variants
                        were completed when
                        production ceased in 1987.
Flying or in service: Many still in military service.

Aérospatiale SOCATA TBM-700

Subject: Aérospatiale SOCATA TBM-700. Registration F-WTBM.
Statistics: Aérospatiale SOCATA TBM-700.

The TBM-700 high-performance executive transport was designed to compete against the traditional piston business market leaders such as the King Air and the Gulfstream Commander. Providing all of the performance and the mission reliability of a larger business twin, the TBM-700's single-turboprop powerplant allows high-performance business-class travel at greatly reduced running costs. The type has won a substantial share of the newly formed single-turboprop market and it now competes against such new offerings as the single-turboprop Piper Malibu, larger Cessna 208 and the Pilatus PC-XII. This is a capable and sophisticated aircraft with the very highest levels of equipment, avionics and pressurization. Construction is of bonded and riveted aluminium sections with some new, lightweight composite parts, especially within the flight control system.

Country of Origin:	France
First Flight:	1988
Accommodation:	1 + 6
Wingspan:	41ft 7in (12.68m)
Length:	34ft 11in (10.64m)
Height:	14ft 3in (4.35m)
Empty Weight:	4,101lb (1,860kg)
Max Take Off:	6,578lb (2,984kg)
Powerplant:	1 X 700hp (522kW) Pratt & Whitney Canada PT6A-64 Turboprop.
Cruise Speed:	280mph (450km/h)
Max Speed:	345mph (555km/h)
Service Ceiling:	30,000ft (9,144m)
Range:	1,784 miles (2,870km)
Number Manufactured:	130 of all variants.
Flying or in service:	125 in service.

Aero Vodochody L-39 Albatross

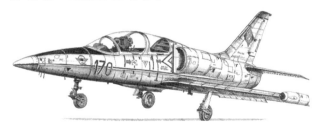

Subject: L-39V was actually a target tug of the former East German Air Force, based at Peenemünde, East Germany.
Statistics: Aero Vodochody L-39 Albatross.

Surely one of the greatest toys of all time, the legendary Aero L-39 advanced trainer and light attack aircraft can now be bought for personal use. Operating a sophisticated ex-military aircraft of this type requires high levels of skill and large amounts of cash.

Country of Origin:	Czechoslovakia
First Flight:	1968
Accommodation:	1 + 1
Wingspan:	31ft 4in (9.54m)
Length:	40ft 0in (12.2m)
Height:	15ft 8in (4.77m)
Empty Weight:	8,866lb (4,030kg)
Max Take Off:	15,400lb (7,000kg)
Powerplant:	1 X 4,850lb (21.57kN) Povazski Strojarne/ZMK DV-2 turbofan.
Max Speed:	543mph (875km/h)
Service Ceiling:	38,470ft (11,730m)
Range:	750 miles (1,210km)
Number Manufactured:	Over 3,000 of all variants.
Flying or in service:	The L-39 is flown by many former Warsaw Pact countries. Several in private ownership.

Aero Vodochody L-29 Delfin

Subject: Ex-military L-29 Delfin.
Statistics: Aero Vodochody L-29 Delfin.

The L-29 Delfin was designed to replace the ageing piston-powered training aircraft of the Czechoslovakian air force. The prototype flew for the first time in 1959 and the type went on to be adapted by the Soviet Union as an advanced jet trainer and light ground attack aircraft. Indeed, the Delfin was a most capable military performer and it was sold to many military operators right across the world. Today an L-29 can be bought for much the same price as a luxury sportscar and the type is beginning to appear at air shows and airfields piloted by private pilots and jet warbird enthusiasts.

Country of Origin:	Czechoslovakia
First Flight:	1959
Accommodation:	1 + 1
Wingspan:	33ft 9in (10.29m)
Length:	35ft 5in (10.81m)
Height:	10ft 3in (3.1m)
Empty Weight:	5,027lb (2,279kg)
Max Take Off:	7,800lb (3,540kg)
Powerplant:	1 X M 701C500 turbojet engine rated at 1,960lb (8.72kN).

Max Cruise:	407mph (655km/h)
Service Ceiling:	36,100ft (11,003m)
Range:	555 miles (894km)
Number Manufactured:	More than 3,000 built including 2,000 supplied to the USSR.
Flying or in service:	Now frequently flown in the jet warbird category.

Airbus A330

Subject: Airbus A330 of national carrier Air France.
Statistics: Airbus A330.

Airbus's highly efficient A330 set new standards of technical and ergonomic comfort when the type was unveiled to the world in 1992. Indeed, the A330 has gone on to become one of the major choices for large-volume airlines which must balance the economies of capital cost, fuel burn, aircraft maintenance and passenger payload when committing to an aircraft type.

Country of Origin:	EU
First Flight:	1992
Accommodation:	2 + Cabin crew + 335 two-class passengers or 444 all-economy passengers.
Wingspan:	197ft 9in (60.3m)
Length:	208ft 9in (63.65m)
Height:	54ft 11in (16.74m)
Empty Weight:	264,374lb (120,170kg)
Max Take Off:	506,000lb (230,000kg)
Powerplant:	2 x 67,500lb (300kN) General Electric CF6-80E1A2 turbofans.
Cruise Speed:	624mph (999km/h)
Max Cruise:	Mach. 0.86
Service Ceiling:	39,370ft (12,000m)
Range:	5,140 miles (8,982km)
Number Manufactured:	Manufacture ongoing.
Flying or in service:	Widely in service.

Airbus A319

Subject: Airbus A319 of US carrier Frontier Airways.
           Registration N914FR.
Statistics: Airbus A319 series.

Airbus had already secured 1,500 orders for its highly successful A320 series before it began the production of its trimmed-down A319 variant. Designed to carry reduced numbers of passengers over greater distances, the A319 has been selected by many of the world's largest and most cost-sensitive airliners. The type has been designed to have near-complete commonality with the Airbus A320 and its stablemate the A321, facilitating great reductions in piloting and maintenance costs.

Country of Origin:	USA
First Flight:	1995
Accommodation:	2 + 122 passengers.
Wingspan:	111ft 10in (34.09m)
Length:	111ft 0in (33.84m)
Height:	38ft 7in (11.76m)
Empty Weight:	88,400lb (40,100 tonnes)
Max Take Off:	141,100lb (64,000 tonnes)
Powerplant:	2 X CFM56-5A4 turbofans rated at 22,025lb (97.9kN) thrust each.
Cruise Speed:	560mph (903km/h)
Max Cruise:	609mph (980km/h)
Service Ceiling:	31,170ft (9,500m)
Range:	3,040 miles (4,892km)
Number Manufactured:	Still in series production.
Flying or in service:	Widely in service.

Airbus A340

Subject: A340-200 airliner. Registration unknown.
Statistics: Airbus A340-200.

The introduction of the Airbus A340 into the long range wide-body market caused massive changes of allegiance within that sector. Operators were being pressed from all sides to reduce their costs and to provide faster turn-around times. The A340, hot off the press, had all of the advantages of an all-new design, and its reduced costing forecasts proved very popular with operators right across the world. Within months of the first A340 entering service with Lufthansa, the order book for the new wide-body transport was filling up and, indeed, the type has been in continuous production since that time. Airbus continues to update and enhance its A340 on a continuous and ongoing basis in order to ensure that new A340s reflect the very latest and best technologies available today.

Country of Origin:	EU
First Flight:	1991
Accommodation:	2 + 295 to 335
Wingspan:	197ft 0in (60.3m)
Length/Height:	194ft 10in (59.39m)
Height:	54ft 11in (16.74m)
Empty Weight:	277,770lb (126,000kg)
Max Take Off:	573,200lb (260,000kg)
Powerplant:	4 X 31,200lb (138.8kN) or 4 X 32,550lb (145kN) CFM turbofans.
Cruise Speed:	547mph (880km/h)
Max Speed:	569mph (914km/h)
Service Ceiling:	39,000ft (11,887m)
Range:	6,700nm (12,415km) with full complement of passengers.
Number Manufactured:	Approximately 350 to date.
Flying or in service:	Widely in service.

Airbus A380

Subject: Prototype Airbus A380 registration F-WWOW (con 001) now flying for Qantas.
Statistics: Airbus A380.

The all-new Airbus A380 is now the world's largest passenger carrier and its introduction into commercial usage will require the making of very large changes to the infrastructures of existing airport facilities. The type is configured to carry a staggering 555 passengers, but as additional floor space is already available on the aircraft, it is expected that this capacity figure will increase as larger and more powerful engines are developed.

Country of Origin:	EU
First Flight:	2005
Accommodation:	2 pilots + cabin crew + 555 three-class passengers.
Wingspan:	261ft 10in (79.8m)
Length:	2328ft 8in (72.75m)
Height:	79ft 0in (24.08m)
Empty Weight:	610,700lb (277,000kg)
Max Take Off:	1,234,600lb (560,000kg)
Powerplant:	4 X 70,000lb (311kN) Rolls-Royce Trent 900 turbofans.
Cruise Speed:	Mach 0.85
Max Speed:	Mach 0.88
Service Ceiling:	43,000ft (13,100m)
Range:	5,600miles (10,370km)
Number Manufactured:	Over 150 on order.
Flying or in service:	1

Airbus A300-600ST Beluga

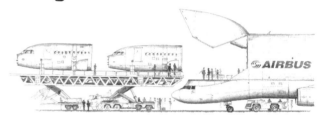

Subject: Airbus A300-B4-608 ST Super-Transporter being loaded with A-319 fuselage plugs. Registration F-GSTB/2.
Statistics: Airbus A300-600 ST Super-Transporter.

Built on the chassis of a standard Airbus A300-600, the giant Airbus Beluga was developed to replace the ageing Super Guppy programme. The type was designed to ferry wing assemblies, fuselage sections and other outsize loads between the various Airbus plants. Loads of up to 103,516lb (47 tonnes) can be carried and individual components can be up to 123ft (37.7m) in length and 24ft 3in (7.4m) in diameter. The type entered service in January of 1996 facilitating a much-deserved retirement of the Super Guppy in late 1997.

Country of Origin:	EU
First Flight:	1994
Accommodation:	2 crew plus a payload with volume of up to 49,440 cubic ft (1,400 cu m)
Wingspan:	147ft 0in (44.84m)
Length:	184ft 3in (56.16m)
Height:	56ft 6in (17.23m)
Empty Weight:	241,372lb (109,500kg)
Loaded:	341,700lb (155,000kg)

Powerplant:	2 x 59,000lb (262.4kN) General Electric CF6-8002A8 turbofans.
Cruise Speed:	485mph (780km/h)
Max Speed:	567mph (912km/h)
Service Ceiling:	35,000ft (10,670m)
Range:	2,160nm (4,000km)
Number Manufactured:	5
Flying or in Service:	5

Airco/de Havilland DH-2

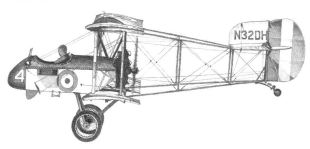

Subject: N32DH is a full-size flying replica of the original DH-2.
Statistics: Airco/de Havilland DH-2.

The skies over the battlefields of Europe were in the grip of the Fokker scourge when the Aircraft Manufacturing Company (or Airco) introduced its new DH-2 model. Designed by none other than Geoffrey de Havilland, the new pusher aircraft was more manoeuvrable and agile than the German aircraft of the day and so the technical advantage was won in the short term. Shortly afterwards, however, the synchronous machine gun appeared for the first time on the German aircraft fleet and this advantage was immediately lost. So it was, then, that the DH-2 had its brilliant but very short career.

Country of Origin:	UK
First Flight:	1915
Accommodation:	1
Wingspan:	28ft 3in (8.61m)
Length:	25ft 2in (7.68m)
Height:	9ft 6in (2.91m)
Empty Weight:	942lb (428kg)
Max Take Off:	1,441lb (653.6kg)
Powerplant:	1 x 9-cylinder air-cooled rotary Gnome Monosoupape rated at 100hp.
Max Cruise:	93mph (150km/h)
Service Ceiling:	14,000ft (4,267m)
Range:	344 miles (553km)
Number Manufactured:	Approximately 400 built.
Preserved:	Australian War Memorial Museum, Canberra, Australia. Museum of Flying, Santa Monica, California, USA.

Airco/de Havilland DH-4

Subject: DH-4 replica registration N981RN marked with the decals of the United States Mail service.
Statistics: Airco/de Havilland DH-4 (replica).

With the entry of the USA into the First World War the tried and trusted de Havilland DH-4 airframe was redesigned in the USA to meet the needs of the mobilizing US forces. It was the incorporation of the superb 412hp Liberty engine, however, which breathed new life into the type. A total of 4,846 of 'The Flaming Coffin' were built, with 1,213 of these being shipped to the frontlines in Europe. Arriving late in the war, the DH-4 marque saw only limited action and, although more than 400 combat sorties are recorded, only 33 of the type were actually lost to the enemy.

Country of Origin:	UK and USA
First Flight:	1916 and 1917
Accommodation:	Pilot & Gunner/Observer
Wingspan:	43ft 6in (13.29m)
Length:	30ft 6in (9.3m)
Height:	10ft 4in (3.17m)
Empty Weight:	2,391lb (1,084kg)
Max Take Off:	3,557lb (1,613kg)
Powerplant:	Liberty 12 rated at 412hp.
Cruise Speed:	90mph (145km/h)
Max Cruise:	128mph (206km/h)
Service Ceiling:	19,600ft (5,974m)
Range:	400 miles (644km)
Number Manufactured:	4,846
Flying or in service:	1
Preserved:	US Air Force Museum, Dayton, Ohio, USA.

Air Tractor AT-802 Fireboss

Subject: Air Tractor AT-802 registration N6159F scoops water into its hopper.
Statistics: Air Tractor AT-802 Fireboss.

In its water-bombing role the Fireboss was designed to facilitate rapid uploading of water by way of scoop-filling its panniers during the on-water landing roll. In practice the AT-802 skims onto the water's surface and, opening its fill doors, takes on a full load of water within seconds before accelerating back into the air. While each fill of water is not massive in volume the rapid turnabout system ensures that a steady flow of water is delivered to the firefront. With its 1,424hp (1,062kW) Pratt & Whitney turboprop powerplant the Fireboss is perhaps the largest and most powerful single engined agricultural and water-bombing aircraft in the world.

Country of Origin:	USA
First Flight:	1973
Accommodation:	1
Wingspan:	58ft 0in (17.68m)
Length:	36ft 4in (11.07m)
Height:	11ft 0in (3.35m)
Empty Weight:	6,300lb (2,860kg)
Max Take Off:	16,000lb (7,260kg)
Powerplant:	1 Pratt & Whitney PT6A-67R turboprop rated at 1,424hp (1,062kW).
Cruise Speed:	209mph (338km/h)
Max Speed:	206mph (331km/h)
Service Ceiling:	18,000ft (5,486m)
Range:	500 miles (805km)
Number Manufactured:	Over 1,500 of all models.
Flying or in service:	In service.

Antonov An-2 Colt

Subject: Antonov An-2 registration CCCP-02660 of state carrier Aeroflot.
Statistics: Antonov An-2.

The Soviet Union's wonderful biplane utility transport and world's biggest flying biplane. The An-2, despite its age, is a rugged and versatile performer. Whether ferrying essential supplies to remote oil-industry communities or providing logistical support to a Paris-Dakar rally team, the An-2 is a superbly mannered and capable workhorse.

Country of Origin:	USSR and Poland
First Flight:	1947
Accommodation:	1 or 2 + 12
Wingspan:	59ft 8in (18.18m)
Length:	40ft 8in (12.4m)
Height:	13ft 2in (4.1m)
Empty Weight:	7,605lb (3,450kg)
Max Take Off:	12,125lb (5,500kg)
Powerplant:	1 X 1,000hp (745kW) PZL Kalisz ASz61R nine-cylinder radial engine.
Cruise Speed:	115mph (185km/h)
Max Speed:	138mph (220km/h)
Service Ceiling:	14,435ft (4,399m)
Range:	455nm (845km) with full complement of passengers.
Number Manufactured:	Over 5,000 built in the Ukraine, with a further 12,000 built in Poland. 1,000 further examples built by SAMC of China as the Y-5.
Flying or in service:	Many still in active service.
Preserved:	March Field Air Museum. Riverside, California, USA. Planes of Fame Air Museum, Chino, California, USA. Russian Central Air Force Museum, Monino, Moscow.

Antonov An-12 Cub

Subject: Antonov An-12. Registration CCCP 11105. Cub of Russian state carrier Aeroflot.
Statistics: Antonov An-12 Cub.

Widely used by both Aeroflot and the Soviet armed forces, the An-12 was an efficient turboprop freighter and utility transport. The type was also built under licence by Shaanxi of China and, in this format, it was given the designation Y-8A. The Cub's glazed nose was designed to facilitate the navigator's workstation and to provide clear vistas of the terrain ahead.

Country of Origin:	USSR
First Flight:	1958
Accommodation:	4 + 90 fully laden troops
Wingspan:	124ft 8in (38m)
Length:	108ft 7in (33.1m)
Height:	34ft 7in (10.53m)
Empty Weight:	61,730lb (28,000kg)
Max Take Off:	134,480lb (61,000kg)
Powerplants:	4 X 3,495hp (2,490kW) Ivchenko AI20K turboprops.
Cruise Speed:	416mph (670km/h)
Max Speed:	483mph (777km/h)
Service Ceiling:	33,500ft (10,200m)
Range:	1,940nm (3,600km) with full payload.
Number Manufactured:	Approximately 1,243 ex-Soviet Union and a further 75 Y-8s licence-built in China.
Flying or in service:	Still widely used.
Preserved:	Russian Central Air Force Museum, Monino, Moscow.

Antonov An-14 Clod

Subject: Antonov An-14 of former East German air force.
Statistics: Antonov An-14 Clod.

While NATO applied the derogatory codename Clod to the diminutive An-14, the type was more favourably nicknamed the 'Little Bee' at home in the Eastern Bloc countries. Designed to be able to fly out of short and uneven airfields, the type was a useful freighter and feederliner, which could be flown by a single pilot.

Country of Origin:	USSR
First Flight:	1958
Accommodation:	1 + 7
Wingspan:	72ft 2in (21.99m)
Length:	37ft 6in (11.44m)
Height:	15ft 3in (4.63m)
Empty Weight:	5,700lb (2,600kg)
Max Take Off:	8,000lb (3,630kg)
Powerplant:	2 X 1,300hp (224kW) Ivchenko AI-14RF radial piston engines.
Cruise Speed:	120mph (193km/h)
Max Speed:	138mph (222km/h)
Service Ceiling:	16,400ft (5,000m)
Range:	497 miles (800km) with full complement of passengers.
Number Manufactured:	Approximately 300 built.
Preserved:	Russian Central Air Force Museum, Monino, Moscow.

Antonov An-28 Cash

Subject: Antonov An-28 Cash of Soviet carrier Aeroflot. Registration 000P-28776.
Statistics: Antonov An-28 Cash.

Developed by the Antonov design bureau and flown for the first time in the Ukraine, the An-28 was manufactured entirely by PZL-Mielec in Poland. On receiving its type certificate in April of 1986 deliveries began to Aeroflot and to other state carriers of the Eastern Bloc countries. The Cash was built around a tough and robust airframe. Its duties involved, for the most part, accessing small, remote airstrips and rural communities and so much emphasis was placed on simplicity of systems and ease of maintenance. Low capital acquisition costs and low maintenance outlays make the An-28 a popular choice with operators today.

Country of Origin:	USSR and Poland
First Flight:	1969
Accommodation:	2 + 17 passengers or density layout of 2 + 20 passengers.

Wingspan:	72ft 5in (22.06m)
Length:	43ft 0in (13.1m)
Height:	16ft 1in (4.9m)
Empty Weight:	8,598lb (3,900kg)
Max Take Off:	14,330lb (6,500kg)
Powerplant:	2 X 1,100hp (820kW) Pratt & Whitney Canada PT6A65Bs.
Cruise Speed:	Economy. 208mph (335km/h)
Max Speed:	218mph (350km/h).
Service Ceiling:	16,400ft (5,000m)
Range:	800 miles (1,300km)
Number Manufactured:	More than 200 of various models delivered and still under manufacture.
Flying or in service:	Many An-28s in service.
Preserved:	National Military Museum, Warsaw, Poland.

Antonov
An-72 Coaler

Subject: An-72 Coaler of Soviet carrier Aeroflot.
                 Registration OOOP-72000.
Statistics: Antonov An-72 Coaler.

The Coaler's large rear-opening ramp door and robust bogie undercarriage arrangement allow for easy loading and for the carriage of large loads. Most of the 160 (-plus) An-72s produced were supplied to military customers and many continue in use in this role today.

Country of Origin:	USSR
First Flight:	1977
Accommodation:	3 + 68 passengers
Wingspan:	104ft 8in (31.89m)
Length:	92ft 1in (28.07m)
Height:	28ft 5in (8.65m)
Empty Weight:	41,998lb (19,050kg)
Max Take Off:	76,059lb (34,500kg)
Powerplant:	2 X 14,330lb (63.7kN) ZMKB Progress D36 turbofans.
Cruise Speed:	340mph (550km/h)
Max Speed:	374mph (600km/h)
Service Ceiling:	35,000ft (10,668m)
Range:	2,590nm (4,800km)
Number Manufactured:	Approx 160 of all variants.
Flying or in service:	Approx 25 still in service.

Armstrong Whitworth Apollo

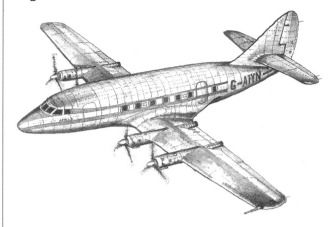

Subject: Armstrong Whitworth Apollo G-AIYN.
Statistics: Armstrong Whitworth Apollo.

The Apollo was at the cutting edge of civilian aviation technology at the time of its first flight in 1949. Using new turboprop technology derived during the war years, Armstrong Whitworth produced an airliner which was quiet, comfortable and reliable. Despite all of these attributes, however, the Apollo was not adopted by the airlines in sufficient quantity to maintain production. This was a time of rapidly developing technology and rival manufacturers were offering aircraft of similar and even higher standards. In this highly charged environment the Apollo project became a casualty.

Country of Origin:	UK
First Flight:	1949
Accommodation:	Crew of 3 and 31 passengers
Wingspan:	93ft 0in (28.35m)
Length:	71ft 6in (21.79m)
Height:	26ft 0in (7.92m)
Empty Weight:	30,800lb (13,970kg)
Max Take Off:	45,000lb (20,411kg)
Powerplant:	4 X 1,010hp Armstrong Siddeley Mamba turboprops.
Max Speed:	330mph (531km/h)
Service Ceiling:	28,000ft (8,500m)
Range:	940 miles (1,513km)
Preserved:	Nottingham East Midlands Aeropark, Derbyshire, UK. Yankee Air Museum, Belleville, Michigan, USA.

Armstrong Whitworth 101 Argosy

Subject: Argosy 101 registration N896U is on open air display at the Yankee Air Museum, Belleville, Michigan.
Statistics: Armstrong Whitworth 101 Argosy.

The Argosy's outsize twin-boom configuration was designed around the need to facilitate the loading and unloading of artillery pieces, military freight, and armoured vehicles. Its large rear-facing freight doors could be opened in flight to allow the delivery by parachute of supply pallets and, indeed, its huge loading ramp provided the perfect launchplatform for mass dispersal of paratroop forces. Fifty-six Royal Air Force Argosys served throughout Britain and many other parts of the world until their eventual retirement in the mid 1970s.

Country of Origin:	UK
First Flight:	1959
Accommodation:	3 crew + 69 fully equipped troops or one laden Saracen armoured car or equivalent.
Wingspan:	115ft 0in (35.05m)
Length:	89ft 0in (27.13m)
Empty Weight:	69,000lb (31,298kg)
Max Take Off:	105,000lb (47,610kg)
Powerplant:	4 X 2,470hp (1,841kW) Dart RDa.8 Mark 101 turboprops.
Cruise Speed:	241mph (390km/h)
Max Speed:	269mph (433km/h)
Service Ceiling:	20,013ft (6,100m)
Range:	3,250 miles (5,220km)
Number Manufactured:	73
Preserved:	Nottingham East Midlands Aeropark, Derbyshire, UK. Yankee Air Museum, Belleville, Michigan, USA.

Arrow Aircraft Active II

Subject: Arrow Active G-ABVE is maintained in airworthy condition by the Shuttleworth Trust and is flown periodically.
Statistics: Arrow Aircraft Active MK. II.

Arrow Aircraft of Leeds was principally involved in the manufacture of aircraft components but it did apply itself to a brief series of aircraft developments in the early 1930s. Under the expert direction of designer Arthur Thornton the Active I and Active II were first flown in 1931 and 1932 respectively. Intended as primary trainers and aerobats, Arrow always hoped that they would be adopted by military customers and, in particular, by the various British military forces. When no substantial orders were placed, however, Arrow's aircraft manufacturing workshop was scaled down and Arrow returned to its former business.

Country of Origin:	UK
First Flight:	1932
Accommodation:	1
Wingspan:	24ft 0in (7.3m)
Length:	18ft 10in (5.7m)
Height:	7ft 6in (2.3m)
Empty Weight:	925lb (420kg)
Max Take Off:	1,325lb (602kg)
Powerplant:	1 x 120hp (89.4kW) Gipsy III inverted air-cooled engine.
Cruise Speed:	129mph (206km/h)
Max Speed:	144mph (230km/h)
Range:	400 miles (640km)
Number Manufactured:	Only 2 manufactured.
Flying or in service:	1

Arrow Sport

Subject: I came across this wonderful airworthy Arrow A2-60 Sport in Florida during 2004.
Statistics: Arrow A2-60 Sport.

These were the wonderful days when a company could build both cars and aircraft in one workshop. Everything was built by hand and clients were allowed an extraordinary level of personal involvement in the selection and the detailing of their personal travelling machines. At Nebraska's tiny Arrow Aircraft and Motor Corporation things were no different. Aircraft were built to order for particular clients and, in the main, these clients were involved in the specification and finishes from the outset. The Arrow Sport, with its unusual side-by-side seating arrangement, was a popular and much sought-after sports biplane in its day. Approximately 100 of the type were built before Arrow closed its doors for good in 1940.

Country of Origin:	USA
First Flight:	1926
Accommodation:	2 side by side.
Wingspan:	25ft 9in (7.8m)
Length:	19ft 3in (5.8m)
Height:	7ft 5in (2.2m)
Empty Weight:	900lb (408kg)
Powerplant:	5-cylinder 60hp Le Blond engine, or 100hp Kinner radial.
Cruise Speed:	95mph (153km/h)
Max Speed:	110mph (177km/h)
Range:	280 miles (449km)
Number Manufactured:	Approx. 100 built before Arrow closed its doors in 1940.
Flying or in service:	Several still airworthy.
Preserved:	Arrow s/n 341 is preserved at the Smithsonian National Air and Space Museum, Steven F. Udvar-Hazy Center. Ottumwa Airpower Museum, Iowa, USA.

Auster AOP-9

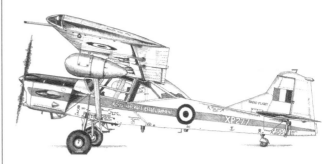

Subject: Ex-Royal Aircraft Establishment XP277 later sold into the USA.
Statistics: Auster AOP-9.

In the later years of the Second World War accurate aerial target and acquisition reporting made it possible for the Allied forces to greatly improve the effectiveness of their ground artillery offensives. While some of this information was gleaned from fast-moving fighters overhead it was found that trained personnel in small observation aircraft could provide more accurate data when deployed immediately behind and above such massed ground forces. In 1946 the Auster 'Aerial Observation Post' AOP-6 was introduced, followed in 1955 by the slightly larger and more powerful AOP-9.

Country of Origin:	UK (from original US design)
First Flight:	1955
Accommodation:	Pilot and observer or stretcher.
Wingspan:	36ft 5in (11.13m)
Length:	23ft 9in (7.24m)
Height:	8ft 11in (2.47)
Empty Weight:	1,590lb (721.2kg)
Max Take Off:	2,330lb (1057kg)
Powerplant:	1 x 180hp (134kW) Blackburn Cirrus Bombardier 203 in-line piston.
Cruise Speed:	110mph (177km/h)
Max Speed:	127mph (204.3km/h)
Service Ceiling:	19,500ft (5,943m)
Range:	242 miles (389.4km)
Number Manufactured:	400 AOP-6s and 145 AOP-9s.
Flying or in service:	Approximately 50.
Preserved:	US Army Aviation Museum, Fort Rucker, Ozark, Alabama, USA.

Auster B-4 Ambulance/Freighter

Subject: Auster's B-4 freighter.
Statistics: Auster B-4 Ambulance/Freighter.

The B-4 ambulance/freighter was a high-wing strutted monoplane with a broad fuselage of square cross section which was designed to facilitate the carriage of stretchers, military supplies and other bulky loads.

Country of Origin:	UK.
First Flight:	1955
Accommodation:	Pilot and observer or stretcher.
Wingspan:	36ft 5in (11.11m)
Length:	23ft 9in (7.24m)
Height:	8ft 11in (2.71m)
Empty Weight:	1,590lb (721.2kg)
Max Take Off:	2,330lb (1,056kg)
Powerplant:	1X 180hp (134kw) Blackburn Cirrus Bombardier 203 in-line piston.
Cruise Speed:	110mph (177km/h)
Max Speed:	127mph (204.3k/h)
Service Ceiling:	19,500ft (4,943m)
Range:	242 miles (389km)

AVE Mizar Flying Car

Subject: AVE Mizar N-88X crashed fatally in 1973.
Statistics: AVE Mizar Flying Car.

The AVE Mizar Flying Car comprised a standard Ford Pinto mated with the rear portion of a Cessna 337 Skymaster. Two prototypes were completed and a further three were under construction. Flight testing was undertaken at Van Nuys in California and the type caused a small media sensation with its promise of bringing flight to the ordinary motorist. A countrywide dealership network was established with a major Ford franchise holder and certification of the type was commenced. The 1973 purchase price from your local Ford dealer's forecourt was expected to be US $18,300 for the basic model and US $29,000 for the fully loaded saloon. The project was abandoned after the car and the aircraft separated in mid-air with tragic consequences.

Country of Origin:	USA
First Flight:	1973
Accommodation:	1 + 4
Wingspan:	38ft 0in 11.58m
Length:	28ft 6in (8.69m)
Height:	8ft 6in (2.59m)
Empty Weight:	4,700lb (2,132kg)
Powerplant:	1 X Continental IO-360-C.
Cruise Speed:	130mph (209km/h) target
Max Speed:	170mph (273km/h) target
Service Ceiling:	16,000ft (4,877m) target
Range:	764 miles (1,223km) target
Number Manufactured:	2 (+ 3 partially completed).

Avro 652-A Anson

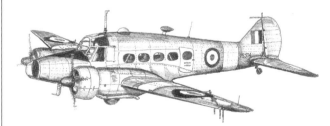

Subject: Glass-fronted Anson T-20 navigational training aircraft of the Royal Air Force.
Statistics: Avro Anson 19.

Avro was not slow to follow the pioneering work of Fokker of The Netherlands and incorporated the latest lightweight steel tube technology into the 1933 design for the Avro Anson. Based on the earlier Avro 652, the Anson adopted the dual innovations of single low cantilevered wing technology and fully retractable landing gear. The new airframe was sleek and clean by 1930s standards and Avro went on to build very large numbers of the type with production running from 1935 right up until 1949 when the last export variants were delivered to Afghanistan and India.

Country of Origin:	UK
First Flight:	1935
Accommodation:	2 + 7
Wingspan:	56ft 6in (17.22m)
Length:	42ft 3in (12.88m)
Height:	13ft 1in (4.0m)
Empty Weight:	7,420lb (3,366kg)
Max Take Off:	10,400lb (4,717kg)
Powerplant:	2 X 420hp (313.2kw) Armstrong Siddeley Cheetah XV.
Cruise Speed:	168mph (270km/h)
Max Speed:	182mph (293km/h)
Service Ceiling:	20,500ft (6,248m)
Range:	820 miles (1,312km)
Number Manufactured:	More than 7,155 of all types.
Preserved:	British Columbia Aviation Museum, Victoria International Airport (MK II). Commonwealth Air Training Plan Museum, Manitoba (MK V).

Avro Athena

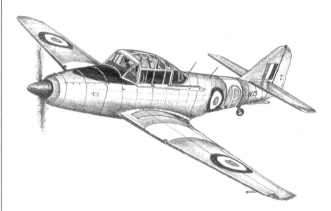

Subject: Royal Air Force Avro 701 Athena.
Statistics: Avro 701 Athena.

A.V. Roe & Co. Ltd developed the Athena to a Royal Air Force specification for a high performance cantilever monoplane advanced trainer which would also be required to fulfil the difficult roles of day and night navigational training. The solution entailed developing a sleek and well-faired airframe which would house Rolls-Royce's powerful 1,280hp (954kW) Merlin 35 engine as well as instructor and student in side-by-side configuration. The Athena trainer was sleek and fast for its day and Avro went on to build 15 airframes for its Royal Air Force base customer.

Country of Origin:	UK .
First Flight:	1948
Accommodation:	2 crew side by side.
Wingspan:	40ft 0in (12.2m)
Length:	37ft 4in (11.38m)
Height:	12ft 11in (3.9m)
Empty Weight:	6,611lb (2,999kg)
Max Take Off:	8,213lb (3,725kg)

Powerplant:	1 x Rolls-Royce Merlin 35
	12-cylinder V. Liquid cooled.
Max Speed:	297mph (478km/h)
Service Ceiling:	29,500ft (8,992m)
Range:	550 miles (885km)
Number Manufactured:	4 prototypes and 15 production.

Range:	5,140 miles (8,982km)
Number Manufactured:	7,377 Lancasters but only a small number of Lancastrians.
Preserved:	Greenwood Military Museum, Nova Scotia, Canada.
	RAF Museum, Hendon, London, UK.

Ayers
Thrush Turbo

Subject: Ayers Turbo Thrush S2RT34 registration N3094M.
Statistics: Statistics for Ayers Turbo Thrush S2RT34.

Ayers (absorbed into North American Rockwell in 1967) has specialized in the area of agricultural cropdusting and aerial crop spraying and has, over the years, developed a series of ever more powerful and sophisticated ag-planes. The original Ayers Thrush was developed into the Ag Commander and later again became the Rockwell Thrush Commander. This is a powerful and sophisticated specialist cropspraying platform with its massive 750hp Pratt & Whitney turboprop powerplant and its sophisticated uniform spray approach and delivery system. The type has won a very large segment of the aerial cropspraying sector within the USA, its main rival in recent years being a ready supply of cheaper ex-Eastern Bloc dusting machines.

Country of Origin:	USA
First Flight:	1956
Accommodation:	1
Wingspan:	44ft 4in (13.5m)
Length:	29ft 5in (8.95m)
Height:	9ft 2in (2.79m)
Empty Weight:	3,600lb (1,633kg)
Max Take Off:	6,000lb (2,720kg)
Powerplant:	1 x 750hp (560kW) Pratt & Whitney Canada PT6A34AG turboprop.
Cruise Speed:	115mph (185km/h)
Max Speed:	158mph (256km/h)
Range:	403 miles (648km)
Number Manufactured:	1,300 built by Rockwell and 350 by Ayers.
Flying or in service:	Several still in active service.

Avro
Lancastrian

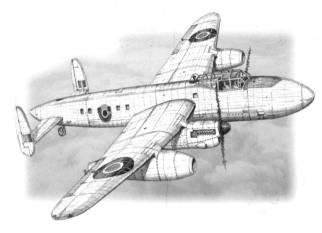

Subject: Lancastrian airframe as jet engine test platform.
Statistics: Avro Lancastrian (with piston powerplants).

Victory Aircraft Ltd of Canada was first to convert war-surplus Lancaster bombers into high-speed long-range transports and mail freighters. The conversions were operated by carrier Trans-Canada Airlines on behalf of the Canadian Government and they carried postal freight and small numbers of passengers on a scheduled route between Montreal and Prestwick in Scotland. Avro, too, saw the merit in converting war-surplus airframes and began a programme which saw the conversion of 87 former Lancasters into high-speed Lancastrians of various designations. The featured Lancastrian was operated as a test bed for various jet propulsion programmes.

Country of Origin:	UK
First Flight:	1949
Accommodation:	3 crew and 8 to 13 passengers.
Wingspan:	102ft 0in (31.09m)
Length:	69ft 4in (21.13m)
Height:	20ft 4in (6.2m)
Empty Weight:	35,167lb (15,985kg)
Max Take Off:	64,864lb (29,484kg)
Powerplant:	Avro conversions powered by 4 x Rolls-Royce Merlin engines.
Max Speed:	272mph (438km/h)
Service Ceiling:	24,600ft (7,498m)

Avro
Shackleton MR-3-3

Subject: Royal Navy Avro Shackleton MR-3-3.
Statistics: Avro Shackleton MR-3-3.

Many of the tried and tested components of the Lincoln and Tudor were incorporated into the Shackleton and, as such, remained in operational service until the type's long overdue retirement in the mid 1990s.

Country of Origin:	UK
First Flight:	1949
Accommodation:	2 + specialist technicians.
Wingspan:	119ft 10in (36.52m)
Length:	87ft 4in (26.62m)
Height:	16ft 9in (5.11m)
Empty Weight:	56,800lb (25,759kg)
Max Take Off:	98,000lb (44,444kg)
Powerplant (Varies):	4 x 2,455hp (1,829kW) Rolls-Royce Griffon 57As.
Max Speed:	273mph (439km/h)
Service Ceiling:	20,200ft (6,200m)
Range:	2,900 miles (4,665km)
Number Manufactured:	185 built between 1951 & 1958.
Flying or in service:	12 intact. 1 still airworthy.
Preserved:	Newark Air Museum, Nottingham, Nottinghamshire, UK.

Avro Tudor

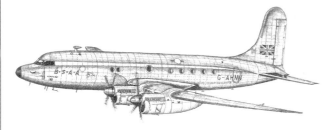

Subject: Avro Tudor G-AHNN in the colours of British carrier BSAA.

Statistics: Avro Tudor 1.

The early Mark 1 Tudors were designed with shortened fuselage and long-range fuel tanks to maximize range for the new scheduled North Atlantic crossings. These design decisions, however, ensured that only 24 passengers could be carried on this long sector. The later Mark 2 Tudor was tailored very differently for BOAC's long routes to South Africa and Australia, where refuelling was possible. This stretched configuration accommodated up to 60 passengers, a massive jump in capacity and a wonder to air travellers of the late 1940s. Other specialized Tudor variants were developed, too, including luxury VIP transport airframes which were built by Armstrong Whitworth for ministerial transport and other VIP-related duties. Those were the days.

Country of Origin:	UK
First Flight:	1945
Accommodation:	3 crew + 24 passengers.
Wingspan:	120ft 0in (36.58m)
Length:	79ft 6in (24.23m)
Height:	21ft 11in (6.7m)
Max Take Off:	71,000lb (32,205kg)
Powerplant:	4 x Rolls-Royce Merlin 621 or 623 powerplants.
Cruise Speed:	298mph (480km/h)
Max Speed:	344mph (554km/h)
Service Ceiling:	31,529ft (9,610m)
Range:	3,630 miles (5,842km)
Number Manufactured:	Approx 74 of all variants.

Avro 685 York

Subject: Avro York 685 in Royal Air Force markings MW295.

Statistics: Avro 685 York.

The York was intended as an interim RAF transport only pending completion of some of the large-scale transport projects already in progress by British design shops. To ensure rapid delivery of the new type, Avro decided to mate a new large-volume fuselage to the earlier Lancaster wingfoils, undercarriage, and tail sections. The new fuselage, with its all-metal square cross section, would accommodate larger loads and greater numbers of troops without all of the design complexities of an ab initio project. The York was rushed into service but, far from being a temporary measure, remained in operation with the RAF right up to 1957 and thereafter with many small airline operators well into the 1960s.

Country of Origin:	UK
First Flight:	1942
Accommodation:	5 + 24 passengers (varied).
Wingspan:	102ft 0in (31.09m)
Length:	78ft 6in (23.93m)
Height:	16ft 6in (5.0m)
Empty Weight:	33,200lb (15,060kg)
Max Take Off:	68,000lb (30,844kg)
Powerplant:	4 x 1,620hp (1,207kW) Rolls-Royce Merlin 24s.
Cruise Speed:	233mph (375km/h)
Max Speed:	298mph (479km/h)
Service Ceiling:	23,000ft (7,010m).
Range:	2,700 miles (4,345km)
Number Manufactured:	255 plus of all variants.
Preserved:	RAF Museum, Cosford Airfield, Shropshire, UK (TS798 York C1).

BAe 146 Whisper Jet

Subject: BAe 146 of carrier Flybe at London City Airport 2004.

Statistics: BAe 146-100.

Hawker Siddeley's 1973 announcement of its HS-146 Hush Jet was greeted with mixed enthusiasm in those times of economic gloom. Changes in environmental awareness over its protracted development period, however, meant that it was much better received by the time of its first flight in 1981. The Whisper Jet went on to serve many airlines and national carriers in many of the most noise-sensitive city-centre airport sites in the world.

Country of Origin:	UK
First Flight:	1981
Accommodation:	2 crew + 70 to 82 passengers.
Wingspan:	86ft (26.21m)
Length:	101ft 8in (31m)
Height:	28ft 3in (8.61m)
Empty Weight:	51,342lb (23,288kg)
Max Take Off:	84,000lb (38,100kg)
Powerplant:	4 x 6,700lb (30.0kN) Textron Lycoming ALF 502R-3s.
Cruise Speed:	445mph (716km/h)
Max Speed:	476mph (766km/h)
Service Ceiling:	31,167ft (9,500m).
Range:	1,620 miles (3,000km)
Number Manufactured:	In excess of 370.
Flying or in service:	Widely in operational service.

Beagle A-61 Terrier 2

Subject: Beagle A-61 Terrier registration G-ASAN.

Statistics: Beagle A-61 Terrier 2.

The A-61 Terrier, A-61 Terrier 2 and 6A Tugmaster were derived from the long-serving military Auster AOP-6 and AOP-9 range. The A-61 Terrier 2 was built to particularly high levels of specification with the intention of appealing to military customers.

Country of Origin:	UK
First Flight:	1962
Accommodation:	2
Wingspan:	36ft 5in (11.11m)
Length:	23ft 9in (7.25m)
Height:	8ft 11in (2.47m)
Empty Weight:	1,590lb (721kg)
Max Take Off:	2,330lb (1,057kg)
Powerplant:	1 x Gipsy Major 7
Cruise Speed:	110mph (177km/h)
Max Speed:	127mph (204km/h)

Service Ceiling:	19,500ft (5,943m)
Range:	242 miles (389km)
Flying or in service:	Small numbers still in service.
Preserved:	A regular at air shows worldwide.

BAC Jet Provost

Subject: Transair owned ex-Royal Air Force Jet Provost.
Statistics: BAC/Hunting Jet Provost.

The retirement of the Provost from operational service has led to the dispersal of many Provost airframes among private warbird pilots and collectors. For the price of an upmarket sports car you can own an airworthy Provost warbird. Keeping it flying, of course, is another matter and deep pockets and strong nerves are a mandatory prerequisite of ownership.

Country of Origin:	UK.
First Flight:	1954
Accommodation:	2
Wingspan:	35ft 4in (10.77m)
Length:	33ft 9in (10.28m)
Max Take Off:	8,524lb (3,866kg)
Powerplant:	1 x 2,500lb (11.12KN) Rolls-Royce Viper MK 202 turbojet.
Max Speed:	404mph (650km/h)
Service Ceiling:	34,500ft (10,515m)
Range:	900 miles (1,450km)
Number Manufactured:	More than 450 manufactured.
Flying or in service:	Many now privately owned.

BAe Harrier T-10

Subject: Harrier T-10 a/f ZH653 of Royal Air Force based at Wharton.
Statistics: BAe Harrier T-10.

From the very first days of powered flight, engineers have tried to master the art of taking off vertically. The extremely delicate balance of forces required to achieve controllability in the take-off stage, however, is immensely difficult to achieve and, until recent years, only the BAe Harrier Jump Jet had managed to make it into large-scale production. Developed from the Hawker Siddeley Kestrel VTOL prototype of 1958-1960 the Harrier project evolved into a potent strike attack platform under the leadership of new owner British Aerospace. A variant with greatly increased weapons payload is licence-built by US manufacturer McDonnell Douglas.

Country of Origin:	UK.
First Flight:	1966
Accommodation:	1 or 2
Wingspan:	30ft 4in (9.4m)
Length:	46ft 4in (14.12m)
Height:	13ft 8in (4.17m)
Empty Weight:	12,500lb (5,700kg)
Max Take Off:	29,750lb (13,494kg)
Powerplant:	1 x Rolls-Royce Pegasus (Various) vectored thrust turbofans.
Cruise Speed:	609mph (975km/h)
Max Speed:	661mph (1,065km/h)
Service Ceiling:	50,000ft (15,000m)
Range (with drop tanks):	3,310 miles (5,382km)
Number Manufactured:	Approx. 815 of all variants.
Flying or in service:	Operational with the armed forces of UK, USA, Spain, India, Australia and others.

BAe/Aérospatiale Concorde

Subject: British Airways Concorde 102 registration G-BOAB overflies the south coast of Ireland. This aircraft now sits on open display on the ramp area at London's Heathrow Airport.
Statistics: BAe/Aérospatiale Concorde.

The introduction of Concorde caused great controversy in early January of 1976 with widespread outcry about the likelihood of sonic-boom pollution and broken windows on a wide scale. In reality, however, few of these problems arose and the type operated with great distinction for almost 25 years. London and Paris were now only 3 hours away from New York and Concorde carried a host of celebrities, VIPs, and well-heeled travellers who had reason or money enough to cross the North Atlantic in the most stylish and technically advanced airliner of all time. The tragic Air France Paris Concorde disaster of 2000, which ultimately led to the retirement of the type, is notable for having been caused not by the aircraft itself, but by items of debris which were lying on the runway in its path as it took off.

Country of Origin:	France and UK
First Flight:	1969
Accommodation:	3 + 128 passengers.
Wingspan:	83ft 10in (25.56m)
Length:	203ft 9in (62.1m)
Max Take Off:	408,000lb (185,065kg)
Powerplant:	4 x 38,050lb (169.3KN) Rolls-Royce/SNECMA Olympus 593 Mk 610 turbojets (with reheat).
Cruise Speed:	Mach 2.02
Max Speed:	Mach 2.04
Service Ceiling:	61,000ft (18,592m)
Range:	4,090 miles (6,580km)
Number Manufactured:	2 prototypes. 2 pre-production models. 10 production models.
Flying or in service:	Retired from service October 2003.
Preserved:	Duxford Aviation Museum, UK (G-AXDN (101)). Steven F. Udvar-Hazy Center, Chantilly, Virginia, USA (F-BVFA). Fleet Air Arm Museum, Somerset, UK (G-BSST).

BAe (de Havilland) HS-125

Subject: de Havilland DH-125 prototype G-ARYA.
Statistics: BAe (de Havilland) HS-125-700.

Hawker Siddeley, and later BAe, were careful to ensure that their evolving 125 series would appeal to military operators as well as to executive and charter companies. So it was, then, that this sleek corporate transport was adopted by armed forces across the world to fulfil a wide variety of roles including communication work, airways inspection, air-ambulance duties, advanced pilot training and specialized radar operations. In these roles the BAe-125 has been operated by the armed forces of the UK, Brazil, Ghana, Malaysia, Mexico, South Africa, Argentina and Australia.

Country of Origin:	UK
First Flight:	1962
Accommodation:	2 + 8
Wingspan:	47ft 0in (14.33m)
Length:	50ft 9in (15.46m)
Height:	18ft (5.49m)
Empty Weight:	15,557lb (7,056kg)
Max Take Off:	24,200lb (10,977kg)
Powerplant:	2 X Garrett AiResearch TFE 731-3-1H turbofan engines.
Max Speed:	368mph (592km/h)
Service Ceiling:	41,000ft (12,497m)
Range:	2,683 miles (4,318km)
Flying or in service:	Large numbers still in service.

Beagle 206 Basset

Subject: G-GFTR is maintained in airworthy condition and is a regular visitor to Private Flying Assocation meetings across Britain.
Statistics: Beagle Aircraft Ltd Beagle 206.

The Beagle 206C twin was developed to satisfy a Royal Air Force specification and all of the systems incorporated into the airframe were built to meet the RAF's rugged and onerous military requirements. Its 2 Continental geared and fuel-injected flat-six piston engines provided 310hp (230kW) to drive a pair of 3-blade constant-speed propellers. The uprated 206S model with its turbocharged powerplant was rated at 340hp (253kW). Designed in troubled Cold War times to position RAF V-bomber crews to their remote stand-by sites, the Beagle 206 could accommodate 8 persons on sectors of up to 1,550nm (2,870km), that is, anywhere within the British Isles. In its later years an 8-seat civil transport variant was produced in small numbers followed by an enlarged 10-seat commuter airliner. Although flown in prototype form, this development came to a swift end when Beagle Aircraft Ltd went into voluntary liquidation on 27 February 1970.

Country of Origin:	UK
First Flight:	1961
Accommodation:	2 + 6
Wingspan:	45ft 10in (13.95m)
Length:	33ft 8in (10.25m)
Height:	11ft 4in (3.45m)
Empty Weight:	5,400lb (2,450kg)
Max Take Off:	7,500lb (3,400kg)
Powerplant:	2 X Continental GIO470A fuel injected flat-six.
Cruise Speed:	160Kt (298km/h)
Max Speed:	191Kt (354km/h)
Range:	1,784 miles (2,870km)
Number Manufactured:	79 of various configurations.
Flying or in service:	Several examples still flying.
Preserved:	Royal Army and Military History Museum, Brussels, Belgium.

Beagle B-121 Pup

Subject: Beagle B-121 Pup registered G-AXPN.
Statistics: Beagle B-121 100 Series Pup.

Three versions of the Pup were built. The standard 100 Series Pup was designed for civilian use and, with its 100 horsepower Continental engine, it provided a good economical touring and training aircraft. The larger 150 Series Pup has an additional 50 horses under the hood and it was favoured by its military customers for its faster cruising speeds and its enhanced climbing ability. Only 9 of the 160 Series Pups were built, these being developed specially for the Iranian Civil Air Training Programme which required additional power to cope with the extremely high air temperatures and resultant low air densities which would be encountered in the Middle East. In recent years large numbers of Pups have been released from military service and sold into private ownership. Given the robust nature of the type and given the very high levels of airframe maintenance provided by its military operators, it is likely that these Pups will be with us for many many years to come.

Country of Origin:	UK .
First Flight:	1967
Accommodation:	2 with marginal capacity for a third person behind.
Wingspan:	31ft 0in (9.45m)
Length:	22ft 11in (6.99m)
Height:	7ft 6in (2.29m)
Empty Weight:	1,063lb (482kg)
Max Take Off:	1,600lb (725kg)
Powerplant:	100 Series: 1 X 100hp (75kW) Rolls-Royce Continental. 150 Series: 1 X 150hp (110kW) Lycoming O-320 flat-four. 160 Series: 1 X 160hp (120kW) Lycoming IO-320 flat-four.
Cruise Speed:	118mph (190km/h)
Max Speed:	126mph (204km/h)
Range:	495 miles (916km)
Number Manufactured:	173 of all types.
Flying or in service:	Large numbers now released to civilian ownership.
Preserved:	Aero Venture, South Yorkshire Aircraft Museum, UK.

Bede BD-5 Micro

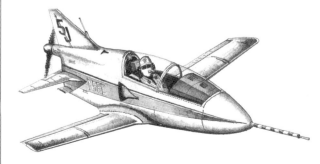

Subject: Bede BD-5 Micro US n-number N58D.
Statistics: Bede BD-5 Micro.

When James Bond used his diminutive BD-5 jet to decimate his villainous enemies it threw even more fuel on the fires of Jim Bede's media hype. The Micro was the homebuild which was always waiting for an engine. Aerodynamically it was a superb performer with excellent flying characteristics and superb cruising speed, stall speed and range. The problem was, however, that all of the many engines investigated seemed to resist sitting compatibly into the airframe. Bede spent years trying to find an engine to mate with his wonder plane. Continually under pressure from the thousands of builders who had paid good money for kits which could not be completed, Bede tried every combination of engine and driveshaft with only moderate success. Eventually Bede could not resist the financial pressures any longer and was forced to declare bankruptcy. Only a small proportion of BD-5s were completed, many of those in later years when it was found that Honda's smaller turbocharged automotive engines could be used to power the Micro with relative success.

Country of Origin:	USA
First Flight:	1971
Accommodation:	2
Wingspan:	21.5ft (6.55m)
Length:	13.9ft (4.24m)
Height:	5.6ft (1.71m)
Empty Weight:	460lb (209kg)
Max Take Off:	830lb (376kg)
Powerplant:	Various experimental engines including Keikaefer, Hirth, Polaris, Kawasaki and, in recent years, Honda automobile engines.
Cruise Speed:	167mph (268km/h)
Max Speed:	200mph (321km/h)
Service Ceiling:	12,000ft (3,657m)
Range:	720 miles (1,158km)
Number Manufactured:	Over 7,000 kits sold but only 650 to 700 were completed.
Flying or in service:	Approximately 200.
Preserved:	Prototype N500BD is on display at the EAA Museum. Oshkosh, USA. Ottumwa Airpower Museum, Iowa, USA. Seattle Museum of Flight, Washington, USA.

Beechcraft Model 35 Bonanza

Subject: Beechcraft 35 Bonanza.
Statistics: Beechcraft Model 35 Bonanza.

The Bonanza's distinctive V-shaped tail is still found to this day at airfields right across the world. In 1945, when it was first flown, however, it was at the very cutting edge of the civil aviation market with its retractable undercarriage, its competent avionics package and its superb constant-speed propeller installation. Indeed, the Bonanza remained in manufacture right up until 1982, by which time 10,400 of the type had been built.

Country of Origin:	USA
First Flight:	1945
Accommodation:	1 + 3
Wingspan:	32ft 10in (10.0m)
Length:	25ft 2in (7.65m)
Height:	14ft 6in (4.42m)
Empty Weight:	1,675lb (760kg)
Max Take Off:	2,725lb (1,236kg)
Powerplant:	1 x 205hp (153kW) Continental E18511 flat-six piston.
Cruise Speed:	152kt (281km/h)
Max Speed:	165kt (306km/h)
Service Ceiling:	18,000ft (5,486m)
Range:	1,056nm (1,955km)
Number Manufactured:	10,400 of all variants built between 1945 and 1982.
Flying or in service:	Many still actively flying.
Preserved:	Model 35 Bonanza preserved at Pima Air and Space Museum, Tucson, Arizona, USA. Mid-America Air Museum, Liberal, Kansas, USA.

Beechcraft Model 55 Baron

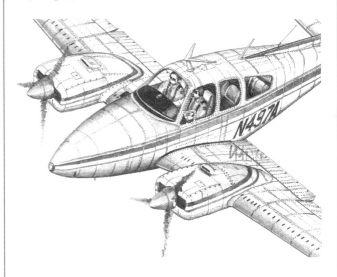

Subject: Beechcraft 55 Baron, US registration N497A.
Statistics: Beechcraft 55 Baron.

In 1965 the US Army selected the Model 95-B55 Baron as the winner of its twin-engine advanced-trainer competition. Following this success the type was adopted as an advanced instrument trainer by the air forces of Spain and Turkey, and by the Civil Air Bureau of Japan. The Baron went on to outlast and outsell its competitors and, indeed, won a very substantial share of the commercial and executive transport sector. Its two 260hp Continental flat-six fuel-injected horizontally opposed engines provide a high level of performance with good climbing ability, a high service ceiling and an economy cruising speed of 173kt. Throughout the type all finishes are presented to the very highest of standards with carefully faired joints and a superbly appointed Bonanza-type interior.

Country of Origin:	USA
First Flight:	1960
Accommodation:	1 + 3
Wingspan:	37ft 10in (11.53m)
Length:	28ft 0in (8.53m)
Height:	9ft 7in (2.92m)
Empty Weight:	3,236lb (1,468kg)
Max Take Off:	5,100lb (2,313kg)
Powerplant:	2 x 260hp (140kW) Continental fuel-injected flat-six pistons.
Cruise Speed:	173kt (320km/h)
Max Speed:	188kt (348km/h)
Service Ceiling:	19,200ft (5,852m)
Range:	900nm (1,836km)
Number Manufactured:	3,155 of all variants between 1961 and 1983.
Flying or in service:	Still widely in service.

Beechcraft 99 Airliner

Subject: Beech 99 Airliner registered in Germany as D-IEXB is operated by specialist freight/courier carrier Night Express.

Statistics: Beech 99 Airliner.

The Beech 99 Airliner was developed from the earlier Beech Queen Air series and, although it had a greatly increased seating capacity, its basic airframe configuration and powerplant specification were unchanged. The Beech 99 was designed to meet an industry requirement for a cost effective regional transport and feederliner to serve smaller and more remote rural communities, particularly those of the US and Canada. The Model 99, known initially as the 'Commuter 99' brought greatly improved levels of efficiency over earlier aircraft types and it went on to be adapted by a wide range of operators leading to a total production run of 239 airframes. Power was provided by a pair of Pratt & Whitney Canada PT6A-28 turboprop powerplants turning a pair of 3-blade constant-speed Hartzell propellers. More than half of the total production run of the type remain in operational service to this day.

Country of Origin:	USA
First Flight:	1966
Accommodation:	Flight crew of 1 or 2 and 14 to 15 passengers or equivalent quantities of freight.
Wingspan:	45ft 11in (14.0m)
Length:	44ft 7in (13.58m)
Height:	14ft 4in (4.38m)
Empty Weight:	5,777lb (2,620kg)
Max Take Off:	10,900lb (4,944kg)
Powerplant:	2 x 680hp (507kW) Pratt & Whitney Canada PT6A-28 turboprops
Cruise Speed:	285mph (456km/h)
Max Speed:	308mph (493km/h)
Range:	1,035 miles (1,665km)
Number Manufactured:	239 of all variants built between 1967 and 1987.
Flying or in service.	Still widely in service today.

Beechcraft 390 Premier 1

Subject: Beechcraft 390 Premier, listed on the German civil register as D-IBBB (con. RB-82).

Statistics: Beechcraft 390 Premier 1.

Examination of the corporate transport market confirmed that most executive jets are flown with very low levels of seat occupancy. Large jets, therefore, are often flown over very long sectors with just 1 or 2 executive occupants resulting in extraordinarily high operating costs per seat. The Raytheon (Beech/Hawker) Premier is among the first of a new generation of compact executive transports which offers full corporate jet status at cost levels which are more akin to those of entry level aircraft. Small, light, and sporting just 6 passenger places, the Premier provides buckets of status and attitude. Its certification for single-pilot operation, too, greatly simplifies the logistics and the costs involved in operating a corporate runabout. The Premier's all-new lightweight composite fuselage shell uses new filament-wound-carbon-fibre technology which was first developed for the Beech Starship programme. The result is a stronger, lighter, and more adaptable fuselage structure which can be turned out by the manufacturer's automated machines in a single day.

Country of Origin:	USA
First Flight:	1998
Accommodation:	Flight crew of 1 or 2 and up to 6 passengers in standard configuration or 4 in full club configuration.
Wingspan:	44ft 6in (13.56m)
Length:	45ft 4in (13.81m)
Height:	15ft 4in (4.66m)
Empty Weight:	7,996lb (3,626kg)
Max Take Off:	12,500lb (5,670kg)
Powerplant:	2 x 2,300lb (10.2kN) Williams Rolls turbofans.
Cruise Speed:	530mph (854km/h)
Service Ceiling:	41,000ft (12,497m)
Range:	1,727 miles (2,780km)
Number Manufactured:	Currently in production at an estimated delivery rate of 50 airframes per year.
Flying or in service.	In service.

Beechcraft Starship

Subject: Beechcraft Starship 2000. Registration number N8285Q.

Statistics: Beechcraft Starship 2000.

Teaming up with Burt Rutan's radical Scaled Composites aviation think-tank was a brave step for Beechcraft. This choice alone determined that the new corporate and executive transport would be radical in configuration, with a heavy reliance on new, lightweight composite structural materials. Rutan was true to form and his prototype was brilliant and radically different to what had gone before. For Beechcraft, however, the venture was an expensive and troubled one. The Starship, which was intended to replace the company's prolific but ageing King Air, cost it 300 million dollars for just 53 airframes, a near-disaster by any count.

Country of Origin:	USA
First Flight:	1983
Accommodation:	2 pilots + 6 or 8
Wingspan:	54ft 5in (16.6m)
Length:	46ft 1in (14.05m)
Height:	12ft 11in (3.69m)
Empty Weight:	10,085lb (4,574kg)
Max Take Off:	14,900lb (6,758kg)
Powerplant:	2 x 1,200hp (895kW) Pratt & Whitney Canada PT6A67A turboprops.
Cruise Speed:	295kt (546km/h)
Max Speed:	335kt (622km/h)
Range:	1,634nm (2,630km)
Number Manufactured:	53
Flying or in service:	Only 4 in operational service.
Preserved:	7 donated to museums including the Mid-America Air Museum, Liberal, Kansas, USA.

Beechcraft T-34 Mentor

Subject: This stunning blue/white Mentor N34YK turned up at Sun 'n Fun 2005 having flown from nearby Daytona.

Statistics: Beechcraft. T-34B and YT-34C Mentor.

The T-34 was developed from the Beechcraft Bonanza as a low-cost tandem 2-seat primary trainer. After extensive flight trials the type was adopted by the US Air Force and later by the US Navy. It served, too, with many other air forces including the Japanese Air Defense Force which flew a licence-built variant designated the T-3 Harukaze or Breeze. By 1973 the T-34B had been in service with the US Navy for many years and its future was becoming uncertain. The Navy's training procedures for ab initio training were moving away from piston-powered training airframes towards more sophisticated jet and turboprop aircraft. And so the YT-34C was born. Beechcraft installed Pratt & Whitney Canada's PT6A-25 turboprop into a beefed-up airframe and added the latest in electronic wizardry. The new YT-34C was a massive improvement on the original T-34 and the US Navy was impressed. The type was ordered in large quantities and, indeed, a small number of these YT-34Cs remain in service with the US Civil Air Patrol to this day. Many others have been released to civil ownership and are much valued and sought after as veterans and warbirds.

Country of Origin:	USA
First Flight:	1948
Accommodation:	2 in a tandem arrangement.
Wingspan:	32ft 10in (9.78m)
Length:	25ft 10in (7.65m)
Height:	10ft 0in (3.05m)
Empty Weight:	2,055lb (932kg)
Max Take Off:	2,900lb (1,315kg)
Powerplant:	T-34B. 1 x 225hp (168kW) Continental O-470-13 flat-six. Later YT-34C. 400hp (298kW) Pratt & Whitney Canada PT6A-25 turboprop.
Cruise Speed:	225mph (362km/h)
Max Speed:	257mph (413km/h)
Service Ceiling:	25,000ft (7,620m)
Range:	750 miles (1,205km)
Number Manufactured:	More than 1,350 of all types.
Flying or in service:	Many warbirds still airworthy.
Preserved:	National Museum of the US Air Force, Wright-Patterson AFB, Dayton, Ohio, USA.

Beechcraft Model 17 Staggerwing

Subject: Beechcraft civilian Model 17 Staggerwing.

Statistics: Statistics for USAAF's Beechcraft UC-43.

The Staggerwing must be one of the most handsome and inspired aircraft designs of all time. Beechcraft's Model 17 made headlines from the start when it collected a bevy of prestigious aviation awards. The world-famous aviator and socialite Jacqueline Cochran was quick to recognize its many merits and it was the Staggerwing she used to set a new US women's closed-circuit record in 1937. With the coming of the War the type was made in huge numbers for the US Army Air Force, its dedicated variant being the uprated UC-43 Staggerwing Traveller. Perhaps the most fascinating delivery by Beechcraft was that in 1939 of one Model 17 each to the beleaguered US military attaches of London, Paris and Rome.

Country of Origin:	USA
First Flight:	1932
Accommodation:	4
Wingspan:	32ft 0in (9.75m)
Length:	26ft 2in (7.97m)
Height:	8ft 6in (2.5m)
Empty Weight:	1,825lb (827kg)
Max Take Off:	4,700lb (2,132kg)
Powerplant:	Earlier Model 17s powered by Jacobs or Wright engines. Later by P & W Wasp Juniors.
Cruise Speed:	202mph (325km/h)
Max Speed:	212mph (341km/h)
Service Ceiling:	20,000ft (6,096m)
Range:	500 miles (805km)
Number Manufactured:	781 of all variants.

Flying or in service:	Several airworthy today.
Preserved:	Model 17 preserved at National Air & Space Museum, Washington, USA. International Sport Aviation Museum, Lakeland Linder Regional Airport, Lakeland, Florida, USA. Planes of Fame Air Museum, Chino, California, USA. Mid-America Air Museum, Liberal, Kansas, USA.

Bell Model 30 Genevieve

Subject: Bell's prototype Model 30 Genevieve.

Statistics: Bell Model 30.

Bell's prototype Genevieve was the forerunner of the Bell Model 47 helicopter, one of the world's earliest and most long-lasting production helicopter designs. The Genevieve's cone shaped tail was destroyed in a handling accident just 6 months after its first flight and Bell replaced it with the rudimentary toblerone-trussed tail boom which would later become the trademark of its Model 47 series. Developed from drawing board to flying prototype in a period of 6 months, the Genevieve perhaps did more to advance the development of rotary flight than any other helicopter. From it, Bell developed the Model 47, which they submitted for US Army trials. Selected by the US Army, the Model 47 was built, and served, in large numbers over the course of the Korean War. On 6 March 1946 the Model 47 became the world's first certified helicopter and it continued to be manufactured in very large numbers for both military and commercial customers.

Country of Origin:	USA
First Flight:	1942
Accommodation:	1
Rotor diameter:	32ft 4in (9.98m)

Length: 26ft 10in (8.19m)
Height: 8ft 7in (2.62m)
Empty Weight: 1,150lb (522kg)
Powerplant: 1 x 160hp Franklin piston engine.
Max Speed: 93mph (150km/h)
Service Ceiling: 10,800ft (3,292m)
Number Manufactured: Prototypes only.
Preserved: Steven F. Udvar-Hazy Center, Washington, DC, USA.

Bensen
B-8M Autogyro

Subject: Bensen B-8M Autogyro.
Statistics: Bensen B-8M.

Bensen's B-8 autogyro was well designed and engineered and, with a reasonably modest build cost, it quickly won the admiration and the favour of the home-building community. Most of the components were easily sourced or engineered and the most complex assemblies could be purchased ready-built from a list of approved specialist engineering workshops.

Country of Origin: USA
First Flight: 1957
Accommodation: 1
Rotor Diameter: 20ft 0in (6.1m)
Length: 11ft 4in (3.45m)
Height: 6ft 3in (1.9m)
Max Take Off: 500lb (227kg)
Powerplant: 1 x 72hp (53.7kW) McCulloch 4318E.
Cruise Speed: 60mph (96km/h)
Max Speed: 85mph (136km/h)
Service Ceiling: 7,000ft (2,133m)
Range: 100 miles (160km)
Number Manufactured: Large numbers completed from plans by home-builders.

Flying or in service: Some B-8Ms still airworthy.
Preserved: March Field Air Museum, Riverside, California, USA.
New England Air Museum, Windsor Locks, Connecticut, USA.
Steven F. Udvar-Hazy Center, Washington, DC, USA.
International Sport Aviation Museum, Lakeland Linder Regional Airport, Lakeland, Florida, USA.
The Helicopter Museum, USA.
American Helicopter Museum, Philadelphia, USA.

Bell
Model 47-G-2A (on floats)

Subject: Bell 47G (H-13G), best helicopter award, at Sun 'n Fun, Florida.
Statistics: Bell 47-G-2A (on floats).

One of the first truly workable and versatile helicopters which was produced by Bell in very large numbers in a production run which ran from the late 1940s right through to 1976. While initial production aircraft featured an open-cockpit arrangement, all later airframes were provided with an enclosed bubble-canopy cabin.

Country of Origin: USA
First Flight: 1945
Accommodation: 2
Rotor Diameter: 37ft 2in (11.32m)
Length: 32ft 6in (9.9m)
Height: 9ft 3in (2.82m)
Empty Weight: 1,888lb (858kg)
Max Take Off: 2,950lb (1,338kg)
Powerplant: 1 x 280 hp Lycoming TVO-435.
Cruise Speed: 84mph (135km/h)

Max Speed: 105mph (168km/h)
Service Ceiling: 20,000ft (6,096m)
Range: 248 miles (396km)
Number Manufactured: 4,000 by Bell. 1,200 by Agusta/Bell Italy. 239 by Kawasaki and 239 by Westland UK.
Flying or in service: Small numbers of military 47Gs maintained by enthusiasts.
Preserved: The Helicopter Museum, Weston-Super-Mare, Somerset, UK (Bell 47H, G-AZYB).
Canada Aviation Museum, Ottawa, Ontario, Canada (Bell HTL-6 (47G)).
Norwegian Aviation Museum, Bodø, Norway (47-G (632)).

Bell Model 206 LT
Twin Ranger

Subject: Spanish Police Force Bell 206 LT Twin Ranger registered EC-HCT.
Statistics: Bell Model 206 LT Twin Ranger.

While Bell Helicopters did produce a prototype twin-turbined Model 400 Twin Ranger in late 1984, the project encountered substantial difficulties and was eventually abandoned. The current Bell 206 LT Twin Ranger, then, is based, not on a Bell product, but a third-party upgrade of the original Bell 206 airframe which was offered by Tridair Helicopters through its Gemini ST conversion programme. This Federal Aviation Authority-certificated conversion allowed the Twin Ranger to operate on either one turbine or two through all stages of flight, thus allowing it to reduce its fuel-burn figures on ferry flights and low-occupancy trips, where only reduced levels of power were required. Having monitored the success of the Tridair conversion Bell decided to produce a new-build Twin Ranger and so developed an equivalent twin-turbine-powered variant based on the Long Ranger airframe.

Country of Origin: USA
First Flight: 1991
Accommodation: 1 + 6
Rotor diameter: 37ft 0in (11.28m)
Length: 42ft 9in (13.02m)

Height:	10ft 4in (3.14m)
Empty Weight:	2,748lb (1,246kg)
Max Take Off:	4,450lb (2,018kg)
Powerplant:	2 X 450shp (335kW) Allison 250-C20R turboshafts.
Cruise Speed:	108kt (200km/h)
Max Speed:	117kt (217km/h)
Service Ceiling:	20,000ft (6,096m)
Range:	347nm (643km)
Number Manufactured:	1,150 by 1987.
Flying or in service:	Widely in service.

Bell Model 209 Huey Cobra

Subject: Bell prototype airframe.
Statistics: Bell AH-1S.

The 209 Cobra was developed using many of the engine and transmission components of the long-standing HU-1A Huey helicopter. The nature of warfare conducted by the Vietcong had required the US to make huge changes to the way in which hostile forces were engaged. Suddenly fleets of helicopters became central to the battle plan with their ability to insert combat troops into any given location and to withdraw them again after short firefights. This plan of battle, however, required these relatively exposed helicopter fleets to be provided with potent escort helicopters complete with ground-attack firepower. It was with this purpose that the 209 Cobra was developed. A number of specialized single-turbine variants were developed for the US Army while the US Navy opted for a much weightier and greatly more powerful twin-turbine version.

Country of Origin:	USA
First Flight:	1965
Accommodation:	Pilot and co-pilot/gunner.
Rotor Diameter:	44ft 0in (13.4m)
Length:	44ft 7in (13.6m)
Height:	13ft 5in (4.1m)
Empty Weight:	6,598lb (2,993kg)
Max Take Off:	10,000lb (4,535kg)
Powerplant:	1 X 1,800shp (1,300kW) Avco Lycoming T53-L-13 Turboshaft.
Cruise Speed:	166mph (267km/h)
Service Ceiling:	12,200ft (3,718km/h)

Combat Range:	315 miles (507km)
Number Manufactured:	More than 1,116 of all Variants.
Flying or in service:	Operated by many armed forces across the world.
Preserved:	US Army Aviation Museum, Fort Rucker, Ozark, Alabama, USA.

Bell 412

Subject: Bell 412 Search-and-Rescue helicopter registered EC-1XX of Spain.
Statistics: Bell 412.

Bell's tried and trusted 412 has, over the years, etched out a substantial segment of the medium/heavy civilian turbine helicopter market. Its Pratt & Whitney twin-turbine powerplant provides greatly enhanced levels of reliability and assurance for long overwater flight and has caused the type to be very popular for oil-rig supply flights and for the transfer of personnel teams to and from oil-processing platforms.

Country of Origin:	USA
First Flight:	1979
Accommodation:	Pilot + 14 passengers.
Rotor Diameter:	46ft 0in (14.02m)
Length:	41ft 9in (12.7m)
Height:	15ft 0in (4.57m)
Empty Weight:	6,759lb (3,066kg)
Max Take Off:	11,900lb (5,397kg)
Powerplant:	1 X 1,800hp (1,350kW) P&W Canada PT6T-3B Turbo-Twin-Pac comprising 2 interlinked PT6 turbines.
Cruise Speed:	127kt (235km/h)
Max Speed:	130kt (240km/h)
Service Ceiling:	16,300ft (4,968m)
Range:	245nm (455km)
Flying or in service:	Current Variant 412EP is still in production.

Bell P-63 Kingcobra

Subject: Bell P-63 Kingcobra.
Statistics: Bell P-63 Kingcobra.

Although it saw little or no frontline service with the US Air Force, the Bell P-63 Kingcobra was delivered in large numbers for use on the battlefields of Europe. Out of the 3,303 airframes manufactured no fewer than 2,400 were shipped to the Soviet Union with a further 300 being shipped to the beleagured Mediterranean area for use by Free French forces. Even as the type was entering production it was becoming outclassed and outdated by the latest offerings from the USA. The P-63 Kingcobra was a substantial upgrade of the earlier P-39 Airacobra design with a larger airframe, all new laminar flow-wing technology, a more powerful powerplant, and greatly improved performance figures. Within the USA itself large numbers of P-63 Kingcobras continued to be used in the role of advanced trainers for the remainder of the war years.

Country of Origin:	USA
First Flight:	1942
Accommodation:	1
Wingspan:	38ft 4in (11.68m)
Length:	32ft 8in (9.96m)
Height:	12ft 8in (3.86m)
Empty Weight:	6,385lb (2,896kg)
Max Take Off:	10,500lb (4,763kg)
Powerplant:	1 X 1,325hp (988kW) centrally mounted Allison V-1710-93.
Cruise Speed:	315mph (507km/h)
Max Speed:	410mph (660km/h)
Range:	2,100 miles (3,380 km)
Number Manufactured:	3,303 of all P-63 variants manufactured inclusive of 2,400 airframes which were delivered to the Soviet Union.
Flying or in service:	Small numbers still operable with flying museums today.
Airframes Preserved:	Fantasy of Flight Museum, Polk County, Florida, USA.

Bell X-14
Research Prototype

Subject: Bell X-14 research prototype undertaking
           a landing.
Statistics: Bell X-14. Research prototype.

Following the success of Bell's private venture VTOL
prototype of 1954, the US Air Force contracted Bell
Aerosystems to develop an all new VTOL programme.
The project began with the selection of a pair of powerful
and compact British built Armstrong Siddeley ASV8 engines
combined with a system of rudimentary thrust deflectors.
The prototype flew well and produced large volumes of
invaluable research data right up until its eventual
retirement in 1981.

Country of Origin:	USA
First Flight:	1957
Accommodation:	1
Wingspan:	34ft 0in (10.36m)
Length:	25ft 1in (7.65m)
Height:	8ft 1in (2.47m)
Empty Weight:	Not established.
Max Take Off:	3,100lb (1,406kg)
Powerplants:	2 x Armstrong Siddeley ASV8 Viper engines.
Cruise Speed:	Not established.
Max Speed:	180mph (290km/h)
Service Ceiling:	18,000ft (5,486km)
Range:	300miles (483km)
Number Manufactured:	1
Preserved:	X-14 prototype preserved at US Army Aviation Museum, Fort Rucker, Alabama, USA.

Blackburn
Iris

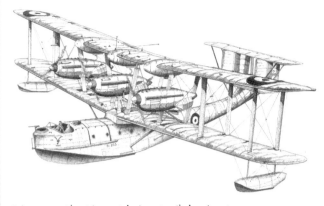

Subject: Blackburn Iris heavy flying boat.
Statistics: Blackburn Iris.

The Iris was Blackburn's first flying boat. Designed to
provide the Royal Navy with a long-range reconnaissance
facility, the Iris could remain airborne for hours on end.
Aviation was still in its early days and the separation of
aviation from naval design was still far from complete.
Indeed, the Blackburn Iris was heavily influenced by the
naval architecture of the day.

Country of Origin:	UK
First Flight:	1926
Accommodation:	2 + 3
Wingspan:	97ft 2in (29.6m)
Length:	83ft 4in (25.4m)
Height:	25ft 3in (7.7m)
Empty Weight:	19,047lb (8,640kg)
Max Take Off:	29,489lb (13,376kg)
Powerplants:	3 x 674hp (503kW) Rolls-Royce Condor IIIB powerplants.
Cruise Speed:	118mph (190km/h)
Service Ceiling:	10,600ft (3,230m)
Range:	800 miles (1,280km)
Number Manufactured:	3 prototypes and 4 production airframes built.

Blackburn
Beverley

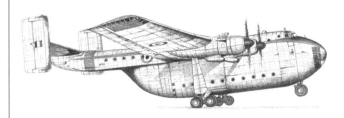

Subject: Blackburn Beverley XB261, of the UK's Aircraft
           & Armament Evaluation Establishment was
           displayed outdoors for many years at Southend
           until corrosion caused it to be scrapped in 1991.
Statistics: Blackburn Beverley.

Though only 47 Beverleys were built, the type had a
long and successful career with the Royal Air Force,
serving in many parts of the world from 1956 to 1967.
The Beverley specialized in moving heavy and outsized
loads and in delivering parachute-drop loads to military
field and other difficult sites. Many small trucks and
Land Rovers met their end during a protracted series
of parachute-drop trials which saw various military loads
and pallets being jettisoned from the backs of low-flying
Beverleys. With such parachute drop technology still in its
infancy, many of these jettison programmes were beset
by extraordinarily high levels of hardware loss.

Country of Origin:	UK
First Flight:	1950
Accommodation:	2 + 58 in the freight bay and a further 36 in the tail boom.
Wingspan:	162ft 0in (49.38m)
Length:	99ft 5in (30.3m)
Height:	38ft 9in (11.8m)
Empty Weight:	82,000lb (37,194kg)
Max Take Off:	135,000lb (61,236kg)
Powerplants:	4 x 2,850hp (2,125kW) Bristol Centaurus.
Cruise Speed:	173mph (278km/h)
Max Speed:	238mph (383km/h)
Service Ceiling:	16,000ft (4,877m)
Range:	3,690 miles (5,938km)
Number Manufactured:	47
Preserved:	Fort Paull Museum, Hull, UK. Newark Air Museum, Nottingham, Nottinghamshire, UK (cockpit).

Blackburn B-24 Skua

Subject: B-24 Skua in the colours of the Royal Air Force.
Statistics: Blackburn B-24 Skua.

With the coming of war in Europe the pace of development of aircraft technology began to accelerate to such an extent that aircraft were nearing obsolescence even as they were reaching operational service. So it was with the Skua. Germany's powerful aircraft industry was employing the latest innovations in aviation technology and mass production techniques while, at the same time, small design shops like Blackburn were grappling for the first time with retractable undercarriage systems and variable-pitch propellers. The Skua was a sophisticated concept which was simply outpaced even as it was being developed.

Country of Origin: UK .
First Flight: 1937
Accommodation: Pilot + Gunner/Bombardier.
Wingspan: 46ft 2in (14.07m)
Length: 35ft 6in (10.85m)
Height: 12ft 5in (3.79m)
Empty Weight: 5,490lb (2,490kg)
Max Take Off: 8,228lb (3,732kg)
Powerplant: 1 x 905hp (675kW) Bristol Perseus XII radial.
Max Speed: 225mph (362km/h)
Service Ceiling: 19,100ft (5,822m)
Range: 800 miles (1,287km)
Number Manufactured: 192 built.
Preserved: Norwegian Aviation Museum, Bodø, Norway (under restoration).

Boeing L-15 Scout

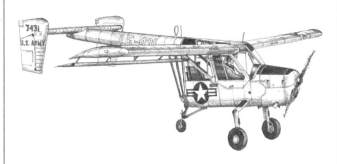

Subject: Boeing L-15 Scout. LE-431. Airframe no 7431 of the US Army.
Statistics: Boeing L-15 Scout LE-431.

The L-15 Scout was Boeing's last single-engine light aircraft design. Developed to meet a US Army specification, the Scout was specifically designed to serve as a ground observation platform. The airframe was designed to be towed behind a jeep or loaded onto a 2-ton truck for transit alongside frontline troops. When advance aerial reconnaissance or gunnery acquisition data was required the L-15's wings would be folded out into position and the type flown off roadways or very short, unprepared areas of ground. In flight the Scout had excellent slow-speed characteristics and a good loiter endurance. The observer, in particular, had unparalleled views all around and could transmit necessary intel to the ground forces below. Twin floats and, indeed, skis could be fitted and the type was carefully proportioned to allow it to be transported to remote locations inside Boeing's massive C-97 transport. Only 12 of the type were manufactured for appraisal by the US Army and, although the type was much favoured by forward forces, no substantial orders followed.

Country of Origin: USA .
First Flight: 1947
Accommodation: 1 + 1
Wingspan: 40ft 0in (12.19m)
Length: 25ft 2in (7.68m)
Height: 8ft 8in (2.65m)
Max Take Off: 2,050lb (930kg)
Powerplant: 1 x Lycoming 0-290 flat-four rated at 125hp (93.2kW).
Cruise Speed: 98mph (158km/h)
Max Speed: 112mph (180km/h)
Service Ceiling: 16,400ft (4,998m)
Range: 699 miles (1,125km)
Number Manufactured: 12
Preserved: United States Army Aviation Museum, Fort Rucker, USA.

Boeing Model 100

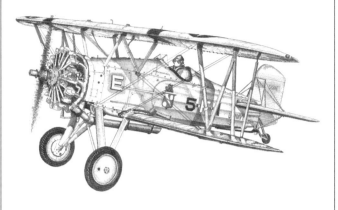

Subject: Boeing Model 100 of the US Navy.
Statistics: Boeing 100.

A variant of the prolific F4B series, the Model 100 was a single-seat biplane version with all items of weaponry and military equipment removed. In their place a new upper wing fuel tank gave enhanced endurance in the air. Only 4 of the Model 100 were built and one of these was retained by Boeing as a factory demonstrator and engine test bed. A single 2-seat Model 100A was built for millionaire businessman Howard Hughes.

Country of Origin: USA .
First Flight: 1928
Accommodation: 1
Wingspan: 30ft 0in (9.14m)
Length: 20ft 5in (6.23m)
Height: 9ft 10in (3.0m)
Max Take Off: 3,611lb (1,638kg)
Powerplant: 1 x 550hp (410kW) R-1340-16 Wasp radial engine.
Cruise Speed: 142mph (228km/h)
Max Speed: 188mph (303km/h)
Service Ceiling: 27,500ft (8,380m)
Range: 370 miles (595km)
Number Manufactured: 4 of Model 100.

Boeing F4B-3

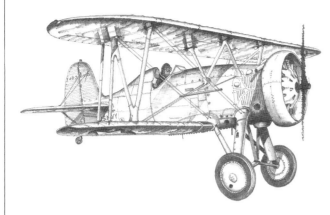

Subject: US Navy Boeing F4B-3 powered by the 525hp
Pratt & Whitney R-1340-17 radial. USN
airframe 8910.
Statistics: Boeing F4B-3 biplane fighter.

The F4B series was one of Boeing's most reliable products
and it helped to maintain the fledgling Wichita company
through some of the most difficult depression years. The
US Navy, in particular, was impressed during its 1928
evaluation of the type and ordered 27 airframes for
service aboard the USS Lexington.

Country of Origin: USA
First Flight: 1928
Accommodation: 1
Wingspan: 30ft 2in (9.2m)
Length: 20ft 4in (6.2m)
Height: 9ft 6in (2.9m)
Empty Weight: 2,354lb (1,070kg)
Loaded: 2,918lb (1,323kg)
Powerplant: 1 x 525hp (392kW) Pratt &
                           Whitney R-1340-17 radial.
Max Speed: 186mph (299km/h)
Service Ceiling: 27,500ft (8,380m)
Range: 370 miles (595km)
Number Manufactured: 586 of all F4B variants.
Preserved: Smithsonian National Air and
                           Space Museum, Washington,
                           DC, USA (F4B-4).

Boeing KC-97F Stratotanker

Subject: Boeing KC-97F Stratotanker No 51-0381 sold to
scrap at Davis-Monthan AFB, Arizona.
Statistics: Boeing KC-97G Stratotanker.

The introduction of Boeing's massive C-97 Stratofreighter
would have radically changed the nature of the Pacific
War had the events at Hiroshima and Nagasaki not brought
about the sudden capitulation of Japan. The C-97 flew for
the first time in November of 1944, just too late to reach
operational status before the war came to an end. If the
Pacific War had dragged on, however, the cavernous
interior of the Stratofreighter would have allowed the US
Forces to supply military supplies, troops, and even fighting
vehicles by air rather than by sea. The KC-97 tanker
variant, too, allowed the ferrying of fuel supplies by air
rather than by sea and therefore greatly reduced the
effectiveness of the Japanese stranglehold on the waters
of the Pacific.

Country of Origin: USA
First Flight: 1944
Accommodation: Crew of 6
Wingspan: 141ft 3in (43.05m)
Length: 117ft 5in (35.81m)
Height: 38ft 3in (11.67m)
Empty Weight: 82,500lb (37,450kg)
Max Take Off: 175,000lb (79,450kg)
Powerplants: 4 x 3,500hp (2,610kW) Pratt
                           & Whitney Wasp Major
                           28-cylinder radials.
Cruise Speed: 300mph (483km/h)
Max Speed: 325kt (523km/h)
Service Ceiling: 30,000ft (9,144m)
Range: 2,300 miles (3,701km)
Number Manufactured: More than 800 manufactured.
Preserved: Castle Air Museum, Atwater,
                           California, USA.

Boeing 737-500

Subject: Boeing 737-500 in the livery of Irish carrier
AerLingus prior to its recent switch to an
all-Airbus fleet.
Statistics: Boeing 737-300.

Boeing hit the jackpot when it decided to borrow
components from the 707 and 727 programmes to build
a new twin-engined airliner which would have a reduced
seating capacity and proportionally lower running costs.
The new 737 jet was every airline operator's dream and
the type became one of the highest-selling commercial
liners of all time. Despite its 1967 vintage the 737's ongoing
upgrades are such that the type continues to be a strong
and much favoured market leader.

Country of Origin: USA
First Flight: 1967
Accommodation: 2 + 152 passengers.
Wingspan: 94ft 9in (28.8m)
Length: 109ft 7in (33.4m)
Height: 36ft 6in (11.13m)
Empty Weight: 69,400lb (31,474kg)
Max Take Off: 138,500lb (62,812kg)
Powerplant: 2 x 20,000lb (88.97kN) CFM
                           International CFM56-3B1
                           turbofans.
Cruise Speed: 510mph (816km/h)
Max Speed: 530mph (855km/h)
Range: 2,784 miles (4,455km)
Number Manufactured: Manufacture ongoing.
Flying or in service: Widely in service.
Preserved: Kansas Aviation Museum,
                           Wichita, Kansas, USA (737-200).

Boeing 747
NASA 905 Shuttle Carrier

Subject: NASA 905 Shuttle Carrier with Shuttle and
          aerodynamic rear fairing in place.
Statistics: Boeing 747 NASA 905 Shuttle Carrier.

The NASA 905, a heavily modified Boeing 747-123, was
commissioned by NASA to facilitate ferrying the Shuttle
between Edwards AFB, California and Cape Canaveral,
Florida. The first combination flight was made from the
Dryden Flight Research Centre, Edwards AFB, in February
of 1977. In addition to transporting the Shuttle between
NASA sites the 905 was intended to facilitate a programme
whereby the Shuttle Orbiter would be air-launched 6 times
as part of its flight development trials.

Country of Origin:	USA .
First Combined Flight:	1977
Accommodation:	Flight crew of 4
Wingspan:	195ft 8in (59.67m)
Length:	231ft 10in (70.67m)
Height:	63ft 5in (19.34m)
Empty Weight:	318,053lb (144,266kg)
Max take off:	713,000lb (323,411kg)
Powerplant:	4 X Pratt & Whitney JT9D-7J Turbofans.
Cruise Speed (with load):	288mph (463km/h)
Max Speed:	Varies depending on configuration and load.
Service Ceiling:	15,000ft (4,572m) with Shuttle. 26,000ft (7,925m) without.
Range (with Shuttle):	1,000 miles (1,852km)
Number Manufactured:	2: NASA 905 and NASA 911.
Flying or in service:	2
Preserved:	In service at NASA Johnson Space Center, Houston, Texas, USA.

Boeing B-17
Flying Fortress

Subject: B-17G Flying Fortress, Gusto, fails to
          make it home.
Statistics: Boeing B-17G Flying Fortress.

With the massive industrial might of the USA mobilized to
the production of aircraft, tanks, battleships and other
weapons of war, it was only a matter of time before
the onslaught of the Axis powers would be halted. Heavy
bombers, in particular, were required to bring the war
directly to the home territories of the protagonist nations
and so began an extraordinary effort which saw the
completion of 12,731 Flying Fortresses alone. It was this
extraordinary level of industrial might that allowed the
Allied forces to range 250, 500 and even 750 aircraft
against enemy targets night after night.

Country of Origin:	USA .
First Flight:	1935
Accommodation:	2 pilots + 7 crew/gunners.
Wingspan:	103ft 9in (31.6m)
Length:	74ft 9in (22.8m)
Height:	19ft 1in (5.8m)
Empty Weight:	32,720lb (14,855kg)
Max Take Off:	49,500lb (22,475kg)
Powerplant:	4 X 1,200hp (295kW) Wright R-1820-97 nine-cylinder exhaust-driven turbo supercharged engines.
Max Speed:	293mph (472km/h)
Service Ceiling:	35,000ft (10,668m)
Range:	955nm (1,770km) with fully laden bomb bay.
Number Manufactured:	12,731 of all variants.
Flying or in service:	15 airworthy including Duxford's Sally B.
Preserved:	Flying Fortress preserved at the Royal Air Force Museum, London, UK (Boeing B-17G). USAF Armament Museum, Elgin Air Force Base, Shalimar, Florida, USA. Castle Air Museum, Atwater, California, USA. National Museum of the US Air Force, Wright-Patterson AFB, Dayton, Ohio, USA.

Boeing B-52
Stratofortress

Subject: Boeing B-52H Stratofortress of US
          Strategic Command.
Statistics: Boeing B-52H Stratofortress.

The notion that a nuclear alert could have caused
the US to despatch its massive fleet of 744 B-52
Stratofortresses against the Soviet Union seems remote
today but it was a very real and frightening threat in
the 1960s and 1970s. Each of the B-52 aircraft which
made up the USA's nuclear deterrent force was capable
of being laden with 8 nuclear-warhead-equipped Cruise
Missiles in its internal bomb bay and another 12 missiles
on underwing pods. Assuming that the Soviet Union was
equipped with similar numbers of aircraft and nuclear
warheads, the outcome of any nuclear exchange between
the 2 longstanding protagonists could only bring death
and misery on a biblical scale.

Country of Origin:	USA .
First Flight:	1952
Accommodation:	3 crew members. 8 cruise missiles stored within bomb bay and 12 externally.
Wingspan:	185ft 0in (56.39m)
Length:	160ft 11in (49.05m)
Height:	40ft 8i (12.4m)
Empty Weight:	449,998lb (204,081kg)
Max Take Off:	505,000lb (229,025kg)
Powerplant:	8 X 17,000lb (75.6kN) Pratt & Whitney TF33-P-3 Turbofans.
Cruise Speed:	510mph (816km/h)
Max Speed:	595mph (952km/h).
Service Ceiling:	49,400ft (15,056m)
Range:	7,500 miles (12,000km)
Number Manufactured:	744
Flying or in service:	In service to this day. Very large numbers in storage by US for recommissioning if required.
Preserved:	Preserved in over 19 aviation museums including National Museum of the US Air Force, Wright-Patterson AFB. Castle Air Museum, Atwater, California, USA.

Boeing KC-135 Tanker

Subject: Boeing KC-135 tanker of the Brazilian Air Force.
Statistics: Boeing KC-135 Tanker.

The KC-135 tanker is derived from the conversion of
retired commercial 707s airliners to meet the role of
air-to-air refuelling tankers. Some of these complex
military conversions have extended the operational lives
of their host airframes by many years.

Country of Origin:	USA
First Flight:	1954 (KC-135)
Accommodation:	5
Wingspan:	145ft 0in (44.42m)
Length:	153ft 1in (46.61m)
Height:	42ft 5in (12.93m)
Powerplant:	4 X Pratt & Whitney JT3C-6 turbojets.
Cruise Speed:	530mph (853km/h)
Max Speed:	585mph (941km/h)
Service Ceiling:	21,500ft (6,553m)
Flying or in service:	Many KC-135s and KC-137s still in operational service.

Boeing C-17 Globemaster III

Subject: Boeing C-17 Globemaster III of US Air Force.
           Registration unknown.
Statistics: Boeing C-17 Globemaster III.

The C-17 Globemaster's impressive intercontinental range
presents new military options when combined with its
ability to land into short, unprepared airfields. Heavy
tanks, Bradley armoured fighting vehicles and other
outsize military loads can now be delivered directly to any
required location without staging through existing airports
or centres of population. Paratroop drops, too, can now
be made over intercontinental distances and, with the

assistance of staged in-flight refuelling, theoretically, over
any part of the world. This form of ultralong-distance
paratroop deployment was used in the course of Operation
Enduring Freedom in Afghanistan in 2000 when a group of
8 C-17s flew all the way from the USA to Afghanistan and
dropped 800 combat-equipped troops after more than 19
hours in flight.

Country of Origin:	USA
First Flight:	1995
Accommodation:	Flightcrew of 3 + 3 Bradley fighting vehicles or 102 fully equipped troops.
Wingspan:	169ft 8in (51.74m)
Length:	174ft 0in (53.04m)
Height:	55ft 1in (16.79m)
Empty Weight:	281,500lb (127,664kg)
Max Take Off:	585,000lb (265,306kg)
Powerplant:	4 X Pratt & Whitney PW2040 turbofans each rated at 40,440lb (179.7kN).
Cruise Speed:	560mph (901km/h)
Max Speed:	585mph (941km/h)
Service Ceiling:	45,000ft (13,716m)
Range:	6,250 miles (10,000km)
Number Manufactured:	144 airframes delivered of a total order of 180.
Flying or in service:	144

Boeing 747-4J6

Subject: Boeing 747-4J6 of Air China hauls itself off the
           deck at London's Heathrow Airport.
Statistics: Boeing 747-400.

Boeing's iconic Jumbo Jet has maintained its position at
the forefront of the high-volume intercontinental airline
market because there was simply no other aircraft in
its class and because Boeing regularly reinvented its
extraordinary flagship. Now as the operational debut of
the giant Airbus 380 nears, the Jumbo may at last lose its

place as queen of the skies. Boeing, however, is not about
to let the European interloper steal the title without
putting up a good fight. New, improved variants of the
old bird are being developed, among them the Boeing
747-400XQLR an ultralong-range carrier with a reduced-
noise footprint and more polished avionics.

Country of Origin:	USA
First Flight:	1969
Accommodation:	2 flightcrew + cabin crew + up to 568 passengers.
Wingspan:	211ft 5in (64.44m)
Length:	231ft 10in (70.67m)
Height:	63ft 8in (19.41m)
Empty Weight:	400,100lb (181,451kg)
Max Take Off:	875,000lb (396,825kg)
Powerplant:	4 X Pratt & Whitney or General Electric or Rolls-Royce turbofans.
Cruise Speed:	490kt (907km/h) economy.
Max Speed:	507kt (939km/h)
Service Ceiling:	45,000ft (13,716m)
Range:	7,284nm (13,491km)
Number Manufactured:	c.1,500 manufactured to date and order book still open.
Flying or in service:	Widely in service.

Boeing 757

Subject: Boeing 557-400 of American Airlines.
Statistics: Boeing 757-200.

Boeing's 757 uses the same fuselage cross section as the
earlier 727 trijet that it was designed to replace. Now
greatly elongated and with all-new wings, flightdeck and
high-bypass turbofan engines, the 575 has graduated to
plug the gap between Boeing's smaller airliners and its
very large 747 series.

Country of Origin:	USA
First Flight:	1982
Accommodation:	Flightcrew of 2 + cabin crew + up to 239 passengers.
Wingspan:	124ft 10in (38.05m)
Length:	155ft 3in (47.3m)
Height:	44ft 6in (13.56m)
Empty Weight:	127,520lb (57,832kg)
Max take off:	240,000lb (108,843kg)

Powerplant:	2 X Rolls-Royce or Pratt & Whitney turbofans.
Cruise Speed:	460kt (850km/h) economy.
Max Speed:	493kt (914km/h)
Service Ceiling:	39,000ft (11,877m)
Range:	4,470 miles (7,195km)
Number Manufactured:	1,050 up to October of 2004.
Flying or in Service:	Widely operational.

Boeing 767

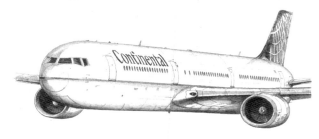

Subject: Boeing 767 of Continental Airlines.
Statistics: Boeing 767-200.

The sweepback component of the 767 was increased by the Boeing engineers in order to facilitate enhanced cruise speeds at high altitude, where the air is less dense and where air traffic is less likely to be encountered. All of the big American airlines were looking for an aircraft which could perform efficiently at altitude and Delta, American, TWA and United Airlines all signed up for early deliveries. The project programme provided for the initial 767-100 base model to be stretched progressively to produce a 200 series, a 300 series and a 400 series. In the end, however, the 100 series was abandoned in favour of the larger 767 family members.

Country of Origin:	USA
First Flight:	1981
Accommodation:	2 + up to 290 economy at 8 abreast (767-200).
Wingspan:	156ft 1in (47.5m)
Length:	159ft 2in (48.5m)
Height:	52ft 0in (15.85m)
Empty Weight:	178,400lb (80,920kg)
Max Take Off:	315,000lb (142,857kg)
Powerplant:	2 X Pratt & Whitney or General Electric turbofans.
Cruise Speed:	531mph (854km/h)
Max Speed:	568mph (914km/h)
Range:	6,625nm (12,269km)
Number Manufactured:	c.900
Flying or in service:	In service.

Boeing 777-300

Subject: Boeing 777-300 of carrier Emirates Airlines.
Statistics: Boeing 777-300.

In response to ever increasing levels of competition from Europe, Boeing has introduced an unprecedented number of innovations into its 777 airliner. The fuselage is of all-new widebody cross section and more than 10% of the airframe weight is comprised of new, lightweight carbon-composite materials. The flightdeck, too, introduces a new generation of liquid crystal display systems and flight management tools. The control system has been completely replaced by an extraordinarily sophisticated fly-by-wire system. Lastly, the new airliner's 2 massive high-bypass turbofans powerplants operate with a level of efficiency previously unheard of in any airliner.

Country of Origin:	USA
First Flight:	1994
Accommodation:	2 + cabin crew + up to 550 in a high density layout.
Wingspan:	199ft 11in (60.93m)
Length:	242ft 4in (73.86m)
Height:	60ft 9in (18.51m)
Loaded:	580,000lb (263,080kg)
Powerplant:	2 X Pratt & Whitney or Rolls-Royce or General Electric turbofans each rated between 90,000lb and 115,300lb.
Cruise Speed:	623mph (1,002km/h)
Max Speed:	659mph (1,062km/h)
Service Ceiling:	43,100ft (13,136m)
Range:	6,582 miles (10,593km)
Number Manufactured:	Currently in production.
Flying or in service:	Widely in service.

Boeing Stearman PT-17 Kaydet

Subject: Boeing Stearman PT-17 of the US Navy.
Statistics: Boeing PT-17 Stearman Kaydet.

Lloyd Stearman himself designed the big biplane that was to become the primary training aircraft of the US Army Air Corps and US Navy. Indeed, the majority of American pilots who served in the Second World War received their first weeks of training on the Stearman. The type was widely used by Canada, Britain and several of the other Allied countries and, to this day, PT-17s can be found at airfields right across the world.

Country of Origin:	USA
First Flight:	1934
Accommodation:	Student + Instructor.
Wingspan:	32ft 2in (9.8m)
Length:	24ft 9in (7.5m)
Height:	9ft 8in (2.9m)
Empty Weight:	1,935lb (878kg)
Max Take Off:	2,635lb (1,195kg)
Powerplant:	1 X 220hp (164kW) R-670-5 piston radial.
Cruise Speed:	106mph (170km/h)
Max Speed:	130mph (208km/h)
Service Ceiling:	11,200ft (3,414m)
Range:	375 miles (600km)
Number Manufactured:	More than 10,000.
Flying or in service:	c.2,250 on US register and 40 on British register but perhaps only 1,000 airworthy.
Preserved:	Castle Air Museum, Atwater, California, USA. Planes of Fame Air Museum, Chino, California, USA. US Army Aviation Museum, Fort Rucker, Ozark, Alabama, USA.

Boeing 307 Stratoliner

Subject: Pan American Airways Boeing 307 Stratoliner Clipper Flying Cloud NC19903 is on display at Washington Dulles International.
Statistics: Boeing 307 Stratoliner.

The world's first pressurized airliner to enter operational service, the Stratoliner was designed to cruise high above atmospheric turbulence and weather patterns. Its ratio of 5 crew members to just 30 paying passengers is as much a reflection on the upmarket nature of flying in the 1930s as it is of the need to provide flight engineering skills alongside the flight crew. Only 10 Model 307s were built, 1 as a development prototype, 5 for Transcontinental & Western Airlines, 3 for Pan Am and one as a luxurious runabout for Howard Hughes.

Country of Origin:	USA
First Flight:	1938
Accommodation:	5 + 33 passengers.
Wingspan:	107ft 3in (32.69m)
Length:	74ft 4in (22.66m)
Height:	20ft 10in (6.34m)
Empty Weight:	30,000lb (13,608kg)
Max Take Off:	42,000lb (19,051kg)
Powerplant:	4 X 1,100hp (820kW) Wright R-1820 radials.
Cruise Speed:	220mph (354km/h)
Max Speed:	246mph (396km/h)
Service Ceiling:	26,200ft (7,985m)
Range:	2,390 miles (3,846km)
Number Manufactured:	10

Boeing-Vertol CH-47 Chinook

Subject: CH-47 Chinook of the Royal Air Force.
Statistics: Boeing-Vertol CH-47 Chinook.

The CH-47 originated from a US Army specification for a new heavy battle mobility helicopter. The brief set out an ambitious array of requirements for the new type, which included an ability to carry 40 fully equipped combat troops, to accommodate a 2-ton internal payload, and to lift jeeps, field guns and other outsized slung loads up to a maximum weight of 8 tons. Deployment in a hostile battlefield environment would require rapid loading and unloading and so a broad ramp arrangement was incorporated into the rear of the airframe. The Chinook has been continually uprated and enhanced over the years to maintain its place as a potent and versatile battlefield tool.

Country of origin:	USA
First Flight:	1961
Accommodation:	2 pilots + 40 laden troops.
Rotor Diameter:	60ft 0in (18.29m)
Length:	52ft 1in (15.87m)
Height:	18ft 11in (5.78m)
Empty Weight:	11,585lb (5,254kg)
Max take off:	24,300lb (11,020kg)
Powerplant:	2 X 1,432hp (1,068kW) LHTEC T800-LHT-801 turboshafts.
Cruise Speed:	155mph (249km/h)
Max Speed:	166mph (267km/h)
Service Ceiling:	14,750ft (4,496m)
Range:	635 miles (1,016km)
Number Manufactured:	In excess of 350 of all types.
Flying or in service:	In service with US, Netherlands, UK, Spain, Canada and others.
Preserved:	United States Army Aviation Museum, Fort Rucker, USA.

Boulton Paul Defiant NF Mk II

Subject: Royal Air Force Boulton Paul NF Mk 3 Defiant.
Statistics: Boulton Paul NF Mk I Defiant.

As the likelihood of hostilities grew across Europe the leading aircraft manufacturers rushed to replace the ageing stocks of traditional fabric-covered aircraft with new all-metal types. The German design shops had long ago pioneered the use of aluminium structures in airframe design starting as far back as 1915 with their Junkers D1 Tin Donkey. Now their Messerschmitt and Heinkel all-metal fighters and bombers were more advanced than those of any other European nation. In this pressurized and troubled environment the designers at Boulton Paul rushed to cram a host of new technologies into the new Defiant airframe with all-metal skin construction, a retractable undercarriage system and a rotating-turret gunnery station.

Country of Origin:	UK
First Flight:	1937
Accommodation:	Pilot + Gunner.
Wingspan:	39ft 4in (11.9m)
Length:	35ft 4in (10.7m)
Height:	12ft 2in (3.71m)
Empty Weight:	264,374lb (120,170kg)
Max Take Off:	8,350lb (3,787kg)
Powerplant:	1 X 1,030hp (767.6kW) Rolls-Royce Merlin III.
Cruise Speed:	250mph (402km/h)
Max Speed:	303mph (488km/h)
Service Ceiling:	30,350ft (9,250m)
Range:	465 miles (743km)
Number Manufactured:	1,064
Preserved:	RAF Museum, London, UK (Mk I).

Bristol Beaufighter

Subject: Bristol Beaufighter of the Royal Air Force.
Statistics: Bristol Beaufighter TFX.

So desperate was the Air Ministry for a multi-engine long range fighter that an order for 300 was placed with Bristol two weeks before its first flight. The existing RAF fighters, the Spitfire and the Hurricane, were excellent performers but neither had the range and endurance required to undertake incursions into Germany's heartland or, indeed, to provide effective standing patrol cover over the South of England. In just 8 short months the engineers at Bristol designed and flew their prototype airframe, a task that would surely have taken years in less uncertain times. The Beaufighter proved to be a powerful and reliable long-range fighter with a particularly vicious 4-gun cannon. Equipped with some of the earliest radar sets it became a superb night hunter lurking high in the night skies over the South of England and picking off unsuspecting German bombers as they crossed the coast under cover of darkness and cloud.

Country of Origin:	UK,
First Flight:	1939
Accommodation:	2
Wingspan:	57ft 10in (17.64m)
Length:	41ft 4in (12.59m)
Height:	15ft 10in (4.84m)
Empty Weight:	15,592lb (7,072kg)
Max Take Off:	25,400lb (11,521kg)
Powerplant:	2 X Bristol Hercules XVII 1,725hp (1,285kW) 14 cylinder radial engines.
Max Speed:	320mph (514km/h)
Service Ceiling:	20,000ft (6,096m)
Range:	1,400 miles (2,253km)
Number Manufactured:	5,562
Preserved:	RAF Museum, Hendon, London, UK.

Bristol Beaufort Mk 1

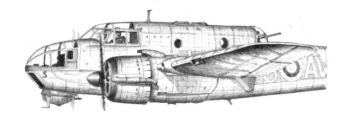

Subject: Bristol Beaufort Mk 1 of the Royal Air Force.
Statistics: Bristol Beaufort Mk 1.

Bristol's Beaufort torpedo bomber was used extensively to defend the coasts of Britain and to frustrate the efforts of Germany's battleships and submarines all along the coasts of occupied Europe. Its 4-hour endurance and its substantial weapons payload allowed it to be used for maritime reconnaissance, minelaying and torpedo bombing

at extreme ranges. The Beaufort took part in many of the great maritime skirmishes of the war in both Northern waters and the Mediterranean and served with distinction until its replacement in 1944.

Country of Origin:	UK .
First Flight:	1938
Accommodation:	4
Wingspan:	57ft 10in (17.64m)
Length:	44ft 7in (13.59m)
Height:	14ft 3in (4.34m)
Empty Weight:	13,107lb (5,945kg)
Max take off:	21,228lb (9,629kg)
Powerplant:	2 X 1,130hp (842kW) Bristol Taurus VI radial engines.
Cruise Speed:	255mph (410km/h)
Max Speed:	265mph (426km/h)
Service Ceiling:	16,500ft (5,030m)
Range:	1,035 miles (1,666km)
Number Manufactured:	2,100
Preserved:	RAF Museum, Hendon, London, UK. Canadian Aviation Museum, Ottawa, Ontario, Canada.

Bristol F-2B Brisfit

Subject: Stunning Bristol F-2B Fighter D.8084 after its 10-year restoration.
Statistics: Bristol F-2B Fighter.

With the cessation of hostilities in November of 1918 many of the Brisfits which had served in Europe were shipped out to India for operational and policing service on India's North Western Frontiers. Indeed, one unfortunate squadron was shipped directly from Europe to India without leave to return home. The Brisfit was widely used in India and in the Middle East for many years to ruthlessly quell all signs of civil disorder and opposition to British rule.

Country of Origin:	UK
First Flight:	1916
Accommodation:	Pilot + Observer/Gunner.
Wingspan:	39ft 3in (11.96m)
Length:	25ft 10in (7.87m)
Height:	9ft 9in (2.97m)

Empty Weight:	2,145lb (975kg)
Max Take Off:	2,848lb (1,292kg)
Powerplant:	1 X 275hp (205kW) Rolls-Royce Falcon piston.
Max Speed:	120mph (193km/h)
Service Ceiling:	18,000ft (5,485m)
Range:	300 miles (483km)
Number Manufactured:	More than 5,100.
Flying or in service:	Shuttleworth Trust maintains its F-2B in airworthy condition.
Preserved:	Shuttleworth Collection, Old Warden, UK. The Fighter Collection, Duxford. RAF Upper Heyford, UK (F-111E).

Bristol Britannia

Subject: Bristol Britannia 312F of the British Aircraft & Armament Evaluation Establishment. Registration XX367 was based Boscombe Down.
Statistics: Bristol Britannia 312.

In 1947 BOAC laid down the specification for a new Medium-Range Empire airliner which was to serve to link Britain with the many capitals of its far-flung interests. In its first draft the Model 175 was a piston-powered aircraft with seating for just 36 passengers but the project and the size of the aircraft grew steadily once the piston engines were abandoned in favour of Bristol's brand-new Proteus turbine powerplants. In its eventual configuration the Britannia was stretched to accommodate no less than 139 passengers over sectors of more than 5,000 miles, a superb achievement for its day. The Britannia presented a great leap in the short evolution of airliner development but its success was quickly overtaken by the advent of turbojet propulsion and the consequent arrival of the first jet airliners.

Country of Origin:	UK
First Flight:	1952
Accommodation:	2 + 139 passengers.
Wingspan:	142ft 3in (43.35m)
Length:	124ft 3in (37.87m)
Loaded:	185,000lb (84,345kg)
Powerplant:	4 X 4,120hp (3,070kW) Proteus 755 turbine powerplants.

Cruise Speed: 357mph (574km/h)
Range: 5,310 miles (8,545km)
Number Manufactured: 85
Flying or in service: Nil. Last flight was in 1991.
Preserved: Britannia Aircraft Preservation
Trust, UK.
RAF Museum Cosford Airfield, UK.

British Aerospace BAe Hawk 100

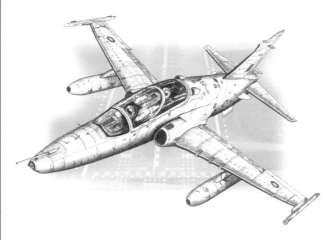

Subject: Royal Air Force BAe Hawk 100 with wingtip
missile rails and elongated nose housing
FLIR sensors.
Statistics: BAe Hawk T Mk 1.

Hawker developed the HS-1182 Hawk to fill the void which
would be brought about by the retirement of the ageing
Gnat trainer. The Hawk was a far more sophisticated
and capable aircraft with the added facility to carry
Sidewinder and other missiles which were mounted and
deployed in the same manner as on the big fighting jets.
The type won great favour with the armed forces of
many countries and it went on to serve with the air
forces of Switzerland, Oman, Finland, Indonesia, South
Korea and Saudi Arabia. The type was licence-built in both
Switzerland and Finland and also in the USA where it was
given the title, 'Goshawk'.

Country of Origin: UK
First Flight: 1974
Accommodation: 2
Wingspan: 30ft 9in (9.39m)
Length: 35ft 4in (10.77m)
Height: 13ft 0in (3.98m)
Empty Weight: 8,041lb (3,647kg)
Max Take Off: 12,566lb (5,699kg)
Powerplant: 1 x 5,200lb (23.1KN) Rolls-
Royce Turbomeca Adour 151-01.
Cruise Speed: 580mph (928km/h)

Max Speed: 615mph (990km/h)
Service Ceiling: 42,250ft (12,875m)
Range: 1,810 miles (2,895km)
Flying or in service: Generally in service.

BAe Nimrod MR-2 Maritime Patrol

Subject: Royal Navy BAe Nimrod MR-2P (with in-flight
refuelling probe).
Statistics: BAe Nimrod MR-2.

Although based closely on the trusted de Havilland Comet
airframe, the BAe Nimrod is an all-new-build aircraft
which has been designed around the needs of specialist
maritime reconnaissance operations. Other Nimrod variants
have been developed to gather electronic intelligence and
to provide an airborne early warning capability. Very little
of the original Comet can be seen apart from its integral
wing mounted engines. Much of the rest of the original
airframe is concealed by the Nimrod's full-length
underbelly equipment pannier and by its striking all-new
nose profile. Britain's independent Nimrod programme is set
to continue into the medium future with the refurbishment
and upgrading of 21 of the existing Nimrod inventory to
Nimrod 2000 MRA-4 standard.

Country of Origin: UK
First Flight: 1967
Accommodation: 2 + up to 9 specialist
systems technicians.
Wingspan: 114ft 10in (35.0m)
Length: 126ft 9in (38.6m)
Height: 29ft 9in (9.08m)
Empty Weight: 86,000lb (39,002kg)
Max Take Off: 192,000lb (87,075kg)
Powerplant: 4 x 12,140lb (54KN) Rolls-
Royce RB168-20 Spey turbofans.
Cruise Speed: 545mph (880km/h)
Max Speed: 575mph (925km/h)
Service Ceiling: 36,000ft (10,972m)
Range: 6,000 miles (9,600km)
Number Manufactured: 46
Flying or in service: In service with Royal Navy.

British Aerospace BAe 1000

Subject: BAe 1000 launch ship appropriately
registered N1258A.
Statistics: BAe 1000.

The BAe 1000 was an enlarged and uprated development
of the earlier BAe (HS) 125 series. With the 1993 purchase
of British Aerospace's corporate jet division by Raytheon
the BAe title was removed and the type was rechristened
the Hawker 1000. Its stretched fuselage and its uprated
Pratt & Whitney turbofan engines were designed to
enhance its appeal to international corporations and to
long-range executive charter companies. The type, however,
was somewhat eclipsed by some of the lighter and more
efficient corporate jets which were beginning to appear,
and only 52 orders materialized before Raytheon closed
the production line.

Country of Origin: UK
First Flight: 1990
Accommodation: 2 + up to 8 passengers.
Wingspan: 51ft 4in (15.68m)
Length: 53ft 10in (16.42m)
Height: 17ft 1in (5.21m)
Empty Weight: 17,900lb (8,119kg)
Max Take Off: 31,100lb (14,061kg)
Powerplant: 2 x 5,225lb Pratt &
Whitney PW-305 turbofans.
Cruise Speed: 452mph (727km/h)
Max Speed: 538mph (867km/h)
Service Ceiling: 43,000ft (13,107m)
Range: 3,525 miles (5,672km)
Number Manufactured: 52.
Flying or in service: Widely in service.

Bücker Bü-133 Jungmeister

Subject: Bücker Bü-133 Jungmeister. Registration D-PRKR.
          Also carrying the US markings N45BJ.
Statistics: Bücker Bü-133 Jungmeister.

Germany's aviation industry was becoming increasingly advanced as the 1920s gave way to the 1930s. In comparison to programmes like the massive Do-X the development of the Jungmeister must have seemed like a simple task for the Bücker design team. They were to design an aircraft which would sweep up all of the aerobatic trophies across Europe while, at the same time, quietly training new pilots in the techniques of aerial combat. When the Jungmeister first flew in 1935 it greatly exceeded its design goals and the new type was immediately put into production. On delivery, the Luftwaffe used the type for many years in a variety of roles from primary trainer to observation and liaison platform. The Bü-133 is an excellent aerobatic performer, with a rich and fascinating history.

Country of Origin: Germany
First Flight: 1935
Accommodation: 1
Wingspan: 21ft 8in (6.61m)
Length: 19ft 8in (6.0m)
Height: 7ft 9in (2.36m)
Empty Weight: 902lb (409kg)
Max Take Off: 1,287lb (584kg)
Powerplant: 1 x Siemens Sh-14A piston rated at 160hp (119kW). 1 x Franklin 220hp (164kW) 6A-350-C1 piston on later models.
Cruise Speed: 137mph (220km/h)
Max Speed: 157mph (253km/h)
Service Ceiling: 15,000ft (4,572m)
Range: 356 miles (574km)
Flying or in service: Small numbers still flying. A highly prized collectable.
Preserved: Air Venture Museum, Oshkosh, Wisconsin, USA.

CAP 231-EX

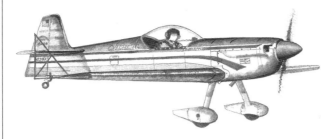

Subject: Avions Mudry CAP 232 British registration G-GFTR.
Statistics: Avions Mudry CAP 232.

One of the most sophisticated and specialized aerobatic aircraft in the world, the CAP 232 is tailored specifically for the onerous loads imposed by unlimited aerobatic competition. The type is capable of withstanding the very highest levels of wing loading, both positive and negative and can be flown through even the most violent of aerobatic manoeuvres, flick rolls, and prolonged inverted displays. A true thoroughbred, the CAP 232 is not an aircraft for the average pilot. With 300 horsepower under the hood and a sleek, undersized airframe a lot of skill and judgement is required in all aspects of the flight envelope. In aerobatic flight, however, it comes into its own and the extraordinary CAP 232 has been selected by many of the world's greatest competition pilots against superb offerings from Sukhoi of Russia and Extra of Germany. With a base price tag of US $250,000 before pilot customization these aircraft reflect serious levels of commitment from their pilots.

Country of Origin: France
First Flight: 1981
Accommodation: 1
Wingspan: 24ft 3in (7.39m)
Length: 22ft 2in (6.77m)
Height: 6ft 3in (1.9m)
Empty Weight: 1,290lb (585kg)
Max Take Off: 1,810lb (821kg)
Powerplant: 1 x Lycoming AE10 540 L1 B.
Cruise Speed: 200mph (322km/h)
Max Speed: 217mph (349km/h)
Service Ceiling: 16,400ft (5,000m)
Range: 650 miles (1,046km)
Number Manufactured: In excess of 47 custom-built for competition flying.
Flying or in service: Widely in service.

Caproni Stipa

Subject: Caproni Stipa prototype airframe of 1932.
Statistics: Caproni Stipa.

The logic behind the Caproni Stipa may look to us today to be flawed and ridiculous but back in the early 1930s the science of aeronautics was only finding its feet and there was considerable interest and excitement in the little-known areas of ducted fan propulsion. The concept was simple. If a cylindrical duct could be built around a propeller it would cause all of the thrust to be directed straight backwards rather than backwards and outwards in a conical shape, as is the pattern with standard propeller arrangements. But would the additional thrust be worth the extra penalties caused by increased weight, additional induced drag, and all of the complexities which would be introduced into the airframe by the addition of such a large and necessarily hollow structure? Without computers and sophisticated airframe design software there was no way forward but to build a prototype airframe. While the Stipa was much less than successful in its own right it did provide invaluable data in the area of ducted-fan propulsion and shrouded-propeller configurations.

Country of Origin: Italy
First Flight: 1932
Accommodation: 2
Powerplant: 1 x 120hp (89.48kW) de Havilland Gipsy engine.
Max Speed: 81mph (130km/h)
Service Ceiling: Never established.
Range: Never established.
Number Manufactured: 1 prototype only.
Flying or in service: In 1995 a 65% scale replica was built and flown by a group of Falco home-builders.
Preserved: Stipa replica flying in the USA.

Capella XS

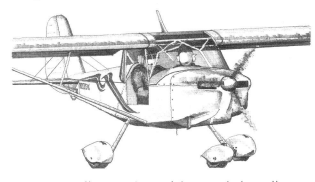

Subject: Capella XS. Private Flying Association Rally, Cranfield, 1998.
Statistics: Capella XS.

An attractive and popular ultralight-category home-build sportplane. The Capella's simplicity and efficiency have attracted many home-builders over the years. Few other aircraft projects provide so much fun for so little cost. The type is generally seen in tricycle or taildragger configuration but it can also be fitted with floats for water-based operations.

Country of Origin:	USA
First Flight:	1996
Accommodation:	2
Wingspan:	28ft 6in (8.72m)
Length:	18ft 5in (5.62m)
Height:	5ft 8in (1.77m)
Empty Weight:	480lb (217.7Kg)
Max Take Off:	1,100lb (498.9Kg)
Powerplant:	1 X 65hp (48.47kW) Rotax 582.
Cruise Speed:	111mph (178km/h)
Max Speed:	116mph (186km/h)
Service Ceiling:	10,000ft (3,048m)
Flying or in service:	In service.

Catalina II Home-build

Subject: Catalina II home-built amphibian.
Statistics: Catalina II.

Catalina II is a 2-seat amphibious sport-plane with a high parasol wing and a 1-piece stepped hull structure. As with all water-based aircraft the engine and propeller are kept high above the waterline. Seating is arranged in a side-by-side format in the lexan screened open cockpit. The Catalina II is an experimental category ultralight and plans are available for home-building.

Country of Origin:	USA
First Flight:	1996
Accommodation:	2
Wingspan:	35ft 0in (10.67m)
Length:	19ft 4in (5.9m)
Height:	5ft 9in (1.75m)
Empty Weight:	660lb (299kg)
Max Take Off. Land:	1,200lb (544kg)
Max Take Off. Water:	1,100lb (498kg)
Cruise Speed:	80mph (128km/h)
Max Speed:	90mph (145km/h)
Service Ceiling:	12,500ft (3,810m)
Range:	364 miles (586km)
Flying or in service:	In service.

CASA/IPTN CN-235

Subject: CASA/IPTN CN-235 of Carrier Binter-Canarias Airlines. Registration EC-012.
Statistics: CASA/IPTN. CN-235.

CASA of Spain and IPTN of Indonesia teamed up to share the development costs of the CN-235 programme. Indonesia, in particular, was keen to foster its fledgling aeronautics industry and to improve its stature in its region. Throughout all stages of the development and production great care has been taken to ensure that both countries are equally represented. Indeed pre-production prototypes of the type were simultaneously rolled out in Indonesia and Spain although the Spanish-produced CN-235 did make it into the air some months before that of Indonesia.

Country of Origin:	Spain and Indonesia
First Flight:	1983
Accommodation:	2 flightcrew + 45 passengers or specialist military equipment
Wingspan:	84ft 8in (25.81m)
Length:	70ft 3in (21.4m)
Height:	26ft 10in (8.18m)
Empty Weight:	21,605lb (9,800kg)
Max Take Off:	33,290lb (15,100kg)
Powerplant:	2 X 1,870hp (1,395kW) General Electric CT7-9C turboprops.
Cruise Speed:	282mph (454km/h)
Max Speed:	316mph (509km/h)
Service Ceiling:	20,000ft (6,096m)
Range:	807 miles (1,300km)
Number Manufactured:	In excess of 220.
Flying or in service:	Generally in service.

Caudron G-4

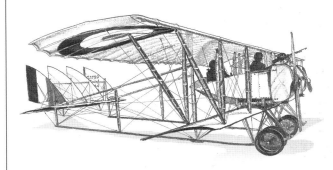

Subject: Caudron G-4 biplane of 1915.
Statistics: Caudron G-4.

It was 1915 and France was in serious trouble. Much of the country had been turned into a quagmire of filthy trenches where massive numbers of Frenchmen were daily sacrificed to hold the enemy at bay. But neither disease nor the combined forces of half a dozen Allied armies could drive the intruders back. But with the two opposing ground forces locked in near-stalemate it fell to the technical advances of the war, the tank and the aeroplane, to break the impasse. It was in this perilous environment that brothers Gaston and Rene Caudron began the development of their twin-engined G-4 fighter bomber. On its introduction to the Western Front the type was a great improvement over the existing single-engined fighters with its greatly increased bomb payload and extended range.

Country of Origin:	France
First Flight:	1915
Accommodation:	Pilot + bombardier/gunner.
Wingspan:	39ft 1in (11.9m)
Length:	23ft 7in (7.2m)
Empty Weight:	1,499lb (680kg)
Max Take Off:	2,601lb (1,180kg)
Powerplant:	2 X 80hp (59.66kW) Le Rhones or 2 X 100hp (74.57kW) Anzani powerplants.
Cruise Speed:	67mph (108km/h)

Max Speed: 77mph (124km/h)
Service Ceiling: 14,750ft (4,500m)
Range: 198 miles (320km)
Number Manufactured: 1,358 by Caudron as well as an unknown number of additional G-4s by Bleriot and SPAD.

Preserved: Steven F. Udvar-Hazy Center, Chantilly, Virginia, USA.

Cessna Super Stol 150

Subject: Cessna 150, registration N9225U, with Super-Stol stall-speed reduction kit fitted to the upper wing surfaces.
Statistics: Cessna 150.

With a total production run of 29,078 Model 150s and Model 152s, the Cessna Aircraft Company's diminutive trainer and sportplane has permeated the world of light aviation and is to be found at airfields right across the globe. It may be basic in specification and rather cramped inside but it is about the cheapest way to get into the air. The subject of this sketch has been retro-fitted with the Super-Stol stall-speed reduction system which reduces the aircraft's stall-speed and, consequently, the length of runway it requires for take-off and landing.

Country of Origin: USA
First Flight: 1957
Accommodation: 2
Wingspan: 32ft 9in (9.98m)
Length: 23ft 11in (7.29m)
Height: 8ft 6in (2.59m)
Empty Weight: 1,034lb (469kg)
Max Take Off: 1,600lb (726kg)
Powerplant: 1 x 100hp (74.5kW) Continental O-200-A flat-four piston.
Cruise Speed: 115mph (184km/h)
Max Speed: 125mph (206km/h)
Service Ceiling: 12,250ft (3,734m)
Range: 391 miles (629km)
Number Manufactured: 29,078 of both the Models 150 and 152 together.
Flying or in service: Still widely in service to this day.

Preserved: 150H Air Venture Museum, Oshkosh, Wisconsin, USA.

Cessna 172 Skyhawk

Subject: Cessna 172, first sketched at Cranfield, England, 1995. Registration unknown.
Statistics: Cessna 172M Skyhawk.

When Cessna released the 172 Skyhawk it could not have known that the type would go on to become the world's biggest-selling sport-plane of all time. With 4 spacious seats, a powerful engine, a rugged build quality and impeccable flying manners the type was an obvious choice for generations of pilots, flight schools and fractional ownership syndicates. A policy of continual improvement, too, helped to maintain the interest of pilots and media alike, and ensured that the 172 retained its place as market leader. Many new variants and upgrades have been offered over the years including the retractable Model 172RG.

Country of Origin: USA
First Flight: 1955
Accommodation: 2 + 2
Wingspan: 36ft 0in (10.97m)
Length: 26ft 11in (8.2m)
Height: 8ft 9in (2.61m)
Empty Weight: 1,300lb (589kg)
Max Take Off: 2,300lb (1,043kg)
Powerplant: 1 x 150hp (111.8kW) Textron Lycoming O-320-E2D piston.
Cruise Speed: 125mph (200km/h)
Max Speed: 140mph (224km/h)
Service Ceiling: 13,500ft (4,115m)
Range: 695 miles (1,112km)
Number Manufactured: More than 42,500 of all variants (including Reims) had been built by 1999.
Flying or in service: Widely in service.

Cessna Model 140

Subject: Pristine Cessna Model 140 attended the PFA fly-in event, Kemble.
Statistics: Cessna 140.

Clyde Cessna combined all-metal monocoque construction with mass production techniques, 2 by-products of war-time technology, to turn out more than 4,900 of his Model 140 aircraft between 1945 and 1949. The predicted market of returning pilots, however, never materialized. Most of them were simply too hard-pressed for money or, indeed, wished to forget all about their wartime experiences. Notwithstanding the early abandonment of the Model 140 production line the type was a remarkably attractive and well-mannered aeroplane and many hundreds of 140s are flown and treasured by their owners to this day.

Country of Origin: USA
First Flight: 1945
Accommodation: 2
Wingspan: 33ft 4in (10.16m)
Length: 21ft 6in (6.55m)
Height: 6ft 7in (2.01m)
Empty Weight: 860lb (390kg)
Max Take Off: 1,450lb (658kg)
Powerplant: 1 x 85hp (63.38kW) Continental C85-12 piston engine.
Cruise Speed: 105mph (168km/h)
Max Speed: 120mph (192km/h)
Service Ceiling: 15,500ft (4,700m)
Range: 450 miles (720km)
Number Manufactured: 4,905
Flying or in service: Many examples flying in private ownership.
Preserved: Mid-America Air Museum, Liberal, Kansas, USA.

Cessna 404
Titan

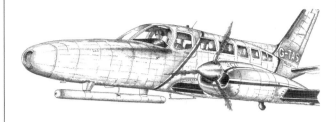

Subject: Cessna 404 Titan II, registration G-TASK
          (c/n 404-0829), is operated in a specialist
          surveying role by Bravo Aviation of
          Coventry, England.
Statistics: Cessna 404 Titan.

Cessna built 378 of its Model 404 Titan for use in a wide
variety of specialist roles. The Titan Ambassador was the
base model with seating for pilots and 8 passengers while
the Titan Freighter was a dedicated cargo variant with an
abundance of tie-down points but no seating. The 404 Titan
shared the same fuselage structure as the turbine-powered
Cessna 441 Conquest but it differed in having the lesser
375hp (280kW) geared piston engines and it was not, of
course, pressurized. The 404 was well received by both
commuter and the freighting operators and Cessna went
on to deliver 378 of all variants before manufacture
ceased in 1982.

Country of Origin: USA
First Flight: 1976
Accommodation: Flightcrew of 1 or 2 and
                         upwards of 8 passengers.
Wingspan: 46ft 4in (14.12m)
Length: 39ft 6in (12.04m)
Height: 13ft 3in (4.04m)
Empty Weight: 4,834lb (2,192kg)
Max Take Off: 8,400lb (3,810kg)
Powerplant: 2 x 375hp (280kW) Continental
                         GTSIO-520-M turbocharged,
                         geared, and fuel injected
                         flat-six piston engines.
Cruise Speed: 187mph (302km/h)
Max Speed: 267mph (430km/h)
Service Ceiling: 26,000ft (7,925m)
Range: 2,115 miles (3,404km)
Number Manufactured: 378 of all Titan variants
                         built between 1976 and 1982.
Flying or in service: Many examples still in service.

Cessna 190/195
Businessliner

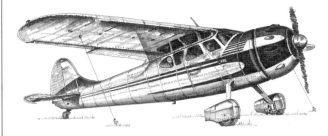

Subject: Cessna 195 Businessliner G-BTBJ has
          flown from its base at Compton Abbas to the
          PFA Fly-In at Cranfield on several occasions.
Statistics: Cessna 190B Businessliner.

There are few sights in aviation as beautiful as that
of a well-cared-for and highly polished classic aircraft,
and the wonderful Cessna 195 must surely sit at the
upper end of this elite category. Of course, all 195s were
not presented in the original polished aluminium finish.
Maintaining such a lustre and sparkle is, in itself, almost
as onerous as keeping the aircraft in airworthy condition.
But Model 195s of this pedigree and standard are labours
of love and are always a source of great fascination and
intrigue at air shows and fly-in events.

Country of Origin: USA
First Flight: 1947
Accommodation: 4 to 5
Wingspan: 36ft 2in (11.02m)
Length: 27ft 4in (8.33m)
Height: 7ft 1in (2.16m)
Empty Weight: 2,230lb (920kg)
Max Take Off: 3,350lb (1,519kg)
Powerplant: 1 x 275hp (205hW)
                         Jacobs R-755B-2 Piston.
Cruise Speed: 157mph (251km/h)
Max Speed: 173mph (277km/h)
Service Ceiling: 18,300ft (5,578m)
Range: 680 miles (1,088km)
Number Manufactured: 1,183
Flying or in service: Small numbers in service.
Preserved: Mid-America Air Museum,
                         Liberal, Kansas, USA (Civilian
                         and Military Models).

Cessna 208
Caravan 1 (on floats)

Subject: Cessna 208. Caravan 1 flying the United States
          n-number N9382F at Lakeland Linder Regional
          Airport, Florida.
Statistics: Cessna 208A Caravan 1.

Cessna's 208 Caravan workhorse was designed as a multi-
purpose civil and military transport and as a tough and
versatile cargo freighter. Ideal for operations into short
and unprepared airfields, the type has been used in large
numbers to service communities and industries in remote
areas. Certified for operations in floatplane format or
on skis, the 208 can access some of the most remote and
inhospitable locations on Earth and even older airframes
with very high numbers of hours will tend to be handed
down from operator to operator, generally ending up in
peripheral or Third World countries.

Country of Origin: USA
First Flight: 1982
Accommodation: 1 + 9 passengers.
Wingspan: 52ft 1in (15.88m)
Length: 37ft 7in (11.46m)
Height: 14ft 2in (4.32m)
Empty Weight: 3,800lb (1,725kg)
Max Take Off: 7,300lb (3,310kg)
Powerplant: 1 x 600hp (450kW) Pratt &
                         Whitney Canada PT6A-114
                         turboprop powerplant.
Cruise Speed: 201mph (322km/h)
Max Speed: 212mph (340km/h)
Service Ceiling: 26,608ft (8,110m)
Range: 1,104 miles (1,767km)
Flying or in service: Generally operational.

Cessna Model 318/T-37 Tweet

Subject: Cessna T-37B primary jet trainer.
Statistics: Cessna T-37B.

The Tweety Bird was Cessna's answer to the US Air Force's 1952 primary jet trainer competition and it went on to be built in large numbers for both the US armed forces and as a designated training/attack aircraft under the controversial US Military Assistance Program. For the project team at Cessna this was an entirely new challenge and they responded by designing a compact and streamlined airframe with side-by-side seating and twin Turbomeca Marbore turbojets integrated neatly into the wing roots. The first flight and subsequent systems and armaments development proceeded well and the US Air Force placed its first large-scale orders. In service the initial T-37A series was found to be an extremely agile and responsive mount in all areas of performance although a little underpowered in the climb. A new T-37B variant was developed and its Continental J69-T25 turbojet engines remedied that shortcoming with approximately 10% more power. The Cessna A-37 (318E) Dragonfly counter-insurgency platform was a further development of the type but, with radically increased weights and performance figures, it is considered to be a separate type.

Country of Origin:	USA
First Flight:	1954
Accommodation:	2
Wingspan:	33ft 9in (10.3m)
Length:	29ft 3in (8.93m)
Height:	9ft 2in (2.8m)
Empty Weight:	3,874lb (1,757kg)
Max Take Off:	6,574lb (2,981kg)
Powerplant:	2 x 1,026lb (4.65KN) Continental J69-T25 turbojets.
Cruise Speed:	360mph (576km/h)
Max Speed:	425mph (680km/h)
Service Ceiling:	25,000ft (7,620m)
Range:	870 miles (1,392km)
Number Manufactured:	1,272 of all T-37A, T-37B and T-37C variants completed when production ended in 1977.
Flying or in service:	Small numbers still in military service across the world.
Preserved:	Valiant Air Command Museum, Titusville, Florida, USA. US Army Aviation Museum, Fort Rucker, Ozark, Alabama, USA. Mid-America Air Museum, Liberal, Kansas, USA (XT-37).

Cessna L-19A-0-1 Bird Dog

Subject: Cessna O-1 Bird Dog. Serial No 14726 of the US Army.
Statistics: Cessna O-1 Bird Dog.

The O-1 Bird Dog was a developed by mating the wings and undercarriage of the commercial Cessna 170 with the tail empennage of the Model 195. The all-new fuselage structure was designed to provide maximum visibility with large plexiglass windows that seemed to lean outwards in order to enhance downward visibility. Given that speed is the pilot's ally in any hostile environment the powerplant, too, was given a substantial boost in the form of Continental's new 213-horsepower O-470-11 piston. The resulting airframe was tough and fast, and, provided with excellent 360-degree visibility, became one of the most prolific observation aircraft of all time.

Country of Origin:	USA
First Flight:	1949
Accommodation:	Pilot + observer.
Wingspan:	36ft 11in (11.25m)
Length:	29ft 6in (8.99m)
Height:	9ft 11in (3.02m)
Empty Weight:	3,125lb (1,417kg)
Max Take Off:	5,200lb (2,358kg)
Powerplant:	1 x 213hp (159kW) Continental O-470-11 piston single.
Cruise Speed:	219mph (352km/h)
Max Speed:	237mph (381km/h)
Service Ceiling:	20,300ft (6,187)
Range:	770 miles (1,240km)
Number Manufactured:	3,400 built by 1962 when production ceased.
Flying or in service:	Many L-19 and O-1 veterans and warbirds still flying.
Preserved:	Steven F. Udvar-Hazy Center, Washington, DC, USA. US Army Aviation Museum, Fort Rucker, Ozark, Alabama, USA. National Museum of the US Air Force, Wright-Patterson AFB, Dayton, Ohio, USA. Norwegian Aviation Museum, Bodø, Norway. Valiant Air Command Museum, Titusville, Florida, USA. Memorial Air Park, Hurlburt Field AFT, Florida, USA.

Cessna 210 Centurion

Subject: Cessna 210. Waterford Airport, Ireland.
Statistics: Cessna 210L Centurion.

With the light plane market practically cornered, Cessna set about introducing a new high-performance sport and touring aircraft to rival some of the long-standing high-end marques. Staying with its winning formula, Cessna's new Model 210 was an all-metal high-wing monoplane. Introduced for the first time, however, were its retractable tricycle landing gear and its fuel-injected 300-horsepower engine. The result was a powerful and capable personal transport with high cruise speeds and excellent endurance. Again, Cessna had designed exactly what the market wanted and the 210 went on to be built in large numbers. As before, a programme of on-going modifications and refinements helped to maintain the type's position in the general aviation marketplace. Among these improved variants were the Centurion II and Turbo Centurion II as well as a number of later pressurized Centurion models.

Country of Origin:	USA
First Flight:	1957
Accommodation:	2 + 4
Wingspan:	36ft 9in (11.2m)
Length:	28ft 2in (8.59m)
Max Take Off:	3,800lb (1,723kg)
Powerplant:	1 x 300hp (225kW) Continental IO-520-L fuel-injected flat-six piston with constant-speed propeller.
Max Speed:	202mph (325km/h)
Service Ceiling:	17,300ft (5,273m)
Range:	1,226 miles (1,973km)
Number Manufactured:	9,336 of all variants.
Flying or in service:	In widespread service.
Preserved:	Planes of Fame Air Museum, Chino, California, USA. Air Venture Museum, Oshkosh, Wisconsin, USA.

Cessna CJ3 Citation Jet

Subject: Cessna displayed this CJ3 Citation Jet registration N51HF at the Experimental Aircraft Association's Sun 'n Fun 2005.

Statistics: Cessna CJ3 Citation Jet.

Cessna's policy of ongoing and continual improvement of its executive jet series ensures that the Citation marque is always exciting and vital to that small but well-heeled market of executive jet buyers. Its CJ3 Citation is yet another stage in the evolution of its earlier Citation series, this time an upgrade of the Model CJ2. With a 20-inch fuselage stretch, larger wing area, more powerful engines and a state-of-the-art flight deck, the CJ3 brings new levels of sophistication to corporate flying and executive transport.

Country of Origin: USA
First Flight: 1969 (first of models).
Accommodation: 1 + 7 passengers.
Wingspan: 53ft 4in (16.26m)
Length: 50ft 2in (15.29m)
Height: 15ft 2in (4.62m)
Empty Weight: 8,590lb (3,896Kg)
Max Take Off: 14,070lb (6,382Kg)
Powerplant: 2 X 2,780lb (12.37KN) Williams FJ44-3A turbofans.
Cruise Speed: 480mph (768km/h)
Max Speed: 455mph (733km/h)
Service Ceiling: 45,000ft (13,716m)
Range: 2,160 miles (3,475Km)
Flying or in service: In service.
Preserved: Steven F. Udvar-Hazy Center, Washington, DC, USA.

Cessna 337 Skymaster

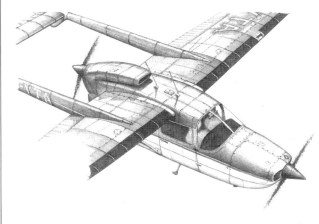

Subject: Cessna 337 Skymaster.

Statistics: Cessna 337d Super Skymaster.

Cessna's fixed-gear Model 336 with its highly unusual push/pull configuration carried the best qualities of Cessna's 210 series to a new level of sophistication. Its slightly later Model 337 continued this progress but replaced the fixed landing gear with a new retractable undercarriage system. As a comfortable touring aircraft, and as a stepup to the more complex twin-engine types, the Skymaster excelled and very large numbers were ordered by small taxi/charter operators and private users alike. Its many merits were not missed by the US Army and Air Force, either, and more than 532 specialist O-2A and O-2B observation and liaison derivatives were delivered, mostly to the American forces but also to the forces of Iran and other Military Assistance recipients. The Model O-2A was later manufactured under licence by Reims Aviation of France which was then 49% owned by Cessna. The French-built O-2 variants were widely exported to third-party countries under the revised title FTB337G Milirole.

Country of Origin: USA
First Flight: 1961
Accommodation: 1 + 5 passengers.
Wingspan: 38ft 0in (11.58m)
Length: 29ft 9in (9.07m)
Height: 9ft 4in (2.84m)
Empty Weight: 2,655lb (1,164Kg)
Max Take Off: 4,400lb (1,995Kg)
Powerplant: 2 X 210hp (157kW) Continental IO-360-C pistons.
Cruise Speed: 190mph (304km/h)
Max Speed: 231mph (370km/h)
Service Ceiling: 19,500 (5,945m)
Range: 1,345 miles (2,152km)
Flying or in service: Still widely in service.
Preserved: Steven F. Udvar-Hazy Center, Chantilly, Virginia, USA (O-2A Super Skymaster 337M). Mid-America Air Museum, Liberal, Kansas, USA.

Champion Lancer 402

Subject: Champion Lancer 402.

Statistics: Champion Lancer 402.

The Lancer had none of the affectations and excesses of standard twins. It was rudimentary and noisy, and its climb rate was embarrassingly, even dangerously, poor. It did excel in one area, however: providing the most inexpensive means of building multi-engine hours or keeping one's multi-engine rating current.

Country of Origin: USA
First Flight: 1960
Accommodation: 2 in tandem arrangement.
Wingspan: 34ft 6in (10.52m)
Length: 22ft 3in (6.78m)
Powerplant: 2 X 100hp Continental O-200 piston engines.
Service Ceiling: 17,500ft (5,334m)
Range: 744 miles (1,197km)
Number Manufactured: 26
Flying or in service: Up to 5 airworthy.

Chrislea CH-3 Super Ace

Subject: Chrislea CH-3 Super Ace, registration G-AKFO.

Statistics: Chrislea CH-3 Super Ace.

Mr Richard Christopherides, designer of the CH-3, closed his eyes to simple commercial realities and designed a single steering wheel control system for his new sport-plane. The Super Ace was a very fine aircraft but it had one serious and insurmountable flaw. With its unique and eccentric control system it forced all pilots to relearn their flying and landing skills practically from scratch. Prospective buyers were, of course, greatly troubled by this simple detail and were slow to invest in the type. Despite the obvious charms and capabilities of the Super Ace only 15 examples were built before production was abandoned.

Country of Origin:	UK
First Flight:	1946
Accommodation:	4
Wingspan:	36ft 0in (10.97m)
Length:	21ft 6in (6.55m)
Height:	7ft 7in (2.31m)
Empty Weight:	1,350lb (612kg)
Max Take Off:	2,350lb (1,066kg)
Powerplant:	1X Lycoming 125hp (93kW)
	1X 145hp (108kW) de Havilland
	Gipsy Major 10 piston.
Cruise Speed:	110mph (176km/h)
Max Speed:	126mph (202km/h)
Range:	400 miles (640km)
Number Manufactured:	15
Flying or in service:	2 still airworthy.

Comper CLA-7 Swift

Subject: The Shuttleworth Collection's superb 1932 Comper Swift bears the registration G-ACTF and is still flown periodically to this day.
Statistics: Comper CLA-7 Swift.

The tiny Comper Swift made worldwide media headlines in November of 1931 when it completed a remarkable journey from England to Australia in just 10 days. Others of the marque served in India, Egypt, Argentina and New Zealand. Compact and streamlined, the Swift was a wonderful performer and a most reliable and well-mannered aircraft.

Country of Origin:	UK
First Flight:	1929

Accommodation:	1
Wingspan:	24ft 0in (7.0m)
Length:	21ft 9in (6.63m)
Height:	6ft 7in (2.0m)
Empty Weight:	540lb (245kg)
Max Take Off:	985lb (447kg)
Powerplant:	1 X 120hp (89.4kW) de
	Havilland Gipsy III or 75hp
	(56kW) Pobjoy piston.
Cruise Speed:	120mph (192km/h)
Max Speed:	140mph (224km/h)
Range:	380 miles (608km)
Number Manufactured:	41
Flying or in service:	2 genuine Swifts and one
	amateur-built replica.
	G-ACTF is preserved in
	airworthy condition by the
	Shuttleworth Trust.
Preserved:	

Christen Eagle

Subject: Christen Eagle registration G-EGLE.
Statistics: Christen Eagle.

Frank Christensen was a highly successful entrepreneur long before he became involved in the production of inverted oil recovery systems for the Pitts series of aerobatic sports-planes. Christensen was fascinated with the world of aviation and he began to dream up his own aircraft project, a new unlimited-class aerobatic aircraft which could be home-built by even the most inexperienced builders from a series of superbly presented and documented plan kits. The aircraft was a superb performer and the Eagle kits were wonderfully complete and well supported by Christensen's distribution company, Aviat Aviation. Over 1,000 Christen Eagles have been completed and the type, with its stunning multicoloured Eagle paint scheme, is always a showstopper.

Country of Origin:	USA
First Flight:	1977
Accommodation:	1 + 1
Wingspan:	19ft 11in (5.82m)
Length:	18ft 6in (5.64m)
Height:	6ft 6in (1.98m)
Empty Weight:	978lb (443kg)
Max Take Off:	1,478lb (670kg)

Powerplant:	1 X 200hp (194kW) Lycoming
	AEIO-360-A1 flat-six.
Cruise Speed:	165mph (265km/h)
Max Speed:	184mph (296km/h)
Service Ceiling:	25,000ft (7,620m)
Range:	402nm (647km)
Number Manufactured:	Over 1,000.
Flying or in service:	Many still actively flying.
Preserved:	The Frontiers of Flight Museum, Dallas, Texas, USA.

Civilian Aircraft Co Coupé

Subject: Civilian Coupé prototype EI-AAV (formerly G-AAIL) was based in Ireland for some years from 1933.
Statistics: Civilian Coupé.

This diminutive Civilian Coupé was based in the Republic of Ireland for some years in the mid-1930s. It was one of just 6 that were built by the tiny Civilian Aircraft Company at Burton-on-Trent in England. EI-AAV may have been the prototype Coupé because its engine appears to be the 75hp ABC Hornet and not the Armstrong Siddeley Genet Major which was fitted to all post-prototype Coupés.

Country of Origin:	UK
First Flight:	1929
Accommodation:	2
Wingspan:	37ft 7in (10.85m)
Length:	19ft 4in (5.89m)
Height:	6ft 3in (1.9m)
Empty Weight:	918lb (416kg)
Max Take Off:	1,500lb (680kg)
Powerplant:	1 X 100hp (74.5kW) Armstrong Siddeley Genet Major 1.
Cruise Speed:	96mph (154km/h)
Max Speed:	110mph (177km/h)
Range:	300 miles (480km)
Number Manufactured:	6
Flying or in service:	Just one airworthy Coupé. Biggin Hill-based G-ABNT is a regular flier.

Commonwealth Wirraway

Subject: Commonwealth Wirraway 652 of the Royal
          Australian Air Force.
Statistics: Commonwealth Wirraway.

As one of the Commonwealth countries Australia, too,
began to expand its army and air force in response to the
ever more alarming signals coming from Germany. By 1937
a high-level Australian government commission had visited
many of the principal American aircraft manufacturers
and had secured, among other projects, the licence to
build an all-Australian version of the North American
NA-33. Back in Australia work commenced on the project
and changes were made to take into account the abundant
stocks of quality natural spruce which were readily
available to the aircraft industry. The Wirraway, in its
final configuration, was constructed of timber longerons
from the firewall to the tail. A total of 755 of the type
were produced.

Country of Origin: Australia
First Flight: 1939
Accommodation: Pilot + gunner or student
                        and instructor.
Wingspan: 43ft 0in (13.11m)
Length: 29ft 0in (8.84m)
Height: 8ft 9in (2.67m)
Empty Weight: 3,992lb (1,810kg)
Max Take Off: 6,353lb (2,882kg)
Powerplant: 1 x 600hp (447kW) Australian-
                        built Pratt & Whitney
                        Wasp radial powerplant.
Cruise Speed: 182mph (293km/h)
Max Speed: 200mph (322km/h)
Number Manufactured: 755
Preserved: RAAF Association Museum, Bull
                        Creek, Perth, Australia.
                        Temora Aviation Museum,
                        Menzies Street, Temora, New
                        South Wales, Australia (CA-16).
                        Caboolture Warplane and Flight
                        Heritage Museum, Caboolture,
                        Queensland, Australia.

Consolidated-Vultee Convaircar

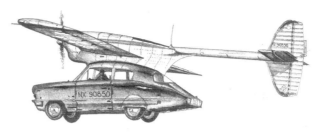

Subject: Consolidated-Vultee. Model 118 Convaircar.
          Registration NX90850.
Statistics: Consolidated-Vultee Convaircar.

Consolidated built its flying car around the body shell of
a 26hp Crossley 2-door coupé automobile. The prototype
was intended to be the first of a new breed of flying cars
that would revolutionize private transport and let the
ordinary man take to the air. The success was short lived,
however. When the prototype Convaircar crashed in the
desert outside San Diego the pilot was mortally wounded
and, despite the construction of a second prototype, the
project floundered in a flurry of media misgivings.

Country of Origin: USA
First Flight: 1947
Accommodation: 2
Wingspan: 34ft 0in (10.36m)
Length: 27ft 4in (8.32m)
Height: 8ft 7in (2.62m)
Empty Weight: 725lb (329kg)
Powerplant: 1 x 90hp Franklin 4AG.
                        Later 190hp Lycoming O-435O.
Cruise Speed: 130mph (209km/h)
Max Speed: 150mph (241km/h)
Service Ceiling: Never established.
Range: Never established.
Number Manufactured: Model 116 and 118 flying
                        prototype airframes only.

Consolidated PB4Y-2 Privateer

Subject: Consolidated PB4Y-2 Privateer in post war
          commercial usage was registered PT-BEG on the
          Brazilian register.
Statistics: Consolidated PB4Y-2 Privateer.

The Privateer was a development of the PB4Y-1, the US
Navy's version of the Liberator. It had a longer fuselage,
additional machine-gun turrets, more powerful engines
and an entirely revised tail structure. On the cessation
of hostilities many of these Privateers were sold off to
small charter companies and freight handlers. Others of
the type were converted for use as firebombers and,
indeed, a small number of Privateer firebombers remained
in service right up to the mid-1990s.

Country of Origin: USA
First Flight: 1943
Accommodation: 2 pilots + navigator + 5 to 8
                        gunners/bombardiers.
Wingspan: 110ft 0in (33.53m)
Length: 74ft 7in (22.73m)
Height: 30ft 1in (9.17m)
Empty Weight: 37,485lb (17,000kg)
Max Take Off: 65,000lb (29,478kg)
Powerplant: 4 x 1,350hp (1,007kW) Pratt
                        & Whitney R-1830-94 radials.
Cruise Speed: 224mph (360km/h)
Max Speed: 237mph (381km/h)
Service Ceiling: 21,000ft (6,400m)
Range: 2,800 miles (4,480km)
Preserved: National Museum of Naval
                        Aviation, NAS Pensacola,
                        Florida, USA.
                        Yankee Air Museum, Belleville,
                        Michigan, USA.

Consolidated B-24 Liberator

Subject: Consolidated B-25 Liberator of the US Air Force.
Statistics: Consolidated B-24M Liberator.

The Consolidated B-24 bomber was ordered by both France and Britain even before orders were placed by the United States. With a massive bomb-bay enclosure and a host of innovations, from de-icing boots to sophisticated new bomb aiming sights, the B-24 promised to be a huge improvement on earlier Allied bomber types. It was. Over the course of the war, vast numbers of B-24 bombers went on to drop countless tons of bombs and incendiaries over the cities of the Axis countries. Indeed, the B-24 took part in all theatres of war and played its part in many of the major offensive operations in both Europe and the Pacific. Among its best-remembered actions of the war was its low-level attack on the German-occupied oilfields of Ploesti in Romania. On the 1st of August 1943 a formation of 177 B-24s departed from Benghazi in Libya and undertook a 2,700-mile round trip to destroy the oilfields which were providing the German mechanized war machine with much of its petroleum. Of the 177 Liberators that set out on the mission no less than 57 aircraft and 570 airmen were lost.

Country of Origin:	USA
First Flight:	1939
Accommodation:	2 pilots + navigator + 5 to 7 gunners/bombardiers.
Wingspan:	110ft 0in (33.53m)
Length:	67ft 2in (20.47m)
Height:	30ft 1in (9.17m)
Empty Weight:	36,985lb (16,779kg)
Max Take Off:	64,500lb (29,257kg)
Powerplant:	4 X 1,200hp (894kW) Pratt & Whitney R-1830-65 radials.
Max Speed:	300mph (483km/h)
Combat Range:	2,100 miles (3,380km)
Number Manufactured:	18,188 of all B-24 variants.
Preserved:	Castle Air Museum, Atwater, California, USA. National Museum of the US Air Force, Wright-Patterson AFB, Dayton, Ohio, USA.

Consolidated PBY-5A Catalina

Subject: Netherlands-registered Consolidated PBY-5A Catalina PH-PBY.
Statistics: Consolidated PBY-5A Catalina.

It was Consolidated engineer Isaac Laddon who designed the remarkable PBY-5A in response to a US Navy competition brief of 1933. In this one design Laddon bent all of the rules and preconceptions which had followed the design of seaplanes and amphibians from the first decade of flight. Gone were all the draggy struts and braces. Instead a sleek, new parasol-wing arrangement provided instant clarity to the design and helped to keep the engines well up above the waterline. Packed with innovations and improvements, it re-examined all of the earlier thinking on flying-boat design and provided new ways of resolving old needs. Even its outboard stabilizing floats, a source of great turbulence on earlier flying-boats, were designed to retract upwards and to become an integral part of the wingtip.

Country of Origin:	USA
First Flight:	1935
Accommodation:	2 + 4
Wingspan:	104ft 0in (31.7m)
Length:	63ft 10in (19.46m)
Height:	20ft 2in (6.15m)
Empty Weight:	21,030lb (9,540kg)
Max Take Off:	35,420lb (16,066kg)
Powerplant:	2 X 1,200hp (894kW) Pratt & Whitney R-1830-92 radials.
Cruise Speed:	120mph (192km/h)
Max Speed:	175mph (282km/h)
Range:	2,350 miles (3,782km)
Number Manufactured:	3,281 of all PBY variants.
Flying or in service:	Small numbers still in service.
Preserved:	National Museum of Naval Aviation, NAS Pensacola, Florida, USA. Atlantic Canada Aviation Museum, Nova Scotia, Canada.

Cozy Mk IV

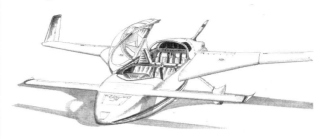

Subject: Cozy Mk IV, registration N14CZ, as flown to Sun 'n Fun 2005 by designer Nat Puffer.
Statistics: Cozy Mk IV.

In aviation circles there is a distinct difference between an 'air show' and a 'fly-in'. At an air show you see impressive aircraft from behind barriers. At a fly-in, however, you can get very close to a vast selection of aircraft ranging from antique to classic and experimental. Individually they may not be as noisy or as spectacular as the air show types but you can get right up close to them and, if you don't mind sounding like a prat, you can ask silly questions of their pilots and sometimes even their designers. This Cozy Mk IV was flown into the Experimental Aircraft Association's massive Sun 'n Fun fly-in event by Nat Puffer, aircraft designer and founder of the remarkable Cozy series.

Country of Origin:	USA
First Flight:	1982
Accommodation:	2 + 2
Wingspan:	28ft 1in (8.57m)
Length:	16ft 10in (4.91m)
Height:	7ft 10in (2.16m)
Empty Weight:	1,050lb (476kg)
Max Take Off:	2,050lb (930kg)
Powerplant:	1 X 180hp (134.2kW) Lycoming O-360 piston.
Cruise Speed:	185mph (297km/h)
Max Speed:	220mph (354km/h)
Service Ceiling:	20,000ft (6,096m)
Range:	1,100 miles (1,770km)
Number Manufactured:	Many projects in progress.
Flying or in service:	More than 350.

Convair
XFY-1 Pogo

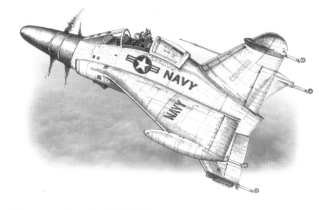

Subject: Convair XFY-1 flying prototype.
Statistics: Convair XFY-1.

Convair test pilot James 'Skeets' Coleman flew more than 70 accident-free experimental flights in the XFY-1 Pogo, an extraordinary achievement given that each sortie entailed taking off vertically, transitioning into horizontal flight, transitioning back into vertical flight, and 'reversing' back to the ground in a precarious vertical-landing manoeuvre. Throughout all of these flights he never closed the canopy and he was, at all times, ready to take to his parachute.

Country of Origin:	USA
First Flight:	1954
Accommodation:	1
Wingspan:	25ft 8in (7.8m)
Length:	34ft 11in (10.5m)
Height:	23ft 11in (7.2m)
Empty Weight:	13,000lb (5,850kg)
Max Take Off:	16,250lb (7,371kg)
Powerplant:	1 X 5,850hp (4,362kW) Allison YT-40-A-6 turboprop comprising 2 smaller T-38 powerplants feeding into one gearbox.
Cruise Speed:	592mph (953km/h)
Max Speed:	610mph (981km/h)
Range:	Not established.
Number Manufactured:	1
Preserved:	The XFY-1 Pogo is preserved at the Smithsonian National Air and Space Museum, Washington, DC, USA.

Curtiss P-40
Kittyhawk

Subject: Curtiss Kittyhawk Sneak Attack of the Old Flying Machine Co.
Statistics: Curtiss P-40 N Kittyhawk.

The P-40 may not have been as powerful as some of the leading-edge Allied fighters but it was far heavier, faster and sturdier than many of the Japanese and the German fighting aircraft. At low level, in particular, it was a potent weapon and, at these altitudes, it built up a most respectable reputation. Perhaps its greatest attribute was that it built up terrific speed in a dive and that it could out-run most of its enemies. Pilots were directed to dive steeply into an intercepting attack, picking up great speed before unleashing the P-40s massive 4 machine guns on the target aircraft. Dogfighting and tight manoeuvres were avoided and the Kittyhawk used its considerable speed advantage to escape its foe and ultimately make it back to high flight levels.

Country of Origin:	USA
First Flight:	1935 (as the P-36). 1938 as the P-40.
Accommodation:	1 or 2
Wingspan:	37ft 4in (11.38m)
Length:	33ft 4in (10.16m)
Height:	10ft 7in (3.24m)
Max Take Off:	8,850lb (4,014kg)
Powerplant:	1 X 1,360hp (1,013kW) Allison V-1710-81 in-line piston.
Cruise Speed:	300mph (483km/h)
Max Speed:	378mph (608km/h)
Service Ceiling:	34,400ft (10,485m)
Range:	600 miles (965km)
Number Manufactured:	13,738 of all P-40 Variants.
Flying or in service:	Small numbers in service.
Preserved:	RAF Museum, Hendon, London, UK. Canada Aviation Museum, Ottawa, Ontario, Canada. Steven F. Udvar-Hazy Center, Chantilly, Virginia, USA (Kittyhawk P-40E).

Curtiss BF2-C-1
Hawk

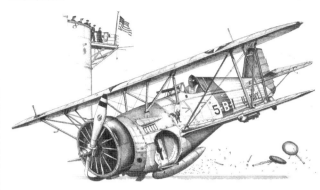

Subject: Curtiss BF2-C-1 of the United States Navy lands heavily on the deck of USS Ranger c.1937.
Statistics: Curtiss BF2-C-1 Hawk.

The Curtiss BF2-C-1 Hawk served on board some of the USA's flagship aircraft carriers for just one year from October of 1936 until November of 1937. In that short time technology progressed at such a rate that the Hawk rapidly became obsolete and was replaced by a new generation of sleek monoplane fighters and dive bombers.

Country of Origin:	USA
First Flight:	1935
Accommodation:	1
Wingspan:	31ft 6in (9.6m)
Length:	23ft 0in (7.0m)
Height:	10ft 10in (3.3m)
Empty Weight:	3,371lb (1,529kg)
Max Take Off:	5,089lb (2,307kg)
Powerplant:	1 X 700hp (522kW) Wright R-1820-04.
Cruise Speed:	220mph (354km/h)
Max Speed:	230mph (370km/h)
Range:	795 miles (1,280km)

Curtiss
H-75A-1 Hawk/Mohawk

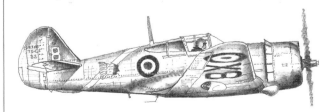

Subject: Curtiss H-75.C1 Hawk No 82 is preserved at Duxford.
Statistics: Curtiss H-75A-1.

244

Developed from the earlier Curtiss Hawk biplane series, the P-36 was one of the evolutionary steps on the way to the remarkable P-40 fighter. Essentially the P-40 was a P-36 airframe with a new 1,360hp in-line Allison powerplant instead of the earlier Pratt & Whitney radial. A small modification, perhaps, but with the advantages of both additional power and a new, streamlined nose profile the new aircraft was a stunning improvement over the original and it went on to make history. The P-36, too, in its own right, saw much action in the early years of the war in the hands of several of the hard-pressed Allied nations.

Country of Origin:	USA
First Flight:	1935
Accommodation:	1
Wingspan:	37ft 4in (11.36m)
Length:	28ft 10in (8.78m)
Height:	8ft 5in (2.57m)
Max Take Off:	6,010lb (2,726kg)
Powerplant:	1 x 1,050hp (782.5kW) Pratt & Whitney R-1830-13 Twin Wasp.
Cruise Speed:	250mph (402km/h)
Max Speed:	300mph (483km/h)
Service Ceiling:	32,700ft (9,966m)
Range:	825 miles (1,330km)
Flying or in service:	At least 1
Preserved:	4 surviving airframes.

Curtiss C-46 Commando

Subject: The Confederate Air Force's Curtiss C-46 Commando China Doll.
Statistics: Curtiss C-46 Commando.

The Curtiss C-46 and the Douglas C-47 worked side by side on many of the great military campaigns of the Second World War carrying troops, freight and military supplies into all of the theatres of war. From island-jumping across the Pacific to the large-scale delivery

of paratroopers and equipment into France, the 2 big freighters could be counted on. Their next great challenge was the remarkable Berlin Airlift which saw every type of freighter and airliner pressed into service to carry essential supplies and foodstuffs into that beleaguered city. In all of these situations the C-46 Commando proved itself to be a reliable and well-rounded performer.

Country of Origin:	USA
First Flight:	1940
Accommodation:	Flight crew of 4 + up to 50 passengers.
Wingspan:	108ft 0in (32.92m)
Length:	76ft 4in (23.27m)
Height:	21ft 8in (6.6m)
Empty Weight:	29,300lb (13,290kg)
Max Take Off:	50,000lb (22,680kg)
Powerplant:	2 x 2,000 hp (1,495kW) Pratt & Whitney R-2800-34 Double Wasp piston radials or similar P&W equivalent.
Cruise Speed:	187mph (300km/h)
Max Speed:	236mph (378km/h)
Service Ceiling:	22,300ft (6,797m)
Range:	1,564 miles (2,897km)
Number Manufactured:	3,182 of all C-46 variants.
Flying or in service:	c.15
Preserved:	Castle Air Museum, Atwater, California, USA. Yanks Air Museum, Chino Airport, California, USA. National Museum of the US Air Force, Wright-Patterson AFB, Dayton, Ohio, USA.

Curtiss SBC-4 Helldiver

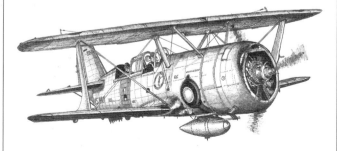

Subject: Curtiss SBC-4 Helldiver biplane of the United States Navy.
Statistics: Curtiss SBC-4 Helldiver.

From the earliest days of flight Curtiss had been the primary supplier of aircraft to the US Navy but by the early 1930s Grumman's superbly designed naval series had

substantially usurped this venerable position. Curtiss was anxious to retain its large US Navy orders and designed its SBC series to compete directly with Grumman's carrier-based fighting aircraft. The SBC-4 was ordered by the US Navy, by France and by Britain (as the Cleveland). Although it did serve in the war effort it saw little frontline action and had few, if any, direct engagements with the enemy.

Country of Origin:	USA
First Flight:	1934
Accommodation:	2
Wingspan:	34ft 0in (10.36m)
Length:	27ft 5in (8.37m)
Height:	8ft 7in (2.64m)
Empty Weight:	4,841lb (2,196kg)
Max Take Off:	6,632lb (3,008kg)
Powerplant:	1 x 950hp (708kW) Wright R-1820-34 Cyclone.
Max Speed:	235mph (378km/h)
Service Ceiling:	27,300ft (8,321m)
Range:	855 miles (1,376km)
Number Manufactured:	307
Preserved:	Steven F. Udvar-Hazy Center, Chantilly, Virginia, USA.

Dassault-Breguet Atlantic 1150

Subject: Dassault-Breguet 1150 Atlantic of the German Air Force.
Statistics: Dassault-Breguet 1150 Atlantic ATL2.

A long-distance reconnaissance and anti-submarine patrol aircraft designed primarily for use by NATO countries but now in service in many parts of the world. Specialist personnel on a typical patrol mission might comprise 2 pilots, 1 aircraft commander, 2 observers, 1 navigator, 1 radio operator, 1 electronic warfare officer, 1 computer technician, 1 tactical co-ordinator, and up to 3 specialist sub-marine detection operators.

Country of Origin:	France
First Flight:	1961
Accommodation:	2 pilots + up to 12 specialist operators/technicians.
Wingspan:	122ft 11in (37.46m)
Length:	104ft 0in (31.75m)
Height:	37ft 1in (11.3m)

Empty Weight:	56,663lb (25,698kg)
Max Take Off:	101,853lb (46,192kg)
Powerplant:	2 x 6,100hp (4,549kW) Rolls-Royce Tyne Turboprops.
Cruise Speed:	345mph (556km/h)
Max Speed:	403mph (648km/h)
Service Ceiling:	33,000ft (10,058m)
Range:	4,861 miles (7,778km)
Number Manufactured:	82
Flying or in service:	Operated by France, Italy, Germany, Belgium, Netherlands and others. In use to this day.

Dassault-Breguet-Dornier Alpha Jet

Subject: Dassault-Breguet-Dornier Alpha Jet of the German Luftwaffe.
Statistics: Dassault-Breguet-Dornier Alpha Jet.

One of the world's most popular and efficient advanced jet trainers, the Alpha Jet was a collaborative venture by Dassault-Breguet of France and Dornier of Germany. While designed to fulfil a lead-in instructional role for heavy military fighters, the Alpha Jet is, in its own right, a potent and formidable weapons platform. Indeed, while most of its customers have employed it as an advanced jet trainer, Germany has configured its Alpha Jets for a light attack role, being intended primarily to counter the threat posed by helicopter gunships. The Alpha Jet is flown by Germany, Egypt, Morocco, Cameroon, Belgium, Ivory Coast and by the famous French national aerobatic team, the Patrouille de France.

Country of Origin:	France/Germany
First Flight:	1973
Accommodation:	2
Wingspan:	29ft 11in (9.11m)

Length:	38ft 7in (11.75m)
Height:	13ft 9in (4.19m)
Empty Weight:	7,376lb (3,345kg)
Max Take Off:	17,640lb (8,000kg)
Powerplant:	2 x 2,976lb (13.24kN) Turbomeca SNECMA Larzac 04-C6 Turbojets.
Cruise Speed:	597mph (960km/h)
Max Speed:	621mph (1,000km/h)
Range:	1,800 miles (2,880km)
Flying or in service:	Widely in service.

Dassault Mirage III

Subject: Dassault Mirage IIIEA of the Argentine Air Force.
Statistics: Dassault Mirage IIIE.

France's superb Dassault Mirage III has been one of the most prolific and successful fighter designs of modern times and has served with the air forces of many nations. It has been operated at various stages by France, Argentina, Australia, Brazil, Chile, Egypt, Israel, Lebanon, Pakistan, South Africa, Spain and Switzerland. The type has played a decisive role in a number of the great military battles of the 20th century including the Six Day War of 1967, the Yom Kippur War of 1973 and the Falklands War of 1982. The type has been configured to perform a variety of mission-specific roles from long-range strategic bombing to strike/attack duties and close air support. It has been licence-built in several third party countries including Israel, where it was copied as the Israel Aircraft Industries Nesher, which served with the Israeli Air Force and the military forces of Argentina. The IAI Nesher was itself upgraded to produce the potent IAI Kfir C2, which now serves with the military forces of Israel, Colombia, Ecuador and South Africa. The Mirage itself, meanwhile, has undergone a succession of comprehensive avionics and weapons-systems upgrades to ensure that it remains a potent and effective component of France's substantial military might.

Country of Origin:	France
First Flight:	1956
Accommodation:	1
Wingspan:	26ft 11in (8.2m)
Length:	49ft 3in (15.03m)

Height:	14ft 9in (4.5m)
Empty Weight:	15,540lb (7,050kg)
Max Take Off Weight:	30,205lb (13,700kg)
Powerplant:	1 x 13,670lb (60.8kN) SNECMA Atar 9C turbojet with afterburner.
Cruise Speed:	600mph (957km/h)
Max Speed:	1,460mph (2,350km/h) or Mach 2.2
Service Ceiling:	55,755ft (17,000m)
Range:	1,490 miles (2,400km)
Number Manufactured:	More than 1,422 of all Mirage III variants built.
Flying or in service:	Continues in service with the military forces of many nations including France, Argentina, Brazil, Chile, Egypt, Israel and South Africa.

de Havilland (Airco) DH-9A Ninak

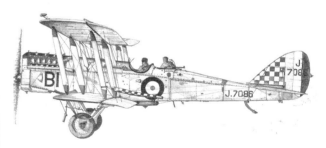

Subject: de Havilland DH-9A Ninak J7086.
Statistics: de Havilland (Airco) DH-9A Ninak.

The combination of the earlier de Havilland DH-9 airframe with the powerful American-built Packard Liberty engine brought about the remarkable DH-9A Ninak. Although the type was introduced only in the last months of the war it did see considerable action over France, Russia, and Germany. Production continued after the war with DH-9As being built for use by the British armed services in the Middle East and India. Others of the type were used to establish a first scheduled airmail service between Cairo and Baghdad.

Country of Origin:	UK
First Flight:	1917
Accommodation:	Pilot + gunner.
Wingspan:	45ft 11in (14m)
Length:	30ft 3in (9.2m)
Height:	11ft 4in (3.45m)
Max Take Off:	4,645lb (2,107kg)
Powerplant:	1 x 400hp (298kW) Packard Liberty 12.

Max Speed:	114mph (185km/h)
Service Ceiling:	16,400ft (5,000 m)
Range:	525 miles (845km)
Number Manufactured:	In excess of 800.
Flying or in service:	Small numbers of highly treasured DH-9As airworthy.
Preserved:	RAF Museum, Hendon, London, UK.

de Havilland DH-91 Albatross

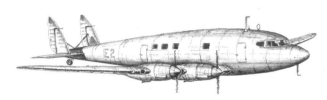

Subject: Prototype de Havilland DH-91 Albatross airframe G-AEVV.
Statistics: de Havilland DH-91 Albatross.

The Albatross was a remarkably sleek and clean aircraft given its early vintage. Throughout its detailing every element of the airframe was superbly faired and rounded to ensure clean and efficient passage through the air. Indeed, the seamless fairing of the spinner into the engine cowling was wonderfully ahead of its time in this 1937 aircraft. The traditional de Havilland feature tail has been doubled up but is otherwise unchanged. Only 7 of the type were produced before the onset of the war diverted de Havilland to more pressing lines of production. Two of these 7 airframes were impressed into military service and used on the important UK to Iceland route which was a vital lifeline to the USA for most of the war years.

Country of Origin:	UK
First Flight:	1937
Accommodation:	3 + 22 passengers.
Wingspan:	105ft 0in (32.0m)
Length:	71ft 6in (21.79m)
Height:	22ft 3in (6.78m)
Empty Weight:	21,230lb (9,630kg)
Max Take Off:	29,500lb (13,381kg)
Powerplant:	4 x 525hp (391kW) de Havilland Gipsy 12.
Cruise Speed:	210mph (338km/h)
Max Speed:	225mph (362km/h)
Service Ceiling:	17,900ft (5,455m)
Range:	905 miles (1,680km)
Number Manufactured:	7

de Havilland DH-94 Moth Minor

Subject: de Havilland DH-94 Moth Minor G-AFNG.
Statistics: de Havilland DH-94 Moth Minor.

A 2-seat primary training aircraft developed as a private venture by de Havilland to replace the Tiger Moth. The Moth Minor was a departure from de Havilland's usual biplane format and it resulted from de Havilland's need to compete with the highly successful Miles Hawk series of monoplane trainers which were clearly pointing the way forward. Most DH-94s were built in open-cockpit format but a closed cockpit or coupé variant was also offered. As for replacing the Tiger Moth? No aircraft has been quite able to replace it to this day.

Country of Origin:	UK
First Flight:	1937
Accommodation:	2
Wingspan:	36ft 7in (11.15m)
Length:	24ft 5in (7.44m)
Height:	6ft 4in (1.93m)
Empty Weight:	960lb (435kg)
Max Take Off:	1,550lb (703kg)
Powerplant:	1 x 80hp (59.65kW) de Havilland Gipsy Minor.
Cruise Speed:	100mph (160km/h)
Max Speed:	118mph (189km/h)
Service Ceiling:	18,400ft (5,608m)
Range:	300 miles (480km)
Number Manufactured:	74 at de Havilland, Hatfield. 44 at de Havilland, Australia.
Preserved:	G-AFOJ at de Havilland Centre, Hertfordshire, UK.

de Havilland DH-89 Dragon Rapide

Subject: Caernarfon Air Park of Wales is home to this stunningly well-presented de Havilland DH-89 Dragon Rapide.
Statistics: de Havilland DH-89A Dragon Rapide.

Constructed of wood and ply with fabric-covered wings, the de Havilland DH-84 Dragon was one of the finest and most beautiful aircraft of its era. The Dragon and the later DH-89 Dragon Rapide were built in substantial numbers and were exported to many parts of the world. To this day small numbers of both types are maintained in airworthy condition and make regular appearances at public air shows and fly-ins. One of the finest of these vintage airframes is the superb EI-ABI Dragon DH-84 which is maintained in flying condition by a dedicated group of Aer Lingus operatives and flown regularly by ex-Aer Lingus Captain J.J. O'Sullivan.

Country of Origin:	UK
First Flight:	1934
Accommodation:	1 pilot + 6 passengers.
Wingspan:	48ft 0in (14.63m)
Length:	34ft 6in (10.52m)
Height:	10ft 3in (3.12m)
Empty Weight:	2,276lb (1,486kg)
Max Take Off:	5,500lb (2,495kg)
Powerplant:	2 x 200hp (149kW) de Havilland Gipsy Queen 3s.
Cruise Speed:	132mph (212km/h)
Max Speed:	157mph (251km/h)
Service Ceiling:	19,500ft (5,944m)
Range:	578 miles (925km)
Number Manufactured:	202 DH-84s completed. Over 700 Dragon DH-89s completed.
Flying or in service:	c.31 airworthy at this time.
Preserved:	Caernarfon Air Park, Wales. Aer Lingus Collection, Dublin. Israeli Air Force Museum, Hatzerim, Beer Sheeva, Israel.

de Havilland DH-100 Vampire

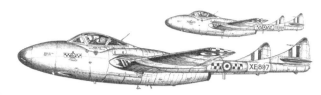

Subject: de Havilland DH-100 Vampire XE897 (G-DHVV) and Wingman.
Statistics: de Havilland DH-100 Vampire.

The DH-100 Vampire was taking shape on the drawing boards at de Havilland as early as 1941 but it was not until April of 1945 that the first completed airframes began to roll off the production lines. Designed around an aspirational RAF specification for a turbojet interceptor fighter, the Vampire used many of the components and the construction techniques developed for the Mosquito. Its unusual pod fuselage and its twin-boom configuration were essentially dictated by the early de Havilland Goblin turbojet powerplant, which was extremely short on power and therefore required a very short tailpipe installation to minimize power loss. The DH-100 Vampire went on to be manufactured in large numbers and it served the armed services of many countries until the mid-1960s.

Country of Origin:	UK
First Flight:	1943
Accommodation:	1
Wingspan:	38ft 0in (11.58m)
Length:	30ft 9in (9.37m)
Height:	6ft 2in (1.88m)
Empty Weight:	8,620lb (3,910kg)
Max Take Off:	12,390lb (5,620kg)
Powerplant:	1 X de Havilland Goblin turbojet.
Cruise Speed:	480mph (768km/h)
Max Speed:	540mph (869km/h)
Service Ceiling:	40,000ft (12,192m)
Range:	1,220 miles (1,963km).
Number Manufactured:	4,342 of all variants.
Flying or in service:	Small numbers finding their way into civilian ownership.
Preserved:	RAAF Association Museum, Bull Creek, Perth, Australia. Fighter World, New South Wales, Australia. RAF Museum, Hendon, London, UK (Vampire F3).

de Havilland DH-104 Devon

Subject: de Havilland DH-104 Devon is preserved at Cosford.
Statistics: de Havilland DH-104 Devon.

The de Havilland Devon was developed from the commercial feederliner DH-104 Dove. Ninety-five of the type were delivered to the Royal Air Force as the Devon C1s while a further 33 Devon C2s were manufactured for the Royal Navy. In these roles the Devon saw service in many parts of the world and, when the types were finally retired, they continued to provide service to smaller carriers and airfreight carriers alike.

Country of Origin:	UK
First Flight:	1945
Accommodation:	2 pilots + up to 10 passengers.
Wingspan:	57ft 0in (17.4m)
Length:	39ft 3in (11.9m)
Height:	13ft 3in (4.0m)
Empty Weight:	5,878lb (2,666kg)
Max Take Off:	8,950lb (4,059kg)
Powerplant:	2 X 400hp (298kW) de Havilland Gipsy Queen 70 Mk 3.
Cruise Speed:	210mph (336km/h)
Max Speed:	230mph (368km/h)
Service Ceiling:	21,800ft (6,644m)
Range:	880 miles (1,408km)
Number Manufactured:	542 of all Dove/Devon types.
Flying or in service:	Circa 22 currently flying.
Preserved:	Air Force Museum, Christchurch, New Zealand.

de Havilland DH-106 Comet

Subject: de Havilland DH-106 Comet 4C, reg G-BDIW, of former carrier Dan-Air London is based at the Hermaskeil Museum, Germany.
Statistics: de Havilland DH-106 Comet 1.

BOAC's Comets, the first off the production line, allowed the airline to inaugurate the first ever passenger turbojet service on the London to Johannesburg route. The service marked a massive advance in airline evolution, knocking days off the journey time and providing passengers with a pressurized and comfortable environment. For almost a year BOAC led the field in turbojet airline travel until a series of mid-air structural failures led to the withdrawal of all Comet 1s from operational service. There followed a long period of investigation as well as much public and political debate. In 1957 it was decided that a modified and strengthened Comet could be returned to service but, despite the fact that BOAC ordered 19 of the new Comet Series 4, the revolutionary Boeing 707 airliner was about to enter service and the day of the Comet had passed.

Country of Origin:	UK
First Flight:	1949
Accommodation:	Flight crew of 3 + 36 to 101 passengers.
Wingspan:	115ft 0in (35.0m)
Length:	93ft 0in (28.35m)
Height:	29ft 6in
Empty Weight:	75,400lb (34,201kg)
Max Take Off:	105,000lb (47,627kg)
Powerplant:	4 X 4,450lb (19.8kN) de Havilland Ghost centrifugal-flow turbojets.
Cruise Speed:	490mph (788km/h)
Range:	2,500 miles (4,024km)
Number Manufactured:	112 of all variants.
Preserved:	Transport Aircraft Collection, Cosford. RAF Museum, Cosford Airfield, Shifnal, Shropshire, UK.

de Havilland DH-108 Swallow

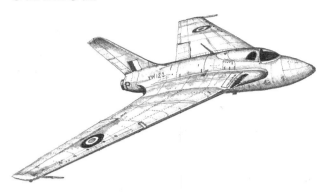

Subject: de Havilland 108 Swallow. Registration TG306, the second prototype.
Statistics: De Havilland DH-108 Swallow.

De Havilland's unfortunate experimental DH-108 research prototype was based on the fuselage of the earlier de Havilland Vampire. Indeed, the first 2 airframes were former Vampires that were heavily converted to Swallow status by the removal of the Vampire's trademark twin-boom tail assembly and the addition of the new prototype's highly suspect swept wings. Designed to progress experimental research into highly swept wing configurations and to collect aerodynamic data on related stability and control thresholds, the Swallow was designed to sit on the very edge of proven aerodynamics. This was a highly dangerous and unstable aircraft that led to the tragic loss of all 3 test prototypes along with their unfortunate test pilots, among them the great Geoffrey Raoul de Havilland himself.

Country of Origin:	UK
First Flight:	1946
Accommodation:	1
Wingspan:	39ft 0in (11.89m)
Length:	24ft 6in (7.47m)
Max Take Off:	8,960lb (4,064kg)
Powerplant:	1 x 3,300lb de Havilland Goblin 3
Max Speed:	640mph (1,030km/h)
Number Manufactured:	3
Flying or in service.	Nil
Preserved:	Nil. All 3 airframes lost.

de Havilland Tiger Moth/Sea Tiger

Subject: de Havilland DH-82 Tiger Moth/Sea Tiger.
Statistics: de Havilland Tiger Moth/Sea Tiger.

The specification for de Havilland's legendary DH-82 biplane trainer was set down by the Royal Air Force and the type became the basic training aircraft for tens of thousands of the pilots who took part in the Second World War. An immensely successful and much loved icon, the type must surely hold the record for being manufactured in more countries than any other aircraft with separate production lines in England, Australia, New Zealand, Canada, Norway, Portugal and Sweden.

Country of Origin:	UK
First Flight:	1931
Accommodation:	2
Wingspan:	29ft 4in (8.94m)
Length:	23ft 11in (7.29m)
Height:	8ft 9in (2.67m)
Empty Weight:	1,115lb (506kg)
Max Take Off:	1,825lb (828kg)
Powerplant:	1 x 130hp (97kW) de Havilland Gipsy Major.
Cruise Speed:	90mph (145km/h)
Max Speed:	104mph (167km/h)
Service Ceiling:	13,600ft (4,145m)
Range:	300 miles (483km)
Number Manufactured:	8,811
Flying or in service.	Upwards of 450 airworthy.
Preserved:	Airworthy Tiger Moth DH82a preserved at Temora Aviation Museum, New South Wales, Australia. Canada Aviation Museum, Ottawa, Ontario, Canada (DH82C). RAF Museum, Hendon, London, UK (Tiger Moth I). Newark Air Museum, Nottingham, Nottinghamshire, UK. Norwegian Aviation Museum, Bodø, Norway.

de Havilland DH-110 Sea Vixen

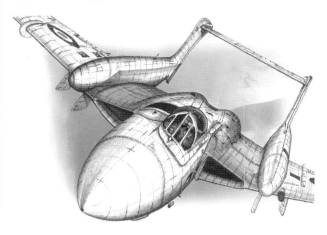

Subject: DH-110 Sea Vixen XP924. Lady Fox in airworthy condition again.
Statistics: de Havilland DH-110 Sea Vixen.

With its sleek swept configuration and its 2 10,000lb thrust Rolls-Royce Avon 208 turbojets, the de Havilland Sea Vixen was a capable and potent carrier-based weapons platform for the Royal Navy and, indeed, it saw action in many far-flung areas of the world. In the summer of 1961 when the forces of President Kassem of Iraq were threatening the invasion of Kuwait, the British government sent 2 modern aircraft carriers to patrol the skies over The Gulf. With the carriers' complements of Sea Vixen fighters patrolling the skies over Kuwait the threat from Iraq quickly dissipated and conflict was averted or, indeed, as history would later prove, postponed for future years. Equipped with hardpoints to carry a wide range of ballistic missiles and defensive armaments, the Sea Vixen was constantly upgraded to maintain its position as a world-class all-weather day-and-nightfighter. It served in many of the world's most troubled areas from its introduction until its retirement from service in 1972.

Country of Origin:	UK
First Flight:	1951
Accommodation:	2
Wingspan:	50ft 00in 15.24m
Length:	55ft 3in (16.95m)
Height:	10ft 9in (3.28m)
Empty Weight:	26,000lb (11,795kg)
Max Take Off:	35,000lb (15,875kg)
Powerplant:	2 x Rolls-Royce Avon 208 turbojets.
Max Speed:	645mph (1,038km/h)
Service Ceiling:	48,200ft (14,700m)
Range:	808 miles (1,300km)
Number Manufactured:	148 of various configurations.
Preserved:	Queensland Air Museum, Australia. Newark Air Museum, Nottingham, Nottinghamshire, UK. Fleet Air Arm Museum, Somerset, UK.

de Havilland DH-114 Heron

Subject: de Havilland DH-114 Heron formerly of the Queen's Flight.
Statistics: de Havilland DH-114 Heron 2C.

The DH-114 was a 14-seat commuter airliner, a stretched 4-engine development of de Havilland's successful DH-104 Dove. Design work on the Heron began in the late 1940s and made as much use of existing Dove components as possible. Both types are easily recognized by the raised cockpit detail, forward nose-gear assembly, separate passenger cabin, and all-metal construction techniques. The Heron was widely exported to those parts of the world where British influence prevailed, and especially to Australia and New Zealand.

Country of Origin:	UK
First Flight:	1950
Accommodation:	2 pilots + up to 14 passengers. An 8-seat executive variant was also available.
Wingspan:	71ft 6in (21.8m)
Length:	48ft 6in (14.8m)
Height:	15ft 7in (4.75m)
Empty Weight:	8,484lb (3,848Kg)
Max Take Off:	13,500lb (6,124Kg)
Powerplant:	4 x 250hp (186KW) de Havilland Gipsy Queen 30 Mk 2 6-cylinder in-line engines.
Cruise Speed:	180mph (288Km/h)
Max Speed:	200mph (320Km/h)
Service Ceiling:	17,200ft (5,242m)
Range:	1,550 miles (2,480Km)
Number Manufactured:	149 of all variants.
Flying or in service:	c.3 airworthy.
Preserved:	Prototype preserved in RAAF Association Museum, Bull Creek, Perth, Australia.

de Havilland Canada DHC-1 Chipmunk

Subject: de Havilland Canada DHC-1 Chipmunk.
Statistics: de Havilland Canada DHC-1 Chipmunk MK 22.

Canada's Chipmunk became the basic training airframe for many nations including Ireland, Egypt, Ceylon, Syria, Burma, Britain and, of course, Canada itself. With a robust build quality and forgiving manners in the air, it was an ideal training aircraft for young and inexperienced pilots in their first years of tuition. When the Chipmunks of the Royal Air Force were eventually retired from military service the Ministry of Defence disposed of them into private ownership and the type began to appear at air shows and aerodromes across Britain and Ireland.

Country of Origin:	Canada
First Flight:	1946
Accommodation:	Instructor + Student.
Wingspan:	34ft 4in (10.46m)
Length:	25ft 5in (7.75m)
Height:	7ft 0in (2.13m)
Empty Weight:	1,425lb (646Kg)
Max Take Off:	2,014lb (913Kg)
Powerplant:	1 x 145hp (108KW) de Havilland Gipsy Major 10.
Cruise Speed:	119mph (190Km/h)
Max Speed:	138mph (221Km/h)
Service Ceiling:	15,800ft (4,815m)
Range:	280 miles (451Km)
Number Manufactured:	1,283 manufactured in Canada, Britain and Portugal.
Flying or in service:	Still frequently seen at fly-in events and aerodromes.
Preserved:	RAF Museum, Hendon, London, UK (DHC-1). Steven F. Udvar-Hazy Center, Chantilly, Virginia, USA (DHC-1A). Canada Aviation Museum, Ottawa, Ontario, Canada (DHC-2).

de Havilland Canada DHC-2 Beaver

Subject: de Havilland Canada Beaver N146KS.
Statistics: de Havilland Canada DHC-2 Beaver.

De Havilland's Canadian-designed Beaver has become the workhorse of cold and remote locations over many years. Servicing some of the coldest and the most remote outposts of Alaska, Canada and, indeed, the world, the Beaver is, to this day, depended on by many small and isolated communities as their sole link to civilization and vital supplies. This is a virtual flying truck, rugged and durable in the extreme. Equipped with large tundra tyres it can land on some of the roughest of airstrips while, fitted with floats, it can serve locations and communities which are close to rivers and lakes. The Beaver's 450-horsepower Pratt & Whitney R-985-AN Wasp Junior 9-cylinder radial piston provided the power required to lift its 5,090lb (2,309kg) all-up weight off water with additional power in reserve to deal with mountainous terrain and its associated downdraft weather patterns.
In 1963 the Turbo Beaver, an uprated and turbocharged development of the Beaver, was flown. Its larger Pratt & Whitney PT6A6 turboprop powerplant brought with it greatly enhanced performance figures and, indeed, even improved its shortfield landing characteristics.

Country of Origin:	Canada
First Flight:	1947
Accommodation:	5/6
Wingspan:	48ft 0in (14.63m)
Length:	30ft 4in (9.25m)
Height:	9ft 0in (2.75m)
Empty Weight:	3,316lb (1,506Kg)
Loaded:	5,090lb (2,309kg)
Powerplant:	Pratt & Whitney R985-AN Wasp Junior radial rated at 450hp (335KW)
Cruise Speed:	125mph (201Km/h)
Max Speed:	134mph (217Km/h)
Service Ceiling:	18,000ft (5,486m)
Range:	775 miles (1,252Km)
Number Manufactured:	1,692 of all configurations built between 1948 and 1968.
Flying or in service:	Yes
Preserved:	Canada Aviation Museum, Ottawa, Ontario, Canada. US Army Aviation Museum, Fort Rucker, Ozark, Alabama, USA.

Delanne Duo-Mono

Subject: Delanne Duo-Mono prototype.
Statistics: Delanne Duo-Mono.

Not unlike the Mignet Flying Flea tandem-wing, the Delanne Duo-Mono was designed by Frenchman Maurice Delanne during 1937 and 1938. The first prototype was lost in a crash but the second prototype flew well and logged more than 600 hours in the cause of research into the aerodynamic advantages of tandem-wing configurations. Unfortunately for Delanne the Germans occupied France just as his first production model was completed and he spent much of the remainder of the war trying to prevent his data getting into the hands of the German information mill.

Country of Origin:	France
First Flight:	1937
Accommodation:	Pilot + gunner.
Wingspan:	33ft 2in (10.11m)
Length:	24ft 1in (7.33m)
Height:	9ft 10in (3.0m)
Max Take Off:	6,349lb
Powerplant:	1 x 1,010hp (753kW) Hispano-Suiza in-line piston.
Max Speed:	342mph (550km/h).
Service Ceiling:	32,810ft (10,000m).
Number Manufactured:	2 prototypes + 1 production.

de Pischoff Flycycle

Subject: Alfred de Pischoff (nee Alfred Ritter Von Pischoff) Flycycle.
Statistics: de Pischoff Flycycle.

In 1922 the Flycycle was designed by Alfred Ritter de Pischoff in yet another unsuccessful attempt to put an aircraft in every garage. With its miniature fuselage and its fold-up wings the Flycycle was designed to be stowed cheaply and easily by the average man. De Pischoff's dream never did come true as he was killed test-flying one of his many prototypes in 1923.

Country of Origin:	Austria/France
First Flight:	1922
Accommodation:	1
Number Manufactured:	1
Preserved:	One of de Pischoff's flying machines (but not the Flycycle) is displayed in the Empire State Aerosciences Museum, New York.

Diamond Aircraft DA20C-1 Katana

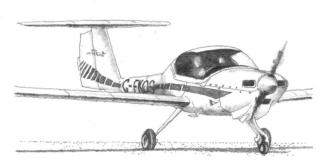

Subject: Diamond Aircraft DA20C-1 Katana. Canadian registration C-FKOS.
Statistics: Diamond Aircraft DA20C-1 Katana.

Hoffman Flugzeugbau of Austria produced a much-refined and improved derivative of its long-running Super Dimona and designated it the DA20 Katana. Now under the new 'Diamond' banner, Hoffman went on to build the type in large numbers to meet a steady demand from flying clubs and private owners alike. With its venerable motorglider ancestry it is not surprising that the Katana retains all of the virtues of its past to create a most efficient and aerodynamic sports aircraft. Its cruise speed is fast compared to other aircraft of its size, and its handling qualities and manners in the landing phase are second to none. It is no wonder, then, that the type has been a resounding success for Diamond, which took the confident step of relocating its Katana production line to Canada so that it could be located near to its main North American and Canadian markets.

Country of Origin:	Canada/Austria
First Flight:	1992
Accommodation:	2
Wingspan:	35ft 8in (10.87m)
Length:	23ft 6in (7.16m)
Height:	7ft 2in (2.18m)
Empty Weight:	656lb (300kg)
Max Take Off:	1,652lb (750kg)
Powerplant:	1 x 125hp (93kW) Teledyne Continental IO-240 piston.
Cruise Speed:	152mph (243km/h)
Max Speed:	172mph (275km/h)
Service Ceiling:	14,000ft (4,267m)
Range:	600 miles (960km)
Number Manufactured:	600 by end of 2000.
Flying or in service:	In service.

Diamond Aircraft DA-40 Diamond Star

Subject: Diamond Aircraft DA-40 demonstrator.
Statistics: Diamond Aircraft DA-40 TDI Diamond Star.

The DA-40 Diamond Star combines aerodynamic efficiency and practical ergonomic design like no other light sport-plane on the market today. Its 169mph cruise speed, its 800-mile range and its spacious, well-appointed interior, together, comprise a package that few pilots can resist. The DA-40's avionics suite, too, is a superbly well-appointed installation which, at the top end of the marque, is only short of glass-cockpit status. The feature of the Diamond Star which most captured the imagination of the general aviation market, however, was its diesel-burning powerplant. Here, for the first time, was a certified aircraft which burned low-cost Jet-A1 (diesel) instead of AVGas, a huge first for general aviation and for Diamond Aircraft.

Country of Origin:	Austria
First Flight:	1997
Accommodation:	4
Wingspan:	39ft 2in (11.94m)
Length:	26ft 5in (8.06m)
Height:	6ft 6in (1.97m)
Empty Weight:	1,720lb (780kg)
Max Take Off:	2,535lb (1,150kg)
Powerplant:	1 x 135hp (100.7kW) Thielert Centurion 1.7 litre turbodiesel powerplant.
Max Speed:	178mph (285km/h)
Flying or in service.	In service.

Diamond Aircraft DA-42 Twin Star

Subject: Diamond Aircraft DA-42 Twin Star demonstrator.
Statistics: Diamond Aircraft DA-42 Twin Star.

Building on the success of the DA-40, Diamond lost no time in unveiling its superb all-new DA-42 twin-engined personal transport. Again, aerodynamic efficiency, as well as practical ergonomic comfort, and a stunningly well-appointed interior, are the hallmarks of the type. Again, its unique ability to operate on low-cost AVtur instead of AVGas has been a revelation to the marketplace. Indeed, throughout the 2005 season the Diamond sales stands at each of the major general aviation events have been surrounded by pilots, admirers and prospective purchasers. With 3 highly successful certified aircraft now in the marketplace and with a manufacturing facility on the North American continent it seems that Diamond Aircraft is set to become one of the great forces in general aviation.

Country of Origin:	Austria
First Flight:	December 2002
Accommodation:	4
Wingspan:	44ft 0in (13.42m)
Length:	27ft 8in (8.5m)
Height:	8ft 5in (2.6m)
Empty Weight:	2,270lb (1,030kg)
Max Take Off:	3,673lb (1,650kg)
Powerplant:	2 x 135hp (100kW) Thielert Centurion 1.7 AVtur burning turbodiesel 4-cylinder piston.
Cruise Speed:	174 mph (280 km/h)
Max Speed:	1198 mph (318 km/h)
Service Ceiling:	20,000ft (6,096m).
Range:	1,188 miles (1,912km)
Number Manufactured:	First deliveries 2006.
Flying or in service:	In service.

Dornier Do-228

Subject: Dornier Do-228 of Icelandic regional operator Landsflug. Registered in Iceland as TF-ELF.
Statistics: Dornier Do-228-200.

The Dornier 228s highly developed wing design is one of the main contributors to the type's remarkable range and load capability. Following its initial introduction in the early 1980s the type has made substantial inroads into some of the regional feederliner markets, particularly those of the less developed world. The development of the 228 itself began with the fuselage cross section of Dornier's immediate post-war designs but Dornier, keen to reflect its sophisticated aerodynamic engineering resources, brought the technology behind that airframe right up to date. This is a skillfully contoured and well-faired airframe with an attractively designed and extremely efficient retractable landing-gear arrangement. The gear retracts cleverly into a swollen under-fuselage pannier without affecting the floor space inside the aircraft.

Country of Origin:	Germany
First Flight:	1981
Accommodation:	2 pilots, flight attendant, + up to 19 passengers.
Wingspan:	55ft 8in (16.97m)
Length:	54ft 4in (16.56m)
Height:	15ft 11in (4.86m)
Empty Weight:	7,800lb (3,547kg)
Max Take Off:	12,640lb (5,700kg)
Powerplant:	2 x 715hp (533kW) Garrett Ai Research turboprops.
Max Speed:	273mph (428km/h)
Service Ceiling:	28,000ft (8,535m)
Range:	1,675 miles (2,703km)
Number Manufactured:	230 manufactured.
Flying or in service:	Generally in service.

Dornier 328

Subject: Do-328, registration OE-LKA of Innsbruck-based carrier Air Alps.
Statistics: Dornier Do-328-110.

Dornier's turboprop-powered Do-328 provides a compact and efficient feederliner and regional transport which combines all the advantages of a small lightweight airframe with the interior fittings and ambience normally only found on larger airliners. For the pilot, too, its 5-screen Honeywell Primus 2000 EFIS avionics system provides a complete flight management system. With a high usage of new lightweight composite materials, and an efficient aerodynamic envelope, the Do-328 can fly higher and further than most of its market contemporaries. The new jet development of the type finally brings the Dornier 328 into the jet airliner category and ensures its place for future years.

Country of Origin:	Germany
First Flight:	1991
Accommodation:	2 pilots, 1 flight attendant, + 32 passengers.
Wingspan:	68ft 8in (20.97m)
Length:	69ft 7in (21.24m)
Height:	23ft 1in (17.04m)
Empty Weight:	19,952lb (9,050kg)
Max Take Off:	27,558lb (12,500kg)
Powerplant:	2 x Pratt & Whitney Canada PW306B turbofans.
Cruise Speed:	397mph (639km/h)
Service Ceiling:	33,000ft (10,050m)
Range:	700 miles (1,126km)
Flying or in service:	In service.

Dornier Do-X Flying Boat

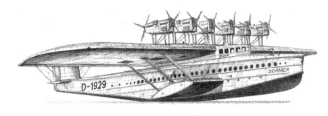

Subject: Prototype Dornier Do-X heavy flying boat, registration D-1929 of 1929.
Statistics: Dornier Do-X Flying Boat.

When it first flew in 1929 the Dornier Do-X was by far the world's largest aircraft. On 21 October 1929 the mammoth flying boat, powered by its 12 Bristol Jupiter radial engines, lifted 169 persons aloft for a full one-hour period, a truly extraordinary technical achievement for Germany given that it was only 26 years since the first tentative flight by Wilbur and Orville Wright. The Do-X went on to create waves right across Europe and, indeed, Germany might have taken the lead in the race into the air had it not been for the intervention of the Great Wall Street Crash of 1929 which led to the great depression. Suddenly nobody wanted to invest in a commercial airliner, even one as obviously promising as the Do-X. In a brave attempt to bring the giant flying boat to the forefront of media attention, Claude Dornier decided to fly the aircraft all the way to New York. His media coup turned into a nightmare, however, when the Do-X was beset by technical difficulties and ill-fortune, eventually taking 10 months to complete its journey.

Country of Origin:	Germany/Switzerland
First Flight:	1929
Accommodation:	Carried 169 passengers on one occasion in 1929.
Wingspan:	157ft 0in (48.0m)
Length:	131ft 4in (40.05m)
Height:	34ft 0in (10.1m)
Empty Weight:	72,600lb (33,000kg)
Max take off weight:	123,460lb (56,000kg)
Powerplant:	12 x Siemens-built Bristol Jupiter radials (later Curtiss Conquerors)
Cruise Speed:	118mph (190km/h)
Max Speed:	125mph (210km/h)
Range:	1,055nm (1,700km)
Number Manufactured:	3

Dornier Do-335A-6 Pfeil

Subject: Dornier Do-335A-6 Pfeil underwent much scrutiny by its captors after the war.
Statistics: Dornier Do-335A-6 Pfeil.

Dornier Flugzeugwerke of Stuttgart developed the Pfeil or 'Arrow' in response to a Luftwaffe specification for a new heavy gunship to be used as a daylight fighter/interceptor and ground attack gunship. Under the expert leadership of Dr Claude Dornier the Pfeil began to take shape around some of his earlier push/pull studies. The result was a radical new arrangement where the aircraft's 2 massive Daimler Benz powerplants were positioned one front and one back, symmetrically on the fuselage centreline. The Pfeil was a stunningly good performer with an impressive 474mph max speed and an ability to absorb punishingly high levels of combat damage. Only a small number of the type saw operational service during the war years.

Country of Origin:	Germany
First Flight:	1943
Accommodation:	2
Wingspan:	45ft 3in (13.81m)
Length:	45ft 5in (13.84m)
Height:	16ft 5in (5.0m)
Empty Weight:	16,005lb (7,260kg)
Max Take Off:	21,165lb (9,600kg)
Powerplant:	2 x 1800hp (1,342KW) Daimler Benz DB603E-1 12 cylinder inverted-Vee piston engines.
Cruise Speed:	426mph (685km/h)
Max Speed:	474mph (763km/h)
Service Ceiling:	20,000ft
Range:	967 miles (1,556km)
Number Manufactured:	Over 80 of all variants.
Preserved:	Steven F. UdVar-Hazy Center, Chantilly, Virginia, USA (Do-335A-1 Pfeil).

Douglas C-124 Globemaster II

Subject: Douglas C-124 Globemaster II of the US Air Force, Tennessee Air Guard, registration 0- 21022.
Statistics: Douglas C-124C Globemaster II.

The Globemaster's 6,820-mile range and its double-deck flooring arrangement were remarkable achievements for 1949. This was the C-17 of its day, an extraordinarily capable aircraft which opened new doors of opportunity to the US Air Force in terms of long-distance logistics and combat-readiness. A total of 446 Douglas C-124s were built and the type went on to be operated by the US armed services in many parts of the world until its eventual retirement in 1972. At that time large numbers of the Globemaster were shipped off to the Davis Monthan Air Force Base 'Desert Boneyard' where thousands of decommissioned military aircraft are stored at any given time. Sadly, records show that the majority, if not all, of these Globemasters were sold off to scrap-metal dealers during the 1980s.

Country of Origin:	USA
First Flight:	1949
Accommodation:	4 crew + 200 fully laden troops or 127 stretchers, outsize loads or pallets.
Wingspan:	174ft 2in (53m)
Length:	130ft 5in (39.75m)
Height:	48ft 3in (14.7m)
Empty Weight:	101,165lb (45,879kg)
Max Take Off:	194,500lb (88,223kg)
Powerplant:	4 x 3,800hp (2,832KW) Pratt & Whitney (Ford) R-4360-63A.
Cruise Speed:	230mph (370km/h)
Max Speed:	320mph (515km/h)
Service Ceiling:	34,000ft (10,363m)
Range:	6,820 miles (10,975km)
Number Manufactured:	446
Preserved:	National Museum of the US Air Force, Wright-Patterson AFB, Dayton, Ohio, USA.

Douglas SBD Dauntless

Subject: Douglas SBD Dauntless of the US Navy.
Statistics: Douglas SBD-5 Dauntless.

The Dauntless was the US Navy's version of the famous Japanese Nakajima B-5N dive-bomber and it was a potent and formidable means of delivering torpedo ordnance to enemy ships on the high seas. While the Dauntless served on many fronts over the course of the war, it was for its sterling work during the Pacific War that it will always be best known. Dive-bombers differ from all other aircraft because their central mission requires that they achieve very steep dive angles, often as much as 80 degrees, in the lead-in to their bombing/torpedo runs. In order to achieve these extraordinary dive angles, the leading edges of the aircrafts wings are fitted with full-length perforated brakes and spoilers which effectively remove the aircraft's lift for the duration of the dive. With massive speed and a small frontal area, the diving aircraft is difficult to shoot down but ordnance delivered in this way is far more likely to hit its target than ordnance dropped by freefall from a greater height.

Country of Origin: USA
First Flight: 1938
Accommodation: Pilot + gunner/bombardier.
Wingspan: 41ft 6in (12.65m)
Length: 33ft 0in (10m)
Height: 12ft 10in (3.9m)
Empty Weight: 6,410lb (2,908kg)
Max Take Off: 9,360lb (4,246kg)
Powerplant: 1 x 1,200hp (895kW) Wright R-1820-60 piston radial.
Cruise Speed: 185mph (296km/h)
Max Speed: 255mph (408km/h)
Service Ceiling: 25,197ft (7,680m)
Range: 1,115 miles (1,784km)
Number Manufactured: 5,938 of all variants.
Preserved: Palm Springs Air Museum, Florida, USA.
Smithsonian Air and Space Museum, Washington, DC, USA.
National Museum of Naval Aviation, NAS Pensacola, Florida, USA.
Planes of Fame Air Museum, Chino, California, USA.

Douglas R4-D

Subject: Douglas R4-D a/f 50819 transport.
Statistics: Douglas R4-D.

All of 70 years after its first flight more than 300 DC-3 and R4-D aircraft are still in service with civil operators and military forces in many countries across the world. The US Navy's R4-D was developed from the DC-3 airliner with the addition of a strengthened floor structure and other modifications to facilitate the carriage of heavy loads and large numbers of personnel. The type was used in large numbers throughout the Second World War and in particular in the later years of the war as the US Navy fought its way across the Pacific Ocean.

Country of Origin: USA
First Flight: 1935
Accommodation: 3 crew + 28 passengers.
Wingspan: 95ft 0in (28.96m)
Length: 64ft 5in (19.63m)
Height: 16ft 1in (5.16m)
Empty Weight: 16,000lb (7,530kg)
Max Take Off: 28,000lb (12,700kg)
Powerplant: 2 x Wright Cyclone or Pratt & Whitney Twin Wasp engines varying in power from 1,000hp (742kW) to 1,200hp (894kW).
Cruise Speed: 170mph (274km/h)
Max Speed: 224mph (360km/h)
Service Ceiling: 24,000ft (7,315m)
Range: 1,025 miles (1,650km)
Number Manufactured: 10,654 of all R4-D and DC-3 variants.
Flying or in service: c.300 still in service.
Preserved: National Museum of Naval Aviation, Pensacola, Florida, USA.
Pima Air and Space Museum, Tucson, Arizona, USA.

Douglas DC-4

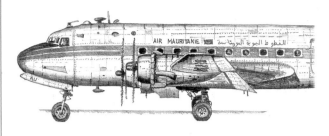

Subject: DC-4-1009 of carrier Air Martinique. Registration unknown.
Statistics: Douglas DC-4-1009.

The DC-4 flew for the first time in 1942 and it would have immediately revolutionized airline travel except that the onset of the Second World War caused manufacture to be postponed. Instead of producing the DC-4, the assembly staff at Douglas found themselves turning out the C-54 military transport variant which was capable of carrying 50 laden paratroopers over sectors of up to 2,500 miles. The type saw extensive service in the later years of the war and, indeed, over the course of the Berlin Airlift, where its 32,000lb freight capacity was an invaluable asset. With the cessation of hostilities in 1945 production of civilian DC-4 airliners was resumed and the type found its way into the inventories and folklore of many national airlines across the world. In later years, many of these airframes were handed down to smaller regional carriers and, later again, they were converted for cargo use.

Country of Origin: USA
First Flight: 1939
Accommodation: Flight crew of 3 + 2 flight attendants + up to 44 passengers or 22 passengers in a sleeping arrangement.
Wingspan: 117ft 6in (35.8m)
Length: 93ft 10in (28.6m)
Height: 29ft 2in (8.38m)
Empty Weight: 43,299lb (19,640kg)
Max Take Off: 72,846lb (33,112kg)
Powerplant: 4 x 1,450hp (1,081kW) Pratt & Whitney R-2000 Twin Wasp.
Cruise Speed: 226mph (365km/h)
Max Speed: 280mph (451km/h)
Service Ceiling: 22,300ft (6,800m)
Range: 2,500 miles (4,023km)
Number Manufactured: 1,312 of all DC-4/C-54 variants (incl Canadair built C-54 North Stars).
Flying or in service: Small numbers still used for freighting operations.
Preserved: March Field Air Museum, March AFB, California, USA (DC-54Q Skymaster).

Douglas DC-3
Dakota

Subject: DC-3 registration NC28341 of US carrier Delta Airlines has been superbly restored by the Delta Air Museum, Atlanta, Georgia.
Statistics: Douglas DC-3A Dakota.

American Airlines was the first operator to receive the new DC-3 and its newly established international routes astounded travellers with new and unprecedented levels of comfort and convenience. Indeed, on some of the longer routes passengers were even provided with sleeping couchettes, rather like those provided on trains. Then came the war and, like the youth of America, the wonderful Douglas DC-3 was conscripted for military service. And what a service it was! Over 10,600 DC-3s and C-47s were built and went on to serve with almost all of the Allied nations. General Dwight Eisenhower, in his summation of the war, included the DC-3/C-47 as one of the 4 most influential weapons of the conflict. Dubbed the Dakota, the Skytrain, the Biscuit Bomber, the Sky Sleeper, the Bullshit Bomber, or the Gooniebird, the DC-3 is without doubt one of the best-known and most loved aircraft of all time.

Country of Origin:	USA
First Flight:	1935
Accommodation:	2 crew, 2 flight attendants, + up to 28 passengers.
Wingspan:	95ft 0in (28.95m)
Length:	64ft 6in (19.7m)
Height:	16ft 11in (5.16m)
Empty Weight:	16,865lb (7,648kg)
Max Take Off:	25,200lb (11,428kg)
Powerplant:	2 x 1000hp (746kW) Pratt & Whitney R-1830 radial engines.
Cruise Speed:	198mph (317km/h)
Max Speed:	230mph (368km/h)
Service Ceiling:	24,000ft (7,315m)
Range:	2,000 miles (3,200km)
Number Manufactured:	10,654 of all DC-3 variants.

Flying or in service:	Over 300 in service. Some still operated commercially as freighters and transports.
Preserved:	Smithsonian National Air and Space Museum, Washington, DC, USA. Canadian Aviation Museum, Ottawa, Ontario, Canada. Queensland Air Museum, Australia. Seattle Museum of Flight, Washington, USA. Swiss Museum of Transport, Lucerne, Switzerland.

Edgley Aircraft
EA-7 and OA-7 Optica

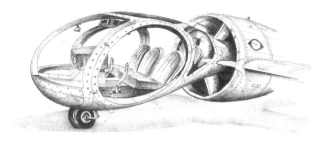

Subject: Edgley Aircraft EA-7 Optica.
Statistics: Edgley Aircraft OA-7-300 Optica.

Ducted-fan propulsion is based on the principle that thrust generated by a propeller is directed more efficiently when the propeller is placed in the centre of a circular duct or shroud. The forces (air) generated by the propeller aerofoil are pushed directly rearwards in a near cylindrical pattern rather than rearwards and outwards in a conical pattern. The result is a greatly increased return in terms of thrust. Ducted-fan systems are not without penalties in aircraft situations, however, and installations do need to be very carefully designed in terms of both additional induced drag and in terms of increased weight. The superb Optica is one of the most thorough and well-designed ducted-fan installations in any aircraft and one of only a few that have made it into production.

Country of Origin:	UK
First Flight:	1979
Accommodation:	Pilot + 2 observers.
Wingspan:	39ft 4in (12.0m)
Length:	26ft 9in (8.15m)
Height:	6ft 6in (1.98m)
Empty Weight:	2,090lb (948kg)
Max Take Off:	2,900lb (1,315kg)

Powerplant:	1 x 260hp (194kW) Textron Lycoming IO-540-V4A5D piston.
Cruise Speed:	119mph (191km/h)
Max Speed:	132mph (213km/h)
Service Ceiling:	14,000ft (4,267m)
Range:	656 miles (1,050km)
Number Manufactured:	23

Embraer
ERJ-135

Subject: Embraer ERJ-135 of former Cork-based carrier JetMagic.
Statistics: Embraer ERJ-135 LR.

Embraer's long-established reputation for cost-effective solid aeroplanes was very much in its favour when it came to the launch of the new ERJ-135. The new regional carrier and feederliner was immediately snapped up by its longstanding customers who had been more than satisfied with their previous Embraer products. The new 135 Legacy, too, is a cost-efficient corporate version of the type with executive seating for 10 passengers as well as pilot and co-pilot. The ERJ-140 is a new commuter/feederliner variant which aims to close the gap between the ERJ-145 and the ERJ-135.

Country of Origin:	Brazil
First Flight:	1998
Accommodation:	2 crew + 37 passengers.
Wingspan:	65ft 9in (20.04m)
Length:	85ft 5in (26.34m)
Height:	22ft 2in (6.75m)
Empty Weight:	25,176lb (11,420kg)
Max Take Off:	44,092lb (20,000kg)
Powerplant:	2 x 7,426lb (33kN) Rolls-Royce AE-3007A1/3 turbofans.
Max Speed:	518mph (834km/h)
Service Ceiling:	37,000ft (11,277m)
Range:	1,700 miles (3,138km)
Number Manufactured:	235
Flying or in service:	In service.

English Electric Wren

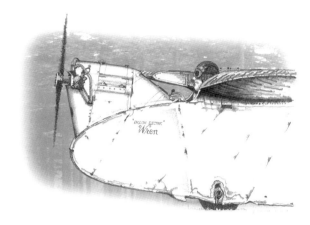

Subject: English Electric Wren, J6973 of the Shuttleworth Collection.
Statistics: English Electric Wren.

It is hard to imagine the engineers at English Electric taking the tiny Wren down to the beach at Laytham for its first flight. But it was on the sands of Laytham beside the English Electric flying boat base that the lightweight Wren first took to the air. It flew well, and quickly proved that its tiny 7.5hp ABC motorcycle engine was a most frugal and efficient powerplant. Indeed the type was able to stay in the air for a full 68 minutes on just one gallon of fuel. The Wren went on to win the Daily Mail Lympne competition, which entailed pouring one gallon of fuel into the aircraft's tank and then flying along a course until the aircraft literally ran out of fuel. Times have certainly changed!

Country of Origin:	UK
First Flight:	1923
Accommodation:	1
Wingspan:	37ft 0in (11.28m)
Height:	5ft 4in (1.65m)
Empty Weight:	232lb (105kg)
Max Take Off:	360lb (163kg)
Powerplant:	1 x 7.5hp (5.6kW) 398cc ABC flat-twin motorcycle engine.
Max Speed:	49mph (79km/h)
Service Ceiling:	Never established.
Range:	c.150 miles (241km).
Number Manufactured:	Prototype + small numbers of trainers built for the RAF.
Preserved:	The Shuttleworth Trust keeps the only surviving Wren air worthy but grounded.

Erco Ercoupé 415C

Subject: Erco Ercoupé 415C registration ZS-UDO.
Statistics: Erco Ercoupé 415C.

Fred Weick wanted to produce the perfect aircraft for the average consumer and, realizing that the average consumer would quickly come to grief in a conventional aircraft, he decided to start out by redesigning the control system so as to do away with the rudder pedals. The completed Ercoupé, then, received all of its control inputs through the yoke. The rudder was connected to the yoke, and yaw correction was automatic. The steerable nose-wheel, too, was linked into the yoke so that you taxied exactly as you drove. The system was simple and easy to understand and it had the added advantage of ensuring that the aircraft could not enter into a spin. The most interesting aspect of Weick's unusual control arrangement was its behaviour during strong crosswind landings. The procedure entailed crabbing the aircraft into the wind all the way down onto the runway and landing in full crab. A sure recipe for disaster in any other aircraft but the Ercoupé would straighten itself out and roll to a stop.

Country of Origin:	USA
First Flight:	1937
Accommodation:	2
Wingspan:	30ft 0in (9.14m)
Length:	20ft 2in (6.15m)
Height:	6ft 3in (1.9m)
Empty Weight:	800lb (362kg)
Max Take Off:	1,260lb (571kg)
Powerplant:	1 x 75hp (55.9kW) Continental C-75-12 piston.
Cruise Speed:	100mph (160km/h)
Max Speed:	117mph (187km/h)
Range:	400 miles (640km)
Number Manufactured:	5,554 of all Ercoupé 415 variants were manufactured by Erco and later by Forney.
Preserved:	Steven F. Udvar-Hazy Center, Chantilly, Virginia, USA. International Sport Aircraft Museum, Lakeland Linder Regional Airport, Florida, USA.

Eurocopter EC-120B Colibri

Subject: Eurocopter EC-120B Colibri of the Spanish Ministry of the Interior. Registered in Spain as EC-HZZ.
Statistics: Eurocopter EC-120B Colibri.

The Colibri was designed by Eurocopter to fulfil a variety of private transport and parapublic missions from executive transport to police observation and medevac duties. With its aerodynamically sophisticated rotor blades and its hushed turbine powerplant installation, the Colibri's noise footprint is well below the limits set down by ICAO, thus making the type a natural choice for police forces and other customers who operate over built-up areas for long periods of time.

Country of Origin:	France/Germany
First Flight:	1995
Accommodation:	1 + 4
Rotor Diameter:	32ft 10in (10.0m)
Length:	31ft 6in (9.6m)
Height:	11ft 2in (3.4m)
Empty Weight:	1,970lb (893kg)
Max Take Off:	3,700lb (1,678kg)
Powerplant:	1 x 504hp (376kW) Turbomeca TM319 Arrius turboshaft.
Cruise Speed:	125mph (200km/h)
Max Speed:	147mph (237km/h)
Service Ceiling:	20,000ft (6,096m)
Range:	480 miles (770km)
Flying or in service:	In service.

Eurocopter EC-145B

Subject: F-MJBH is registered to the French Gendarmerie.
Statistics: Eurocopter EC-145B.

The 145 series is Eurocopter's new middleweight utility transport twin. Designed to accommodate 7 passengers as well as the pilot, it is a development of the earlier EC-135. The 145 has found much favour with the civil police and customs forces of several European countries and it continues to expand its share of the advanced helicopter market.

Country of Origin:	France/Germany/Japan
First Flight:	1999
Accommodation:	Pilot + 7 passengers (11-seat variant planned).
Rotor Diameter:	36ft 1in (11.0m)
Length:	42ft 9in (13.03m)
Height:	13ft 0in (3.96m)
Max Take Off:	7,904lb (3,585kg)
Powerplant:	2 x Turbomeca Arriel 1E2 turboshaft powerplants.
Cruise Speed:	152mph (245km/h)
Max Speed:	172mph (278km/h)
Service Ceiling:	18,000ft (5,485m)
Range:	416 miles (670km)
Flying or in service:	In service.

Eurocopter AS-350B Ecureuil

Subject: Eurocopter AS-350B Ecureuil registration G-WHAM.
Statistics: Eurocopter AS-350B Ecureuil.

The Squirrel is Europe's best selling helicopter and it is to be found in all parts of the world in a variety of mission-specific roles. An AVco Lycoming-powered version of the type flew for the first time in June of 1974 but this powerplant was soon dropped in favour of the Turbomeca Arriel. Customer deliveries began in 1978 and the Squirrel soon became a favourite with police and customs forces across the world. Other mission-specific versions of the type have been developed by Eurocopter and sales remain buoyant to this day.

Country of Origin:	France/Germany
First Flight:	1974
Accommodation:	Pilot + 5 passengers
Rotor Diameter:	35ft 1in (10.7m)
Length:	35ft 11in (10.93m)

Height:	10ft 4in (3.14m)
Empty Weight:	2,590lb (1,175kg)
Max Take Off:	4,960lb (2,250kg)
Powerplant:	1 x 848hp (632kW) Arriel 2B turboshaft.
Max Speed:	154mph (248km/h)
Service Ceiling (in hover):	12,240ft (3,792m)
Range:	414 miles (666km)
Number Manufactured:	In excess of 3,000 of all types.
Flying or in service:	In service.

Eurofighter Typhoon

Subject: Eurofighter Typhoon hangs from the ceiling of the RAF Museum, Hendon, London.
Statistics: Eurofighter Typhoon.

The Eurofighter consortium estimates a total production run of over 620 aircraft for the 4 participating countries alone. Sales to third-party countries would further boost this figure. At approximately 60M euro per aircraft the figures involved are staggering by any count. Perhaps, then, the many difficulties of a group of disparate nations jointly developing a jet fighter will prove its worth. The theory is that the many complex aerodynamic and electronics skills developed over the course of the Eurofighter project will reap rewards in other aviation-related projects and in other fields of technology for many years to come.

Country of Origin:	EU
First Flight:	1994
Accommodation:	2
Wingspan:	36ft 11in (10.95m)
Length:	52ft 5in (15.96m)
Height:	17ft 4in (5.28m)
Empty Weight:	22,050lb (10,000kg)
Max Take Off:	46,305lb (21,000kg)
Powerplant:	2 x 20,000lb (89kN) Eurojet Turbo EJ200 turbofans.

Max Speed:	1,522mph (2,435km/h)
Service Ceiling:	60,000ft (18,000m)
Range:	2,300 miles (3,680km)
Flying or in service:	In service.
Preserved:	RAF Museum, Hendon, London, UK.

Europa Aviation Europa XS

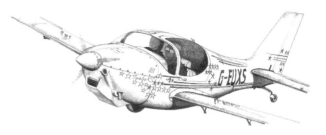

Subject: Europa G-EUXS has been a constant visitor to the Private Flying Association's air rallies at Cranfield and Kemble over the years.
Statistics: Europa Aviation Tricycle XS with Rotax 914.

Ivan Shaw's wonderful touring Europa brought lightweight efficient composite flying to thousands of pilots across Europe and the USA. Released first with a bulbous centre monowheel, news of the Europa revolution spread like wildfire across the home-build market and projects were soon underway in many countries. Shaw, himself a homebuilder of many years, understood the tribulations and frustrations of the amateur builder and he tailored the kit to make it substantially easier for pilot/builders to realize their goal. Soon a large fleet of completed Europa monowheels began to appear on the flying circuit. But all was not well. The skill levels of the average pilot fell far short of those of the Europa test pilots and the unusual monowheel arrangement which was the Europa's trademark soon become its greatest liability. A new fixed tricycle landing-gear arrangement was designed and released as a retrofit kit. Today most new Europas are built with the tricycle landing-gear configuration and, indeed, many of the original monowheel airframes have since been retrofitted.

Country of Origin:	UK
First Flight:	1992
Accommodation:	2
Wingspan:	27ft 2in (8.28m)
Length:	19ft 2in (5.84m)
Height:	7ft 0in (2.13m)
Empty Weight:	780lb (340kg)
Loaded:	1,370lb (623kg)
Powerplant:	80bhp Rotax 912, 100bhp 912S, and 115hp (take-off only) Rotax 914 Turbo.

Cruise Speed: 160mph (257km/h)
Max Speed: 190mph (305km/h)
Service Ceiling: 16,000ft (4,877m)
Range: 1,050 miles (1,689km)
Preserved: Fleet Air Arm Museum, Somerset, UK.

Extra 300L

Subject: Extra EA 300L at Lakeland-Linder, Florida, 2005. Registration N192EX.
Statistics: Extra EA 300L.

I came across this beautifully chequered Extra 300 in the trade exhibitors area at Sun 'n Fun 2005 and immediately knew that it would make an interesting drawing. To draw it closer to the viewer and fill the page, however, I had to chop off its lanky mainwheels, insert myself and launch the lot into the air. I wonder if I could log the hours in my log book. The Extra 300 was conceived by Walter Extra to serve as an unlimited aerobatic competition flyer and to ensure that his earlier aerobatic series retained its place at the very cutting edge of aerobatic competition flying. The extraordinary Extra 300L does just that. Even on the ground the type is a stunningly handsome sight. Its superb 300hp Lycoming engine is so finely balanced and its power so raw that even those spectators who know little of aerobatic racing will understand that it was designed with some thoroughbred intent in mind. At home in the air, however, it is even more impressive.

Country of Origin: Germany
First Flight: 1983 for the 230 series.
1988 for the 300 series.
Accommodation: 1
Wingspan: 26ft 3in (8.0m)
Length: 23ft 4in (7.12m)
Height: 8ft 7in (2.62m)
Empty Weight: 1,389lb (630kg)
Max Take Off: 2,094lb (950kg)
Powerplant: 1 x 300hp (225kW) Textron Lycoming IO-360 flat-four.
Cruise Speed: 207mph (331km/h)
Max Speed: 213mph (343km/h)
Service Ceiling: 16,000ft (4,877m)
Range: 605 miles (974km)
Number Manufactured: In excess of 220 of all Variants.
Flying or in service: In service.

Fairchild C-82 & C-119 Packet & Flying Boxcar

Subject: Fairchild C-82 Packet with civilian markings N9701F continues to carry commercial freight but still bears its US Army Air Force decals.
Statistics: Fairchild C-119G Packet.

Immediately after the attack on Pearl Harbor the US Government called for the production of more than 50,000 new aircraft per year. Knowing that the US would have to battle its way across the Pacific Ocean, they decided that a large proportion of these aircraft should be heavy transports, bombers and gunships. So it was, then, that each of the major manufacturers began the onerous task of developing new heavy transport programmes. Fairchild, too, found itself heavily drawn into this massive effort when its C-82 design and mock-up of 1942 were accepted by the US Army Air Force. The type took to the air for the first time in 1944 and its square fuselage section and twin boom configuration were found to be eminently suitable for rapid and efficient loading of materials. 220 of the C-82 Packet were built up to 1948, when the new and improved C-119 Flying Boxcar variant replaced it on the production line.

Country of Origin: USA
First Flight: 1944
Accommodation: Crew of 5 + payload.
Wingspan: 109ft 3in (33.3m)
Length: 85ft 2in (26m)
Height: 26ft 3in (8m)
Empty Weight: 40,000lb (18,140kg)
Max Take Off: 74,400lb (33,740kg)
Powerplant: 2 x 3,400hp (2,535kW) Wright R-3350-89W pistons.
Cruise Speed: 200mph (320km/h)/
Max Speed: 297mph (475km/h)
Service Ceiling: 27,000ft (8,230m)
Range: 2,275 miles (3,640km)
Number Manufactured: 220 of the C-82 and 1,151 of the C-119 (all variants). Flying or in service. Up to 12 still in service as firebombers, freighters, and as part of warbird collections.
Preserved: National Museum of the US Air Force, Wright-Patterson AFB, Dayton, Ohio, USA.

Evans VP-1 Volksplane

Subject: Mick Donoghue of Wicklow built his Volksplane, EI-AYY, from Bud Evans' plans to become one of Ireland's earliest home-built aircraft.
Statistics: Evans VP-1 Volksplane.

Bud Evans estimates that up to 7,000 sets of VP-1 plans have been purchased since he unveiled his remarkable VP-1 back in 1969. Since he reckons that only 1 in 10 home-builders will have the tenacity to bring their projects to completion, this gives his Volksplane an approximate fleet strength of 700 aircraft. The normal completion rate for home-built aircraft is even less at 1 completion per 25 projects but Bud's experience has shown that the simplicity of the VP-1, as well as its low materials cost, has greatly helped to increase these odds. Bud Evans' tiny VP-1 was a major shot in the arm for the home-building movement and it drew many thousands of enthusiasts into the field of general aviation. Plans for the type can still be bought on the internet to this day.

Country of Origin: UK
First Flight: 1969
Accommodation: 1
Wingspan: 24ft 0in (7.32m)
Length: 18ft 1in (5.5m)
Height: 5ft 0in (1.55m)
Empty Weight: 450lb (204kg)
Max Take Off: 740lb (336kg)
Powerplant: 1 x 40hp (30kW) Volkswagen 1,500cc piston engine with double ignition installation.
Cruise Speed: 75mph (120km/h)
Max Speed: 85mph (136km/h)
Service Ceiling: 10,500ft (3,200m)
Range: 200 miles (320km)
Number Manufactured: c.600
Flying or in service: Generally in service.

Fairchild Republic A-10 Thunderbolt

Subject: Fairchild Republic A-10 Thunderbolt.
Statistics: Fairchild Republic OA-10A Thunderbolt II.

The Thunderbolt's 7-barrel Gatling-type cannon is so powerful when fired that it slows the aircraft down and so can only be fired in short bursts. The USAF's A-10 is a formidable and ominous ground-attack aircraft which is designed primarily as a tank buster. The volume and the ferocity of its ground-attack weaponry is, however, so large that it is difficult to imagine combat operations without massive collateral damage. Somehow it seems acceptable to target hostile tanks and mobile weapons but in practice most operations by A-10s are against concealed troop formations where unfortunate infantry soldiers are entirely without defence against such efficient high-volume killing machines. Even more controversy surrounds the use of A-10 Thunderbolts and similar weaponry near to built up areas and areas of population.

Country of Origin:	USA
First Flight:	1972
Accommodation:	1
Wingspan:	57ft 0in (17.53m)
Length:	53ft 0in (16.25m)
Height:	15ft 0in (4.47m)
Empty Weight:	21,500lb (10,977kg)
Max Take Off:	49,900lb (21,500kg)
Powerplant:	2 X 9,042lb (40.3 kN) General Electric TF34-GE-100 turbofans.
Max Speed:	438mph (682km/h)
Service Ceiling:	34,500ft (10,515m)
Range:	Operational radius is 620 miles.
Number Manufactured:	713
Flying or in service:	In service.
Preserved:	National Museum of the US Air Force, Wright-Patterson AFB, Dayton, Ohio, USA.

Fairey Flycatcher

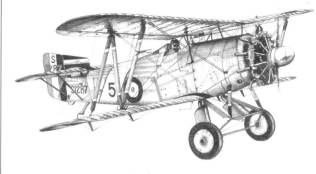

Subject: John Fairey's Fairey Flycatcher replica G-BEYB in markings S1287.
Statistics: Fairey Flycatcher Mk 1.

The Flycatcher could never be described as a good-looking aircraft but it was an extremely manoeuvrable and capable fighter. Designed as a front-line carrier-based fighter, the type served aboard every Royal Navy carrier in the late 1920s and, as such, saw service in many parts of the world. On board its aircraft carrier the Flycatcher was designed to be rapidly disassembled for stowage below the ship's deck. The aircraft's wings, therefore, were not just folded up but actually dismantled and derigged. Ground crews went through extensive exercises in rigging and dismantling Flycatcher airframes to ensure that the type could be rapidly launched when required. Fairey's Flycatcher may have been eccentric but it was greatly loved and trusted by its pilots.

Country of Origin:	UK
First Flight:	1922
Accommodation:	1
Wingspan:	29ft 0in (8.84m)
Length:	23ft 0in (7.0m)
Height:	12ft 0in (3.6m)
Empty Weight:	2,032lb (922kg)
Max Take Off:	3,018lb (1,369kg)
Powerplant:	1 X 400hp (298kW) Armstrong Siddeley Jaguar III radial.
Cruise Speed:	130mph (209km/h)
Max Speed:	133mph (214km/h)
Service Ceiling:	19,000ft (5,790m)
Range:	310 miles (500km)
Number Manufactured:	192
Preserved:	Replica Fleet Air Arm Museum, Somerset, UK.

Fairey Fulmar Mk 1

Subject: Fulmar Mk. 1 N2062 of the Royal Navy.
Statistics: Fairey Fulmar Mk 1.

Fairey's Fulmar was designed to fulfil a variety of vital roles for Britain's Royal Navy, including those of interceptor fighter, and convoy escort. In the latter role the Fulmar spent countless hours over the waters of the Atlantic and the Barents Sea often operating in appalling weather conditions off dangerous carrier decks. Although it carried no less than 8 forward-facing cannon the Fulmar was most unusual in being the only 2-seat fighter not to be equipped with a rear-facing machine gun. Indeed, the observer/radio operator must have felt redundant and helpless when under enemy attack from the rear.

Country of Origin:	UK
First Flight:	1940
Accommodation:	2
Wingspan:	46ft 4in (14.14m)
Length:	40ft 3in (12.2m)
Height:	14ft 0in (4.27m)
Empty Weight:	6,915lb (3,136kg)
Max Take Off:	9,800lb (4,445kg)
Powerplant:	1 X 1,145hp (853kW) Rolls-Royce Merlin VIII.
Cruise Speed:	235mph (378km/h)
Max Speed:	280mph (450km/h)
Service Ceiling:	26,000ft (7,925m)
Range:	800 miles (1,288km)
Number Manufactured:	600
Preserved:	Fleet Air Arm Museum, Somerset, UK.

Fairey Gannet T-2

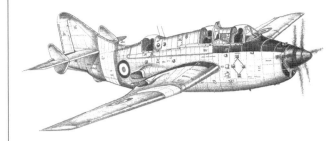

Subject: Fairey Gannet T-5 registration XT-752 of the Royal Navy.
Statistics: Fairey Gannet T-2.

With the advent of the Cold War, huge efforts were made by both the Soviets and the Western powers to develop new maritime patrol aircraft which could track the passage of surface ships and, more importantly, submarines. Paranoia flourished and each of the powers believed that the other was busily engaged in positioning its fleet of nuclear-powered submarines in preparation for the first salvo of Armageddon. But the same paranoia on the other side was such that it was entirely true. For years a deadly game of nuclear chess was played beneath the seas and in the skies above the polar ice caps of the northern hemisphere. It was in this environment of extreme political uncertainty that the Gannet operated from the mid-1950s right up until the late 1970s. The Gannet AEW-3 series, which commenced service on board HMS Ark Royal in 1970 was the last of the naval fixed wing AEW types, this role being filled from then on by a variety of helicopter types.

Country of Origin:	UK
First Flight:	1949
Accommodation:	Pilot, observer/navigator, + radio/radar operator.
Wingspan:	54ft 4in (16.5m)
Length:	43ft 0in (13.1m)
Height:	16ft 10in (5.13m)
Max Take Off:	19,600lb (8,890kg)
Powerplant:	1 x 3,035hp (2,262kW) Armstrong Siddeley Double Mamba double turboprop driving a pair of contra-rotating propellers.
Max Speed:	299mph (481km/h)
Range:	662 miles (1,065km)
Number Manufactured:	304 maritime patrol Gannets. 44 AEW-3 Gannets.
Flying or in service:	3 flying in private ownership.
Preserved:	Newark Air Museum, Nottingham, Nottinghamshire, UK (AEW-3). Fleet Air Arm Museum, Somerset, UK (AEW-3).

Fairey Primer

Subject: Fairey Primer, registration G-ALBL.
Statistics: Fairey Primer.

Ernest Tips of Gosselies, Belgium, designed and flew the Primer in 1939 but all drawings and design material were lost when the Avions Fairey workshops were bombed on 10 May 1940. With the Germans advancing through the Low Countries, Tips assembled all of his company personnel and materials and fled through France to England. His convoy reached St Nazaire just in time to board a ship for England but the ship was sunk by German bombers as it pulled out of the harbour. Although some of the Avions Fairey staff were killed in the attack, most were rescued from the water and went on to join Fairey in the UK. By 1948, however, Tips had resurrected the project and it became the basis of the Fairey Primer, a light-training and liaison aircraft which came up against the de Havilland Canada DHC-1 Chipmunk in its military evaluation trials. The DHC-1 Chipmunk was the successful contender and the Fairey Primer was relegated to the uncertainties of the post-war civilian market, being built in only small numbers before production was abandoned.

Country of Origin:	Belgium
First Flight:	1939 and 1948
Accommodation:	2
Powerplant:	Tips's original was fitted with a 145hp (108kW) de Havilland Gipsy Major X while Fairey Primers were fitted with the 155hp (155kW) Blackburn Cirrus Major 3.
Flying or in service:	1

Fairey Rotodyne Convertiplane

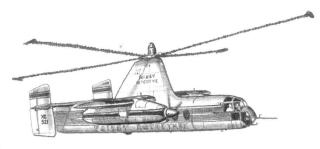

Subject: Fairey Rotodyne Convertiplane prototype.
Statistics: Fairey Rotodyne Convertiplane.

Fairey's Rotodyne compound helicopter was an extraordinary achievement for its day. Indeed it is only in recent years with massive investment from Boeing and the US Government that the development of convertiplane technology and tilt-wing aircraft has finally been cracked. But back in 1957 the engineers at Fairey had done it all. The Rotodyne prototype achieved reliable and controllable flight and met all of the design goals set down by the 3 project partners, British European Airways, the UK Ministry of Supply and, of course, Fairey itself. The project was not without its share of technical difficulties, however, especially in the area of noise abatement, but Fairey was quite confident that these problems would be solved with time. The take-over of Fairey by Westland, however, delivered the fatal blow to the Rotodyne project when Westland's cost accountants descended on the Fairey works and terminated the project.

Country of Origin:	UK
First Flight:	1957
Accommodation:	2 pilots + between 54 and 70 passengers.
Rotor Diameter:	90ft 0in (27.43m)
Stub Wing Span:	46ft 4in (14.17m)
Length:	58ft 7in (17.88m)
Height:	22ft 1in (6.76m)
Empty Weight:	22,000lb (10,000kg)
Max Take Off:	33,000lb (15,000kg)
Powerplant:	2 x 2,800hp (2,088kW) Napier Eland NE1.7 turboprops. Pressure jets on rotor blades.
Cruise Speed:	185mph (298km/h)
Max Speed:	190mph (305km/h)
Service Ceiling:	12,200ft (4,000m) estimate.
Range:	450 miles (725km)
Number Manufactured:	1

Fairey Swordfish

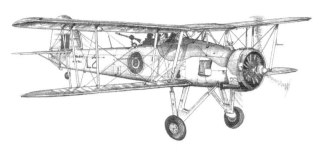

Subject: Royal Navy Historic Flight Fairey Swordfish
          Mk II LS326.
Statistics: Fairey Swordfish Mk II.

On 11 November of 1940 a substantial portion of the Italian naval fleet anchored at Taranto was decimated by a flight of 21 Swordfish which were launched off the British aircraft carrier HMS Illustrious. This was a daring raid, the first of its kind to be launched off an aircraft carrier, and it sank 2 battleships, a battlecruiser and a destroyer. Most of all, however, the raid was a major blow to the morale of Italy's armed forces and an immense embarrassment in front of its Axis partners. The Swordfish was slow and dated but, nonetheless, it developed a superb reputation as a torpedo bomber and it was much loved and trusted by its crews.

Country of Origin: UK
First Flight: 1934
Accommodation: 2 or 3.
Wingspan: 45ft 0in (13.87m)
Length: 36ft 0in (10.87m)
Height: 12ft 1in (3.8m)
Empty Weight: 4,690lb (2,132kg)
Max Take Off: 7,493lb (3,406kg)
Powerplant: 1 x 750hp (559kW) Bristol
                        Pegasus 9-cylinder radial.
Max Speed: 139mph (222km/h)
Service Ceiling: 10,700ft (3,261m)
Range: 1,028 miles (1,658km)
Number Manufactured: 2,392 of all Variants.
Preserved: Canadian Aviation Museum,
                        Ottawa, Ontario, Canada.
                        Museum of Flying, Santa Monica,
                        California, USA.
                        Fleet Air Arm Museum,
                        Somerset, UK.

Fiat G-59B

Subject: Fiat G-59B, formerly of the Italian air force.
Statistics: Fiat G-59B.

A single and 2-seat advanced military trainer based on the earlier Fiat G-55 series. Complete with the 1,100hp (842kW) Rolls-Royce Merlin engine, the type served the Italian air force and with the air forces of various other nations.

Country of Origin: Italy
First Flight: 1951
Accommodation: 1 or 2
Wingspan: 38ft 10in (11.85m)
Length: 27ft 5in (8.37m)
Max Take Off: 8,179lb (3,710kg)
Powerplant: 1 x 1,130hp (842kW) Rolls-
                        Royce Merlin.
Max Speed: 385mph (620km/h)
Service Ceiling: 42,980ft (13,100m)
Range: 1,025 miles (1,650km)
Number Manufactured: over 100

Fieseler Fi-103 Piloted flying bomb

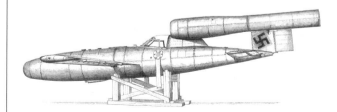

Subject: Fieseler Fi-103 piloted flying bomb.
Statistics: Fieseler Fi-103.

Germany's piloted flying-bomb programme was the macabre progeny of Hanna Reitsch, and SS-Hauptsturmführer Otto Skorzeny. Flugkapitan Hanna Reitsch was an internationally celebrated woman pilot before the outbreak of the war,

and Otto Skorzeny the extraordinary German officer who masterminded and led the daring raid that snatched Mussolini from captivity in the Gran Sasso. Indeed, while the project was under way for some months, it was Skorzeny himself who suggested modifying the Fieseler Fi-103 pilotless missile to accommodate its sacrificial pilot. The conversion of the Fi-103 took only 14 days, which is either a measure of Fiesler's efficiency or else a symptom of Germany's increasing desperation. In September of 1944 the first two prototype Fi-103 flying bombs were dropped from their Heinkel He-111 motherships but both were destroyed on landing. Hanna Reitsch herself then, being no shrinking violet, took the controls of the third flying-bomb prototype and nursed it through its freefall glide to a safe landing below. The flying bomb was now a reality and Germany began to recruit pilots for special training and indoctrination. Demand to join this elite group was naturally less than overwhelming.

Country of Origin: Germany
First Flight: 1944
Accommodation: 1 pilot + one 1,874lb
                        explosive warhead.
Wingspan: 18ft 9in (5.7m)
Length: 26ft 3in (8.0m)
Weight: 4,960lb (2,250kg)
Powerplant: 1 x 660lb (497kN)
                        Argus As-014 pulse jet.
Max Speed: 497mph (800km/h)
Service Ceiling: Not established.
Range: 205 miles when released at
                        8,000ft, or 32 minutes
                        endurance.
Number Manufactured: 175

Fieseler Fi-156 Storch

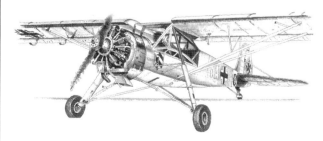

Subject: Fieseler Fi-156C-1 Storch in the colours of
          the Luftwaffe.
Statistics: Fieseler Fi-156C-1 Storch.

Fieseler's Fi-156 STOL army cooperation aircraft has entered the annals of history for its many daring and remarkable exploits over the course of the war years. Developed especially for slow-speed flying and for operation out of unprepared and restricted spaces, the Storch's strut-braced high wing and its long shock-absorbing legs were highly effective when it came to landing on unprepared surfaces. The type was widely employed throughout the war years as a quick-launch reconnaissance platform and as a personnel transport for moving officers around the areas immediately behind the battle lines. Other uses of the Storch included the covert placement of intelligence personnel into remote areas or behind enemy lines.

Country of Origin:	Germany
First Flight:	1936
Accommodation:	Pilot + 1 or 2 passengers.
Wingspan:	46ft 9in (14.25m)
Length:	32ft 6in (9.9m)
Height:	9ft 10in (3.0m)
Empty Weight:	2,050lb (930kg)
Max Take Off:	2,910lb (1,320kg)
Powerplant:	1 x 240hp (179kW)
	Argus As.10C piston.
Cruise Speed:	90mph (144km/h)
Max Speed:	110mph (176km/h)
Service Ceiling:	15,000ft (4,600m)
Range:	240 miles (384km)
Number Manufactured:	2,549 of all variants.
Flying or in service:	Small numbers still in service.
Preserved:	Fantasy of Flight Museum, Polk City, Florida, USA.
	RAF Museum, Hendon, London, UK.
	Swiss Museum of Transport, Lucerne, Switzerland.

Flug & Fahrzeugwerke Ag C-3605

Subject: The superbly presented Technik Museum Speyer C-3605, which is maintained in airworthy condition. Registration D-FOXY.
Statistics: Flug & Fahrzeugwerke C-3605.

Switzerland's 1968 turboprop conversion of the earlier EKW C-3603 fighter bomber resulted in an unusually stretched and pointed airframe. Its new Lycoming turboprop powerplant was positioned well forward of the existing firewall in order to make up for the reduced weight of the new turboprop engine. With this unusually exaggerated movement arm the balance of forces was again restored and the C-3605 went on to serve a long operational career with the Swiss armed services.

Country of Origin:	Switzerland
First Flight:	1939/1968
Accommodation:	2
Wingspan:	45ft 1in (13.74m)
Length:	42ft 5in (12.93m)
Height:	13ft 5in (4.1m)
Empty Weight:	5,808lb (2,634kg)
Max Take Off:	8,193lb (3,716kg)
Powerplant:	1 x 1,100hp (820kW) Lycoming T53-L-7 turboprop powerplant.
Max Speed:	255mph (410km/h)
Service Ceiling:	16,404ft (5,000m)
Range:	621 miles (1,000km)
Number Manufactured:	144 of the original C-3605 built up to 1944.
	23 converted to turboprop status between 1968 and 1970.
Preserved:	Technik Museum Speyer, Germany, G-FOXY.

Flettner Fl-265

Subject: Flettner Fl-265 Synchropter D-EFLV complete with Nazi roundel.
Statistics: Flettner Fl-265.

Throughout the 1930s the German State fostered a broad range of sophisticated technological programmes, both in the field of weapons development and in general industrial science. The other European countries, during these years, applied little in the way of political incentive and public funding for such development programmes and so fell far behind in many areas of technology and industrial production. Frank Whittle's ground-breaking discovery of the jet engine, for example, lay dormant in England for years before funding was secured for its development. Meanwhile, in Germany, projects like Anton Flettner's synchropter and many other promising innovations were being generously plied with research grants and public funding.

Country of Origin:	Germany
First Flight:	1939

Accommodation:	2
Wingspan:	36ft 0in (10.97m)
Length:	22ft 6in (6.89m)
Height:	11ft 1in (3.36m)
Empty Weight:	2,319lb (1,052kg)
Max Take Off:	2,969lb (1,347kg)
Powerplant:	1 x 245hp (183kW)
	Franklin 0-405-9.
Cruise Speed:	85mph (136km/h)
Max Speed:	100mph (160km/h)
Service Ceiling:	6,725ft (2,050m)
Preserved:	Kansas Air Museum, Wichita, USA.

Fokker Dr1 Triplane

Subject: Fokker Dr1 Triplane of Germany's Luftstreikrafte, Jasta 11.
Statistics: Fokker Dr1 Triplane.

Each of the German Jagdstaffeln flying combat groups had its own distinctive colour scheme, and that of Jasta JD11, commanded by 25-year-old Manfred Von Richthofen, was red. So it was, then, that Germany's top ace became known as the legendary Red Baron. Flying high over the seething trenches of the Western Front, Richthofen and his battle-hardened Jasta 11 engaged the biplanes and triplanes of the RFC in a daily game with frightening consequences. On both sides life expectancy was short, as their flimsy aircraft twisted and rolled in mortal combat. At all times they were at risk of pot-shots from the ground troops in the trenches below.

Country of Origin:	Germany
First Flight:	1917
Accommodation:	1
Wingspan:	23ft 8in (7.2m)
Length:	18ft 11in (5.7m)
Height:	9ft 8in (2.95m)
Empty Weight:	948lb (430kg)
Max Take Off:	1,380lb (626kg)

Powerplant:	1 X 110hp (82KW) Oberursel UR II rotary engine or 9
cylinder	Le Rhône rotary engine.
Max Speed:	103mph (165Km/h)
Service Ceiling:	20,000ft (6,096m)
Range:	135 miles (217Km)
Preserved:	National Museum of the US Air Force, Wright-Patterson AFB, Dayton, Ohio, USA.

Fokker F-VII

Subject: Fokker F-VII of 1928.
Statistics: Fokker F-VII.

The Fokker F-VII was a development of the earlier Fokker F-III parasol monoplane. Just 5 of the type were built for the fledgling KLM Airlines and they were used on routes across the Netherlands, Poland, Switzerland and Germany. The seating configuration was perhaps a hangover from the days of chauffeurs and carriages, with the pilot raised up at the front of the aircraft and the 8 passengers accommodated in a small cabin beneath the wing. A record flight by D. Bernard from Karachi to London in less than four and a half days brought the type much media attention and adulation. The Fokker F-VIIb-3m was a 3-engined development of the type and, for a period in the 1930s, it was one of the world's best-known commercial airliners.

Country of Origin:	Netherlands
First Flight:	1928
Accommodation:	Pilot + 8 passengers.
Powerplant:	1 X 360hp (268KW) Rolls-Royce Eagle IX powerplant.
Number Manufactured:	5 for KLM + others for civilian and military use.
Preserved:	Smithsonian National Air and Space Museum, Washington, DC, USA. Canadian Aviation Museum, Ottawa, Ontario, Canada.

Fokker F-70

Subject: Fokker F-70 of Netherlands carrier KLM registration PH-KZI.
Statistics: Fokker F-70.

A twin-engined jet airliner and feederliner, the F-70 was developed from Fokker's long-standing and highly successful F-100 series. Shorter in length by 15ft 2in (4.63m) the Fokker F-70 was intended to meet the needs of lighter routes and smaller carriers. Forty-five of the type were built before a Fokker entered a protracted period of financial turmoil which eventually forced it to cease trading in 1996. Despite the demise of the Fokker marque the F-70 jet continues in operation with many commercial carriers, both in Europe and across the world.

Country of Origin:	Netherlands
First Flight:	1993
Accommodation:	2 pilots, flight attendants + up to 79 passengers.
Wingspan:	92ft 2in (28.08m)
Length:	101ft 5in (30.91m)
Height:	27ft 11in (8.5m)
Empty Weight:	49,985lb (22,673Kg)
Max Take Off:	81,000lb (36,740Kg)
Powerplant:	2 X 67,500lb (300KN) Rolls-Royce Tay turbofans.
Cruise Speed:	461mph (743Km/h)
Max Speed:	532mph (856Km/h)
Service Ceiling:	35,000ft (10,668m)
Range:	1,267 miles (2,040Km)
Number Manufactured:	48
Flying or in service:	In service.

Gee-Bee Model Y

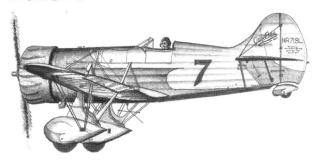

Subject: Gee-Bee Model Y Sportster.
Statistics: Gee-Bee Model Y.

The Model Y was a high-performance single-seat and 2-seat sports monoplane. Being a Granville brothers project the very last in performance was always being squeezed out of the aircraft and so the many different powerplants were tried, from Menasco to Warner Scarab to Lycoming and various others. Although considered a company runabout for use in support of the larger R-1 and R-2 racers, the Model Y was regularly entered in air races in its own right. Model Y registration NR718Y won many prestigious air race titles for Maud Tait, the well-known female racing pilot and longtime Granville Brothers backer.

Country of Origin:	USA
First Flight:	1931
Accommodation:	1
Wingspan:	30ft 0in (9.14m)
Length:	21ft 0in (6.4m)
Empty Weight:	1,400lb (635Kg)
Powerplant:	215hp (160.3KW) Lycoming R680.

Gee Bee R-1 and R-2 Racer

Subject: Gee Bee NR2101 which won the 1932 Thompson Trophy in the hands of Jimmy Doolittle.
Statistics: Gee Bee R-1 Racer.

The Granville brothers of Springfield Massachusetts were thrown into the media spotlight by the successes of their remarkable Gee Bee series of unlimited racers. Without doubt their competition aircraft were the fastest and the most impressive of all of the racing types. The difficulty was, however, that they were also the most precarious. With massive engines and diminutive airframes, all of the Gee Bee airframes flew on the very edge of controllability and, as several of their unfortunate pilots found, beyond.

Country of Origin:	USA.
First Flight:	1932
Accommodation:	1
Wingspan:	25ft 6in (7.7m)
Length:	15ft 1in (4.6m)
Height:	5ft 8in (1.73m)
Empty Weight:	880lb (399kg)
Max Take Off:	2,280lb (1,034kg)
Powerplant:	1 x 535hp (399kW) Pratt & Whitney Wasp Junior radial piston.
Cruise Speed:	230mph (370km/h)
Max Speed:	270mph (435km/h)
Range:	1,000 miles (1,600km)
Preserved:	Replica New England Air Museum, Connecticut, USA.

General Aircraft GAL-56

Subject: General Aircraft prototype GAL-56 research airframe.
Statistics: General Aircraft GAL-56.

General Aircraft Ltd founded its design office and workshop at Croydon Airport in 1931 and went on to acquire the rights from the Mono-Spar Company to employ its system of airframe construction. Thereafter, General Aircraft went on to develop and build a number of single and twin-type aircraft including the well-known Cygnet monoplane. With the coming of hostilities GAL built a number of military gliders including the Hotspur training glider and the later Hamilcar heavy assault glider. The GAL-56 was one of a series of specialist research

airframes produced over the course of the war years. In 1949 General Aircraft Ltd merged with Blackburn to become Blackburn and General Aircraft Ltd.

Country of Origin:	UK.
First Flight:	1944
Accommodation:	1
Number Manufactured:	1

General Aircraft Hamilcar X

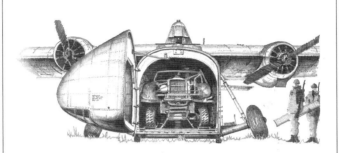

Subject: General Aircraft Hamilcar X rests on its skids to assist in disgorging its military payload.
Statistics: General Aircraft Hamilcar X.

The GAL Hamilcar's loading platform was designed to accommodate vehicles and outsize loads of up to 25ft 6in in length and 8ft in width, enough to accommodate some of the lighter British tanks, self-propelled guns and armoured personnel carriers. The intention was that large groups of battle tanks could be dropped silently and covertly into any hostile environment to be joined by paratroopers and other specialist forces. Large numbers of Hamilcars were deployed in several of the large-scale Allied offensives in both Europe and the Mediterranean. Perhaps the greatest drawback of this form of offensive transport was the very high levels of casualty among the glider groups and the tendency for the attacking forces to become separated and disoriented in the moments immediately after release from their Lancaster and Stirling tug aircraft. Another problem, too, was the likelihood that any minor impact during the landing roll would cause the vehicles to break free of the lightweight glider structure and run over the troops and pilot immediately in front of them.

Country of Origin:	UK.
First Flight:	1942
Accommodation:	Pilot + Tetrarch tank with crew or 2 Universal carriers with crews or combat troops.
Wingspan:	110ft (33.52m)
Length:	68ft (20.72m)
Height:	20ft 3in (6.09m)

Powerplant:	The Hamilcar X was the only powered version with 2 Bristol Mercury 31 radials.
Number Manufactured:	390 without power. 22 Hamilcar Xs powered by Bristol Mercury 31s.

General Dynamics F-16 Fighting Falcon

Subject: General Dynamics F-16 Fighting Falcon.
Statistics: General Dynamics F-16C Fighting Falcon.

The General Dynamics F-16 Fighting Falcon is a fast, agile, and relatively inexpensive front-line fighter and intercept platform. With a dash speed in excess of Mach 2 and the very latest in target acquisition systems, the Fighting Falcon is a formidable combat weapon. Initial F-16A models were limited to daylight intercept roles only but the later F-16C was upgraded to provide all-weather capability and a range of highly developed electronic systems. The type has been adopted by the armed services of the United States and by many of the NATO countries. Despite its 1974 vintage the F-16 looks set to remain in use as a front-line weapon for many years to come.

Country of Origin:	USA.
First Flight:	1974
Accommodation:	1
Wingspan:	31ft 0in (9.45m)
Length:	47ft 8in (14.52m)
Height:	16ft 5in (5.0m)
Max Take Off:	37,500lb (17,010kg)
Powerplant:	1 x 27,600lb (12,538kN) Pratt & Whitney F100-PW-100 turbofan with reheat.
Max Speed:	1,333mph (2,145km/h) or Mach 2.02.
Service Ceiling:	55,000ft (16,764m)
Tactical Radius:	575 miles (925km) without jettisonable fuel tanks.
Number Manufactured:	In excess of 2,500.
Flying or in service:	In service.

GlasAir III

Subject: GlasAir III Kitplane, N90GG.
Statistics: GlasAir III.

The GlasAir III Kitplane provides some of the highest performance figures in the world of home-building and, as such, it has always enjoyed a high level of popularity. The types introduction into the kitbuilding market in 1980 was as noted for Glasair's immense attention to detailing as for the new kit's superbly crafted premoulded components. A programme of continuous upgrading and improvement and a faultless builder support programme have helped Glasair to maintain its market position over the years. All of this sophistication, however, does come at a cost and the GlasAir kit is one of the most expensive on the home-build market.

Country of Origin: USA
First Flight: 1979
Accommodation: 2
Wingspan: 23ft 3in (7.09m)
Length: 21ft 4in (6.49m)
Height: 7ft 6in (2.29m)
Powerplant: 1 X 300hp (223.7KW) Lycoming
                        IO-540 piston.
Range: 1,220 miles (1,963km)
Number Manufactured: A highly popular kit with many
                        projects still in progress.
Flying or in service: Approximately 1,200 in service.

GlasAir GlaStar

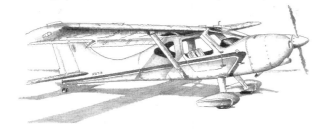

Subject: GlasAir GlaStar.
Statistics: GlasAir GlaStar.

GlasAir had already cornered a sizeable segment of the high-performance kitplane market when it decided to expand into the lower-end utility sector. To achieve this it developed the GlaStar, an all-composite 2-seat light-plane with excellent flying manners, respectable performance figures and a high build quality. With a spacious side-by-side cabin and a generous 250lb (113.4kg) baggage allowance the GlaStar provides its pilots with a comfortable flying and touring environment. Other innovations include folding wings and a removable tail section for ease of trailering and storage.

Country of Origin: USA
First Flight: 1994
Accommodation: 2
Wingspan: 35ft 0in (10.67m)
Length: 22ft 4in (6.8m)
Height: 9ft 1in (2.77m)
Empty Weight: 1,200lb (544kg)
Max Take Off: 2,100lb (952kg)
Powerplant: 1 X Continental IO-240.
Cruise Speed: 151mph (243km/h)
Max Speed: 156mph (251km/h)
Service Ceiling: 17,000 to 21,000ft (5,181m
                        to 6,400m).
Range: 597 miles (960km)
Preserved: Glassair RG International Sport
                        Aviation Museum, Lakeland
                        Linder Regional Airport, Florida,
                        USA.

Glass Goose Amphibian

Subject: Glass Goose Amphibian, Registration N30GG.
           Lakeland Linder, Florida, 2005.
Statistics: Glass Goose Amphibian.

The Glass Goose is a capable and attractive option for home-builders who wish to fly off both land and water. With good performance figures in all areas of flight the type offers a host of unusual water-based opportunities that other sports-planes simply cannot offer. Fishing, exploration, and access to the most remote of terrains are possible. The Glass Goose's configuration, too, is most unusual. The type is essentially a biplane although, without the need for inter-wing struts, its look is certainly more contemporary than classic. A beautifully designed amphibious aircraft which takes on an air of great aerodynamic efficiency when the landing-gear is retracted.

Country of Origin: USA
Accommodation: 2 in side by side configuration.
Wingspan: 27ft 0in (8.23m)
Length: 19ft 6in (5.94m)
Height: 7ft 6in (2.29m)
Empty Weight: 900lb (408kg)
Max Take Off: 1,800lb (816kg)
Powerplant: 1 X 160hp to 180hp (119KW to
                        134KW) Lycoming O-320 piston.
Cruise Speed: 140mph (225km/h)
Max Speed: 160mph (257km/h)
Range: 1,100 miles (1,770km)

Globe Aircraft Corp Swift

Subject: Globe Swift.
Statistics: Globe GC-1B Swift.

The Globe Swift was designed in early 1940 even as the vast bulk of resources within the aviation industry began to be channelled into war production. Reputed to be based closely on the earlier Culver Cadet, the Globe was a 2-seat touring aircraft and sports-plane which set very high performance standards for its day. Despite a first flight in 1941, however, production was delayed until after the war, by which time several of the first post-war aircraft designs began to catch up with the Swift. The type was, nonetheless, very popular with pilots and owners, and a total of 589 was completed, firstly by the Texas Engineering and Manufacturing Company and later, by Temco Aircraft Corporation.

Country of Origin: USA
First Flight: 1941
Accommodation: 2
Wingspan: 29ft 4in (8.94m)
Length: 20ft 10in (6.35m)
Height: 6ft 2in (1.88m)
Empty Weight: 1,125lb (511kg)
Max Take Off: 1,710lb (776kg)

Powerplant:	1 x 125hp (93.2kW) Continental piston powerplant.
Cruise Speed:	138mph (222km/h)
Max Speed:	150mph (241km/h)
Service Ceiling:	18,000ft (5,486m)
Range:	420 miles (672km)
Number Manufactured:	1,505 built by 1951.
Flying or in service:	Many still in service.
Preserved:	Mid-America Air Museum, Liberal, Kansas, USA.

Gloster E-28/39

Subject: Gloster E-28/39.
Statistics: Gloster E-28/39.

Frank Whittle's revolutionary turbojet engine patents had languished in obscurity since 1930 when the 23-year-old had first designed his ground-breaking turbojet engine. Now, almost a decade later, the quietly-spoken Royal Air Force officer became a central figure in the survival of Britain as resources were finally found to develop a new turbojet interceptor around his theories on propulsion. Under the top secret Air Ministry specification E-28/39 Gloster began to develop the airframe while Power Jets Ltd began to build the first prototype turbojet powerplants. The type was designed to perform the role of a high-altitude intercept fighter but in reality the principal aim of the project was to derive a serviceable configuration for incorporation of a turbojet engine into a flying airframe. As such the E-28/39 programme was highly successful all round and, indeed, it set the general configuration for generations of jet fighters after it.

Country of Origin:	UK
First Flight:	1941
Accommodation:	1
Wingspan:	29ft 0in (8.84m)
Length:	25ft 4in (7.72m)
Height:	9ft 3in (2.7m)
Max Take Off:	3,700lb (1,678kg)
Powerplant:	Each of the 4 first prototypes had different turbojet engines. Prototype 2 had a Rover W2 turbojet.

Cruise Speed:	357mph (574km/h)
Max Speed:	466mph (749km/h)
Service Ceiling:	32,000ft (9,756m)
Number Manufactured:	Development prototypes only.
Preserved:	Science Museum, London, UK.

Grob G-115 & G-115T

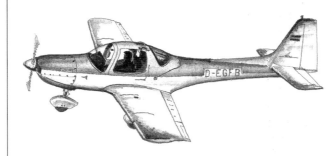

Subject: Grob G-115 based at Weston Aerdrome, Dublin, Ireland.
Statistics: Grob G-115E.

In setting out the design parameters for the G-115 series, Grob adapted the lightweight composite construction techniques which it had earlier used in its sailplanes and motor gliders. This knowledge, built up over the years, provided Grob with a distinct advantage and allowed it to produce an aircraft which was strong, light and aerodynamically efficient. The type was built in a number of variants from the basic G-115 (115hp) 2-seat sportsplane to the G-115B and G-115C (160hp) touring and training models. Finally in an unusual move Britain's Royal Air Force ordered 99 of a newly upgraded G-115E (180hp) trainer to replace its ageing Beagle Bulldog fleet.

Country of Origin:	Germany
First Flight:	1985
Accommodation:	2
Wingspan:	32ft 9in (10.0m)
Length:	25ft 5in (7.75m)
Height:	9ft 0in (2.75m)
Empty Weight:	1,522lb (690kg)
Max Take Off:	2,183lb (990kg)
Powerplant:	1 x 180hp (134kW) Textron Lycoming IO-360 piston engine.
Cruise Speed:	143mph (230km/h)
Max Speed:	155mph (250km/h)
Range:	780 miles (1,255km)
Number Manufactured:	260 completed by December 2000.
Flying or in service:	Still widely in service.

Gloster F-8 Meteor

Subject: Gloster F-8 Meteor.
Statistics: Gloster F-8 Meteor.

The pioneering E-28/39 programme led directly and rapidly to the Gloster Meteor series of twin turbojet fighters which was to become a vital and central part of Britain's defence system right up until their eventual withdrawal in 1957. The Meteor saw its first action in August of 1944 when 20 early production F-1 models were flown by No 616 Squadron on operational sorties against German V-1 flying bombs over the South of England. From that time onwards the Meteor went through a continuous programme of improvement and enhancement which touched on every part of its airframe and performance. In particular, however, the rapid pace of turbojet development meant that the Meteor was being provided with new and more powerful powerplants with every new issue. By the time the F-8 was introduced its new Rolls-Royce Derwent turbojets were turning out 15.57 kiloNewtons of thrust per side and the Meteor was capable of reaching almost 600mph in level flight.

Country of Origin:	UK
First Flight:	1943
Accommodation:	1 or 2
Wingspan:	37ft 2in (11.3m)
Length:	44ft 7in (13.6m)
Height:	13ft 1in (4.0m)
Empty Weight:	10,684lb (4,845kg)
Max Take Off:	15,700lb (7,120kg)
Powerplant:	2 x 3,500lb (15.57kN) Rolls-Royce Derwent 8 turbojets.
Cruise Speed:	420mph (676km/h)
Max Speed:	598mph (962km/h)
Range:	690 miles (1,104km)
Number Manufactured:	3,181 of all Meteor variants.
Flying or in service:	Small numbers maintained in airworthy condition.
Preserved:	RAF Museum, Cosford Airfield, Shifnal, Shropshire, UK. Classic Fighter Jets Museum, Parafield Airport, South Australia. Israeli Air Force Museum, Hatzerim, Beer Sheeva, Israel.

Gloster Gamecock II

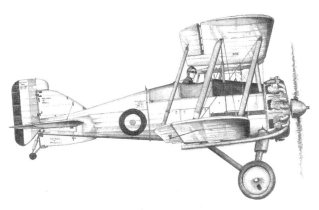

Subject: Gloster Gamecock II.
Statistics: Gloster Gamecock II.

Developed directly from the Gloster Grebe, the Gamecock was flown by the RAF until 1931, when most of its number were withdrawn from use. Although it eventually proved itself to be a reliable fighter its first years were fraught with problems, and quick-fix remedies were being sought for serious flutter problems even as the aircraft was in operational service. The Gamecock II was exported to Finland and formed an important part of the Finnish air force, serving as a fighter and training aircraft until the outbreak of the Second World War.

Country of Origin:	UK
First Flight:	1925
Accommodation:	1
Wingspan:	29ft 9in (9.08m)
Length:	19ft 8in (5.99m)
Height:	9ft 8in (2.95m)
Empty Weight:	1,929lb (875kg)
Max Take Off:	2,742lb (1,244kg)
Powerplant:	1 x 425hp (317kW) Bristol Jupiter VI radial.
Max Speed:	145mph (233km/h)
Service Ceiling:	21,981ft (6,700m)
Range:	325 miles (523km)

Gloster SS-37 Gladiator

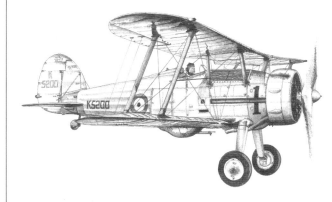

Subject: Gloster SS-37 Gladiator.
Statistics: Gloster SS-37 Gladiator II.

H.P. Folland's design for the Gloster Gladiator represents the very pinnacle of biplane development in Britain and the type exhibited superb flying characteristics which were invaluable in military flying and the execution of carrier-borne landings. In attempting to deliver the requirements set down by the Air Ministry's F.7/30 specification Folland opted to build his new biplane fighter around the airframe of the earlier Gloster Gauntlet and the powerful new range of Bristol Mercury radial powerplants. In July of 1935 the Air Ministry ordered the first of 23 production Gladiators and the rest is history. The Gladiator went on to serve as a biplane in an era of fast monoplanes and yet it managed to serve with great distinction on many fronts over the course of the war years. The Gloster Gladiator continued to serve with both the Royal Navy and the Royal Air Force until 1945, when the cessation of hostilities and the abundance of more capable aircraft types brought about its withdrawal from service.

Country of Origin:	UK
First Flight:	1934
Accommodation:	1
Wingspan:	32ft 3in (9.83m)
Length:	27ft 5in (8.36m)
Height:	11ft 9in (3.58m)
Empty Weight:	3,062lb (1,398kg)
Max Take Off:	4,750lb (2,155kg)
Powerplant:	1 x 840hp (618.5kW) Bristol Mercury radial powerplant.
Max Speed:	250mph (402km/h)
Service Ceiling:	27,000ft (8,229m)
Range:	410 miles (660km)
Number Manufactured:	747 of all Variants.
Preserved:	Norwegian Aviation Museum, Bodø, Norway.

Grumman F9-F Cougar

Subject: Grumman TAF-9J Cougar 131167 of the US Navy was retired to Davis-Monthan AFB in 1969 and sold for scrap in July of 1974.
Statistics: Grumman F9-F-8T Cougar.

The Cougar was a swept-wing development of Grumman's earlier G-79 Panther carrier-borne fighter. With its 35-degree wing sweep the new Cougar was capable of greatly increased performance and it quickly found its way into active service. Production ran for a period of 4 years, by which time 1,985 of all types had been completed. Specialist Cougar variants included an electronic countermeasures platform and a dedicated photographic and reconnaissance ship.

Country of Origin:	USA
First Flight:	1951
Accommodation:	1 + 2
Wingspan:	34ft 6in (10.5m)
Length:	48ft 6in (14.78m)
Height:	12ft 3in (3.7m)
Max Take Off:	20,600lb (9,344kg)
Powerplant:	1 x 8,500lb (37.81 kN) Pratt & Whitney J48-P-8A turbojet.
Max Speed:	705mph (1,135km/h)
Service Ceiling:	42,000ft (12,800m)
Range:	1,000 miles (1,610km)
Number Manufactured:	1,985 of all variants.
Preserved:	Steven F. Udvar-Hazy Center, Chantilly, Virginia, USA. National Museum of Naval Aviation, NAS Pensacola, Florida, USA.

Granger Brothers Archaeopteryx

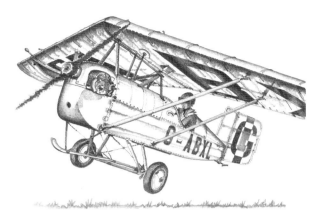

Subject: Granger Archaeopteryx G-AXBL of the Shuttleworth Trust.
Statistics: Archaeopteryx.

Brothers R.F.T. Granger and R.J.T. Granger, lacemakers by trade, were stunned when they saw the Westland-Hill Pterodactyl and they befriended C.H. Latimer-Needham, its designer. With some help from Needham the brothers set about designing their own tailless aircraft and by 1927 the inner framework for their extraordinary Archaeopteryx was ready. It took another 3 years, however, to complete the project and so it was only in October of 1930 that the type finally lifted off the ground at Hucknall, Nottingham. The Archaeopteryx was an immediate success and a widely reported curiosity in the world of aviation. Although it was not registered in its first years of flight the introduction of early Certificate of Airworthiness regulations in 1932 saw it taking on the markings of G-ABXL, the registration it bears today.

Country of Origin: UK
First Flight: 1930
Accommodation: 1
Wingspan: 30ft 0in (9.14m)
Empty Weight: 450lbs (204kg)
Powerplant: 1 x 32hp (23.86kW) Bristol Cherub 1 flat-twin driving a two-blade hand-carved propeller.
Max Speed: 90mph (149km/h)
Number Manufactured: 1 prototype only.
Flying or in service: G-ABXL airworthy but grounded.
Preserved: 1 preserved in airworthy but grounded condition by the Shuttleworth Collection, Bedfordshire, UK.

Grumman U-16 Albatross

Subject: Grumman U-16 Albatross.
Statistics: Grumman HU-16B Albatross.

By the end of the war years Grumman had become firmly established as the foremost designer of flying boats and amphibious maritime patrol aircraft. While the world was awash with decommissioned aircraft and amphibians a new threat was emerging in the form of the Cold War and the US began to ramp up its development of anti-submarine and maritime patrol aircraft. It was in this environment that the specification for the Albatross was laid down. By July of 1949 the first HU-16A (designated SA-16A) search-and-rescue amphibians were in operational service. Thereafter followed a continuous progression of airframe and powerplant upgrades as well as mission-specific variants. More than 488 of all types were produced for the US Air Force, US Navy, and the US Coast Guard.

Country of Origin: USA
First Flight: 1947
Accommodation: Crew of 3 to 5 + 22 passengers.
Wingspan: 96ft 8in (29.46m)
Length: 62ft 10in (19.18m)
Height: 25ft 10in (7.87m)
Max Take Off: 37,500lb (17,010kg)
Powerplant: 2 x 1,425hp (1,062kW) Wright R-1820-76A radials.
Max Speed: 236mph (379km/h)
Service Ceiling: 24,800ft (7,558m)
Range: 2,850 miles (4,587km)
Number Manufactured: 466 for US Forces and 22 for export to third party countries.
Flying or in service: Up to 100 still airworthy with commercial operators and private owners.
Preserved: Castle Air Museum, Atwater, California, USA (SA-16). National Museum of the US Air Force, Wright-Patterson AFB, Ohio, USA (HU-1B).

Grumman (McKinnon) TurboGoose

Subject: Grumman (McKinnon) TurboGoose, bearing the US civil registration N70AL.
Statistics: Grumman (McKinnon) TurboGoose.

Immediately after the war large numbers of Grumman's amphibious Goose began to find their way onto the civilian and commercial markets across the world. Within months the type had found itself a new life in the hands of the many commercial operators who found it ideal for ferrying cargo and blazing new passenger routes into remote and inaccessible locations. By 1953 McKinnon Enterprises Inc. of Oregon began to offer newly uprated variants of the Goose in the form of the McKinnon G-21C Goose with its 4 Lycoming piston engines, and the later McKinnon TurboGoose with its 2 UACL or P&W turboprop powerplants.

Country of Origin: USA
First Flight: 1937
Accommodation: 2 pilots + 8 to 10 passengers.
Wingspan: 50ft 10in (15.49m)
Length: 39ft 7in (12.06m)
Empty Weight: 6,700lb (3,040kg)
Max Take Off: 12,500lb (5,670kg)
Powerplant: 2 x 860hp (505kW) Pratt & Whitney Canada PT6A-27 turboprops driving 3-blade propellers.
Max Speed: 243mph (391km/h)
Service Ceiling: 20,000ft (6,096m)
Range: 1,600 miles (2,575km)
Flying or in service: Small numbers of both radial and turbine versions still in service.

Grumman JF/J2F Duck

Subject: Grumman JF/J2F Duck.
Statistics: Grumman J2-F6 Duck.

Grumman's JF/J2F Duck series was descended directly from Grover Loening's long line of amphibious aircraft. When Loening was absorbed into the Curtiss Wright Works in 1929 several of its key design employees left the company to set up the new Grumman Engineering Corporation. Among their earliest projects was the development of a powerful and heavy single-hulled amphibian which became known as the Duck. Built for both the US Navy and Coast Guard, the type was manufactured in 9 main versions ranging in powerplant size, armaments and mission-specific equipment. As a search-and-rescue ship the Duck served on many fronts over the course of the war years and many a downed airman owed his life to the type.

Country of Origin:	USA
First Flight:	1933
Accommodation:	2
Wingspan:	39ft 0in (11.89m)
Length:	34ft 0in (10.36m)
Height:	14ft 6in (4.4m)
Max Take Off:	7,700lb (3,492kg)
Powerplant:	1 x 900hp (670.7kW) Wright R-1820-54 radial powerplant.
Cruise Speed:	155mph (249km/h)
Max Speed:	190mph (305km/h)
Service Ceiling:	25,750ft (7,848m)
Range:	780 miles (1,255km)
Number Manufactured:	Over 600 of all 9 variants.
Flying or in service:	Several still flown by private collections and owners.
Preserved:	National Museum of Naval Aviation, NAS Pensacola, Florida, USA. Fantasy of Flight Museum, Polk City, Florida, USA.

Grumman F3F-2 Fighter

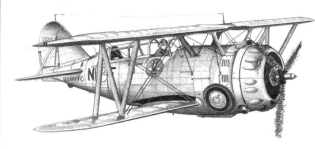

Subject: Grumman F3F.
Statistics: Grumman F3F.

The F3F was the last biplane interceptor to operate from the deck of any American aircraft carrier. The production run of 216 aircraft (both F2F and F3F types) served with front-line Navy and Marine Corps units between 1936 and 1941. Many of the best-known US fighter pilots cut their teeth in the F3F in the years immediately leading up to 1941 and the US's involvement in the war.

Country of Origin:	USA
First Flight:	1935
Accommodation:	1
Wingspan:	32ft 0in (9.75m)
Length:	23ft 3in (7.09m)
Height:	9ft 4in (2.83m)
Empty Weight:	3,254lb (1,476kg)
Max Take Off:	4,750lb (2,154kg)
Powerplant:	1 x 750hp (559kW) Wright R-1820 radial.
Max Speed:	264mph (425km/h)
Service Ceiling:	33,200ft (10,119m)
Range:	980 miles (1,577km)
Number Manufactured:	216 of both F2F & F3F series.
Flying or in service:	Several F3Fs still airworthy.
Preserved:	Planes of Fame Air Museum, Chino, California, USA.

Grumman G-21A Goose

Subject: Grumman G-21 Goose registered N86639 on the US civil register.
Statistics: Grumman G-21 Goose.

The Grumman Goose was designed initially as an executive transport but the darkening political climate of the late 1930s saw it being ordered by the US Navy and the US Coast Guard. Indeed, the type provided a superb maritime patrol platform and it was delivered in large numbers throughout the war years. In response to detailed US Navy and Coast Guard requests Grumman developed several specialist Goose variants including a long-range photographic survey aircraft and a super-long-range polar patrol variant complete with de-icing equipment and autopilot.

Country of Origin:	USA
First Flight:	1937
Accommodation:	Aircrew of 2 + 6 passengers.
Wingspan:	49ft 0in (14.94m)
Length:	38ft 3in (11.66m)
Height:	12ft 2in (3.71m)
Empty Weight:	4,905lb (2,223kg)
Max Take Off:	7,500lb (3,400kg)
Powerplant:	2 x 450hp (335.5kW) Pratt & Whitney Wasp Junior pistons.
Cruise Speed:	175mph (282km/h)
Max Speed:	195mph (314km/h)
Service Ceiling:	21,000ft (6,400m)
Range:	1,150 miles (1,840km)
Number Manufactured:	345 of all variants between 1937 and 1945.
Flying or in service:	Small numbers still in service.
Preserved:	Steven F. Udvar-Hazy Center, Chantilly, Virginia, USA. Canada Aviation Museum, Ottawa, Ontario, Canada (G21A II). Palm Springs Air Museum, California, USA.

Grumman F-14D Tomcat

Subject: Grumman F-14D Tomcat.
Statistics: Grumman F-14A Tomcat.

On 15 January 1969 Grumman's design was announced as competition winner for the US Navy's carrier-based VFX fighter programme. Under the designation F-14A Tomcat the new aircraft entered a period of intense development and appraisal leading to a first flight in 1970. Throughout all stages of development great emphasis was placed on producing an aircraft of comparatively low weight and size with massive levels of performance which would present a significant advantage over the then current F-4 Phantom. Grumman had a complex design problem on its hands. It needed to achieve Mach 2 fighter performance while at the same time ensuring that the aircraft could be brought in to land safely and slowly in difficult conditions on a carrier deck. To achieve these two diverse aims a variable geometry wing was selected. The F-14 continues to provide front-line carrier-based service to the US Navy and, indeed, almost half of the type's inventory remains operational to this day.

Country of Origin:	USA
First Flight:	1970
Accommodation:	1 + 2
Wingspan:	64ft 1in (19.55m)
Length:	62ft 4in (19.0m)
Height:	16ft 1in (4.88m)
Empty Weight:	34,245lb (15,530kg)
Max Take Off:	74,350lb (33,718kg)
Powerplant:	2 x 12,350lb (54.95kN) Pratt & Whitney TF30-P-414A turbofans.
Cruise Speed:	610mph (982km/h)
Max Speed:	1,540mph (2,480km/h)
Service Ceiling:	50,000ft (15,240m)
Range:	2,400 miles (3,840km)
Number Manufactured:	656 of all variants.
Flying or in service:	In operational service.
Preserved:	National Museum of Naval Aviation, NAS Pensacola, Florida, USA (F-14A). Yanks Air Museum, Chino Airport, California, USA.

Grumman E-2 Hawkeye

Subject: Grumman E-2 Hawkeye.
Statistics: Grumman E-2C Hawkeye.

The Grumman E-2 Hawkeye is essentially a flying radar station, which serves aboard each of the US fleet's aircraft carriers with the purpose of providing complete AWACS (Airborne Warning and Control System) capability on station. In this way it can provide the carrier battle group with continuous real-time advance warning of all movements and threats within its area, while at the same time doubling as a sophisticated command and control platform for the carrier group's forward combat aircraft. When not in use, the Hawkeye's wings can be folded compactly behind its airframe to minimize its footprint on the carrier deck.

Country of Origin:	USA
First Flight:	1971
Accommodation:	5
Wingspan:	80ft 7in (24.56m)
Length:	57ft 7in (17.54m)
Height:	18ft 3in (5.58m)
Max Take Off:	51,900lb (23,556kg)
Powerplant:	2 x 4,910hp (3,661kW) Allison T56-A425 turboprops.
Max Speed:	374mph (598km/h)
Service Ceiling:	30,000ft (9,390m)
Endurance:	Greater than 6 hours.
Flying or in service:	In service.

Grumman S-2 Tracker

Subject: Grumman S-2E Tracker, 152822, served with the US Navy until 1974, at which time it was sent to Davis Monthan AFB, Arizona, for storage. It later served with the South Korean navy.
Statistics: Grumman G-89 Tracker S-2E.

The Tracker was the first anti-submarine patrol aircraft to combine the roles of submarine detection and submarine hunter/killer in one. Designed to counter the threat of the Soviet Union's vast fleet of attack submarines, the Tracker became a vital component of the US carrier battle group. Operated both from on board aircraft carriers and from dry land, the Tracker could search vast tracts of open sea in the course of its 9-hour-long patrol tour. The type was widely operated by the US Navy, but was also exported to Brazil, Australia, Turkey, Taiwan, and Argentina. Canada, too, operated a version of

the type built by de Havilland Canada. In later years Marsh Aviation of Arizona developed a turboprop-powered water-bomber variant from surplus Navy airframes.

Country of Origin:	USA
First Flight:	1952
Accommodation:	2 pilots + 2 mission specialist operators.
Wingspan:	72ft 7in (22.12m)
Length:	43ft 6in (13.26m)
Height:	16ft 7in (5.05m)
Empty Weight:	18,711lb (8,505kg)
Max Take Off:	29,088lb (13,222kg)
Powerplant:	2 x 1,525hp (1,137kW) Wright R-1820-82WA Cyclone radial.
Patrol Speed:	149mph (241km/h)
Max Speed:	264mph (426km/h)
Service Ceiling:	21,000ft (6,400m)
Endurance:	9 hours
Number Manufactured:	1,169 S-2A Trackers built by Grumman, with a further 100 CS2F-1s completed by de Havilland Canada.
Preserved:	National Museum of Naval Aviation, NAS Pensacola, Florida, USA. Canada Aviation Museum, Ottawa, Ontario, Canada (CP121 Tracker).

Grumman X-29A

Subject: Grumman X-29A prototype.
Statistics: Grumman X-29A.

Germany's Junkers Ju-287 bomber of 1944 proved that forward-swept wings could provide improved performance at high speeds and became the inspiration for a brave effort by NASA to further investigate the aerodynamic qualities of forward-swept-wing configurations. Awarding a contract to Grumman for the construction of 2 FSW prototype airframes, NASA set in motion the X-29 project, which was to provide invaluable research data over its 242 test flights. In order to achieve flight at supersonic speeds in a forward-swept configuration, however, advances in the areas of composite materials, flight control computers, and fly-by-wire technology were necessary. The X-29 took to the air for the first time in December 1984, and there followed a 7-year flight-test programme that demonstrated that forward-swept-wing technology could produce greater levels of manoeuvrability, flight at extreme angles of attack, and vastly reduced levels of fuel burn.

Country of Origin:	USA
First Flight:	1984
Accommodation:	1
Wingspan:	27ft 0in (8.29m)
Length:	54ft 0in (16.44m)
Height:	14ft 0in (4.26m)
Empty Weight:	13,772lb (6,260kg)
Max Take Off:	17,763lb (8,074kg)
Powerplant:	1 X 15,965lb (71.17kN) General Electric turbofan.
Max Speed:	1,180mph (1,900km/h)
Service Ceiling:	50,000ft (15,300m)
Range:	347 miles (560km)
Number Manufactured:	2 prototypes.
Preserved:	Both prototypes stored by NAS at the Dryden Flight Research Facility, California, USA.

Grumman J4F/G-44 Widgeon

Subject: Grumman J4F Widgeon.
Statistics: Grumman G-44 Widgeon.

The Widgeon was again designed for personal touring and executive travel, but, as before, such was the demand for maritime patrol aircraft that much of its production was absorbed into the growing war effort. It was only after the war that Grumman finally began to produce civilian Widgeons in large numbers. Smaller and less expensive than the Grumman Goose, the Widgeon was an affordable and cost-effective means of reaching some of the more remote and exotic resorts of the Caribbean and the US seaboards. To this day, substantial numbers of Widgeons continue to be maintained in airworthy condition by small operators, private owners, and dedicated collectors.

Country of Origin:	USA
First Flight:	1940

Accommodation:	1 + 4 passengers.
Wingspan:	40ft 0in (12.19m)
Length:	31ft 1in (9.47m)
Height:	11ft 5in (3.48m)
Empty Weight:	3,240lb (1,469kg)
Max Take Off:	4,525lb (2,052kg)
Powerplant:	2 X 200hp (149kW) Ranger 6-440C-5 piston engines.
Cruise Speed:	138mph (222km/h)
Max Speed:	153mph (246km/h)
Range:	920 miles (1,472km)
Number Manufactured:	277 built by Grumman and 40 built in France by SCAN.
Flying or in service:	Up to 100 still in service with small operators and private owners.
Preserved:	National Museum of Naval Aviation, NAS Pensacola, Florida, USA.

Guimbal Cabri G-2 Helicopter

Subject: Guimbal's prototype Cabri, F-PILA.
Statistics: Guimbal Cabri G-2.

Bruno Guimbal's Cabri design was intended to form the basis of a kitbuild helicopter that would first be offered to amateur builders for home construction, but would ultimately enter commercial series production. The immense complexities of developing any helicopter design, however, even a light and compact one, are so great that few new projects ever make it to the market place. In this difficult environment the unusual Cabri, although displaying excellent flying qualities, has still not yet made it into production. The project is still very much alive, however, and Hélicoptères Guimbal are currently at an advanced stage of development with EASA certification expected in 2006.

Country of Origin:	France
First Flight:	1992
Accommodation:	2
Rotor diameter:	20ft 11in (6.4m)
Height:	7ft 3in (2.2m)
Empty Weight:	727lb (330kg)
Loaded:	1168lb (530kg)

Powerplant:	150hp (111.8 kW) Lycoming piston powerplant.
Cruise speed:	98mph (157km/h)
Max speed:	109mph (176km/h)
Range:	435 miles (700km)
Number Manufactured:	1
Flying or in service:	Nil
Preserved:	1

Handley Page HP-65 Hermes

Subject: Handley Page HP-65 Hermes.
Statistics: Handley Page HP-65 Hermes.

The Hermes was a civilian airliner, almost identical in external appearance and size to the military Hastings. Handley Page had originally intended to introduce the Hermes before the Hastings, but the loss of the prototype aircraft on its maiden flight was a blow to the Hermes project and it was not until 1947 that the type finally took to the air. The Hastings was initially powered by the Bristol Hercules 763 powerplant, but all of these aircraft were later fitted with the larger Bristol Hercules 773s to give them the revised designation Hermes 4. Twenty-five of the type were delivered to BOAC for use on its arduous Commonwealth routes to Africa, India, and Australia.

Country of Origin:	UK
First Flight:	1942. Crashed on maiden flight. 1947. Successfully flown.
Accommodation:	7 flight crew + 40 to 74 passengers.
Wingspan:	113ft 0in (34.4m)
Length:	81ft 9in (24.9m)
Height:	22ft 6in (6.9m)
Empty Weight:	41,689lb (18,910kg)
Max Take Off:	75,000lb (34,010kg)
Powerplant:	4 X 2,100hp (1,565kW) Bristol Hercules 763 powerplants all later replaced with 2,125hp (1,583,5kW) Bristol 773s.
Max Speed:	350mph (563km/h)
Number Manufactured:	25 delivered to BOAC for use on its Commonwealth routes.
Preserved:	Imperial War Museum, Duxford, Cambridgeshire, UK.

Handley Page HP-42

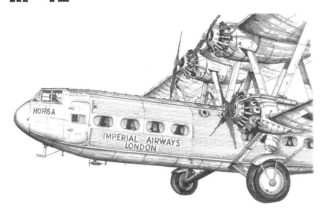

Subject: Handley Page HP-42 Horsa of Imperial
Airways, London.
Statistics: Handley Page HP-42.

The Helena, Hadrian, Horatius, and the Horsa were all
names given to Handley Page's massive HP-42 Empire route
airliners of 1930. Handley Page built 8 of these monsters
for the fledgling Imperial Airways, which used them on its
long-range routes to Europe, India, and South Africa. With
a wingspan of 130ft, the HP-42 was an extraordinary
achievement for its time. Up to 24 passengers were
carried on the South African routes, while a full
complement of 38 passengers could be carried on the
shorter European routes. The type was not without its
critics, and Anthony Fokker famously declared that it
had its own built-in headwinds. In 10 years of scheduled
international flights, however, the HP-42 series maintained
a superb safety record and was much loved and trusted
by its crews.

Country of Origin: UK.
First Flight: 1930
Accommodation: 2 pilots + 24 to 38 passengers
in separate fore and aft
cabins.
Wingspan: 130ft 0in (39.62m)
Length: 89ft 9in (27.36m)
Max Take Off: 29,500lb (13,381kg)
Powerplant: 4 x 555hp (413.6kW) Bristol
Jupiter XFBMs.
Cruise Speed: 105mph (168km/h)
Max Speed: 127mph (204km/h)
Range: 500 miles (805km)
Number Manufactured: 8

Hatfield Little Bird

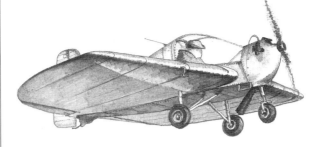

Subject: Milt Hatfield at the controls of his remarkable
Little Bird.
Statistics: Hatfield Little Bird.

Milt Hatfield built his experimental 'Little Bird' light plane
in the late 1980s. In choosing its configuration it is thought
that he was inspired by the Arup S-2 of 1933, which had
an aspect ratio so low that it was close to being a lifting-
body aircraft. Hatfield's Little Bird, too, had an
extraordinarily low aspect ratio. Little is known of how
it behaved in the air or what became of the airframe.

Country of Origin: UK.
First Flight: 1980s
Accommodation: 1
Number Manufactured: 1

Handley Page Victor B-2 and K-2

Subject: Handley Page Victor K-2, XM715, air-to-air
refuelling tanker.
Statistics: Handley Page Victor B-2 strategic nuclear
bomber.

Design development on the Handley Page Victor began
in 1947 with the intention of providing Britain with a
strategic nuclear deterrent. When the prototype
airframe flew for the first time in December 1952, its
configuration was most unconventional with swept crescent
wings and large engine intakes buried into the wing roots.
The Victor B-1 was designed to penetrate hostile territory
at extreme altitudes and speeds to deliver freefall
nuclear weapons or large numbers of conventional freefall

bombs. The Victor B-2, which entered operational service in
1962, had an increased wingspan and larger engines, and
was designed to penetrate enemy territories at both high
and low levels. All of these Victor B-2s have since been
converted to in-flight refuelling tankers under the
designation Victor K-2.

Country of Origin: UK.
First Flight: 1952
Accommodation: Flightcrew + 35 x 1,000lb
conventional freefall bombs
or equivalent weight of
freefall nuclear weapons.
Wingspan: 120ft 0in (36.58m)
Length: 115ft 0in (35.05m)
Max Take Off: 175,000lb (79,379kg)
Powerplant: 2 x 20,600lb (91.63kN) Rolls-
Royce Conway RCo.17 Mk 201
turbojets.
Max Speed: 660mph (1,062km/h)
Range: 4,600 miles (7,403km)

Hawker Hurricane

Subject: Hawker Hurricane.
Statistics: Hawker Hurricane MkIIC.

When Sydney Camm's diminutive fighter took to the air
for the first time on 6 November 1935, the assorted Air
Ministry observers could not possibly have understood the
important part that it would shortly play in the defence
of Britain. But it was the Hurricane fighter, more than
any other aircraft, that managed to hold Germany's
relentless Luftwaffe at bay throughout the Battle of
Britain. Consisting generally of a timber framework with
a stretched fabric covering, the Hurricane was surprisingly
strong and able to absorb reasonable levels of battle
damage. It was the combination of the type's sleek,
lightweight airframe with its superb Rolls-Royce Merlin
powerplant that made it such a potent weapon. A total
of 12,780 of all variants were manufactured in Britain and
a further 1,451 examples in Canada. The type served on
all fronts throughout the war, both from Allied land bases
and from Royal Navy carriers.

Country of Origin:	UK
First Flight:	1935
Accommodation:	1
Wingspan:	40ft 0in (12.19m)
Length:	32ft 0in (9.75m)
Height:	13ft 2in (4.0m)
Empty Weight:	5,350lb (2,427Kg)
Max Take Off:	8,250lb (3,742Kg)
Powerplant:	1 X 1,280hp (954kW) Rolls-Royce Merlin XX powerplant.
Cruise Speed:	320mph (515km/h)
Max Speed:	334mph (538km/h)
Service Ceiling:	36,000ft (10,970m)
Range:	460 miles (740km)
Number Manufactured:	12,780 manufactured in Britain and 1,451 in Canada.
Preserved:	Steven F. Udvar-Hazy Center, Chantilly, Virginia, USA (MK IIC). Canada Aviation Museum, Ottawa, Ontario, Canada (XII). RAF Museum, Hendon, London, UK. Museum of Flying, Santa Monica, California, USA. National Museum of the US Air Force, Wright-Patterson AFB, Dayton, Ohio, USA.

Hawker Siddeley C-1 Andover

Subject: Hawker Siddeley C-1 Andover XS606 spent much of its operational life with 52 Squadron in Singapore before joining the Empire Test Pilots School at Boscombe Down, Wiltshire.
Statistics: Hawker Siddeley C-1 Andover.

Following the success of the Hawker Siddeley 748 airliner and its adoption by the military forces of many third-party countries, a mission-specific freighter variant 780, later the Andover C-1, was developed for Britain's Royal Air Force. Inheriting many of the components and features of the HS-748, the Andover's spacious interior was dominated by a large rear-loading ramp that allowed outsize loads and other military supplies to be quickly and efficiently stowed. The Andover served the Royal Air Force and the Royal New Zealand Air Force for many years before being sold into commercial usage.

Country of Origin:	UK
First Flight:	1965
Accommodation:	3 to 4 flight crew of + specialist outsize payload.
Wingspan:	98ft 6in (30.02m)
Length:	67ft 0in (20.42m)
Height:	24ft 10in (7.57m)
Empty Weight:	25,988lb (11,786kg)
Max Take Off:	45,095lb (20,451kg)
Powerplant:	2 X 2,105hp (1.569kW Rolls-Royce Dart turbofans).
Cruise Speed:	250mph (402km/h)
Max Speed:	287mph (462km/h)
Range:	1,910 miles (3,056km)
Number Manufactured:	31
Preserved:	RAF Museum, Hendon, London, UK.

Hawker Siddeley HS-748 Srs 2-A

Subject: Hawker Siddeley HS-748 Srs 2-A.
Statistics: Hawker Siddeley HS-748 Srs-2.

The 748 series was first developed by Avro, but when that venerable manufacturer was absorbed into the Hawker Siddeley Group in 1963, the type was rechristened the HS-748. The prototype airframe flew for the first time in June 1960, and Hawker Siddeley went on to build a total of 326 of the type. A further 89 HS-748 Srs 2-M military variants were built by Hindustan Aeronautics for the Indian air force.

Country of Origin:	UK
First Flight:	1960
Accommodation:	2 + 44 to 51 passengers.
Wingspan:	98ft 6in (30.02m)
Length:	67ft 0in (20.42m)
Height:	24ft 10in (7.57m)
Empty Weight:	25,899lb (11,785Kg)
Max Take Off:	45,095lb (20,450kg)
Powerplant:	2 X 2,105hp (1,569kW) Rolls-Royce Dart turboprops.
Cruise Speed:	250mph (402km/h)
Max Speed:	287mph (462km/h)
Range:	1,910 miles (3,056km)
Number Manufactured:	326 by Hawker Siddeley and 89 by Hindustan Aeronautics for the Indian air force.

Hawker Siddeley Buccaneer

Subject: Hawker Siddeley Mk.2 Buccaneer XN875 spent its last operational years with the Royal Radar Establishment at Pershore, Worcestershire.
Statistics: Hawker Siddeley Buccaneer.

Blackburn Aircraft first laid down the design parameters for the Buccaneer, but the new type continued its development under the Hawker Siddeley Group banner. Designed to deliver a single nuclear warhead deep into the heart of enemy territory, the Buccaneer was intended to fly the later portions of its deadly mission at extremely low levels and to outmanoeuvre its enemies through sheer performance and speed over the ground.

Country of Origin:	UK
First Flight:	1958
Accommodation:	1
Wingspan:	44ft 0in (13.41m)
Length:	63ft 5in (19.33m)
Height:	16ft 3in (4.95m)
Max Take Off:	62,000lb (28,122kg)
Powerplant:	2 X 11,100lb (49.4 kN) Rolls-Royce RB.168 Spey turbofans.
Max Speed:	645mph (1,038km/h)
Service Ceiling:	40,000ft (12,190m)
Range (striking range):	2,300 miles (3,700km)
Number Manufactured:	206
Preserved:	RAF Museum, Hendon, London, UK.

Heinkel He-III

Subject: Heinkel He-III.
Statistics: Heinkel He-III.

With the creation of the Third Reich in 1933, elaborate measures were taken to conceal the real extent to which rearmament was taking place in Germany. Almost immediately it began the development of a broad range of dual-purpose aircraft, civilian transports that were really, in essence, military bombers. Heinkel's He-III, too, was passed off as a 10-passenger civilian transport, but its purpose was, of course, far more sinister. Its press debut on 10 January 1936 was a much-choreographed affair, and the prototype displayed to the public was a civilian passenger transport and not a military type.

Country of Origin:	Germany
First Flight:	1935
Accommodation:	5 flight crew
Wingspan:	74ft 2in (22.6m)
Length:	53ft 10in (16.4m)
Height:	13ft 1in (4.0m)
Empty Weight:	19,136lb (8,680kg)
Max Take Off:	30,865lb (14,000kg)
Powerplant:	2 x 1,350hp (1,006kW) Junkers Jumo 211F-2 in-line pistons.
Max Speed:	270mph (435km/h)
Service Ceiling:	27,890ft (8,500m).
Range:	1,212 miles (1,850km)
Number Manufactured:	Over 5,000 of He-111H, excluding other variants.
Preserved:	Cavanaugh Flight Museum, Addison, Texas, USA.

Heinkel He-162A-2

Subject: Heinkel He-162A-2 Salamander is preserved at RAF Museum, Hendon, London.
Statistics: Heinkel He-162A-2.

The He-162 took to the air just 38 days after the detailed design blueprints were issued to the production team. It was December 1944 and Germany was in deep trouble. On all sides the armies of the Allied forces were closing in and only some new wonder weapon could now save the day. At Heinkel the engineers worked round the clock to prepare the extraordinary He-162 turbojet for operational status. There was no time for assessment or refinement. Mass production of the type began in the vast underground salt mines of Magdeburg, and plans were laid

to produce up to 5,000 airframes per month. The speed of the Allied advances into Germany, however, caught the Salamander programme off guard and the Magdeburg plant was overrun by US troops long before its full potential was reached. Indeed, over the last months of the war up to 800 partially finished He-162 airframes were captured as the Allies closed in on Berlin.

Country of Origin:	Germany
First Flight:	1944
Accommodation:	1
Wingspan:	23ft 7in (7.2m)
Length:	29ft 8in (9.05m)
Height:	8ft 6in (2.6m)
Empty Weight:	3,868lb (1,758kg)
Max Take Off:	6,171lb (2,805kg)
Powerplant:	1 x 1,755lb (7.8kN) BMW 003E-1 axial-flow turbojet.
Max Speed:	490mph (890km/h)
Service Ceiling:	27,890ft (8,500m)
Range:	384 miles (620km)
Number Manufactured:	270 completed, many of which made it to operational status. Up to 800 partially completed airframes captured.
Preserved:	RAF Museum, Hendon, London, UK. Canada Aviation Museum, Ottawa, Ontario, Canada.

Hughes Model 269-300

Subject: Hughes Model 269-300 on floats.
Statistics: Hughes Model 300.

The Model 269 began life on the drawing boards of the Hughes Tool Company in 1955, and the first prototype took to the air just 1 year later. In a bid to sell the type to the US Army, the first 5 pre-production airframes were presented for military evaluation leading to its selection in 1964 as the primary army training helicopter. It was a major coup for Hughes, and a total of 792 were purchased under the designation TH-55A. In 1961 the first commercial deliveries of the Model 269 were made and the type quickly gained a reputation as an efficient, reliable utility

transport. The Model 300, meanwhile, was developed from the Model 269B. With a substantially improved payload capacity and a reduced noise footprint, the Hughes 300 continues in use to this day.

Country of Origin:	USA
First Flight:	1956
Accommodation:	2
Rotor Diameter:	26ft 10in (8.18m)
Length:	22ft 2in (9.4m)
Height:	8ft 9in (2.66m)
Empty Weight:	1,043lb (473kg)
Max Take Off:	2,046lb (928kg)
Powerplant:	1 x 225hp (168kW) Lycoming IO-360 piston powerplant.
Max Speed:	95mph (152.8km/h)
Range:	225 miles (360km)
Flying or in service:	In service.

Hughes Model 369E

Subject: Hughes Model 369E registration ZK-HTN in Greenpeace colours.
Statistics: Hughes Model 369E.

The Model 369 derived from the US Army's Light Observation Helicopter (LOA) competition of the early 1960s. Emerging as the victor over 12 rival entries, the 'Flying Egg' went on to be built in a number of variants and mission-specific roles. The type was built for the US Army as the OH-6A Cayuse, a light attack helicopter with further roles in the areas of reconnaissance, artillery observation, and escort gunship, and in large numbers for civilian use as a utility transport, for pipeline inspection duties, and for customs, police, and TV work.

Country of Origin:	USA .
First Flight:	1963
Accommodation:	4
Rotor Span:	26ft 4in (8.0m)
Length:	23ft 2in (7.1m)
Empty Weight:	1,087lb (493kg)
Max Take Off:	3,000lb (1,361kg)
Powerplant:	1 x 317hp (236kW) Allison T63-A turboshaft.
Cruise Speed:	135mph (217km/h)

Max Speed: 152mph (244km/h)
Mission Radius: 376 miles (606km)
Flying or in service: In service.
Preserved: The Helicopter Museum, Weston-Super-Mare, Somerset, UK (YOH-6A).

Hunting Pembroke

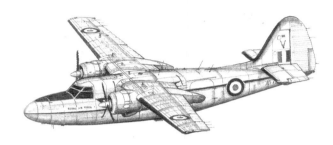

Subject: Hunting P-66 Pembroke of the Royal Air Force.
Statistics: Hunting P-66 Pembroke.

The Percival Pembroke twin-engined light transport was manufactured for the Royal Air Force, as well as for the air forces of Sweden, Belgium, West Germany, Denmark, and Sudan. The type was based on the earlier and smaller P-50 Percival Prince, which was flown by the Royal Navy as the P-57 Sea Prince. A total of 128 Pembrokes were built, as well as 5 civilian P-66 'President' executive transports. The Pembroke served in a wide variety of military roles for many years before being retired and sold on to commercial operators. Thereafter, many of the type went on to provide years of further service in the roles of freighter, taxi, and utility transport.

Country of Origin: UK
First Flight: 1952
Wingspan: 64ft 6in (19.66m)
Length: 46ft 0in (14.0m)
Height: 16ft 1in (4.9m)
Empty Weight: 9,178lb (4,162kg)
Max Take Off: 13,500lb (6,122kg)
Powerplant: 2 X 540hp (402.5kW) Alvis Leonides Mk 127 piston.
Cruise Speed: 209mph (336km/h)
Max Speed: 224mph (360km/h)
Range: 1,150 miles (1,840km)
Number Manufactured: 128 manufactured as the C.Mk1 military variant. 5 of the civilian P-66 President variant also built.
Flying or in service: Up to 4 in airworthy condition.

Hunting Percival Provost T-1

Subject: Hunting Percival Provost T-1.
Statistics: Hunting Percival P-56 Provost.

Percival Aircraft designed the P-56 Provost to meet with Specification T-16/48 of the Royal Air Force and, after the production of 3 prototype airframes, the type was selected as the new RAF standard basic trainer. The Provost was a rugged and well-built airframe, and later airframes were fitted with hardpoints for a variety of weapons systems under the designation Provost T-3. While the majority of airframes produced went to the RAF, small numbers of the type were supplied to the Irish Air Corps and to the air forces of Rhodesia, Burma, Iraq, Sudan, Ceylon, Malaysia, and Oman. The Provost was an ideal training aircraft allowing instructor and student to sit side-by-side throughout the basic training stages. Its ability to carry armaments facilitated ab initio training in a variety of weapons systems.

Country of Origin: UK
First Flight: 1950
Accommodation: 2
Wingspan: 35ft 2in (10.72m)
Length: 29ft 0in (8.85m)
Height: 11ft 9in (3.58m)
Empty Weight: 3,350lb (1,519kg)
Max Take Off: 4,400lb (1,995kg)
Powerplant: 1 X 550hp (410kW) Alvis Leonides 126 piston power-plant.
Cruise Speed: 177mph (285km/h)
Max Speed: 200mph (322km/h)
Range: 690 miles (1,110km)
Number Manufactured: 461
Preserved: Newark Air Museum, Nottingham, Nottinghamshire, UK (AR-107). RAF Museum, Cosford Airfield, Shifnal, Shropshire, UK.

Ilyushin Il-12 Coach

Subject: Ilyushin Il-12 Coach.
Statistics: Ilyushin Il-12 Coach.

With the cessation of hostilities in Europe, the Soviet Union's airline network became immediately dependent on the vast numbers of army-surplus Douglas DC3s and Lisunov Li-2s that were being released to commercial operators. Increasing numbers of civilians were expressing interest in airline travel, and Aeroflot, the long-time national carrier, set out requirements for a new airliner with an increased capacity and range. The resulting aircraft, flown for the first time in 1946, was designated the Ilyushin Il-12.

Country of Origin: USSR
First Flight: 1946
Accommodation: 4 flight crew + 27 to 32 passengers
Wingspan: 103ft 11in (31.67m)
Length: 69ft 11in (21.31m)
Max Take Off: 38,030lb (17,250kg)
Powerplant: 2 X 1,775hp (1,323kW) ASh82FNV piston radials.
Max Speed: 217mph (350km/h)
Service Ceiling: 22,000ft (6,705m)
Range: 1,865 miles (3,000km)

Ilyushin Il-14 Crate

Subject: Ilyushin Il-14 Crate.
Statistics: Ilyushin Il-14 Crate.

The Il-14 Crate was an improved version of the earlier Il-12 airliner. Complete with a new and more efficient wingfoil, more powerful Shvetsov powerplants, and a more streamlined airframe, the type was manufactured in large numbers to provide Aeroflot and the other carriers of the Eastern Bloc countries with the capacity they required. The Crate was a tough and capable performer that was as much at home in the frozen wastes of Siberia as it was in the intense heat of Kazakhstan. A tough and versatile workhorse that continued in service up until the late 1980s.

Country of Origin:	USSR
First Flight:	1953
Accommodation:	3 flight crew + up to 32 passengers.
Wingspan:	103ft 11in (31.67m)
Length:	73ft 3in (22.34m)
Max Take Off:	38,030lb (17,250kg)
Powerplant:	2 x 1,900hp (1,416kW) Shvetsov ASh-82T radials.
Cruise Speed:	198mph (320km/h)
Max Speed:	258mph (415km/h)
Service Ceiling:	24,280ft (7,400m)
Range:	932 miles (1,500km)
Number Manufactured:	Total production of 1,276 including 80 by VEB of East Germany and 203 by Avia of former Czechoslovakia.
Flying or in service:	Small numbers operational.
Preserved:	Pacific Coast Air Museum, Santa Rosa, California, USA. Khodynskoe Pole, Central Airfield, Moscow, Russia.

Ilyushin Il-18 Coot

Subject: Ilyushin Il-18 Coot.
Statistics: Ilyushin Il-18E Coot.

The 4-engined Coot passenger airliner and freighter entered service with Aeroflot in 1959 and went on to be built in massive numbers over many years. In its military guise it was built for the Soviet air force and for the air forces of Afghanistan, Algeria, Bulgaria, Czechoslovakia, China, Poland, Syria, and Yugoslavia. Initial production Il-18 Coots were configured to carry 75 passengers, but later examples were stretched and tweaked to bring passenger capacity up to 122 persons. The Ilyushin Il-38 May is a maritime patrol variant of the type, while the the Coot A is an electronic intelligence-gathering platform. Up to 45 Il-18s remain operational and airworthy at this time.

Country of Origin:	USSR
First Flight:	1957
Accommodation:	3 flight crew + 90 to 122 passengers.
Wingspan:	122ft 8in (37.3m)
Length:	117ft 9in (35.9m)
Height:	33ft 4in (10.17m)
Empty Weight:	77,160lb (35,000kg)
Max Take Off:	134,925lb (61,200kg)
Powerplant:	4 x 4,250hp (3,169kW) AI-20M powerplants.
Max Speed:	419mph (675km/h)
Service Ceiling:	32,800ft (10,000m)
Range:	3,230 miles (5,200km)
Number Manufactured:	In excess of 700.
Flying or in service:	Up to 45.

Ilyushin Il-76 Candid

Subject: Ilyushin Il-76 Candid.
Statistics: Ilyushin Il-76TD Candid.

Like many of the other Soviet airliners, the Il-76 was designed with 2 distinct purposes in mind. Although designed to fulfil the needs of Aeroflot, the state carrier, the type could be adapted immediately if required for a wide range of military purposes. It was provided with an all-glass navigational cabin immediately beneath the pilot's station, a massive overkill for a civilian aircraft. Following its introduction to service in 1975 the type was given the NATO codename 'Candid'. Production ran to more than 900 airframes, most of them for the air forces of the Soviet Union and its Eastern Bloc neighbours. Up to 300 of the type continue to serve with Aeroflot and other civilian carriers.

Country of Origin:	USSR
First Flight:	1971
Wingspan:	165ft 8in (50.5m)
Length:	152ft 10in (46.58m)
Height:	48ft 5in (14.76m)
Empty Weight:	209,475lb (95,000kg)
Max Take Off:	418,950lb (190,000kg)

Powerplant:	4 x 26,466lb (117,7kN) AviadVigatel (Soloviev) turbofan powerplants.
Cruise Speed:	470mph (756km/h)
Max Speed:	528mph (850km/h)
Range:	4,163 miles (6,660km)
Number Manufactured:	In excess of 920.
Flying or in service:	Up to 300.

Ilyushin Il-86 Camber

Subject: Ilyushin Il-86-300 in the livery of Soviet state carrier Aeroflot.
Statistics: Ilyushin Il-86.

The Il-86 Camber was intended to revolutionize the Soviet Union's airline fleet, but the type fell far short of its design goals in terms of both fuel burn and range. As a result, the type was manufactured in modest numbers only before production was abandoned. This was the Soviet Union's very first wide-body airliner and it differed from its western counterparts in that passengers entered from ground level and, passing through a large lower-deck luggage room, would climb up a further internal staircase to the main passenger deck. The Il-82 'Maxdome' is a military airborne command post variant of the type.

Country of Origin:	USSR
First Flight:	1976
Accommodation:	3 to 4 flight crew + up to 350 passengers.
Wingspan:	157ft 8in (48.06m)
Length:	195ft 4in (59.9m)
Height:	51ft 10in (15.81m)
Max Take Off:	458,560lb (208,000kg)
Powerplant:	4 x 28,660lb (127.5kN) KKBM (Kuznetsov) NK-86 turbofans.
Cruise Speed:	560mph (900km/h)
Max Speed:	590mph (950km/h)
Range:	2,875 miles (4,629km)
Number Manufactured:	103 built inclusive of 4 military command posts.
Flying or in service:	Widely in service.

Ilyushin Il-96

Subject: Ilyushin Il-96, again in the colours of Aeroflot.
Statistics: Ilyushin Il-96-300.

The development of the Il-86 to the Il-96 was so thorough and so successful that the Il-96 is generally considered as an all-new airline type. In all of the areas where the earlier aircraft failed to meet its design targets, the new airliner excels. Throughout the design a wide range of new technologies has been introduced, from a new supercritical wing to new winglet technology and a triplex fly-by-wire flight control system. Other changes include a new generation of low-burn turbofan powerplants and a new 6-screen EFIS flight deck and flight management system. In all areas the new offering from Ilyushin delivers the standard and the performance expected of a modern and sophisticated airliner. Export orders have, nonetheless, failed to materialize and only 17 of the type have been built to date.

Country of Origin:	USSR
First Flight:	1988
Accommodation:	3 flight crew and seating for up to 300 passengers in a high-density configuration.
Wingspan:	197ft 1in (60.1m)
Length:	181ft 7in (55.34m)
Height:	57ft 8in (17.58m)
Empty Weight:	262,395lb (119,000kg)
Max Take Off:	529,200lb (240,000kg)
Powerplant:	4 X 35,274lb (156.9kN) AviadVigatel PS-90A turbofans.
Cruise Speed:	530mph (850km/h)
Max Speed:	559mph (900km/h)
Range:	8,700 miles (13,920km)
Number Manufactured:	17
Flying or in service:	In service.

Jungster 1 Biplane

Subject: Jungster 1 Biplane, registration N458J.
Statistics: Jungster 1 Biplane (with basic 85hp powerplant).

Designed by aeronautical engineer Rim Kaminskas of Los Angeles, the Jungster 1 Biplane was designed closely around the airframe of Germany's superb Bücker Jungmeister. Fully aerobatic and complete with 11 degrees of wing sweepback, the Jungster was classified as an experimental aircraft and plans were made available to amateur builders for home construction. Kaminskas's structure was simple and efficient, comprising aircraft-grade spruce and plywood with a fabric covering. The resulting airframe was tough and capable with permissable wing loadings ranging from 10.6Gs positive right through to 6Gs negative. As with many other projects that are targeted at the amateur market, the Jungster is capable of accepting a wide range of aircraft and automotive engines, ranging in power output from 85hp to 150hp.

Country of Origin:	USA
First Flight:	1962
Accommodation:	1
Wingspan:	16ft 8in (5.08m)
Length:	16ft 0in (4.87m)
Height:	9ft 3in (2.81m)
Empty Weight:	606lb (275kg)
Max Take Off:	1,000lb (454kg)
Powerplant:	Designed for use with a range of 85hp to 150hp aviation and automotive powerplants
Cruise Speed:	119mph (191km/h)
Max Speed:	125mph (202km/h)
Number Manufactured:	Plans sold for construction by amateur builders
Flying or in service:	Small numbers flying in Europe and the USA.

Junkers D1 (J9)

Subject: Junkers D1.
Statistics: Junkers D1.

A single-seat cantilever monoplane fighter of 1918 vintage, which was revolutionary in its time for its all-corrugated metal construction. The Junkers D1 was a most effective and unusual fighter in an era of biplanes, and it quickly built a reputation for itself in the skies above the trenches of France. Behind the diminutive fighter was Professor Hugo Junkers, the academic and lateral thinker who pioneered the science of corrugated-metal construction in airframe design. Junkers quickly realized that the strength provided by his new construction method was such that a cantilevered wing was possible without the need for either braces or struts. An additional advantage of the type, too, was its ability to absorb large amounts of small arms ground fire, always a great danger for pilots operating above the seething enemy trench network.

Country of Origin:	Germany
First Flight:	1918
Accommodation:	1
Wingspan:	29ft 6in
Length:	23ft 9in
Height:	7ft 4in
Empty Weight:	1,439lb (654kg)
Max Take Off:	1,835lb (834kg)
Powerplant:	1 X 185hp (138kW) BMW III piston engine.
Max Speed:	116mph (185km/h)
Number Manufactured:	41

Junkers
Ju-52

Subject: Junkers Ju-52M.
Statistics: Junkers Ju-52M.

The Ju-52 was no beauty, but it did make a massive mark on European aviation throughout the 1930s. This was the aircraft that Lufthansa used to establish its extensive network of of air routes, and the type plied the skies of Europe, Africa, and even South America. Professor Junkers' corrugated stressed-skin construction techniques were again used to produce a tough and reliable airframe, and again the type established a superb reputation among pilots and passengers alike. At that time flying with any airline, and particularly with Lufthansa's Ju-52s, was a stylish and fashionable experience, even for the well-to-do. The build-up to war in Europe, however, changed everything. Suddenly the Ju-52 became a paratroop transport and a mainstay of the German Luftwaffe's communications wing. Junkers began a massive programme of expansion and thousands of the type were produced. Thereafter it served tirelessly on all fronts of the War. From Crete to the Low Countries, and from North Africa to Norway, the Ju-52s of the Luftwaffe's paratroop and communications divisions were never far from the battlefront.

Country of Origin:	Germany
First Flight:	1930
Accommodation:	2 pilots + 17 passengers.
Wingspan:	95ft 10in (29.2m)
Length:	62ft 0in (18.9m)
Height:	14ft 10in (4.52m)
Empty Weight:	12,568lb (5,700kg)
Max Take Off:	23,152lb (10,500kg)
Powerplant:	3 x 830hp (619kW) BMW-132A piston powerplants.
Cruise Speed:	155mph (249km/h)
Max Speed:	175mph (280km/h)
Range:	550 miles (880km)
Number Manufactured:	430 commercial Ju-52s built before the war, as well as 2,804 German-built military examples. 415 later built in France and 170 in Spain.

Flying or in service:	Up to 9 still airworthy.
Preserved:	RAF Museum, Hendon, London, UK (Ju52/3m).
	Steven F. Udvar-Hazy Center, Chantilly, Virginia, USA.
	Fantasy of Flight Museum, Polk City, Florida, USA.
	National Museum of the US Air Force, Wright-Patterson AFB, Dayton, Ohio, USA.

Junkers
Ju-87 Stuka

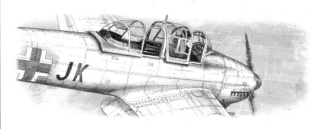

Subject: Junkers Ju-87 G-2 Stuka is preserved at the RAF Museum, Hendon, London.
Statistics: Junkers Ju-87 D-1 Stuka.

The effectiveness of dive-bombing over gravity-bombing techniques was first demonstrated in the late 1920s by American military pilots, who were acting in support of the Nicaraguan government against leftist rebels. The theory was that any missile launched from an aircraft as it dived steeply towards a target was much more likely to impact that target than gravity ordnance dropped from a height. The difficulty was, however, that the loads imposed on the aircraft during its 60- to 80-degree dives were such that the airframe had to be substantially strengthened throughout. Now this additional weight slowed the dive-bomber significantly and left it at the mercy of the lighter and faster pedigree fighters. German air ace and Luftwaffe officer Ernst Udet witnessed US dive-bombers in simulated exercises in 1934. On returning to Germany, he championed the idea and quickly became the driving force behind the Luftwaffe's dive-bomber programme. The prototype Ju-87 Stuka flew for the first time in early 1935, powered, ironically, by a British Rolls-Royce Kestrel V engine. The aircraft that would terrorize Europe had been born.

Country of Origin:	Germany
First Flight:	1935
Accommodation:	1 or 2
Wingspan:	45ft 3in (13.8m)
Length:	37ft 9in (11.5m)
Max Take Off:	17,517lb (6,585kg)

Powerplant:	1 x 1,400hp (1,043kW) Junkers Jumo 211J-1.
Max Speed:	255mph (410km/h)
Range:	621 miles (1,000km)
Number Manufactured:	In excess of 5,700 built.
Preserved:	RAF Museum, Hendon, London, UK (Ju-87R-1).

Kamov
Ka-32S

Subject: Kamov Ka-32S of Murmansk Aviation Company. Registration RA-31019 (c/n 6002).
Statistics: Kamov Ka-32T.

The Ka-32 series was designed originally as a shipborne anti-submarine helicopter, but it has been subsequently developed into a wide range of mission-specific airframes for use by various Soviet military forces and commercial operators. The Ka-32T is a basic utility version used for basic transport work and lifting of underslung loads. The Ka-32S is provided with an all-weather avionics suite and is designed for maritime patrol duties, search-and-rescue work, oil-rig support duties, and back-up support for the Soviet Union's large fleet of ice breakers. Historically the Soviet Union has always been slow to allow its more advanced helicopter types to find their way to the West, but in recent years large numbers of Kamov Ka-32s have begun commercial operations in Canada, Turkey, Malaysia, South Korea, Greece, Spain, and Switzerland. The Ka-32 is a very capable and cost-effective helicopter platform, and is likely to provide its wide range of military and civilian operators with the highest levels of service for many years to come.

Country of Origin:	USSR
First Flight:	1980
Accommodation:	2 + 16 passengers or freight or stretchers.
Rotor Diameter:	52ft 2in (15.9m)
Length:	37ft 1in (11.3m)
Height:	17ft 9in (5.4m)
Empty Weight:	14,330lb (6,500kg)
Max Take Off:	27,775lb (12,600kg)
Powerplant:	2 x 2,190hp (1,633kW) Klimov TV3-117V turboshafts driving 2 contra-rotating rotors.

Cruise Speed:	143mph (230km/h)
Max Speed:	155mph (250km/h)
Service Ceiling:	16,400ft (4,000m)
Range:	497 miles (800km)
Flying or in service:	Generally in service.

Karman-Petroczy Captive Helicopter

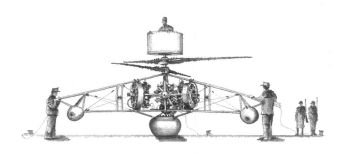

Subject: Karman-Petroczy Captive Helicopter.
Statistics: Karman-Petroczy Captive Helicopter.

Stephen Petroczy and Theodore Von Karman designed the extraordinary Karman-Petroczy captive helicopter as an aerial observation post, rather than as a freeflying rotor craft. The type was flown in trials for the Austrian army, but only under tethered conditions. Its 2 huge, carved rotors thrashed about dangerously with their brave human cargo overhead. The Karman-Petroczy had absolutely no flight controls and its vertical ascents and descents were controlled by simple winches and cables. It flew on many occasions, and on one of these flights ascended to a height of 165 feet (50m), and maintaining that altitude for more than 1 hour. On its 15th flight, control was lost and the captive helicopter crashed to the ground. Little is known of the fate of the unfortunate crow's-nest observer.

Country of Origin:	Austria
First Flight:	1918
Accommodation:	1
Rotor Diameter:	20ft 0in (6.1m)
Length:	20ft 0in (6.1m)
Height:	12ft 0in (3.66m)
Powerplant:	3 x 120hp (89kW) Le Rhône radial powerplants.
Cruise Speed:	No forward speed.
Max Speed:	No forward speed.
Service Ceiling:	165ft (50m)
Number Manufactured:	2

Keuthian Solaris

Subject: Keuthian Solaris, Merrit Island Airport, Florida.
Statistics: Keuthian Solaris.

Keuthian Aircraft, makers of the Solaris light sport-plane, was based at Merrit Island Airport, Florida until 1996, when its assets were sold to Arnet Pereyra, Inc. and distribution of the Solaris kit ceased. An unusual sporting ultralight with a slightly swept wing, a pusher propeller, and a canard foreplane.

Country of Origin:	USA
Accommodation:	1
Number Manufactured:	Unknown

Kolb Firestar

Subject: Kolb Firestar Ultralight.
Statistics: Kolb Firestar.

With a take-off distance of just 225ft, the Kolb Firestar can be operated off almost any level piece of ground. Classified as an ultralight aircraft, the Firestar is shipped as a kit and assembled by its owner/pilot. Options include a fully enclosed cabin for flight in colder climates and a ballistic parachute-recovery system that can be deployed if things get really out of hand.

Country of Origin:	USA
First Flight:	1993
Accommodation:	1
Wingspan:	27ft 8in (8.47m)
Length:	20ft 4in (6.17m)
Height:	6ft 3in (1.91m)
Empty Weight:	280lb (127kg)
Max Take Off:	725lb (329kg)
Powerplant:	1 x 41hp (30.57kW) Rotax 447
Cruise Speed:	60mph (96.5km/h)
Max Speed:	70mph (112km/h)

KIS TR-1 Cruiser

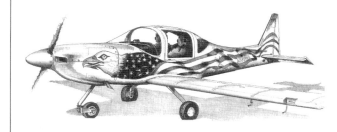

Subject: KIS TR-1, reg N240X, flew into Sun 'n Fun, Florida, 2005.
Statistics: KIS TR-1 Cruiser with Lycoming O-360 powerplant.

A 4-place lightplane and touring aircraft which uses the very latest in lightweight composite construction techniques. The Cruiser is an experimental category kitbuild aircraft that was designed by Rich Trickel and Vance Jaqua of Oxnard, California. Its sleek, aerodynamic contours and powerful engine allow it a maximum speed of 180mph, a most respectable tally for any home-build project. The Cruiser's flight envelope is designed for the lower end of the scale, too, with a 70mph approach speed and superb flying manners in the landing stages. A good all-rounder with an attractive level of specification.

Country of Origin:	USA
First Flight:	1991
Accommodation:	4
Wingspan:	29ft 0in (8.84m)
Length:	23ft 5in (7.15m)
Height:	7ft 5in (2.27m)
Empty Weight:	1,280lb (580kg)
Max Take Off:	2,380lb (1,079kg)
Powerplant:	1 x 180hp (134kW) Lycoming O-360 or 200hp (149kW) Continental IO-360.
Cruise Speed:	165mph (265km/h)
Max Speed:	180mph (289km/h)
Range:	950 miles (1,523km)

Kitfox Speedster

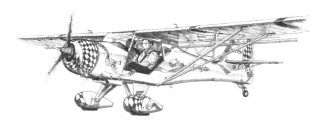

Subject: Kitfox Speedster.
Statistics: Kitfox Speedster.

The Kitfox is marketed as a kitbuild lightplane for amateur builders and home constructors. Designed to carry 2 pilots in side-by-side configuration, the Kitfox is simple to fly and relatively easy to build. The advertised build time is between 600 and 1,000 hours, but most inexperienced builders will take the full 1,000 hours to reach completion. After completion, the type's good air-handling qualities and short take-off/landing roll allow operation off even the shortest of unpaved landing strips, thus keeping costs to a minimum. A great side-by-side 2-seat aircraft for sociable flying and all-round fun.

Country of Origin:	USA
First Flight:	1984
Accommodation:	2
Wingspan:	32ft 0in (9.75m)
Length:	18ft 3in (5.56m)
Height:	6ft 6in (1.98m)
Empty Weight:	640lb (290.3kg)
Max Take Off:	1,200lb (544.3kg)
Powerplant:	1 X 80hp (59kW) Rotax 912
Cruise Speed:	115mph (185km/h)
Max Speed:	120mph (193km/h)
Range:	640 miles (1,030km)
Flying or in service:	Many projects completed and privately operated.
Preserved:	International Sport Aviation Museum, Lakeland Linder Regional Airport, Florida, USA.

Kugisho Ohka 22 Flying Bomb

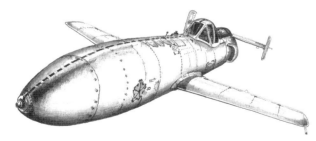

Subject: Kugisho Ohka 22 Flying Bomb.
Statistics: Kugisho Ohka 22 Flying Bomb.

The Ohka 22 was a human-guided missile designed to allow pilots with even rudimentary training to impact at high speed into the Allied fleet, which was getting ever closer to the Japanese mainland. At this late stage of the war the Allied aircraft carriers had become used to kamikaze attacks by standard Japanese fighting aircraft, and the numbers of anti-aircraft guns on the carriers now often exceeded 100. The resulting pom-pom barrage was so intense that the Japanese fighters were having immense difficulty getting through, and Vice Admiral Onishi Takijino

of the Japanese navy recommended adoption of the new jet-powered Model 22 programme. Although commonly referred to as kamikaze attacks, the Japanese referred to them as 'Tokko', meaning 'special attacks'. A number of philosophical concepts motivated the Tokko pilots: the ultimate sacrifice to save homeland, countrymen, and emperor; duty to Bushido, the warrior code of honour and conduct; and the belief that these ultimate Tokko missions would rekindle the miracle of the 'divine wind', a typhoon that destroyed a Mongol invasion fleet in the year 1281. The first Ohka prototype was plagued with a very short range, and so the Ohka Model 22 with a reduced warhead and increased range was developed.

Country of Origin:	Japan
First Flight:	1945
Accommodation:	1 + 1,323lb (600kg) Warhead.
Wingspan:	13ft 6in (4.11m)
Length:	22ft 7in (6.88m)
Height:	3ft 9in (1.14m)
Empty Weight:	1,202lb (545kg)
Powerplant:	1 X Tsu-11 hybrid reciprocating/ rocket motor (like a primitive jet engine afterburner).
Max Speed (Estimated):	In excess of 500mph (804km/h)
Range:	80.7 miles (130km)
Number Manufactured:	50 airframes built but only 3 engines completed.
Preserved:	Steven F. Udvar-Hazy Center, Washington, DC, USA.

Lake Sport Mermaid Amphibian

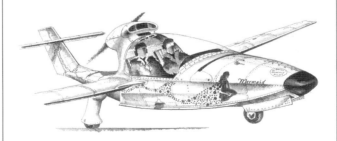

Subject: Lake Sport Mermaid Amphibian.
Statistics: Lake Sport Mermaid Amphibian.

The Czech Aircraft Works' little Mermaid amphibian is a most appealing aircraft on every front. Beautifully contoured and superbly detailed, the type comprises an aluminium hull with mid-level wings and a 2-person side-by-side cockpit. The Mermaid is one of a new generation of light planes that are emerging from the countries of eastern Europe, where massive state-funded aviation projects are being replaced by smaller and more

pragmatic privately funded aviation ventures. These projects clearly demonstrate the very high levels of design and manufacturing skills that have become available to the eastern European aviation industry, and these skills are likely to play an even greater role in general aviation in future years. The Mermaid is form and function rolled into one, a piece of flying art.

Country of Origin:	Czech Republic
First Flight:	2005
Accommodation:	2
Wingspan:	31ft 2in (9.51m)
Length:	24ft 0in (7.3m)
Empty Weight:	727lb (330kg)
Max Take Off:	1,370lb (621kg)
Powerplant:	1 X Rotax 912 ULS.
Cruise Speed:	115mph (185km/h)
Max Speed:	132mph (213km/h)
Range:	497 miles (800km)
Number Manufactured:	First production examples now coming on stream.
Flying or in service:	Prototypes only.

Lancair IV P

Subject: Lancair IV P (pressurized).
Statistics: Lancair IV.

Lance Neibauer's all-new Lancair IV takes the wing of the earlier Lancair 320/360 design and combines it with an all-new carbon-fibre composite fuselage structure and greatly more powerful 350hp Continental powerplant. The result is the Lancair IV with its impressive 365mph top speed, an extraordinary performance for any home-built aircraft. This is the top end of the kitbuild market, a hugely expensive but thrilling hobby. Neibauer's fully pressurized Lancair IV P brought the type to even greater heights, facilitating high-speed travel at altitude where weather conditions and air traffic are less likely to disturb the aircraft's flightpath.

Country of Origin:	USA
First Flight:	Lancair 200 first flown in 1984. Lancair IV first flown in 1991.
Accommodation:	4

Wingspan:	30ft 2in (9.19m)
Length:	25ft 0in (7.62m)
Height:	8ft 0in (2.44m)
Empty Weight:	2,000lb (907kg)
Max Take Off:	3,400lb (1,542kg)
Powerplant:	1 X 350hp (261kW) Continental IO-550 piston.
Cruise Speed:	330mph (531km/h)
Max Speed:	365mph (587km/h)
Range:	1,450 miles (2,300km)
Flying or in service:	Many examples now complete and in operation with private owners.

Lavochkin LA-156

Subject: Lavochkin LA-156.
Statistics: Lavochkin LA-156 (Type 5).

The years immediately following the end of the Second World War saw huge advances in the development of jet fighters right across Europe, the USA, and the USSR. The speed at which aircraft designers adjusted to the all-new configurations required by jet engines was extraordinary. The Lavochkin LA-156 was one of the first Soviet jet fighters. Even as it was being built it was being adjusted to take into account the latest improvements in its RD-10F afterburning turbojet. At the same time Lavochkin was experimenting with swept-wing configurations. So it was, then, that the Lavochkin LA-156 was essentially outdated even before it had completed its flight evaluation.

Country of Origin:	USSR
First Flight:	1947
Accommodation:	1
Wingspan:	27ft 11in (8.52m)
Length:	29ft 11in (9.12m)
Empty Weight:	5,286lb (2,398kg)
Max Take Off:	7,762lb (3,521kg)
Powerplant:	1 X RD-10F turbojet with afterburner.
Max Speed:	562mph (905km/h)
Service Ceiling:	35,104ft (10,700m)
Range:	410 miles (660km)

LET Aero 145 and Super Aero

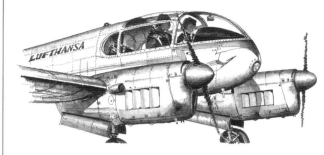

Subject: LET Super Aero 145 wearing the livery of carrier Lufthansa.
Statistics: LET Super Aero 145.

The Aero 145 was an all-metal, twin-engine, 4- to 5-seat utility transport that was manufactured by Prague-based Aero Tovarna Letadel immediately after the war. With a first flight in 1947 the type was manufactured until 1951, by which time up to 200 had been completed and delivered to various Eastern Bloc state bodies for use in the roles of air taxi and airline training. In 1951, under the new LET banner, the type was given a thorough facelift and again introduced to the marketplace, this time as the Aero 45S Super, with new engines, improved avionics, and a greatly increased all-up weight. Later still the new Super Aero 145 was introduced, this time bringing more powerful engines, better cruise speeds, and increased range. A total of 570 of all variants was delivered.

Country of Origin:	Czechoslovakia
First Flight:	1947
Accommodation:	4 to 5
Wingspan:	40ft 3in (12.24m)
Length:	25ft 6in (7.77m)
Height:	7ft 6in (2.3m)
Empty Weight:	2,115lb (959kg)
Max Take Off:	3,305lb (1,499kg)
Powerplant:	2 X 140hp (104.3kW) Walter M-332 pistons.
Cruise Speed:	155mph (249km/h)
Max Speed:	175mph (282km/h)
Range:	1,050 miles (1,680km)
Number Manufactured:	200 Aero 145s were built. 228 Aero 45S Super were built. 142 Super Aero 145s were built.
Flying or in service:	Several of the type still in service with private owners and collections.

LET L-40 Meta-Sokol

Subject: LET L-40 Meta-Sokol is registered G-ARSP on the UK civil register.
Statistics: LET L-40 Meta-Sokol.

Developed from the LET Mraz M.1 Sokol of the late 1940s, the L-40 Meta-Sokol was one of the lesser-known aircraft to emerge from behind the Iron Curtain. Used in the main as a training aircraft, the Meta-Sokol was often the very first aircraft on which student airline pilots would log hours. While the M.1 featured wooden construction and a taildragger undercarriage arrangement, the Meta-Sokol was an all-metal airframe with an unusual reverse tricycle undercarriage. Its new all-metal construction gave it great strength to face the rigours of imperfect student landings, and, indeed, many of the type demonstrated extraordinary longevity in the face of such ritual abuse. Up to 200 of the type were built between 1954 and 1961, and several are still flying in private ownership to this day.

Country of Origin:	Czechoslovakia
First Flight:	1956
Accommodation:	4
Wingspan:	32ft 10in (9.98m)
Length:	28ft 9in (8.76m)
Height:	8ft 1in (2.47m)
Empty Weight:	1,147lb (520kg)
Max Take Off:	2,030lb (920kg)
Powerplant:	1 X 140hp (104kW) Walter M-332 inverted inline 4-cylinder piston powerplant.
Cruise Speed:	129mph (208km/h)
Max Speed:	147mph (237km/h)
Service Ceiling:	14,750ft (5,000m)
Range:	527 miles (850km).
Number Manufactured:	Up to 200 airframes built between 1954 and 1961.
Flying or in service:	Several still flying including G-ARSP, which is based in the UK.

LET L-410 Turbolet

Subject: LET L-410 Turbolet.
Statistics: LET L-420 Turbolet.

The L-410 Turbolet was developed by LET to serve the needs of Aeroflot and the other Eastern Bloc carriers. It was designed to carry between 16 and 19 passengers on short-sector routes, and to serve isolated and remote communities where larger aircraft types could not be justified. Several variants were developed over the years, including the initial batch of 30 Pratt & Whitney PT6A-powered L-410As and a wide assortment of later Motorlet M601A-powered versions. The Turbolet filled an important niche in the transportation networks of the Eastern Bloc countries, and up to 1,100 of all variants have been manufactured to date. In recent years the type has been marketed in the West as the LET L-420, with more powerful 778hp (580kW) Motorlet M601F turboprop engines and a greatly upgraded avionics suite.

Country of Origin:	Czechoslovakia
First Flight:	1969
Accommodation:	2 flight crew + up to 19 passengers or 14 parachutists, or 6 stretchers + 5 sitting casualties + attendant.
Wingspan:	65ft 7in (20.0m)
Length:	47ft 4in (14.42m)
Height:	19ft 2in (5.85m)
Empty Weight:	8,960lb (4,064kg)
Max Take Off:	14,550lb (6,599kg)
Powerplant:	2 X 778hp (580kW) Motorlet M601F turboprop powerplants.
Cruise Speed:	230mph (370km/h)
Max Speed:	239mph (384km/h)
Service Ceiling:	24,300ft (7,406m)
Range:	844 miles (1,350km)
Number Manufactured:	In excess of 1,100 of all variants to date.
Flying or in service:	Many examples still in operational service.

Lockheed SR-71 Blackbird

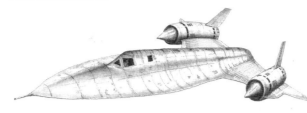

Subject: Lockheed SR-71 Blackbird.
Statistics: Lockheed SR-71 Blackbird.

Clarence 'Kelly' Johnson joined Lockheed in 1933 and became its chief engineer while still in his twenties. His extraordinary Skunk Works think-tank became one of America's greatest resources and one of its most closely guarded secrets. Here Johnson and his team of experts designed a succession of groundbreaking aircraft, including the F-104 Starfighter, the U-2 Spyplane, and, of course, the high-altitude SR-71 Blackbird. When it first flew in 1964 the Blackbird represented the very leading edge of aerodynamic technology and, indeed, in many ways it still does today. With a top speed of over Mach 3 and an 85,000ft mission ceiling, the type has pushed back the given boundaries of a whole range of technologies, from ultra-high-altitude aerodynamic profiling to powerplant development, metallurgy, high-altitude surveillance systems, and the design of low-radar-signature airframes.

Country of Origin:	USA
First Flight:	1964
Accommodation:	2
Wingspan:	55ft 7in (16.9m)
Length:	107ft 5in (32.7m)
Height:	18ft 6in (5.64m)
Max Take Off:	67,500lb (30,618kg)
Powerplant:	2 X 32,500lb (144.6kN) Pratt & Whitney J58 turbojets with afterburners.
Max Speed:	2,250mph (3,620km/h) or Mach 3.03.
Service Ceiling:	85,000ft (25,900m)
Range:	2,982 miles (4,800km)
Number Manufactured:	50
Flying or in service:	Small numbers still in operational service.
Preserved:	Castle Air Museum, Atwater, California, USA. Steven F. Udvar-Hazy Center, Chantilly, Virginia, USA (SR-71A).

Lockheed L-049 Constellation

Subject: Lockheed L-049 Constellation.
Statistics: Lockheed L-1049E Super Constellation.

Lockheed began the development of the Constellation in 1939, but the coming of the war meant that all of the first 22 completed airframes were requisitioned by the US Army Air Force as the C-69 transport. The first Constellation flew in 1943, and the type went on to serve Air Transport Command for the rest of the war. With the cessation of hostilities, the production of civilian Constellations began in earnest and TWA received its long-promised Constellation L-049s in October 1945. Within months the first scheduled flights to Paris via Gander and Shannon were established and the rest is history. The Constellation became an icon of style and prestige as a new generation of confident airline passengers were ferried across oceans in sumptuous comfort. Continuous improvements to the type produced upgraded L-649 and L-749 variants, but it was the L-1049 Super Constellation of 1950 that really brought a new level of sophistication to the type. The L-1049 had a longer fuselage, more powerful engines, and a greatly increased payload that allowed larger numbers of passengers and even greater range. The final chapter in the development of the type was the L-1649A Starliner, a Super Connie airframe with longer wings, stretched fuselage, and even more powerful turbo-compound engines.

Country of Origin:	USA
First Flight:	1943
Accommodation:	4 to 5 flight crew + 3 flight attendants + up to 109 passengers.
Wingspan:	123ft 0in (37.49m)
Length:	113ft 4in (34.54m)
Height:	24ft 7in (7.54m)
Empty Weight:	76,500lb (34,665kg)
Max Take Off:	133,000lb (60,328kg)
Powerplant:	4 X 3,165hp (2,435kW) Wright turbo-compound radial engines.
Cruise Speed:	323mph (520km/h)
Max Speed:	370mph (590km/h)
Service Ceiling:	23,700ft (7,223m)

Range: 5,000 miles (7,950km)
Flying or in service: Very small numbers still flying or regularly taxied with flying museums and preservation societies.
Preserved: National Aeronautical Museum Aviodrome, Lelystad, The Netherlands

Lockheed P-38 Lightning

Lockheed F-104G Starfighter

Subject: Lockheed F-104G Starfighter of the Netherlands Air Force.
Statistics: Lockheed F-104S Starfighter.

Lockheed HC-130J Hercules

Subject: Lockheed HC-130J Hercules of the US Coast Guard.
Statistics: Lockheed EC-130H Hercules electronic warfare platform.

The Lockheed Hercules was originally designed to fulfil the duties of assault transport and freighter, but its roles have been greatly expanded over the years to include electronic warfare, close air support, troop transport, Coast Guard duties, and paratroop deployment. The Hercules' high-mounted wing keeps the cargo area clear of obstacles and ensures that the engines are kept high up off the ground for operations off short and unprepared landing sites. On landing, the aircraft's large rear-loading ventral ramp opens downwards to facilitate rapid loading and unloading of all manner of supplies, from Jeeps to humanitarian aid.

Country of Origin: USA
First Flight: 1954
Accommodation: 3 flight crew + 8 electronic warfare operators or a total of 90 troops.
Wingspan: 133ft 0in (40.4m)
Length: 98ft 0in (29.7m)
Height: 38ft 0in (11.66m)
Empty Weight: 75,030lb (34,105kg)
Max Take Off: 163,244lb (74,202kg)
Powerplant: 4 x 4,050hp (3,020kW) Allison T56-A-15 turboprops.
Max Speed: 379mph (611km/h)
Service Ceiling: 43,400ft (13,225m)
Range: 2,540 miles (4,100km)
Number Manufactured: In excess of 2,200 of all variants completed and still under construction.
Flying or in service: Widely in service.

Subject: Lockheed P-38 Lightning.
Statistics: Lockheed P-38 Lightning.

The P-38 Lightning was developed to provide an interceptor fighter that could accompany standard bombing aircraft over very long distances. With its 2 1,475hp powerplants and its sleek twin-boom configuration, the Lightning was a powerful and potent weapon. In the course of the war years it served on all fronts, from Europe to Africa and the Pacific islands. Built in very large numbers, the Lightning is the only US aircraft that continued in production from before the war years right through to VJ day.

Country of Origin: USA
First Flight: 1939
Accommodation: 1
Wingspan: 52ft 0in (15.85m)
Length: 37ft 10in (11.53m)
Height: 9ft 10in (3.0m)
Empty Weight: 12,800lb (5,806kg)
Max Take Off: 21,600lb (9,798kg)
Powerplant: 2 x 1,475hp (1,099kW) Allison V-1710 12-cylinder pistons.
Max Speed: 414mph (666km/h)
Service Ceiling: 44,000ft (13,410m)
Range: 450 miles (724km)
Number Manufactured: 10,037 of all variants built.
Preserved: Steven F. Udvar-Hazy Center, Chantilly, Virginia, USA. Planes of Fame Air Museum, Chino, California, USA. National Museum of the US Air Force, Wright-Patterson AFB, Dayton, Ohio, USA.

Often described as a 'human missile', the awesome F-104 Starfighter, again from Kelly Johnson's Skunk Works, stretched the limits of aerodynamics to the very edge of what was possible in 1954. The type was an air superiority fighter and interceptor, based on the premise of applying massive doses of power to achieve great speed and height in readiness for engagements with enemy aircraft. The first full fighter to achieve Mach 2 status, the Starfighter, went on to serve in large numbers with the US Air Force and with the air forces of Germany, Italy, Belgium, the Netherlands, Turkey, Canada, and Japan. Perhaps the most unusual Starfighter ever built was the home-built version constructed by amateur builder Darryl Greenamyer over a 10-year period out of discarded and army-surplus 'non-serviceable' parts. Greenamyer's F-104RB Red Baron Starfighter was without doubt the fastest and the most sophisticated home-built project ever attempted, and he went on to establish the world speed record over a 3km closed circuit at 988.26mph (1,590.45km/h).

Country of Origin: USA
First Flight: 1954
Accommodation: 1
Wingspan: 21ft 11in (6.68m)
Length: 54ft 9in (16.69m)
Height: 13ft 5in (4.09m)
Empty Weight: 13,995lb (6,348kg)
Max Take Off: 31,000lb (14,061kg)
Powerplant: 1 x 17,900lb (79.62kN) General Electric J79-GE-19 turbojet with afterburner.
Cruise Speed: 610mph (982km/h)
Max Speed: 1,483mph (2,386km/h) or Mach. 2.
Range: 775 miles (1,247km)
Number Manufactured: In the region of 1,718 built, most of them under licence by European manufacturers.
Preserved: Canada Aviation Museum, Ottawa, Ontario, Canada. Smithsonian National Air and Space Museum, Washington, DC, USA. Castle Air Museum, Atwater, California, USA. Planes of Fame Air Museum, Chino, California, USA (F-104B).

Lockheed U-2 and TR-1A

Subject: Lockheed U-2.
Statistics: Lockheed U-2R.

Today's U-2R high-altitude 'Dragon Lady' is larger and more powerful than the original U-2 in which Gary Powers made world headlines in May 1960. Although flown for the first time in 1955, the type remains an important tool much favoured by elements of the US security network for the monitoring of hostile threats and for screening large tracts of third-party territories. It carries a sophisticated suite of electronic, photographic, and radar sensors that relay large volumes of sensitive military and industrial information to one of the US military satellite chains and thereafter to one of several US command posts where the information can be monitored or analyzed in real time. Even after 50 years and several redesigns, the U-2 is a delicate and sensitive aircraft that is difficult to land. To this day its pilots wear full space suits to protect them from the hazards of flight at such extreme altitudes.

Country of Origin:	USA
First Flight:	1955
Accommodation:	1
	2 (U2-RT training variant).
Wingspan:	103ft 0in (31.4m)
Length:	62ft 9in (19.13m)
Height:	17ft 0in (5.18m)
Empty Weight:	12,700lb (5,760kg)
Max Take Off:	19,000lb (8,617kg)
Powerplant:	1 x 17,000lb (75.6kN) Pratt & Whitney J75-P-13B turbojet.
Cruise Speed:	400mph (644km/h)
Max Speed:	430mph (692km/h)
Service Ceiling:	81,459ft (24,835m) can be maintained for several hours.
Range:	3,000 miles (4,800km)
Number Manufactured:	102 completed by the time production ceased in 1989.
Flying or in service:	Still in service.
Preserved:	Smithsonian National Air and Space Museum, Washington, DC, USA.

Lockheed L-1011 TriStar

Subject: Lockheed L-1011 TriStar.
Statistics: Lockheed L-1011-500 TriStar.

The TriStar was the great rival of the McDonnell Douglas DC-10, and the 2 airliners fought it out over many years in the airline marketplace. Financial difficulties at Lockheed nearly ended the project before production started, but they were resolved and the type was saved, only to be rocked for a second time when Rolls-Royce experienced its own monetary problems. Again a restructuring plan resolved the immediate difficulties and production of the TriStar resumed, but not before the DC-10 began to eat into the TriStar's market share. The last TriStar was rolled out of Lockheed's Palmdale plant in 1983, by which time 250 had been built. The type was operated by TWA, Eastern Airlines, Cathay Pacific, Delta, British Airways, and many of the other great world airlines. In 1983 the Royal Air Force bought 6 TriStars from British Airways for conversion to tanker status, and many of these tankers are in service to this day.

Country of Origin:	USA
First Flight:	1970
Accommodation:	4 flight crew + flight attendants + up to 315 passengers.
Wingspan:	164ft 5in (50.11m)
Length:	164ft 2in (50.04m)
Height:	55ft 10in (17.02m)
Empty Weight:	243,000lb (110,204kg)
Max Take Off:	496,000lb (224,943kg)
Powerplant:	3 x 50,000lb (222.4 kN) Rolls-Royce RB211-524B turbofans.
Cruise Speed:	485mph (781km/h)
Max Speed:	545mph (877km/h)
Range:	4,310 miles (6,896km)
Number Manufactured:	250
Flying or in service:	Up to 125 TriStars still in commercial service.

Lockheed Martin F-117 Nighthawk

Subject: Lockheed Martin F-117 Nighthawk.
Statistics: Lockheed Martin F-117A Nighthawk.

For many years it was known that US forces were flying some sort of top-secret stealth aircraft around the night skies of Nevada, but it was only in the opening hours of the Gulf War that the full capabilities of the F-117 became known to the world. Indeed, in the first days of that war the F-117 Nighthawk was intensively used to target military control centres, communications equipment, surface-to-air missile sites, and airfields, using a range of smart munitions and highly accurate laser-guided bombs. Despite spending considerable amounts of time above some of Iraq's fiercely guarded built-up areas, the F-117's stealth-cloaking systems functioned perfectly and not one of the aircraft was hit.

Country of Origin:	USA .
First Flight:	Prototype flown in 1981.
Accommodation:	1
Wingspan:	43ft 4in (13.2m)
Length:	65ft 11in (20.08m)
Height:	12ft 5in (3.78m)
Empty Weight:	29,983lb (13,600kg)
Max Take Off:	52,500lb (23,814kg)
Powerplant:	2 x 10,800lb (48.04kN) General Electric turbofans without afterburners.
Cruise Speed:	685mph (1,102km/h) estimated.
Max Speed:	755mph (1,215km/h) estimated.
Combat Radius:	746 miles (1,200km) without use of in-flight refuelling.
Number Manufactured:	6 prototypes and 58 production examples delivered.
Flying or in service:	In service.

Loening OA-1A Amphibian

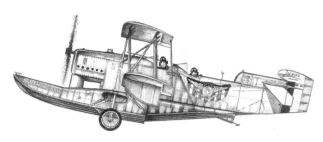

Subject: Loening OA-1A.
Statistics: Loening OL-8.

The OA-1A amphibian was one of a series of flying-hull biplane observation aircraft that was built by Grover Loening for the US Navy, Army, Marine Corps, and Coast Guard. The type went through a long succession of airframe and powerplant upgrades and was given designations from OA-1A right up to OL-8 accordingly. The series was central to many of the great pioneering and military adventures of the time, from Commander Byrd's famous 6,000-mile flight over the Arctic to the US Navy's historic 20,000-mile flight around South America. Throughout all of these extraordinary adventures, Loening's aircraft performed admirably given the fledgling nature of both aircraft and powerplant development.

Country of Origin:	USA
First Flight:	1923
Accommodation:	2
Wingspan:	45ft 0in (13.72m)
Length:	35ft 3in (10.74m)
Max Take Off:	5,253lb (2,383kg)
Powerplant:	1 X 425hp (317kW) Pratt & Whitney Wasp.
Max Speed:	124mph (200km/h)
Range:	650 miles (1,046km)
Number Manufactured:	Approx 136 of all variants.
Preserved:	National Museum of the US Air Force, Wright-Patterson AFB, Dayton, Ohio, USA.

LoPresti Piper Swift Fury

Subject: LoPresti Piper Swift.
Statistics: LoPresti Piper Swift.

The LoPresti Swift Fury was introduced as a prototype in 1988 after Roy LoPresti, with backing from Piper, was granted a licence to modify the Globe Swift light plane of 1942. Starting with the basic Globe Swift GC-1B design, LoPresti updated the entire aircraft, reworking the control system and improving the fuel system until the finished Swift Fury exemplified his personal motto, 'life is short, so fly fast'. Unfortunately for LoPresti, the general aviation industry fell on hard times and Piper was forced to withdraw its offer of funding. Despite an order book for 569 aircraft, the Swift Fury was now fully shelved. LoPresti diversified and formed LoPresti Speed Merchants, a company that would become famous for its high-performance engine induction systems, where propeller pulses were synchronized with engine intake strokes to produce better engine 'breathing' and increased power.

Country of Origin:	USA
First Flight:	1988
Accommodation:	2
Wingspan:	29ft 3in (8.92m)
Length:	22ft 6in (6.86m)
Height:	7ft 2in (2.19m)
Empty Weight:	1,450lb (657kg)
Max Take Off:	2,300lb (1,043kg)
Powerplant:	1 X Lycoming IO-360-A1B6 piston powerplant.
Cruise Speed:	215mph (346km/h)
Max Speed:	222mph (357km/h)
Service Ceiling:	21,000ft (6,400 m)
Range:	1,000 miles (1,609km)

Luft-Verkehrs Gesellschaft CV-1

Subject: Hendon's LVG CV-1 was captured almost intact in Germany in 1918.
Statistics: Luft-Verkehrs Gesellschaft CV-1.

The Luft-Verkehrs Gesellschaft CV-1 was employed in large numbers by Germany over the trenches of France and it is estimated that by the beginning of 1918 up to 175 of the type were being produced monthly. This was a handsome and beautifully designed fighter powered by a 230hp (171.5kW) Benz upright in-line piston engine. Airframe No. 7198/18 was captured almost intact in Germany during 1918 and was shipped back to Martlesham Heath, Suffolk, for evaluation by the A&AEE. This very airframe was displayed in mock aerial combat with a Bristol Fighter during the 1937 Hendon Air Pageant. Model 7198/18, the oldest surviving German aircraft, is now preserved in flying condition by the Shuttleworth Trust.

Country of Origin:	Germany
First Flight:	1917
Accommodation:	Pilot + gunner/observer.
Wingspan:	42ft 8in (13.0m)
Length:	24ft 5in (7.45m)
Max Take Off:	2,890lb (1,310kg)
Powerplant:	1 X 230hp (171.5kW) Benz upright in-line piston engine.
Max Speed:	105mph (170km/h)
Range:	370 miles (595km)
Number Manufactured:	Up to 1,100 manufactured with production of 175 per month during the war years.
Flying or in service.	1
Preserved:	Shuttleworth Trust, Old Warden, Bedfordshire, UK.

Luscombe Model 8 Silvaire

Subject: Luscombe Model 8 Silvaire is registered G-BTCH on the UK register.
Statistics: Luscombe Model 8F Renaissance (1998).

Luscombe's wonderful Model 8 Silvaire began life in 1937, but production was halted in 1942 when America entered the war. With the coming of peace in 1945, production of the Model 8 was immediately resumed and the type went on to be built in large numbers for private owners and returning pilots alike. Financial pressures within the sport-aircraft manufacturing industry have always been huge and Luscombe was forced into receivership in 1949. US manufacturer Temco Aircraft then took up the rights to production and manufactured a small number of the type before it, too, began to experience financial turbulence. Between 1956 and 1960 Colorado-based Silvaire Aircraft Company completed a total of 80 Silvaire Model 8Fs. The final chapter in the Silvaire story began in 1998 when Renaissance Aircraft of Maryland set about relaunching an updated Silvaire. Despite the development of a prototype airframe and a production agreement with the Czech Aircraft Works, the new Silvaire never made it past the prototype stage.

Country of Origin: USA
First Flight: 1937
Accommodation: 2
Wingspan: 35ft 1in (10.7m)
Length: 22ft 0in (6.71m)
Height: 7ft 0in (2.13m)
Empty Weight: 950lb (431kg)
Max Take Off: 1,400lb (635kg)
Powerplant: 1 X 150hp (111.8kW) Lycoming
                        0-320 piston powerplant.
Cruise Speed: 140mph (225km/h)
Max Speed: 150mph (241km/h)
Range: 600 miles (960km)
Number Manufactured: 5,980
Flying or in service: Many still in active service.
Preserved: Ottumwa Airpower Museum,
                        Iowa, USA.

Marchetti Avenger Gyrocopter

Subject: Marchetti Avenger displays US civil registration number N189A.
Statistics: Marchetti Avenger Gyrocopter.

Experimental category 2-seat gyrocopter which was made available to enthusiasts and amateur builders for home construction.

Country of Origin: USA
Accommodation: 2
Rotor Diameter: 28ft 6in (8.7m)
Powerplant: 1 X 150hp (112kW) Lycoming
                        0-320 piston powerplant.
Number Manufactured: Built by kitbuilders in large
                        numbers.
Flying or in service: Small numbers still in service.

Martin SP-5B Marlin

Subject: Martin SP-5B Marlin, s.n 135533 in the markings of the US Navy.
Statistics: Martin P-5M Marlin.

The Marlin submarine hunter and maritime patrol aircraft was developed to counter the perceived threat from the submarine fleet of the Soviet Union. In an environment where accurate information was not available the Americans came to the conclusion that the Soviets had a submarine fleet of up to 600 ocean-going vessels, a massive exaggeration of its actual strength and a frightening prospect for America. In this climate of fear and uncertainty the Martin Marlin was developed as one of a number of measures to counter this threat. Designed to operate over vast tracts of open water, the Marlin was packed full of sensors and detection equipment to help it locate hostile submarines beneath the ocean's surface. The Marlin also had the weaponry required to attack and destroy its prey on finding it. The type served with the US Navy and US Coast Guard from 1952 until 1967, when it was finally retired.

Country of Origin: USA
First Flight: 1948
Accommodation: 11 flight crew + specialist
                        operators.
Wingspan: 118ft 2in (36.02m)
Length: 100ft 7in (30.66m)
Height: 32ft 8in (9.97m)
Empty Weight: 50,380lb (22,900kg)
Max Take Off: 84,821lb (38,555kg)
Powerplant: 2 X 3,450hp (2,573kW) Wright
                        R-3350-32WA Turbo-Compound
                        radial powerplants.
Max Speed: 250mph (402km/h)
Service Ceiling: 24,000ft (7,315m)
Range: 2,050 miles (3,300km)
Preserved: National Museum of Naval
                        Aviation, NAS Pensacola,
                        Florida, USA.

Martin 4-0-4

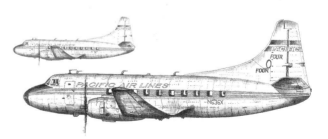

Subject: Martin 4-0-4, N636X, of Pacific Air Lines.
Statistics: Martin 4-0-4.

The Martin 4-0-4 airliner was a pressurized and stretched development of the earlier Martin 2-0-2. Glenn Martin's manufacturing plants had been absorbed in filling US military contracts for many years before he turned his attention to producing a new civilian aircraft to capture a portion of the lucrative post-war airline market. His first effort was the unpressurized Martin 2-0-2 of 1946 but, following weak sales, Martin introduced his improved and more successful 4-0-4 airliner of 1950. Purchased by both Eastern Airlines and TWA, the 4-0-4 airliner was modestly successful in the marketplace and the type went on to serve for many years, later again being sold on to smaller operators and freight carriers. One 4-0-4 airframe was converted into an executive transport and used as the personal aircraft of none other than Frank Sinatra.

Country of Origin:	USA
First Flight:	Martin 2-0-2 flown 1946. Martin 4-0-4 flown 1950.
Accommodation:	Flight crew of 3 + up to 40 passengers.
Wingspan:	93ft 3in (28.42m)
Length:	74ft 7in (22.73m)
Height:	28ft 5in (8.66m)
Empty Weight:	29,064lb (13,211kg)
Max Take Off:	44,805lb (20,366kg)
Powerplant:	2 x 2,400hp (1,790kW) Pratt & Whitney R-2800-CB16 radial engines.
Cruise Speed:	225mph (362km/h)
Max Speed:	311mph (502km/h)
Service Ceiling:	29,000ft (8,840m)
Range:	892 miles (1,738km)
Number Manufactured:	60 built for Eastern Airlines. 41 built for TWA. 2 built for the US Coast Guard.
Flying or in service:	Up to 10 still operational.
Preserved:	Mid-Atlantic Air Museum, Reading, Pennsylvania, USA.

Martin B-26 Marauder

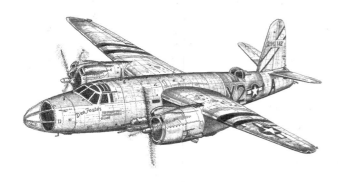

Subject: Martin B-26 Marauder.
Statistics: Martin B-26G Marauder.

Responding to a US Army specification for a high-speed bomber the Glenn L. Martin Company developed its B-26 Marauder over a period of 16 months and achieved first flight in November of 1940. By February of 1941 the type was being mass-produced and a total of 5,157 were

completed before production ceased at the end of 1944. The Marauder was a capable and potent weapon with a maximum 5,800lb (2,631kg) bomb load and five 0.50in. machine guns positioned around its airframe. Despite a rash of landing accidents in its first months of operations the Marauder went on to build a reputation as a reliable and well-fortified penetration bomber.

Country of Origin:	USA
First Flight:	1940
Accommodation:	Crew of 7.
Wingspan:	71ft 0in (21.64m)
Length:	56ft 1in (17.1m)
Height:	20ft 4in (6.2m)
Empty Weight:	25,300lb (11,477kg)
Max Take Off:	38,200lb (17,327kg)
Powerplant:	2 x 1,920hp (1,431.5kW) Pratt & Whitney R-2800-43 pistons.
Cruise Speed:	265mph (410km/h)
Max Speed:	283mph (455km/h)
Service Ceiling:	19,800ft (6,035m)
Range:	1,100 miles (1,760km)
Number Manufactured:	5,157 of all variants.
Flying or in service:	One B-26 airworthy today and several extensive refurbishments in progress.
Preserved:	USAF Museum, Dayton, Ohio, USA.

Martin Marietta X-24A

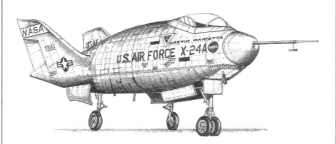

Subject: Martin Marietta X-24A prototype bearing USAF markings.
Statistics: Martin Marietta X-24A.

By the late 1960s several of the larger US aircraft design shops had been commissioned to carry out detailed research into the aerodynamics of lifting bodies, and Martin Marietta began work on its unmanned X-23 and piloted X-24 series of lifting-body prototypes. The X-23A was a small, unmanned research prototype which was built to gather basic data on lifting-body airframes. The X-24A, however, was a much more complete piloted aircraft prototype which was built to provide an insight into the complex aerodynamics of lifting-body airframes of compound shape. Powered by its internal rocket engine,

the X-24A was launched at altitude from the underside of a specially modified Boeing B-52 bomber and found to behave well in all stages of flight. Martin Marietta then went on to build the X-24B, an entirely new lifting-body shape built off the stripped down structural frame of the original X-24A. Again the type flew with distinction and much invaluable aerodynamic data was collected.

Country of Origin:	USA
First Flight:	1970
Accommodation:	1
Wingspan:	13ft 8in (4.17m)
Length:	24ft 6in (7.47m)
Height:	10ft 4in (3.15m)
Max launch:	10,700lb (4,853kg)
Powerplant:	1 x 8,000lb Thiokol XLR-11 rocket-powered engine with 2 optional 400lb (1.78kN) Bell LLRV landing rockets.
Max Speed:	1,200mph (1,931km/h) or Mach. 1.62.
Service Ceiling:	71,410ft (21,765m)
Number Manufactured:	Only 1 X-24A was built and this prototype was later stripped down and rebuilt as the X-24B.

MBB Bö-105 CBS-4

Subject: MBB Bö-105 CBS-4, registered N915SH on the US civil register.
Statistics: MBB (Eurocopter) Bö-105 LSA-3.

The MBB Bö-105 flew for the first time in 1967 and since that time more than 1,500 of all variants have been built. The Bö-105 has been manufactured, not only by MBB of Germany, but also by PT Nurtanio of Indonesia, CASA of Spain, PADC of the Philippines, and Eurocopter Canada on the North American continent. The Bo-105 has been adapted for a wide variety of specialist roles but it has always been popular as an air-ambulance on account of its clear floorplate and its rear loading doors. The MBB Bö-105 CBS-4 is a stretched variant with additional windows and an increased payload.

Country of Origin:	EU
First Flight:	1967
Accommodation:	5
Rotor Diameter:	32ft 4in (9.84m)
Length:	38ft 11in (11.86m)
Height:	9ft 10in (3.0m)
Empty Weight:	3,153lb (1,430kg)
Max Take Off:	5,733lb (2,600kg)
Powerplant:	2 x 500hp (373kW) Allison 250 turboshafts.
Cruise Speed:	140mph (225km/h)
Max Speed:	149mph (240km/h)
Range:	320 miles (512km)
Number Manufactured:	Over 1,500 of all variants built by Germany, Indonesia, Philippines, Spain and Canada.
Flying or in service:	Widely in service.

McDonnell Douglas MD-11

Subject: McDonnell Douglas MD-11 of Thai Airlines.
Statistics: McDonnell Douglas MD-11.

The MD-11 is an updated, stretched and entirely re-engined development of the long-standing DC-10 trijet airliner. With new Winglet technology, an 18ft 9inch stretch, an all-new 6-screen EFIS flight deck, and new low-burn engines, the MD-11 is a most attractive prospect for large-volume long-range operators and airlines alike. As well as its state-of-the-art flight deck the MD-11's passenger cabin has been entirely restyled to ensure that the new type cannot be confused with what went before. Other MD-11 variants which have been proposed by McDonnell Douglas include furtherstretches as well as one MD-11 with a unique underfloor panorama seating deck and greatly increased passenger capacity.

Country of Origin:	USA
First Flight:	1990
Accommodation:	Flightcrew of 2 + up to 410 economy passengers.
Wingspan:	169ft 6in (51.66m)

Length:	200ft 10in (61.21m)
Height:	57ft 9in (17.6m)
Empty Weight:	286,965lb (130,165kg)
Max Take Off:	602,555lb (273,314kg)
Powerplant:	3 x 60,000lb (266.9kN) Pratt & Whitney PW4460s or General Electric CF6 turbofans.
Cruise Speed:	544mph (876km/h)
Max Speed:	587mph (945km/h)
Range:	7,849 miles (12,632km).
Flying or in service:	In service.

McDonnell Douglas F-4 Phantom

Subject: McDonnell Douglas F-4 Phantom.
Statistics: McDonnell Douglas F-4E Phantom II.

Although it flew for the first time all of 48 years ago the mighty F-4 is still a leading contender among the superfighters of the world. The Phantom has now retired from the armed services of the US but it remains on strength with many other air forces including those of Germany, Egypt, Japan, Israel and many others. Now faced with the rising costs of purchasing new aircraft types, many F-4 operators are turning to the option of upgrading their existing F-4s and, in particular, are turning to the F-4F ICE (Improved Combat Efficiency) upgrade of the original airframe, which brings the type right back into the front line in the fighter supremacy class.

Country of Origin:	USA
First Flight:	1958
Accommodation:	2
Wingspan:	38ft 5in (11.72m)
Length:	63ft 0in (19.2m)
Height:	16ft 6in (5.03m)
Empty Weight:	31,855lb (14,447kg)
Max Take Off:	61,795lb (28,025kg)
Powerplant:	2 x 17,900lb (79.6kN) General Electric J79-GE-17A turboprops.
Max Speed:	1,485mph (2,390km/h) or Mach. 2.
Service Ceiling:	62,250ft (18,975m)
Range:	1,975 miles (3,160km)

Number Manufactured:	5,195 of all variants including Japanese-built airframes
Flying or in service:	In service with many air forces across the world.
Preserved:	Smithsonian National Air and Space Museum, Washington, DC, USA (FH1 Phantom 1). National Museum of Naval Aviation, NAS Pensacola, Florida, USA (F4N Phantom II). Norwegian Aviation Museum, Bodø, Norway (F4E).

McDonnell Douglas F-15 Eagle

Subject: McDonnell Douglas F-15E Strike Eagle, based at Coltishall, UK.
Statistics: McDonnell Douglas F-15E Eagle.

Designed to replace the F-4 Phantom, the F-15 Eagle is a potent and capable air superiority fighter. Highly manoeuvrable and bristling with sophisticated electronics, the Eagle achieves dominance in air combat through a combination of awesome power and low wing loading. Initial climb rate, for example, is an unprecedented 61,000 feet per minute. The notion of such sophisticated aircraft actually engaging in close air combat, of course, is now almost inconceivable, as air-to-air missiles are now designed to be launched at distances of up to 80 miles. The F-15E Strike Eagle fighter bomber version of the F-15 gives the type a new and powerful ground attack capability without losing any of its air-to-air capability and over 200 now serve with the US Air Force.

Country of Origin:	USA
First Flight:	1972
Accommodation:	2
Wingspan:	42ft 9in (13.03m)
Length:	63ft 9in (19.43m)
Height:	18ft 5in (5.61m)
Empty Weight:	32,000lb (14,513kg)
Max Take Off:	81,000lb (36,735kg)
Powerplant:	2 x 14,670lb (65.3kN) Pratt & Whitney F100-P-220 turbofan powerplants.

Cruise Speed: 915mph (1,473km/h)
Max Speed: 1,900mph (3,057km/h)
Service Ceiling: 60,000ft (18,288m)
Range: 2,760 miles (4,416km)
Number Manufactured: 1,500
Flying or in service: In service.
Preserved: Tyndall Museum, Tyndall AFB, Florida, USA.

McDonnell Douglas
F/A-18B Hornet

Subject: McDonnell Douglas F/A-18B Hornet of the Spanish Air Force.
Statistics: McDonnell Douglas F/A-18C Hornet.

Built for the US Navy as a carrier-based fighter bomber, the F/A-18 provides both high-level fleet protection and strike capability in one. This is a complex and extremely capable fighting aircraft which can be used in conjunction with a wide array of electronic aids and smart weapons to remove threats to the carrier group or to attack military targets with pinpoint accuracy. In addition to serving with the US Navy fleet carriers the F/A-18 is operated from land bases by Canada, Finland, Kuwait, Spain and Switzerland. The Royal Australian Air Force, too, operates an Australian assembled version of the type.

Country of Origin: USA
First Flight: 1978
Accommodation: 2
Wingspan: 37ft 6in (11.43m)
Length: 56ft 0in (17.07m)
Height: 15ft 3in (4.66m)
Empty Weight: 23,049lb (10,455kg)
Max Take Off: 49,225lb (22,328kg)
Powerplant: 2 X 16,020lb (71.2kN) General Electric F404-GE-400 turbofans with afterburners.
Max Speed: 1,190mph (1,915km/h) or Mach 1.8.
Service Ceiling: 50,000ft (15,240m)
Range: 2,070 miles (3,312km)
Number Manufactured: In excess of 1,400 of all F-18 variants.
Flying or in service: In service.
Preserved: National Museum of Naval Aviation, NAS Pensacola, Florida, USA.

McDonnell Douglas
Model 79

Subject: McDonnell Douglas Model 79 prototype ramjet helicopter.
Statistics: McDonnell Douglas Model 79.

The Model 79, 'Big Henry', was designed to investigate the possibilities of ramjet-powered helicopter flight. This was the second venture by McDonnell Douglas into the area of ramjet helicopters. Its earlier XH-20 flying prototype 'Little Henry' had behaved well in the air and had proved the basic concept. Now the Model 79 was intended to explore the remaining aerodynamic issues and, by way of trial and error, to find workable solutions. Throughout a protracted flight evaluation programme Big Henry displayed excellent flying qualities but McDonnell Douglas were unable to find any practical solution to the ear-splitting levels of noise which emanated from the 2 ramjet motors. In the end, defeat had to be accepted and the Model 79 project was abandoned.

Country of Origin: USA
First Flight: 1952
Accommodation: 1
Rotor Diameter: 27ft 0in (8.23m)
Length: 15ft 6in (4.72m)
Height: 8ft 4in (2.54m)
Empty Weight: 647lb (293kg)
Max Take Off: 1,800lb (816kg)
Powerplant: 2 X 8RJ4 ramjet powerplants.
Max Speed: 86mph (138km/h)
Service Ceiling: 10,000ft (3,050m)
Endurance: 62 minutes
Number Manufactured: 1

McDonnell Douglas
XF-85 Goblin

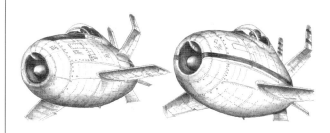

Subject: McDonnell Douglas XF-85 Goblins would work in packs to keep hostile aircraft at bay.
Statistics: McDonnell Douglas XF-85 Goblin.

The XF-85 Goblin was a miniature single-seat jet-propelled parasite fighter which was developed by McDonnell Douglas with the intention of providing an instant defensive capability to the US fleet of ultra-long-range heavy bombers. The XF-85 was a wonder of miniature engineering. Its tiny airframe housed all of the complex installations required to sustain its jet engine, its weapons systems and its vital pilot life support systems. The prototype Goblin was launched from its specially modified B-36 mothership on up to 12 occasions and it managed to return to its 'trapeze'-like hook-up point on at least half of these test flights. The test programme was a highly dangerous time for programme test pilot Ed Schoch, who had to land the craft on its underbelly whenever turbulence in the wake of the massive B-36 caused the hook-up to be missed. An extraordinary aviation concept for extraordinary times.

Country of Origin: USA
First Flight: 1948
Accommodation: 1
Wingspan: 21ft 0in (6.44m)
Length: 14ft 1in (4.30m)
Height: 11ft 0in (3.35m)
Empty Weight: 3,975lb (1,807kg)
Max Take Off: 5,580lb (2,531kg)
Powerplant: 1 X 2,995lb (13.35kN) Westinghouse turbojet engine.
Max Speed: 650mph (1,046km/h)
Service Ceiling: 48,200ft (14,691m)
Range: 350 miles (563km)
Number Manufactured: 2

McDonnell Douglas 500-D

Subject: McDonnell Douglas 500-D.
Statistics: McDonnell Douglas 500 MD. Defender II.

The Model 500 series is the commercial and foreign military counterpart of the US Army's long-standing OH-6 Cayuse. Built in large numbers and purchased by military authorities and civil operators across the globe, the Model 500 is a complex and capable helicopter platform which can be adapted to fulfil a wide variety of roles. In its civilian guise the type is used for pipeline inspection, TV-related work and turbine training. In its military guise its roles are far more specific, requiring dedicated airframe modifications and the provision of an assortment of weapons hard points, surveillance aids and communications equipment.

Country of Origin:	USA
First Flight:	First prototype flew in 1963.
Accommodation:	5
Rotor Diameter:	26ft 5in (8.05m)
Length:	21ft 5in (6.52m)
Empty Weight:	1,295lb (588kg)
Max Take Off:	3,000lb (1,362kg)
Powerplant:	1 x 420hp (313kW) Allison 250-C20B turboshaft.
Cruise Speed:	160mph (257km/h)
Max Speed:	175mph (282km/h)
Range:	263 miles (423km)
Number Manufactured:	Almost 5,000 of all variants.
Flying or in service:	Widely in service.

McDonnell Douglas MD-900

Subject: McDonnell Douglas MD-900, registration SE-JCG.
Statistics: McDonnell Douglas MD-900 Explorer.

McDonnell Douglas carried out a survey of 177 helicopter operators in order to produce a clear picture of what it was looking for in terms of mechanical specifications, flight performance and general layout. The result was the MD-900 utility helicopter and general transport. Built largely of new, lightweight composite materials, the MD-900 incorporates a range of new technologies to improve flight safety and performance while at the same time reducing operating costs. They include McDonnell Douglas's simple and effective NOTAR yaw control system, as well as an all-new flight management and instrument display system.

Country of Origin:	USA
First Flight:	1992
Accommodation:	2 pilots + 6 passengers.
Rotor Diameter:	33ft 10in (10.3m)
Length:	32ft 4in (9.85m)
Height:	12ft 0in (3.66m)
Empty Weight:	3,265lb (1,481kg)
Max Take Off:	6,740lb (3,057kg)
Powerplant:	2 x 630hp (470kW) Pratt & Whitney PW206B turboshafts.
Cruise Speed:	155mph (249km/h)
Max Speed:	167mph (269km/h)
Range:	363 miles (581km)
Flying or in service:	Widely in service.

McDonnell Douglas XV-1 Convertiplane

Subject: McDonnell Douglas XV-1 Convertiplane.
Statistics: McDonnell Douglas XV-1.

A convertiplane or a compound helicopter, the XV-1 pushed back the boundaries of VTOL flight with its confident lines and its capable performance in transitioning from vertical to horizontal flight. McDonnell Douglas's XV-1 programme began in 1949 under the watchful eye of the US Army which was immediately aware of the military applications of such a machine. Although the prototype performed admirably throughout its flight evaluation programme the US Army was of the opinion that, while the basic concept was sound, the existing range of piston powerplants could not provide the necessary power. The project was then shelved pending developments in the area of turbine engines.

Country of Origin:	USA
First Flight:	1955
Accommodation:	4 to 5.
Wingspan (fixed wing):	25ft 9in (7.9m)
Length:	29ft 6in (9.0m)
Height:	9ft 8in (3.0m)
Empty Weight:	3,626lb (1,645kg)
Max Take Off:	4,762lb (2,160kg)
Powerplant:	1 x 525hp (391kW) Continental R-975-19 7-cylinder radial.
Cruise Speed:	118mph (190km/h)
Max Speed:	200mph (322km/h)
Service Ceiling:	11,800ft (3,600m)
Number Manufactured:	2
Preserved:	Army Aviation Centre Museum, Fort Rucker, Alabama, USA. Smithsonian National Air and Space Museum, Washington, DC, USA.

Messerschmitt Bf-109

Subject: Messerschmitt Bf-109.
Statistics: Messerschmitt Bf-109G-6.

It was Willy Messerschmitt of the Bayerische Flugzeugwerke who laid down the design for the aircraft that would change aerial combat for ever. Germany's Bf-109 was a particularly powerful and successful weapon of war, especially when used in conjunction with highly mechanized and well-equipped ground forces and its contribution to the Blitzkrieg against Europe shocked complacent government leaders and civilian populations right across the world. Cinema newsreels captured tiny segments of the horror that was being unleashed in Europe. In many of these films the Bf-109 seemed to be invincible and its pilots, blooded during the Spanish civil war, applied unprecedented levels of force with stunning accuracy and effectiveness. The type went on to be built in massive numbers for the entire duration of the war years.

Country of Origin:	Germany
First Flight:	1935
Accommodation:	1
Wingspan:	32ft 6in (9.92m)
Length:	29ft 0in (8.84m)
Height:	8ft 6in (2.59m)
Max Take Off:	8,109lb (3,678kg)
Powerplant:	1 x 2,000hp (1,490kW) Daimler-Benz DB605.
Cruise Speed:	290mph (466km/h)
Max Speed:	386mph (621km/h)
Service Ceiling:	36,500ft (11,130m)
Range:	350 miles (563km)
Number Manufactured:	35,000 (estimated) of all Messerschmitt Bf-109 variants.
Flying or in service:	One Messerschmitt Bf-109E is currently active as well as 6 Spanish-built Hispano HA-1112.
Preserved:	Canada Aviation Museum, Ottawa, Ontario, Canada. Smithsonian National Air and Space Museum, Washington, DC, USA. RAF Museum, Hendon, London, UK. Valiant Air Command Museum, Titusville, Florida, USA. National Museum of the US Air Force, Wright-Patterson AFB, Dayton, Ohio, USA.

Messerschmitt Me-262

Subject: Messerschmitt Me-262.
Statistics: Messerschmitt Me-262A-1a.

The world's first turbojet-powered fighting aircraft to enter operational service, the Me-262 arrived just too late in the war to influence the course of aerial combat. Its operational debut in June of 1944 was hampered by the speed with which it was rushed into combat and by the absolute lack of tactics for dealing with opponents with lower airspeeds and greater manoeuvrability. The Me-262 was an extraordinary feat of engineering for its time and a ringing endorsement of the technical abilities of wartime Germany. The fact that it would have been available to the Luftwaffe 2 years earlier if properly supported by Hitler is also, however, a testament to the clouded political thinking of the day.

Country of Origin:	Germany
First Flight:	1942 (jet-powered).
Accommodation:	1
Wingspan:	41ft 0in (12.5m)
Length:	34ft 10in (10.61m)
Height:	12ft 7in (3.84m)
Empty Weight:	9,800lb (4,445kg)
Max Take Off:	15,531lb (7,045kg)
Powerplant:	2 x 1,984lb (8.825kN) Junkers Jumo 109-004B-1 or 109-004B-4 turbojets.
Max Speed:	539mph (868km/h)
Service Ceiling:	37,565ft (11,450m)
Range:	652 miles (1,050km)
Preserved:	RAF Museum, Hendon, London, UK (Me-262A-2a). National Museum of the US Air Force, Wright-Patterson AFB, Dayton, Ohio, USA.

Meyer P-51 Scaled Replica

Subject: Meyer P-51 (Plans-built scaled replica).
Statistics: Meyer P-51 (Plans-built scaled replica).

The Meyer P-51 is a plans-built scale replica of the mighty North American P-51 warbird. Designed for construction by amateur home-builders, the Meyer presents a superb likeness of the original Mustang with just a tiny taste of its flying prowess. A beautifully turned-out sportsplane and a most interesting and worthwhile project for amateur construction.

Country of Origin:	USA
Accommodation:	1

Meyers M-200C

Subject: Meyers M-200C N108M, flew into Lakeland Linder Regional Airport, Florida, 2005.
Statistics: Meyers M-200C.

Fifty-two years after its first flight Alan H. Meyers' enthusiastic followers are still quick to claim the M-200 as the fastest normally aspirated aircraft in the world. Indeed, the Meyers M-200A did hold the group speed record over a 3km closed circuit for almost 18 years with a 227.24mph average, a superb return from a non-turbocharged, non-supercharged, engine. The real merit behind the Meyers M-200, however, lies in its stunning build quality. There is simply no other aircraft which is as well built or as beautifully detailed as the Meyers. Pilots and owners do not talk about 'owning' a Meyers but rather 'taking care of a Meyers'. In 53 years the airframe has not had one FAA-mandated Airworthiness Directive issued against it, another aviation first.

Country of Origin:	USA
First Flight:	1953
Accommodation:	4
Wingspan:	24ft 4in (7.42m)
Length:	30ft 6in (9.3m)
Height:	7ft 4in (2.24m)
Empty Weight:	1,940lb (822kg)
Max Take Off:	3,330lb (1,500kg)
Powerplant:	300hp (220kW) Continental IO-550 piston powerplant.
Service Ceiling:	18,500ft (5,600m)
Range:	1,200 miles (1,930km)
Number Manufactured:	Estimated as 33 Meyers M-200 variants with a further 83 built by Rockwell as the Aero Commander 200D.
Flying or in service:	Up to 102 Meyers M-200s still registered in the US today.

Mignet
Flying Flea

Subject: Mignet Flying Flea G-AEBB, of the Shuttleworth
          Collection, was originally powered by a 1,300cc
          Henderson motorcycle engine but later fitted
          with a 25hp Scott Squirrel powerplant.
Statistics: Mignet Flying Flea HM-14.

Henri Mignet's tiny Pou-du-Ciel became an instant media
sensation when it was introduced for the first time in
1935. For the first time ever an aircraft could be built
by the average man for less than 140 pounds sterling.
No special tools were needed and only a rudimentary
knowledge of basic joinery techniques was expected. Within
a month of its unveiling, Mignet had sold over 6,000 sets
of plans in Britain alone. A fever of Flying Flea
construction followed and many airframes did reach
completion. The Flea was not without in-built control
problems, however, and within months a series of tragic air
accidents had tarnished its name for ever. The Mark II Flea
is a modified variant of the original Flying Flea of 1933.

Country of Origin: France
First Flight: 1933
Accommodation: 1
Wingspan: 18ft 8in (6.00m)
Length: 16ft 9in (5.1m)
Height: 5ft 1in (1.6m)
Empty Weight: 315lb (143kg)
Max Take Off: 243lb (535kg)
Powerplant: 1 X 35hp (26kW) Bristol.
Max Speed: 81mph (130km/h)
Range: 281 miles (450km)
Number Manufactured: Very large numbers of plans
                        sold across the world but
                        there is little information on
                        the number of Fleas that
                        made it to completion.
Preserved: G-AEBB preserved by the
                        Shuttleworth Trust, Old Warden.
                        Mignet HM Pou-du-Ciel 'La
                        Cucaracha', Steven F. Udvar-
                        Hazy Center, Chantilly, Virginia,
                        USA.
                        RAF Museum, Hendon, London, UK.
                        Newark Air Museum,
                        Nottingham, Nottinghamshire, UK.

Mil
Mi-2S Hoplite

Subject: Mi-2s air-ambulance of the former East German
          air force.
Statistics: Mil (PZL) Mi-2 Hoplite.

The Mi-2 Hoplite was designed and developed to prototype
stage by the Soviet Mil design bureau. Then, following its
flight evaluation programme, all further Mi-2 development,
production and marketing was gifted exclusively to the
Polish aviation industry. It was a prestigious, if politically
motivated, gesture to decentralization but it did provide
years of employment to Poland's skilled aviation workers,
who turned out more than 5,080 of the type.

Country of Origin: USSR/Poland.
First Flight: 1961
Accommodation: 2 pilots + 7 passengers
Rotor Span: 47ft 7in (14.5m)
Length: 37ft 5in (11.4m)
Height: 12ft 3in (3.73m)
Empty Weight: 5,183lb (2,351kg)
Max Take Off: 8,160lb (3,701kg)
Powerplant: 2 X 437hp (325.8kW) Isotov
                        GTD-350 turboshafts.
Cruise Speed: 124mph (200km/h)
Max Speed: 132mph (213km/h)
Service Ceiling: 13,125ft (4,000m)
Range: 360 miles (576km)
Number Manufactured: In excess of 5,080 of all
                        Mi-2 variants.
Flying or in service: Small numbers still airworthy.
Preserved: Russian Central Air Force
                        Museum, Monino, Moscow.

Mil
Mi-4 Hound

Subject: Mi-4 of Soviet carrier Aeroflot, airframe no
          CCCP-03586.
Statistics: Mil Mi-4 Hound.

When the Mi-4 Hound appeared for the first time in the
early 1950s its rotor blades were comprised of wood and
bakelite. The technology gap between the Soviet Union and
the West was closing but the Soviet Union had some way to
go in the area of helicopter design. The resemblance of the
Mi-4 to the American Sikorsky S-55 of 1949 is most likely
to be less than a coincidence unless, of course, that the
very best solutions to any difficult problem will tend to
throw up the same solution.

Country of Origin: USSR
First Flight: 1952
Accommodation: 2 + 14 fully equipped troops
                        or 3,800lb (1,723kg) of
                        freight.
Rotor Diameter: 68ft 10in (20.96m)
Length (with rotors):   82ft 1in (25.0m)
Height: 14ft 5in (4.4m)
Empty Weight: 14,608lb (6,626kg)
Max Take Off: 16,600lb (7,529.6kg)
Powerplant: 1 X 1,700hp (1,268kW)
                        Shvetsov ASh-82V radial piston.
Cruise Speed: 115mph (185km/h)
Max Speed: 124mph (200km/h)
Service Ceiling: 18,000ft (5,486m)
Range: 370 miles (590km)
Number Manufactured: Over 3,000 built in the Soviet
                        Union and a further 545 built
                        by Harbin in China.
Flying or in service: Small numbers of later Harbin
                        types still in service.
Preserved: Luftwaffenmuseum Flugplatz,
                        Germany.
                        The Helicopter Museum, Weston-
                        Super-Mare, Somerset, UK.
                        Russian Central Air Force
                        Museum, Monino, Moscow.

Mil
Mi-8 Hip

Subject: Mil Mi-8 Hip wearing United Nations colours.
Statistics: Mil Mi-8T Hip.

Design of the Mi-8 began in 1960 with the development of a large-diameter fuselage of circular cross section. All of the necessary fuel tanks and powerplants were located outside and above the fuselage shell with the intention of ensuring that the fuselage would be entirely clear and free of internal obstructions. A large pair of clamshell doors at the rear of the helicopter ensured maximum access to the large interior and facilitated the rapid deployment of assault troops. The Mi-17 of 1976 was a development of the type with uprated powerplants, increased payload and, in some cases, a large rear loading ramp in lieu of the clamshell doors.

Country of Origin:	USSR
First Flight:	1961
Accommodation:	2 + 28 fully equipped troops or equivalent weaponry or freight.
Rotor Diameter:	69ft 10in (21.3m)
Length:	82ft 9in (25.22m)
Height:	18ft 6in (5.64m)
Empty Weight:	15,750lb (7,144kg)
Max Take Off:	26,400lb (12,000kg)
Powerplant:	2 X 1,480hp (1,104kW) klimov (Isotov) TV-2-117A turboshafts.
Cruise Speed:	140mph (225km/h)
Max Speed:	155mph (250km/h)
Service Ceiling:	14,750ft (4,495m)
Range:	575 miles (930km)
Number Manufactured:	Over 10,000 of all variants of the Mi-8 and Mi-17 have been constructed.
Flying or in service:	Widely in service.
Preserved:	Luftwaffenmuseum Flugplatz, Germany. Russian Central Air Force Museum, Monino, Moscow.

Mil Mi-9

Subject: East German Mi-9 specialist mobile control centre of HFSA-3 based at Basepohl.
Statistics: Mil Mi-9.

Similar in configuration and specification to the Mi-8, the Mi-9 was used as a mobile command centre complete with specialist communications equipment, and additional radio antennas. This East German air force example was flown by the Armeefliegerkrafte HSFA-3 based at Cottbus and Basepohl.

Country of Origin:	USSR
First Flight:	1961
Accommodation:	2 + 28 to 40 fully equipped troops or equivalent freight.
Rotor Diameter:	69ft 10in (21.3m)
Length:	82ft 9in (25.22m)
Height:	18ft 6in (5.64m)
Empty Weight:	15,750lb (7,144kg)
Max Take Off:	26,400lb (12,000kg)
Powerplant:	2 X 1,480hp (1,104kW) klimov (Isotov) TV-2-117A turboshafts.
Cruise Speed:	140mph (225km/h)
Max Speed:	155mph (250km/h)
Service Ceiling:	14,750ft (4,495m)
Range:	575 miles (930km)
Flying or in service:	In service.

Mil
Mi-14 Haze

Subject: Mi-14BT Search-and-Rescue ship of former East Germany.
Statistics: Mil Mi-14PL Haze.

Developed from the earlier Mil Mi-8, the Mi-14 Haze is a specialist maritime patrol variant which has been designed around the needs of shipboard anti-submarine operations. Its fuselage has been enlarged and fitted with a full boat hull to facilitate water landings and to provide a measure of safety for long-duration flights over water. The Mi-14PS is a Search-and-Rescue variant with an enlarged door and an electronic winch system. The Mi-14BT minesweeper is a specialized mine-clearing variant which tows a large water-skimming sled which uses sound and electrical pulses to activate mines. The Mi-PL anti-submarine patrol variant is the most prolific of the type and is fitted with a towed magnetic-anomaly detector and multiple sonobuoy dispensers.

Country of Origin:	USSR
First Flight:	1974
Accommodation:	Flightcrew of 3 + 26 fully laden troops.
Rotor Diameter:	69ft 10in (21.29m)
Length:	60ft 3in (18.37m)
Height:	31ft 7in (9.63m)
Empty Weight:	19,584lb (8,902kg)
Max Take Off:	30,800lb (14,000kg)
Powerplant:	2 X 1,925hp (1,434kW) (klimov Isotov) TV3-117MT turbofans.
Cruise Speed:	130mph (209km/h)
Max Speed:	143mph (230km/h)
Range:	704 miles (1,135km)
Number Manufactured:	273 built by the time production ceased in 1986.
Flying or in service:	In service.

Mil
Mi-24-P

Subject: Again from East Germany, the Mi-24P heavy assault gunship.
Statistics: Mil Mi-24V.

The Mi-24 is a powerful and capable assault helicopter which is designed to suppress hostile forces en route to its drop zone, where it can deposit up to 8 fully laden combat troops. Working in groups, the Mi-24 can deposit clusters of ground forces into any location with extraordinary effectiveness and speed. The type is essentially a flying armoured personnel carrier which is further armed with one 12.7mm rapid-firing machine gun as well as four AT-2

Swatter anti-tank missiles. As well as serving with the Soviet Forces, the Mi-24 has been exported to Afghanistan, Algeria, Libya and Vietnam.

Country of Origin:	USSR
First Flight:	1970
Accommodation:	Pilot, gunner + up to 8 fully laden troops.
Rotor Diameter:	56ft 9in (17.3m)
Length:	57ft 5in (17.5m)
Height:	17ft 11in (5.64m)
Empty Weight:	18,480lb (8,400kg)
Max Take Off:	27,500lb (12,500kg)
Powerplant:	2 x 2,225hp (1,659kW) klimov (Isotov) TV3-117VMA turboshafts.
Cruise Speed:	175mph (281km/h)
Max Speed:	210mph (338km/h)
Service Ceiling:	14,765ft (4,500m)
Range:	700miles (1,120km)
Number Manufactured:	2,500 completed and still in production.
Flying or in service:	In service with many countries.
Preserved:	The Helicopter Museum, Weston-Super-Mare, Somerset, UK. Russian Central Air Force Museum, Monino, Moscow.

Mikoyan-Gurevich MiG-3

Subject: MiG-3.
Statistics: MiG-3.

The Mikoyan-Gurevich MiG-3 was designed as a single-seat high-altitude fighter and following a first flight in April of 1940 the type was operational by the time the Germans invaded the Soviet Union. Flying first as the MiG-1, the new fighter was quickly developed to MiG-3 status with a more powerful engine, increased range and an enclosed cockpit. The first encounters between the MiG-3 and the Luftwaffe's Bf-109s took place in early 1942 and Germany's intelligence services were sharply criticized for providing no advance warning of this superb high-altitude performer.

Country of Origin:	USSR
First Flight:	1940 (MiG-1).
Accommodation:	1
Wingspan:	33ft 9in (10.3m)
Length:	26ft 9in (8.15m)
Height:	8ft 8in (2.64m)
Empty Weight:	5,950lb (2,699kg)
Max Take Off:	7,385lb (3,350kg)
Powerplant:	1 x 1,350hp Mikulin AM-35A liquid-cooled V12.
Cruise Speed:	314mph (505km/h)
Max Speed:	398mph (640km/h)
Service Ceiling:	39,370ft (12,000m)
Range:	777 miles (1,250km)
Number Manufactured:	2,100 of all MiG-1 and MiG-3 Variants completed.
Preserved:	Full scale replica Russian Central Air Force Museum, Monino, Moscow.

Mikoyan-Gurevich MiG-15 Fagot

Subject: Mikoyan-Gurevich MiG-15 UTI of the Russian air force.
Statistics: Mikoyan-Gurevich MiG-15UTI 2-seat 'Midget' trainer.

In the last months of the war, operational jet fighters began to appear for the first time in the skies of Europe and the Soviet Union were most keen to develop their own indigenous jet-fighter programme. Their first efforts were built with mixed success around the technologies of captured German powerplants but it was the introduction of the Rolls-Royce Nene engine of 1946 that transformed the Soviet Union's jet programme forever. Within months the Nene engine was being produced in the Soviet Union as the klimov RD45 and the combination of this powerplant and the MiG-15 airframe proved to be a formidable and inspired match.

Country of Origin:	USSR
First Flight:	1947
Accommodation:	1
Wingspan:	33ft 4in (10.16m)
Length:	33ft 2in (10.11m)

Height:	12ft 4in (3.76m)
Empty Weight:	8,262lb (3,747kg)
Max Take Off:	11,900lb (5,397kg)
Powerplant:	1 x 5,950lb (26.47kN) klimov RD-45FA turbojet.
Cruise Speed:	550mph (885km/h)
Max Speed:	630mph (1,014km/h)
Service Ceiling:	39,370ft (12,000ft)
Range:	650 miles (1,040km)
Number Manufactured:	12,000 of all Variants and all production lines completed.
Flying or in service:	Small numbers now operated by private enthusiasts.
Preserved:	RAF Museum, London (MiG 15bis). Steven F. Udvar-Hazy Center, Chantilly, Virginia, USA (MiG 15bis FAgot B). Szolnok Museum, Hungary. Belgium Air Force Hall, Brussels. Fantasy of Flight Museum, Polk City, Florida, USA.

Mikoyan-Gurevich MiG-21 M Fishbed

Subject: Mikoyan-Gurevich MiG-21 Fishbed of the Vietnamese air force is displayed at the Hanoi Museum.
Statistics: Mikoyan-Gurevich MiG-21MF Fishbed.

The MiG-21 air superiority fighter was designed to take advantage of the extraordinary developments which were taking place in the area of turbojet technology and airframe design. In the short few years since the launch of the MiG-15, cruise speeds had almost doubled and had passed the 1,000mph mark. The MiG-21 became one of the most widely used of all jet fighters, serving for many years with the Soviet Union, China, Czechoslovakia, India, Romania and many other countries that fell within the Soviet Union's sphere of influence.

Country of Origin:	USSR
First Flight:	1955 (E-2 prototype).
Accommodation:	1 or 2
Wingspan:	23ft 5in (7.14m)
Length:	40ft 4in (12.29m)

Height:	14ft 9in (4.5m)
Empty Weight:	12,895lb (5,850kg)
Max Take Off:	21,605lb (9.800kg)
Powerplant:	1 x 9,350lb (41.59KN) Tumansky turbojet.
Cruise Speed:	1,200mph (1,931km/h)
Max Speed:	1,355mph (2,180km/h) or Mach 1.83
Service Ceiling:	50,030ft (15,250m)
Range:	1,100 miles (1,770km)
Number Manufactured:	10,900 MiG-21s built as well as 2,500 of the Chinese-built Chengdu J-7/F-7 Version.
Preserved:	Steven F. Udvar-Hazy Center, Chantilly, Virginia, USA (MiG 21-F). Indian Air Force Museum, Palam Air Station (MiG 21M). Belgian Air Force Hall, Brussels.

Mikoyan-Gurevich MiG-25 Foxbat

Subject: Mikoyan-Gurevich MiG-25 Foxbat of the Russian air force.
Statistics: Mikoyan-Gurevich MiG-25RB.

The Soviets were absolutely incensed that they could do nothing to stop the routine reconnaissance overflights by the USA and so they began the development of a series of diverse projects to ensure that such high-flying aircraft could never again operate with impunity above their territories. The MiG-25 Foxbat was the first of a new generation of ultra-high-altitude intercept fighters. With a top speed in excess of Mach 2.5, a service ceiling of almost 70,000ft and the latest AA-6 missiles, the MiG-25 was a formidable defensive weapon.

Country of Origin:	USSR
First Flight:	1964
Accommodation:	1
Wingspan:	43ft 11in (13.39m)
Length:	70ft 9in (21.56m)
Height:	19ft 9in (6.02m)
Empty Weight:	74,970lb (34,000kg)
Max Take Off:	145,530lb (66,000kg)
Powerplant:	2 x 24,690lb (109.8KN) Tumanski R-15BD-300 turbo fans.

Max Speed:	1,864mph (3,000km/h) or Mach 2.51.
Service Ceiling:	68,900ft (21,000m).
Range:	1,300 miles (2,092km).
Number Manufactured:	1,200 of all MiG-25 Variants.
Preserved:	Russian Central Air Force Museum, Monino, Moscow. Khodynskoe Pole, Central Airfield, Moscow, Russia.

Mikoyan-Gurevich MiG-29 Fulcrum

Subject: Mikoyan-Gurevich MiG-29 Fulcrum of the German Air Force.
Statistics: Mikoyan-Gurevich MiG-29S Fulcrum.

The Soviet Mikoyan-Gurevich bureau's MiG-29 is a superbly manoeuvrable and capable air defence fighter which was developed to counter the threat posed by the American F-16 and other contemporary high-technology fighters. The type provides the very highest levels of power, agility and weapons technology at costs which are far below those of Western fighting aircraft, and this approach alone has won for the MiG-29 a wide following. The MiG-29 Fulcrum is, however, no cheap second-rate fighter. It is perhaps the most potent and versatile fighter in the world today. The type is operated by the Soviet Union, Bulgaria, Iran, Czech Republic, Germany, Cuba, India, Poland and North Korea.

Country of Origin:	Russia
First Flight:	1977
Accommodation:	1 or 2
Wingspan:	37ft 3in (11.35m)
Length:	53ft 5in (16.28m)
Height:	15ft 6in (4.72m)
Empty Weight:	24,536lb (11,134kg)
Max Take Off:	43,940lb (19,934kg)
Powerplant:	2 x 18,300lb (81.4KN) Klimov RD-33 turbofans.
Max Speed:	930mph (1,497km/h)
Service Ceiling:	60,000ft (18,288m)
Range:	1,300 miles (2,080km)
Number Manufactured:	Production estimated at 1,500.
Flying or in service:	In service.
Preserved:	Prototype Russian Central Air Force Museum, Monino, Moscow. Khodynskoe Pole, Central Airfield, Moscow, Russia.

Miles M-57 Aerovan 1

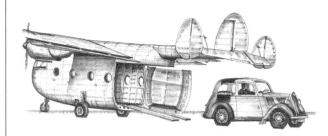

Subject: Miles M-57 Aerovan.
Statistics: Miles M-57 Aerovan.

The Aerovan flew for the first time in January of 1945 and its introduction to service marked the standard for a whole new generation of efficient and functional civilian freight carriers. Simple and pragmatic, the Aerovan's high tail and large rear access door facilitated the loading of small vehicles or equivalent freight. Its 12ft 3in (3.73m) freight cabin was just large enough to accommodate a small car, and its 2 155hp (115.5kW) engines were just powerful enough to lift it. With its introduction to service in late 1945 the Aerovan presented a range of new possibilities to many of Britain's islands and more remote communities who could, for the first time, airlift freight and other outsize loads at an affordable level of cost.

Country of Origin:	UK
First Flight:	1945
Accommodation:	1 pilot + 6 to 9 passengers or 1 small automobile or equivalent freight payload.
Wingspan:	50ft 0in (15.24m)
Length:	36ft 0in (10.97m)
Height:	13ft 5in (4.1m)
Empty Weight:	3000lb (1,361kg)
Max Take Off:	5,800lb (2,631kg)
Powerplant:	2 x 155hp (115.5kW) Blackburn Cirrus Major pistons.
Cruise Speed:	109mph (175km/h)
Max Speed:	127mph (204km/h)
Range:	400 miles (644km)
Number Manufactured:	48 completed before Miles closed its doors for ever.
Flying or in service:	Last known working M-57 was a Mark VI Aerovan operating out of Italy in 1968.
Preserved:	Section of fuselage at Museum of Berkshire Aviation, UK.

Miles M-65 Gemini

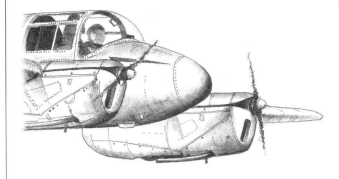

Subject: Miles M-65 Gemini.
Statistics: Miles M-65 Gemini.

The M-65 Gemini was a twin-engine development of Miles's successful M-38 Messenger of 1942. Its fuselage, wings and tail empennage were generally adapted from the Messenger and the new type was provided with retractable landing-gear which folded neatly into the undersides of the wing-mounted engine cowlings. Given that it was powered by just 100hp per engine the Gemini's 146mph top speed was quite respectable. Only 149 were completed, however, before Miles Aircraft Ltd collapsed in 1947.

Country of Origin: UK.
First Flight: 1945
Accommodation: 2 + Cabin Crew
Wingspan: 36ft 1in (11.00m)
Length: 22ft 2in (6.75m)
Height: 7ft 6in (2.29m)
Empty Weight: 1,930lb (876kg)
Max Take Off: 3,000lb (1,361kg)
Powerplant: 2 x 100hp (74.57kW) Blackburn Cirrus Minor II piston engines.
Cruise Speed: 131mph (211km/h)
Max Speed: 146mph (235km/h)
Range: 1,000 miles (1,609km)
Number Manufactured: 149 completed by 1947 when Miles ceased trading.
Flying or in service: Small numbers still airworthy.
Preserved: Airworthy: Belgium, Bristol Plane Preservation Unit, UK. Museum of Transport & Technology Auckland, New Zealand. Miles Aircraft Collection, Woodley, UK.

Miles M-25 Martinet

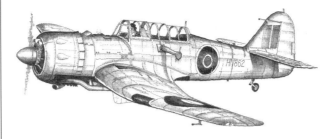

Subject: Miles M-25 Martinet.
Statistics: Miles M-25 Martinet.

The Martinet was designed from scratch as a target tug, perhaps the first ever tug to be designed from the outset rather than simply adapted. Based on the earlier Miles Master, the M-25 is distinctive for its large, cowled radial powerplant and its unusual side-mounted winch assembly. The Martinet is designed to trail a variety of drogues and flags for use as aerial targets. The prototype flew for the first time in April of 1942 and up to 1,790 were completed for use in preparing Allied combat pilots and gunners. Miles went on to produce a radio-controlled variant, the M-50 Queen Martinet, for similar target-training duties and 65 of this type were completed.

Country of Origin: UK.
First Flight: 1942
Accommodation: 1 or 2 (without winch)
Wingspan: 39ft 1in (11.89m)
Length: 30ft 11in (9.42m)
Height: 11ft 6in (3.53m)
Empty Weight: 4,640lb (2,105kg)
Max Take Off: 6,750lb (3,062kg)
Powerplant: 1 x Bristol Mercury XXX radial.
Max Speed: 240mph (386km/h)
Range: 695 miles (1,120km)
Number Manufactured: More than 1,790 of the M-25 Martinet were completed. A further 65 Queen Martinets were built.
Preserved: Museum of Berkshire Aviation, UK.

Miles M9-A Master

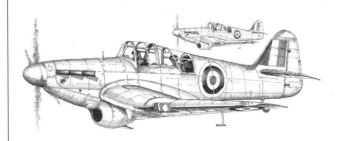

Subject: Miles M9-A Master.
Statistics: Miles M9-A Master Mk 1.

The Master Mk 1 was first demonstrated at the Hendon Air Show in July of 1937 but it was only in June of 1939, 3 months before Hitler's invasion of Poland, that the Air Ministry placed an order for the type. The Master was to be used as an advanced training airframe and, for that purpose, a lower airspeed was required. To this end the order, as placed, called for the installation of a derated 715hp Kestrel engine which gave a substantial reduction in airspeed and overall performance. Despite these changes the Master was an ideal training aircraft for pilots who would shortly graduate to Hurricanes and Spitfires.

Country of Origin: UK..
First Flight: First flown in 1937 but series production not flown until 1939.
Accommodation: Instructor + Student
Wingspan: 39ft 0in (11.89m). Later, generally clipped to 35ft 9ins (10.89m) to increase airspeed.
Length: 30ft 5in (9.29m)
Empty Weight: 4,370lb (1,982kg)
Max Take Off: 5,573lb (2,528kg)
Powerplant: 1 x 715hp Rolls Royce Kestrel XXX piston engine (Mk 1).
Cruise Speed: 160mph (257km/h)
Max Speed: 226mph (363km/h)
Range: 393 miles (632km)
Number Manufactured: 900 Master Mk 1 completed. 1,748 Master Mk 2 completed. 602 Master Mk 3 completed.
Preserved: None surviving. Replica Newark Air Museum, UK.

Miles M-17 Monarch

Subject: Miles M-17 Monarch, registered G-AFLW on the UK civil register.
Statistics: Miles M-17 Monarch.

Whitney Straight was a wealthy aviation enthusiast whose encouragement and financial support led Miles to produce 50 examples of a club training aircraft which would become known as the Miles M-11 Whitney Straight. The type was superbly received but by 1938 Miles had improved it even further and, in this form, it became known as the Miles M-17 Monarch. A most graceful and beautifully proportioned taildragger, the Monarch was luxuriously detailed, both inside and out. Despite its huge appeal only 11 of the type were completed because Miles was heavily involved in the production of wartime aircraft for the Air Ministry.

Country of Origin:	UK
First Flight:	1938
Accommodation:	3
Wingspan:	35ft 7in (10.84m)
Length:	26ft 0in (7.92m)
Height:	8ft 9in (2.67m)
Empty Weight:	1,389lb (630kg)
Max Take Off:	2,150lb (975kg)
Powerplant:	1 x 130hp (97kW) de Havilland Gipsy Major piston engine.
Cruise Speed:	125mph (201km/h)
Max Speed:	139mph (224km/h)
Service Ceiling:	17,400ft (5,303m)
Range:	620 miles (998km)
Number Manufactured:	Only 11 manufactured.
Preserved:	Museum of Flight, East Fortune, Scotland.

Miles M-2L Speed Hawk Six

Subject: Miles M-2 Speed Hawk Six.
Statistics: Miles M-2E Speed Hawk Six.

The Miles Speed Hawk Six was a single-seat racing version of the Hawk Major. Built by Phillips & Powis Aircraft Ltd of Woodley, Reading, forerunner to Miles Aircraft, the Speed Hawk Six was a low-wing monoplane of all-spruce construction with plywood and fabric covering. Although reputed to be quite a handful in the air, the Speed Hawk Six won many of the great air races of its day.

Country of Origin:	UK
First Flight:	1934
Accommodation:	1
Wingspan:	33ft 0in (10.06m)
Length:	24ft 0in (7.32m)
Height:	6ft 8in (2.04m)
Empty Weight:	1,355lb (614.6kg)
Max Take Off:	1,900lb (861.8kg)
Powerplant:	1 x 200hp (149kW) de Havilland Gipsy 6 piston.
Max Speed:	195mph (313.8km/h)
Flying or in service:	At least one airworthy M-2 Speed Hawk Six today.
Preserved:	160 G-ADGP Airworthy: Fairoaks, UK.

Miles & Atwood Special

Subject: Miles & Atwood Special Miss Tulsa.
Statistics: Miles & Atwood Special.

Leland Miles and Leon Atwood designed and financed the Miles & Atwood racing monoplane of 1933. The actual building, however, was undertaken by one Larry Brown of Los Angeles. The Miles & Atwood Special was a capable pedigree racing aircraft which achieved excellent speeds with its humble 150hp (111.85kW) Menasco powerplant. Its two designers entered it in many of the great air races of its day and won many accolades for sheer gusto on such a small engine. Leland Miles was killed in 1937 when one of the Special's wing-cable fittings snapped and the aircraft plunged to earth.

Country of Origin:	USA
First Flight:	1933
Accommodation:	1
Wingspan:	16ft 8in (5.09m)
Length:	16ft 9in (5.11m)
Powerplant:	1 x 150hp (111.85kW) Menasco C piston powerplant.
Max Speed:	189.5mph (305km/h)
Number Manufactured:	1
Preserved:	Owls Head Transportation Museum, Maine, USA.

Minimaster

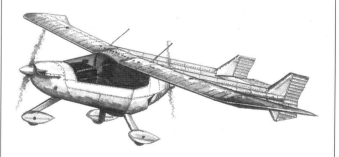

Subject: Minimaster Prototype.
Statistics: Minimaster.

Powers-Bashforth Aircraft Corp. was formed to develop and market the Minimaster, an ultralight version of the well-known twin-engined Cessna Skymaster. As principal designer for the type Bruce Bashforth was responsible for the aircraft's configuration with its 2 Rotax push/pull engines. Like the Skymaster, the Minimaster was designed with its two engines on the airframe centreline, thus ensuring that, if one engine was lost, asymmetric flight would not cause controllability problems. Although the prototype was successfully flown, Powers and Bashforth were unable to raise the large amounts of funding required to bring the Minimaster to production.

Country of Origin:	USA
First Flight:	1989
Accommodation:	2

Wingspan: 33ft 2in (10.05m)
Length: 23ft 9in (7.02m)
Powerplant: 2 X Rotax 532
piston powerplants.
Number Manufactured: 1 prototype only.

Mooney Ranger (M-20J) 201 series

Subject: Mooney Ranger 201 sporting the US N
number N201M.
Statistics: Mooney Ranger M-20R Ovation.

It was veteran aircraft designer Al Mooney who laid down the design for the M-20 utility transport monoplane series. With its distinctive forward-swept tail and its clean lines the type stands out in any gathering of light aircraft. Performance figures are impressive throughout the range but especially in the more recent models, where an array of aerodynamic improvements and an uprated powerplant give the type a cruise speed of over 200mph and a range of 1,300 miles. The Mooney M-20 series has been built in a wide range of variants over the years from the basic utility and training models through to complex stretched and turbocharged versions of the type.

Country of Origin: USA .
First Flight: 1953
Accommodation: 4
Wingspan: 36ft 1in (11.0m)
Length: 26ft 9in (8.15m)
Height: 8ft 5in (2.57m)
Empty Weight: 2,223lb (1,008kg)
Max Take Off: 3,368lb (1,527kg)
Powerplant: 1 X 280hp (208.7kW)
Continental IO-550G piston.
Cruise Speed: 191mph (307km/h)
Max Speed: 215mph (345km/h)
Service Ceiling: 19,500ft (5,943m)
Range: 1,300 miles (2,082km)
Number Manufactured: 10,000 of all M-20 series built by the beginning of year 2,000.
Flying or in service: Widely in service.

Morane-Saulnier MS-230

Subject: Morane-Saulnier MS-230, registered G-AVEB on the UK civil register.
Statistics: Morane-Saulnier MS-230.

The Morane-Saulnier MS-230 was designed to meet a French air ministry specification for an observation, gunnery and training aircraft. The prototype flew for the first time in February of 1929 and the type proved itself well in a long evaluation programme leading to large order books and eventually to production of more than 1,000 of the type. The MS-230 was an excellent performer with good handling and aerobatic qualities and it remained in service as an advanced military trainer for many years. Approximately 12 examples of the type remain airworthy and in civilian ownership to this day.

Country of Origin: France
First Flight: Prototype flew in 1929.
Accommodation: 2
Wingspan: 35ft 1in (10.7m)
Length: 22ft 11in (6.7m)
Height: 8ft 6in (2.59m)
Empty Weight: 1,828lb (829kg)
Max Take Off: 2,535lb (1,150kg)
Powerplant: 1 X 230hp (171.4kW) Salmson 9Ab radial powerplant.
Max Speed: 127mph (205km/h)
Service Ceiling: 16,400ft (5,000m)
Range: 500 miles (800km)
Number Manufactured: 1,080 of all MS-230 variants.
Flying or in service: Approximately 12 in airworthy condition to this day.
Preserved: Yanks Air Museum, Chino Airport, California, USA.

Morane-Saulnier D-3801

Subject: Morane D-3801.
Statistics: Morane-Saulnier MS-406 C1.

As the political clouds gathered over Europe it was becoming clear that Germany's ambitions were such that war in Europe was at least likely if not inevitable. Despite a policy of appeasement on all sides Germany was clearly building a massive military machine and its immediate neighbours began to become increasingly alarmed. All too late, France began to build up its air strength by purchasing new fighters from Britain and the US and by mass-producing whatever indigenous aircraft it could muster. The Morane-Saulnier was one such project and more than 1,000 were produced despite the fact that it was greatly outpaced and outgunned by the German Messerschmitt Bf-109 fighters. Switzerland built a number of D-3801 fighters, a development of the MS-406, with larger powerplant, enhanced instrumentation and more efficient propeller. The D-3801 continued to serve with Switzerland's defence forces right up until 1959.

Country of Origin: France
First Flight: MS-405 first flew in 1935. MS-406 first flew in 1939.
Accommodation: 1
Wingspan: 34ft 10in (10.62m)
Length: 26ft 10in (8.18m)
Height: 10ft 10in (3.3m)
Empty Weight: 4,682lb (2,124kg)
Max Take Off: 5,996lb (2,719kg)
Powerplant: 1 X 1,050hp (783kW) Hispano-Suiza 12Y51.
Max Speed: 303mph (488km/h)
Range: 497 miles (800km)
Number Manufactured: 15 MS-405s completed as well as 1,080 MS-406s by 1940 when France fell to the Germans.
Flying or in service: At least one flying to this day.
Preserved: Flieger-Flab Museum, Dubendorf, Switzerland.

Murphy Rebel

Subject: Murphy Rebel. Canadian registered C-FMUQ.
Statistics: Murphy Rebel.

Darryl Murphy founded Murphy Aircraft Manufacturing of British Columbia and went on to produce a series of popular and successful kitbuild aircraft for amateur homebuilders. The Rebel was a two-seat sport plane which was, and still is, available to builders in kit form. The entire kit could be purchased in one go or the cost of the project could be staged over time by purchasing mini-kits for individual sub-elements of the aircraft, such as the tail, the undercarriage or the fuselage. As with all homebuild aircraft projects, only a portion of the kits which are purchased ever make it to completion and first flight and despite the fact that the Rebel kit was sold in large numbers, only 250 of the type have flown to date. Once flown, however, the Rebel becomes a superb lifestyle aircraft which can be flown on tundra wheels, standard wheels, floats or even skis.

Country of Origin:	Canada
First Flight:	1990
Accommodation:	2 + 1
Wingspan:	30ft 1in (9.17m)
Length:	21ft 4in (6.5m)
Height:	6ft 8in (2.03m)
Empty Weight:	825lb (374kg)
Max Take Off:	1,650 0lb (748kg)
Powerplant:	1 X 116hp (86.5kW) Lycoming O-235 piston engine.
Cruise Speed:	110mph (177km/h)
Max Speed:	124mph (200km/h)
Service Ceiling:	15,000ft (4,572m)
Range:	800 miles (1,287km)
Number Manufactured:	Approximately 250 Murphy Rebel kits have reached completion.
Flying or in service:	Up to 250 airworthy.

Murphy Renegade Spirit

Subject: Murphy Renegade Spirit, registered in Belgium as OO-D29.
Statistics: Murphy Renegade Spirit.

Another popular light plane of Canadian origin, the Murphy Renegade was developed for amateur constructors. Offering open-cockpit flying and all of the fun of a biplane, the Renegade was immediately successful and up to 600 avid home-builders ordered their kits and set to work. By 1988 the first completed kits began to appear at airfields and aerodromes and, within a few years, the Renegade had achieved a good spread across the American continent and Europe. The Renegade Spirit is an improved and uprated version of the type with an 80hp Rotax engine in place of the earlier 53hp Rotax. Performance, range and payload are all increased and the Renegade Spirit has become a regular sight at airfields and flying events.

Country of Origin:	Canada
First Flight:	Prototype flew in 1985.
Accommodation:	2
Wingspan:	21ft 3in (6.48m)
Length:	18ft 5in (5.61m)
Height:	6ft 10in (2.08m)
Empty Weight:	460lb (208.9kg)
Max Take Off:	950lb (430.9kg)
Powerplant:	1 X 80hp (59.66kW) Rotax 912 piston engine.
Cruise Speed:	85mph (136.7km/h)
Max Speed:	125mph (201km/h)
Service Ceiling:	10,000 ft (3,048m)
Range:	300 miles (483km)
Number Manufactured:	Over 600 Renegade kits sold.
Flying or in service:	Many examples flying in the US, Canada and Europe.

Myasishchev M-4 Bison

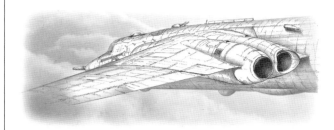

Subject: Myasishchev M-4 Bison of the Russian air force.
Statistics: Myasishchev M-4 Bison.

The M-4 Bison is a relic of the frightening days when both the Soviets and the Americans maintained nuclear bomber patrols, complete with live nuclear weapons, in the air above the Bering Sea and other far northerly parts of the world. The Bison had 3 large internal bomb bays each capable of accommodating nuclear or conventional weapons. With a maximum speed of 560mph and a range of up to 7,000 miles the type was a potent threat to the US. Indeed, with the assistance of in-flight refuelling, large fleets of Bisons armed with nuclear weapons posed a threat to many of America's main centres of population.

Country of Origin:	USSR
First Flight:	1953
Wingspan:	165ft 7in (50.47m)
Length:	154ft 10in (47.19m)
Max Take Off:	350,000lb (158,750kg)
Powerplant:	4 X 19,180lb (85.3 kN) Mikulin AM-3D turbojet powerplants.
Max Speed:	560mph (900km/h)
Service Ceiling:	41,000ft (12,500m)
Range:	7,000 miles (11,265km)

Nanchang CJ-6

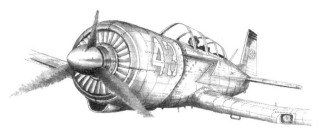

Subject: Nanchang CJ-6A bearing the n-number N556TR flew from its California base to Sun 'n Fun, Lakeland Linder, Florida, 2005.
Statistics: Nanchang CJ-6A.

The People's Republic of China had earlier flown the CJ-5, a licence-built variant of the Soviet Union's long-standing

Yakovlev Yak-18. Its success led in time to the development of improved variants and upgrades and by 1958 to the introduction of the Nanchang CJ-6. With tandem seating, a retractable undercarriage and generous dihedral on the outer wings, the CJ-6 was a capable and stable training aircraft which was designed to take punishing treatment from students and instructors alike. So successful was its formula that no less than 1,900 airframes were produced for training applications for the military forces of China, Albania, Bangladesh, Cambodia, North Korea, Tanzania and Zambia and, indeed, a small number of these airframes continue in operational service to this day. Others of the type have discovered that there is life after military service and have found their way into the hands of private pilots and collectors who are increasingly drawn by the lure of operating original warbirds at reasonable levels of cost.

Country of Origin:	People's Republic of China
First Flight:	1958
Accommodation:	2
Wingspan:	33ft 5in (10.18m)
Length:	27 ft 9in (8.46m)
Height:	10ft 8in (3.25m)
Empty Weight:	2,600lb (1,180kg)
Max Take Off:	3,130lb (1,420kg)
Powerplant:	1 x 285hp (212.5kW) Quzhou Huosai HS6A radial piston.
Cruise Speed:	160mph (257km/h)
Max Speed:	185mph (298km/h)
Service Ceiling:	17,000ft (5,181m)
Range:	640 miles (1,024km)
Number Manufactured:	In excess of 1,900 of all CJ-6 types manufactured.
Flying or in service:	Still in service with the air forces of Albania, Bangladesh, North Korea and Zambia. Up to 70 examples flying with private owners in Australia, Europe and the US.
Airframes Preserved:	Museum of Aviation, Warner Roberts AFB, Georgia, USA.

Nakajima B-5N Kate

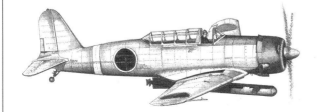

Subject: Nakajima B-5N Kate with torpedo.
Statistics: Nakajima B-5N2 Kate.

Japan's Nakajima works produced approximately 1,200 of the B5N Kate carrier-borne torpedo bomber. Early aircraft of the series were powered by a 770hp (574kW) Nakajima Hikari nine-cylinder radial but later B-5N2 airframes were provided with the more powerful 1,020hp (760kW) Nakajima Sakae II powerplant, which greatly boosted the type's weapons payload capacity and performance. By December of 1941 when Japan launched its devastating attack on Pearl Harbor the B-5N and the uprated B-5N2 torpedo bombers were an integral part of the Imperial Japanese Navy and they partook in that extraordinary attack with deadly precision. Although no comprehensive records of B-5N production survived the war it is estimated that total production reached 1,200 of all variants.

Country of Origin:	Japan
First Flight:	1937
Accommodation:	2 or 3
Wingspan:	50ft 10in (15.5m)
Length:	33ft 9in (10.3m)
Empty Weight:	4,645lb (2,106kg)
Max Take Off:	9,039lb (4,100kg)
Powerplant:	1 x 1,020hp (760kW) Nakajima Sakae II piston powerplant.
Max Speed:	236mph (380km/h)
Service Ceiling:	25,000ft (7,620m)
Range:	610 miles (980km)
Number Manufactured:	Estimated at 1,200 aircraft.

NAMC YS-11

Subject: NAMC YS-11.
Statistics: NAMC YS-11-100.

Japanese giants Fuji, Kawasaki, Mitsubishi and Shin Meiwa pooled their considerable resources to develop the NAMC YS-11 short-haul domestic airliner. With seating for up to 60 passengers the type was designed to satisfy the short- to medium-haul requirements of Japan's many civil carriers. The YS-11 was adopted by many of Japan's best-known airline operators from All Nippon Airways to Toa Airways but it was also exported to third-party countries such as Greece, the Philippines and the United States. The Japanese Self Defense Forces, too, selected the type as a VIP transport, freighter, utility transport, and electronic countermeasures platform.

Country of Origin:	Japan
First Flight:	1962
Accommodation:	Crew of 3 + 60 passengers or equivalent payload.
Wingspan:	105ft 0in (32.0m)
Length:	86ft 3in (26.3m)
Height:	29ft 6in (8.99m)
Empty Weight:	33,290lb (15,097kg)
Max Take Off:	51,800lb (23,492kg)
Powerplant:	2 x 3,060 hp (2,281kW) Rolls-Royce Dart turboprops.
Cruise Speed:	280mph (450.6km/h)
Max Speed:	295mph (475km/h)
Service Ceiling:	25,000ft (7,620m)
Range:	860 miles (1,376km)
Number Manufactured:	180 of all variants built.
Flying or in service:	Up to 80 still active.

NASA Space Shuttle

Subject: NASA Space Shuttle 'Discovery'.
Statistics: NASA Space Shuttle.

The Shuttle programme was launched in 1972. The world's first re-usable low-cost spacecraft was to be called 'Constitution' but a massive campaign of letters by fans of the Star Trek television series caused the White House to change the first Orbiter's name to 'Enterprise'. By 1976 the 'Enterprise' was partaking in glide-descent trials to prove its air-handling qualities and to train the first batch of Shuttle astronauts. By April of 1981 the first fully functional Shuttle, 'Columbia' was ready for lift-off and, with much of the world glued to their television screens, the Shuttle blasted into space for the first time. There followed a golden age of near space exploration for the US. NASA's 'Columbia', 'Challenger', 'Discovery' and 'Atlantis' carried out to date a total of 114 missions, flew 430 million miles, and spent all of 1,045 days in space. They deployed 61 military and civilian satellites, docked with the Soviet MIR station 9 times and with the International Space Station 17 times. Together they orbited the earth 16,577 times and gave real space experience to no less than 703 astronauts. Despite the terrible 'Challenger' and 'Columbia' disasters of 1986 and 2003, the Shuttle continues to be one of the greatest space exploration programmes of our time and one of the greatest technical achievements of mankind.

Country of Origin:	USA
First Flight:	1976 (glide descents) 1981 (into space)
Accommodation:	Generally up to 7 astronauts but the Shuttle can accommodate 10 if required.
Wingspan:	78ft 1in (23.79m)
Length:	122ft 2in (37.23m)
Max Take Off:	4.5 million lb (2,040,000kg)
Max Speed:	17,321mph (27,875km/h)
Service Ceiling:	115 to 600 miles above earth.
Range:	Longest mission so far has been 17 days.
Number Manufactured:	7 built (including 'Pathfinder' mock-up and 'Enterprise' test bed).
Flying or in service:	'Discovery', 'Atlantis', and 'Endeavour' are active.

Nimrod AEW-3

Subject: As part of the abortive AEW-3 programme ex BOAC Comet 4, G-APDS, was fitted with this massive radome. When the programme was abandoned, XW626, its new designation, never flew again.
Statistics: Nimrod MR-2 Maritime Patrol Variant.

The Nimrod series has undergone a programme of constant revision and upgrading since its first tentative flight in 1967. Developed from the airframe of the de Havilland Comet 4C, the Nimrod has had a difficult and protracted evolution with delays, cost overruns, and much intervention and interruption by politicians of every persuasion. Despite all of these tribulations, however, the first Nimrods have been in operational service now for about 40 years and continue to present a viable solution to Britain's maritime patrol and early warning system requirements.

Country of Origin:	UK
First Flight:	1967
Accommodation:	Flight crew of 4 + specialist submarine detection + radar operators.
Wingspan:	114ft 10in (35.0m)
Length:	126ft 9in (38.63m)
Height:	29ft 9in (9.07m)
Empty Weight:	86,000lb (39,000kg)
Max Take Off:	192,000lb (87,075kg)
Powerplant:	4 x 12,140lb (54KN) Rolls-Royce Spey turbofans.
Cruise Speed:	545mph (880km/h)
Max Speed:	575mph (925km/h)
Range:	6,000 miles (9,600km)
Flying or in service:	In service.

Nord N-1203 Norecrin II

Subject: Nord (SNCAN) N-1203 Norecrin II, registered in Germany as D-EKIC.
Statistics: Nord (SNCAN) N-1203 Norecrin II.

After the cessation of hostilities in 1945 the French Ministère de l'Air lost no time in advertising a limited competition to establish which was the greatest private sportplane of the time. Against stiff competition from a wide array of post-war contenders it was Nord's N-1203 Norecrin which won the day and the type then went on to be manufactured in large numbers for use by French flying clubs, private owners and for export to third-party countries. Distinctive for its slightly eccentric nose profile and exaggerated dihedral, the Norecrin's superb build quality has provided it with great longevity and approximately 20 examples of the type remain in active service to this day.

Country of Origin:	France
First Flight:	1945
Accommodation:	4
Wingspan:	33ft 5in (10.2m)
Length:	23ft 8in (7.21m)
Height:	9ft 5in (2.87m)
Empty Weight:	1,435lb (650.91kg)
Max Take Off:	2,315lb (1,050kg)
Powerplant:	1 x 135hp (100kW) Regnier 4L piston.
Cruise Speed:	140mph (225km/h)
Max Speed:	175mph (281km/h)
Service Ceiling:	16,400ft (5,000m)
Range:	560 miles (900km)
Number Manufactured:	378 completed.
Flying or in service:	Up to 20 still actively flying.
Preserved:	Flieger-Flab Museum, Dubendorf, Switzerland.

Nord N-2501 Noratlas

Subject: Nord (SNCAN) N-2501 Noratlas, registration F-AZVM.
Statistics: Nord (SNCAN) N-2501 Noratlas.

In the late 1940s the French SNCA du Nord company began development of a new military transport and freighter to replace the ageing Douglas C-47s and Junkers Ju-52s then in service with the Armée de l'Air. The N-2500 design was a twin-engined general transport and cargo freighter with a twin-boom arrangement similar in configuration to the American Fairchild C-82 Packet. The improved N-2501 was an even more satisfactory performer and the type went on to be manufactured in large numbers, mostly for the Armée de l'Air, but also in smaller numbers for civil operations. The N-2501 Nordatlas also served with the air forces of Chad, Niger and Greece. When the type was finally retired from military service the airframes were far from exhausted and Nord's Noratlas began a new life as a commercial freighter. In this role it remained active in Africa and South America until recent years when it began at last to be replaced by more recent freighter types. A small number of Nord Noratlas remain in operation to this day.

Country of Origin:	France
First Flight:	1949.
Accommodation:	Flight crew of 3 + 45 paratroopers or up to 14,990lb (6,800kg) of freight.
Wingspan:	106ft 7in (32.49m)
Length:	72ft 0in (21.95m)
Height:	19ft 8in (5.99m)
Empty Weight:	28,821lb (13,075kg)
Max Take Off:	50,706lb (23,000kg)
Powerplant:	2 x 2,090hp (1,558kW) SNECMA Bristol Hercules 738.
Cruise Speed:	200mph (322km/h)
Max Speed:	273mph (440km/h)
Service Ceiling:	24,600ft (7,500m)
Range:	1,615 miles (2,584km)
Number Manufactured:	418 of all variants by Nord of France and by Flugzeugbau Nord of Germany.
Flying or in service:	Several still airworthy and appearing on the air show circuit to this day.
Preserved:	Israeli Air Force Museum, Hatzerim, Beer Sheva, Israel.

Nord N-1101 Noralpha

Subject: Nord N-1101 Noralpha F-BLQU is actively flying to this day.
Statistics: Nord N-1101 Noralpha.

With the fall of France the Germans began the task of adapting its industries and raw-material stocks to the advantage of the Reich. To make best usage of the Nord Aviation works, Messerschmitt was called in and it designed a larger derivative of its earlier Bf-108 and progressed the project to the point where 2 prototypes were flown, but production was not undertaken. Thereafter, the Noralpha remained in limbo while the war raged back and forth around Les Mureaux. With the liberation of France the Nord Aviation works began once again to look to the future and decided to build Messerschmitt's Me-208 design as the Nord N-1101 Noralpha civilian sportplane and the Nord Ramier military utility transport. Approximately 200 airframes were produced in all.

Country of Origin: France
First Flight: 1946
Accommodation: 4
Wingspan: 37ft 8in (11.48m)
Length: 28ft 0in (8.53m)
Height: 10ft 6in (3.2m)
Empty Weight: 2,090lb (948kg)
Max Take Off: 3,630lb (1,646kg)
Powerplant: 1 x 233hp (173.7kW) Renault piston powerplant.
Cruise Speed: 175mph (282km/h)
Max Speed: 188mph (302.5km/h)
Range: 750 miles (1,207km)
Number Manufactured: 200 completed.
Flying or in service: Up to 6 still airworthy today.

Noorduyn Aviation Norseman

Subject: Noorduyn Aviation Norseman.
Statistics: Noorduyn Aviation Norseman V.

Both the Canadian Air Force and the United States Air Force purchased large quantities of Robert B. Noorduyn's superb bushplane, the Norseman. A tough and versatile civilian or military utility transport, the Noorduyn Norseman was ideal for operations on tundra wheels, standard wheels, floats, or even on skis. Throughout the war the type was widely used for communications duties as well as for the patrolling of isolated and remote areas. In the immediate aftermath of the war, large numbers of the type were released onto the civilian market and many of these airframes found their way to where they were needed most, that is northern Canada, Alaska, Norway and Sweden. Indeed even today there are many examples of the Noresman in operation with private owners and small commercial operators.

Country of Origin: Canada
First Flight: 1935
Accommodation: Pilot + 7 passengers.
Wingspan: 51ft 8in (15.75m)
Length: 32ft 4in (9.85m)
Height (without floats): 10ft 0in (3.05m)
Empty Weight: 4,660lb (2,113.7kg)
Max Take Off: 7,500lb (3,402kg)
Powerplant: 1 x 550hp (410kW) Pratt & Whitney Wasp.
Cruise Speed: 140mph (225km/h)
Max Speed: 155mph (249km/h)
Service Ceiling: 17,000ft (5,181m)
Range: 464 miles (742km)
Number Manufactured: 902 of all variants.
Flying or in service: Many still in service.
Preserved: Alberta Aviation Museum, Edmonton, Canada.
National Museum of the US Air Force, Wright-Patterson AFB, Dayton, Ohio, USA.

Nord N-1002 Pingouin II

Subject: Nord (SNCAN) 1002 Pingouin II G-ETME (c/n 274) is part of the Shuttleworth Trust flying museum.
Statistics: Nord (SNCAN) 1002 Pingouin II.

Using incomplete airframes and parts left over from the German-controlled French production line, Nord continued to produce the Messerschmitt Bf-108 reconnaissance light plane as the Nord 1000 Pingouin. The Argus aircraft engine works had been heavily bombed in the last months of the war and so Nord selected the 233hp (174kW) Renault piston to power the type. When the stocks of surplus airframes and assorted parts had been used up, Nord continued to produce the type, this time from all-new manufactured parts, under the title Nord N-1002 Pingouin II and the type was primarily used by the French Armée de L'Air.

Country of Origin: France
First Flight: 1945
Accommodation: 4
Wingspan: 34ft 5in (10.49m)
Length: 27ft 3in (8.31m)
Height: 7ft 6in (2.29m)
Empty Weight: 1,940lb (880kg)
Max Take Off: 3,050lb (1,383kg)
Powerplant: 1 x 233hp (174kW) 6-cylinder Renault piston powerplant.
Max Speed: 186mph (299km/h)
Service Ceiling: 16,400ft (5,000m)
Range: 620 miles (998km)
Preserved: Flugzeugmuseum, Frankfurt, Germany.

North American
P-51 Mustang

Subject: P-51, N472218, 'Big Beautiful Doll' of the US
          Air Force.
Statistics: North American P-51D. Mustang.

The Mustang derived from a 1940 request by the British
Purchasing Commission for a high-speed long-range escort
fighter which would be able to accompany Britain's bombers
on their long-haul missions into middle Europe. Designed by
the engineers of North American Aviation over the summer
months of 1940, the P-51 reached flying prototype stage
by October of 1940 and first deliveries were made to the
RAF in October of 1941. Immediately the potential of the
new fighter was apparent. It excelled in every area of
flight except at the very highest of altitudes and even
this shortcoming was remedied when the P-51 Mustang was
matched with the Packard Merlin powerplant, a US-built
version of the venerable Rolls-Royce Merlin. With its superb
mission radius and its ability to carry extraordinary
amounts of ammunition, the Mustang was a potent and
effective escort fighter.

Country of Origin: USA
First Flight: 1940
Accommodation: 1
Wingspan: 37ft 0in (11.28m)
Length: 32ft 3in (9.83m)
Height: 13ft 8in (4.17m)
Empty Weight: 7,125lb (3,232.6kg)
Max Take Off: 11,600lb (5,261.6kg)
Powerplant: 1 X 1,490hp (1,111.09kW)
                        Packard Merlin V-1650-7.
Cruise Speed: 380mph (611km/h)
Max Speed: 435mph (700km/h)
Service Ceiling: 40,000ft (12,192m)
Range: 2,300 miles (3,680km)
Number Manufactured: 15,586 of all variants
                        completed when production
                        ceased in 1946.
Flying or in service: Upwards of 140 still flying.
Preserved: Steven F. Udvar-Hazy Center,
                        Chantilly, Virginia, USA (P-51C
                        Excalibur III).
                        RAF Museum, London (P-51D).
                        Fantasy of Flight Museum, Polk
                        City, Florida, USA.
                        US Army Aviation Museum, Fort
                        Rucker, Ozark, Alabama, USA.
                        National Museum of the US Air
                        Force, Wright-Patterson
                        AFB, Dayton, Ohio, USA.

North American
B-25 Mitchell

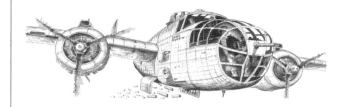

Subject: North American B-25 Mitchell.
Statistics: North American B-25J Mitchell.

North American's B-25 Mitchell was built in larger numbers
than any of the other American twin-engined bombers.
With a bomb load of over 2,400lb and a range of 1,275
miles the Mitchell was an effective and potent weapon.
Used in groups of up to 1,000 bombers with accompanying
fighters and pathfinders the Mitchell was particularly
effective in the later stages of the war, and its
relentless bombing of the Axis powers' most important
cities and industrial areas was a major component of
the Allied offensive. The B-25 was heavily defended with
a combination of gun turrets and heavy cannon guarding
every part of the air space around it. Its most effective
defensive weapons however, were sheer numbers and high-
performance fighter cover. With the end of the war large
numbers of B-25s were released onto the civilian market
for use as transports and freight planes, and many of
these airframes continue to operate in some of the
countries of South America until relatively recent years.

Country of Origin: USA
First Flight: 1940
Accommodation: 3 + up to 7
Wingspan: 67ft 7in (20.6m)
Length: 52ft 11in (16.1m)
Height: 15ft 10in (4.83m)
Max Take Off: 41,800lb (18,960kg)
Powerplant: 2 X 1,850hp (1,378kW) Wright
                        R-2600-29 Cyclone radials.
Cruise Speed: 233mph (375km/h)
Max Speed: 275mph (443km/h)
Service Ceiling: 23,800ft (7,255m)
Range: 1,275 miles (2,052km)
Number Manufactured: Over 10,000 manufactured.
Flying or in service: Up to 40 examples are still in
                        airworthy condition.
Preserved: Carol Jean Steven F.
                        Udvar-Hazy Center, Chantilly,
                        Virginia, USA (B-25J).
                        Castle Air Museum, Atwater,
                        California, USA.

North American
Navion Rangemaster

Subject: North American Navion Rangemaster H,
          registration N2548T.
Statistics: North American Navion Rangemaster H.

When Navion Aircraft of Harlingen, Texas, began building
the Navion H in 1961 it made many changes to North
American's long-established design. Perhaps the most
noticeable of these modifications was the replacement
of the trademark sliding bubble canopy with a more
integrated and streamlined canopy arrangement. Beneath
its cowlings, too, the Rangemaster H housed the greatly
more powerful 285hp (212.5kW) Continental IO-520B
powerplant giving higher cruise speeds and substantially
increased range. The Rangemaster H is the ultimate
progression of the Navion design and it had been passed
from manufacturer to manufacturer many times over the
years. Designed originally by North American, the type was
sold to Ryan Aeronautical in 1947 when North American
became bogged down with the logistics of building the F-86
Sabre jet. In its later years it would be owned also by
Tulsa Manufacturing Co. (Tusco), by the American Navion
Society, by the Rangemaster Aircraft Corporation and by
Consolidated Holdings. Total production of all Navion
variants by all manufacturers is 2,811 and of these
the Rangemaster H series airframes are among the
most treasured and sought after of the marque.

Country of Origin: USA
First Flight: First Navion flew in 1946.
                        First Navion Rangemaster H
                        flew in 1971.
Accommodation: 5
Wingspan: 34ft 9in (10.59m)
Length: 27ft 6in (8.38m)
Height: 8ft 4in (2.5m)
Empty Weight: 1,950lb (884kg)
Max Take Off: 3,317lb (1,504kg)
Powerplant: 1 X 285hp (212kW)
                        Continental IO-520-B piston.
Cruise Speed: 173mph (278km/h)
Max Speed: 180mph (289km/h)
Service Ceiling: 20,500ft (6,248m)
Range: 1,858 miles (2,990km)
Number Manufactured: 2,631 Navions built by North
                        American and Ryan, a further
                        172 Rangemaster Hs by Navion
                        and 8 more by Consolidated.
Flying or in service: Many of all variants in service.

North American AT-6D Harvard/Texan

Subject: North American AT-6D Harvard III, G-ELMH / 42-84555 is based in the United Kingdom and is a regular visitor on the air show circuit.
Statistics: North American AT-6D Harvard/Texan.

The US Army Air Corps called it the Texan, while the Royal Air Force and the Canadian Air Force called it the Harvard. The AT-6 advanced combat trainer was a cantilever low-wing monoplane with a tandem cockpit, retractable undercarriage and a powerful 600hp (447kW) Pratt & Whitney radial piston powerplant. With a total production of almost 16,000, the Harvard/Texan became the trainer for a whole generation of wartime pilots and, indeed, it became the last aircraft that young pilots flew before they transitioned on to the frontline fighters. Tough, rugged and with built-in longevity, many examples of the Harvard/Texan continue to fly with private owners and with Warbird collections to this day.

Country of Origin: USA
First Flight: 1937
Accommodation: 2
Wingspan: 42ft 0in (12.8m)
Length: 29ft 1in (8.86m)
Height: 11ft 8in (3.56m)
Empty Weight: 4,158lb (1,886kg)
Max Take Off: 5,300lb (2,404kg)
Powerplant: 1 x 600hp (447kW) Pratt & Whitney piston powerplant.
Cruise Speed: 170mph (273km/h)
Max Speed: 205mph (329km/h)
Service Ceiling: 21,500ft (6,553m)
Range: 750 miles (1,207km)
Number Manufactured: Almost 16,000 of all AT-6 variants completed.
Flying or in service: Several hundred T-6s continue flying to this day.
Preserved: Israeli Air Force Museum, Hatzerim, Beer Sheeva, Israel. Fleet Air Arm Museum, Somerset, UK.

Northrop XP-56 Black Bullet

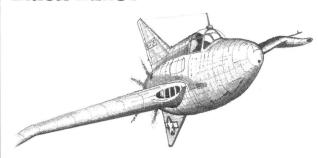

Subject: Northrop XP-56 Black Bullet.
Statistics: Northrop XP-56.

The XP-56 Black Bullet was an attempt by Jack Northrop to revolutionize the performance of fighting aircraft by the use of near all-wing aircraft configurations and unusual pusher propeller arrangements. Northrop had the ability to push the boundaries on every front and, for the XP-56, he pioneered the use of pure magnesium airframe components and Heliarc structural welding. The XP-56 was not successful in its flight test programme, the first of the 2 prototypes being destroyed in high-speed taxi trials before even leaving the ground. The second prototype XP-56 was slightly larger and had been modified aerodynamically as a result of losing its sister ship. It did fly, although its behaviour in the air was far from confidence-building for test pilot Harry Crosby. After a short and dramatic evaluation period it was decided that the Black Bullet was basically not safe to fly and the project was formally abandoned.

Country of Origin: USA
First Flight: 1943
Accommodation: 1
Wingspan: 42ft 7in (12.98m)
Length (First prototype): 23ft 7in (7.19m)
Height (First prototype): 9ft 9in (2.97m)
Empty Weight: 8,700lb (3,946kg)
Max Take Off: 12,145lb (5,509kg)
Powerplant: 1 x 2,000hp (1,491kW) Pratt & Whitney R-2800-29 18-cylinder radial engine.
Max Speed: 465mph (748km/h). Estimated.
Service Ceiling: 33,000ft (10,058m). Estimated.
Range: 660 miles (1,062km). Estimated.
Number Manufactured: 2 prototypes completed.

Northrop F-5E Tiger II

Subject: Northrop F-5E Tiger II of the Brazilian air force.
Statistics: Northrop F-5E Tiger II.

The F-5 tactical interceptor fighter was very similar in appearance to the T-38 Talon trainer but with just 1 pilot, a greatly strengthened airframe, more powerful afterburning turbojets and an assortment of weapons hardpoints, it was a much more pointed and potent combat weapon. The type was intended for use by US forces and by the forces of US-friendly nations and it was originally given the title 'Freedom Fighter'. In August of 1972 Northrop flew an upgraded development of the type, which was designated the F-5E Tiger II, a greatly improved variant which continues to serve as a tactical fighter and reconnaissance platform with the air forces of many countries.

Country of Origin: USA
First Flight: F-5 first flown in 1959. F-5E Tiger II first flown 1972.
Accommodation: 1
Wingspan: 26ft 8in (8.13m)
Length: 48ft 2in (14.68m)
Height: 13ft 5in (4.09m)
Empty Weight: 9,575lb (4,344kg)
Max Take Off: 24,675lb (11,192kg)
Powerplant: 2 x 5,000lb (22.24kN) General Electric J85-GE-21A turbojets with afterburner.
Max Speed: 1,208mph (1,945km/h) or Mach 1.63.
Service Ceiling: 51,800ft (15,790m)
Range: 2,310 miles (3,696km)
Number Manufactured: 1,145 delivered.
Flying or in service: Still in operational service.
Preserved: Polish Aviation Museum, Cracow.

North American F-86 Sabre

Subject: North American F-86 Sabre FU25222 of the US Air Force.
Statistics: North American F-86F Sabre.

When North American flew the Sabre for the first time in 1947 the new type demonstrated extraordinary speed and faultless handling. The first production Sabres followed only 7 months later and the type entered service with the US Air Force the following year. The F-86 incorporated a wide array of aerodynamic and control innovations which had never before been collected in any one airframe, from hydraulically-assisted flight controls, to full-span leading edge slats, and large air-brakes which could be extended out of the rear fuselage to reduce aircraft speed when required. The Sabre was a massive step in the evolution of military aviation and it went on to be built in large numbers for the US armed services and for several of the other NATO air forces.

Country of Origin: USA
First Flight: 1947
Accommodation: Cabin Crew + 2 passengers
Wingspan: 39ft 1in (11.91m)
Length: 37ft 6in (11.43m)
Height: 14ft 9in (4.5m)
Empty Weight: 11,143lb (5,057kg)
Max Take Off: 20,610lb (9,350kg)
Powerplant: 1 x 5,970lb (26.56kN) General Electric J47-GE-27 turbojet.
Cruise Speed: 520mph (837km/h)
Max Speed: 687mph (1,105km/h)
Service Ceiling: 49,000ft (14,935m)
Range: 925miles (1,485km) for the F-86F up to 1,615miles (2,584km) for the F-86F-30.
Number Manufactured: 6,720 of all F-86 variants.
Flying or in service: Several flying with private owners and warbird collections.
Preserved: Steven F. Udvar-Hazy Center, Chantilly, Virginia, USA (F-86A). Tyndall Museum, Tyndall Air Force Base, Florida, USA.

Northrop XB-35 Flying Wing

Subject: Northrop XB-35 Flying Wing.
Statistics: Northrop XB-35 Flying Wing.

The year was 1941 and in the darkest days of the Second World War it looked as if both Britain and the Soviet Union could shortly fall to the Axis powers. In preparation for such a scenario the US Army Air Corps began to lay plans for a heavy bomber of intercontinental range which could attack targets in central Europe from bases in the US. To produce an aircraft which could accomplish such a mission, however, would require a new and radical approach and the USAAC turned to Northrop for a solution. Aviation pioneer Jack Northrop had spent many years developing the concept of the flying wing aircraft, which he believed would trade the weight and drag of a conventional fuselage and tail for greatly increased speed and range. The resulting XB-35 flying wing was an enormous aircraft by the standards of its day but its new and radical nature presented many new technical challenges which had to be resolved before production of operational aircraft could begin. By the time of its first flight in June of 1946 the war was long over and the XB-35 project was effectively cancelled in favour of the YB-49 programme, which saw the prototypes converted to turbojet status.

Country of Origin: USA
First Flight: 1946
Accommodation: 9 + up to 6 relief crewmen.
Wingspan: 172ft 0in (52.43m)
Length: 53ft 1in (16.18m)
Height: 20ft 0in (6.1m)
Max Take Off: 180,000lb (81,646kg)
Powerplant: 4 x 3,000hp (2,237kW) Pratt & Whitney R-4360 supercharged radial powerplants.
Cruise Speed: 183mph (294km/h)
Max Speed: 391mph (629km/h)
Service Ceiling: 39,700ft (12,100m)
Range: 8,150 miles (13,116km)
Number Manufactured: 2 completed.
Preserved: Both prototypes scrapped in August of 1949.

North American T-39D Sabreliner

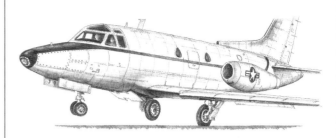

Subject: North American T-39D Sabreliner 150969 of the US Navy.
Statistics: North American T-39D Sabreliner.

The T-39 was developed by North American Aviation as a speculative private venture to meet the US Air Force's need for a twin-turbofan utility transport and trainer. The USAF was impressed with the performance of the prototype and by June of 1960 the first of its 143 orders had been delivered. Now, with the US military market tied up, North American turned its attention to the highly lucrative civilian market. The new civilian Sabreliner jet was fitted out with de-icing boots, autopilot and additional communications and navigational aids which the USAF had not required on their military airframes. Seating capacity, too, was increased to accommodate 7 passengers as well as the 2-man flight crew. The Sabreliner went on to become one of the most influential and popular aircraft of its era and North American's only successful commercial aircraft.

Country of Origin: USA
First Flight: 1958
Accommodation: 2 + 4 passengers (military). 2 + 7 passengers (civilian).
Wingspan: 44ft 6in (13.56m)
Length: 44ft 0in (13.41m)
Height: 16ft 0in (4.88m)
Empty Weight: 9,260lb (4,200kg)
Max Take Off: 18,340lb (8,319kg)
Powerplant: 2 x 3,000lb (13.34kN) Pratt & Whitney J60s.
Cruise Speed: 500mph (805km/h)
Max Speed: 538mph (866km/h)
Service Ceiling: 42,000ft (12,800m)
Range: 1,348 miles (2,169km)
Number Manufactured: 212 military T-39s and more than 388 civilian Sabreliners manufactured.
Flying or in service: Small numbers still operational.
Preserved: T-39A US Army Aviation Museum, Fort Rucker, Ozark, Alabama, USA.

North American F-82 Twin Mustang

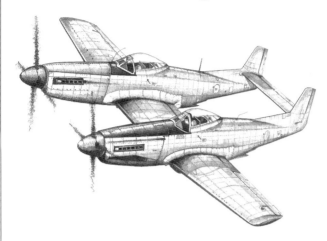

Subject: North American F-82 Twin Mustang without markings.
Statistics: North American F-82B Twin Mustang.

The need to develop a long-range fighter to accompany bomber groups all the way to their targets in central Europe, and the immense distances between the islands of the Pacific, were the 2 reasons for the development of the F-82 Twin Mustang. With 2 Merlin powerplants but the weight of only 1 airframe the P-82's range was a great improvement on the earlier P-51. Its 2 pilots, too, could more easily share the workload of ultra-long-distance flight while still remaining fresh for engagement in aerial combat with enemy fighters. The first production airframes were delivered just too late to take part in the Second World War but the F-82 went on, nonetheless, to serve with the US Air Force until June of 1953.

Country of Origin:	USA
First Flight:	1945
Accommodation:	2
Wingspan:	51ft 3in (15.62m)
Length:	38ft 1in (11.61m)
Height:	13ft 8in (4.17m)
Max Take Off:	24,800lb (11,250kg)
Powerplant:	2 x 1,380hp (1,029kW) Packard-built Merlin powerplants.
Cruise Speed:	280mph (450km/h)
Max Speed:	482mph (775km/h)
Service Ceiling:	40,000ft (12,192m)
Range:	2,200 miles (3,540km)
Number Manufactured:	272 completed including 22 prototype, test, and early production airframes.
Preserved:	National Museum of the US Air Force, Wright-Patterson AFB, Dayton, Ohio, USA.

Northrop/Grumman B-2A Spirit

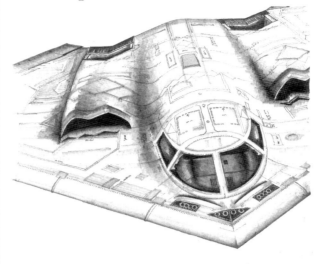

Subject: Northrop/Grumman B-2A Spirit.
Statistics: Northrop/Grumman B-2A Spirit.

When all of the associated development costs are taken into account, the 21 Northrop Grumman B-2 bombers delivered to date come with a price tag of 2.2 billion dollars each, an extraordinary amount of public funds by any count. Whether the investment was worthwhile will depend on the length of time it takes for radar search technology to catch up with the trademark low-signature stealth technology of the B-2. With a 593mph cruise speed the B-2 is not a particularly fast aircraft and the type relies almost entirely on its stealth characteristics while flying in hostile environments. Its 11,100-mile range and its capacity to carry up to 75,000lb of missiles or conventional bombs in its 2 internal bomb bays, however, sets the type apart and provides the aircraft with the ability to deliver large amounts of ordnance to almost any location on earth.

Country of Origin:	USA
First Flight:	1990
Accommodation:	3
Wingspan:	172ft 0in (52.4m)
Length:	69ft 0in (21.0m)
Height:	17ft 0in (5.18m)
Empty Weight:	153,500lb (69,640kg)
Max Take Off:	336,500lb (152,633kg)
Powerplant:	4 x 19,000lb (84.52kN) General Electric F118-GE-110 turbofans.
Cruise Speed:	590mph (950km/h)
Max Speed:	610mph (982km/h)
Service Ceiling:	50,000ft (15,240m)
Range:	11,100 miles (17,863km).
Number Manufactured:	21 manufactured to date.
Flying or in service:	In service.

Panavia Tornado IDS

Subject: Panavia Tornado IDS of the German Luftwaffe.
Statistics: Panavia Tornado GR MK 1B.

A 2-seat variable-geometry supersonic fighter which was developed to fill the roles of close air support, battlefield interdiction, air superiority interceptor, air defence fighter and naval strike platform. The Tornado was developed jointly between DASA of Germany, Alenia of Italy and BAE Systems of the UK, and the project was designed throughout to meet the agreed operational requirements of the 3 sponsoring countries. The first of 6 Tornado prototypes and pre-production airframes flew in Germany in August of 1974 and the first completed airframes went into operational service some months later. Like all frontline combat aircraft, the Tornado is subject to a programme of constant review and upgrading, and recent changes to the type include the addition of new head-up/head-down displays, forward-looking infra-red (FLIR) systems, and the ability to carry the Sea Eagle anti-shipping missile.

Country of Origin:	Germany, Italy and UK
First Flight:	1974
Accommodation:	2
Wingspan:	28ft 3in (8.61m) when swept. 45ft 7in (13.89m) spread.
Length:	54ft 9in (16.69m)
Height:	20ft 0in (6.1m)
Empty Weight:	29,983lb (13,600kg)
Max Take Off:	59,862lb (27,153kg)
Powerplant:	2 x 16,008lb (71.21kN) Turbo-Union R.B.199-34R turbofans with afterburners.
Max Speed:	919mph (1,482km/h)
Service Ceiling:	In excess of 70,000ft (21,335m).
Combat Radius:	828 miles (1,332km).
Number Manufactured:	Over 990 of all variants manufactured.
Flying or in service:	In service with the air forces of Germany, Italy, UK and Saudi Arabia.
Preserved:	RAF Museum, Hendon, London, UK (GR1A).

Panzl S-330 Aerobat

Subject: Panzl S-330 Aerobat at Lakeland Linder, Florida, 2005. S/n 005. American registration N541FC.
Statistics: Panzl S-330 Aerobat.

Developed from the earlier Staudacher, Greg Panzl's S-330 is a highly specialized aerobatic aircraft which has been designed for use at the very highest levels of unlimited aerobatic competition flying. A pedigree aircraft like the S-330 is a serious handful in the air and its tricky flying characteristics would present immense difficulty to any average pilot even when flying basic procedures. Designed to fly on a knife edge, the S-330's superb aerobatic displays are made possible by its rapid response to control system inputs, its ability to drop a wing when required and its extraordinary ability to twist, turn, invert, and hang on its massive Lycoming IO-540 piston powerplant. Indeed, all of the flight characteristics which make the S-330 an excellent aerobat are the very ones which are undesirable in normal transport and utility aircraft.

Country of Origin: USA
First Flight: 2003
Accommodation: 1
Wingspan: 24ft 4in (7.42m)
Length: 21ft 9in (6.63m)
Height: 5ft 11in (1.8m)
Empty Weight: 1,289lb (585kg)
Max Take Off: 1,600lb (725kg)
Powerplant: 1 x 330hp (246kW)
                          Lycoming IO-540 SER
Cruise Speed: 161mph (259km/h)
Max Speed: 200mph (322km/h)
Range: 700 miles (1,126km)
Flying or in service: Small numbers flying in specialized aerobatic circles.

Payne Knight Twister

Subject: Payne Knight Twister, registration N5DF.
Statistics: Payne Knight Twister KT-85.

Vernon Payne designed the Twister back in 1928 in an effort to generate enthusiasm and interest among the students in his class. It worked! The Payne Knight Twister was a groundbreaking aircraft for its day. Miniature in size yet capable of great speeds and a full range of aerobatic manoeuvres, the Knight Twister went on to influence a whole generation of aircraft designers. Vernon Payne, meanwhile, went on to offer plans of his aircraft to amateur constructors for home-building and it is estimated that at least 75 of the type were completed and flown.

Country of Origin: USA
First Flight: Vernon Payne's prototype first flew in 1929.
Accommodation: 1
Wingspan: 15ft 0in (4.57m)
Length: 14ft 0in (4.27m)
Height: 5ft 3in (1.6m)
Empty Weight: 535lb (242kg)
Max Take Off: 960lb (435kg)
Powerplant: 1 x 90hp (67.11kW) Continental C90 piston. (also 50hp, 70hp, and 125hp).
Cruise Speed: 130mph (209km/h)
Max Speed: 160mph (257.5km/h)
Range: 610 miles (982km)
Number Manufactured: In excess of 75 completed.

Piaggio P-180 Avanti

Subject: Piaggio P-180 Avanti registration N1808P makes a dramatic approach.
Statistics: Piaggio P-180 Avanti.

Piaggio's beautifully packaged Avanti turboprop gives all of the performance and finish of a jet for the running costs of a standard turboprop. Its sleek, aerodynamic fuselage is perfectly contoured to provide maximum width within the cabin area while still presenting a superbly honed profile to the oncoming airflow. A highly efficient high-aspect-ratio wing mounted towards the rear of the fuselage is matched at the front of the aircraft by a small canard wing which brings the centre of gravity of the loaded aircraft back into an acceptable centre of gravity range. Finally the P-180 Avanti's rear-facing 5-blade propellers deliver as much thrust as can possibly be wrung out of a pair of 1,480hp (1,103.5kW) P&W powerplants.

Country of Origin: Italy
First Flight: 1986
Accommodation: 2 + up to 10 passengers.
Wingspan: 37ft 6in (11.43m)
Length: 47ft 3in (14.4m)
Height: 12ft 11in (3.94m)
Empty Weight: 7,500lb (3,401kg)
Max Take Off: 11,550lb (5,238kg)
Powerplant: 2 x 1,480hp (1,103.5kW) Pratt & Whitney PT6A-66 turboprops.
Cruise Speed: 440mph (708km/h)
Max Speed: 455mph (732km/h)
Range: 1,980 miles (3,168km)
Flying or in service: Generally in service.

Piaggio P-136L-1

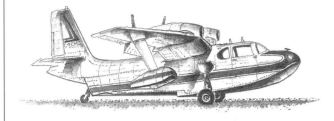

Subject: Piaggio P-136 5-seat light amphibian, registration C-FCMC.
Statistics: Piaggio P-136L-2.

The P-136 light amphibian was one of Piaggio's first post-war offerings and it was built both as a training airframe for the Italian air force and as a civilian utility and sport-plane. The type was introduced to the USA in 1955 as the Piaggio Royal Gull and, under that title, it enjoyed reasonable sales. The P-136L-2 was a slightly upgraded variant with a larger 320hp (238.6kg) powerplant and minor aerodynamic and airframe revisions. Eighty-one of all P-136 variants had been completed by 1967 when production ceased.

Country of Origin:	Italy .
First Flight:	1948
Accommodation:	5
Wingspan:	44ft 5in (13.5m)
Length:	35ft 5in (10.8m)
Height:	12ft 7in (3.84m)
Empty Weight:	4,652lb (2,110kg)
Max Take Off:	6,600lb (2,993kg)
Powerplant:	2 X 320hp (238.6kW) rear facing Textron Lycoming GSO-480-B1C6 pusher pistons.
Cruise Speed:	190mph (306km/h)
Max Speed:	208mph (335km/h)
Range:	900 miles (1,440km)
Number Manufactured:	81 of all variants including 23 for the Italian air force.
Flying or in service:	Several Royal Gulls still in airworthy condition.

Pilatus Britten Norman Trislander

Subject: Pilatus Britten Norman BN-2A MK 3 Trislander, registered G-BAXD of Channel Islands-based Aurigny Airlines.
Statistics: Pilatus Britten Norman BN-2A MK 3 Trislander.

Britten Norman's Islander operators had been requesting a stretched development with greater seating capacity and so BN began the development of the Trislander. Rather than increasing the output of the Islander's 2 existing engines, however, the decision was made to add a third powerplant above the tail, rather in the style of the DC-10 or the TriStar. The first Trislander was, in fact, a conversion of the second Islander prototype with significant structural changes to the tail unit and rear fuselage, and a new 7ft 6-inch plug inserted immediately to the front of the wing. Thereafter, the Trislander was built on the same production line as the Islander.

Country of Origin:	UK .
First Flight:	1970 (converted from the second Islander prototype).
Accommodation:	1 pilot and 1 passenger on the flight deck and 16 passengers in the cabin behind them.
Wingspan:	53ft 0in (16.15m)
Length:	49ft 3in (15m)
Height:	14ft 2in (4.32m)
Empty Weight:	6,100lb (2,767kg)
Max Take Off:	10,000lb (4,536kg)
Powerplant:	3 X 260hp (194kW) Lycoming O-540-E4C5 flat-six pistons.
Cruise Speed:	161mph (259km/h)
Max Speed:	180mph (290km/h)
Service Ceiling:	13,125ft (4,000m)
Range:	1,000 miles (1,609km)
Number Manufactured:	73 produced in the UK. One additional aircraft assembled in Guernsey, UK.

Pilatus P-2

Subject: Pilatus P-2.
Statistics: Pilatus P-2.

First flown in 1945, the Pilatus P-2 served as a primary trainer with the Swiss Air Force until 1982 when the last serviceable airframes were sold into private ownership in Europe and the USA. The P-2 was a robust and sturdily built aircraft of all-metal construction and its powerful Argus piston engine required all of its 465hp to climb out of Switzerland's many valley-bound airfields. Total production amounted to 56 aircraft, 26 of which were fitted with a 7.9mm forward-firing machine gun as well as hardpoints for conventional gravity bombs and rockets.

Country of Origin:	Switzerland
First Flight:	1945
Accommodation:	2
Wingspan:	36ft 1in (11.0m)
Length:	29ft 9in (9.07m)
Height:	8ft 10in (2.69m)
Empty Weight:	3,335lb (1,513kg)
Max Take Off:	4,335lb (1,966kg)
Powerplant:	1 X 465hp (346.75kW) Argus As.410A-2 piston powerplant.
Cruise Speed:	195mph (313km/h)
Max Speed:	210mph (338km/h)
Service Ceiling:	21,654ft (6,600m)
Range:	530 miles (853km)
Number Manufactured:	56 built and delivered to the Swiss Air Force.
Flying or in service:	Most retired and sold off in 1982. Many flying with private owners to this day.
Preserved:	Flieger-Flab Museum, Dubendorf, Switzerland.

Pilatus PC-6 B2/H4 Turbo Porter

Subject: Pilatus PC-6 B2/H4 Porter of MS Air, registered D-FFBZ on the German Civil Register.

Statistics: Pilatus PC-6 B2/H4 Porter.

The Pilatus Porter was designed for STOL operations off short or unprepared landing strips or for flight under harsh environmental conditions. The first 45 Porters were fitted with Lycoming's 350hp (261kW) IO-540 piston powerplant but all further production airframes were provided with the considerable advantages of turboprop power. A number of turboprop powerplants have been tried over the years with all recent airframes receiving Pratt & Whitney's popular and versatile PT6A line of powerplants while the licence-built Fairchild Hiller Heli-Porter received the 575hp (428.7kW) Garrett AiResearch turboprop. The Pilatus PC-6 Porter is operated by civilian and military operators in almost 50 countries and the type has served with, among others, the air forces of France, Australia, Switzerland, Peru, the USA and Argentina.

Country of Origin:	Switzerland
First Flight:	Flown with piston in 1959. Flown as turboprop in 1961.
Accommodation:	Flight crew of 1 or 2 + 10 passengers.
Wingspan:	52ft 1in (15.87m)
Length:	35ft 9in (10.9m)
Height:	10ft 5in (3.17m)
Empty Weight:	2,800lb (1,270kg)
Max Take Off:	6,174lb (2,800kg)
Powerplant:	1 x 680hp (507kW) Pratt & Whitney PT6A-27 turboprop.
Cruise Speed:	135mph (217km/h)
Max Speed:	165mph (265.5km/h)
Service Ceiling:	28,000ft (8,535m)
Range:	575 miles (925km)
Number Manufactured:	45 piston Porters built. 520 turboprop powered Porters built and still in production.
Flying or in service:	Widely in service.

Piper PA-22 Tri Pacer

Subject: Piper PA-22 Tri Pacer.

Statistics: Piper PA-22-160 Tri Pacer.

The Tri Pacer was a tricycle version of Piper's earlier 4-seat PA-20 high-wing monoplane taildragger. Airline design had moved over from taildragger to tricycle configurations and Piper followed suit with the PA-22 Tri Pacer. Although it had to compete directly with the revolutionary Cessna 172, the Tri Pacer fared well in the marketplace and a total of 7,629 of the type were manufactured.

Country of Origin:	USA
First Flight:	1951
Accommodation:	4
Wingspan:	29ft 5in (8.97m)
Length:	20ft 6in (6.25m)
Height:	8ft 4in (2.54m)
Empty Weight:	1,130lb (512.5kg)
Max Take Off:	2,000lb (907kg)
Powerplant:	1 x 160hp (119kW) Lycoming O-320 flat-four piston.
Cruise Speed:	130mph (209km/h)
Max Speed:	140mph (225km/h)
Service Ceiling:	15,000ft (4,572m)
Range:	536 miles (858km)
Number Manufactured:	7,629 completed.
Flying or in service:	Large numbers of Tri Pacers still flying to this day.
Preserved:	Mid-America Air Museum, Liberal, Kansas, USA.

Piper PA-28 Cherokee

Subject: Piper Cherokee PA-28 registration EI-WRN operated by Waterford Aeroclub and based at Waterford Airport, Ireland.

Statistics: Piper Cherokee PA-28-161.

Piper's PA-28 family of touring and training aircraft underwent many upgrades over the years and in excess of 30,200 of all PA-28 variants have been delivered. At the bottom of the range was Piper's PA-28 Cherokee 140 with its 140hp Lycoming engine while, at the top of the range, was the Piper PA-28R-201 Arrow IV with its 200hp Lycoming engine, retractable undercarriage and greatly improved aerodynamics.

Country of Origin:	USA
First Flight:	1960
Accommodation:	4
Wingspan:	35ft 0in (10.67m)
Length:	23ft 10in (7.25m)
Height:	7ft 4in (2.22m)
Empty Weight:	1,352lb (613kg)
Max Take Off:	2,440lb (1,105kg)
Powerplant:	1 x 160hp (110kW) Lycoming O-320 flat-four piston engine.
Cruise Speed:	120mph (195km/h)
Max Speed:	146mph (235km/h)
Service Ceiling:	11,000ft (3,353m)
Range:	733 miles (1,179km)
Number Manufactured:	In excess of 30,200 of all PA-28 variants completed and still in production.
Flying or in service:	Widely in service with private owners and flying clubs across the world.

Piper
PA-31 Chieftain

Subject: Piper PA-31 Chieftain.
Statistics: Piper PA-31-350 Chieftain.

Piper's PA-31 Chieftain 8- to 10-seat corporate transport and commuter airliner is a stretched version of the earlier Navajo. Designed to compete against the Cessna 401 and the Queen Air, the Chieftain has always appealed to the value-conscious business market, and over 1,000 of the type have been delivered. The PA-31T Cheyenne of 1972 was a further pressurized and turboprop-powered development of the type.

Country of Origin: USA
First Flight: The Navajo first flew in 1964 while the Chieftain derivative first flew in 1973.
Accommodation: Pilot + 7 to 9 passengers
Wingspan: 40ft 8in (12.39m)
Length: 34ft 7in (10.54m)
Height: 13ft 0in (3.96m).
Empty Weight: 4,383lb (1,988kg)
Max Take Off: 7,000lb (3,175kg)
Powerplant: 2 x 350hp (261kW) Lycoming L/TIO-540-J2BD piston engines.
Cruise Speed: 254mph (408km/h)
Max Speed: 272mph (437km/h)
Service Ceiling: 24,000ft (7,315m)
Range: 1,087 miles (1,750km)
Number Manufactured: 3,944 of all Navajo/Chieftain derivatives completed including 1,051 Piper PA-31-350 Chieftains.
Flying or in service: Many later airframes still operational.

Piper PA-32
Saratoga II TC

Subject: Piper PA-32 Saratoga II TC, was on display at the Experimental Aircraft Association's Sun 'n Fun convention, 2005.
Statistics: Piper PA-32R-301 Saratoga II HP.

The PA-32 Saratoga was developed from the Cherokee Six of 1964. Designed to meet the needs of top-end personal users and small corporate or taxi operators, the Saratoga is a capable and well-appointed aircraft with a 175mph cruise speed and a range of 920 miles. Other associated aircraft of the PA-32 family are the Piper Lance, the Cherokee Lance, and the Turbo Saratoga SP, and the type continues in production to this day.

Country of Origin: USA
First Flight: 1980
Accommodation: 6
Wingspan: 36ft 3in (11.05m)
Length: 27ft 1in (8.25m)
Height: 8ft 6in (2.59m)
Empty Weight: 2,360lb (1,070kg)
Max Take Off: 3,600lb (1,633kg)
Powerplant: 1 x 300hp (223.7kW) Lycoming IO-540 piston.
Cruise Speed: 175mph (281km/h)
Max Speed: 190mph (305km/h)
Range: 920 miles (1,480km)
Number Manufactured: Over 7,842 of all PA-32 models completed to date and the type is still in production.
Flying or in service: Widely in service.

Piper
PA-25-235 Pawnee B

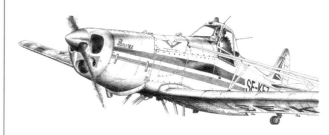

Subject: Piper PA-25-235 Pawnee B has found a new life in Uppsala, Sweden, as a glider tug. Swedish civil registration SE-KEZ.
Statistics: Piper PA-25-235 Pawnee C.

It was veteran Fred Weick of Weick W-1 fame who designed the AG-1 agricultural cropsprayer, which later became the PA-25 Pawnee. A robust and capable workhorse, the Pawnee was designed around the exacting needs of commercial cropdusting contractors who required an aircraft that could be loaded quickly, could carry large quantities of pesticide, could land on unprepared fields and strips, and could be repaired easily on station. Weick's AG-1 prototype flew for the first time in 1954 but it was not until 1959 that Piper's first Pawnee rolled off the production line. Thereafter, the type continued to be built in quantity until 1981, by which time 5,167 had been built. Many PA-25s remain in service to this day as agricultural cropsprayers or as glider tugs.

Country of Origin: USA
First Flight: 1954 (as Fred Weick's AG-1).
Accommodation: 1
Wingspan: 36ft 3in (11.05m)
Length: 24ft 8in (7.52m)
Height: 7ft 3in (2.21m)
Empty Weight: 1,400lb (635kg)
Max Take Off: 2,900lb (1,315kg)
Powerplant: 1 x 235hp (175kW) Lycoming O-540 piston powerplant.
Cruise Speed: 112mph (180km/h)
Max Speed: 124mph (200km/h)
Service Ceiling: 13,000ft (3,962km)
Range: 290 miles (466.7km)
Number Manufactured: 5,167 of all variants completed by 1981 when manufacture was discontinued.
Flying or in service: Many still in active service.

Piper PA-34 Seneca

Subject: Piper PA-34 Seneca.
Statistics: Piper PA-34-220T Seneca V.

Again based on Piper's Cherokee Six airframe, the PA-34 Seneca is a 6-seat twin-engine transport which cruises well in excess of 200mph over a range of almost 1,000 miles. In order to minimize the effects of adverse torque Piper's early PA-34 Seneca twins were provided with one standard 200hp Lycoming IO-360 piston engine and one contra-rotating version of the same powerplant. From 1975 onwards the type was rebranded as the PA-34 Seneca II with a newly streamlined airframe, larger turbocharged engines and an improved avionics suite. Very large numbers of PA-34s have been built by Piper in the USA and further licence-built versions have been produced in Argentina, Brazil, Colombia and Poland.

Country of Origin:	USA
First Flight:	1969
Accommodation:	6
Wingspan:	39ft 0in (11.89m)
Length:	28ft 7in (8.71m)
Height:	9ft 11in (3.02m)
Empty Weight:	3,422lb (1,552kg)
Max Take Off:	4,750lb (2,154kg)
Powerplant:	2 x 220hp (164.05kW) Continental IO-360 pistons.
Cruise Speed:	215mph (346km/h)
Max Speed:	225mph (362km/h)
Range:	950 miles (1,529km)
Number Manufactured:	4,790 PA-34s completed by Piper USA, with further licence-built versions by third country manufacturers.
Flying or in service:	Widely in service.

Pitts Special S-1 and S-2

Subject: Pitts Special S-1, registered G-BGSE on the UK civil register.
Statistics: Pitts Special S-1T.

Even as the Second World War was raging, Curtis Pitts was laying down the design for what was to become the world's best-known aerobatic biplane. The Pitts Special of 1943/44 is remarkably small with a wingspan of just 17ft and a height of only 6ft. In the air, however, the Special is an extraordinary performer, being able to throw loops and rolls like the most powerful competition aircraft, and dazzling spectators with its nostalgic biplane format. Without the extensive commercial infrastructure required to manufacture his aircraft, Pitts offered his plans for sale to amateur constructors. Its tube-and-fabric construction was ideal for home-building and large numbers of projects began to take shape across the USA and Europe. In later years, the Pitts Special was available in kit form or, indeed, as a fully completed aircraft. A superb aerobatic performer which is still manufactured to this day.

Country of Origin:	USA
First Flight:	1944
Accommodation:	1 or 2
Wingspan:	17ft 4in (5.28m)
Length:	15ft 6in (4.72m)
Height:	6ft 2in (1.88m)
Empty Weight:	845lb (383.3kg)
Max Take Off:	1,165lb (528.4kg)
Powerplant:	1 x 200hp (149.14kW) Lycoming AEIO-360-A1E flat-six piston.
Cruise Speed:	175mph (281.6km/h)
Max Speed:	185mph (297.7km/h)
Service Ceiling:	20,100ft (6,126m)
Range:	308 miles (496km)
Flying or in service:	Large numbers in service across the world.
Preserved:	Curtis Pitts's 1966 2-seat S-2 'Big Stinker' is preserved at the EAA Air Museum, Oshkosh, Wisconsin, USA.

Portsmouth Aviation Co. Aerocar

Subject: Portsmouth Aviation Co. Aerocar prototype s/n 002, registration G-AGTG, which perished in 1950.
Statistics: Portsmouth Aviation Co. Aerocar.

Portsmouth Aviation, formerly The Portsmouth Southsea and Isle of Wight Aviation Company Ltd, is notable for being the pre-war employer of pioneer aviator Amy Johnson. With the coming of the Second World War, Amy Johnson left to join the Air Transport Auxiliary while Portsmouth Aviation expanded its operations to service and repair large numbers of combat aircraft for the Royal Air Force and Royal Navy. With the cessation of hostilities in 1945 Portsmouth Aviation found itself to have a most experienced and skilful workforce and the decision was made to develop an all-new aircraft type for series manufacture. So it was that the Portsmouth Aerocar was born. G-AGTG, the single flying prototype, was a twin-engined twin-boomed, high-wing monoplane with a fully retractable tricycle undercarriage. A second, and smaller, prototype was added to the civil register as G-AGNJ but was never completed.

Country of Origin:	UK
First Flight:	1947
Accommodation:	2 + Cabin Crew
Number Manufactured:	1 prototype Aerocar Major, s/n 002, registration G-AGTG, completed. 1 prototype Aerocar Minor, s/n 001, registration G-AGNJ, was never completed.
Preserved:	G-AGTG was unfortunately scrapped in 1950.

Pitcairn AC-35

Subject: Pitcairn AC-35 is preserved at the Smithsonian National Air and Space Museum, Washington, DC.
Statistics: Pitcairn AC-35.

The Autogiro Company of America, a subsidiary of Pitcairn, entered the AC-35 autogiro into the 1935 roadable aircraft competition of the US Bureau of Air Commerce. The AC-35 was a fully roadable aircraft with folding rotors and a 25mph top speed on public roadways. Pitcairn's intention, and that of the Bureau of Air Commerce, was that anybody could fly the type after rudimentary training; that is, that the average man could aspire to having a simple roadable aircraft in his garage. The AC-35 prototype went through a protracted series of evaluation flights over the course of 1937 before Pitcairn sold the manufacturing rights to the Skyway Engineering Company of Carmel, Indiana. Skyway built one 135hp (100.6kW) Lycoming 0-290-powered manufacturing prototype before internal problems caused the project to be abandoned.

Country of Origin: USA
First Flight: 1936
Accommodation: 2
Rotor Diameter: 36ft 4in (11.07m)
Length: 21ft 8in (6.4m)
Height: 8ft 0in (2.44m)
Max Take Off: 1,330lb (603kg)
Powerplant: 1 x 90hp (67.1kW) Pobjoy Cascade piston engine.
Max Speed: 70mph (112.6km/h) in the air. 25mph (40km/h) on the road.
Number Manufactured: 1 by Pitcairn/Autogiro Co. of America and 1 by Skyway Eng Company of Carmel, Indiana.
Preserved: Smithsonian National Air and Space Museum. Washington, DC, USA.

Pushy Galore

Subject: Pushy Galore, registered N189BB.
Statistics: Pushy Galore.

Bruce Bohannon's superb interpretation of Jim Miller's 1973 JM-2 racing aircraft became legendary in aviation circles as a prolific collector of Formula One racing titles. From Reno to Oshkosh, Bohannon's dubiously named Pushy Galore scooped up trophies wherever it competed. Bohannon himself modified the aircraft as he thought necessary between races, often adding up to 3ft to his wingspan or making radical changes to his engine induction or cooling systems for any particular challenge. By 1994 Bohannon turned his attentions to setting 'time-to-height' records and Pushy Galore set a long series of new records to given heights, some of them in excess of 33,000 ft (10,058m).

Country of Origin: USA
First Flight: 1989
Accommodation: 1
Max Speed: 237.1mph (381.5km/h)
Service Ceiling: In excess of 33,000 ft (10,058m).
Number Manufactured: 1
Preserved: Bruce Bohannon's 1989 Miller JM-2 Pushy Galore is preserved at the EAA Air Museum, Oshkosh, Wisconsin, USA.

PZL M-28B-1-TD Bryza

Subject: PZL-Mielec M-28B-1-TD Bryza of the Polish navy.
Statistics: PZL-Mielec M-28 Bryza-1R BIS maritime patrol platform.

The latest development of the M-28 Skytruck, the Bryza is a dedicated maritime patrol and reconnaissance aircraft with a sophisticated submarine detection capability. Complete with a state-of-the-art 360-degree surface surveillance radar installation and a MAG-10 magnetometer system, the Bryza is a most capable maritime search weapon. The type is designed for coastal border patrol, Search-and-Rescue duties, tracking of cross-border immigration, protection of national economic sea zones and detection of submarines.

Country of Origin: Poland
Accommodation: 6. Comprised of flight crew + specialist operators.
Wingspan: 72ft 4in (22.06m)
Length: 42ft 11in (13.1m)
Height: 16ft 1in (4.9m)
Empty Weight: 9,590lb (4,350kg)
Max Take Off: 15,432lb (7,000kg)
Powerplant: 2 x 960hp (716kW) PZL-10S turboprops.
Cruise Speed: 168mph (270km/h)
Max Speed: 217mph (350km/h)
Service Ceiling: 19,685ft (6,000m)
Range: 764 miles (1,230km)
Flying or in service: In service.

PZL 230F Skorpion

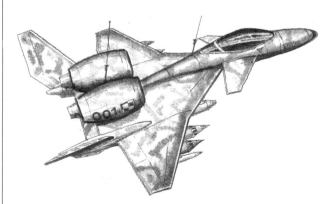

Subject: PZL-Mielec 230F Skorpion, which reached flying prototype stage only.
Statistics: PZL-Mielec 230FI Skorpion.

A close air support fighter and battlefield attack aircraft, the 230F was developed by PZL in the 1990s in an effort to replace its traditional Soviet military customer base, which was fast contracting. The Skorpion design reflected a host of new and emerging technologies, from canard foreplanes to blending the fuselage with the wings and utilizing new lightweight composite materials. Unfortunately, military users have always favoured sophisticated high-end combat aircraft over simple low-cost fighters and so the Skorpion did not attract the orders that PZL-Mielec had hoped for.

Country of Origin:	Poland
First Flight:	1990
Accommodation:	1
Wingspan:	29ft 5in (9.0m)
Length:	30ft 4in (9.3m)

PZL-Mielec
M-26 Iskierka

Subject: PZL-Mielec M-26 Iskierka bearing US civilian register markings.
Statistics: PZL-Mielec M-26 Iskierka.

PZL-Mielec of Poland developed the M-26 Iskierka advanced military and civilian trainer as a result of the experience and expertise it had gained as a licensed manufacturer of the Piper PA-34 Seneca. Using many of the Seneca's airframe components, a shortened Seneca wing, and the Seneca's tail empennage, PZL-Mielec developed a superb low-cost training aircraft which promises much of the performance of other military training types for a fraction of the cost.

Country of Origin:	Poland
First Flight:	1986
Accommodation:	2
Wingspan:	28ft 3in (8.6m)
Length:	27ft 2in (8.29m)
Height:	9ft 9in (2.96m)
Empty Weight:	2,293lb (1,040kg)
Max Take Off:	3,086.5lb (1,400kg)
Powerplant:	1 x 300hp (223.7kW) Lycoming AEIO-540-L1B5 six-cylinder air-cooled piston powerplant.
Cruise Speed:	195mph (313.8km/h)
Max Speed:	205mph (330km/h)
Range:	584 miles (940km)
Number Manufactured:	Very small numbers manufactured to date.
Flying or in service:	2 in service with Bolivian air force. Small numbers flying in USA.

PZL Mielec
M-15-01 Belphegor

Subject: PZL-Mielec M-15-01 Belphegor in the livery of Aeroflot.
Statistics: PZL-Mielec M-15-01 Belphegor.

Using jet-powered aircraft to lay agricultural chemicals may seem rather extravagant, but the M-15 Belphegor turbofan-powered biplane cropduster was capable of carrying 5 times the amount of chemicals that the earlier dusters had been able to lift. The type, too, must surely have been among the slowest jet-powered aircraft of all time with its 112mph cruise speed. The Belphegor was designed to replace the ageing fleet of Antonov An-2 cropdusters which had served the state farms. Its complex maintenance requirements, however, caused the type to be spectacularly unsuccessful in the role of cropduster, and examples of the extraordinary M-15 Belphegor jet biplane were abandoned all over the Eastern Bloc countries. Meanwhile, the Antonov An-2, which it was meant to replace, is still widely used.

Country of Origin:	Poland
First Flight:	1973
Accommodation:	1 + 2
Wingspan:	72ft 2in (22m)
Length:	41ft 0in (12.5m)
Height:	17ft 1in (5.2m)
Max Take Off:	11,686lb (5,300kg)
Powerplant:	1 x 3,306lb (14.7kN) Ivchenko AI-25 turbofan powerplant.
Max Speed:	112mph (180km/h)
Service Ceiling:	14,763ft (4,500m)
Range:	248 miles (400km)

PZL 104
Wilga 35

Subject: PZL 104 Wilga 35.
Statistics: PZL 104 Wilga 35.

The Wilga is a 4-seat light utility aircraft designed for a wide variety of general purpose, military and flying-club duties. With its high-lift wing and its cranked undercarriage the Wilga is designed for STOL operations off short and unprepared fields and for a variety of related missions. The type can be configured for air-ambulance work, agricultural spraying, glider towing, border patrol duties, or fitted with forward-looking infra red sensors for a variety of military applications. Like many of the other former Warsaw Pact manufacturers, PZL found its traditional customer base contracting radically as the political climate changed, and it began to develop variants of the Wilga for export to the West. A variety of Lycoming- and Continental-powered Wilga 80 and 2000 models are now certified and offered for sale on Western markets.

Country of Origin:	Poland
First Flight:	1962
Accommodation:	4
Wingspan:	36ft 9in (11.2m)
Length:	26ft 7in (8.1m)
Height:	9ft 8in (2.95m)
Empty Weight:	1,988lb (901.7kg)
Max Take Off:	2,866lb (1,300kg)
Powerplant:	1 x 260hp (193.88kW) PZL AI-14RA piston radial.
Cruise Speed:	105mph (167km/h)
Max Speed:	120mph (193km/h)
Range:	350 miles (563km)
Number Manufactured:	More than 1,000 completed and production is still ongoing.
Flying or in service:	Widely in service in former Warsaw Pact countries with small numbers flying in Europe and the USA.
Preserved:	Wilga 43, Polish Aviation Museum, Cracow.

PZL Swidnik Mi-2 Hoplite

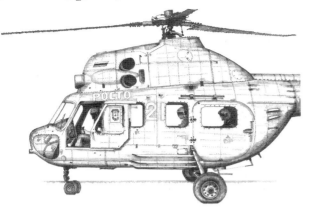

Subject: PZL Swidnik Mi-2.
Statistics: PZL Swidnik Mi-2.

A Soviet-designed helicopter which became a bestseller for PZL's Swidnik-based production line. Over 5,080 of all Mi-2 types were manufactured, most of them being exported to the Soviet Union, but others remaining in Poland or the other Warsaw Pact countries. North Korea, Syria, Nicaragua and Iraq, too, operated the type and in recent years a specially uprated Mi-2 Kania (Kittyhawk) variant has been offered on the US and European markets.

Country of Origin:	USSR/Poland
First Flight:	1961
Accommodation:	2 pilots + 7 passengers.
Rotor Diameter:	47ft 7in (14.5m)
Length:	37ft 5in (11.4m)
Height:	12ft 3in (3.73m)
Empty Weight:	5,183lb (2,351kg)
Max Take Off:	8,160lb (3,701kg)
Powerplant:	2 X 437hp (325.8kW) Isotov GTD-350 turboshafts.
Cruise Speed:	124mph (200km/h)
Max Speed:	132mph (213km/h)
Service Ceiling:	13,125ft (4,000m)
Range:	360 miles (576km)
Number Manufactured:	In excess of 5,080 of all Mi-2 variants.
Flying or in service:	Small numbers still airworthy.
Preserved:	The Helicopter Museum, Weston-Super-Mare, Somerset, UK.

Potez 60 and 600 Sauterelle

Subject: Potez 60 registered in Switzerland as HB-SPM.
Statistics: Potez 600 Sauterelle.

155 of the Potez 600 Sauterelle were provided to French flying clubs and training institutions under the 1930s French-government-sponsored 'Popular Aviation Movement'. Henri Potez designed the type to provide a reliable and forgiving environment for flight training and for touring. With a remarkably high mounted parasol wing and superb low-speed handling qualities, the Potez Sauterelle almost falls into the same category as the Storch or the Wilga, although it must be admitted that no other aircraft can quite surpass the handling characteristics of the Storch.

Country of Origin:	France
First Flight:	1935
Accommodation:	2
Wingspan:	32ft 9in (9.98m)
Length:	22ft 10in (6.95m)
Height:	7ft 9in (2.36m)
Empty Weight:	630lb (285kg)
Max Take Off:	1,234lb (560kg)
Powerplant:	1 X 60hp (44.7kW) Potez 3B radial piston.
Cruise Speed:	65mph (96.5km/h)
Max Speed:	90mph (145km/h)
Range:	400 miles (643km)
Number Manufactured:	155 completed.
Flying or in service:	1 in France and 1 in Switzerland.

Questair Venture

Subject: Questair Venture, registered N62V.
Statistics: Questair Venture.

Jim Griswold's incredibly short-coupled Questair Venture is a high-performance personal transport which can carry its 2 occupants in great comfort and speed over sectors of up to 1,000 miles. Griswold's previous experience on the design team of the Piper Malibu is clearly apparent throughout the Questair Venture, from the new type's high-end target group to many of the subassemblies and technologies employed in the design. In 1991 Questair began marketing the Questair Spirit, a new 3-seat variant with an optional third seat and a fully fixed and faired undercarriage.

Country of Origin:	USA
First Flight:	1987
Accommodation:	2
Wingspan:	27ft 6in (8.38m)
Length:	16ft 3in (4.95m)
Height:	7ft 8in (2.34m)
Empty Weight:	1,185lb (537.51kg)
Max Take Off:	2,000lb (907.18kg)
Powerplant:	1 X 280hp (208.7kW) Continental IO-550-G piston.
Cruise Speed:	275mph (442km/h)
Max Speed:	305mph (490km/h)
Range:	1,150 miles (1,851km)
Number Manufactured:	In excess of 30 completed by amateur constructors.
Flying or in service:	30-plus.

Quickie Aircraft Corp. Quickie

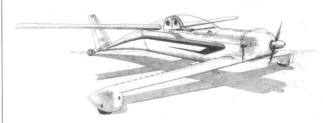

Subject: Quickie Aircraft Corp. Quickie N3QS, visited Lakeland Linder, Florida, 2005. Roy cruises at 100mph and uses just one and a half gallons of fuel per hour.
Statistics: Quickie Aircraft Corp. Quickie Q-200.

Aircraft designer Burt Rutan was asked by Gene Sheehan and Tom Jewett of the Mojave-based Quickie Aircraft Corporation to use his vast knowledge of epoxy composite materials and unorthodox airframe configurations to design an all-new advanced composite light plane for construction by amateur builders. Rutan took on the challenge and his off-beat and eccentric stamp is clearly visible throughout the aircraft. The original Quickie 1 was able to achieve a 100mph cruise speed on its 22hp Onan B48M chainsaw engine, an extraordinary achievement by any standards and a superb tribute to Rutan's design skills. Later Quickies tended to be fitted with larger engine types such as the Rotax 582 or equivalent. The Quickie Q-2 of 1980 was an enlarged 2-seat derivative with a greatly uprated powerplant. The Quickie Q-200 is more powerful again with a possibility to have up to a 115hp Lycoming O-235 engine and a 205mph cruise speed.

Country of Origin:	USA
First Flight:	1977
Accommodation:	Quickie 1 seats 1.
	Quickie Q-2 seats 2.
	Quickie Q-200 seats 2.
Wingspan:	16ft 8in (5.079m)
Length:	19ft 10in (6.04m)
Height:	5ft 0in (1.52m)
Empty Weight:	500lb (226.7kg)
Max Take Off:	1,100lb (499kg)
Powerplant:	1 x 100hp (74.56kW) Continental O-200-A piston.
Cruise Speed:	205mph (330km/h)
Max Speed:	220mph (354km/h)
Range:	1,000 miles (1,609km)
Preserved:	International Sport Aviation Museum, Lakeland Linder Regional Airport, Florida, USA.

Republic RC-3 Seabee

Subject: Republic RC-3 Seabee at Lakeland Linder, Florida, 2005. US registration NC 6240K.
Statistics: Republic RC-3 Seabee.

The Republic Aviation Corp. (formerly Seversky) bought the rights to the Seabee flying boat from designer P.H. Spencer in 1943 and went on to manufacture more than 1,000 of the type. It was an attractive deal for Republic and an astute deal for Spencer too, as he received a royalty payment for every Seabee delivered. This was a revolutionary aircraft for its day, perhaps the first truly practical flying boat for use by private pilots. Its spacious, comfortable, fully enclosed cockpit could accommodate, for the first time, touring pilots and their families. The Seabee opened new doors to a whole generation of pilots and would-be explorers, and substantial numbers were sold throughout North America and Canada. Robust, forgiving, and blessed with extraordinary longevity, large numbers of the Seabee are still in service today.

Country of Origin:	USA
First Flight:	1944
Accommodation:	4
Wingspan:	37ft 8in (11.48m)
Length:	27ft 11in (8.5m)
Height:	9ft 7in (2.9m)
Empty Weight:	1,900lb (862kg)
Max Take Off:	3,000lb (1,360kg)
Powerplant:	1 x 215hp (160kW) Franklin 6A8-215-B8F piston.
Cruise Speed:	105mph (169km/h)
Max Speed:	120mph (193km/h)
Service Ceiling:	12,000ft (3,657m)
Range:	550 miles (885km)
Number Manufactured:	1,060 of all types built during 1946 and 1947.
Flying or in service:	Large numbers of Seabee RC-3s still in service.
Preserved:	Steven F. Udvar-Hazy Center, Chantilly, Virginia, USA. Canadian Bushplane Heritage Centre, Ottawa, Canada. Southern Museum of Flight, Alabama, USA.

Republic P-47D Thunderbolt

Subject: Republic P-47D Thunderbolt.
Statistics: Republic P-47D Thunderbolt.

When the first batch of P-47s reached the 8th Air Force in Britain in 1943 the type quickly won the trust and respect of its pilots. Its sheer bulk and momentum, combined with its massive firepower, caused the Thunderbolt to be regarded with trepidation by the Axis pilots. If you did get onto the tail of a P-47 it could withstand fearsome firepower and still continue flying. If a Thunderbolt got onto your tail its 8 heavy machine guns would finish you off in seconds. As well as operating in the role of long-range escort fighter, the P-47 was designed to undertake ground strafing and bombing missions. In the strafing role its 8 forward-firing machine guns were designed to cut a wide swathe through any area of hostile activity while its 3-to-5 hardpoints could accommodate a wide variety of freefall munitions.

Country of Origin:	USA
First Flight:	1941
Accommodation:	1
Wingspan:	40ft 9in (12.42m)
Length:	36ft 1in (10.99m)
Height:	14ft 2in (4.31m)
Max Take Off:	19,400lb (8,800kg)
Powerplant:	1 x 2,535hp (1,889kW) Pratt & Whitney R-2800-59 Double Wasp radial powerplant.
Cruise Speed:	350mph (563km/h)
Max Speed:	428mph (690km/h)
Range:	590 miles (950km)
Number Manufactured:	15,676 of all Variants.
Flying or in service:	Up to 12 airworthy with private owners and collections.
Preserved:	Steven F. Udvar-Hazy Center, Chantilly, Virginia, USA. Thunderbolt II, RAF Museum, London, UK (P-47D). USAF Armament Museum, Elgin Air Force Base, Shalimar, Florida, USA (PN-47N). National Museum of the US Air Force, Wright-Patterson AFB, Dayton, Ohio, USA.

Ritter SDSC Floatplane

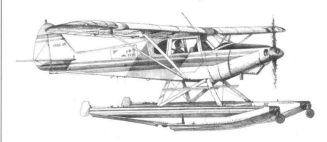

Subject: Frank Ritter's SDSC Floatplane.
Statistics: Ritter SDSC Floatplane.

A one-off amateur-built amphibious sports-plane by US Experimental Aircraft Association member John Ritter of Wyoming, USA. John's garage-built Ritter Floatplane has proved itself over 10 years and 1,100 hours of flying pleasure.

Country of Origin:	USA
First Flight:	1996
Accommodation:	2
Wingspan:	38ft 8in (11.78m)
Length:	23ft 2in (7.01m) (with floats)
Height:	9ft 2in (2.74m) (with floats)
Empty Weight:	1,604lb (727kg) (with floats)
Max Take Off:	2,321lb (1052kg) (with floats)

Powerplant:	1 x 180hp (134.2kW) Lycoming O-360 C1G horizontally opposed piston engine.
Cruise Speed:	130mph (209km/h) without floats. 110mph (177km/h) with floats.
Max Speed:	138mph (222km/h) without floats. 115mph (185km/h) with floats.
Number Manufactured:	1
Flying or in service:	1

Robinson
R-44 Astro

Subject: Robinson R-44 Astro 4-seat helicopter.
Statistics: Robinson R-44 Astro.

The Robinson Helicopter Company of Torrance, California, was greatly encouraged by the continued popularity of its R-22 series and so began the development of a larger and more powerful 4-seat variant. Following its first flight in 1990 it was clear that the R-44 Astro held great appeal for Robinson's existing R-22 customer base as well as for a host of small helicopter operators, owners and training schools. With capital and operating costs which are only a fraction of those of other helicopter types, the R-44 Astro will continue to grow and expand its sizeable segment of the market. When Robinson does eventually enter the lucrative turbine helicopter market it will cause much upset and soul-searching to an industry which has shown little or no interest in producing cost-effective low-technology helicopters.

Country of Origin:	USA
First Flight:	1990
Accommodation:	4
Rotor Diameter:	33ft 0in (10.05m)
Length:	29ft 9in (9.06m)
Height:	10ft 9in (3.27m)
Empty Weight:	1,397lb (633kg)
Max Take Off:	2,394lb (1,086kg)

Powerplant:	1 x 260hp (194kW) Lycoming O-540 horizontally opposed 6-cylinder piston engine.
Cruise Speed:	130mph (209km/h)
Max Speed:	150mph (241km/h)
Service Ceiling:	14,000ft (4,267m)
Range:	400 miles (643km)
Number Manufactured:	Over 1,000 manufactured.
Flying or in service:	Widely in service.
Preserved:	Steven F. Udvar-Hazy Center, Chantilly, Virginia, USA.

Rockwell 690
Turbo Commander

Subject: Rockwell 690 Turbo Commander, which flies with operator Helicargo and is registered in Colombia as HK-4370.
Statistics: Rockwell 690B Turbo Commander.

Rockwell's 690 Turbo Commander is a pressurized corporate, utility and military transport. Derived from the earlier Strike Commander 500S, the new 690 Turbo Commander was designed to cruise at higher levels with all of the reliability and smoothness that turboprop powerplants provide. In its military and public service roles the 690 Turbo Commander has been used for tasks as diverse as VIP transport, customs patrol, and airborne snow surveying.

Country of Origin:	USA
First Flight:	1968
Accommodation:	Pilot + 7 passengers.
Wingspan:	46ft 8in (14.22m)
Length:	44ft 4in (13.51m)
Height:	14ft 9in (4.49m)
Empty Weight:	6,830lb (3,098kg)
Max Take Off:	10,325lb (4,683kg)
Powerplant:	2 x 700hp (522kW) Garrett AiResearch TPE 331-5-251K turboprop engines.
Max Speed:	327mph (526.2km/h)
Service Ceiling:	31,000ft (9,449m)
Range:	1,689 miles (2,718km)
Flying or in service:	In service.

Rockwell
B-1A and B-1B

Subject: Rockwell B-1B Lancer of the United States Air Force.
Statistics: Rockwell B-1B Lancer.

Rockwell's B-1B Lancer is a low-altitude penetration bomber which was designed in the early 1970s to deliver gravity-fall nuclear weapons deep into enemy territories. Although it is not known for its stealth characteristics its ultra-low-level flightpath and its shielded turbofan arrangement gives it a radar signature which is only 1/5 that of the B-52. Flying immediately above ground level gives the Lancer every advantage in hostile environments, where its reduced radar signature is likely to be lost in ground clutter or to be indistinguishable from other low-level returns. To make such sustained low-level flight possible the B-1B is provided with an advanced terrain-following radar system which surveys the contours of the terrain ahead and ensures that the aircraft hugs them at all times. In this low-level environment where hostile missiles are unlikely to be able to engage it, the Lancer has a very good chance of penetrating any nation's defensive systems to deliver its cargo of up to 24 B61/B83 nuclear bombs.

Country of Origin:	USA
First Flight:	1974
Accommodation:	4
Wingspan:	136ft 8in (41.65m) unswept. 78ft 2in (23.82m) swept.
Length:	147ft 0in (44.8m)
Height:	34ft 10in (10.61m)
Empty Weight:	192,000lb (87,090kg)
Max Take Off:	477,000lb (216,363kg)
Powerplant:	4 x 30,780lb (136.9kN) General Electric F101-GE-102 turbofans.
Cruise Speed:	630mph (1,014km/h)
Max Speed:	825mph (1,327km/h)
Range:	7,455 miles (11,997km)
Number Manufactured:	4 B-1A development aircraft and 100 B-1B production airframes.
Flying or in service:	In service.

Rotorway Exec Home-build Helicopter

Subject: Rotorway Exec 162F.
Statistics: Rotorway Exec 162F.

There are several kitbuild helicopters available to amateur constructors but, among these, the RotorWay Exec is by far the most sophisticated. In choosing any helicopter project it is important to examine the numbers of hours flown by each of the helicopter types and in this test the RotorWay Exec always proves its higher levels of reliability and serviceability. The RotorWay 162F, introduced in 1995, is an upgraded variant of the marque with an all-new FADEC digital control system and improved performance.

Country of Origin:	USA
First Flight:	1980
Accommodation:	2
Rotor Diameter:	25ft 0in (7.62m)
Length:	28ft 10in (8.78m)
Height:	8ft 0in (2.43m)
Empty Weight:	975lb (442kg)
Max Take Off:	1,500lb (680kg)
Powerplant:	1 x 152hp (113.3kW) Rotorway RW-152 piston.
Cruise Speed:	95mph (152km/h)
Max Speed:	115mph (185km/h)
Range:	180 miles (290km)
Number Manufactured:	Approximately 500 kits sold and up to 300 examples completed.
Flying or in service:	Up to 300 Execs in service.
Preserved:	Southern Museum of Flight, Alabama, USA.

Rubik R-11B Cimbora Glider

Subject: Rubik R-11B Cimbora Glider, registered in Hungary as HA-5035.
Statistics: Rubik R-11B Cimbora Glider.

Glider design is an art form, and Erno Rubik's Model R-11B competition glider of 1938 is among the most beautiful and perfectly detailed gliders of all time. At this specialist level of aeronautical design every tiny screw and stitch has to be carefully considered and its weight balanced against its function. Rubik's R-11B glider wraps all of this thought and care into a sleek and beautifully finished airframe which is still an excellent gliding performer to this day.

Country of Origin:	Hungary
First Flight:	1938
Accommodation:	2
Wingspan:	45ft 11in (14.0m)
Length:	29ft 6in (9.0m)
Powerplant:	No powerplant.
Flying or in service:	1

Rutan Long Ez

Subject: Dave Ryan's superbly presented Long Ez is based at Waterford Airport. Registered in Ireland as EI-CPI.
Statistics: Rutan Long Ez.

Burt Rutan's Varieze caused a sensation when it first appeared at Oshkosh in the mid-1970s. Despite its eccentric appearance it could fly faster, higher and further than any other aircraft of similar engine size and within months the type was being built by enthusiasts and home-builders

across the USA. By 1979 Rutan had turned his attentions to the design of a larger touring aircraft with longer range. The Long Ez was identical in configuration to the Varieze save that its swept inboard strake sections were enlarged to facilitate larger 52-gallon fuel tanks and additional baggage space. Up to 4,000 sets of Long Ez plans were sold to amateur builders from which some 800 aircraft have reached completion. The Long Ez is a superb touring aircraft in which the pilot and passenger can sit in a comfortable semi-reclined position over sectors of up to 8 hours' duration (16 hours with pilot only). Like the Varieze, the Long Ez has won, and continues to hold, many aviation titles and records over the years.

Country of Origin:	USA
First Flight:	1979
Accommodation:	2
Wingspan:	26ft 1in (7.95m)
Length:	16ft 9in (5.1m)
Height:	7ft 10in (2.38m)
Empty Weight:	740lb (335kg)
Max Take Off:	1,325lb (601kg) 1,425lb (646kg) with waiver.
Powerplant:	1 x 115hp (85.74kW) Lycoming O-235 piston engine.
Cruise Speed:	187mph (301km/h)
Max Speed:	200mph (321km/h)
Service Ceiling:	26,000ft (7,924m)
Range:	2,010 miles (3,235km)
Preserved:	The prototype Varieze, from which the Long Ez has been developed, is on display at the EAA Air Museum, Oshkosh, Wisconsin, USA.

Rutan VariViggen

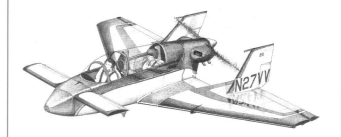

Subject: Rutan VariViggen registered N27VV.
Statistics: Rutan VariViggen.

The VariViggen prototype flew for the first time on 27 February 1972 and so began Rutan's long association with canard foreplanes and unorthodox aircraft configurations. Composed of wood and fabric, the Viggen's configuration was shockingly different to the other light aircraft of the time. Rutan released the VariViggen plans for sale to the many amateur builders who requested them and in the following years a small fleet of VariViggens began to reach completion in workshops and garages across America.

Country of Origin:	USA
First Flight:	1972
Accommodation:	2
Wingspan:	19ft 0in (5.79m)
Length:	20ft 0in (6.09m)
Height:	5ft 6in (1.67m)
Empty Weight:	1,020lb (462kg)
Max Take Off:	1,700lb (771kg)
Powerplant:	1 x 150hp (111.8kW) Lycoming O-320 pusher powerplant.
Cruise Speed:	150mph (241km/h)
Max Speed:	165mph (265km/h)
Service Ceiling:	14,900ft (4,541m).
Range:	300 miles (483km).
Number Manufactured:	Close to 1,000 sets of plans sold but relatively few projects reached completion.
Preserved:	International Sport Aviation Museum, Lakeland Linder Regional Airport, Florida, USA.

Royal Aircraft Factory SE-5A

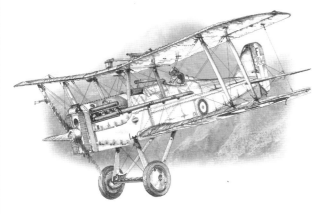

Subject: RAF SE-5A of the Shuttleworth Collection, registered F904 in military life and G-EBIA in its post-military life.
Statistics: Royal Aircraft Factory SE-5A.

British flying ace Edward Mannock scored 50 of his 73 kills in the SE-5A, while celebrated ace Albert Ball clocked up 34 of his 44 victories in the type. The SE-5A was undoubtedly one of the best fighting aircraft of its time and it made a deep impression when it was introduced to the Western Front in the hands of Ball, Mannock and some of the other great aerial fighters of the day.

Country of Origin:	UK
First Flight:	1916
Accommodation:	1
Wingspan:	26ft 7in (7.92m)
Length:	20ft 11in (6.37m)
Height:	9ft 6in (2.89m)
Empty Weight:	1,397lb (633kg)
Max Take Off:	1,988lb (901kg)
Powerplant:	1 x 200hp (194kW) Hispano-Suiza 8 cylinder piston or 1 x Wolseley Viper piston.
Max Speed:	135mph (217km/h)
Service Ceiling:	22,000ft (6,705m)
Range:	340 miles (547km)
Number Manufactured:	5,205 built.
Preserved:	Shuttleworth Trust, Old Warden, UK. RAF Museum, Hendon, London, UK. US Army Aviation Museum, Fort Rucker, Ozark, Alabama, USA.

Ryan B-1 Brougham

Subject: Ryan B-1, 'Spirit of St Louis'.
Statistics: Ryan B-1, 'Spirit of St Louis'.

The Ryan B-1 Brougham was a commercial variant of the 'Spirit of St Louis', the tiny aircraft that famously carried Lindbergh across the Atlantic. Lindbergh's aircraft was developed under his own watchful direction from the Ryan M-2 Mailplane of 1926. After Lindbergh's historic flight the 'Spirit of St Louis' became a household name across the world and the Ryan B-1 Brougham, by association, became a bestseller for Ryan. In all, a total of 150 of the type was built and delivered to operators in both the USA and abroad.

Country of Origin:	USA
First Flight:	1927
Accommodation:	5
Wingspan:	42ft 0in (12.8m)
Length:	27ft 9in (8.45m)
Height:	9ft 10in (2.99m)
Empty Weight:	2,150lb (975kg)
Max Take Off:	5,135lb (2,330kg)
Powerplant:	1 x 225hp (168kW) Wright J-5

	Whirlwind radial engine.
Max Speed:	126mph (202.6km/h)
Range:	In excess of 3,600 miles.
Number Manufactured:	150
Preserved:	Smithsonian National Air and Space Museum, Washington, DC, USA. Yanks Air Museum Chino Airport, California, USA.

Ryan L-17 Navion

Subject: Ryan L-17 Navion flew into Lakeland Linder Regional Airport, Florida, during the EAA's 2005 fly-in event.
Statistics: Ryan Navion B Super 260.

The Navion was produced in many different configurations by its long line of manufacturers for various duties, from basic utility transport to high-performance personal touring, to military liaison and aerial observation duties. Tough and reliable, forgiving and capable, the Navion was built in large numbers with production by various aircraft manufacturers stretching from mid-1947 right up to 1976. Today, Navions of all vintage are a regular sight at airfields and flying events across the US and Europe, and military Navion L-17s tend to be particularly sought after and cared for by their proud owners.

Country of Origin:	USA
First Flight:	1946
Accommodation:	4
Wingspan:	33ft 5in (10.19m)
Length:	27ft 6in (8.38m)
Height:	8ft 8in (2.64m)
Empty Weight:	1,930lb (875kg)
Max Take Off:	2,850lb (1,292kg)
Powerplant:	1 x 260hp (194kW) Lycoming GO-435-C2 piston engine.
Cruise Speed:	155mph (249km/h)
Max Speed:	17mph (280km/h)
Service Ceiling:	21,500ft (6,553m)
Range:	750 miles (1,200km)

Number Manufactured:	2,631 NaVions built by North American and Ryan. A further 172 Rangemaster HS by NaVion and 8 more by Consolidated.
Flying or in service:	Many NaVions still flying with private owners & enthusiasts.
Preserved:	US Army Aviation Museum, Fort Rucker, Ozark, Alabama, USA.

Ryan STM Trainer

Subject: Ryan STM Trainer.
Statistics: Ryan PT-22.

Claude Ryan's ST (sport-trainer) series was developed by the Ryan Aeronautical Company and flew for the first time on 8 June 1934. A low-wing braced monoplane with tandem open cockpits, the ST series was developed and uprated by Ryan with a succession of more powerful engine types to meet the requirements of sports flying, club training and various military applications. Variants included the S-T, the STA, the STM and various PT models for the USAAC. Over 1,500 of all models were completed for private owners, aeroclubs, military training schools and for export to the air forces of several South American countries.

Country of Origin:	USA
First Flight:	1934
Accommodation:	1 or 2
Wingspan:	30ft 1in (9.17m)
Length:	22ft 5in (6.83m)
Height:	7ft 2in (2.18m)
Empty Weight:	1,310lb (594kg)
Max Take Off:	1,860lb (844kg)
Powerplant:	1 x 160hp (119kW) Kinner R-540-1 piston powerplant.
Cruise Speed:	110mph (177km/h)
Max Speed:	130mph (209km/h)
Service Ceiling:	21,500ft (6,553m)
Range:	352 miles (566km)
Number Manufactured:	Over 1,500 of all S-T, STA, STM and PT series completed.
Flying or in service:	Small numbers still airworthy.

Saab J-29F

Subject: Saab J-29F of the Swedish air force.
Statistics: Saab J-29F.

Saab's J-29 was the first swept-wing fighter to be put into series production after the war. Europe was beginning to find its feet again after years of unprecedented destruction but there was a new chill in international politics and Sweden was all too aware of its vulnerable position immediately adjacent to the USSR. So it was that, in this environment of uncertainty, Sweden rushed to get its first jet-powered interceptor fighter into the air. With the assistance of the British de Havilland Ghost turbojet powerplant the first flight of the J-29 took place in September of 1948. Thereafter, all J-29 variants were provided with an all-Swedish-built version of the Ghost powerplant. The J-29F was a later interceptor fighter development of the type.

Country of Origin:	Sweden
First Flight:	1948
Accommodation:	1
Wingspan:	36ft 1in (10.99m)
Length:	33ft 2in (10.11m)
Height:	12ft 3in (3.73m)
Max Take Off:	13,360lb (6,060kg)
Powerplant:	1 x 5,000lb (22.24kN) Swedish built version of the de Havilland Ghost turbojet.
Max Speed:	659mph (1,060km/h)
Range:	1,678 miles (2,700km)
Preserved:	Austrian Air Force Museum, Graz, Austria.

Saab 35 Draken

Subject: Saab J-35 Draken of the Danish air force.
Statistics: Saab J-35F Draken.

With its highly swept double delta platform and its 76.52kN Volvo Flygmotor turbojet, the Saab Draken is a stunningly powerful interceptor fighter with near-Mach 2 performance and an enormous rate of climb. A total of 657 of the type was built for use by the air forces of Sweden, Denmark, Austria and Finland.

Country of Origin:	Sweden
First Flight:	1955
Accommodation:	1 or 2
Wingspan:	30ft 11in (9.42m)
Length:	50ft 4in (15.34m)
Height:	12ft 9in (3.88m)
Empty Weight:	18,190lb (8,250kg)
Max Take Off:	33,075lb (15,000kg)
Powerplant:	1 x 17,200lb (76.52kN) Volvo Flygmotor turbojet.
Max Speed:	1,320mph (2,124km/h)
Service Ceiling:	60,040ft (18,300m)
Range:	1,720 miles (2,768km)
Number Manufactured:	657 manufactured.
Flying or in service:	Up to 24 still in service with the Austrian air force.
Preserved:	Austrian Air Force Museum, Graz, Austria. Newark Air Museum, Nottingham, Nottinghamshire, UK. Norwegian Aviation Museum, Bodø, Norway.

Saab JA-37 Viggen

Subject: Saab JA-37 Viggen of the Swedish air force.
Statistics: Saab JA-37 Viggen.

Sweden's unique defensive order of battle is built around deploying the fastest and the most agile second- and third-generation supersonic fighters from disbursed preselected roadways and unprepared sites right across the country. To succeed with this plan, however, a new-generation high-performance interceptor fighter with full STOL capabilities was required. Effectively Sweden's new fighter would have to operate from short lengths of public roadway and yet be able to compete at the highest levels with the very best fighters of the East and the West. Sweden's independent JA-37 Viggen fighter, developed by Saab, fulfils this role with distinction.

Country of Origin:	Sweden
First Flight:	1967
Accommodation:	1 or 2
Wingspan:	34ft 9in (10.59m)
Length:	53ft 10in (16.40m)
Height:	19ft 4in (5.89m)
Empty Weight:	20,950lb (9,500kg)
Max Take Off:	37,485lb (17,000kg)
Powerplant:	1 x 28,110lb (125kN) Volvo Flygmotor turbofan with afterburner.
Cruise Speed:	913mph (1,469km/h)
Max Speed:	1,320mph (2,125km/h)
Service Ceiling:	60,000ft (18,288m)
Range:	1,250 miles (2,000km)
Number Manufactured:	329 of all production variants plus prototypes.
Flying or in service:	Still on force with the Swedish air force.

Scaled Composites Pond Racer

Subject: Scaled Composites Pond Racer prototype, registered N221BP.
Statistics: Scaled Composites Pond Racer.

The Pond Racer was an unlimited-class racing aircraft which was financed by Bob Pond with the intention of finding an alternative to the unfortunate and shortsighted practice of butchering the scarce remaining stocks of warbird powerplants for use in pylon-racing aircraft. To succeed in this noble venture, however, Pond would need to produce a new unlimited-class aircraft which would far out-perform all of the existing racers and so he turned to designer Burt Rutan. The Pond Racer began to take shape at Rutan's Mojave-based Scaled Composites 'Skunk Works' and it appeared at the world-famous Reno Air Races for the first time in 1991. While the Pond Racer airframe showed much promise, the Electromotive-Nissan powerplants never reached their full potential and fell far short of

delivering the 1,000hp promised. Tragically, the Pond Racer crashed while undertaking a forced landing on 14 September 1993 and test pilot Rick Brickert was killed. Following this tragedy the project was abandoned.

Country of Origin:	USA
First Flight:	1990
Accommodation:	1
Wingspan:	25ft 5in (7.74m)
Length:	20ft 0in (6.09m)
Powerplant:	2 x Electromotive-Nissan VG-30 3-litre GTP powerplants.
Number Manufactured:	1

Saunders Roe SR-A/1

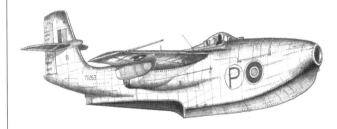

Subject: Saunders Roe SR-A/1 in the markings TG263, the first of the 3 prototypes and the only one to survive.
Statistics: Saunders Roe SR-A/1

The Saunders Roe SR-A/1 jet-powered flying boat was developed as a result of an Air Ministry specification for a high-performance jet fighter which would support the massive naval drive across the Pacific towards Japan. The type was the first ever jet-powered flying boat and the first flying boat to exceed 500mph in level flight. The SR-A/1 prototype, TG263, flew for the first time in 1947 and put up a remarkable display of high-speed flight. A total of 3 prototypes was completed and, while the 2 later aircraft were lost in accidents during the test programme, the third remains intact and preserved to this day.

Country of Origin:	UK
First Flight:	1947
Accommodation:	1
Wingspan:	46ft 0in (14.02m)
Length:	50ft 0in (15.24m)
Height:	16ft 9in (5.10m)
Max Take Off:	19,000lb (8,618kg)
Powerplant:	3,237lb (14.4kN) Metropolitan Vickers F-2/4 Beryl turbojets.
Max Speed:	510mph (820km/h)

Service Ceiling:	43,000ft (13,110m)
Range:	650 miles (1,046km)
Number Manufactured:	3 flying prototypes only.
Preserved:	The 1 surviving airframe is preserved at the Imperial War Museum, London, UK.

Saunders Roe AOP-12 Skeeter

Subject: Saunders Roe AOP-12 Skeeter.
Statistics: Saunders Roe AOP-12 Skeeter.

When Saunders Roe acquired the Cierva Autogyro Company in 1951 they inherited its superb Skeeter light helicopter programme which, having achieved first flight in 1948, was in an advanced state of development. SARO continued development of the diminutive helicopter for both military and civilian usage and, in so doing, established a reliable and competent helicopter platform that would dominate the lightweight helicopter market for many years to come. The Skeeter served with the observation and training wings of the UK Army Air Corps and, in smaller numbers, with the Royal Air Force. Germany, too, selected the type and operated 10 Skeeter MK-50s and MK-51s. Surplus military Skeeters have been offered to the civilian market on several occasions over the years and a number of the type continue to operate on the civilian register to this day.

Country of Origin:	UK
First Flight:	1948
Accommodation:	2
Rotor Diameter:	32ft 0in (9.75m)
Length:	26 ft 6in (8.08m)
Height:	7ft 6in (2.31m)
Empty Weight:	1,656lb (751kg)
Max Take Off:	2,200lb (998kg)
Powerplant:	1 x 215hp (160kW) de Havilland Gipsy Major.
Cruise Speed:	101mph (162km/h)
Max Speed:	109mph (175km/h)

Range: 215 miles (344km)
Number Manufactured: 64 of the AOP-12 Variant alone as well as substantial numbers of other Variants.
Flying or in service: A sizeable number of army surplus Skeeters are flying in private ownership to this day.

Scaled Composites Proteus

Subject: Scaled Composites Proteus N281PR displays an under-fuselage radome disc.
Statistics: Scaled Composites Proteus.

Scaled Composites Inc. developed the long-endurance Proteus high-altitude aircraft for use as a systems platform for relaying of cellular phone signals for project sponsor Angel Technologies Corp. Highly efficient and cost effective, the Proteus is capable of remaining on station for up to 14 hours, and as such it presents a whole new array of possibilities in terms of signal relaying, border control, mapping and police work. The configuration of the Proteus is unique and highly unorthodox, its tandem wing arrangement allowing for the insertion of large fuselage plugs and sensors as required to facilitate the specific requirements of individual customers and governmental agencies.

Country of Origin: USA
First Flight: 1998
Accommodation: Flightcrew of 2 + Various mission-specific pods/plugs.
Wingspan: 77ft 7in (23.64m)
Length: 56ft 3in (17.14m)
Height: 17ft 7in (5.35m)
Empty Weight: 5,860lb (2,658kg)
Max Take Off: 12,500lb (5,669kg)
Powerplant: 2 x 2,293lb (10.2kN) Williams FJ44 turbofans.
Cruise Speed: 219mph (352km/h)
Service Ceiling: 61,920ft (18,873m)
Range: 2,648 miles (4,261km) or up to 14 hours on station.
Number Manufactured: 1 prototype completed but fleet production planned.
Flying or in service: 1
Preserved: Can be seen at Mojave Airport and air shows.

Scaled Composites Space Ship One

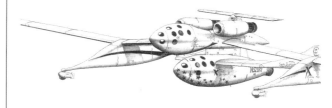

Subject: Scaled Composites White Knight registration N318SL, and Space Ship One registration N328KF: surely the only spacecraft on the US Federal Aviation Administration register of aircraft.
Statistics: Scaled Composites White Knight.

The White Knight was developed by Scaled Composites for the sole purpose of providing a suitable launch platform for Space Ship One. As with many of Burt Rutan's designs the White Knight is highly unorthodox in its configuration with a unique landing-gear arrangement, twin tail booms and the remarkable Space Ship One slung beneath its fuselage. The White Knight and Space Ship One were designed to have identical cockpit layouts in order to facilitate the training of Space Ship One pilots/astronauts, a simple and effective design decision which provided considerable benefits during the Space Ship One flight development programme and the subsequent flights into space.

Country of Origin: USA
First Flight: 2004
Accommodation: Pilot + 2 passengers in White Knight. Up to 3 astronauts in Space Ship One.
Powerplant: 2 x 3,850lb (17.1kN) General Electric J85-GE-5 turbofans.
Number Manufactured: 1
Flying or in service: 1
Preserved: Smithsonian National Air and Space Museum, Washington, DC, USA.

Scottish Aviation Jetstream T2

Subject: Jetstream T2 instructional airframe of the Royal Navy.
Statistics: Scottish Aviation Jetstream T1.

Developed originally by Handley Page, the Jetstream flew for the first time in 1967. Following the closure of Handley Page in 1970, however, the Jetstream project was purchased by Scottish Aviation, which went on to build 26 Jetstream T1s for Britain's Royal Navy. The T1 was an advanced-training aircraft which was fitted out internally with 2 highly sophisticated training consoles for Royal Navy observation instructors and their students. 16 of the 26 original Royal Navy airframes were upgraded to Jetstream T2 standard with improved radar systems and electronics suites, and small numbers of the type continue in operational service to this day.

Country of Origin: UK
First Flight: First Handley Page Jetstream flew in 1967. First Scottish Aviation T2 flew in 1973.
Accommodation: Flight crew + 2 tuition consoles.
Wingspan: 52ft 0in (15.84m)
Length: 47ft 1in (14.35m)
Height: 17ft 11in (5.46m)
Max Take Off: 12,566lb (5,700kg)
Powerplant: 2 x 996hp (743kW) Turbomeca Astazou XVI.D turboprops.
Max Speed: 282mph (453km/h)
Service Ceiling: 26,000ft (7,924m)
Range: 1,380 miles (2,224km)
Number Manufactured: 26 of the T1 Variant built for the Royal Navy and 16 of these converted to T2 status.
Flying or in service: Still operated by the Royal Navy.

Schweizer BD-2 Phoenix

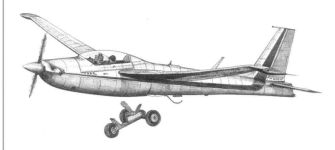

Subject: Schweizer BD-2 Phoenix discarding its take-off bogie.
Statistics: Schweizer BD-2 Phoenix.

A high-altitude research aircraft from long-time sailplane manufacturer Schweizer.

Country of Origin: USA
First Flight: 1967
Accommodation: 1

Schweizer 330 Sky Knight

Subject: Schweizer 330 Sky Knight.
Statistics: Schweizer 330.

Developed from the Hughes 300 series, the Schweizer 330 is a turbine-powered general utility helicopter. Schweizer had been manufacturing the Hughes 300 under licence from McDonnell Douglas since 1983, and in November of 1986 they purchased the rights to the type and began the development of a new turbine-powered version. The Schweizer 330 was designed to fill a number of military and utility roles from aerial observation to training, border patrol, general transport and law enforcement.

Country of Origin: USA
First Flight: 1st Schweizer 330 flew in 1988.
Accommodation: Pilot + 2 passengers.
Rotor Diameter: 26ft 7in (8.16m)
Length: 22ft 4in (6.82m)
Height: 9ft 6in (2.89m)
Empty Weight: 1,117lb (506kg)

Max Take Off: 2,226lb (1,009kg)
Powerplant: 1 x 420hp (313.2KW) Allison
                          250-C-20 turboshaft.
Max Speed: 115mph (185km/h)
Range: 309 miles (498km)
Number Manufactured: Still under construction
Flying or in service: Flying with civilian operators
                          and with the Venezuelan army.

Shavrov Sh-2 Amphibian

Subject: Shavrov Sh-2 amphibian.
Statistics: Shavrov Sh-2.

More than 700 of this Soviet flying boat were built in the early 1930s and the type was used as a training airframe and light observation aircraft. Its role was expanded in more remote and isolated areas to take in light transport duties and air-ambulance work. In many cases the Sh-2 was the only connection between isolated rural communities and civilization. After the type passed its state acceptance trials in 1931 production began, and more than 700 had been completed by 1934 when the type was abandoned in favour of more advanced designs.

Country of Origin: USSR
First Flight: 1930
Accommodation: Pilot + 1 passenger.
Wingspan: 42ft 7in (13.0m)
Length: 26ft 10in (8.2m)
Empty Weight: 1,455lb (660kg)
Max Take Off: 2,066lb (937kg)
Powerplant: 1 x 100hp (74.5KW) M-11
                          powerplant.
Cruise Speed: 87mph (140km/h)
Service Ceiling: 13,120ft (4,000m)
Range: 807 miles (1,300km)
Number Manufactured: In excess of 700 completed.
Flying or in service: At least one airworthy and
                          flying to this day.
Preserved: 1

Short Brothers S-10 Gurnard

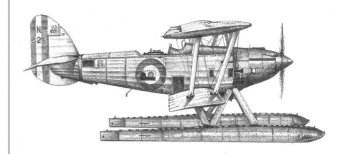

Subject: Short Brothers S-10 Gurnard.
Statistics: Short Brothers S-10 Gurnard.

Brothers Horace, Eustace and Oswald Short founded Short Brothers Ltd in 1909 and commenced designing and manufacturing aircraft at their Isle of Sheppey base. The brothers' excellent folding-wing biplanes quickly won favour with the Royal Navy and Short Brothers Ltd soon began to build a solid reputation. The Short Gurnard of 1929 was a 2-seat carrier-borne fighter biplane of wood and fabric covering. With its relatively clean airframe and its well-faired engine, the Gurnard had a maximum speed of 166mph and an endurance of 3.5 hours.

Country of Origin: UK
First Flight: 1929
Accommodation: 2
Wingspan: 37ft 0in (11.27m)
Length: 31ft 6in (9.60m)
Empty Weight: 3,660lb (1,660kg)
Max Take Off: 5,194lb (2,356kg)
Powerplant: 1 x 525hp (391KW) Rolls-Royce
                          Kestrel 12-cylinder engine.
Max Speed: 166mph (267km/h)
Endurance: 3.5 hours

Shin Meiwa PS-1 and US-1

Subject: Shin Meiwa PS-1 and US-1.
Statistics: Shin Meiwa US-1A.

Developed to meet the requirements of Japan's Maritime Self Defense Force, the Shin Meiwa US-1A is a heavy long-range flying boat which is used to patrol the seas around Japan's lengthy chain of islands. During the Cold War years Japan became greatly alarmed at the immense size of the Soviet submarine fleet and began the development of a large anti-submarine flying boat. The SS-2 flying boat was given the designation PS-1 when it became operational with the Japanese Maritime Self Defense Force. Of the 2 early prototypes and the 42 production PS-1 airframes which were delivered, just 16 were selected to be upgraded to US-1A status.

Country of Origin:	Japan
First Flight:	1967 for the prototype PS-1. 1974 for the US-1 upgrade.
Accommodation:	Flight crew of 5 on the US-1A. Crew of up to 10 on the PS-1.
Wingspan:	108ft 9in (33.14m)
Length:	109ft 9in (33.45m)
Height:	32ft 6in (9.9m)
Empty Weight:	56,220lb (25,500kg)
Max Take Off:	99,200lb (44,996kg)
Powerplant:	4 x 3,400hp (2,535kW) Ishikawajima turboprops.
Cruise Speed:	265mph (426km/h)
Max Speed:	318mph (511km/h)
Range:	2,370 miles (3,814km)
Number Manufactured:	44 of all Variants, 16 of which have been upgraded to US-1A status.
Flying or in service:	16 still operational with JMSDF.

Short Solent III

Subject: Short Solent III registered G-AHIY.
Statistics: Short Solent II.

The civil version of the Short Seaford flying boat, the Solent was operated by BOAC on some of its long-distance over-sea routes. A total of 18 of the type served with the carrier, 12 of the earlier Solent II model with seating for 30 passengers, and 6 of the 34-seat Solent III model. The rapid development of large land-based airliners, however, was causing the large flying boats to look greatly less attractive to the main airline operators, and the days of the great flying boats were drawing to a close. In 1950 BOAC retired all of its flying boats in favour of land-based airliners.

Country of Origin:	UK
First Flight:	1946
Accommodation:	Flight crew of 3 + between 30 and 42 passengers.
Wingspan:	112ft 9in (34.36m)
Length:	87ft 8in (26.7m)
Empty Weight:	47,760lb (21,663kg)
Max Take Off:	78,000lb (35,380kg)
Powerplant:	4 x 1,690hp (766kW) Bristol Hercules 637 radials.
Max Speed:	273mph (439km/h)
Range:	1,800 miles (2,896km)
Number Manufactured:	18 of all Variants including prototype.
Preserved:	Former Tasman Airways Solent Mk IV is preserved at the Museum of Transport & Technology, Auckland, Australia. EX-BOAC Solent preserved at Western Aerospace Museum, Oakland, California, USA. Yanks Air Museum, Chino Airport, California, USA.

Short SC-1 VTOL

Subject: Short SC-1 prototype XG900, which is preserved at the Fleet Air Arm Museum, Yeovilton.
Statistics: Short SC-1.

Single-seat delta wing VTOL research airframe developed by Short to investigate the fledgling sciences of vertical lift and vectored thrust. The Short SC-1 made its first public appearance at the Farnborough Air Show of 1959 and the type generated huge public interest. The first prototype, XG900, was displayed at the Paris Air Show of 1961 and, in so doing, it became the first VTOL aircraft to cross the English Channel. After a difficult and protracted flight evaluation programme, during which test pilot J.R. Green tragically lost his life, the SC-1 was retired to storage.

Country of Origin:	UK
First Flight:	1957
Accommodation:	1
Wingspan:	23ft 0in (7.01m)

Length:	30ft 0in (9.14m)
Height:	11ft 0in (3.35m)
Empty Weight:	5,984lb (2,714kg)
Max Take Off:	7,689lb (3,487kg)
Powerplant:	5 x 2,000lb (8.89kN) Rolls-Royce RB.108 turbojets.
Max Speed:	184mph (296km/h)
Range:	150 miles (240km)
Number Manufactured:	2 prototypes built by Shorts of Belfast.
Preserved:	Fleet Air Arm Museum, Yeovilton, UK (Short SC-1 prototype XG900). Ulster Folk & Transport Museum, Hollywood, Northern Ireland (Short SC-1 prototype XG905).

Short 360

Subject: Short 360-300.
Statistics: Short 360-300.

The success of the Short SC-7 Skyvan of 1963 led to the development of the Short 330 commuter liner of 1974 and finally to the Short 360 commuter and feederliner of 1981. With their squared-off, spacious fuselages and their simple configuration, both the Short 330 and the Short 360 were very popular with regional airlines and smaller commuter operators. The Short 360 was the largest of the marque with capacity for 36 seats as well as the flight crew. A total of 164 of the type were delivered and many continue in operation to this day. Up to 17 of these ex-airline Short 360 airframes have been repurchased and upgraded to C-23B Sherpa configuration for the US Army with large rear loading ramp and modified twin-tail empennage.

Country of Origin:	UK
First Flight:	Short 360 first flew in 1981.
Accommodation:	Short 360 seats 36 + crew.
Wingspan:	74ft 9in (22.78m)
Length:	70ft 9in (21.56m)
Height:	23ft 10in (7.26m)
Empty Weight:	17,325lb (7,858kg)
Max Take Off:	27,042lb (12,266kg)
Powerplant:	2 x 1,425hp (1,062kW) Pratt & Whitney Canada PT6A-65AR turboprops.
Max Speed:	248mph (399km/h)

Range: 732 miles (1,178km)
Number Manufactured: 139 production Short 330s and 164 production Short 360s.
Flying or in service: Over 100 still in service across the world.

Short TT-2 Sturgeon

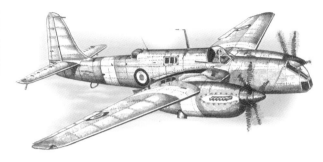

Subject: Short TT-2 Sturgeon.
Statistics: Short TT-2 Sturgeon.

The Sturgeon was first designed as a twin-engined naval reconnaissance bomber for deck operations off the Royal Navy's 'Ark Royal' and 'Hermes' Class aircraft carriers. With the cessation of hostilities in Europe, however, the type was deemed to be surplus to requirements and those airframes which had already been completed were converted for the purposes of carrier-based target towing, radar calibration and photographic surveillance.

Country of Origin: UK
First Flight: 1946
Accommodation: 2
Wingspan: 59ft 11in (18.26m)
Length: 44ft 0in (13.41m)
Height: 13ft 2in (4.01m)
Empty Weight: 18,126lb (8,222kg)
Powerplant: 2 X 2,080hp (1,551kW) Rolls-Royce Merlin powerplants.
Max Speed: 366mph (589km/h)
Number Manufactured: 22

Sikorsky R-4 Helicopter

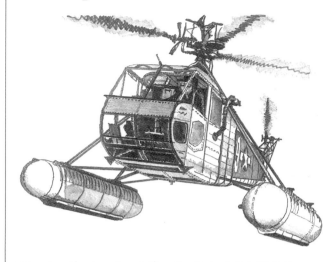

Subject: Float-equipped Sikorsky R-4 of the US Navy.
Statistics: Sikorsky R-4B.

The world's first helicopter to be put into series production, the prototype XR-4 flew for the first time in January of 1942. It was a superb effort given that Igor Sikorsky had managed to launch his first successful rotary-winged VS-300 aircraft only 3 years earlier. Now, using data gleaned from his VS-300, he had developed the R-4 to the point where it could be manufactured for issue to operational units. A total of 130 of the type was built before production was switched to Sikorsky's larger and more capable R-5 series. A small number of Sikorsky R-4 helicopters did see action in the last months of the war, primarily in the role of air-ambulances, but also as transports.

Country of Origin: USA
First Flight: 1942
Accommodation: 2
Rotor diameter: 38ft 1in (11.6m)
Length: 48ft 1in (14.65m)
Height: 12ft 5in (3.78m)
Empty Weight: 2,008lb (911kg)
Max Take Off: 2,537lb (1,150kg)
Powerplant: 1 X 185hp (138kW) Warner R-550-3 Super Scarab piston.
Max Speed: 74mph (120km/h)
Service Ceiling: 8,000ft (2,438m)
Range: 130 miles (209km)
Number Manufactured: 130 manufactured before production switched to the R-5.
Preserved: RAF Museum, Hendon, London, UK (R-4B Hoverfly 1).

SIAI-Marchetti SF-260

Subject: Civilian registered SIAI SF-260 Marchetti in borrowed US Air Force markings.
Statistics: SIAI SF-260 Marchetti.

Designer Stelio Frati developed the SF-260 civilian touring aircraft and sports-plane for Aviamilano, which then licensed SIAI-Marchetti to manufacture the type. It was fast, agile, and a superb aerobatic performer but it was too expensive to succeed on the civilian market and its first years were lean ones for its manufacturer. It was only when its huge potential as a military trainer was exploited that sales of the SF-260 really took off. By comparison with other military training aircraft the Marchetti represented excellent value and it quickly found its way into the inventories of up to 19 air forces across the world, including Ireland, Zambia, Belgium, Somalia, Tunisia and Ceylon.

Country of Origin: Italy
First Flight: 1964 (F-250 prototype).
Accommodation: 2
Wingspan: 27ft 5in (8.35m)
Length: 23ft 4in (7.11m)
Height: 7ft 11in (2.41m)
Empty Weight: 1,694lb (768kg)
Max Take Off: 2,860lb (1,297kg)
Powerplant: 1 X 260hp (194kW) Avco-Lycoming O-540 -E4A5 piston.
Max Speed: 189mph (304km/h)
Service Ceiling: 14,700ft (4,480m)
Range: 684 miles (1,100km)
Number Manufactured: More than 1,000.
Flying or in service: In service with many air forces across the world.

Sikorsky S-38B

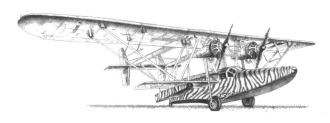

Subject: Sikorsky S-38B registration NC28V flew into the Experimental Aircraft Association convention at Lakeland Linder Regional Airport, Florida, 2005.
Statistics: Sikorsky S-38C.

A truly extraordinary sight on the ground or in the air, the Sikorsky S-38 carried Pan American's well-heeled passengers to their many Caribbean haunts. Given its 1924 vintage it was a superb achievement despite its virtual forest of booms, struts, braces, cables and ties. In recent years 2 beautifully detailed S-38C replicas have been built by Born Again Restorations and both make regular appearances on the US and Canadian air show circuit.

Country of Origin:	USA.
First Flight:	1924
Accommodation:	S-38B pilot + 8 passengers.
	S-38C pilot + 10 passengers.
Wingspan:	71ft 8in (21.84m)
Length:	40ft 3in (12.26m)
Height:	13ft 10in (4.21m)
Empty Weight:	6,460lb (2,930kg)
Max Take Off:	10,480lb (4,753kg)
Powerplant:	2 x 420hp (313kW) Pratt & Whitney Wasp pistons.
Cruise Speed:	110mph (177km/h)
Max Speed:	125mph (201km/h)
Service Ceiling:	16,000ft (4,876m)
Range:	600 miles (965km)
Number Manufactured:	101 of all variants built.
Flying or in service:	2 superb S-38C replicas flying.

Sikorsky S-39

Subject: Sikorsky S-39.
Statistics: Sikorsky S-39 B.

Igor Sikorsky's S-39 was a smaller, single-engined version of the 8- to 10-seat S-38 flying boat. Seating just 4 passengers as well as the pilot, the S-39 was intended as a personal transport and sports-plane. Again there was an abundance of struts and braces but with reduced spans and reduced loads the airframe was somewhat cleaner than its S-38 sibling.

Country of Origin:	USA.
First Flight:	1929
Accommodation:	1 pilot + 4 passengers.
Wingspan:	52ft 0in (15.84m)
Length:	31ft 11in (9.72m)
Empty Weight:	2,678lb (1,214kg)
Max Take Off:	4,000lb (1,814kg)
Powerplant:	1 x 300hp (223.7kW) Pratt & Whitney Wasp Junior.
Cruise Speed:	100mph (161km/h)
Max Speed:	119mph (191km/h)
Service Ceiling:	18,000ft (5,486m)
Range:	400 miles (643km)
Number Manufactured:	26 including prototypes.
Flying or in service:	1 restored by Dick Jackson of Rochester, New Hampshire, USA.
Preserved:	New England Air Museum, Bradley International Airport, Connecticut, USA.

Sikorsky S-51 Dragonfly

Subject: Sikorsky S-51 Dragonfly of the Royal Navy.
Statistics: Sikorsky R-5B.

The US Air Force was greatly encouraged by its first batch of Sikorsky R-4 helicopters and it rapidly issued a revised specification for a new and larger helicopter with increased capacity and range for observation duties and Search-and-Rescue work. From this specification Sikorsky developed a series of prototypes which culminated in the R-5, a narrow fully enclosed helicopter with a tandem seating arrangement. The S-51 was developed from the R-5 and it became the first Sikorsky helicopter to be certified by Britain's CAA for commercial operations. The S-51 was a most capable and serviceable helicopter and it

served for many years with both the US Navy and the Royal Canadian Air Force. The type was licence-built in the UK by Westland Helicopters and it was supplied in quantity to the Royal Air Force as the S-51 Dragonfly.

Country of Origin:	USA
First Flight:	1946
Accommodation:	4
Rotor Diameter:	48ft 0in (14.63m)
Length:	57ft 0in (17.37m)
Height:	13ft 0in (3.96m)
Empty Weight:	3,781lb (1,715kg)
Max Take Off:	4,826lb (2,189kg)
Powerplant:	1 x 450hp (336kW) Pratt & Whitney R-985-AN-5 radial.
Cruise Speed:	85mph (136km/h)
Max Speed:	106mph (170km/h)
Service Ceiling:	14,400ft (4,389m)
Range:	360 miles (579km)
Number Manufactured:	Over 200 of all S-51 variants manufactured.
Preserved:	US Army Aviation Museum, Fort Rucker, Ozark, Alabama, USA (H-5G).
	American Helicopter Museum, Philadelphia, USA.

Sikorsky MH-60G Pave Hawk

Subject: Sikorsky MH-60G Pave Hawk awaits its moment.
Statistics: Sikorsky MH-60G Pave Hawk.

The MH-60G Pave Hawk is a shortened version of the UH-60A which is equipped for use by the Special Forces of the US Air Force. Up to 4 MH-60Gs can be airlifted within the cargo hold of a C-5 Galaxy for deployment to any part of the world within a matter of hours. Once on station the MH-60G's advanced navigation systems, defensive armaments, and in-flight refuelling probe allow it to operate many hundreds of miles inside hostile territory on covert missions or in support of special forces. The MH-60K is the US Army equivalent of the type and it is essentially identical save that it has the advantage of additional terrain-following radar which allows it to travel at high speeds in close proximity to ground level, where radar reflections are likely to be confused with ground clutter.

Country of Origin:	USA
First Flight:	1974
Accommodation:	2 + 12 fully laden troops.
Rotor Diameter:	53ft 8in (16.35m)
Length:	57ft 0in (17.37m)
Height:	16ft 9in (5.10m)
Empty Weight:	13,480lb (6,110kg)
Max Take Off:	22,000lb (9,979kg)
Powerplant:	2 X 1,622hp (1,210kW) General Electric turboshaft power plants.
Cruise Speed:	173mph (278km/h)
Max Speed:	18mph (296km/h)
Service Ceiling:	19,000ft (5,790m)
Operational Radius:	Estimated 600 miles (960km)
Number Manufactured:	In excess of 2,000 of all collected Sikorsky S-70 types built by Sikorsky and by other foreign licenced manufacturers.
Flying or in service:	MH-60G and MH-60K in service with US Air Force and US Army.

Sikorsky S-64 Skycrane and CH-54 Tarhe

Subject: Sikorsky CH-54A Tarhe of the US Army.
Statistics: Sikorsky CH-54A Tarhe.

In its military role it bears the designation CH-54 Tarhe while in its civilian role it passes as the S-64 Skycrane. An extraordinary heavy-lift helicopter from the prolific Igor Sikorsky, the CH-64 is designed to carry outsize loads and it can accommodate a wide variety of specially designed pods, control rooms, mobile hospital components, etc. Even the largest and most awkward of loads can be carried and the CH-65 was used during the Vietnam War to retrieve no less than 380 crashed or downed aircraft. An remarkable helicopter with a unique configuration and an ability to lift loads of up to 9 tonnes.

Country of Origin:	USA
First Flight:	1962
Accommodation:	Flight crew of 2 + 1 load master. 45 troops in purpose-designed pod.
Rotor Diameter:	72ft 0in (21.94m)
Length:	88ft 6in (26.97m)
Height:	18ft 7in (5.66m)
Empty Weight:	19,240lb (8,727kg)
Max Take Off:	42,000lb (19,051kg)
Powerplant:	2 X 4,559hp (3,400kW) Pratt & Whitney T73-1 turboshafts.
Cruise Speed:	105mph (169km/h)
Max Speed:	126mph (203km/h)
Range:	300 miles (482km)
Number Manufactured:	80
Flying or in service:	20 still in service.
Preserved:	United States Army Aviation Museum, Fort Rucker, Alabama, USA.

Sikorsky VH-60N White Hawk

Subject: Sikorsky VH-60N White Hawk of the US Marine Corps. S/N 163261.
Statistics: Sikorsky VH-60N White Hawk.

The US Marine Corps' VH-60N White Hawk helicopter is the main helicopter transport of the president, vice president and the US heads of state. The type is essentially a much-modified UH-60 Black Hawk with a soft upholstered interior to reduce noise transfer, and an enhanced communications suite, greater range, and other non-disclosed defensive systems.

Country of Origin:	USA
First Flight:	1974 (as the UH-60).
Accommodation:	Flight crew of 3 + presidential passengers.

Rotor Diameter:	54ft 0in (16.36m)
Length:	65ft 0in (19.76m)
Height:	17ft 0in (5.13m)
Powerplant:	2 X General Electric turboshafts.
Cruise Speed:	150mph (241km/h)
Max Speed:	184mph (296km/h)
Service Ceiling:	19,000ft (5,790m)
Range:	580 miles (933km)
Flying or in service:	Operated by US Marine Corps HMX-1 presidential unit from Quantico AFB, USA.

Sikorsky S-65/H-53 Sea Stallion

Subject: Sikorsky CH-53D of the German Luftwaffe.
Statistics: Sikorsky CH-53E Super Stallion.

The S-65 is a twin-turbine heavy assault helicopter with a capacity for between 38 and 44 fully laden troops. The type is used by the US Marine Corps for heavy assault operations, minesweeping and electronic countermeasures, and by the US Air Force for general transport, positioning of special forces, and recovery/rescue missions. An extraordinarily powerful and capable assault support helicopter which has been adopted in a wide range of variants and designations by the military forces of the US, Austria, Israel and Germany.

Country of Origin:	USA
First Flight:	1964
Accommodation:	Flight crew + between 38 and 44 fully laden troops.
Rotor Diameter:	79ft 0in (24.07m)
Length:	73ft 4in (22.38m)
Height:	17ft 5in (5.30m)
Empty Weight:	33,228lb (15,071kg)
Max Take Off:	69,750lb (31,638kg)
Powerplant:	2 X 4,380hp (3,266kW) General Electric turboshafts.
Cruise Speed:	173mph (278km/h)
Max Speed:	196mph (315km/h)
Range:	540 miles (864km)

Number Manufactured: Up to 750 of all variants manufactured to date.
Flying or in service: Widely in service.
Preserved: Flying Leatherneck Aviation Museum, San Diego, California, USA.

Sikorsky S-61N

Subject: Sikorsky S-61N registration EI-RCG is operated by CHC Ireland out of Waterford Airport on behalf of the Irish Coast Guard.
Statistics: Sikorsky S-61N.

Built in huge quantities in the US, Japan, and the UK, the S-61 was produced in many different variants including the S-61N. With a sealed hull for amphibious operations the S-61N can accommodate up to 26 passengers in addition to its flight crew. Most Search-and-Rescue examples, however, are flown with much smaller numbers of fixed seats as required to keep the cabin floor free for a large, sealed First-Aid pad and all of its associated medical equipment. The Paymaster is a stripped-down commercial, construction and logging variant with a payload capacity of 11,000lb (4,990kg).

Country of Origin: USA
First Flight: 1959 (as the YSH-3A prototype). 1962 (as the sealed-hull S-61N).
Accommodation: 2 + up to 28.
Rotor Diameter: 62ft 0in (18.89m)
Length: 72ft 10in (22.19m)
Height: 18ft 5in (5.61m)
Empty Weight: 12,510lb (5,674kg)
Max Take Off: 20,500lb (9,297kg)
Powerplant: 2 x 1,500hp (1,118kW) General Electric CT58-140-1 turboshafts.
Cruise Speed: 138mph (222km/h)
Max Speed: 146mph (234km/h)
Range: 495 miles (792km)
Number Manufactured: 827 of all variants built by Sikorsky, 185 by Mitsubishi, and 328 (Sea Kings) by Westland.
Flying or in service: In service with many countries.

Sikorsky S-70/UH-60A Black Hawk

Subject: Sikorsky UH-60A Black Hawk of the US Air Force.
Statistics: Sikorsky UH-60A Black Hawk.

Another derivative of the S-70 marque, the UH-60 Black Hawk is the primary medium assault helicopter of the US Army and Air Force. The type replaces the Bell Huey in the role of battle assault and support helicopter with greater capacity, better performance and greatly higher levels of armour protection than its predecessor. A versatile and capable assault helicopter which has been built in large quantities.

Country of Origin: USA
First Flight: UH-60A prototype flew in 1974.
Accommodation: 2 + 11 fully equipped troops.
Rotor Diameter: 54ft 0in (16.36m)
Length: 65ft 0in (19.76m)
Height: 17ft 0in (5.13m)
Empty Weight: 13,620lb (6,177kg)
Max Take Off: 21,837lb (9,905kg)
Powerplant: 2 x 1,690hp (1,261kW) General Electric T700-GE-700/701/ or 401 turboshafts.
Cruise Speed: 173mph (278km/h)
Max Speed: 184mph (296km/h)
Range: 370 miles (595km)
Number Manufactured: In excess of 2,000 of all collected Sikorsky S-70 types built by Sikorsky and by other foreign licensed manufacturers.
Flying or in service: In service.

Sikorsky S-76

Subject: Sikorsky S-76 VH-HRP, which is operated on behalf of the Royal Australian Air Force.
Statistics: Sikorsky S-76B.

The S-76 is Sikorsky's 12-seat civil transport helicopter and its strongest performer on the high-end civil, corporate and general helicopter market. Sikorsky's chief rivals in this range, the Agusta A-109 and the Bell Model 222 are superb helicopters but the Sikorsky's larger cabin interior and its excellent performance have ensured that the type continues to retain a very large segment of the market. The S-76 can be fitted out for executive and corporate transport, oil-rig support, air-ambulance work and Search-and-Rescue duties.

Country of Origin: USA
First Flight: 1977
Accommodation: 2 + up to 12 passengers.
Rotor Diameter: 44ft 0in (13.41m)
Length: 44ft 1in (13.43m)
Height: 14ft 5in (4.39m)
Empty Weight: 6,640lb (3,012kg)
Max Take Off: 11,700lb (5,307kg)
Powerplant: 2 x 980shp (731kW) Pratt & Whitney PT6B-36A turboshafts.
Cruise Speed: 167mph (268km/h)
Max Speed: 180mph (289km/h)
Range: 410 miles (656km)
Number Manufactured: In excess of 600 of all S-76 variants completed to date.
Flying or in service: Widely in service.

Skandinavisk Aero Ind KZ VIII

Subject: ScandinaVisk Aero Ind KZVIII, registered HB-EPB in Switzerland.
Statistics: ScandinaVisk Aero Ind KZVIII.

Again from Viggo Kramme and Karl Zeuthen, the KZ VIII was a high-performance aerobatic monoplane designed to order for Sylvest Jensen's Aerobatic Circus. Only 2 of the type were built and both are in good condition to this day.

Country of Origin:	Denmark
First Flight:	1949
Accommodation:	1
Wingspan:	23ft 7in (7.2m)
Number Manufactured:	2
Flying or in service:	One flying in private ownership in UK.
Preserved:	Danish Collection of Vintage Aircraft, Skjern, Denmark.

Skandinavisk Aero Ind KZ II

Subject: ScandinaVisk Aero Ind KZ II Sport, registered in Denmark as OY-FAK.
Statistics: ScandinaVisk Aero Ind KZ II Kupe.

Kramme and Zeuthen's pre-war KZ II open-cockpit sports-plane and military trainer was unusual for being built both before and after the Second World War. Fourteen of the type were built before Europe was engulfed in conflict and

a further 16 were built after the cessation of hostilities in 1945. The type was an excellent primary-training aircraft and most of the output of the KZ assembly line was delivered to the Danish air force, which operated it right up to 1955. Thereafter, the remaining inventory of KZ II's airframes were disposed of to private owners and at least 4 of type remain airworthy to this day.

Country of Origin:	Denmark
First Flight:	1937
Accommodation:	2
Wingspan:	33ft 6in (10.21m)
Length:	24ft 7in (7.49m)
Height:	7ft 4in (2.23m)
Max Take Off:	1,875lb (850kg)
Powerplant:	1 x 145hp (108kW) de HaVilland Gipsy Major piston.
Cruise Speed:	130mph (209km/h)
Max Speed:	145mph (233km/h)
Range:	560 miles (896km)
Number Manufactured:	30
Flying or in service:	4 still airworthy.

Solar Challenger

Subject: Dr Paul MacCready's groundbreaking Solar Challenger.
Statistics: Solar Challenger.

The Solar Challenger was developed by AeroVironment Inc., which was founded in 1971 by inventor and radical sailplane designer Dr Paul MacCready of Los Angeles. Constructed of Mylar, foam sheeting, lightweight alloy tubing and even balsa wood, the Solar Challenger was powered by no less than 16,128 photovoltaic cells which generated, between them, 2.7kW (3.6hp) of power to drive a highly efficient motor and propeller. The Solar Challenger set an absolute altitude record of 14,300ft using solar power only, without the assistance of batteries or other storage devices. In July of 1981 it surpassed even that record by flying a distance of 163 miles from Paris to the southern outskirts of London in 5 hours and 23 minutes.

Country of Origin:	USA
First Flight:	1980
Accommodation:	1
Wingspan:	46ft 6in (14.17m)
Length:	30ft 4in (9.24m)
Empty Weight:	336lb (152.4kg)
Max Take Off:	486lb (220.4kg)
Max output:	Max 2,700 watts from cells.
Powerplant:	Powered by 16,128 photo voltaic cells generating 2.7kW (3.6hp) of power to drive a high-efficiency propeller.
Cruise Speed:	25mph (40km/h)
Max Speed:	34mph (54km/h)
Service Ceiling:	14,300ft (4,358m)
Range:	163 miles (262km)
Number Manufactured:	1

Spartan 7W Executive

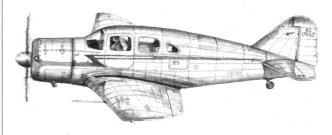

Subject: Spartan 7W Executive, registration NC17667, was a Texaco corporate transport in its early life. It now flies in private ownership.
Statistics: Spartan 7W Executive.

In 1936 the Spartan Executive represented the pinnacle of personal transport aircraft. Its beautiful detailing and its gleaming, polished aluminium finish were far ahead of any of the other personal aircraft of the day and it went on to be built right up until 1939, when the changing political climate deemed that production of military aircraft should be given precedence over civilian aircraft. Indeed, many Executives were impressed into the US Air Force as UC-71s and served Stateside as general communications aircraft and utility transports for the duration of the war.

Country of Origin:	USA
First Flight:	1936
Accommodation:	5
Wingspan:	39ft 0in (11.88m)
Length:	26ft 10in (8.18m)
Height:	8ft 0in (2.43m)
Empty Weight:	2,987lb (1,354kg)
Max Take Off:	4,400lb (1,996kg)
Powerplant:	1 x 400hp (298kW) Pratt & Whitney Wasp Junior SB piston.
Cruise Speed:	205mph (330km/h)
Max Speed:	212mph (341km/h)

Range:	850 miles (1,360km)
Number Manufactured:	35 built between 1937 and 1939.
Flying or in service:	Up to 20 surviving airframes but not all are airworthy.
Preserved:	Air Venture Museum, Oshkosh, Wisconsin, USA.

Stearman Hammond

Subject: Stearman Hammond.
Statistics: Stearman Hammond Y-125.

Designer Dean Hammond and chief engineer Carl Hadden of the Hammond Aircraft Corporation developed the Stearman Hammond Y with the intention of meeting all of the requirements set down by the Bureau of Air Commerce in its competition to find the ideal safe and affordable personal transport aircraft. The promise displayed in the Stearman Hammond was such that it was awarded joint first prize even though it far exceeded the cost target set down by the Bureau. In practice the type was not able to compete against the incumbent volume market leaders and the Stearman Hammond Y never did enter series production, but was built only in small numbers.

Country of Origin:	USA
First Flight:	1936
Accommodation:	2
Wingspan:	40ft 0in (12.19m)
Length:	26ft 11in (8.2m)
Height:	7ft 7in (2.31m)
Empty Weight:	1,400lb (635kg)
Max Take Off:	2,150lb (975kg)
Powerplant:	1 X 125hp (93.21kW) Menasco 4-cylinder piston engine.
Max Speed:	120mph (193km/h)
Number Manufactured:	Prototypes plus 15 delivered.
Preserved:	Smithsonian National Air and Space Museum, Paul Garber Facility, USA.

Stits Sky Baby

Subject: Just a step above a child's pedal car, the Stits Sky Baby.
Statistics: Stits Sky Baby.

The Stits Sky Baby, once the world's smallest aircraft, is preserved on static display at the Experimental Aircraft Association Museum, Oshkosh. With a wingspan of just 7ft 2 inches it is a wonder that it could support the weight of a pilot, but it could, and it was a sprightly performer, clocking up a maximum speed of 185mph. The extraordinary Stits Sky Baby remained unchallenged until the 1980s, when its former pilot Robert Starr built the even smaller Bumble Bee.

Country of Origin:	USA
First Flight:	1952
Accommodation:	1
Wingspan:	7ft 2in (2.18m)
Length:	9ft 6in (2.89m)
Empty Weight:	425lb (193kg)
Max Take Off:	666lb (303kg)
Powerplant:	1 X 85hp (63.38kW) Continental C-65 powerplant.
Cruise Speed:	165mph (265.5km/h)
Max Speed:	185mph (297.7km/h)
Range:	165 miles (265.5km)
Number Manufactured:	1
Preserved:	Experimental Aircraft Association Museum, Wittman Airfield, Oshkosh, USA.

Stout Amphibian

Subject: William B. Stout's fascinating Stout Amphibian of 1927.
Statistics: Stout Amphibian.

The Stout Amphibian was an all-metal flying boat which was designed and built by William B. Stout whose later designs led to the Ford Trimotor. With its full flying hull, and its most unusual wing configuration the Stout was forward thinking and radical for its 1927 vintage. The Stout Metal Aeroplane Company was bought by Henry Ford and, with the assistance of its former proprietor William Stout, went on to develop and manufacture the famous Ford Trimotor.

Country of Origin:	USA
First Flight:	1927
Accommodation:	1
Powerplant:	2 X 32hp (23.8kW) Bristol Cherub piston engines.

Supermarine Spitfire T-9

Subject: Supermarine Spitfire T-9, registration G-LFIX. Duxford.
Statistics: Supermarine Spitfire Mk.XIV.

R.J. Mitchell, designer of the iconic Spitfire, incorporated the vast wealth of experience he had gained in designing and building high-performance Schneider Trophy seaplanes into the private-venture Spitfire prototype. Prototype F37.34, the result of this design process, flew for the first time in March of 1936 and it was immediately hailed as the fastest military aircraft of its time. A superb fighter and performer, the Spitfire continued to evolve throughout the duration of the war with larger powerplants, improved avionics and a wide array of armament options. Specialized Spitfire applications included escort fighter, high-altitude reconnaissance, defensive fighter patrol and strafing of enemy concentrations. Up to 20,350 of all Spitfire variants were completed as well as 2,408 Seafires with folding wings for carrier-based operations.

Country of Origin:	UK
First Flight:	1936
Accommodation:	1

Wingspan:	36ft 10in (11.22m)
Length:	32ft 8in (9.95m)
Max Take Off:	8,490lb (3,851kg)
Powerplant:	1 x 2,050hp (1,527.7kW) Rolls-Royce Griffon 65 powerplant.
Max Speed:	448mph (721km/h)
Range:	850 miles (1,368km)
Number Manufactured:	20,350 Spitfires of all types and 2,408 Seafires with folding wings for carrier operations.
Flying or in service:	Many airframes survive in museums and collections with perhaps just 45 airworthy.
Preserved:	LF Mk IX/Mk IIB/Mk XVIe Canada Aviation Museum. Smithsonian National Air and Space Museum, Washington, DC, USA (Mk VII). RAF Museum, Hendon, London, UK (F24/I/LF XVIE/Vb).

Supermarine 535 Swift

Subject: Supermarine 535 Swift.
Statistics: Supermarine 535 Swift FR.5.

In July of 1952 the Swift made headlines when it flew from London to Brussels in just 18 minutes, a distance of 200 miles and an average point-to-point speed of 665mph. Supermarine's Swift was a single-seat swept-wing fighter which was built around the latest Rolls-Royce Avon turbojet powerplant. Sleek, fast and extremely capable, the Swift was rushed into operational service while its many technical problems were still being resolved. As a result the aircraft suffered a myriad of problems while in operational service and all Swift variants were speedily retired from the RAF except the later Swift FR.5.

Country of Origin:	UK
First Flight:	1952
Accommodation:	1
Wingspan:	32ft 4in (9.85m)
Length:	42ft 3in (12.87m)
Max Take Off:	21,400lb (9,707kg)
Powerplant:	1 x 9,450lb (42KN) Rolls-Royce Avon turbojet with afterburner.

Max Speed:	685mph (1,102km/h)
Range:	480 miles (772km)
Number Manufactured:	Several prototypes built, 61 delivered to the RAF, one of which crashed on delivery.
Preserved:	RAF Museum, Hendon, London, UK. Newark Air Museum, Nottingham, Nottinghamshire, UK.

Supermarine Scimitar F-1

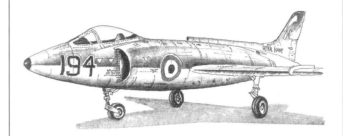

Subject: Supermarine Scimitar F-1, Sn XD332.
Statistics: Supermarine Scimitar F-1.

A single-seat twin-engined interceptor fighter designed to operate off aircraft carrier decks. The Scimitar F-1 flew for the first time in January of 1956 and the first of 76 production airframes lifted into the air just one year later. The Scimitar went on to serve for many years on board both HMS Ark Royal and HMS Victorious seeing action in many parts of the world.

Country of Origin:	UK
First Flight:	1956
Accommodation:	1
Wingspan:	37ft 2in (11.32m)
Length:	55ft 4in (16.86m)
Height:	17ft 4in (5.28m)
Empty Weight:	23,962lb (10,869kg)
Max Take Off:	34,200lb (15,513kg)
Powerplant:	2 x 11,250lb (50KN) Rolls-Royce Avon Mk 202 turbojets.
Max Speed:	710mph (1,142km/h)
Service Ceiling:	46,000ft (14,020m)
Range:	883 miles (1,422km)
Number Manufactured:	Prototypes plus 76 production airframes.
Preserved:	Fleet Air Arm Museum, Somerset, UK.

Supermarine S-5

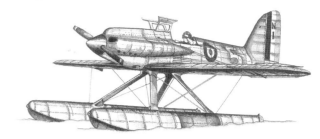

Subject: Supermarine S-5.
Statistics: Supermarine S-5.

In 1912 French businessman and aviation philanthropist Jacques Schneider announced his intention to sponsor a new international competition to foster excellence in the area of seaplane design. In so doing he initiated a new technological race that would last for decades and would have a direct bearing on the evolution of aeronautical science and even on the outcome of the Second World War. Throughout the 1920s and 1930s the Schneider Trophy generated unprecedented levels of interest and national pride as Italy, Germany, the USA, France, Britain and the other competing countries fought over the prestigious title. The Schneider Trophy was one of the primary drivers of aeronautics in the 1920s and 1930s and it was from the experience gained building Schneider Trophy competition aircraft that Supermarine's R.J. Mitchell developed the skills required to produce the Spitfire. The Supermarine S-5 successfully represented Britain in Venice at the 1927 Schneider Cup competition.

Country of Origin:	UK
First Flight:	1926
Accommodation:	1
Wingspan:	26ft 9in (8.15m)
Length:	24ft 2in (7.36m)
Empty Weight:	3,100lb (1,406kg)
Powerplant:	1 x 900hp (671kW) Napier Lion VIIA powerplant.
Number Manufactured:	2

Supermarine Stranraer

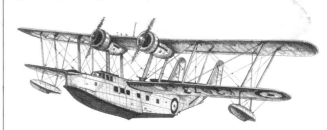

Subject: Supermarine Stranraer.
Statistics: Supermarine Stranraer.

Supermarine's pre-war all-metal long range maritime patrol and submarine-hunting flying boat. The Stranraer was powered by 2 875hp Bristol Pegasus X powerplants and armed by machine guns in the bow, at midship and in the tail. One torpedo could be carried in the lower centre section and gravity-fall munitions could be accommodated. The Stranraer's excellent endurance and its suitability for operations over water were ideal for long-range maritime patrol duties and the type was used by both Britain and Canada.

Country of Origin: UK/Canada
First Flight: 1934
Accommodation: Crew of 6 to 7
Wingspan: 85ft 0in (25.9m)
Length: 54ft 0in (16.45m)
Height: 21ft 9in (6.62m)
Empty Weight: 11,250lb (5,103kg)
Max Take Off: 19,000lb (8,618kg)
Powerplant: 2 X 875hp (652kW) Bristol
                          Pegasus X radial engines.
Max Speed: 165mph (266km/h)
Service Ceiling: 18,500ft (5,639m)
Combat Range: 1,000 miles (1,609km)
Number Manufactured: 23 by Supermarine and 5 by
                          the Canadian arm of Vickers.
Preserved: RAF Museum, Hendon, London, UK.

Swearingen SX-300

Subject: Swearingen SX-300, registered in the US as N2H.
Statistics: Swearingen SX-300.

Ed Swearingen flew the prototype SX-300 in July of 1984 and, having proven its flying qualities, offered the aircraft to amateur builders in the form of modular kits. The SX-300 is a high-performance two-seat aircraft with a retractable tricycle undercarriage and highly efficient aerodynamics. With a 270mph cruise speed and a range of 1,150 miles the SX-300 is a very capable touring aircraft.

Country of Origin: USA
First Flight: 1984
Accommodation: 2
Wingspan: 24ft 4in (7.41m)
Length: 21ft 1in (6.42m)
Height: 7ft 10in (2.38m)

Empty Weight: 1,600lb (726kg)
Max Take Off: 2,400lb (1,088kg)
Powerplant: 1 X 300hp (224kW) Lycoming
                          IO-540-L1C5 piston powerplant.
Cruise Speed: 270mph (434km/h)
Max Speed: 285mph (458km/h)
Range: 1,150 miles (1,850km)
Number Manufactured: In excess of 40 completed and
                          flying. Other projects ongoing.
Flying or in service: Up to 40.

Supermarine Walrus

Subject: Supermarine Walrus MK I.
Statistics: Supermarine Walrus MK II.

Supermarine's Walrus must have looked like a relic among the sleek, fast fighting aircraft of the war years. The type, however, performed a task that few other aircraft could perform, that is the rescue and recovery of pilots who had been shot down over water. Almost 750 of the type were produced for service on catapult-equipped Royal Navy ships, and for patrolling of coastal waters around all theatres of battle. The Walrus plucked countless pilots and seamen from the open seas and from certain death, and one Royal Navy Walrus is recorded as having rescued no less than 16 downed pilots in one day.

Country of Origin: UK
First Flight: 1933 (as the Seagull Mk V).
Accommodation: 4
Wingspan: 45ft 10in (13.97m)
Length: 37ft 3in (11.35m)
Height: 15ft 3in (4.67m)
Empty Weight: 4,890lb (2,218kg)
Max Take Off: 7,185lb (3,259kg)
Powerplant: 2 X 620hp (462kW) Bristol
                          Pegasus VI radial piston engine.
Max Speed: 135mph (217km/h)
Service Ceiling: 17,100ft (5,212m)
Range: 600 miles (965km)

Number Manufactured: 285 Walrus MK Is with metal
                          hulls built by Supermarine.
                          461 Walrus MK IIs with wooden
                          hulls built by Saunders Roe.
Preserved: RAAF Museum, Point Cook,
                          Australia.
                          Fleet Air Arm Museum,
                          Somerset, UK.

Thomas Morse Scout

Subject: Thomas Morse S4C Scout.
Statistics: Thomas Morse S4C Scout.

Commonly known as the 'Tommie' by its pilots and ground crews, the Scout was a single-seat advanced trainer which first appeared as the 100hp Gnome-powered S4B but soon afterwards evolved into the Le Rhône-powered S4C. The Scout was the standard advanced-training aircraft of the US forces and it was built in large numbers and operated by almost all of the military training schools across the USA. After the First World War, many hundreds of Scouts were released onto the general aviation market, where they found new lives as personal sport-planes, show planes and Hollywood props.

Country of Origin: USA
First Flight: 1917
Accommodation: 1
Wingspan: 26ft 5in (8.05m)
Length: 19ft 10in (6.04m)
Height: 8ft 10in (2.69m)
Empty Weight: 961lb (435kg)
Max Take Off: 1,371lb (621kg)
Powerplant: 1 X 80hp (60kW) Le Rhône C-9
                          Licence-built by Union
                          Switch & Signal.
Max Speed: 94mph (151km/h)
Service Ceiling: 16,000ft (4,876m)
Range: 250 miles (402km)
Number Manufactured: Up to 600 of all S4 variants.
Preserved: National Museum of Naval
                          Aviation, NAS Pensacola, Florida.
                          National Museum of the US Air
                          Force, Wright-Patterson
                          AFB, Dayton, Ohio, USA.

Taylor Aerocar

Subject: Taylor Aerocar.
Statistics: Taylor Aerocar 1A.

There have been several attempts over the years to design a fully roadable aircraft, that is, an aircraft that can be used on public roadways as a fully functioning car. Of all these attempts, however, Molt Taylor's 1949 Aerocar is by far the most successful and it happens, too, to be an extraordinarily endearing and attractive combination of engineering and design. Taylor designed the 2-seater so that it could leave its wings behind at the airport and drive the last part of its journey on local roadways. Alternatively the intrepid pilot/owner could tow the wings home for storage in the family garage. The Taylor Aerocar was first flown in 1949, certificated by the FAA in 1956, and put into production in 1957. Only 5 aircraft were built in addition to Taylor's 1949 prototype.

Country of Origin:	USA
First Flight:	1949
Accommodation:	2
Wingspan:	34ft 0in (10.36m)
Length:	21ft 6in (6.55m)
Height:	7ft 6in (2.28m)
Empty Weight:	1,500lb (680kg)
Max Take Off:	2,050lb (929kg)
Powerplant:	1 x 143hp (106.6kW) Lycoming O-320 piston.
Cruise Speed:	100mph (161km)
Max Speed:	117mph (188km/h)
Max Road Speed:	67mph (107.8km/h)
Service Ceiling:	12,000ft (3,657m)
Range:	300 miles (483km)
Number Manufactured:	Prototype and 5 manufactured. 1 modified to become the 4-seat Aero-Plane and a second remodelled in the late 1960s with an updated car body.
Flying or in service:	1
Preserved:	4 Taylor Aerocars in museums, including one in the Museum of Flight, Seattle, Washington, USA. One in the EAA Museum, Oshkosh, Wisconsin, USA.

Thorp T-18

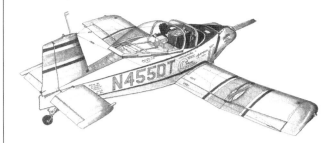

Subject: Don Taylor's Thorp T-18, registration N455DT, which became the first homebuilt aircraft to circumnavigate the globe.
Statistics: Thorp T-18 Tiger.

John Thorp's plan sales for his excellent home-build T-18 touring aircraft were selling well when retired Air Force pilot Don Taylor propelled the type to fame with his solo circumnavigation of the globe. This was the first time that a home-built aircraft had circled the world, and Thorp was inundated with requests for plans. A very large number of plan sets were sold to prospective builders and, from these, around 400 aircraft are known to have reached completion.

Country of Origin:	USA
First Flight:	1964
Accommodation:	2
Wingspan:	20ft 10in (6.35m)
Length:	18ft 2in (5.53m)
Height:	4ft 10in (1.47m)
Empty Weight:	650lb (295kg)
Max Take Off:	1,195lb (542kg)
Powerplant:	1 x 180hp (134.2kW) Lycoming O-360 piston powerplant.
Cruise Speed:	130mph (209km/h)
Max Speed:	144mph (231km/h)
Service Ceiling:	18,000ft (5,486m)
Range:	410 miles (659km)
Number Manufactured:	Around 400 completed by amateur aircraft builders.
Flying or in service:	Large numbers airworthy.
Preserved:	Don Taylor's Thorp, N455DT is preserved at the Experimental Aircraft Association, Museum of Flight, Oshkosh, Wisconsin, USA.

Tipsy Nipper T-66

Subject: Tipsy Nipper T-66 registered G-AWJE flies on the UK register.
Statistics: Tipsy Nipper T-66 Mk 2.

Earnest Tips of Avions Fairey SA, Belgium, began developing the Tipsy Nipper in 1952 but it was not until 1957 that it was ready for flight. Tips's intention was to build an aircraft that was easy to fly and extremely cheap to buy. The Nipper is both. It provides all that is essential for flight but nothing more, and it is this remarkable simplicity that provides its charm. Despite its eccentric appearance, its off-beat name and its diminutive size the Tipsy Nipper is one of the more instantly recognizable aircraft of the last 50 years.

Country of Origin:	Belgium
First Flight:	1957
Accommodation:	1
Wingspan:	19ft 8in (5.99m)
Length:	14ft 9in (4.49m)
Height:	6ft 2in (1.87m)
Empty Weight:	412lb (186kg)
Max Take Off:	660lb (299kg)
Powerplant:	1 x 45hp (33.5kW) Stark Stamo piston engine. Later Mk 3 Nippers were powered by a modified Volkswagen engine.
Cruise Speed:	90mph (145km/h).
Max Speed:	100mph (161km/h).
Range:	200 miles (322km).
Number Manufactured:	110 of all Nipper variants.
Flying or in service:	Up to 42 still actively flying.
Preserved:	Luftfahrt-Museum Laatzen-Hannover, Germany.

Turbine Legend

Subject: Turbine Legend registered in the USA as N42BR.
Statistics: Turbine Legend.

The Turbine Legend provides prop fighter performance and exceptional range without the complex and costly service and certification issues which normally accompany aircraft at this level. The Legend is an amateur-build Kitplane designed to fly under the US experimental category. It is, however, a complex and demanding project and it represents a very serious commitment in terms of both financial resources and construction time.

Country of Origin:	USA
First Flight:	1996
Accommodation:	2
Wingspan:	28ft 5in (8.66m)
Length:	25ft 7in (7.79m)
Height:	9ft 5in (2.87m)
Empty Weight:	2,050lb (930kg)
Max Take Off:	3,300lb (1,497kg)
Powerplant:	1 x Walter M601 turbine powerplant.
Cruise Speed:	300mph (483km/h)
Max Speed:	338mph (544km/h)
Range:	1,143 miles (1,839km)

Tupolev Tu-154 Careless

Subject: Tupolev Tu-154 of Balkan Airlines was registered in Bulgaria.
Statistics: Tupolev Tu-154M.

A 3-engined medium-haul airliner which began service with Aeroflot in February of 1972. The Tu-154 was stretched and improved over the years to increase its passenger capacity from 128 in its earliest models to 167 in its later models. The type has been used extensively throughout the Soviet Union and has been exported to many other countries of Soviet influence. Over 900 Tupolev Tu-154s have been built to date and large numbers remain in commercial service across the world.

Country of Origin:	USSR
First Flight:	1968
Accommodation:	Flightcrew + between 158 and 167 passengers.
Wingspan:	123ft 0in (37.4m)
Length:	157ft 0in (47.8m)
Height:	37ft 5in (11.4m)
Empty Weight:	121,915lb (55,300kg)
Max Take Off:	220,460lb (100,000kg)
Powerplant:	3 x 23,380lb (104kN) AviadVigatel-Perm turbofans.
Cruise Speed:	560mph (900km/h)
Max Speed:	580mph (933km/h)
Service Ceiling:	39,000ft (11,887m)
Range:	4,100 miles (6,598km)
Number Manufactured:	In excess of 900.
Flying or in service:	Widely in service.

Tupolev Tu-4

Subject: Tupolev Tu-4 of the People's Republic of China.
Statistics: Tupolev Tu-4.

The Tupolev Tu-4 heavy bomber first appeared as part of Moscow's 1947 Aviation Day parade. Painstakingly reverse engineered from Boeing's B-29, the Tu-4 was a carbon copy of the original. Western military observers were aware for some time that the Soviets had appropriated 3 examples of the giant US B-29 bomber in the last years of the war as it closed in on Japan. When 3 performed a low-level pass over Moscow's Tushino Airport on the occasion of the 1947 Aviation Day parade there was little surprise, but when a fourth airframe appeared it was immediately apparent that Soviet heavy bomber technology had surreptitiously made a giant leap forward. The revelation brought consternation to western military circles. The Tu-4, if it performed as well as the B-29, would have the range and payload required to wreak havoc on many of North America's cities and, in the light of the latest intelligence reports on the USSR's advancing atomic weapons programme, it led to a massive intensification of investment in US weapons technology.

Country of Origin:	USSR
First Flight:	1947
Accommodation:	Pilot, co-pilot, engineer, radio operator, navigator, and up to 7 gun/weapons operators
Wingspan:	141ft 3in (43m)
Length:	99ft 0in (30.18m)
Height:	29ft 7in (9m)
Empty Weight:	77,756lb (35,270Kg)
Max take off:	145,500lb (65,999kg)
Powerplant:	4 x 9,600hp (7,158kW) Shvetsov Ash-73TK powerplants
Max Speed:	347mph (558km/h)
Range:	3,106 miles (5,000km)
Number Manufactured:	More than 1,200 completed for both the Soviet Union and the People's Republic of China.

Ultravia Aero Pelican

Subject: Ultravia Aero Pelican PL-914, registered in Canada as C-GEPL.
Statistics: Ultravia Aero Pelican PL-912S.

Ultravia Aero of Canada developed the Pelican PL series of light aircraft in response to the sudden demand for ultralight aircraft which came about as a result of changes to legislation governing ultra-light pilot licensing in both Canada and Europe. Starting with the single-seat 'Le Pelican', Ultravia developed a market niche and then expanded its product range with the 80hp two-seat Pelican 912 and the later and more powerful Pelican 914. More than 300 of all Pelican types have been completed to date.

Country of Origin:	Canada
First Flight:	Single-seat Pelican flew 1982. 2-seat Pelican flew 1985.
Accommodation:	2
Wingspan:	29ft 6in (8.99m)

Length:	19ft 9in (6.02m)
Height:	8ft 1in (2.46m)
Empty Weight:	750lb (340.1kg)
Max Take Off:	1,400lb (635kg)
Powerplant:	1 x 80hp (59.6kW) Rotax 912 or 115hp (85.7kW) Rotax 914.
Cruise Speed:	115mph (185km/h)
Max Speed:	142mph (228km/h)
Service Ceiling:	16,000ft (4,877)
Range:	800 miles (1,287km)
Number Manufactured:	Large numbers of kits sold to amateur constructors and over 300 of these completed.
Flying or in service:	Many currently in service in Canada and United States.

Vans RV-9A

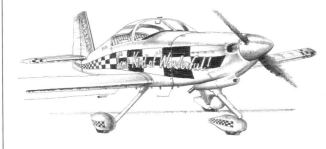

Subject: Vans RV-9A 'Some kind of Wonderful', registration N592RS, flew into Kissimme, Florida, 2003.
Statistics: Vans RV-9A (with 160hp powerplant).

The Vans marque has enjoyed immense popularity with the home-building community since the early 1970s, when the first Van's RV-3 took to the air. Behind the Vans project was home-builder and designer Dick Van Grunsven who went on to market the project with great success over many years. Beginning with the RV-3, the Vans family has been constantly upgraded over the years with larger engines, aerodynamic improvements, tailwheel or tricycle undercarriage options, and wider and more comfortable cockpits.

Country of Origin:	USA
First Flight:	1971 (as the Vans RV-3) 2000 RV-9A (tricycle variant) 2002 RV-9 (tailwheel variant)
Accommodation:	2
Wingspan:	28ft 0in (8.53m)
Length:	20ft 5in (6.22m)
Height:	6ft 0in (1.82m)
Empty Weight:	1,057lb (479kg)
Max Take Off:	1,750lb (793kg)
Powerplant:	1 x 160hp (119kW)
Cruise Speed:	185mph (298km/h)

Max Speed:	197mph (317km/h)
Service Ceiling:	24,500ft (7,467m)
Range:	710 miles (1,142km)
Number Manufactured:	In excess of 10,000 of all RV kits have been sold and up to 2,500 have been completed.
Flying or in service:	Widely in service.

Vickers Type 141 Scout

Subject: Vickers Type 141 Scout.
Statistics: Vickers Type 141 Scout.

The Scout was intended by Vickers to provide both the Royal Air Force and the Royal Navy with a capable and effective fighting platform that could be operated from land bases, as well as from the decks of Britain's new aircraft carriers. Comprising a blend of new aluminium skin technology and older wood and fabric construction, the Scout underwent a protracted trials period on the high seas but was eventually selected despite strong opposition from rival manufacturers.

Country of Origin:	UK
First Flight:	1926
Accommodation:	1
Wingspan:	34ft 0in (10.36m)
Length:	27ft 0in (8.23m)
Height:	8ft 11in (2.72m)
Empty Weight:	2,650lb (1,202kg)
Max Take Off:	3,700lb (1,678kg)
Powerplant:	1 x 465hp (346.7kW) Hispano-Suiza 12Jb.
Max Speed:	177mph (284km/h)

Vickers Varsity

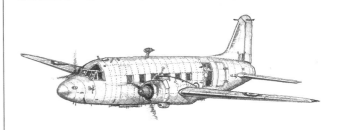

Subject: Vickers Varsity T-1, WF425, of the Meteorological Research Flight.
Statistics: Vickers Varsity.

The Varsity was very similar in configuration and dimension to the Valetta save that it was provided with a tricycle undercarriage and a stretched fuselage. The type entered service as an aircrew trainer with the RAF in 1951 with the intention of replacing the ageing Wellington T10s then in service. For instruction of bombardier crews a bomb bay and a bomb-aiming station were provided in a pannier which was built tight up against the fuselage underbelly. A total of 163 Varsity's of all variants were constructed and the type began operational service with the RAF in 1951.

Country of Origin:	UK
First Flight:	1949
Accommodation:	Flight crew, 4 instructors + 4 students.
Wingspan:	95ft 7in (29.13m)
Length:	67ft 6in (20.57m)
Height:	23ft 11in (7.28m)
Empty Weight:	27,040lb (12,265kg)
Max Take Off:	37,500lb (17,009kg)
Powerplant:	2 x 1,950hp (1,454kW) Bristol Hercules 264 radials.
Max Speed:	288mph (463km/h)
Service Ceiling:	28,700ft (8,748m)
Range:	2,648 miles (4,261km)
Number Manufactured:	163 delivered to the RAF.
Preserved:	RAF Museum, London, UK (T Mk1). Newark Air Museum, Nottingham, Nottinghamshire, UK.

Vickers Valetta C-1

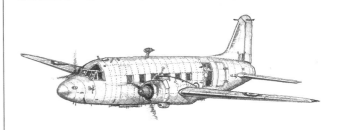

Subject: Vickers Valetta C-1.
Statistics: Vickers Valetta C-1.

The Vickers Valetta military transport was produced in 4 specific variants. The Valetta C-1 was the standard Royal Air Force version which was used for transporting troops, lifting freight, dropping paratroop forces and as a medevac air-ambulance. The C-2 was a comfortably appointed VIP transport with accommodation for between 9 and 15 officer passengers. The T-3 was a specialized flying classroom for navigational training and the T-4 was similar to the T-3 save for the provision of an additional radar suite.

Country of Origin:	UK
First Flight:	1947
Accommodation:	Flightcrew + 34 troops or equivalent freight.
Wingspan:	89ft 3in (27.2m)
Length:	62ft 11in (19.17m)
Height:	19ft 7in (5.96m)
Empty Weight:	24,980lb (11,330kg)
Max Take Off:	36,500lb (16,556kg)
Powerplant:	2 x 1,975hp (1,472kW) Bristol Hercules 230 9-cylinder air-cooled radial engines.
Max Speed:	258mph (415km/h)
Service Ceiling:	21,500ft (6,553m)
Range:	1,460 miles (2,350km)
Number Manufactured:	260 of all 4 Valetta types.

Vickers Viscount

Subject: Vickers 757 Viscount CF-THI (c/n 270) of Trans-Canada Airlines.
Statistics: Vickers Viscount 810.

443 examples of the Viscount were manufactured by Vickers between 1948 and 1963. With its reliable Rolls-Royce Dart engines and its large-capacity interior, the Viscount was a popular choice with airlines. Having British European Airways as its launch customer, too, was an added advantage for the type, and it quickly found itself flying medium-haul routes all over the world. Despite first entering operational service as far back as 1949, small numbers of Viscounts continue to be operated as commercial freighters to this day.

Country of Origin:	UK
First Flight:	1948
Accommodation:	Flightcrew + between 57 and 65 passengers.
Wingspan:	93ft 8in (28.54m)
Length:	85ft 8in (26.11m)
Height:	27ft 9in (8.45m)
Max Take Off:	72,500lb (32,885kg)
Powerplant:	4 x 1,990hp (1,484kW) Rolls-Royce Dart turboprops.
Max Speed:	357mph (574km/h)
Service Ceiling:	25,500ft (7,772m)
Range:	1,585 miles (2,550km)
Number Manufactured:	443 of all variants completed.
Flying or in service:	Small numbers are still used as commercial freighters on the African continent.
Preserved:	RAF Museum, Hendon, London, UK.

Vickers Vildebeest

Subject: Vickers Vildebeest on coastal patrol.
Statistics: Vickers Vildebeest IV.

The Vildebeest entered service with the RAF in 1933 in the role of torpedo bomber and anti-submarine patrol aircraft. An ungainly and eccentric-looking biplane, it overcame huge amounts of inbuilt aerodynamic drag by way of massive horsepower alone. The 810hp Bristol Perseus powerplant of the Mk IV Vildebeest gave it a maximum speed of 156mph, and a patrol mission radius of over 600 miles.

Country of Origin:	UK
First Flight:	1928
Accommodation:	Pilot, gunner and bombardier.
Wingspan:	49ft 0in (14.93m)
Length:	37ft 8in (11.48m)
Empty Weight:	4,773lb (2,165kg)
Max Take Off:	8,500lb (3,855kg)
Powerplant:	1 x 810hp (604kW) Bristol Perseus VIII powerplant.
Max Speed:	156mph (251km/h)
Service Ceiling:	17,000ft (5,181m)
Range:	625 miles (1,006km)
Number Manufactured:	In excess of 200 for the RAF. 27 CASA licence-built examples delivered to Spanish forces and 30 delivered to RNZAF.

Vultee Valiant BT-13 and BT-15

Subject: Vultee Valiant BT-13 basic trainer of the US Air Force.
Statistics: Vultee Valiant BT-13.

The Vultee Valiant was delivered to the US Army Air Corps as the BT-13 and BT-15, and to the US Navy as the SNV. The type served as the standard basic trainer for both the Army and Navy and was built in huge numbers from 1939 right up until 1944. After rudimentary instruction on the Boeing Stearman, students graduated to the Valiant to hone and develop their skills before taking the big step up to flying fighters and transports. More than 11,500 of all variants were built and the type played a vital part in the training of pilots for the Allied war effort.

Country of Origin:	USA
First Flight:	1939
Accommodation:	2
Wingspan:	42ft 2in (12.85m)
Length:	28ft 10in (8.78m)
Height:	11ft 6in (3.5m)
Empty Weight:	3,375lb (1,530kg)
Max Take Off:	4,495lb (2,039kg)
Powerplant:	1 x 450hp (335.5kW) Pratt & Whitney R-985-AN-1 Wasp Junior radial piston engine.
Cruise Speed:	170mph (273km/h)
Max Speed:	180mph (290km/h)
Service Ceiling:	19,400ft (5,913m)
Range:	725 miles (1,167km)
Number Manufactured:	11,537 completed between 1939 and 1944.

Flying or in service: Small numbers still flying in private ownership.
Preserved: Fantasy of Flight Museum, Polk City, Florida, USA.
Steven F. Udvar-Hazy Center, Chantilly, Virginia, USA (BT-13A).
Castle Air Museum, Atwater, California, USA.

Range: Prototype carried 20 gallons of fuel only.
Number Manufactured: One V-173 prototype.
One XF5U prototype completed but not flown.
Preserved: The V-173 prototype is preserved at the Smithsonian National Air and Space Museum, Washington, DC, USA.

Vought
A-7 Corsair II

Subject: Vought A-7E Corsair II of the Greek air force.
Statistics: Vought A-7H Corsair II.

The Vought A-7 Corsair II was based on the earlier F-8 Crusader of 1955. Designed to meet a US Navy specification for a subsonic attack platform with a larger non-nuclear bomb payload, the Corsair II was built in large numbers and operated by the US Navy, by Greece and by Portugal.

Country of Origin: USA
First Flight: First prototype flew in 1965.
Accommodation: 1
Wingspan: 83ft 9in (25.52m)
Length: 46ft 2in (14.07m)
Height: 16ft 0in (4.87m)
Empty Weight: 19,774lb (8,969kg)
Max Take Off: 41,910lb (19,010kg)
Powerplant: 1 x 15,000lb (66.7kN) Allison TF41-A-2 turbofan.
Max Speed: 696mph (1,123km/h)
Range: 2,280 miles (3,669km).
Flying or in service: Still in limited service with the Air Forces of Greece and Portugal.
Preserved: A-7 Corsair II, Iowa Air National Guard, Sioux City Municipal Airport, Iowa, USA.
Vintage Aircraft Museum, Greenfield Municipal Airport, Iowa, USA.

Vought V-173
Flying Pancake

Subject: Vought V-173 Flying Pancake prototype.
Statistics: Vought V-173 Flying Pancake.

The Vought V-173 Flying Pancake must surely be one of the most unusual prototype aircraft of all time. Flown for the first time in 1942, the V-173 was an effort to develop an all-lifting-body interceptor fighter for operation on US naval carriers. The V-173 prototype performed well in all of its test flights, demonstrating an ability to take off and land in very short distances, a promising attribute for a carrier-based fighter. Following the success of the V-173 programme the US Navy commissioned the construction of a full-size XF5U prototype. Although this highly experimental aircraft was completed by 1947 the advent of turbojet technology meant that it was instantly outdated and the entire project was abandoned even before its first flight.

Country of Origin: USA
First Flight: 1942
Accommodation: 1
Wingspan: 23ft 4in (7.11m)
Length: 26ft 8in (8.73m)
Height: 12ft 11in (3.93m)
Max Take Off: 2,258lb (1,024kg)
Powerplant: 2 x 80hp (59.6kW) Continental A-80 pistons.
Max Speed: 132mph (212.4km/h)

Vought-Hiller-Ryan
XC-142A

Subject: Vought-Hiller-Ryan XC-142A.
Statistics: Vought-Hiller-Ryan XC-142A.

A 4-engined experimental tilt-wing flying prototype which was commissioned by the US government in order to investigate the possibility of vertical take-off and landing and hybrid tilt-wing aircraft. The XC-142A made its first hovering ascent in December of 1964 and transitioned to horizontal flight just 2 weeks later.

Country of Origin: USA
First Flight: 1964
Wingspan: 67ft 6in (20.57m)
Length: 58ft 2in (17.72m)
Height: 25ft 8in (7.8m)
Max Take Off: 41,500lb (18,824kg)
Powerplant: 4 x 3,080hp (2,297kW) General Electric T64-GE turboprops.
Cruise Speed: 235mph (378km/h)
Max Speed: 400mph (644km/h)
Service Ceiling: 25,000ft (7,619m)
Range: 820 miles (1,320km)
Number Manufactured: 5
Preserved: United States Air Force Museum, Wright-Patterson AFB, Ohio, USA.

Vought F4U-4 Corsair

Subject: Vought F4U-4 Corsair in US Navy colours.
Statistics: Vought F4U-4 Corsair.

The mighty Corsair was the result of a 1938 United States Navy request to US aircraft manufacturers for a new and powerful fighter for operation off aircraft carriers. The proposal from Vought, initially designated the V-166B, was a novel and promising one and it was selected for development to prototype stage. The nature of carrier-based operations is such that fighter range and endurance are critical to the carrier group's defence and effectiveness. To maximize range, Vought designed the smallest possible airframe around the biggest aircraft powerplant then available, the 2,100hp Pratt & Whitney Double Wasp radial. The other main feature of the type is the unusual gull-wing arrangement which resulted from the designer's need to keep the huge four-blade propeller clear of the aircraft carrier's deck.

Country of Origin: USA
First Flight: 1940
Accommodation: 1
Wingspan: 41ft 0in (12.49m)
Length: 33ft 8in (10.26m)
Height: 14ft 9in (4.49m)
Empty Weight: 9,205lb (4,175kg)
Max Take Off: 14,670lb (6,654kg)
Powerplant: 1 x 2,100hp (1,566kW) Pratt &
                          Whitney R-2800-18W Double
                          Wasp radial powerplant.
Max Speed: 446mph (718km/h)
Service Ceiling: 37,000ft (11,277m)
Range: 1,000 miles (1,609km)
Number Manufactured: 12,204 of all Corsair
                          variants completed.
Flying or in service: Many intact airframes survive
                          to this day but only some 30
                          are still airworthy.
Preserved: National Museum of Naval
                          Aviation, NAS Pensacola,
                          Florida, USA.
                          Mid-America Air Museum,
                          Liberal, Kansas, USA.

Waco CG-4A Hadrian

Subject: Waco Hadrian. If you could walk away it was
          a good landing.
Statistics: Waco CG-4A Hadrian.

The Waco Aircraft Company and 15 other contractors began the mass production of CG-4A Hadrian troop-carrying assault gliders in 1942 and completed more than 13,900 airframes for use in the Allied offensives in Europe. As well as its pilots the Hadrian could accommodate 13 fully laden troops or one quarter-ton jeep and its crew of 4. Other typical loads included a 75mm howitzer with both its ammunition and its 3-man crew, or equivalent quantities of vital supplies and ordnance. The CG-4A Hadrian was used in quantity as part of the Allied airborne assaults on Sicily and France.

Country of Origin: USA
First Flight: 1942
Accommodation: 2 pilots + 13 fully armed
                          troops or one 1/4-ton Jeep.
Wingspan: 83ft 8in (25.5m)
Length: 48ft 4in (14.73m)
Max Take Off: 9,000lb (4,082kg)
Normal speed under tow: 100mph (161km/h)
Range: As towing aircraft.
Number Manufactured: In excess of 13,900 completed.
Preserved: National Museum of the US Air
                          Force, Wright-Patterson
                          AFB, Dayton, Ohio, USA.
                          Yankee Air Museum, Belleville,
                          Michigan, USA.

Waterman Arrowbile

Subject: Waldo Waterman's wonderfully presented
          Waterman Arrowbile 6.
Statistics: Waterman Arrowbile 6.

Waldo Waterman of Santa Monica, California, was convinced that the future of general aviation lay in the development of flying cars. If the family car could be flown safely and cheaply the skies would be opened up to all. Waterman spent much of his life developing his theories and constructing a series of practical and usable aircraft which were simple to fly and yet were fully roadable. The car manufacturing giant Studebaker, suppliers of the Arrowbile's automotive engine, ordered the first 5 production aircraft but only 3 were delivered when Waterman became ill and the Waterman Aeroplane Company had to suspend its operations. After the war, Waterman collected together all of the components required to assemble Airframe No. 4 while William Stout of Ford Trimotor fame purchased what remained of Airframe No. 5. The last of the 6 partially built airframes was rescued by Waterman in the late 1940s and it became the basis for his improved 3-seat Arrowbile No. 6.

Country of Origin: USA
First Flight: 1937
Accommodation: Arrowbiles 1 to 5 had 2 seats.
                          Arrowbile 6 had seating for 3.
Wingspan: 38ft 0in (11.58m)
Length: 20ft 6in (6.24m)
Height: 8ft 8in (2.64m)
Empty Weight: 1,770lb (803kg)
Powerplant: 1 x modified Studebaker
                          automotive engine.
Number Manufactured: A total of 6 completed.
Preserved: Preserved at the Smithsonian
                          National Air and Space Museum,
                          Washington, DC, USA.

Watson GW-1 Windwagon

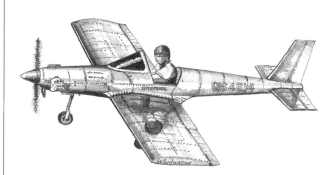

Subject: Watson GW-1 Windwagon.
Statistics: Watson GW-1 Windwagon.

The Watson Windwagon was an all-metal single-seat light aircraft which was offered to amateur builders for home-construction.

Country of Origin:	USA
First Flight:	1977
Accommodation:	1
Wingspan:	21ft 0in (6.4m)
Length:	13ft 2in (4.01m)
Height:	4ft 0in (1.21m)
Empty Weight:	270lb (122.4Kg)
Max Take Off:	550lb (250kg)
Powerplant:	1 x modified Volkswagen automotive engine.
Cruise Speed:	115mph (185km/h)
Max Speed:	135mph (217km/h)
Service Ceiling:	13,000ft (3,962m)
Range:	250 miles (402km).
Number Manufactured:	Many sets of plans sold but little information on numbers actually completed.

Westland Merlin EH-101

Subject: Westland EH-101 Merlin HC.3 of the Royal Air Force.
Statistics: Westland Merlin EH-101.

Developed jointly between Agusta of Italy and Westland of Britain, the EH-101 is a large military and civil helicopter.

Country of Origin:	UK, Italy.
First Flight:	1987
Accommodation:	Flight crew of 4 and up to 24 combat-equipped troops.
Rotor Diameter:	60ft 11in (18.59m)
Length:	74ft 10in (22.81m)
Powerplant:	3 x Rolls-Royce/Turbomeca RTM.322 turboshafts.
Max Speed:	192mph (309km/h)
Range:	621 miles (1,000km)
Number Manufactured:	More than 60 delivered so far of total orders for 140 of the type.
Flying or in service:	60
Preserved:	RAF Museum, Hendon, London, UK.

Weick W-1

Subject: Fred Weick's prototype Weick W-1.
Statistics: Weick W-1.

A twin-boom, twin-tailed experimental aircraft with an unusual tricycle undercarriage and unprecedented low-speed handling characteristics, the Weick W-1 introduced, among other innovations, the slot-lip aileron. Fred Weick went on to work for NACA and wrote the definitive 1920s textbook on propeller design. His 1936 design for the Erco Ercoupé of 1937 is perhaps his best-remembered contribution to aviation, perhaps because of the ease with which it could be flown, or because many Ercoupés remain in service to this day.

Country of Origin:	USA
First Flight:	1934
Accommodation:	1
Wingspan:	30ft 0in (9.14m)
Powerplant:	1 x 85hp (63.3kW) Pobjoy pusher.
Number Manufactured:	1. NACA was carrying out flight trials when the aircraft was damaged. Scrapped in 1938.

Weir W-9 Helicopter

Subject: Weir W-9 prototype, s/n PX-203.
Statistics: Weir W-9.

The Weir W-9 used a powerful multi-bladed fan to cool its powerplant and then ducted the resulting hot air through the tubular tail boom, ejecting it through openings in the port side to compensate for the torque created by the main rotor. An extraordinarily simple and effective arrangement from Weir/Cierva.

Country of Origin:	UK
First Flight:	1944
Accommodation:	1
Number Manufactured:	1 prototype crashed in 1946.

Westland Wessex HC-2

Subject: Wessex HC-2 of the Royal Air Force bears the markings XT674.
Statistics: Wessex HC-2.

The Wessex was a turbine-powered version of the American Sikorsky S-58 helicopter, which was developed under licence for the Royal Navy. A later version designed to meet the requirements of the Royal Air Force was designated the HC-2. Designed to perform the roles of troop transport, ground attack and air-ambulance, the HC-2 has become very familiar over the years in its bright yellow Search-and-Rescue colour scheme.

Country of Origin:	UK
First Flight:	1958
Accommodation:	Flightcrew + 16 passengers.
Rotor Diameter:	56ft 0in (17.06m)
Length:	65ft 10in (20.06m)
Height:	15ft 10in (4.82m)
Empty Weight:	8,340lb (3,783kg)
Max Take Off:	13,500lb (6,123kg)
Powerplant:	2 coupled 1,350hp (1,006kW) Bristol Siddeley Gnome H.1200 turboshafts in helicopter nose.
Max Speed:	132mph (212.4km/h)
Service Ceiling:	12,000ft (3,657m)
Range:	310 miles (499km)
Number Manufactured:	In excess of 380 of all variants.
Preserved:	Ulster Aviation Society, Langford Lodge, Northern Ireland. The Helicopter Museum, Weston-Super-Mare, Somerset, UK. Nottingham East Midlands Aeropark, UK. RAF Museum, London, UK (HCC4). Newark Air Museum, UK.

Westland Lysander III

Subject: Westland Lysander III.
Statistics: Westland Lysander MK I.

Dubbed the 'Lizzie' by its pilots and ground crews, Westland's Lysander is perhaps best remembered for its daring work with the Special Operations Executive, which used its short-field capabilities for covertly infiltrating and retrieving agents from occupied France and the Low Countries. Others of the type served in North Africa and the Middle East, where their ability to operate off the roughest of improvised airstrips allowed them to operate where other aircraft could not. It was its covert and extraordinarily courageous night-time rendezvous in deepest Europe, however, which won the Lizzie its special place in history.

Country of Origin:	UK
First Flight:	Prototype first flew in 1936.
Accommodation:	2
Wingspan:	50ft 0in (15.24m)
Length:	30ft 6in (9.29m)
Height:	14ft 6in (4.41m)
Max Take Off:	5,920lb (2,685kg)
Powerplant:	1 x 890hp (663.2kW) Bristol Mercury XII radial powerplant.
Cruise Speed:	189mph (298km/h)
Max Speed:	229mph (369km/h)
Service Ceiling:	26,000ft (7,923m)
Range:	600 miles (966km)
Number Manufactured:	1,428 built by Westland and 255 built by NSCC in Canada.
Flying or in service:	Small numbers still maintained in airworthy condition by collections and private owners.
Preserved:	Lysander III, V9441 is preserved in flying condition by the Shuttleworth Trust. Replica, Alberta Aviation Museum. Canadian Museum of Flight, Langley, BC (Lysander I). Steven F. Udvar-Hazy Center, Chantilly, Virginia, USA (Lysander IIIa).

Westland AH-1 Scout

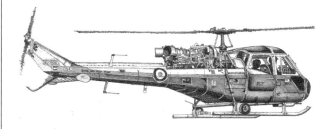

Subject: Westland AH-1 Scout, XP849, served with the Empire Test Pilots' School at Boscombe Down, UK.
Statistics: Westland AH-1 Scout.

Westland's Scout was developed from the Saunders Roe P.531 and the first operational airframes to reach the British Army were designated P.531 Mk Is. The Scout was a versatile, if relatively rudimentary, battle support helicopter which could be used to launch the SS.11 anti-tank guided missile or could be used as a troop transport to ferry groups of soldiers in and out of the battle zone. The Royal Navy, too, included the type in its inventory of weapons, developing a modified variant, the Wasp, with a stretched cabin and 4 wheels in lieu of the Scout's basic tubular steel skids.

Country of Origin:	UK
First Flight:	1959
Accommodation:	2 + 4
Rotor Diameter:	32ft 3in (9.82m)
Length:	30ft 4in (9.24m)
Height:	8ft 10in (2.69m)
Empty Weight:	3,084lb (1,398kg)
Max Take Off:	5,350lb (2,427kg)
Powerplant:	1 x 685hp (510.7kW) Rolls-Royce Nimbus 101 turboshaft.
Cruise Speed:	122mph (196.3km/h)
Max Speed:	131mph (211km/h)
Range:	316 miles (506km)
Number Manufactured:	149 of all Scout variants. 125 of Naval Wasp variants.
Flying or in service:	Small numbers of ex-military Scouts are now finding their way into private ownership.
Preserved:	The Helicopter Museum, Weston-Super-Mare, Somerset, UK.

Westland Delanne Lysander

Subject: Westland Delanne Lysander prototype, s/n K6127.
Statistics: Westland Delanne Lysander.

Placing a heavy machine gun at the rearmost extreme of the Lysander was going to cause catastrophic upset to the aircraft's centre of gravity and so the Westland designers added a second lifting wing at the back of the aircraft. In terms of aerodynamics this was unknown territory and the boffins at Westland thought it prudent to meet up in Paris with the guru of tandem-wing design, Maurice Henri Delanne. Given the impending political and military events of the day, that journey to Paris must have been filled with drama. Only one tandem-wing Delanne Lysander prototype was built before Westland abandoned the project.

Country of Origin:	UK
First Flight:	1940
Accommodation:	2 to 3.
Length:	25ft 7in (7.79m)
Powerplant:	1 x Bristol Perseus XII.
Number Manufactured:	1
Preserved:	Prototype broken up in 1944. Replica, Alberta Aviation Museum, Edmonton, Canada.

Westland-Hill Pterodactyl

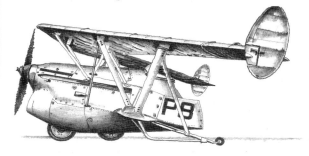

Subject: Westland-Hill Pterodactyl.
Statistics: Westland-Hill Pterodactyl.

A 2-seat tailless fighter prototype based on British experiments of the 1920s. The Pterodactyl was an effort to investigate the flying properties of several radical aeronautical theories from swept-wing design to tailless aircraft. Other novel ideas which were incorporated into the Pterodactyl were the tandem main wheels combined with the wheeled outriggers, and the prophetic twin-winglet arrangement.

Country of Origin:	UK
First Flight:	1925
Accommodation:	2
Wingspan:	45ft 6in (13.87m)
Length:	17ft 0in (5.18m)
Height:	6ft 8in (2.03m)
Empty Weight:	900lb (408.2kg)
Max Take Off:	1,080lb (489.8kg)
Max Speed:	70mph (112km/h)
Number Manufactured:	Pterodactyl I, IA, IV, and V prototypes.
Preserved:	Preserved in the British Science Museum, South Kensington, London, UK.

Westland Sea King

Subject: Westland Sea King Mk.4X ZB506 is temporarily fitted out with the Blue Kestrel radome as part of the development programme for the EH-101 Merlin helicopter.
Statistics: Westland Sea King Mk.42B.

The Sikorsky S-61 helicopter presented an ideal airframe for long range maritime patrol and anti-submarine operations. Its watertight hull was cleverly designed to keep overall weight to a minimum while maintaining endurance and range. In 1959 Westland purchased the rights to build the S-61 in Britain to meet a Royal Navy specification for a helicopter to replace the ageing Westland Wessex. The Sea King, in its final configuration, was very different to the S-61 save for in its outward appearance, but it did satisfy the requirements of the Royal Navy, Egypt, India, Qatar, Belgium, Germany, Pakistan and Australia, and it was built in very large numbers. The sketch illustrates a MK.4X Sea King which has been temporarily modified to carry the Blue Kestrel radome as part of the development programme for the sophisticated EH-101 Merlin helicopter.

Country of Origin:	UK
First Flight:	1969
Accommodation:	Crew + Varying numbers of passengers depending on specialist systems installed.
Rotor Diameter:	62ft 0in (18.89m)
Length:	72ft 8in (22.14m)
Height:	16ft 10in (5.13m)
Empty Weight:	11,865lb (5,382kg)
Max Take Off:	21,454lb (9,731kg)
Powerplant:	1 x 1,465hp (1,092kW) Rolls-Royce Gnome turboshafts.
Cruise Speed:	126mph (203km/h)
Max Speed:	140mph (226km/h)
Range:	920 miles (1,482km)
Number Manufactured:	328 of all Sea King Variants completed.
Flying or in service:	In service.

Wozniak Double Eagle

Subject: Wozniak Double Eagle, registration N2717.
Statistics: Wozniak Double Eagle.

Frank Wozniak's one-off home-built aircraft providing the very best of contemporary cabin comfort with good old-fashioned biplane fun. The beauty of home-building is that you can build what you wish as long as you stay within the laws of aerodynamics, and of your national aviation licensing administration.

Country of Origin:	USA
Accommodation:	2 + 2
Number Manufactured:	1
Flying or in service:	1

Wright Flyer

Subject: Wilbur and Orville Wright's Flyer of 1903.
Statistics: Wright Flyer.

The Wright brothers were made of stern material, and the problems which had dogged would-be aviators for years before them were simply small hurdles to be overcome on the way to a solution. Combining their skills as bicycle makers with an extraordinary level of inventiveness and determination, the two brothers applied logic and science to the the problem and developed a series of gliders and flyers culminating in the Wright Flyer of 1903. While the Flyer of 1903 did achieve the first ever heavier-than-air flight the prototype was caught by strong winds at Kitty Hawk and was badly damaged. Although it was retrieved by the brothers it never did fly again. It is now on display at the Smithsonian National Air and Space Museum, Washington.

Country of Origin:	USA
First Flight:	1903
Accommodation:	1
Wingspan:	40ft 4in (12.3m)
Length:	21ft 1in (6.4m)
Height:	9ft 4in (2.8m)
Empty Weight:	605lb (274kg)
Max Take Off:	Not established.
Powerplant:	1 x 12hp (8.9kW) home-made gasoline piston engine.
Cruise Speed:	Not established.
Max Speed:	Not established.
Service Ceiling:	Not established.
Range:	Not established.
Number Manufactured:	1 original flyer. Later flyers all differed from the original.
Preserved:	The original Wright Flyer is preserved at the Smithsonian National Air and Space Museum, Washington, DC, USA.

X-5 Seabird

Subject: X-5 Seabird Flying Boat.
Statistics: X-5 Seabird.

Experimental home-built flying boat with traditional biplane format. The X-5 Seabird's single powerplant is mounted high on the upper wing, well out of reach of spray from the aircraft's stepped hull.

Country of Origin: USA
Accommodation: 1*

Yakovlev Yak-7B

Subject: Yak-7B, US registration N7YK, at Lakeland Linder, Florida.
Statistics: Yakovlev Yak-1.

This 2-seat training conversion of the trusted Yak-1 was initially designated the UTI-26. When it entered production in 1941, however, it adopted the Yak-7 title and took on the role of converting pilots from advanced-training ships to front-line fighters. The performance of the Yak-7 was a great improvement on the Yak-1 series and variants were developed for night fighting patrols (Yak-7V) and for day fighting (Yak-7B). The Yak-1, Yak-3, Yak-7 and Yak-9, being based on the Yak-1 airframe, were all derivatives of the one family and over 37,000 of all variants were built.

Country of Origin: USSR
First Flight: 1942
Accommodation: 2
Wingspan: 32ft 9in (9.98m)
Length: 27ft 10in (8.48m)

Height: 7ft 11in (2.41m)
Max Take Off: 6,217lb (2,820kg)
Powerplant: 1 x 1,100hp (820kW)
                          Klimov M-105P.
Max Speed: 360mph (580km/h)
Service Ceiling: 33,465ft (10,200m)
Range: 528 miles (850km)
Flying or in service: Yak-7B, N7YK is airworthy and
                          based in USA.

Yakovlev Yak-18T

Subject: Yakovlev Yak-18T registration ZU-BHR.
Statistics: Yakovlev Yak-18T.

Designed as a single-seat and two-seat advanced-trainer, the Yak-18 was powered by the 300hp (223.6kW) Ivchenko radial powerplant. Robust, powerful and forgiving, the type served with training institutions right across the Soviet Union and total production was in excess of 8,700. The Yak-18T, on the other hand, was based on the same airframe but it was greatly modified to accommodate 4 passengers. The extra power required was provided by the larger 360hp (268.5kW) VOKBM Vedeneyev M-14P radial engine, while the cabin area and the turtle were carefully blended into the fuselage to produce an efficient 4-seat liaison and communications aircraft.

Country of Origin: USSR
First Flight: Yak-18 first flown in 1946.
                          Yak-18T first flown in 1967.
Accommodation: 4
Wingspan: 36ft 7in (11.15m)
Length: 27ft 6in (8.38m)
Height: 11ft 2in (3.40m)
Empty Weight: 2,695lb (1,222kg)
Max Take Off: 3,650lb (1,655kg)
Powerplant: 1 x 360hp (268.5kW) VOKBM
                          Vedeneyev M-14P radial.
Cruise Speed: 150mph (241.5km/h)
Max Speed: 183mph (294.5km/h)
Service Ceiling: 18,120ft (5,523m)
Range: 373 miles (600km)
Number Manufactured: In excess of 500 Yak-18Ts
                          completed.
Flying or in service: Many Yak-18Ts still in service.
Preserved: Steven F. Udvar-Hazy Center,
                          Chantilly, Virginia, USA.

Yakovlev Yak-42

Subject: Yak 42, CCCP-42096, in the markings of state carrier Aeroflot.
Statistics: Yak-42.

Developed from the earlier and slightly smaller Yak-40, the Yak-42 employs the same 3-turbofan layout. The type was designed originally for Aeroflot and its sister airlines as a regional airliner and feederliner and it is still used today by many airlines within the former Soviet Union and its many satellite states. Within the Yak-42 family there are many specialist airframes such as the Yak-42A which is fitted out for a combination of passengers and freight, the Yak-42F geological survey aircraft for finding locations of mineral resources, and the Yak-42D, which has greater range but seating for just 90 passengers.

Country of Origin: USSR
First Flight: 1975
Accommodation: Flightcrew + 120 passengers.
Wingspan: 112ft 2in (34.18m)
Length: 119ft 4in (36.37m)
Height: 32ft 4in (9.85m)
Max Take Off: 114,640lb (52,000kg)
Powerplant: 3 x 14,200lb (63.2kN) D-36
                          Lotarev turbofans.
Cruise Speed: 510mph (820km/h)
Range: 620 miles (1,000km)
Number Manufactured: Estimated to be in excess of
                          200 to date.
Flying or in service: Widely in service with airlines
                          of Soviet Union and China.

Yakovlev Yak-52

Subject: Yakovlev Yak-52 appeared at Sun 'n Fun 2005, USA.
Statistics: Yakovlev Yak-52.

While the Yak-52 was initially developed in the Soviet Union, production was transferred to Aerostar in Romania. Intended originally as a basic trainer for the former Warsaw Pact countries, the Yak-52 has become immensely popular in the West, and large numbers of the type appear on the civil aircraft registers of Europe, the UK, USA and Australia. The Yak-52TW is a new tailwheel variant of the trusted Yak-52 marque with revised landing configuration and other aerodynamic modifications.

Country of Origin: USSR/Romania
First Flight: 1979
Accommodation: 2
Wingspan: 30ft 6in (9.29m)
Length: 25ft 5in (7.74m)
Height: 8ft 9in (2.66m)
Empty Weight: 2,228lb (1,010kg)
Max Take Off: 2,867lb (1,300kg)
Powerplant: 1 x 360hp (268kW) Vedeneyev M-14P radial piston.
Cruise Speed: 165mph (265km/h)
Max Speed: 177mph (285km/h)
Range: 311 miles (500km)
Number Manufactured: In excess of 1,800 and production continues.
Flying or in service: Many in Yak-52s in private ownership within UK, USA and across the world.
Preserved: Russian Central Air Force Museum, Monino, Moscow.

Zlin Z-43

Subject: Zlin Z-43 of East German air force, VFK-1, based at Cottbus.
Statistics: Zlin Z-43.

A 4-seat touring and training monoplane which first took to the air in October of 1967. The Zlin Z-43 was supplied in large numbers to training schools and flying clubs across Czechoslovakia and the Soviet Union and, in more recent years, has been widely exported to the West. Robust and forgiving, even if not particularly imaginative, the type represents excellent value on today's Western general aviation market.

Country of Origin: Czechoslovakia
First Flight: 1968
Accommodation: 4
Wingspan: 32ft 0in (9.76m)
Length: 25ft 5in (7.75m)
Height: 9ft 7in (2.91m)
Empty Weight: 1,609lb (730kg)
Max Take Off: 2,976lb (1,350kg)
Powerplant: 1 x 210hp (156.5kW) Avia M-337A powerplant.
Cruise Speed: 130mph (210km/h)
Max Speed: 146mph (235km/h)
Range: 683 miles (1,100km)
Flying or in service: Many still in service with clubs and private owners.

Zlin Z-526F Trener-Master

Subject: Zlin Z-526F, sporting N number N526SB, flew into Lakeland Linder, Florida, 2005.
Statistics: Zlin Z-526F.

The Z-526 Trener-Master was developed from Zlin's long line of Z-26 aerobatic and training aircraft. Tough, rugged and a superb performer in the air, the type was a familiar sight in Eastern Europe and has now begun to appear in small numbers in the West.

Country of Origin: Czechoslovakia
First Flight: 1968
Accommodation: 2
Wingspan: 34ft 9in (10.6m)
Length: 26ft 3in (8.0m)
Height: 6ft 9in (2.06m)
Empty Weight: 1,465lb (665kg)
Max Take Off: 2,150lb (975kg)
Powerplant: 1 x 180hp (135kW) Avia M137A inverted in line piston engine.
Cruise Speed: 130mph (210km/h)
Max Speed: 152mph (244km/h)
Service Ceiling: 17,000ft (5,180m)
Range: 256 miles (475km)
Number Manufactured: 291 completed.
Flying or in service: Small numbers still flying with private owners.

Glossary

Absolute Ceiling The maximum altitude at which a heavier-than-air aircraft can be maintained in level flight.

ACIS Altitude Compensation Induction System.

Aerodynamics That branch of fluid mechanics that deals with the reactions of bodies as they pass through air.

Aerofoil (airfoil) A form or structure that is shaped to generate aerodynamic lift as it moves through the air.

AEW Airborne Early Warning.

AFB Air Force Base.

Afterburner An auxiliary burner of fuel in a turbine powerplant that provides greatly enhanced thrust for short periods of time.

Aileron A movable control surface that is used to control an aircraft's rolling movement. Ailerons are generally located in the trailing edge of the wing.

Airbrake A drag-inducing control surface that is deployed in flight to reduce an aircraft's airspeed or to deliberately reduce its efficiency in the air for purposes of losing height.

Airframe The body of an aircraft as distinct from its powerplants and ancillary systems.

Altimeter A primary flight instrument, generally built around a sensitive aneroid barometer, which is used to indicate an aircraft's height.

Amphibian An aircraft which is capable of being operated from both land and water.

Angle of Attack The angle of attack for a given aerofoil is the angle between an aerofoil chord line and the oncoming airflow.

Angle of Incidence The angle at which an aerofoil is set in relation to the fore and aft axis of an aircraft.

Anhedral The angle at which the wings of an aircraft are set in relation to the fuselage when the wingtips are lower than the wing roots, or the points where the wing is attached to the fuselage.

AOP Air Observation Post.

Aspect Ratio The ratio of span to chord of any particular wing. A high-aspect-ratio wing will have a large span and a narrow chord and is generally slow, but highly efficient. A low-aspect-ratio wing will produce higher cruising speeds but lower levels of efficiency.

ASW Anti-Submarine Warfare.

Attitude The angle of an aircraft in relation to the oncoming airflow or, when in close proximity to the ground, in relation to the surrounding terrain.

Autogyro An aircraft that generates its lift by way of a non-powered rotary wing which autorotates as the aircraft is propelled through the air by a conventional pusher engine arrangement.

AWACS Airborne Warning and Control System.

BAC British Aircraft Corporation.

BAe British Aerospace.

Biplane A fixed-wing aircraft configuration comprising two sets of wings generally arranged one above the other and secured in place by way of a system of struts and wire braces.

Black Box A flight-data-recording device that collects data and voice inputs from many critical sources on a large aircraft. Usually fluorescent orange or yellow in colour. Never black.

BOAC British Overseas Airways Corporation.

Boundary Layer That thin layer of air which lies closest to an aerofoil's surface. The behaviour of the boundary layer on any given aerofoil section will greatly determine the usefulness and efficiency of the finished wing.

Canard An additional lifting surface that is added to an aircraft forward of the main wings for the purposes of providing additional lift, control or stability.

Cantilever Wing A wing structure that requires no external support, struts or braces beyond the line of the fuselage.

CASA Spanish manufacturer Construcciones Aeronauticas SA.

Ceiling The normal maximum operating altitude of an aircraft.

Centre of Gravity That point on the longitudinal axis of an aircraft's structure where the total combined forces of the aircraft's weight appear to act.

Chaff A defensive screen of radar-reflective particles released by a military aircraft to confuse the radar detection systems of enemy aircraft and incoming missiles. Usually released by way of carefully timed explosive dispersal.

Chord The distance measured from the leading to the trailing edge of a given aerofoil.

Coanda Effect The propensity of a fluid or a gas to remain attached to a surface.

COIN Counter Insurgency.

Constant-Speed Propeller A propeller arrangement that provides optimum performance in flight by way of automatically adjusting propeller pitch. Constant-speed propellers can be complex and expensive but they do deliver great advantages in terms of performance.

Control Surfaces The ailerons, elevators and rudder of an aircraft, which can be manipulated by the pilot to determine an aircraft's path through a mass of air.

Cowling The shaped panels enclosing an aircraft engine.

DASA Daimler-Benz Aerospace AG.

DHC de Havilland Aircraft of Canada Ltd.

Dihedral The angle at which the wings of an aircraft are set in relation to the fuselage when the wing tips are higher than the wing roots or the points where the wing is attached to the fuselage.

Dirigible A lighter-than-air aircraft or airship which is capable of being steered and powered through the air.

Dorsal Any surface or appendage that relates to the upper surface of an aircraft's fuselage.

Drag The forces of air resistance that resist the motion of an aircraft through a body of air.

Drone A heavier-than-air pilotless aircraft generally used for research, reconnaissance or military purposes.

Drop Tank A disposable or reusable fuel tank that can be carried externally by an aircraft to provide additional fuel capacity or to extend mission range.

Duralumin A light, strong alloy of aluminium containing small percentages of magnesium, copper and manganese.

EAA Experimental Aircraft Association of the USA.

ECM Electronic countermeasures employed by many sophisticated military aircraft to reduce the effectiveness of an enemy's radar and weapons systems.

EFIS Electronic Flight Instrumentation System.

Elevator A movable control surface that is generally mounted on the trailing edge of an aircraft's tailplane for purposes of controlling pitching movement.

Elevon A control surface that combines the functions of elevator and aileron.

Empty Weight The weight of an aircraft inclusive of all avionics and instrumentation but exclusive of fuel, pilots and payload.

ETOPS Extended Range, Twin Engine Operations.

FAA Federal Aviation Administration, USA.

FADEC Full Authority Digital Electronic Control engine management system.

FAI Fédération Aéronautique Internationale.

Fairing A non-structural cover or jointer that is intended to streamline component parts of an airframe.

Fin A fixed vertical aerofoil surface, usually located at the tail of an aircraft, which provides stability in yaw and is generally used as a mounting point for the rudder assembly.

Flap A moving surface that is generally mounted at the trailing edge of a wing and which can be deployed in full or in part to increase lift or drag for general flight control purposes or for adjustment of attitude and stall speed in the landing configuration.

Flat-Four Generic description of a horizontally opposed 4-cylinder piston engine arrangement.

Flat-Six Generic description of a horizontally opposed 6-cylinder piston engine arrangement.

FLIR Forward-Looking Infra-Red.

Floatplane An aircraft that is supported on the water's surface by way of floats. Not to be confused with seaplanes.

Flutter An unstable and dangerous oscillation of an aerofoil or control surface that can lead to serious in-flight structural failure.

Fly-by-Wire An electronic flight control system rather than a mechanical one. Generally highly dependent on computing power.

Flying Wing An all-wing aircraft whose fuselage and tail have been incorporated or substantially incorporated into the wing structure. Generally efficient in flight.

fpm feet per minute.

Fuselage The main body of an aircraft, to which the wings and powerplants are affixed.

Hardpoint A strengthened attach point on the under-wing or under-fuselage of an airframe that is used for mounting of external weapons, armaments or stores.

Head-up-display A sophisticated display system that projects critical flight and weapons information onto a clear screen which is directly in the military pilot's line of sight.

Horizontally Opposed Engine A reciprocating piston engine that is configured with 2 banks of inline cylinders arranged opposite each other. Generally air-cooled in aviation powerplants.

hp Horsepower.

HUD Head-Up Display.

Hull The boat-like, watertight under-fuselage of a flying boat or seaplane.

Hypoxia A potentially incapacitating condition brought on by oxygen deficiency at high altitudes.

IAI Israeli Aircraft Industries.

IFR Instrument Flight Rules govern flight by reference to on-board instrumentation and radio-navigational aids under conditions of reduced visibility and/or darkness.

IPTN Industri Pesawat Terbang Nusantara of Indonesia.

Inline Engine A reciprocating piston engine that is configured with all cylinders in a straight line, one after the other.

Interrupter Gear A cam-based timing device that allowed machine guns to be fired through the arc of a propeller.

JAR Joint Airworthiness Requirements.

JASDF Japanese Air Self Defense Force.

JMSDF Japanese Maritime Self Defense Force.

km/h Kilometre per hour.

kN Kilonewtons.

kW Kilowatt.

Leading Edge That front portion of an aerofoil that first meets the oncoming airflow.

Lift The force exerted on the upper surface of an aerofoil that causes it to rise as it moves through the air.

Longeron A structural fuselage component that runs fore to aft.

Mach Number Airspeed calibrated as a ratio of the speed of sound.

MAD Magnetic Anomaly Detector.

Max Speed The maximum speed an aircraft can achieve in level flight.

Max Take-off The largest lift-off weight that the designer or the regulator of a given aircraft type has authorized.

MBB Messerschmitt Bölkow Blöhm.

Microlight A small lightweight powered aircraft often built in the form of a hang-glider with undercarriage and pilot seat.

Monocoque A structural system in which the aircraft's outer skin carries the primary stresses with little or no dependence on internal bracing or ribs.

Monoplane A fixed-wing aircraft that derives its lift from just one pair of wings.

NACA US National Advisory Committee on Aeronautics.

Nacelle A streamlined enclosure housing a powerplant or any other component of an aircraft that is likely to induce drag or otherwise require protection from the airflow or elements.

NASA US National Aeronautics and Space Administration.

NATO North Atlantic Treaty Organization.

NOTAR No tail rotor.

OKB Opytno Konstrooktorskoye Byuro (Russian Design Bureau).

Ornithopter An aircraft that derives its lift from a flapping bird-like motion of its wings. A notional rather than a practical route to flight which was much favoured by early pioneers in the field of aviation.

Parasol Wing A single-span wing that is attached to an aircraft above the level of the fuselage and is generally separated from the fuselage by way of pylons, struts and wire bracing.

Payload Passengers or cargo carried by an aircraft or, in a military aircraft, its stock of munitions.

PFA Private Flying Association, UK.

Pitot Tube An open-ended tube that directs a sample of the air pressure caused by the movement of an aircraft through the air straight to a series of sensitive instruments that are configured to display airspeed, etc.

Powerplant Piston engine, turboprop, turbojet or turbofan.

Pressurization The artificial generation of air pressure within an aircraft to compensate for the effects of reduced atmospheric pressure when altitude is increased.

Pusher Propeller An engine/propeller arrangement whereby the propeller is located behind the engine rather than in front of it.

PZL Panstwowe Zaklady Lotnicze, Poland.

RAAF Royal Australian Air Force.

Radar Signature A radar echo that identifies an aircraft in flight.

Radial Engine A reciprocating piston engine whose cylinders are arranged in a circular configuration around a crankshaft.

Radome A radar-transparent protective cover or housing that accommodates specialist radar sensors or emitters.

RAE The UK Royal Aircraft Establishment, formerly the Royal Aircraft Factory.

RAF Royal Air Force.

Ramjet A crude but effective engine comprising an aerodynamic duct into which air is drawn, compressed by the forward motion of the engine, mixed with raw fuel, and ignited to produce a high-velocity propulsive thrust. Simple and effective but immensely inefficient in terms of fuel burn.

Range The maximum distance an aircraft can travel at best economic cruise, minimum payload and no allowances for fuel reserves.

RCAF Royal Canadian Air Force.

RFC UK Royal Flying Corps.

RNAS UK Royal Naval Air Service.

RNZAF Royal New Zealand Air Force.

Rotary Engine A powerplant configuration that is spatially similar to a radial engine arrangement except that the crankshaft remains in a fixed position and the cylinders and crankcase rotate around it.

Rotor The rotating wing of a helicopter or autogyro, generally referred to as the rotor blades or rotor assembly.

Rotorcraft An aircraft that generates its lift by way of a power-driven rotary wing or by way of a rotor wing which autorotates as the aircraft is pushed through the air.

Saab Svenska Aeroplan AB, Sweden.

SAAC The Society of Amateur Aircraft Constructors, Republic of Ireland.

SAI Skandinavisk Aero Industri of Denmark, builders of the KZ series of light aircraft.

SAR Search and Rescue.

Semi-Monocoque A structural system in which the aircraft's outer skin carries some of the primary stresses within the airframe but which requires additional internal longerons and formers to provide reinforcement and hold its shape.

Service Ceiling The greatest height to which an aircraft can be climbed in ordinary use or, more precisely, the height at which an aircraft's rate of climb has been reduced to just 100ft/min.

Skid A tubular sled-type undercarriage on a helicopter or a non-wheeled tail-sled on early aircraft types.

Skin The external fabric, plywood or metal covering of an aircraft's inner structure.

SLAR Sideways-Looking Airborne Radar.

Smart Weapons The use of satellite-based guidance systems or laser targeting devices to ensure precise and accurate delivery of munitions.

SNCAN Société Nationale de Constructions Aéronautiques du Nord.

SNCASE Société Nationale de Constructions Aéronautiques Sud Est.

SOCATA Société de Construction d'Avions de Tourisme et d'Affaires.

Span The dimension from wingtip to wingtip of a given aircraft.

Spar The main span-wise structural component of a wing or a pair of wings.

SRAAM Short-Range Air-to-Air Missile.

Stall A flight condition that arises when the smooth flow of air over the upper surface of an aerofoil changes suddenly from a steady streamlined flow to a violent eddying motion resulting in massive and sudden loss of lift.

Stealth Technology A sophisticated blend of geometric shaping, materials technologies and heat dissipation techniques, all of which are directed at producing an aircraft that has an extremely low radar signature.

STOL Short Take-Off and Landing.

Strut A structural member employed as a brace or spacing device between the upper and lower wings of a biplane or used as a triangulating or stiffening device in more conventional aircraft. Usually shaped or streamlined to facilitate clean airflow.

Supercharger A compressor-type device that supplies air to the cylinders of an internal combustion engine at increased pressure in order to produce additional power.

Swept Wing A wing whose leading edge is biased towards the rear of the aircraft at an angle of less than 90 degrees to the centreline of the fuselage.

Swing Wing See Variable-geometry Wing.

Tab Small secondary control surfaces that can be adjusted in flight to offset the aerodynamic loads which are imposed on the main flying control surfaces as the aircraft changes in speed and configuration.

Max Take-off The largest lift-off weight that the designer or the regulator of a given aircraft type has authorized.

Thrust The forces produced by a powerplant to propel an aircraft through the air.

Thrust Vectoring Control of a jet aircraft's movement by way of adjusting the angle of its propulsive thrust or by way of manipulating adjustable nozzles or jet efflux gates.

Torque A twisting force generated by a propeller or other rotating powerplant component.

Tractor Propeller The standard and commonplace engine/propeller arrangement whereby the propeller is located immediately on the front of the engine.

Trailing Edge The rearmost edge of a wing or aerofoil.

Turbofan Gas turbine powerplant with a large-diameter forward fan arrangement which by-passes air at great speed around the core turbine and adds it to the normal jet efflux to provide a highly efficient and reliable source of propulsion.

Turbojet The gas turbine engine in its simplest form producing thrust in the form of a high-velocity jet efflux.

Turboprop A gas turbine powerplant that uses fast-spinning compressor blades to draw air into a combustion chamber where it is heated with burning fuel. As the expanding gases escape through the exhaust outlet they cause a turbine to rotate, thereby driving the propeller. A highly efficient and reliable source of propulsion.

Turboshaft Again, a gas turbine powerplant that uses fast spinning compressor blades to draw air into a combustion chamber where it is heated with burning fuel. As the expanding gases escape through the exhaust outlet they cause a turbine to rotate at high speeds, thereby driving a helicopters rotor blades or, indeed, any other item of heavy equipment. A highly efficient and reliable source of propulsion.

TWA Trans World Airlines.

UAV Unmanned air vehicle or pilotless aircraft.
USAAC United States Army Air Corps.
USAAF United States Army Air Force.
USAAS United States Army Air Service.
USAF United States Air Force.
USCG United States Coast Guard.
Useful Load Difference between maximum gross weight and empty weight.
USMC United States Marine Corps.
USN United States Navy.
VFR Visual Flight Rules.

Variable-Geometry Wing A sophisticated wing arrangement that is highly swept backwards in flight to facilitate high-supersonic speeds but which can be extended bodily outwards to near-90-degree configuration for slow-speed flight and for the duration of the landing phase.

Variable-Pitch Propeller A propeller whose pitch (and therefore its angle of attack relative to the oncoming airflow) can be altered in flight from fine for the take-off phase to coarse for economic cruising.

Ventral Any surface or appendage that relates to the lower surface of an aircraft's fuselage.

Vee Engine A reciprocating piston engine that is configured with 2 banks of inline cylinders arranged opposite and at an angle to each other.

V/STOL Vertical and Short Take-Off and Landing.

VTOL Vertical Take-Off and Landing.

Widebody An airliner of sufficient cross-sectional area to allow it be configured internally in 3 aisles of multiple seats with 2 walking aisles between.

Winglet A vertical fin-like structure at the outermost point of a wing that is designed to reduce drag by preventing the spillage of high-pressure air around the outer wingtip to the low-pressure zone above.

Wing Loading The maximum take-off weight of an aircraft divided by its wing area expressed in lbs/sq ft.

Wingspan The dimension from wingtip to wingtip of a given aircraft.

Wing Warping A rudimentary system of lateral control made possible by a slight twisting or warping of an aircraft's wings to provide roll control. Wing warping was commonplace in the very earliest of flying machines but it was soon abandoned in favour of ailerons.

Yaw The rotation of an aircraft around its vertical axis generally resulting in a change of heading.

Further Reading

Addison, Colin, 'Oshkosh: The World's Biggest Aviation Event' (London 1990).

Aldrich, Richard J., 'Witness to War: Diaries of the Second World War in Europe' (London 2004).

Aldrin, Buzz, 'Men From Earth' (New York 1997).

Alison, Tom and Dana Bell, eds., 'At The Controls: The Smithsonian National Air and Space Museum Book of Cockpits' (Shrewsbury 2001).

Almond, Peter, 'Aviation: The Early Years' (Cologne 1997).

Ambrose, Stephen E., 'Band of Brothers' (New York 1992).

Ambrose, Stephen E., 'D-Day June 6th, 1944: The Battle for the Normandy Beaches' (London 2002).

Baldry, Dennis and Mike Jerram, 'The DEC Schneider Trophy Race' (Oxford 1987).

Barry, Jim, 'Flying the North Atlantic' (London 1987).

Carpenter, M. Scott, et al 'We Seven' (New York 1962).

Chant, Christopher, 'Aircraft Prototypes: Aerospace Technology from the Light Fighter to the B2 Stealth Bomber' (London 2003).

Davies, David and Mike Vines, 'Antique and Classic Aircraft' (London 1997).

Debay, Yves, 'Combat Helicopters' (Paris 1997).

Ellis, Ken, 'Wrecks & Relics', 10th edition (Hersham, Surrey 1986).

Flack, Jeremy, 'Today's Royal Air Force in Colour' (London 1987).

Grant, R.G., 'Flight: 100 Years of Aviation' (London 2004).

Green, William, ed., 'The New Observer's Book of Aircraft' (London 1985).

Green, William, 'Warplanes of the Third Reich' (London 1992).

Gunston, Bill, ed., 'The Encyclopedia of Modern Warplanes: The Development and Specifications of All Active Military Aircraft' (Leicester 1995).

Hogg, Ian and John Weeks, 'The Illustrated Encyclopedia of Military Vehicles' (London 2003).

Hook, Alex, 'Illustrated History of the Third Reich' (London 2004).

Horton, John, 'The Grub Street Dictionary of Aircraft Nicknames, Variants, and Colloquial Terms' (London 1994).

Humble, Richard, 'Aircraft Carriers' (London 1982).

Jackson, Robert, 'Flying Modern Jet Fighters' (London 1987).

Endres, Günter and Michael J. Getting, eds., 'Jane's Aircraft Recognition Guide', 3rd edition (London 2002).

Jackson, Paul, 'Jane's All the World's Aircraft 2005-2006' (Coulsdon, Surrey 2005).

Gunston, Bill, 'Jane's Fighting Aircraft of World War II' (New Jersey 1997).

Wood, Derek, ed., 'Jane's World Aircraft Recognition Handbook' (Coulsdon, Surrey 1989).

Taylor, Michael J.H., 'Jane's Encyclopedia of Aviation' (Castle Douglas 1993).

Kermode, A.C., 'Flight Without Formulae' 5th edition (London 1989).

Stolley, Richard B., 'Life: World War II: The World's Greatest Conflict in Pictures' (New York 2005).

Mackersey, Ian, 'The Wright Brothers' (London 2003).

Mondey, David, 'The Complete Illustrated Encyclopedia of the World's Aircraft' (London 1988).

Nemecek, Vaclav, 'Vojenska Letadla I' (Prague 1974).

Nemecek, Vaclav, 'Ceskoslovenska Letadla II: 1945-1984' (Prague 1984).

Parker, Matthew, 'The Battle of Britain: July-October 1940' (London 2001).

Rawnsley, C.F. and Robert Wright, 'Night Fighter' (London 1957).

Sebag-Montefiore, Hugh, 'Enigma: The Battle for the Code' (London 2002).

Shores, Christopher, 'Great Air Battles of World War I' (London 2002).

Simpson, Rod, 'Airlife's World Aircraft: The Complete Reference to Civil, Military and Light Aircraft' (Shrewsbury 2001).

Taylor, Michael J.H., 'Planemakers: Boeing' (Coulsdon, Surrey 1987).

Thom, Trevor, 'The Air Pilot's Manual: Air Navigation' Air Pilot's Manual Series, 3 (Shrewsbury 2002).

Thom, Trevor, 'The Air Pilot's Manual: Flying Training' Air Pilot's Manual Series, Volume 1 (Shrewsbury 2003).

Wall, Robert, 'A History of Airliners' (London 1989).

Whitley, M.J., 'German Cruisers of World War II' (Annapolis, Maryland 1985).

Willmott, H.P., 'Pearl Harbor' (London 2001).

Winchester, Jim, 'The Aviation Factfile: Biplanes, Triplanes, and Seaplanes' (Rochester 2004).

Winchester, Jim, 'The Aviation Factfile: Concept Aircraft: Prototypes, X-Planes, and Experimental Aircraft' (Berkeley, California 2005).

Yeager, Chuck and Leo Janos, 'Yeager' (London 1986).

Yeager, Jeana and Dick Rutan, 'Voyager' (London 1987).

Index

Acknowledgments

The Aviation Book could not have come to pass without the assistance of a great number of people whose knowledge and understanding of aviation helped to shape its pages. My thanks especially to the members of the Society of Amateur Aircraft Constructors (Republic of Ireland) whose tireless dedication to aviation helped to develop in me a thorough understanding of aircraft construction techniques which, I hope, is apparent in the detailing of this drawing collection. My thanks too to my great friend Dave Ryan and the other members of Waterford Aeroclub who have in the last years shown me the lighter side of aviation and allowed me to enjoy long Saturdays deep in engine oil, aeronautical charts, and endless discussions on aircraft and aviation trivia. This book would not have been possible, too, without the great airshows, flying events and journals of the Private Flying Association (UK), The Experimental Aircraft Association (USA), the Réseau du Sport de l'Air (RSA, France) and the many other aviation bodies through whom I have been able to access some of the world's most fascinating aircraft, and indeed often their pilots, in closest detail. Aviation museums, too, have been a great source of material and particular thanks must go to the Imperial War Museum, Duxford, the Shuttleworth Collection, Old Warden, the Royal Air Force Museum, Hendon, the Flying Tigers Warbird Restoration Museum, Kissimmee, FL, the Kermit Weeks Fantasy of Flight Museum, Polk City, FL, the EAA Florida Air Museum, the Canada Aviation Museum, Ottawa, and many other museums and aircraft collections across the world. Others who played a vital role in this project were David Ryan Jnr who developed the text fonts from my own handwriting, Dave English who kept my many computers talking to each other, and Nicky Toullier who worked tirelessly through the night when my server hard drive began to self destruct. My thanks also to Petra Barnes who helped to provide the initial text spacings for foreign language versions and to Vanessa O Loughlin-Fox who gave me invaluable assistance in the closing months of the project. To Mike Delaney who was always ready to provide insight and expert advice and to friends Fred and Cheryl Mahan who provided large helpings of encouragement and ensured that their gas guzzling camper van was pre-positioned for me on the flightline of the EAA's annual Sun 'n Fun airshow.

Special thanks are due to my publishers, Thames & Hudson, and in particular to Jamie Camplin who provided invaluable encouragement and enthusiasm from the outset.

Most of all, however, I owe a great debt of thanks to my wonderful wife Carina and to my budding-artists, son and daughter Josh and Aimee, who have put up with my great preoccupation for many years and who patiently allowed their holidays and family outings to be punctuated with explorations of airports, hangars, and aviation museums. My thanks forever.

Fia O Caoimh.